LONELY PLANET PUBLICATIONS

D0174465

GINGER ADAMS OTIS
BETH GREENFIELD
ROBERT REID
REGIS ST LOUIS

NEW YORK CITY

C I T Y   G U I D E

INTRODUCING NYC

In a New York minute: taxis zoom through bustling Times Square (p132)

New York can be anything you want it to be. It's why countless people have pinned their dreams on the place, thrown caution to the wind and shown up on its doorstep.

And it's why visitors keep streaming in from all corners of the globe, grasping at their silver-screen visions – and finding them – but discovering plenty more on the way. New York is a city that's surprising yet malleable, incredibly straightforward yet bafflingly complex. It's got so many sides and so much to offer that it can be intimidating, even to the most urban-minded of visitors. But approach it with a combination of organization and openness, and you'll be met with some staggering and unexpected rewards.

You could decide you'd like your day to be filled with high culture and trendy eating, for example, and – voila! – you're working your way through the Museum of Modern Art, then watching the New York City Ballet perform at Lincoln Center. Or perhaps you like your city grittier, and spend an afternoon wandering through the twisting streets of Chinatown and in the edgy art galleries of Williamsburg. Just don't be too shocked if your day of high culture turns edgy when you come across a gorgeous jazz singer on the subway platform – or if your bohemian day gets fancy when a trendy boutique seduces you, and you're shelling out for perfect shoes before you know it. Whatever. New York is easy that way.

CITY LIFE

Even while, at this writing, the US seemed certain to be sliding into an economic recession, New York City appeared to be holding its own. That's because after decades of battling demons from crime to a failing infrastructure, followed by the terror and fallout of September 11, NYC went through an impressive renaissance, managing to cement itself as an unshakable, shining icon. The year 2007 was

'NYC has gone through an impressive renaissance to cement itself as an unshakable, shining icon'

an economic record setter here, bringing about $25 billion in new construction, a 33% home ownership rate and a whopping 46 million tourists. And the city is setting even higher goals for tourism in the coming years, ramping up its reach by launching campaigns that specifically court folks from Sweden, Russia, China and Brazil – as well as gay and lesbian travelers from across the globe – in an attempt to bring in 50 million annual visitors by 2015.

Luckily, visitors are drawn to new attractions, and a spate of them – the New Museum of Contemporary Art, the relocated Museum of Art and Design and the new Museum of Chinese in America among them – are here to help the cause.

The low crime rate – which dropped to a 40-year low in 2007 – doesn't hurt, either. It's good information for the many out-of-towners who still fear they will visit here and find the New York of the '70s. Though the city's major cleanup has been widely flaunted, sometimes you just have to see something to believe it.

New York is cleaning up its act in other ways, too. It's been attempting to improve the state of public health with various programs, fix the school system and turn this city into the lean, 'green' machine that it should be, by calling for environmentally sound development and transportation policies. It's the city of the future. And it's here right now.

The magnificently marbled main hall of Grand Central Terminal (p128)

HIGHLIGHTS

LOWER MANHATTAN & TRIBECA

Home to icons from Wall Street to the Statue of Liberty, the southern tip of Manhattan pulses with businesslike energy during the day before settling into quiet nights.

❶ Brooklyn Bridge
Walk or bike across this glorious span (p83).

❷ Megu
Wow your senses at this stunning palace of Japanese cuisine (p249).

❸ City Hall
Get inside city government with a free tour under the rotunda (p82).

❹ Statue of Liberty
Get up close and personal with the lovely lady (p70).

❶ Film Forum
Cinema buffs will delight in this indie movie house (p319).

❷ Balthazar
Brunches are all the buzz at this SoHo hotspot (p252).

❸ Soho Grand
Lay your head in boutique-hotel heaven (p351).

❹ Bloomingdale's SoHo
Find a chic department-store vibe at this downtown version of the classic (p220).

SOHO, NOHO & NOLITA

The original industrial-chic feel – a mood set by historic cast-iron buildings – still serves as a subtle backdrop for this trio of neighborhoods gone glossy with coveted boutiques, inns and eateries.

CHINATOWN & LITTLE ITALY

Chinese and Vietnamese markets and restaurants line the bustling streets here, packed and frenzied – and fast moving in on what's left of tiny Little Italy, now just a handful of red-sauce restaurants and classic bakeries.

❶ Mahayana Buddhist Temple
Step on in to meet the city's largest Buddha (p95).

❷ Doyers Street
Slip along the mysterious curve of one of Chinatown's oddest byways (p95).

❸ Ferrara Cafe and Bakery
Little Italy lives on at this pastry-filled shop (p95).

1 Bowery Hotel
Enjoy high style on NYC's former skid row at this new boutique inn (p352).

2 New Museum of Contemporary Art
This sleek Bowery tower is the talk of downtown (p99).

3 WD 50
Creative cuisine thrives at this gourmet temple (p255).

4 Eldridge Street Synagogue
Spectacularly renovated, this house of worship is back from the dead (p97).

EAST VILLAGE & THE LOWER EAST SIDE

Old meets new on every block of this downtown duo – two of the city's hottest 'hoods for nightlife – where Jewish immigrant traditions linger as nostalgic reminders of life here not so long ago.

GREENWICH VILLAGE, WEST VILLAGE & THE MEATPACKING DISTRICT

Quaint, twisting streets and well-preserved brick townhouses mingle with newer architectural wonders and endless options for intimate dining and drinking in the West Village. The neighboring Meatpacking District has trendy nightlife options galore.

❶ Washington Square Arch
Gaze up at the glory of Greenwich Village's stately icon (p108).

❷ Spotted Pig
Don't miss this hot-ticket gastro pub (p258).

❸ Christopher Street Pier
Enjoy breezy, balmy days on this landscaped finger of parkland (p112).

CHELSEA, UNION SQUARE & THE FLATIRON DISTRICT

Though known as a hoppin' gay ghetto, Chelsea's got plenty for everyone – nightclubs and eateries, cafés and parks. Nearby Union Square and the Flatiron District are a bit mellower but no less cool, each anchored by its own lively 'town square.'

❶ Pierpont Morgan Library
Don't miss the impressive holdings at this stellar space (p125).

❷ Union Square Greenmarket
Forage for gorgeous regional produce at this locals' favorite farmers market (p121).

❸ General Theological Seminary
Find a tranquil escape at this silent green space (p114).

MIDTOWN

The pulsing heart and soul of Manhattan, this is the home of fantasy New York: Times Square, Broadway theaters, canyons of skyscrapers and bustling crowds that rarely thin.

❶ Allen Room
Listen to top-notch jazz in a stellar setting (p139).

❷ Museum of Modern Art
Dive into the masters at this well-packed collection (p137).

❸ New York Public Library
This glorious spot is a temple of knowledge (p129).

❹ Top of the Rock
Find million-dollar views on top of the world (p133).

1 Neue Galerie
This mansion-housed collection is a Klimt-filled gem (p145).

2 Frick Collection
Don't miss this hushed and thrilling museum (p144).

3 Lincoln Center
A night of culture here is a must (p152).

4 Metropolitan Museum of Art
'The Met' is the grande dame of the art world (p141).

UPPER EAST SIDE & UPPER WEST SIDE

The Upper East Side's Museum Mile is just about the most cultured strip in the city. Its historic mansions don't hurt the sophisticated feel – nor do the stately old buildings of the Upper West Side, known for its artsy, airy, park-lined vibe.

CENTRAL PARK

An oasis of verdant calm in the city, Central Park is an escape from the madness and an entrance into a whole other world.

❶ Wollman Skating Rink
Slip and slide beneath the stars at this ice-skating spot (p150).

❷ Bethesda Fountain
Settle beneath the angel's wings on a warm and sunny day (p151).

❸ Delacorte Theater
Catch Shakespeare in the Park at this alfresco performance space (p313).

❹ Strawberry Fields
Honor John Lennon with likeminded strangers at this beloved shrine (p148).

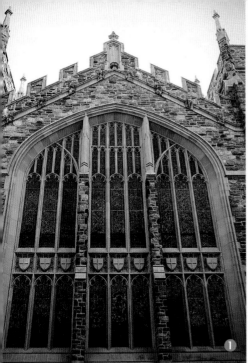

❶ Abyssinian Baptist Church
Get fired up with gospel at this favorite place of prayer (p161).

❷ Studio Museum in Harlem
This museum brings high-quality art way uptown (p161).

❸ Cathedral Church of St John the Divine
Take in the overwhelming glory of this massive house of worship (p157).

❹ Apollo Theater
This is Harlem's legendary entertainment spot (p162).

HARLEM & NORTHERN MANHATTAN

Harlem and upper Manhattan represent African American New York – past, present and future – and its surrounding neighborhoods are ripe for exploring other cultures, far away from the crowds.

BROOKLYN

Big and booming, Brooklyn is a borough of distinct neighborhoods that boast hot restaurants and bars. Much of the fun comes from long walks on shaded sidewalks, where you're much more likely to get a 'hello' (or at least a nod) than in Manhattan.

❶ Williamsburg
You can no longer know NYC's best bars without a night out in this hipster haven (p176).

❷ Coney Island
See its glorious seedy side soon, as its 'shoot the freak' days are numbered (p195).

❸ Tom's Restaurant
Try the egg creams and pancakes at this super-friendly, classic 1930s diner (p281).

❹ Prospect Park
Built by the creators of Central Park, who considered this expanse of forest, lawns and playgrounds far superior (p181).

❺ Brooklyn Heights Promenade
Some of the best Lower Manhattan views come from Brooklyn's riverside walkway (p172).

❻ Brooklyn Children's Museum
The world's first museum for kids has been recently expanded (p193).

❼ Brooklyn Botanic Garden
Free on Saturday mornings, the garden is one of the city's great green spaces (p184).

QUEENS, THE BRONX & STATEN ISLAND

Don't tell the other outer boroughs they're not New York: Queens is the world's most diverse neighborhood, the Bronx is the birthplace of hip-hop and the Yankees, and Staten Island, though more remote, is reached by the best free ferry ride in the world.

❶ New York Yankees
No American sports team has won more championships than the Bronx Bombers (p325).

❷ PS1 Contemporary Art Center
Located in an old school, Queens' PS1 hosts popular 'Warm Up' summer concert evenings (p202).

❸ Rockaway Beach
Queens' beach front inspired the Ramones' classic, Beach Boys–inspired anthem, and now surfers are free to hit the waves, too (p205).

CONTENTS

Continued from previous page.

Ginger Adams Otis

Though not a native daughter, Ginger is proud to call New York City home. This country girl from New Hampshire has finally adapted to life in the fast lane and wouldn't trade it for the world. When not writing Lonely Planet guidebooks, she's a reporter for a New York daily paper. Ginger was the coordinating author and wrote the Sleeping and Day Trips & Excursions chapters.

Beth Greenfield

A New Jersey native, Beth spent her teenage years fantasizing about someday living on the other side of the river, in a Tribeca loft. While she has yet to make it into that coveted space, she's lived in and written about the city for 16 years and counting. She's also a staff editor at *Time Out New York* magazine and a regular contributor to the *New York Times* travel section, with other articles in *Esquire*, the *Village Voice, Budget Travel* and *Out*. For Lonely Planet, Beth contributed to the previous two editions of *New York City* as well as *Miami & the Keys, Mexico* and *USA*. Beth wrote the Introducing NYC, Getting Started, Background, Arts, Gay & Lesbian NYC and Directory chapters, and cowrote the Neighborhoods and Eating chapters.

Robert Reid

Raised in Oklahoma, Robert now lives in Brooklyn, where he writes full-time and occasionally finds an excuse to cross the East River. See his website at www .reidontravel.com. Robert wrote the Drinking & Nightlife, Sports & Activities, Transportation and Brooklyn Unbound chapters, and cowrote the Neighborhoods and Eating chapters.

Regis St Louis

A Hoosier by birth, Regis grew up in a sleepy town where he dreamed of big-city intrigue and small, expensive apartments. He settled in New York, which had all that and more, in 2001. He currently lives in Chelsea and is a full-time travel writer. Regis wrote the Shopping and NYC Style chapters.

PHOTOGRAPHER
Dan Herrick

Dan has lived in NYC for the past seven years after living and studying in Latin America and Europe. He enjoys documenting the city's continual change and frenetic way of life, and pulling himself away to travel abroad or to one of the many different worlds that exist within NYC's boundaries.

New York will lead, and you must follow. Still, it can't hurt to be armed with a well-mapped plan, as the head-spinning number of options in this vibrant city will pull you in all directions. It's a dream destination, after all, and you'll want to know you experienced as much as possible. So budget your time – knowing that everything will take about twice as much time as you'd figured – and you won't be sorry.

WHEN TO GO

New York shines in all seasons. Spring and fall, with their mild temperatures and disarmingly beautiful blossoms and foliage, are optimal times for strolling, which you'll do a lot of here. Summer brings stifling heat and sizzling pavements but other rewards aplenty, from outdoor concerts and festivals to crowd-free weekends, reduced hotel rates and perfect opportunities for side trips to the seashore. Finally, while winter can be chilly, it's nothing that can't be cured by lingering in cozy museums and cafés – or by the fact that hotel rates tend to drop after the fun and frenzied holidays, when the crowds thin out. Plus, experiencing a New York City snowstorm, when noise gets muffled and jaded cityfolk act like wide-eyed kids, is quite a heartwarming treat.

FESTIVALS

It seems as though there's always some sort of celebration going on here. National holidays, religious observances and just plain ol' weekends prompt parades, parties or street fairs, with highlights such as the fireworks on July Fourth and the street parades for Halloween (October), Thanksgiving (November) and Gay Pride (June).

Federal holidays such as Labor Day, Christmas and Thanksgiving may affect business hours and transit schedules. While they won't affect your ability to eat out, explore or be entertained, they could put a crimp in your plans to visit the post office or bank. Check with your hotel concierge (or local host) before setting out.

January

THREE KINGS PARADE
☎ 212-831-7272; www.elmuseo.org
Every year in the first week of January, the streets of Spanish Harlem are filled with parading schoolchildren, donkeys and sheep, celebrating Christmas in the tradition of many Latin American and Caribbean countries. Check the website for route details.

WINTER RESTAURANT WEEK
☎ 212-484-1222; www.nycvisit.com
One of two official Restaurant Weeks (the other is in July), this marks a wonderful opportunity to try the expensive, high-profile restaurant of your dreams – nearly 200 participating eateries offer three-course lunches for $20 or so and three-course dinners for $30.

February

LUNAR (CHINESE) NEW YEAR FESTIVAL
www.explorechinatown.com
One of the biggest Chinese New Year celebrations in the country, this display of fireworks and dancing dragons draws mobs of thrill-seekers into the streets of Chinatown. The date of Chinese New Year fluctuates from year to year, often falling in late January but sometimes in early February.

MERCEDES-BENZ FASHION WEEK
www.mbfashionweek.com/newyork
The infamous Bryant Park fashion shows are sadly not open to the public. But whether you're invited or not, being in the city this week – when the couture world descends upon Manhattan to thrill over new looks – could provide a vicarious thrill, especially if you can find the after-parties. A second fashion week is held in September.

WESTMINSTER KENNEL CLUB DOG SHOW
www.westminsterkennelclub.org
Who will be Best in Show? Catch the oft-mocked parade of pure breeds at this dead-serious canine showcase, held annually at Madison Square Garden (see p326).

March

ST PAT'S FOR ALL PARADE

☎ 718-721-2780; www.stpatsforall.com
Held early in the month in Sunnyside, Queens, this festive community affair is an inclusive answer to the mainstream St Patrick's Day Parade, which bans gay groups from marching.

ST PATRICK'S DAY PARADE   March 17

☎ 718-793-1600
A massive audience, rowdy and wobbly from cups of green beer, lines Fifth Ave on March 17 for this popular parade of bagpipe blowers, sparkly floats and clusters of Irish-lovin' politicians. The event is protested each year by a small but feisty group of LGBT folks, who object to the fact that march organizers specifically ban any gay groups from joining in.

April

EASTER PARADE & EASTER BONNET FESTIVAL

www.saintpatrickscathedral.org
This loosely organized tradition brings mobs of well-clad folks to the stretch of Fifth Ave (closed off to traffic for the day) in front of St Patrick's Cathedral, where they strut in the sun to show off their elaborate bonnets, caps and other headgear.

HAVANA FILM FESTIVAL

☎ 212-946-1839; www.hffny.com
Fast nearing its 10th year, this beloved film fest screens shorts, docs and features from Cuba, the Caribbean, Mexico and Central and South America.

TAX DAY   April 15

April 15 is the deadline for Americans to pay off Uncle Sam. In NYC, it's just another reason to dress up and make some noise. Check out both the partiers and protestors who gather on the grand steps of the General Post Office – kept open round the clock as procrastinators rush to get their postmark – in a quirky, crazy display of free speech.

May

TRIBECA FILM FESTIVAL

☎ 212-941-2400; www.tribecafilmfestival.com
Robert De Niro co-organizes this annual downtown film fest, held in the first week of May. The week of screenings, featuring world and US premieres, has become a prestigious, celeb-studded event, with plenty of red-carpet action.

CHERRY BLOSSOM FESTIVAL

☎ 718-623-7200; www.bbg.org
Known in Japanese as *Sakura Matsuri*, this annual tradition, held the first weekend in May, celebrates the pink, puffy flowering of the Kwanzan cherry trees along the Brooklyn Botanic Garden's famous esplanade. It's complete with entertainment, refreshments and awe-inspiring beauty.

BIKE NEW YORK

☎ 212-932-2453; www.bikemonthnyc.org
May is Bike Month, featuring two-wheelin' tours, parties and other events for pedal-pushing New Yorkers. Bike New York, the main event, sees thousands of cyclists hit the pavement for a 42-mile ride, much of it on roads closed to traffic or waterfront paths through each of the city's five boroughs.

FLEET WEEK

☎ 212-245-0072; www.intrepidmuseum.com
For one week at the end of the month, Manhattan resembles a 1940s movie set as clusters of fresh-faced, uniformed sailors go 'on the town' to look for adventures. The ships they leave behind, docked in the Hudson River, invite the curious to hop aboard for tours.

June

PUERTO RICAN DAY PARADE

www.nationalpuertoricandayparade.org
The second weekend in June attracts thousands of flag-waving revelers for the annual Puerto Rican pride parade. Now in its fifth decade, it runs up Fifth Ave from 44th to 86th Sts.

JVC JAZZ FESTIVAL

☎ 212-501-1390; www.festivalnetwork.com
More than 40 jazz shows go on in clubs around the city for this festival held in mid-June, featuring big names such as Etta James, Branford Marsalis, Keith Jarrett and Eartha Kitt.

LESBIAN, GAY, BISEXUAL & TRANSGENDER PRIDE

☎ 212-807-7433; www.nycpride.org

June is Gay Pride Month, and it culminates in a major march down Fifth Ave on the last Sunday of the month – a five-hour spectacle of dancers, drag queens, gay police officers, leathermen, lesbian soccer-moms and representatives of just about every other queer scene under the rainbow. Various outer-borough Pride events take place on other June weekends, with the Queens Pride March (www.queenspride.com) in Jackson Heights among the most multi-culti. The annual Dyke March (www.nycdykemarch.org), a separate and female-only event, heads down Fifth Ave the evening before the big march, starting at 42nd St and Sixth Ave.

MERMAID PARADE

☎ 718-372-5159; www.coneyisland.com

Celebrating the sand, the sea and the beginning of summer is this wonderfully quirky afternoon parade, now more than 25 years old. It's a flash of glitter and glamour, as elaborately costumed folks display their mermaid finery along the Coney Island boardwalk. Held on the last Saturday of the month.

July

JULY FOURTH FIREWORKS   July 4

☎ 212-494-4495

America's Independence Day is celebrated with fireworks over the East River, starting at 9pm. Good viewing spots include the waterfronts of the Lower East Side and Williamsburg, Brooklyn, or any high rooftop or east-facing Manhattan apartment. Roosevelt Island also hosts a fireworks-viewing festival at its Southpoint Park. The pyrotechnic display, hosted by Macy's and courtesy of the renowned Grucci fireworks company, is an impressive sight to behold (though the accompanying patriotic music is rather on the schmaltzy side).

NATHAN'S FAMOUS HOT-DOG-EATING CONTEST   July 4

www.nathansfamous.com

This bizarre celebration of gluttony brings world-champion food inhalers to Coney Island each Fourth of July. The 2007 winner, Joey Chestnut of California, set a new world record by downing 66 dogs (and buns!) in 12 minutes – despite a jaw injury, no less.

PHILHARMONIC IN THE PARK

☎ 212-875-5656; www.newyorkphilharmonic.org

Free nighttime concerts in the park from the country's premier orchestra are among the most wonderful treats of summer in the city. Grab a blanket, pack a picnic and choose from Central Park, Brooklyn's Prospect Park or parks in Queens, the Bronx or Staten Island; the symphony visits each borough, beginning in early July, and brings a different music program to each.

August

FRINGE FESTIVAL

☎ 212-279-4488; www.fringenyc.org

This annual mid-August theater festival presents two weeks of performances from companies all over the world. It's the best way to catch the edgiest, wackiest and most creative up-and-comers around.

HOWL! FESTIVAL

☎ 212-673-5433; www.howlfestival.com

This week-long celebration, named for Beat writer Allen Ginsberg's famous poem, brings visual art, theater, dance, film and literature to venues around the artsy East Village.

PRIDE IN THE CITY

☎ 718-230-0770; www.prideinthecity.com

This black gay pride festival – meant both for celebration and education about preventing the spread of HIV – brings five event-packed days to various venues around NYC. One highlight is the annual beach-party blowout, featuring live performances, held at Jacob Riis Park in the Rockaways (see p205).

US OPEN TENNIS TOURNAMENT

☎ 718-760-6200; www.usopen.org

Tennis fans turn out en masse for this, one of the four Grand Slam tournaments of professional tennis, to see top-ranked men and women compete in singles and doubles matches. Held at the USTA Billie Jean King National Tennis Center (p328), a sort of miniature tennis universe out in Flushing, Queens.

September
WEST INDIAN AMERICAN DAY CARNIVAL PARADE
☎ 718-467-1797
To most New Yorkers, Labor Day is a wistful day signaling the official end of summer. But for two million Caribbean Americans and other fun-loving onlookers, it's time to head on over to Eastern Pkwy in Brooklyn for the annual Carnival parade – a colorful, day-long march and party featuring over-the-top costumes, delicious Caribbean eats and nonstop music.

SAN GENNARO FESTIVAL
www.sangennaro.org
Rowdy, loyal crowds descend on the narrow streets of Little Italy for carnival games, sausage-and-pepper sandwiches, deep-fried Oreos and more Italian treats than you can stomach in one evening. For more than 75 years, it's remained an old-world tradition.

HOT SUMMER IN THE CITY
The following organizations present frequent events and series, mainly in the summer months.

Bryant Park/HBO Summer Film Series
www.bryantpark.org
Every Monday night from mid-June through August, a mob of New Yorkers bring blankets and picnic dinners to this patch of green in Midtown, trying to catch a good spot for watching the classic films – *Casablanca*, *Annie Hall*, *Psycho* and others – that show on the big outdoor screen.

Celebrate Brooklyn
www.briconline.org/celebrate
From late spring through summer, the Prospect Park band shell in Park Slope, Brooklyn, presents a stellar lineup of concerts, films, spoken-word shows and dance performances. The series, going strong for more than 30 years, hosts shows during the week and on weekends, many of which offer free admission.

Central Park SummerStage
www.summerstage.org
Throughout the summer, the New York City Parks Foundation hosts an incredible series of outdoor performances at its SummerStage (Map p149) – dance, theater, spoken word and music concerts in all genres – many of which are free. Recent talents have included Amiri Baraka, the Philadelphia Dance Company, Neko Case, Café Tacuba, Bob Weir and Cassandra Wilson.

NewFest: The New York LGBT Film Festival
www.newfest.org
In addition to hosting this annual gay film festival in early June, NewFest presents LGBT film programming throughout the year, including NewFest at BAM in Brooklyn, which shows the best of the June fest in one packed weekend, and NewFest at IFC Center, a monthly series in Greenwich Village.

River to River Festival
www.rivertorivernyc.org
Lasting throughout most of summer and offering something to do on almost every night of the week, this is the largest free arts event in NYC, with hundreds of creators and performers bringing theatre, music, dance and film to a slew of downtown parks.

DUMBO ART UNDER THE BRIDGE FESTIVAL

www.dumboartscenter.org

Celebrating and promoting Dumbo's local artist community – with newfound vigor each year, thanks to the neighborhood's growing gentrification – this Brooklyn fest features open studios and galleries, performances and street displays.

October

BLESSING OF THE ANIMALS

www.stjohndivine.org

In honor of the Feast Day of St Francis, which falls early in the month, pet owners flock to the grand Cathedral of St John the Divine with their creatures – poodles, lizards, parrots, donkeys, you name it – to be blessed. It's a wild and wonderful afternoon for participants and onlookers alike.

OPEN HOUSE NEW YORK

☎ 212-991-6469; www.ohny.org

The country's largest architecture and design event, held at the start of the month, features special, architect-led tours, as well as lectures, design workshops, studio visits and site-specific performances.

HALLOWEEN PARADE   October 31

www.halloween-nyc.com

The nation's largest public Halloween celebration lures all sorts of freaks and geeks into the streets of Greenwich Village for a wild night of parading and prancing about in costume. The outfits range from very clever and of-the-moment to over-the-top raunchy, and the spectators lining the streets love one and all.

November

NEW YORK CITY MARATHON

www.nycmarathon.org

Held in the first week of November, this annual 26-mile run through the streets of the city's five boroughs draws thousands of athletes from around the world – and just as many excited viewers, who line the streets to cheer folks on.

ROCKEFELLER CENTER CHRISTMAS TREE LIGHTING CEREMONY

www.rockefellercenter.com

At this traditional mob-scene event, folks flock around the massive spruce tree to watch it come aglow with energy-efficient bulbs before it's taken down and recycled into lumber. It's a green Christmas!

THANKSGIVING DAY PARADE

www.macys.com

This famous cold-weather event, for hardy viewers only, parades its famous floats and balloons (watch your head) along Broadway, from 72nd St to Herald Sq. For an even better view, join the throngs who gather at the southwest corner of Central Park to watch the balloons being inflated the night before.

NEW YORK BOTANICAL GARDENS HOLIDAY TRAIN SHOW

☎ 718-817-8700; www.nybg.org

Opening the day after Thanksgiving and lasting through January, this annual spectacle recreates New York City landmarks in miniature using natural materials like pine cones, cinnamon sticks and poppy pods, with miniature trains wending in and out. Come stroll through the Bronx wonder in the afternoon or – even better – at night, when the display is all lit up.

December

NEW YEAR'S EVE   December 31

www.timessquarenyc.org/nye/

In addition to the world-famous countdown to midnight and dropping of the Waterford Crystal ball held in Times Sq – a raucous, freezing, alcohol-fueled spectacle that you're honestly better off missing – the city has plenty of other celebratory events, namely the Midnight Run in Central Park (☎ 212-860-4455) and midnight fireworks in Central Park, Prospect Park and the South Street Seaport. An unofficial but thoroughly NYC option is the Hot Nude Yoga New Year's Eve (www.hotnudeyoga.com), a spiritual-meets-sensual night for men only.

COSTS & MONEY

The year 2008 brought along with it a financially disturbing trend for New Yorkers: droves of 'weak dollar' tourists descending upon the city's most fashionable shops, eateries and real-estate offices. They were enjoying the sad state of the US dollar, which had dropped 12% against the British pound and 10% against the Euro the year before.

And so, for the first time in recent memory, many New York visitors had come to enjoy bargains, rather than to grin and bear the act of emptying their wallets. Brits and Europeans: congratulations! Enjoy yourselves. Anyone else: prepare thyself. A trip to New York could never be described as cheap – even now.

That said, there are plenty of ways to enjoy the city, with options for just about every budget. Finding deals, whatever the state of the economy, usually just takes a mix of forethought and creativity.

Basic costs for a NYC trip start with accommodations (unless you've got a friend or relative who's willing to put you up in their sure-to-be-cramped apartment). An unavoidable fact is that the average night in a city hotel costs $300, with those on the more desirable end easily going for upwards of $400. The best way to find serious bargain rates is by not being picky about your hotel's location; in other words, look for beds in non-trendy parts of Manhattan (like East Midtown) or, better yet, in Brooklyn, Queens and even across the Hudson River, in New Jersey. If you're patient enough to deal with mass transit to get you into the heart of the city each day, you'll wind up saving a pretty penny (though don't expect your rates to dip too far under $200 a night).

City B&Bs also tend to be more affordable; several in and around the Chelsea area (p354) have rooms with shared bathrooms for about $150 – just book far in advance, as they tend to fill quickly. Another way to bargain hunt is to book through online resources such as tripadvisor.com, orbitz.com, and hotels.com – the sheer number of them keeps prices competitive. Finally, those who can stomach hostel aesthetics are most in luck, as there are several barebones places right in Manhattan, such as those in the Jazz Hostel group (p365), which offer dorm beds for as low as $30.

You'll also have to pay to eat, of course. The absolute cheapest way to go is to forgo the foodies' restaurant-scene paradise and stick to making your own meals (if you have access to a kitchen) or subsist on packaged and prepared foods bought at the city's many markets. Basic non-gourmet delis, found on practically every corner, make egg-and-cheese sandwiches for breakfast ($3 on average), and a range of other basic sandwiches throughout the day, whether it's egg salad on rye for $6 or roast beef on a roll for $7. Street food, while not too healthy, is also way-cheap, with everything from hot dogs for $2 to gyros for $3.

Or you can try to be wholesome by trolling the city's vast array of Greenmarket Farmers Markets (www.cenyc.org) for fresh fruits, breads and cheeses for in-room backpacker picnics.

Eating at restaurants will cost you, but still, the prices range tremendously. The most budget options can get you hearty ethnic meals for under $10, while midrange restaurants with table service start at about $10 to $15 per person for dinner, with the numbers going up from there. Head to a five-star dining establishment, order three courses and throw in a bottle of wine, and you could easily drop $200 per person. Families looking to save should head to diners and other low-key spots with kids menus (see Top Picks, p251), which usually offer dishes for less than half of the normal price.

If you want to shop while you're here – and who doesn't? – then you'll also find extreme price ranges in all categories. For clothing, there are bargain spots aplenty, with stores like Filene's Basement (p234), Century 21 (p217), Loehmann's (p233) and H&M (p237) high on the radar screens of local bargain shoppers looking for knockoffs and discounted labels. You can also try your luck at designers' sample sales (see boxed text, p217).

Entertainment prices can be sky-high, with prime opera or theater tickets easily costing over $100 a piece. But there's plenty for paupers, too. Get your dose of theater for $15 a pop at Off-Off-Broadway productions, or through events like the Fringe Festival (p22) – or try your patience waiting in line for tickets for Shakespeare in the Park (see p313), which offers top-notch theater for free. Broadway tickets can be bought for half price

HOW MUCH?

Bottle (8oz) of water: $1.50

Bottle of Brooklyn Lager beer: $2.25

Venti latte from Starbucks: $4.05

Sunday *New York Times:* $4.50

Hot dog from street vendor: $1.75

Slice of pizza: $2.50

I ♥ NY T-shirt: $10

Movie ticket: $12

Pair of J Brand jeans: $180

NYC postcard: 5 for $1

Taxi ride from Midtown to the Upper West Side: $13

at the two TKTS booths (see the boxed text, p313) in Manhattan. And plenty of venues all over the city – music, comedy, cabaret, dance and theater – frequently offer cheap ($5 to $10) and free performances; check local arts listings in publications such as *Time Out New York* and the *Village Voice* for daily free and cheap activities. Also, while museums like the expensive MoMA (p137) can charge up to $20 for entrance, many have 'pay-what-you-wish' days or times, plus generous discounts for students and seniors.

INTERNET RESOURCES

Curbed.com A real estate, business and neighborhood-obsessed site and blog with up-to-the-minute links to New York publications.

Forgotten-NY.com Kevin Walsh's awesome site about historic NYC, with not-found-elsewhere tales about everything from old subway stations to cemeteries.

Gawker.com Mostly insidery blog for those in the media industry, but its snarky gossip and detailed celebrity sightings (complete with maps) could appeal to anyone.

GoMag.com Online version of a popular lesbian nightlife guide.

GothamGazette.com Top-notch source for city news, politics and heated issues.

Gothamist.com Cool blog site with quirky news and links about everything from local politics to entertainment gossip.

HX.com The online version of the ultimate gay nightlife guide, complete with bar listings organized by neighborhood.

Menupages.com Indispensable guide to New York restaurants, organized by cuisine and neighborhood, with actual menus and locals' opinions.

NewYorkology.com Excellent roundup of NYC travel offers, events and news items.

SUSTAINABLE NEW YORK

Here's some good news for travelers who want to leave a small carbon footprint in their wake: New York City makes it pretty darn easy to do just that, primarily because of its incredible mass-transit system. Walking should (and can easily) be your number-one choice here, but if you can't walk, then hop aboard the aging but efficient subway system or one of New York's public buses (the city claims the largest number of hybrid-electric buses in North America, with more than 550 pollution-free vehicles).

Even taxis – not as efficient as subways and buses, perhaps, but preferable to individually owned cars – are going green: more than a thousand yellow taxis in New York will be hybrids by 2009; by 2012, all of them will be, according to the pledge made by Mayor Bloomberg. Yet another option is to hail a

ADVANCE PLANNING

Procrastinators can do just fine winging it in New York. But if you have specific, must-do goals in mind, being prepared is essential.

It should go without saying that unless you have infinite bucks to spend (or no comfort or cleanliness standards to speak of), booking a hotel room in advance is a must. The same goes for anything else you might want to be a part of that's in high demand, whether it's dinner at a trendy spot or great seats at a popular theater event. For restaurant reservations, use the free, online OpenTable.com system; Broadway theater tickets, meanwhile, can be had through Telecharge.com, Ticketmaster.com or other sites (p310), while ballet and sporting-event tickets are best scored through the website of the individual venue or sports team.

Other outings you might want to plan for include nightclub forays – emailing or calling ahead to have your name placed on the night's guest list could save you from waiting in line behind the velvet ropes; see individual club websites (p300) for guest-list info. You can also avoid lines at some popular tourist sites by buying and printing out tickets in advance; both the Empire State Building (p129) and Top of the Rock (p133) allow you to do this.

A less obvious detail that will benefit from some forethought is that of renting a car for out-of-town side trips – especially on holiday weekends, when it can seem like every rental agency in the city is flat out of automobiles. Just hit the websites in advance to secure your vehicle (see p394).

Finally, before you leave you can start getting details about what will be happening in the city during your trip – just sign up for some email lists. One generally useful bulletin comes from Daily Candy (www.dailycandy.com), offering information on nightlife, shopping and dining. For news about sample sales (p217), sign up to receive updates from Top Button (www.topbutton.com).

WHEN IN NEW YORK CITY, DO AS NEW YORKERS DO

- Only hail a taxi if its roof light is on. Look carefully, though: if the middle light is on, the cab is available; if only the lights on the sides are on, the cab's off-duty; and if no lights are on, there's already a passenger inside. Trying to hail a taxi that's engaged or off-duty is probably the number-one tourist blunder.
- Be aware that most taxis, because of unfathomably ridiculous shift-change hours, are off-duty during rush hour, so avoid needing one between about 4pm and 5pm on weekdays.
- Don't stand on corners waiting for the 'walk' sign. New Yorkers cross against the light as soon as there's a big enough lull in traffic.
- It's How-sten Street. Not Hew-sten. Got it? Good.
- Be politely aggressive when boarding a crowded subway. Don't just stand and wait for your turn to board, or you may miss your chance.
- While waiting for your subway train to arrive, figure out from which end you'll need to disembark (eg uptown or downtown) and walk towards it, thereby assuring the most efficient use of time.
- When walking on the sidewalk, think of yourself as a car on the street: don't stop short, pay attention to the speed limit, and pull off to the side if you need to look at a map or dig through your bag for an umbrella.
- Don't walk down the street saying 'Hello!' to the people you pass. It's sad but true – everyone will think you're crazy.
- Say 'thank you' to the bus driver as you exit a bus from the front door (don't yell it from the back). It's one of a few pleasantries that New Yorkers really love to honor.

pedicab – these pedaled rickshaws can be found primarily around midtown, especially when Broadway shows let out, and are great for traveling short distances when you're too pooped to perambulate.

Finally, sustain NYC's local economy by throwing the big chains (Starbucks, Barnes & Noble, etc) under the bus in favor of trying out the locally owned indie cafés and shops. Isn't that what travel's all about anyway?

HISTORY

LIVING OFF THE LAND

Long before land-grabbing settlers or property-obsessed residents took hold of this area, the swath that would eventually become NYC belonged to Native Americans known as the Lenape – 'original people' – who resided in a series of seasonal campsites. They lived up and down the eastern seaboard, along the signature shoreline, and on hills and in valleys sculpted by glaciers after the Ice Age left New York with glacial debris now called Hamilton Heights and Bay Ridge. Glaciers scoured off soft rock, leaving behind Manhattan's stark rock foundations of gneiss and schist. Around 11,000 years before the first Europeans sailed through the Narrows, the Lenape people foraged, hunted and fished the regional bounty here. Spear points, arrowheads, bone heaps and shell mounds testify to their presence. Some of their pathways still lie beneath streets such as Broadway. In the Lenape language of Munsee, the term Manhattan may have translated as 'hilly island.' Others trace the meaning to a more colorful phrase: 'place of general inebriation.'

1524: A RUDE AWAKENING

The Lenape people lived undisturbed until explorers muscled in, firstly by way of the French vessel *La Dauphine*, piloted by Florentine explorer Giovanni da Verrazano. He explored the Upper Bay in 1524, deemed it a 'very beautiful lake,' and while anchored at Staten Island, he attempted to kidnap some of the Native Americans he encountered. This touched off several decades of European explorers raiding Lenape villages, and cultivated their deep mistrust of outsiders. By the time the Dutch West India Company employee Henry Hudson arrived in 1609, encounters with Native Americans were often dichotomized into two crude stories that alternated between 'delightful primitives' and 'brutal savages.'

BUYING MANHATTAN

The Dutch West India Company sent 110 settlers to begin a trading post here in 1624. They settled in Lower Manhattan and called their colony New Amsterdam, touching off bloody battles with the unshakable Lenape. It all came to a head in 1626, the colony's first governor, Peter Minuit, became the city's first – but certainly not the last – unscrupulous real estate agent. He offered to buy Manhattan's 14,000 acres from the Lenape for 60 guilders, or $24. Unaware of the concept of private land ownership, the Lenape agreed, probably thinking that the exchange was about rent, and permission to hunt, fish and trade, rather than a permanent transfer of property.

From the beginning New Amsterdam's governors displayed more talent for self-enrichment than for administration. As colonists grumbled about the Dutch West India Company's stingy provisions and primitive wood huts, the walls and ramparts of the 'fort' crumbled under the

TIMELINE

c AD 1500	1625–26	1646
About 15,000 Native Americans live in 80 different sites around the island. These included the Iroquois and the Algonquins, who fought among themselves before clashing with Europeans.	As the population of New Amsterdam reaches 200, the Dutch West India Company imports slaves from Africa to New Amsterdam for the fur trade and to work in construction.	The Dutch found the village of Breuckelen on the eastern shore of Long Island, naming it after Breukelen in the Netherlands; it will remain an independent city until 1898.

assault of free-roaming pigs, cattle and sheep. Meanwhile, new Governor Willem Kieft stirred up so much trouble with the surrounding Native Americans that they formed an alliance to subdue the aggressive Europeans. By the time Peter Stuyvesant stomped off a ship to clean up the mess in 1647, the Lenape population had dwindled to around 700, and Kieft had retreated to count his gains in various corrupt transactions.

PEG LEG, IRON FIST

Newly appointed governor Peter Stuyvesant busily set about remaking the demoralized colony, making peace with the Lenape, establishing markets and a night watch, repairing the fort, digging a canal (under the current Canal St) and authorizing a municipal wharf. His vision of an orderly and prosperous trading port was partially derived from his previous experience as governor of Curaçao – and the burgeoning sugar economy in the Caribbean helped to inspire an investment in slave trading that soon boosted New Amsterdam's slave workforce to 20% of the population. After long service, some were partially freed and given 'Negroe Lots' near today's Greenwich Village, the Lower East Side and City Hall; you can see the remnants of their African Burial Ground (see the boxed text, p82), now a national park, on Duane St. The Dutch West India Company encouraged the fruitful connection to plantation economies on the islands, and issued advertisements and offered privileges to attract merchants to the growing port. Although these 'liberties' did not at first extend to the Jews who fled the Spanish Inquisition, the Dutch West India Company turned Stuyvesant's intolerance around. By the 1650s, warehouses, workshops and gabled houses were spreading back from the dense establishments at the river's edge on Pearl St.

But by 1664, the English showed up in battleships, ready for a nasty fight. Stuyvesant was tired, though, and avoided bloodshed by surrendering without a shot. King Charles II promptly renamed the colony after his brother the Duke of York, and instead picked fights with the Lenape, many of whom were killed off before retreating upstate. Over the next few decades, the colony's Dutch look became decidedly English, as elegant townhouses sprouted up. New York becoming a prosperous British port and population rose to 11,000 by the mid 1700s. But at the same time, colonists were becoming resentful over British taxation.

FREEDOM OF PRESS

Evidence of the rising tension could be found in the colonial press, as John Peter Zenger's *New York Weekly Journal* flayed king and royal governor so regularly that the authorities tried to convict Zenger for seditious libel. He was acquitted, though, and that outcome was the beginning of what we now know as 'freedom of press.' Today you can see a marker in front of Federal Hall (p78), where Zenger was tried, honoring that victory. Meanwhile, some 2000 enslaved New Yorkers continued to resist their involuntary servitude, while at the same time trade with the Caribbean accelerated, and wharves lined the East River to accommodate the bulging merchant ships. By the 18th century the economy was so robust the locals were improvising ways to avoid sharing the wealth with London. Smuggling to dodge various port taxes was commonplace, and the jagged coastline, full of coves and inlets, hid illegal activity well (a virtue that 21st-century drug smugglers have discovered). And so New York's being a hotbed of hotheads and tax dodgers provided the stage for the fatal confrontation with King George III.

1754	1784	1789
New York gets its first institution of higher learning in the form of King's College, founded by royal charter from George II; after the American Revolution it's reborn as Columbia University.	Alexander Hamilton founds America's first bank, the Bank of New York, with holdings of $500,000; almost a decade later, it will become the first corporate stock to be traded on the New York Stock Exchange.	Following a seven-day procession from his home in Mount Vernon, greeted by excited crowds in cities from Alexandria to Trenton, George Washington is inaugurated at Federal Hall as the country's first president.

REVOLUTION & WAR

Patriots clashed in public spaces with Tories, who were loyal to the king, while Lieutenant Colonel Alexander Hamilton, an intellectual, became a fierce anti-British organizer. Citizens fled the scene, sensing the oncoming war, and revolutionary battle began in August of 1776, when General George Washington's army lost about a quarter of its men in just a couple of days. He retreated, and fire encompassed much of the colony. But soon the British left and Washington's army reclaimed their city. After a series of celebrations, banquets and fireworks at Bowling Green, General Washington bade farewell to his officers at what is now the Fraunces Tavern Museum (p78), and retired as commander-in-chief.

But in 1789, to his surprise, the retired general found himself addressing crowds at Federal Hall (p78), gathered to witness his presidential inauguration. Alexander Hamilton, meanwhile, began rebuilding New York, and became Washington's secretary of the treasury, working to establish the New York Stock Exchange. But people distrusted a capitol located adjacent to the financial power of Wall St merchants, and New Yorkers lost the seat of the presidency to Philadelphia shortly thereafter.

POPULATION BUST, INFRASTRUCTURE BOOM

There were plenty of setbacks at the start of the 19th century: the bloody Draft Riots of 1863, massive cholera epidemics, rising tensions among 'old' and new immigrants and the serious poverty and crime of Five Points, the city's first slum, located in what is now Chinatown and the City Hall area and dramatized by Hollywood in 2002's *Gangs of New York*. Eventually, though, the city was prosperous, and found mighty resources to build mighty public works. A great aqueduct system brought Croton Water to city dwellers, relieving thirst and stamping out the cholera that was

top picks

HISTORY BOOKS

Check out the ubiquitous street sellers for cheap copies of these books, old and new.

- Gotham: A History of New York City to 1898 (Edwin G Burrows and Mike Wallace, 2003) A hugely entertaining, 1000-page, Pulitzer prize–winning tome that lends itself to chapter-by-chapter sampling. Chock-full of evildoers, absurdity and contention.
- Lowlife (Luc Sante, 2000) A rollicking look at 19th-century criminality, drawing heavily on Herbert Asbury's *Gangs of New York*, that includes characters such as the fat fence Marm Mandelbaum, who gave dinner parties on chairs that her clients stole.
- The Restless City: A Short History of New York From Colonial Times to the Present (Joanne Reitano, 2006) Compact enough for you to tuck into your travel bag, this collection of mini-essays covers diverse eras and struggles in the city's history.
- Gay New York (George Chauncey, 1995) The hidden history of dandies, the docks, drag balls and brief encounters, demonstrating how gay urban habits evolved within surprisingly variable sexual cultures and practices.
- Taxi! A Social History of the New York City Cabdriver (Graham Russell Gao Hodges, 2007) 'Probably the best account of the taxi man ever to be written,' said a *Wall Street Journal* review; this solid history begins with the first medallion cab in 1907 and has tales up through the present.
- The Historical Atlas of New York City: A Visual Celebration of 400 Years of New York City's History (Eric Homberger, 1998) This visually stimulating book describes the city's initial settlement up through Giuliani's New York, enriched with colorful maps, illustrations, charts and photographs.

1795	1811	1825
Just two years after turning away refugees from a Yellow Fever epidemic in Philadelphia, New York finds itself in the midst of its own outbreak, which kills nearly 750 people.	Manhattan's grid plan is developed by Mayor DeWitt Clinton, which leads to reshaping the city by leveling hills, filling in swamps and laying out plans for future streets.	The Erie Canal, considered one of the greatest engineering feats of the era, is ceremoniously completed, greatly influencing trade and commerce in New York.

sweeping the town. Irish immigrants helped dig a 363-mile 'ditch' – the Erie Canal – linking the Hudson River with Lake Erie. The canal's chief backer, Mayor DeWitt Clinton, celebrated the waterway by ceremonially pouring a barrel of Erie water into the sea (Clinton's cask is on view at the New-York Historical Society, p155). Clinton was also the mastermind behind the modern-day grid system of Manhattan's street layout – a plan created by his commission to organize the city in the face of an oncoming population explosion.

And there was yet another grand project afoot: one to boost the health of the people crammed into tiny tenement apartments, in the form of an 843-acre public park. Begun in 1855 in an area so far uptown that some immigrants kept pigs, sheep and goats there, Central Park (p148) was both a vision of green reform and a boon to real-estate speculation. As much as Central Park promised a playground for the masses, the park project also offered work relief for the city when the Panic of 1857 (one of the city's periodic financial debacles) shattered the nation's finance system. Another vision was realized by German-born engineer John Roebling, who sought a solution to a series of winter freezes that had shut down the ferry system connecting downtown Manhattan to Brooklyn, then an independent city. He designed a soaring symphony of spun wire and Gothic arches to span the East River, and his Brooklyn Bridge (p83) accelerated the fusion of the neighboring cities. Soon the city population hit two million, and these urbanites were served by even more new creations – from the elevated railway to trains that pulled into Grand Central Depot, built by rail tycoon Cornelius Vanderbilt and later replaced by today's Grand Central Terminal (p128).

19TH-CENTURY CORRUPTION & IMMIGRATION

Out of such growth and new prosperity came the infamous William 'Boss' Tweed – a powerful and charming politician who had served in the US House of Representatives and had become the leader of political organization Tammany Hall, which basically looked out for the wealthy class. He soon took charge of the city treasury and spent years embezzling funds – perhaps up to $200 million – which put the city in debt and contributed to citizens' growing poverty. His crimes were highlighted by Thomas Nast's biting caricatures in the 1870s, and Boss was eventually caught and thrown in jail, where he died.

By the turn of the 20th century elevated trains carried a million people a day in and out of the city. Rapid transit opened up areas of the Bronx and Upper Manhattan, spurring mini building booms in areas near the lines. At this point, the city was simply overflowing with the masses of immigrants arriving from southern Italy and Eastern Europe, who had boosted the metropolis to around three million. The journey from immigrant landing stations at Castle Garden and Ellis Island led straight to the Lower East Side. There, streets reflected these myriad origins with shop signs in Yiddish, Italian, German and Chinese. Ethnic enclaves allowed newcomers to feel comfortable speaking their home languages, buy both familiar and New World staples from pushcart peddlers and worship varied versions of the Christian and Jewish faiths. You can experience their extremely tight living quarters today at the Lower East Side Tenement Museum (p97).

CLASS LESSONS

All sorts of folks were living in squalor by the late 19th century, when the immigration processing center at Ellis Island opened, welcoming one million newcomers in just its first year. They crammed into packed tenements, shivered in soup lines and shoveled snow for nickels.

1853	1863	1870
The State Legislature authorizes the allotment of public lands, which removes 17,000 potential building sites from the real estate market for what will later become Central Park.	The Civil War Draft Riots erupt in New York, lasting for three days and ending only when President Lincoln dispatches combat troops from the Federal Army to restore order.	After four years of lobbying for a national institution of art by a civic group led by lawyer John Jay, the Metropolitan Museum of Art is founded by a collection of local leaders, philanthropists and artists.

Children collected rags and bottles, boys hawked newspapers, and girls sold flowers to contribute to family income. Family budgets were so meager that it was common to pawn the sheets to raise food money before a payday.

Meanwhile newly wealthy folks – boosted by an economy jump-started by financier JP Morgan, who bailed out sinking railroads and led to New York being the headquarters of Standard Oil and US Steel – began to build increasingly splendid mansions on Fifth Ave. Modeled on European chateaux, palaces such as the Vanderbilt home, on the corner of 52nd St and Fifth Ave, reached for new summits of opulence. Tapestries adorned marble halls, mirrored ballrooms accommodated bejeweled revelers, liveried footmen guided grand ladies from their gilded carriages in a society where Astors, Fricks and Carnegies ruled. Reporter and photographer Jacob Riis illuminated the widening gap between the classes by writing about it in the *New York Tribune* and in his now-classic 1890 book, *How the Other Half Lives*, eventually forcing the city to pass much-needed housing reforms.

1898: BOROUGHS JOIN MANHATTAN

After years of governmental chaos caused by the 40 independent municipalities around the New York area, a solution came in 1898: the ratifying of the Charter of New York, which joined the five boroughs of Brooklyn, Staten Island, Queens, the Bronx and Manhattan into the largest city in America. (Brooklyn, though, already a fiercely independent city, took some cajoling to join the others, and had actually refused the idea five years earlier.) The move – which would be celebrated 100 years later with the biggest fireworks display in history – brought even more development, this time in the form of skyscrapers that made good use of the steel industry and spawned many building contests to see who could reach higher into the sky. The Flatiron Building (p119), Woolworth Building (p83) and Chrysler Building (p124) held the title briefly, all to be eventually outdone by yet another architect with vision. New York was home to nearly 70 skyscrapers by 1902.

FACTORY TRAGEDY, WOMEN'S RIGHTS

Wretched factory conditions – low pay, long hours, abusive employers – in the early 20th century were illuminated with a tragic event in 1911. It was the infamous Triangle Shirtwaist Company fire (see the boxed text, p36) when rapidly spreading flames caught onto the factory's piles of fabrics and killed nearly 150 of 500 women workers who were trapped behind locked doors. The event led to sweeping labor reforms after 20,000 female garment workers marched to City Hall. At the same time, suffragists held street-corner rallies to obtain the vote for women. Nurse and midwife Margaret Sanger opened the first birth-control clinic in Brooklyn, where 'purity police' promptly arrested her. After her release from jail in 1921, though, she formed the American Birth Control League (later Planned Parenthood), providing services for young women and researching methods of safe birth control.

THE JAZZ AGE

All this sassiness paved the way for what came to be known as the Jazz Age, when Prohibition outlawed the sale of alcohol, encouraging bootlegging and speakeasies, not to mention organized crime. James Walker was elected mayor in 1925, ruling with pizzazz during a time when jazz

1883	1886	1904
The Brooklyn Bridge, which was built at a cost of $15.5 million (and 27 lives) opens; 150,000 people to walk across its span at the inaugural celebration.	The Statue of Liberty's pedestal is completed, allowing the large lady to be presented to New York at a dedication ceremony that takes place before thousands of citizens.	Luna Park in Coney Island opens, followed by Dreamland amusement park; meanwhile, the IRT subway carries its first 150,000 passengers – each of whom pay a nickel to ride – on its very first day of operation.

ruled, Babe Ruth reigned at Yankee Stadium and the Great Migration from the South led to the Harlem Renaissance, when the neighborhood became the center of African American culture and society. It turned out poetry, music, painting and an innovative attitude that continues to influence and inspire. This is where the Apollo Theater (p162), still humming on 125th St, began its famous Amateur Night; the venue has boosted the careers of unknowns such as Ella Fitzgerald, James Brown and the Jackson Five. Harlem's daring nightlife in the 1920s and '30s attracted the flappers and gin-soaked revelers that marked the complete failure of Prohibition. Indeed, the Jazz Age seems to have taught women to smoke, drink and dance at speakeasies, a foretaste of the liberated nightlife that New Yorkers still enjoy today (although they are forced to smoke on the street outside bars now).

HARD TIMES

The fun times were not to last, though, as the stock market crashed in 1929, beginning the Great Depression of the 1930s, which the city dealt with through a combination of grit, endurance, rent parties, militancy and a slew of public works projects. The once-grand Central Park blossomed with shacks, derisively called Hoovervilles, after the president who refused to help the needy. But Mayor Fiorello LaGuardia found a friend in President Franklin Roosevelt, and worked his Washington connections to great effect to bring relief money – and subsequent prosperity – home. Riverside Park (p154) and the Triborough Bridge are just two of the still functioning monuments of New Deal projects brought to New York by the Texas-born, Yiddish-speaking son of an Italian bandmaster.

WWII brought troops galore to the city, ready to party down to their last dollar in Times Sq, before being shipped off to Europe. Converted to war industries, the local factories hummed, staffed by women and African American workers who had rarely before had access to these good unionized jobs. The explosion of wartime activity led to a huge housing crunch, which brought New York its much-imitated and tenant-protecting Rent Control Law.

But there were few evident controls on business, as Midtown bulked up with skyscrapers after the war. The financial center marched north, even while the banker David Rockefeller and his brother Governor Nelson Rockefeller dreamed up the Twin Towers to revitalize downtown.

ENTER ROBERT MOSES

Working with LaGuardia to usher the city into the modern age was Robert Moses, an urban planner who would influence the physical shape of the city more than anyone else in the 20th century – either wonderfully or tragically, depending on whom you ask. He was the mastermind behind the Triborough Bridge, Jones Beach State Park (p376), the Verrazano-Narrows Bridge, the West Side Hwy and the Long Island parkway system – not to mention endless highways, tunnels and bridges, which shifted this mass-transit area into one largely dependent on the automobile. His vision was one of doing away with intimate neighborhoods of brownstones and townhouses and of creating sweeping parks and soaring towers. The approach got preservationists fired up, and their efforts to stop him from bulldozing neighborhoods led to the Landmarks Preservation Commission being formed in 1965. His years of work were documented in the 1974 Pulitzer Prize–winning book *The Power Broker*, by Robert Caro, which portrayed Moses as an anti-preservationist who had callously removed huge numbers of residents from ghettos to make way for development. He responded with the following statement: 'I raise my stein to

1919	1931	1941
The Yankees acquire slugger Babe Ruth from Boston, leading to their first championship. Red Sox fans will use 'The Curse of the Bambino' to explain their 85-year-long losing streak, finally reversed in 2004.	The Empire State Building (1454ft tall) is built in 410 days, superseding the Chrysler Building as the world's tallest skyscraper; it will remain as such until the World Trade Center's north tower is completed in 1972.	Duke Ellington's band leader Billy Strayhorn, inspired by the subway line that leads to Harlem, composes 'Take the A Train,' which becomes the band's signature song.

FIVE NEW YORKERS WHO CHANGED HISTORY

- Margaret Sanger (1879–1966), a nurse and midwife who worked with poor women on the Lower East Side, was a birth-control activist who opened the first birth-control clinic in the country here in 1916, causing her arrest for being a 'public nuisance.' Outcries over her many prosecutions helped changed birth-control laws in favor of women's choice. She eventually founded the first World Population Conference in Geneva and what would become today's Planned Parenthood.

- Jane Jacobs (1917–2006), a Greenwich Village resident and organizer with no formal city planning training, was spurred into action by Robert Moses' plan to clear a huge tract of her neighborhood for public housing. She defended preservation, inspired the creation of the Landmarks Preservation Commission (the first such US group) and wrote a much lauded book, *Death and Life of Great American Cities*, the first open attack on Urban Renewal and an inspiration to proponents of New Urbanism everywhere.

- Sylvia Rivera (1951–2002), born Rey Rivera Mendoza, was a transgender activist known for helping to spark the modern gay-rights movement by throwing the first of many Molotov cocktails at police officers following a routine raid on the gay Stonewall Inn (p343). The fighting back sparked the Stonewall Riots and landed the weeklong event in history books. She later worked on a campaign for a gay civil rights bill and housed many queer homeless youths. Upon her deathbed, Rivera had friends promise to continue running the shelter, which still exists, as Sylvia's Place.

- Run-DMC, the three-member rap group – Joseph 'Rev Run' Simmons, Daryl 'DMC' McDaniels and Jason 'Jam Master Jay' Mizell – grew up together in Hollis, Queens, and were extremely influential in the early days of hip-hop in the 1980s. Their 1986 album *Raising Hell* became the best-selling rap album in history (though it was later outdone as rap grew in popularity) and reached number six on the Billboard charts.

- Christine Quinn (b 1967) became the first open lesbian – and female – to become City Council Speaker in 2006, breaking boundaries of both gender and sexuality, as the second most powerful official (after mayor) in the NYC. She first served for seven years as a member of Council, and since the election by her peers she has been an outspoken proponent for equal rights and was expected, at the time of writing, to run for mayor in 2009.

the builder who can remove ghettos without removing people as I hail the chef who can make omelets without breaking eggs.'

BEATS & GAYS

The '60s ushered in an era of legendary creativity and anti-establishment expression, with many of its creators centered right downtown in Greenwich Village. One movement was Abstract Expressionism, a large-scale outbreak of American painters – Mark Rothko, Jackson Pollock, Lee Krasner, Helen Frankenthaler and Willem de Kooning among them – who offended and intrigued with incomprehensible squiggles and blotches and exuberant energy. Then there were the writers, such as Beat poets Allen Ginsberg and Jack Kerouac or novelist/playwright Jane Bowles, who gathered in Village coffeehouses to exchange ideas and find inspiration, which were often found in the form of folk music from some burgeoning big names, such as Bob Dylan. It all created an environment that was ripe for rebellion – a task that gay revelers took on with gusto, finding their political strength and voice in fighting a police raid at the Stonewall Inn (p343) in 1969. The Stonewall Riots, as they are now known, showed the city and the world that the lesbian and gay community would not accept being treated as second-class citizens.

1945	1961	1963
The United Nations, headquartered on Manhattan's east side, is established after representatives of 50 countries meet in San Francisco to agree on a charter.	Nineteen-year-old folk singer Bob Dylan arrives in NYC during a snowstorm, catches a subway to the Village and plays a set of Woody Guthrie tunes at Cafe Wha? on his first night in town.	The original Penn Station – a 1910 Beaux-Arts masterpiece designed by McKim, Mead and White – is demolished to build a new sports arena (today's Madison Square Garden); public outcry leads to the foundation of the Landmarks Preservation Commission.

'DROP DEAD'

By the early 1970s deficits had created serious fiscal crisis here, demoting the elected Mayor Abraham Beame to a figurehead, and turning over the city's real financial power to Governor Carey and his appointees. President Ford's refusal to lend federal aid – summed up nicely by the *Daily News* headline 'Ford to City, Drop Dead!' – marked the nadir of relationships between the US and the city it loved to hate. As massive layoffs decimated the city's working class, untended bridges, roads and parks reeked of hard times. Even the bond raters turned their thumbs down on New York's mountain of debt.

But the traumatic '70s – which reached a low point in 1977 with a citywide blackout and the existence of terrorizing serial killer Son of Sam – actually drove down rents for once. It helped to nourish an exciting alternative culture that staged performances in abandoned schools, opened galleries in unused storefronts and breathed new life into the hair-dye industry. The fees from shooting the movie *Fame* at PS 122 (p314) at 9th St and First Ave, for example, helped pay for the renovation of the still-popular performance space. Blue-haired punks turned former warehouses into pulsing meccas of nightlife, transforming the former industrial precincts of SoHo and Tribeca. Immortalized in Nan Goldin's famous photographic performance piece *The Ballad of Sexual Dependency,* this lowlife renaissance bent gender roles into pretzels and turned the East Village into America's center of tattooing and independent filmmaking.

OUT OF THE ASHES

Meanwhile, in South Bronx, a wave of arson reduced blocks of apartment houses to cinders. But amid the smoke, an influential hip-hop culture was born both here and in Brooklyn, fueled by the percussive rhythms of Puerto Rican salsa. Rock Steady Crew, led by 'Crazy Legs' Richie Colon, pioneered athletic, competitive break-dancing. Kool DJ Herc spun vinyl for break beat all-night dance parties, drawing on his Jamaican apprenticeship in appropriated rhythms. Afrika Bambaataa, another founding DJ of hip-hop, formed Zulu Nation, to bring DJs, break-dancers and graffiti writers together to end violence. Daring examples of the latter dazzled the public with their train-long graphics. Perhaps the best-known 'masterpiece' belied the graf writers' reputation as vandals: Lee 163, with the Fab 5 crew, painted a whole car of trains with the message 'Merry Christmas, New York.' Some of these maestros of the spray can infiltrated the art world, most notably, Jean-Michel Basquiat, once known by his tag 'Samo,' who hung with Andy Warhol and sold with the big boys in the go-go art world of the 1980s.

Some of the easy money snagged in the booming stock markets of the 1980s was spent on art, but even more was blown up the noses of young traders. While Manhattan neighborhoods struggled with the spread of crack cocaine, the city reeled from the impact of addiction, citywide crime, and an AIDS epidemic that cut through communities. Mayor Edward Koch could barely keep the lid on the city as homelessness burgeoned and landlords converted cheap old single-room hotels into luxury apartments. Squatters in the East Village fought back when police tried to clear a big homeless encampment, leading to the Tompkins Sq Park riots of 1988. Hard to imagine that just a few years later, Manhattan would yet again become the shiny apple of prosperity's eye.

DOT-COM DAYS

A *Time* magazine cover in 1990 sported a feature story on 'New York: The Rotting Apple.' Still convalescing from the real estate crash at the end of the 1980s, the city faced crumbling bridges and

1976–7	1977	1980
David Berkowitz, the 'Son of Sam' killer, says a demon in a dog told him to commit a string of murders around the city; using a .44 revolver, he kills six and wounds seven others.	Following a lightning strike at a power substation, a summer blackout leaves New Yorkers in the dark for 24 sweltering hours, which leads to rioting around the city.	Deranged gunman Mark David Chapman kills John Lennon in front of the Beatle's home at the Dakota, on Manhattan's Upper West Side; five years later, the Strawberry Fields memorial to Lennon is dedicated nearby in Central Park.

FIVE TURNING POINTS IN NYC HISTORY

- **Commissioners Plan of 1811** (March 22, 1811) – Orderly but bland, squashing the motley heights and valleys of Manhattan into a flat checkerboard, the plan imposed a grid on a city that had yet to develop above Houston St. It did make city navigation a cinch for strangers. But the plan also forestalled agreeable variety, in the name of creating tidier and more marketable rectangular bundles of real estate.

- **Triangle Shirt Waist Fire** (March 25, 1911) – A tossed cigarette probably ignited the raging inferno in the top stories of a sweatshop full of young immigrant women. The terrified garment makers collapsed at a locked door to the staircase; the owners had fastened it to prevent employee pilfering. Within minutes, dozens of workers had jumped from the 9th floor. The death toll of 146 spurred public sympathy for workers, and new safety codes to prevent a repetition. Today firefighters avoid sleeping on high floors because they know the limits of ladders and hoses.

- **Dodgers Leave Brooklyn** (1957) – The borough's favorite baseball team got its name from fans dodging trolleys that turned around near its playing field. When owner Walter O'Malley moved the team to Los Angeles, cries of pain and rage echoed across the east. Did this mean the end of great cities and their valiant athletic teams? Only two years earlier the Dodgers had finally won the World Series against hated rivals, the Yankees. Since the Dodgers (and Manhattan's Giants) moved to California, many sports-team owners have yanked their teams out to suburban stadiums with big parking lots. And many more threaten to do so, in an intricate game of blackmail to force cities to build new facilities.

- **Demolition of Pennsylvania Station** (1963) – Despite public outcry, the magnificent McKim, Mead and White Pennsylvania Station, built in 1910, was demolished. The grand structure modeled on the Roman baths of Caracalla was replaced by the current underground maze. Architectural historian Vincent Scully summed up the difference saying, 'one entered the city like a god…now one scuttles in like a rat.' The infamous preservation defeat led directly to New York City's Landmarks Law in 1965. Jacqueline Kennedy Onassis was a member of the Landmarks Commission when it prevented a repeat demolition of Grand Central Terminal in the 1970s (p128).

- **The Closing of CBGB** (2006) – For 33 years, Hilly Kristal's East Village dive fostered rockers including Patti Smith, the Ramones, Johnny Thunders and Debbie Harry, while at the same time nourishing the alternative scene in a usually fickle city. Rising rents had threatened to close the club for years, but frequent rallies, often bolstered by the musicians who had come up in the music world with Hilly's help, kept postponing the end. Finally, a doubled rent rate proved to be too much, and masses descended on the place for its final show, which starred Patti Smith. CBGB is still being mourned, and is looked to by many as the final blow to an already gentrified neighborhood where money is now valued more than creativity.

roads, jobs leaking south, and Fortune 500 companies hopping the rivers to suburbia. And then the dot-com market roared in, turning geeks into millionaires and the New York Stock Exchange into a speculator's fun park. Buoyed by tax receipts from IPO (initial public offering) profits, the city launched a frenzy of building, boutiquing and partying unparalleled since the 1920s.

With pro-business, law-and-order Rudy Giuliani as mayor, the dingy and destitute were swept from Manhattan's yuppified streets to the outer boroughs, leaving room for Generation X to score digs and live the high life. Abrasive, aggressive and relentless, Mayor Giuliani grabbed headlines with his campaign to stamp out crime, even kicking the sex shops off notoriously seedy 42nd St. The energetic mayor succeeded in making New York America's safest large city, by targeting high crime areas, using statistics to focus police presence, and arresting subway gate-crashers, people committing a minor infringement of city law but who often had other

1988	2001	2002
Crowds of squatters, who had turned the East Village's Tompkins Square Park into a massive homeless encampment, riot when cops attempt to forcibly remove them from their de facto home.	On September 11, terrorist hijackers fly two planes into the Twin Towers, destroying the World Trade Center and killing nearly 2800 people.	After outliving many of his other mobster contemporaries, Gambino crime family boss John Gotti, aka 'the Dapper Don,' dies of throat cancer in prison, where he was serving a sentence for murder, racketeering, tax evasion and other charges.

charges pending. So, in the 1990s crime dropped, powering a huge appetite for nightlife in the city that never sleeps. Restaurants boomed in the spruced-up metropolis, Fashion Week gained global fame and *Sex and the City* beamed a vision of sophisticated singles in Manolos around the world.

Meanwhile, to the delight of unionized plumbers, electricians and carpenters, real estate prices sizzled, setting off a construction spree of new high-rises, converted warehouses and rejuvenated tenements. Throwing off the uncertainty of the era of David Dinkins, a cautious politician who was NYC's first African American mayor, New Yorkers flaunted the new wealth. Areas of the Lower East Side that housed artist storefront galleries in the 1970s and '80s morphed overnight into blocks of gentrified dwellings with double-door security and maintenance charges equal to normal humans' take-home pay.

Those left behind seldom seemed to bother the mayor. No new housing for ordinary people was built, but plenty of solid apartment stock disappeared from the rent rolls, as landlords converted rentals into pricey cooperative buildings. And yet the city's population grew and grew, as ambitious young graduates flocked to the financial center. At the new Ellis Island – JFK airport – customs officials greeted wave after wave of Southeast Asians, South Americans and other immigrants willing to double up in cramped quarters in the outer boroughs. Still, things were faltering in the New York at the dawn of the new millennium, and when that fateful day came in 2001, it forever changed the perspective of both the city and the world.

SEPTEMBER 11

September 11, 2001, was the day terrorists flew two hijacked planes into the World Trade Center's Twin Towers, turning the whole complex into dust and rubble and killing nearly 2800 people in the process. Downtown Manhattan took months to recover from the ghastly fumes wafting from the ruins of the World Trade Center, as forlorn missing-person posters grew ragged on brick walls. While recovery crews coughed their way through the debris, the city braved constant terrorist alerts and an anthrax scare to mourn the dead. Shock and grief drew people together, and united the oft-fractious citizenry in a determined effort not to succumb to despair. Before the year was out, community groups were already gathering together in 'Imagine New York' workshops, to develop ideas for renewal and a memorial at the World Trade Center site (p56). Still, good times were already faltering before the attack, which ushered in a period of high unemployment and tightened belts for everyone.

SHINY HAPPY HIGHRISES

In 2002 Mayor Michael Bloomberg began the unenviable task of picking up the pieces of a shattered city that had (finally) thrust all its support behind his predecessor, longtime controversial mayor Rudy Giuliani, whose popularity rose after his reaction to September 11. Wrangling for his own rep, Bloomberg found his critics during his four-year campaign to build a huge sports arena atop the West Side Hwy, in order to bring the Jets back from Jersey and score a bid for the 2012 Olympic Games. All three failed after Albany said 'no' to a $2.2 billion project (to the cheer of many a New Yorker fearing traffic build-up and cost), but Bloomberg didn't take a dent in the 2005 elections, comfortably topping the Bronx Democrat Fernando Ferrer.

The boom in NYC probably didn't hurt his bid for re-election. For one thing, tourism picked up its pace by 2005, when receipts beat pre–September 11 levels and hotel prices and

2005	2007	2008
Following a feverish bid by the group NYC 2012, founded by local rich guy Daniel Doctoroff, the city loses its bid for the 2012 Olympics – to the great relief of the majority of New Yorkers.	The New Museum of Contemporary Art – the first and only New York museum dedicated to contemporary art – causes a big buzz when it opens on the Lower East Side.	Former NYC Mayor Rudy Giuliani, who had decided to take on fellow New York Senator Hillary Clinton, ends his campaign bid for the White House after early disappointments in the primary race.

occupancy rates reached record heights. The Museum of Modern Art (p137) refurbished itself into a bigger, more beautiful version of itself. And plenty of 'un–New York' projects rushed out of the gate in the wake of September 11. One, both exotic and controversial, was the boom in malls and Texas-sized department chains. The Shops at Columbus Circle opened in 2003, with 'upscale' boutiques designed to draw in the stroller-pushers from neighboring Central Park. Sixth Ave became, cynics would say, a super-sized ghetto, with Best Buy and Home Depot opening up. Lower East Side hipsters were outraged when Starbucks opened on Delancey St in 2005. Downtown Brooklyn chimed in too, with the 2004 opening of a Target right off Flatbush Ave. The prime example of this un–New York movement, perhaps, was its setting in 2004 for the Republican National Convention, where 400,000 protested the president, the war and the clean-cut suits in Madison Square Garden. But the Republicans carried the victory banner in the national elections anyway.

Preservation of the past has never been a strong New York trait, and in 2006 the landmark downtown-rock shrine CBGB closed its doors after its rent more than doubled. Similar tales are told all around the city, as a massive influx of national chains – banks, drugstores and retail outlets like Old Navy and Dunkin' Donuts – constantly push indie bookstores, cafés and music shops out of business. The entire city seems to be under construction, as luxury high-rise condos are built at an alarming rate in every neighborhood, leaving many longtime New Yorkers wondering just where their diverse, creative and fostering city has gone. Still, they hold onto the hope that it hasn't gone far, planting their feet in harder than ever before until everything swings back their way.

ARTS

Talk to just about anyone in today's NYC art world – anyone on the creative, rather than business end, that is – and you'll tap into sentiments that are rather on the bitter side, with large doses of nostalgia tossed in. Visual-arts folks will tell you that the big contemporary-art museums – the Whitney (p143), MoMA (p137), the Guggenheim (p144) – are aging giants that continually avoid radicalism in favor of what's safe and beautiful and loved by the masses. 'It would be unfair to expect the Modern to play the same cultural role it did in the 1930s, when it was probably the single most powerful force in introducing Americans to European Modernism,' noted a *New York Times* critic in an excited preview of the New Museum of Contemporary Art. 'Yet as these institutions have quietly receded into middle age, they have left a void in the heart of the city.' Folks will almost always add that nothing has been the same since the '80s, when creative types could afford to live here, toiling away until stumbling into their big break and being lauded for having unique, even controversial vision. Talk to theater people and you'll hear a similar tale, about how soaring production costs have pressured producers to take on shows that are 'safe,' and more likely to do well at the box office. It's the same with the music scene, which complains that a lack of great venues (the closing of the legendary CBGB being the most recent example, see the boxed text on p36) has been a struggle for those who want to get their sound out there. It's a conservative tide that's sent many creative types heading for more cutting-edge cities, such as Berlin.

But wait! What about NYC being the arts capital of the world? Don't worry. Because for every negative voice in the creative world, there are 10 positive ones that will point to the amazing up-and-coming artists that *are* here, or to the off-off-Broadway shows that *do* get produced and succeed, or the musicians who create a buzz in the dingiest of venues only to zoom to the forefront of the scene and get reviewers frothing at the mouth in a few month's time. Plus there is a spate of new venues – the New Museum of Contemporary Art (p99), the just-moved Museum of Arts & Design (p138) and the still-under-construction Lincoln Center (p152) among them, along with older, edgy venues that just keep wowing, like Brooklyn's St Ann's Warehouse (p314) and the just-moved Galapagos Art Space (p299), or the ever-expanding Chelsea art galleries (p114) – that keeps the artistic scene fresh and buoyant. You'll quickly learn that it's all just a matter of relativity, and that creative excitement waxes and wanes here as much as politics or the economy.

New Yorkers are also fortunate to have a mayor who is very much a supporter of the arts. Michael Bloomberg has quietly supported the cause ever since he first took office, reviving arts awards that had been forgotten since the '80s, greatly minimizing budget cuts to the Department

of Cultural Affairs, borrowing sculptures and paintings from city museums for p[...]
at Gracie Mansion at City Hall, and, most significantly, making 'anonymous d[...]
groups from his personal fortune to make up for where the city's budget has b[...]

PAINTING & VISUAL ARTS

While the landscape for artists has certainly changed over the decades – with high r[...]
so-called starving artists to be more creative about resources than ever before (o[...] simply
be trust-fund kids from the start) – hot new contemporary works are not so hard to find.
You just have to know where to look. The center of the gallery scene still lies in Chelsea (see
www.chelseaartgalleries.com for a definitive list of what's there), which has close to 250 art
spaces in its neighborhood alone and there are big names such as Matthew Marks and Barbara
Gladstone among them. Many decry the 'Chelseafication' of the gallery scene, though, saying
that it's too slick, too dealer driven and too sprawling; it would take about a week to see every
space. And though the neighborhood's power is undeniable, as well as incredibly diverse, the
backlash (and skyrocketing rents) has led to smaller pockets of edgier galleries popping up in
other neighborhoods, mainly the Lower East Side, Williamsburg, Brooklyn, Long Island City
and other parts of Queens. Soon, some art critics predict, the only galleries left in Chelsea

will be the blue-chip spaces, which own their buildings; scrappier ones will be forced to move out – especially once the High Line (p115) arrives, which is sure to drastically alter the neighborhood's character. Up-and-coming artists will continue to create and show their wares, though, as an always-changing list of ones to watch, including photographer Hanna Liden, sculptor Gedi Sibony and installation artist Josephine Meckseper, continues to thrill viewers, buyers and reviewers alike.

Art museums have seen some excitement of their own recently. The biggest news has been the opening of the New Museum of Contemporary Art (p99), on the Lower East Side, which had reviewers in a tizzy for months after its unveiling. And while there haven't been any other brand-new art palaces, plenty have either expanded, renovated or moved, including the Museum of Art & Design (p138), the Guggenheim (p144), El Museo del Barrio (p162), the Museum of Comic & Cartoon Art (p87) and the Brooklyn Museum (p184), which recently opened a new wing, the Elizabeth A Sackler Center for Feminist Art. But it's still the biggies – the Met (p141), MoMA (p137) and the Whitney (p143) – that generate the most crowds.

The story of the fickle and shifting art gallery scene is not a new one, with the earliest galleries opening on and around 57th St because it was in the vicinity of the immensely popular Museum of Modern Art. Opened in 1929 as a challenge to the conservative policies of traditional museums (such as those of the Met), MoMA spawned a slew of smaller spaces, such as the galleries owned by Julien Levy and Peggy Guggenheim, which showed the progressive work of artists including Mark

top picks

GREAT NYC ART SPACES

The Met and MoMA are world-class art repositories; Chelsea's got 250 galleries in one little area. But some of New York City's premier art moments can also be had at the following local faves.

- New Museum of Contemporary Art (p99) The new Lower East Side home of cutting-edge art is housed in an architectural wonder.
- PS1 Contemporary Art Center (p202) MoMA's cooler cousin, located in Long Island City, Queens, is a hulking old school filled with edgy contemporary works.
- Drawing Center (p90) Located in SoHo since 1977, this is the only nonprofit gallery in the country to focus exclusively on drawing.
- Frick Collection (p144) Skip the crowds, not the classics, at this quiet uptown gem.
- International Center of Photography (p138) Constant stunning exhibitions here are a must for shutterbug fans.
- Jewish Museum (p145) Displaying not only Judaica, this institution has impressive blockbusters of diverse painters and sculptors.
- Neue Galerie (p145) Fans of Klimt and Schiele should not miss this intimate space, housed in a former Rockefeller mansion.
- Socrates Sculpture Park (p202) This alfresco waterfront park is filled with large-scale, climbable works by Mark di Suvero and rotating exhibitors.
- Queens Museum of Art (p205) Located in Flushing Meadows Corona Park in Queens, exhibits here provide a fresh new perspective.

...d Jackson Pollock. The scene moved uptown for a while during the pop-art move-...of the '50s, and then shifted down to the East Village, when showcases for the second ...eration of Abstract Expressionism opened along East 10th St. Andy Warhol gained notoriety for his Marilyn Monroe and Campbell's soup can images during this period, displaying much of his work in the early '60s before opening his infamous Factory. It was during this time and scene that the genre of video art began to build in popularity, with artists like Nam June Paik, Vito Hannibal Acconci and Warhol himself showing that art could truly come to life. Today video art has morphed largely into multimedia art, with installations always found in contemporary retrospectives such as the Whitney Biennial; current New Yorkers working within the genre include Marcin Ramocki and Christian Marclay.

After the East Village art scene had run its course, however, an entrepreneur by the name of Paula Cooper moved all the fun into SoHo when she opened the first commercial gallery on Wooster St in 1969. It launched a neighborhood revolution, as artists flocked to SoHo lofts that worked as both living and working spaces, and galleries opened here en masse. The year 1980 brought the scene back to the East Village for a while, where galleries brandished a highly ironic set of works that actually helped to bring about the swift gentrification of the 'hood. It ended as suddenly as it had begun, jump-starting a brief SoHo revival which ended in 1993, when high rents forced the art crowd into West Chelsea, a barren area that was ripe for taking over. And so it goes.

Public Art

Art that graces public spaces has a rich history in NYC that's getting richer with the support of the Bloomberg administration. It's a tradition that reached its peak most recently in 2008 with *The New York City Waterfalls* – a much-touted installation by Olafur Eliasson that consisted of four artificial waterfalls, created at locations in Brooklyn, Manhattan and Governor's Island, which were all lit up at night for full effect. It had not yet opened at the time of writing, but was expected to make as big a splash, if not a bigger one, than that of 2005's *The Gates*, by Christo and Jeanne-Claude, which unfurled 7500 bright-orange sheets of heavy fabric from high gates suspended over 23 miles of footpaths in Central Park. Not everyone loved it, but it got people talking about art – and going to check it out, if only out of curiosity – turning it into a public-art event of massive proportion.

The Waterfalls was a project of the nonprofit Public Art Fund (www.publicartfund .org) – an organization dedicated to working with both established and emerging artists to

top picks

NYC PUBLIC ART

Nearly every park and neighborhood has something cool to look at in its public spaces – including art! This mini-guide will help you find some of the most notable:

- The Sphere Fritz Koenig's ball of bronze, meant to symbolize world peace through trade, moved to Battery Park from the World Trade Center after it sustained damage but survived the September 11 attacks.
- Alamo Tony Rosenthal's balancing cube, made of 1800 pounds of Cor-Ten steel, is in Astor Place (p109), and it spins if you turn it with some muscle.
- Reclining Figure Henry Moore's form sits within the reflecting pool at Lincoln Center (p152).
- NYC Manhole Covers Lawrence Weiner's collection of 19 arty covers south of Union Square (p120) bear the phrase: 'In direct line with another and the next.'
- Subway Map Floating on a New York Sidewalk Francoise Schein's 87ft-long work is a delight to look down on; it's embedded in a sidewalk in front of 110 Greene St (between Prince and Spring Sts) in SoHo.
- Mohandas K Gandhi Statue This beautiful likeness by Kantilal Patel stands in Union Square Park (p120).
- Fashion Center Information Kiosk (see p132) Claes Oldenburg designed this huge and whimsical button, held upright with a 31ft needle at the kiosk.
- Botero Sculptures Several towering, bulbous nudes by Fernando Botero stand guard within the confines of the Time Warner Center (p139).
- Unisphere A 140ft-high globe created by the US Steel Corporation in honor of the 1964–65 World's Fair, it's a symbol of unity that sits in Flushing Meadows Corona Park (p204), Queens.
- Eleanor Roosevelt Penelope Jencks' figure of the first lady, who lived for a time in NYC, leans contemplatively at the southern end of Riverside Park (p154), at 72nd St and Riverside Dr.

GRAFFITI & STREET ART

Graffiti art, as we know it, is a movement that began in the 1960s, mostly through 'writers' using public property to make political statements, and through gang members marking their turf. Early writers were mostly known for their work on subway cars. Tag styles began to quickly evolve, both in style and scale, as a way for writers to distinguish themselves. Early recognition of graffiti as an art form came from scholars and articles, namely in the *New York Times*. NYC's fiscal crisis of the mid '70s gave rise to the height of graffiti, thanks to a poorly maintained transit system; images from that day have been so long-lasting that it's often those tagged-up cars that many tourists expect to still find.

They won't find them, though, as the Transit Authority made eliminating tag art – known by detractors as vandalism – a priority. Diehards remained throughout the antigraffiti climate of the '80s and '90s and, though many believed that tagging transit spaces was the only real way to go, the hip-hop movement gave rise to writers springing up all over town, adding to the mix colorful mural art on the sides of buildings, bridges, rooftops and various hard-to-reach places. The movement even gave rise to some 'legitimate' pop artists, including Keith Haring and Jean-Michel Basquiat.

Today there's a split between renegade street artists and graffiti that's been co-opted by the art scene and become a serious business. A recent, fascinating example of this occurred in 2007, when a new type of renegade was going around the city and anonymously vandalizing graffiti – formerly known as vandalism – with bold splashes of what seemed to be house paint. The vandal would leave messages about 'Euthanizing your Bourgeois Fad,' and the serial splashings caused quite an uproar among the street-art scene, with some hating the mystery tagger and others impressed by his or her revolutionary vision.

The best places to glimpse renegade street art are in the outer boroughs, mainly in South Bronx and in Queens, from the elevated 7 train before and after the Hunters Point Ave station. There are several options for more organized viewings. Exhibit 1A Gallery (Map pp158–9; 147th St at Eighth Ave) is the city's first all-graffiti art gallery, housed in a residential building, and shows 'Graffiti Uptown: You Can't Shut Us Down' every year in November; check www.graffiti.org for upcoming events. Finally, there's the Graffiti Hall of Fame (Map p142; 106th St & Park Ave, East Harlem), founded by Ray Rodriguez and consisting of murals on walls of the schoolyard of Junior High School 13; special annual exhibits are held here each summer. For more information on tagging artists and history, visit Streets Are Saying Things (www.streetsaresayingthings.com) and @149st (http://at149st.com).

present large-scale works to the public. The fund commissions new projects, works with museums to help expand beyond its gallery space (such as when it collaborates with the Whitney to place sculptures in Central Park as part of its Biennial), has open calls for innovative new works every year, and organizes an ongoing lecture series about public art. To find up-to-date locations of commissioned works, visit the website.

Mayor Bloomberg has been a great supporter of the Public Art Fund, as well as the Department of Cultural Affairs' Percent for Art, initiated in 1982 by then-mayor Edward Koch, and requiring that 1% of the city's budget for construction projects be spent on integrating art into the design or architecture of new facilities. Since its inception there have been nearly 200 such projects at public schools, libraries, parks and police stations, and projects have included Valerie Jaudon's brick-and-granite mosaic at Manhattan's police headquarters, Jorge Luis Rodriguez' bright-orange steel flower in the East Harlem Artpark (Map pp158–9; Sylvan Pl & E 120th St), and a Holocaust Memorial (Map p120; State Supreme Court, 25th St at Madison Ave) by Harriet Feigenbaum.

New Yorkers tend to get excited about public art, whose installations are welcome spots of calm creativity in an otherwise frenzied landscape. Projects also add texture to many of the city's parks, namely Central Park – not only filled with lots of permanent sculptures but hosting the always-changing projects of the Public Art Fund at its corner of Fifth Ave at 60th St. The small Madison Square Park (p121) is also known for its rotating outdoor exhibits, part of a popular 'Mad Sq Art' project that has brought shiny steel trees by Roxy Paine, orange steel-beam sculptures by Mark di Suvero and a concrete wall of towers by Sol Lewitt to the park's grassy areas.

Public art can also be found in spades underground, thanks to the dazzling projects of the ongoing Arts for Transit program of the MTA (find a map with photos at www.mta.info/mta/aft). Every now and then, New Yorkers will be awakened from their commuting slumber when a new tile mosaic or sculpture appears in their regular subway station, prompting smiles and curiosity. A recent addition includes the brilliant green-and-blue glass panels *Crescendo* by Michael Ingui at the E 105th St L station, and a favorite is the collection of whimsical cast-bronze sculptures by Tom Otterness at the 14th St subway station on A, C, E and L lines – consisting of lovable, cartoonish characters that have raised chuckles out of the most jaded New Yorkers.

Still other subway art projects are remnants of the now-defunct 'Creative Stations' project of the Metropolitan Transit Authority (MTA), including a glass-wall-and-mural installation at the 28th St stop on the 6 line; colorful tile mosaics at the Bowling Green 4, 5 station; and the sonic, synthesized-music piece hanging overhead at the 34th St N, R platform.

MUSIC

You may wonder what everyone's bouncing their heads to, listening to iPods on the subway. And it could be anything, which would be in keeping with the fact that so much of the music world has built its muscle in NYC. Many people swoon over the golden days when Charlie Parker put bebop into jazz, camp hit the Broadway stage, and leather jackets and distortion pedals energized punk rock in the East Village. Office buildings have long replaced the jazz clubs of 52nd St, while CBGB has shut its legendary doors for good. But music here is far from over. NYC remains *the* destination for musicians, of all forms, looking to make it big and bend the way music is made. Remnants of all music genres are still in NYC for the taking, in the form of free summer concerts in the parks, noise fests in Red Hook and Brooklyn, indie rock galore in Williamsburg, jazz shows in original Greenwich Village clubs, and Broadway music weaving with the changes in Midtown. NYC's music, both past and present, is a look at the music of the world.

This is where post–Civil War vaudeville exploded – spurred on by 'Tin Pan Alley,' a collection of songwriters and music publishers who changed music with its contributions to ragtime blues, show tunes, folk and jazz. It's the home of Broadway and musical theater, and to composers like Irving Berlin and George Gerswhin. Then there's jazz and New York's endless roster of greats – Louis Armstrong, Duke Ellington, Charlie Parker, Miles Davis, Billie Holiday – all of whom helped establish a scene that still thrives here. Folk had a strong presence from the 1930s to the '70s, with heavy hitters like Bob Dylan and Woody Guthrie playing downtown venues. Then came rock, with up-and-comers from Elvis to Janis Joplin snagging coveted spots on the NYC-based *Ed Sullivan Show*, and other soon-to-be-biggies reigning on stages at downtown hotspots like the now-closed Bottom Line and CBGB. This was also Ground Zero for disco culture, much of it kicked off by gay men at clubs like the defunct Loft, Paradise Garage, Saint and legendary Studio 54. Even rap originated in NYC, through ad-hoc DJ soirees in the Bronx and Queens that gave rise to stars from the Sugar Hill Gang to Run-DMC.

So what's it all about today? For starters, you can still find the best of the best when it comes to all those nostalgic genres – jazz at clubs like the Village Vanguard (p306) and Birdland (p305), dance music at parties like the 718 Sessions (see the boxed text, p302) and clubs like Splash Bar (p343), and vaudeville-inspired burlesque at trendy spots such as Joe's Pub (p303) and Galapagos Art Space (p299). Broadway and classical sounds are yours for the taking at heavy-hitting venues all over town.

But there are plenty of exciting new sounds, too. While the indie-rock scene is not quite as frenzied as it was when the Strokes, Yeah Yeah Yeahs, Clap Your Hands Say Yeah or the Scissor Sisters rose out of NYC into national prominence several years ago, there's been an endless stream of noisemakers who have gained attention nationally and internationally. While the Secret Machines and Interpol are perhaps the biggest New York names these days, others include the Sightings, Yeasayer, MGMT, the Big Sleep and the curious adolescent garage-punk duo called Tiny Masters of Today – all of which are based in Brooklyn, by the way. Brooklyn is the site of several purveyors of cool when it comes to indie sounds – venues that include the fiercely popular McCarren Pool (p176), an empty Williamsburg pool used for outdoor summer shows; Warsaw at the Polish National Home (p304), housed in a Polish cultural center, and intimate rock venues including Southpaw (p304), Union Hall (p298) and Northsix (p304). Hip Manhattan venues are aplenty, with the favorites right now being the Hiro (p301) at the western edge of Chelsea, The Delancey (p303) on the Lower East Side and the new Highline Ballroom (Map p116; ☎ 212-414-5994; www .highlineballroom.com; 431 W 16th St btwn Ninth and Tenth Aves), arriving way before its overhead High Line.

Music festivals such as the No Fun Festival, an annual celebration of noise bands that recently moved from Red Hook to Manhattan's Knitting Factory (p304), and the more establishment CMJ Music Marathon bring hundreds of new bands to venues throughout NYC each October.

THEATER

The biggest, splashiest dramas and musicals are probably what's best associated with NYC's entertainment scene – mainly because the name 'Broadway' is known round the world.

But Broadway shows, while they do make up a significant portion of the local theater scene, refer strictly to productions staged in the 38 official Broadway theaters – lavish, early-20th-century jewels surrounding Times Square. Public opinion about the state of the theater changes drastically every couple of years, with some folks constantly moaning that, with constant revivals, there's just no good, original theater anymore. But then along come the new waves of innovators – musicals like *Spring Awakening*, *Wicked* and *Xanadu*, and dramas including *August: Osage County* and the *Farnsworth Invention* – and theater fans are drawn right back, excitedly wondering what might be next.

That Theater District as we see it today was begun in 1893 by Charles Frohman, who opened the Empire Theater on 40th St, beginning the shift of the district from the '30s to what would later become Times Square. That same year, the first-ever industry trade union – the National Alliance of Theatrical Stage Employees, for stagehands – was formed. By 1901 the flood of lights coming from theater facades in the area was so great that designer OJ Gude deemed the Broadway district the 'Great White Way.' Soon after, the Theater Guild began its long and distinguished history of producing big hits, from Eugene O'Neill, George Bernard Shaw and others, and musicals began to soar in quality and popularity. The first Tony Awards took place in 1947, the Theater Development Fund was established 20 years after and, by the late '80s, nearly every Broadway theater was designated as a historic landmark.

Broadway, though, doesn't tell nearly the whole story. Off-Broadway, more adventurous, less costly theater shown in houses that seat 200 to 500 people, or off-off-Broadway, even edgier, more affordable performances housed in theaters for crowds of less than 100, are both big businesses here. They often provide venues for more established actors to let their hair down a bit, and sometimes produce shows that wind up on Broadway; *Rent*, for example, premiered at the downtown New York Theater Workshop, just as *Angels in America* started at the Public Theater and *The Vagina Monologues* took off at the tiny HERE in SoHo. To see a lot of experimental theater in a short amount of time, watch for the Fringe Festival (p22; www.fringenyc.org), held in various downtown venues every August. Also in summer, usually beginning in June, is the acclaimed Shakespeare in the Park festival, produced by the Public Theater and taking place at the Delacorte Theater in Central Park. Tickets are free, but you do need to line up bright and early that morning to claim yours.

To purchase tickets for any other show in town, you can either head to the box office, or use one of several ticket-service agencies (see p310 for a list). Bargain-hunters can try to score

top pi

NYC LIVE MUSIC SC

It's all a matter of taste, of course, and depends which genres most move you. But here are some good spots for aural pleasures:

- Jazz at Lincoln Center (p139) Gorgeous, intimate spaces hover over Central Park in the Time Warner Center, with top acts from Freddy Cole to kd lang.
- Southpaw (p304) Park Slope's premiere rock spot, showcasing local and visiting bands like Imani Coppola, Dengue Fever and DJ parties like Turntables on the Hudson.
- Smoke (p306) You'll find music pros seven days a week in this tiny house of jazz uptown, near Columbia.
- Joe's Pub (p303) An intimate supper club with great sightlines and sound, this is the place to catch acts such as Erin McKeown, Toshi Reagon, Lucy Wainwright and Holcombe Waller.
- McCarren Pool (p176) This empty outdoor pool holds Billyburg crowds who pile in for big-draw shows by the likes of the Beastie Boys, Disco Biscuit and Feist.
- Hiro (Maritime Hotel, p301) Here's the place to catch acts as diverse as Taylor McFerrin and Grandmaster Flash.
- Carnegie Hall (p315) Settle into this gorgeous concert hall for symphonies, orchestras, pianists and solo artists spanning opera, folk and pop.
- Warsaw (p304) Housed in Williamsburg's Polish National Home, hipsters crowd in to catch performers such as George Clinton, Henry Rollins, Liars and Super Diamond.
- Knitting Factory (p304) Originally a jazz-only club, this multi-space venue now has just about everything else covered, too, from hard rock to punk and blues.
- Prospect Park (p181) Come summer, Celebrate Brooklyn! brings all sorts of favorites to this al fresco band shell, with recent favorites including Ani DiFranco, They Might Be Giants, Dr John and Joan Armatrading.

BACKGROUND ARTS

cks

NYC PLAYLIST

in your iPod and use
ing the city that's in-

lonelyplanet.com   Holiday

- 'Rapture' – Blondie
- 'NYC' – *Annie* musical cast recording
- 'Take the "A" Train' – Duke Ellington
- 'Cradle & All' – Ani DiFranco
- 'Chelsea Hotel No 2' – Leonard Cohen
- 'New York City Cop' – The Strokes
- 'Fight the Power' – Public Enemy
- 'New York City' – They Might Be Giants
- 'Cali to New York' – Black Eyed Peas
- 'Chelsea Morning' – Joni Mitchell
- 'Coney Island Baby' – Tom Waits
- 'Dirty Boulevard' – Lou Reed
- 'Boy From New York City' – Manhattan Transfer
- '42nd Street' – *42nd Street* musical cast recording
- 'Lullaby of Broadway' – *42nd Street* musical cast recording
- 'Frank Mills' – *Hair* musical cast recording
- 'I Happen to Like New York' – Cole Porter
- 'Into the Fire' – Bruce Springsteen
- 'La Vie Boheme' – *Rent* musical cast recording
- 'Leaving New York' – REM
- 'Me and Julio Down by the Schoolyard' – Paul Simon
- 'New York City' – Hanoi Rocks
- 'New York, New York' – Frank Sinatra

same-day standing-room tickets for sold-out shows for about $15. You'll get great views and sore feet, but you can always scope out vacant seats at intermission. In Times Sq, the TKTS booth (p313), run by the Theater Development Fund, sells same-day tickets to Broadway and off-Broadway musicals and dramas.

COMEDY, CABARET & PERFORMANCE ART

Performance art is a sort of catch-all of performance genres, anything that's not a straight-up play counts – while comedy refers to standup or sketch-comedy shows, and cabaret can mean anything from a solo artist singing standards from the piano to a troupe of drag kings and topless gals doing burlesque. And New York's got bucketfuls of all of the above.

As far as comedy goes, this city has a great history of discovering great funny people – it's the town that brought us Jon Stewart and his *Daily Show* as well as Jerry Seinfeld, Eddie Murphy and Chris Rock, who began their careers at Caroline's on Broadway. Jim Belushi, Dennis Miller, Joe Piscopo, Kevin Nealon, Dana Carvey and Tina Fey (along with many others) all had their careers launched on the hit New York series *Saturday Night Live* (p319).

Similar to many other entertainment forms here, the comedy scene is sharply divided between the big-name, big-ticket clubs and the more experimental and obscure places – which often host the best shows in town, sometimes bending the typical stand-up style to include music, burlesque or comedy sketches. For that kind of anything-goes format, check out the Upright Citizens Brigade Theatre (p300), which specializes in improv and often sees comedy celebs in its audience. Rififi Cinema Classics (Map p104; ☎ 212-677-6309; 332 E 11th St) has an innovative series as well, as does newcomer Comix (Map p116; ☎ 212-524-2500; 353 W 14th St at Ninth Ave), showcasing standup, improv, sketch comedy and music performances. Various festivals also keep you up on what's hot and funny, including the Brooklyn Underground Comedy Festival (www.thebushwickstarr.org) and the New York Comedy Festival (www.nycomedyfestival.com), held each November.

Cabaret, while it often has plenty of comedic overtones, is subtler. Usually consisting of a performer at a piano or a microphone holding court in an intimate venue, cabaret often features clever riffs or anecdotes that are just highlights to the real purpose: live music. Jazz and standards are the most popular fare, although at Theater District venues – Danny's Skylight Room, Don't Tell Mama (p299) – you'll get a big dose of Broadway show tunes. Styles also differ depending on the pricing and on whether the venue is considered 'classic,' such as Feinstein's (p299) or Café Carlyle (p299), where cabaret stars including Woody Allen, Betty Buckley and Ann Hampton Callaway sometimes grace the stage. Though all cabaret has a gay bent by its very (campy) nature, the queer feel is more evident at the Duplex (p299), where performers will often be in drag; gay bars and lounges often become ad hoc cabaret venues – such as Therapy (p344) and Splash Bar (p343), among others.

BACKGROUND ARTS

Some of the gay nightspot shows verge on performance art, although there are plenty of other places to go to find that murky genre as well. One of the hottest styles remains burlesque, which can be seen at various multi-themed venues around the city such as Galapagos Art Space (p299) and Joe's Pub (p303). La MaMa ETC (p313) and the all-women WOW Café Theater (Map p104; ☎ 212-696-8904; 59 E 4th St btwn Bowery & Second Ave), both in the East Village, are also excellent places to find burlesque, strange music revues, live soap-opera series and all-around cleverness.

CLASSICAL MUSIC & OPERA

If downtown Manhattan is home to all things contemporary – indie rock bands, clever drag shows, cutting-edge art installations and experimental dance theater – then Uptown is the refuge for more classic, timeless pursuits. A visit to the Upper West Side, a neighborhood for old-school artists, reveals this quickly enough, as musicians who make their living as cellists, bassists or tuba players for orchestras and ensembles can almost always be spotted lugging their instruments, secured in bulky, odd-shaped cases, home from the 72nd or 96th St stops on subway lines 1, 2, or 3. For a good number of them, work has probably included gigs at either the Lincoln Center (p311) complex or Carnegie Hall (p315) at one point or another, just as a fair amount have most likely studied – or at least taken a class – at one of the premier schools for classical music and opera in the country: the Juilliard School or the Manhattan School of Music, which are also host to top-notch concerts.

Lincoln Center was built in the 1960s as part of an urban renewal plan under development commissioner Robert Moses (p33), controversially clearing out a slew of slums (the ones used as the basis for *West Side Story*, actually) in the process. And what started as a questionable project for many preservationists and arts fans has largely won over much of NYC with its incomparable offerings – so much so that it's now in the midst of a massive renovation and redesign, to coincide with its 50th anniversary. Housed in the under-construction miniworld, complete with fountains and reflecting pools and wide-open spaces, are the main halls of Alice Tully, Avery Fisher, the Metropolitan Opera House (the most opulent of all the venues here) and the New York State Theater, as well as the Juilliard School, the Fiorello LaGuardia High School for the Performing Arts, and the Vivian Beaumont and Mitzi Newhouse theaters. Resident companies include the Metropolitan Opera and the New York City Opera, the New York Philharmonic, the New York City Ballet and the Chamber Music Society of Lincoln Center, among others. Its programs are far reaching, with some free offerings – such as the popular summer Concerts in the Parks series of the Philharmonic, itself founded in 1842 and America's premier orchestra, currently directed by Lorin Maazel. The Metropolitan Opera – now in an exciting period thanks to its populist general manager, Peter Gelb – has always been the grand, more classic company, while the New York City Opera is its more unique, imaginative and down-to-earth sibling.

The smaller, more contained and limited Carnegie Hall, meanwhile, is just as beloved a venue – especially since opening Zankel Hall, offering eclectic world-music and jazz sounds, and the likes of Laurie Anderson and Bobby McFerrin – beneath the main Isaac Stern Hall, whose stage has been graced by all the big names. This is the place to experience visiting orchestras from all over the world, acclaimed soloists such as pianist Alfred Brendel, small groups like the Brentano String Quartet, and big concerts including the New York Pops series. A similarly solid classical lineup can be found at the newly redesigned Merkin Concert Hall (p315), known for top-notch piano and chamber music shows.

Outside of these biggie venues, there's plenty more. But one of the main attractions is the Brooklyn Academy of Music (BAM; p315), the country's oldest academy for the performing arts, where you'll find opera seasons and concerts from its resident Brooklyn Philharmonic, which also plays for free in summer, in nearby Prospect Park. (For other classical performance venues, see p314.) To catch quality classical sounds anytime without paying a penny, tune in to one of the local radio stations that serve as community centers for lovers of the genre: the 77-year-old 96.3-FM WQXR, which is all classical all the time; and 93.9-FM WNYC, the city's local National Public Radio (NPR) affiliate, which goes classical weekdays at 2pm and 7pm and weekend evenings at 8pm.

DANCE

The past few years have been exciting for the New York dance world, with new spaces and companies bursting onto the scene like never before. Most recently came the formation of

Morphoses/The Wheeldon Company (www.morphoses.org), started by gifted New York City Ballet chore-ographer Christopher Wheeldon, shortly after he announced he was leaving his post at the ballet. And before that was the **Baryshnikov Arts Center** (450 W 37th St), a three-story interdisciplinary rehearsal and performance space in Hell's Kitchen, and the Cedar Lake Ensemble (p316), which opened a theater and studio. Still to come is a brand new space for the edgy Dixon Place (p313), which offers a healthy dose of dance along with theater, readings and performance art. The new spaces represent a change in tune from the recent past, when all new dance spaces, such as the Mark Morris Dance Group, housed in a relatively new space in Fort Greene, Brooklyn, were sent scrambling for real estate in the outer boroughs.

All dance roads have historically led to NYC. It's a place where the dance scene is really comprised of two separate halves – the classical and the modern – and its split personality is what makes it one of the most renowned dance capitals of the globe. You can see this two-spirited self by browsing dance listings, whether you're a fan or not – or you can experience it firsthand, by taking a dance class while you're in town. Almost any dance school in the city, whether it's Steps on the Upper West Side, Dance Space in SoHo or anything in between, offers a wild blend of classes – modern or jazz or some blend, or ballet, whose students are known as 'bunheads' by the modern folks. And most amateurs pick one side of the line and stick with it, similar to pros and their fans.

It all started here in the 1930s, when American classical ballet took off and laid the founda-tion for what would soon become the world-class American Ballet Theatre (ABT) and New York City Ballet. Lincoln Kirstein envisioned a US ballet for Native American dancers, and wanted them trained by the ballet masters of the world so they could create a repertory that had a built-in cast. Kirstein met the Russian-trained George Balanchine in 1933 in London, and together the two started their now legendary American school, the New York City Ballet, in New York that year, later performing with Jerome Robbins as assistant artistic director. In 1964 they opened the New York State Theater and have been its resident ballet company ever since. Since then, ballet bigwigs, including Balanchine, Robbins and Peter Martins, have choreographed dances for the troupe, which has boasted stars such as Maria Tallchief, Suzanne Farrell and Jacques D'Amboise.

Meanwhile, making its own inroads was the American Ballet Theatre (ABT), founded in NYC in 1937 by Lucia Chase and Rich Pleasant and made famous through works by Balanchine, Antony Tudor, Jerome Robbins *(Fancy Free)*, Alvin Ailey and Twyla Tharp *(When Push Comes to Shove)*. After defecting from the Soviet Union, Mikhail Baryshnikov found fame with ABT as a principal dancer in the '70s, and remained as its artistic director from 1980 to 1989 before founding his own (now-defunct) White Oak Dance Project.

Simultaneously, Martha Graham, Charles Wiedman and Doris Humphrey sowed the seeds of the NYC modern movement, which was continued here after WWII by masters including Merce Cunningham, Paul Taylor, Alvin Ailey and Twyla Tharp. Today both scenes continue to be global forces, with the more experimental, avant-garde dance world constantly growing as well – enabling you to see pretty much anything from muscle-bound women mixing circus-type trapeze acts into their performance to naked troupes rolling around on a bare stage.

Today's up-and-coming dancers continue to move in new directions, bringing their own interpretations to small downtown theaters including the Kitchen, the Joyce Theater and Dance Theater Workshop (see p316 for all venue information). And the dancers themselves, often forced to work other jobs to support themselves and their craft in such an expensive city, are remarkably supportive of each other. Dancers can apply for financial grants, studio space and other creative assistance through organizations such as the Field, Movement Research, Pentacle, New York Foundation for the Arts and Dance Theater Workshop – which hosts the Bessies, a prestigious annual awards ceremony for dancers (named after Bessie Schönberg, a highly regarded dance teacher who died in 1997).

LITERATURE

New York's lit scene goes way beyond a great selection of bookstores – mainly because so many top-notch writers reside here. Famous authors are practically a dime a dozen, as contemporary scribes including Michael Cunningham, Jonathan Ames, Tom Wolfe, Frank McCourt, Joan Didion, Jay McInerney and too many others to name all still live and write in NYC. Throw in the fact of the still-unknowns – everyone and his mother is writing a book in this town, and can be found on the active public-readings circuit – and the fact that New York is the capital of the publishing industry, and you've got yourself quite a bookish city indeed. That should come as no surprise, considering the many sources of inspiration here, coupled with a long and storied literary history.

Greenwich Village has perhaps the most glorified such history in New York, and deservedly so. Literary figures including Henry James, Herman Melville and Mark Twain lived in the Washington Sq area at the turn of the 19th century. And by 1912, the tight-knit, storied clan of John Reed, Mabel Dodge Luhan, Hutchins Hapgood, Max Eastman and other playwrights and poets wrote about bohemian life and gathered at cafés in these parts for literary salons and liquor-fueled tête-à-têtes. But when Prohibition sent too many uptowners searching for hooch downtown, the party broke up, and things remained quiet for a time, until Eugene O'Neill and his cohorts came along, followed by such luminaries as novelists Willa Cather, Malcolm Cowley, Ralph Ellison and poets ee cummings, Edna St Vincent Millay, Frank O'Hara and Dylan Thomas, who is said to have died in this 'hood after downing one too many drinks at the local White Horse Tavern in 1953.

The area is still most closely associated with the late 1950s and '60s, when the wild and wonderful Beat movement was led by William S Burroughs, Allen Ginsberg, Jack Kerouac and

NYC IN LITERATURE

Novels set in New York are naturals, as suspense, drama and action tend to come with the territory. Here, just a handful of examples.

- *Small Town* (Lawrence Block, 2002) Series master Block wrote this chilling thriller about one man's response to losing his wife in the September 11 attacks by becoming a serial killer on a vengeance spree.
- *Beebo Brinker* (Ann Bannon, 1962) As part of the classic lesbian '50s and '60s pulp fiction series, this fun, campy morsel tells the tale of the series' butch heartthrob and her navigation of gay Greenwich Village during a time when being out of the closet was unthinkable.
- *The Invention of Everything Else* (Samantha Hunt, 2008) This Brooklyn author delves back into the 1940s, creating historical fiction out of the adventures of scientist Nikola Tesla, who lived in the Hotel New Yorker. The story revolves around a time machine, a homing pigeon and the love life of a hotel chambermaid.
- *Ellington Boulevard: A Novel in A Flat* (Adam Langer, 2008) This modern-day tale links an eclectic group of New Yorkers by the 106th St building they live in, which is up for sale by a wannabe theater owner who wants to make a major real-estate deal.
- *Bonfire of the Vanities* (Tom Wolfe, 1987) The man who recorded the world of 1960s acid tests and high-class society's love affair with Black Power delved into the status-obsessed '80s with this gripping novel of an uptown investment banker's entanglement with the world of the black South Bronx.
- *Go Tell It on the Mountain* (James Baldwin, 1953) This emotional, lyrical, tight novel shares the details of just one day in the life of 14-year-old John Grimes, bringing readers into Harlem during the Depression.
- *Jazz* (Toni Morrison, 1992) Pulitzer Prize–winner Morrison explores the Harlem Jazz Age through the tales of three tragic, intersecting lives.
- *Among Other Things, I've Taken Up Smoking* (Aoibheann Sweeney, 2007) While the first half of this debut novel takes place on a lonely, atmospheric island in Maine, the second half has the story's heroine – Miranda, who has lost her mother and was raised by her father – shuttled off to NYC, where she learns her own lessons about life by falling in love.
- *Motherless Brooklyn* (Jonathan Lethem, 1999) This genius novel had a quick rise to cult status among north-Brooklyn residents, as its oddly compelling tale – of grown-up orphan Lionel Essrog, a detective with Tourette's syndrome who is investigating the death of his boss – explores crevices and histories of north Brooklyn 'hoods that newcomers never knew existed.
- *Push* (Sapphire, 1996) Brooklyn writer Sapphire's wrenching modern-age story about an abused young Harlem woman, 16-year-old Precious Jones, is almost too much to bear. But her gorgeous, honest prose pulls you through.
- *Slaves of New York* (Tama Janowitz, 1986) This real estate-obsessed collection of deadpan, quirky stories about folks living downtown in the '80s is a nostalgic glance at a time when real-life starving artists could scrape by and find their own little nests, whether in illegal lofts or dilapidated studios.
- *The Story of Junk* (Linda Yablonsky, 1997) Years after her grim existence as a heroin junkie living in the down-and-out, pre-gentrified artists' Lower East Side, Yablonsky recalls all the shocking, seedy details.

their gang. These poets and novelists rejected traditional writing forms and instead adopted rhythms of basic American speech and jazz music for their literary musings. Ginsberg is best known for *Howl,* which he wrote in 1956 as an attack on American values. Kerouac's prose, as seen in novels including *On the Road, The Subterraneans* and *The Dharma Bums,* similar to that of Burroughs *(Naked Lunch),* reflects a disdain for convention and a thirst for adventure.

In 1966 Ginsberg helped found the Poetry Project at St Mark's-Church-in-the-Bowery in the East Village, still an active, poet-staffed literary forum and resource – and sort of all-around community center – for New York writers. Ginsberg gave a historic joint reading here with Robert Lowell, and some of the many other literary legends to read here have included Adrienne Rich, Patti Smith and Frank O'Hara.

That this center took root in the East Village is one of the best proofs that intellectual, writerly activities and inspirations have never been confined to the fabled Greenwich Village. Harlem, for example, has a long literary history. James Baldwin, born in this uptown 'hood, was a black, gay, preacher's son who wrote about conflicts of race, poverty and identity in novels including *Go Tell It on the Mountain* and *Giovanni's Room,* published in the 1950s. Audre Lorde, a Caribbean American lesbian, activist and writer, was raised in Harlem and attended Columbia University. Her poetry, written mostly in the '70s, and memoir, *Zami: A New Spelling of My Name* (1982), dealt with class, race and gay and lesbian issues. Much earlier, in the 1920s, Dorothy Parker held court at the famous Algonquin Round Table – a private clique of writers who hung out and drank and talked endlessly about American culture, politics and literature. Soon, the regular gatherings – which included *New Yorker* founder Harold Ross, author Robert Benchley, playwrights George S Kaufman, Edna Ferber, Noel Coward, Marc Connelly and various critics – turned into a national amusement, as stories were written about the gatherings and tourists often came to gawk at the intellectual bunch.

In the 1980s novelists such as Bret Easton Ellis *(American Psycho)* began expounding upon the greedy, coke-fueled era. At the same time, notable poets and writers of the East Village (where Allen Ginsberg actually lived) included Eileen Myles, whose poetry and unconventional novel *Chelsea Girls* took readers into the rebellious downtown art world, as did poets Gregory Masters and Michael Scholnick.

And way before any of this, of course, came Long Island native Walt Whitman, who wrote from his home in the borough of Brooklyn, publishing *Leaves of Grass* in 1855, paving an early way for more contemporary Brooklyn authors, including Betty Smith, who wrote *A Tree Grows In Brooklyn* in 1943, and modern darling Jonathan Lethem, whose *Motherless Brooklyn* (1999) sparked new interest in the area around Cobble Hill and Brooklyn Heights. Other breakout Brooklynites of this century and the late '90s include Rick Moody *(Purple America, The Ice Storm),* who mixes suburban and urban adventure; Paul Auster *(New York Trilogy, Mr Vertigo, Timbuktu),* who writes about current-day New York; and the Augusten Burroughs *(Running With Scissors, A Wolf at the Table),* who has documented the tales of his life in moving (and amusing) literary-memoir style.

For information regarding venues where you can catch readings by authors both legendary and up-and-coming, see p321.

FILM & TELEVISION

As both a subject and venue, New York has a long and storied life in TV and the movies. At least a dozen films are in production here at any given time, while 20 prime-time TV shows *(Law & Order, Lipstick Jungle, Gossip Girl, Secret Lives of Women, What Not to Wear, 30 Rock)* are regularly produced here, along with 40 daytime and late-night shows *(All My Children, The Today Show, Saturday Night Live)* and about 30 cable shows *(Project Runway, Inside the Actors Studio, Made, The People's Court, Sesame Street).* Many of the shows are filmed not only on the city streets, but at Silvercup Studios in Long Island City, Queens, which is the largest full-service film and TV production facility in the city; it's been here since 1983. (Its large rooftop sign might look familiar – the fight scene at the end of the first *Highlander* movie was filmed here.) And, nestled in with the endless array of TV stations with homes here – NBC, ABC, CNN, MTV, the local NY1 news network, and the Food Network and Oxygen Media, both housed in the Chelsea Market – are now a couple of major film companies, including New Line Cinema (a division of Time Warner), New Yorker Films, and Miramax and Tribeca Productions (owned by Robert De Niro), both housed in the Tribeca Film Center, proving that the entire industry,

NYC ON FILM

There is a very long history of this city starring on the silver screen, with many of the images – King Kong falling from the Empire State Building, Tom Hanks dancing on the massive toy piano at FAO Schwarz in *Big* – burned forever into people's minds.

- *Sex and the City* (Directed by Michael Patrick King, 2008) The eagerly awaited screen continuation of the cult-TV favorite catches up with the famous foursome, witty as ever, whose lives are caught up with new dramas that include cheating, jilting and kids.
- *Spider-Man 3* (Directed by Sam Raimi, 2007) The third in a series of Hollywood blockbusters about the superhero has Tobey Maguire in the lead role, battling villains with NYC as a backdrop in the darkest, most action-packed film of the three.
- *Across the Universe* (Directed by Julie Taymor, 2007) Its plot involves a young man who arrives in 1960s New York and falls in love with a young woman; they wind up entrenched in the antiwar movement and each other. The visuals and the Beatles soundtrack make it quite a nice trip.
- *American Gangster* (Directed by Ridley Scott, 2007) A Harlem-based drug drama, inspired by a true story, that deals with heroin importation and an alliance with the Mafia, as well as the tale of one very honest policeman.
- *Angels in America* (Directed by Mike Nichols, 2003) Starring Al Pacino, Meryl Streep, Jeffrey Wright, this exquisite, HBO-made movie version of Tony Kushner's Broadway play recalls 1985 Manhattan: relationships are on the brink, AIDS is out of control and a closeted Roy Cohn – advisor to President Ronald Reagan – does nothing about it except fall ill himself. Follow characters from Brooklyn to Lower Manhattan to Central Park.
- *Big* (Directed by Penny Marshall, 1988) Starring Tom Hanks and Elizabeth Perkins, this seriously heartwarming tale is of a boy who gets his wish to be big. Hanks plays the bogus grown-up who becomes an executive at a toy company, creating wonderful scenes in loft apartments, glitzy restaurants and other hallmarks of 1980s NYC.
- *Chasing Amy* (Directed by Kevin Smith, 1997) Starring Ben Affleck and Joey Lauren Adams, this breakout film, though far from a cinematic masterpiece, put Meow Mix and other aspects of Manhattan lesbian life on the map.
- *Crossing Delancey* (Directed by Joan Micklin Silver, 1988) Single gal Isabelle (Amy Irving) is set up with Sam the Pickle Man (Peter Riegert) by her grandmother in a romantic comedy showing the Lower East Side before the trendies moved in.
- *Fatal Attraction* (Directed by Adrian Lyne, 1987) Starring Michael Douglas, Glenn Close and Anne Archer, this psycho thriller is about a happily married man whose one-night stand turns into a series of run-ins with his trick-turned-stalker. Catch great glimpses of the pre-gentrification Meatpacking District (and that famous lift scene).
- *Kids* (Directed by Larry Clark, 1995) Starring Leo Fitzpatrick, Chloë Sevigny and Rosario Dawson, this film is shot in documentary style with a bunch of then-unknowns and it's a chilling tale of privileged Manhattan kids growing up with no rules – downtown in the 1990s. It tackles sexual promiscuity, drugs and AIDS.
- *Manhattan* (Directed by Woody Allen, 1979) Starring Woody Allen, Diane Keaton and Mariel Hemingway. A divorced New Yorker dating a high-school student (the adorable, baby-voiced Hemingway) falls for his best friend's mistress in what is essentially a love letter to NYC. Catch romantic views of the Queensboro Bridge and the Upper East Side.
- *Party Monster* (Directed by Fenton Bailey, 2003) Starring Seth Green and Macauley Culkin, who plays the crazed, famed, murderous club kid Michael Alig, this is a disturbing look into the drug-fueled club-kid era of the late '80s in downtown NYC. The former Limelight club is featured prominently.
- *Saturday Night Fever* (Directed by John Badham, 1977) Starring John Travolta and Karen Lynn Gorney. Travolta is the hottest thing in bell-bottoms in this tale of a streetwise Brooklyn kid who becomes king of the dance floor. Great glimpses of '70s Bay Ridge.
- *Summer of Sam* (Directed by Spike Lee, 1999) Starring John Leguizamo, Mira Sorvino and Jennifer Esposito. One of Spike Lee's best films, this sordid tale puts the city's summer of 1977 in historical context by weaving together the Son of Sam murders, the blackout, racial tensions and the misadventures of one disco-dancing Brooklyn couple, including scenes at both CBGB and Studio 54.
- *Taxi Driver* (Directed by Martin Scorsese, 1976) Starring Robert De Niro, Cybill Shepherd and Jodie Foster. De Niro is a mentally unstable Vietnam-war vet whose urges to lash out are heightened by the high tensions of the city. It's a funny, depressing, brilliant classic that's a potent reminder of how much grittier this place used to be.

at least, is not confined to Hollywood. Local cable shows (there are two cable carriers, Time Warner and Cablevision) are popular forms of entertainment, with the public-access Manhattan Neighborhood Network (MNN) channel providing constant cultural programming and just plain weird shows, as the station grants airtime to just about any local resident who wants it (visit www.mnn.org for a schedule).

The Mayor's Office of Film, Theater & Broadcasting (MOFTB) has definitely been a driving force behind the success of the local industry – worth more than $5 billion and 100,000 city jobs. Spend just a little time in this city and you will most likely see the evidence of this for yourself, as it's not uncommon to happen upon on-location shoots, which often close down city blocks, blast them with floodlights at night and surround them with massive trucks and bossy assistants who'll stop you in your tracks if you try to walk through the filming area – much to the dismay of the locals, who are often barred from even going home to make dinner after a long day of work until the scene-in-session has ended! Running into local TV and film stars is also second nature to New Yorkers, who tend to look at local celebs as part of this one big family. Locals turned out in droves to mourn on the doorstep of film star Heath Ledger when he died in 2008; Brooklynites had calmly adopted him and ex-partner Michelle Williams and their baby daughter when they were still living together in Cobble Hill. Others are just as much part of the fabric here, from Julianne Moore and Sarah Jessica Parker to *Project Runway*'s dapper Tim Gunn. See the boxed text, p49, for a rundown of movies filmed on-location here.

As a showcase for film, New York is a star as well. There have been quite a few new movie theaters built over the past several years, most with stadium seating, wide screens and other glamorous amenities, such as gourmet snack stands. And the number of annual film festivals held here throughout the year just keeps rising: the number currently stands at around 30, including Dance on Camera (January), Jewish Film Festival (January), New York Film Festival (January), African American Women in Film Festival (March), Williamsburg Film Festival (March), the fast-rising Tribeca Film Festival (May), Lesbian & Gay Film Festival (June) and the Human Rights Watch Film Festival (June).

New York is home to some of the top film schools in the country – NYU's Tisch Film School, the New York Film Academy, the School of Visual Arts, Columbia University and the New School – and the students get great support from MOFTB, which offers free film permits to students for use of any public property. But you don't have to be a student to learn, as plenty of museums – namely the currently expanding Museum of the Moving Image (p203) in Astoria, Queens, and the Paley Center for Media (p129) – serve as major showcases for screenings and seminars about productions both past and present.

Finally, you can always go and get a glimpse of locations made famous from appearances in TV shows and movies, from the Dakota building (Central Park West at 72nd St), the apartment building used in the classic thriller *Rosemary's Baby*, to Tom's Diner (Broadway at 112th St), the facade of which was used regularly in *Seinfeld*. The best way to find all the spots you want to see is to take a movie- or TV-location guided tour, such as On Location Tours (p404), which takes you to spots where your favorite films and TV shows were filmed, including *The Devil Wears Prada, The Apprentice, Spider-Man* and more.

There are also a few local TV stations worth tuning into (note that the channel number varies depending on the source of programming from the TV that you're watching; options range from Cablevision and Time Warner cable providers to Direct TV satellite TV):

Manhattan Neighborhood Network (MMN; www.mnn.org; various channels) This excellent community TV station is chock-full of local entertainers, talkers and other assorted narcissists.

MSG Network (www.msgnetwork.com) The local sports station, run by Madison Square Garden, broadcasts the games of local teams, including the Yankees, Mets, Knicks, Liberty, Jets and Rangers.

New York 1 (www.ny1.com) This 24-hour local news channel, with hourly one-minute updates and 'weather on the ones', is only on Time Warner Cable's channel 1.

NYC TV (Channel 25) The city's official TV station has an excellent line-up of NYC-based programming, including 'Cool in Your Code,' which looks at the cultural perks of a neighborhood based on its zip code, and 'City Classic,' which shows old footage of protests, press conferences and special events.

Time Out On Demand (www.tony.com, Time Warner Digital channel 1112) This new interactive station of *Time Out New York* magazine has staff editors discussing culture and entertainment picks of the week.

ARCHITECTURE

It's an extremely exciting moment, architecturally speaking, for this city. While there was a time not so long ago when talking about New York architecture meant you were most likely discussing the past – the golden ages of art deco, Gothic and Greek-revival works that managed to have lasting visual impact, even as modern, soulless towers soared around them – more recent years have changed all that. New Yorkers are more interested in architecture than ever before, in part because the post–September 11 planning led to years of public forums that got folks talking and thinking about their surroundings. Architects became admired celebrities with recognized names, the most well known dubbed 'starchitects,' and getting almost as much ink in trendy local magazines as celebrity chefs (who have long achieved rock-star status). And it's been no wonder, as the amount of building going on in this city has been staggering.

A recent exhibit by the city's Architectural League, 'New New York: Fast Forward,' mapped more than 600 new building and planning projects going on throughout the five boroughs: hotels, condos, art institutions, parks and more. It was a stunning visual aid to what has begun to seem like a constant state of flux here. The sight of cranes and building frames and the sound of jackhammers and backhoes has become a permanent part of city life, but getting a grasp on the true scope of what's been getting constructed has not been easy. It proved that NYC is in the midst of an explosion of activity, and that it's looking to be not only industrious about it, but creative and, in many cases, environmentally sound.

Among the most talked-about completed projects (besides the plan for the Freedom Tower, discussed in more depth on p56) has been the New Museum of Contemporary Art (p99) on the Lower East Side, a flurry of grandiose high-end condos (many of which have touched off neighborhood controversies) and several exciting office buildings, including sleek and massive new headquarters for both The New York Times Company and Hearst Publications. Also, there is the stunning glass sculpture along the West Side Hwy in Chelsea, designed by Frank Gehry, which is the home of Barry Diller's IAC/InterActiveCorp conglomerate. But new ones just keep on a-comin', with the most highly anticipated works including 53 W 53rd, a luxury skyscraper by Jean Nouvel that will tower 75 stories above MoMA.

PAST BUILDING THRILLS

Of course, this is not the first time in history that the city has been enlivened by lovely architectural additions. Some of the earliest beauties, such as Dutch Colonial farmhouses from New Amsterdam, still survive, and are on view here. The Pieter Claesen Wyckoff House (Map pp170–1; ☎ 718-629-5400; www.wyckoffassociation.org; 5816 Clarendon Rd, Flatbush; adult/child under 10/student & senior $5/free/3; ☉ 10am-4pm Tue-Sun May-Oct, Tue-Sat Nov-Apr), in Brooklyn, is the oldest house in the city. Its first section, constructed in 1652, is easily recognizable by its shingled exterior and peaked roof, which has flaring eaves.

Later styles were influenced by British rule, with buildings that were rectangular and symmetrical with hipped roofs, tall-end chimneys and, sometimes, topped with a cupola. English originals were created from fine stone; the transplants built of brick or wood. St Paul's Chapel (p80), 1766–94, is a copy of St Martin-in-the-Fields in London, but built of Manhattan fieldstone and brownstone. French architect Pierre L'Enfant designed the high altar, crowned by a golden sunburst, in the sanctuary. And way up north in Inwood is the 1765 Morris-Jumel Mansion (p165), the oldest house in Manhattan and one of the best built in colonial America.

After the Revolutionary War, heavy solid forms of the Georgian period were replaced by refined Federal architecture of the new republic. Diminutive City Hall (p82), 1812, owes its French form to émigré architect Joseph François Mangin and its Federal detailing to American-born John McComb Jr. Originally faced with white marble, the rear was covered in brownstone to cut costs. The interior contains an airy rotunda and curved cantilevered stairway. Gracie Mansion (see p145), 1799, the official residence of the mayor since 1942, was built as a country villa. The cream-colored frame house features Chinese Chippendale railings, a fanlight doorway with leaded glass sidelights and a porch that runs along the length of its river-view facade.

You can recognize Federal row houses by their small size, distinctive Flemish bond (alternating long and short bricks), peaked roofs with dormer windows, and decorative doorways. The Merchant's House (p90), 1832, has a late Federal exterior decorated with Greek-revival ironwork and interior ornament. It's the city's only home preserved intact from the 19th century (and with original furnishings).

GEMS OF THE 19TH CENTURY

Greek fever spread through the US in the 1820s as Americans linked the populist presidency of Andrew Jackson with ancient Greek democracy. Architects and builders who had never stepped foot in Greece cribbed designs from pattern books. Churches and public buildings dressed up like Greek temples with tall columns supporting a horizontal entablature and a classical pediment. Two of the best are still standing. The gray granite St Peter's Church (246 W 20th St), built in 1838, replaced the first Roman Catholic church in the city, erected in 1785 and destroyed by fire. The white-marble Federal Hall National Memorial (p78), 1842, originally the US Custom House, is now a museum.

But in the 1840s, pagan Greek revival was abandoned for the spiritual Gothic, reaching toward the heavens and echoing English and French church architecture of the late Middle Ages. Richard Upjohn jump-started the Gothic revival in New York with his Church of the Ascension (Map p110; Fifth Ave at 10th St), 1841, a square-towered English country church faced in brownstone. Architect Stanford White gathered a group of artists in 1888 to redecorate the interior with paintings, sculptures and stained-glass windows. Upjohn's next project, Trinity Church (p80), 1842, also brownstone, used Gothic forms and ornament but 'modern' building techniques, adding fake buttresses and a plaster ceiling.

Another new style invaded New York in the mid-19th century, evoking links with great wealth and power, based on the imposing palazzi of the Italian Renaissance. McKim, Mead & White designed private hangouts fit for the Medici, such as the Metropolitan Club (Map p126; 1 E 60th St), 1894, and the University Club (Map p126; 1 W 54th St), 1899. Villard Houses (Map p126; Madison Ave at 50th St), 1884, also by McKim, Mead & White and modeled after Rome's Cancelleria, were six splendid brownstone mansions for the super-rich, surrounding a courtyard, like a unified palazzo, now part of the Palace Hotel.

BEAUX-ARTS & HEAVY HITTERS

By the start of the 20th century, somber brownstone was out and gleaming white was the newest fashion. Grand Central Terminal (p128), 1913, engineering by Reed & Stem, facade and interior by Warren and Wetmore, showcases a giant clock and sculptures by Jules Coutan. A high-vaulted ceiling covered with a zodiac mural by Paul Helleu tops the breathtaking concourse. Allegorical sculptural figures decorate the facade of the New York Public Library (p129), 1911, by Carrere and Hastings. Added in 1920 by Edward Clark Potter, two marble lions, nicknamed Patience and Fortitude, guard the steps. The Metropolitan Museum of Art (p141) was built in stages; the Fifth Ave facade in 1902 was by Richard Morris Hunt and the 1926 side wings by McKim, Mead and White. Three giant Roman arches alternate with paired Corinthian columns, topped with uncut blocks of stone, originally planned as massive sculptures.

top picks

ARCHITECTURAL MUST-SEES

- Empire State Building (p128) Perhaps the best-known architectural icon in the city, this is art deco at its finest.
- Chrysler Building (p124) The favorite of many New Yorkers, this art-deco gem boasts gargoyles and a famous stainless-steel crown.
- Flatiron Building (p119) It's a mesmerizing work by Daniel Burnham, built on a unique triangular footprint.
- Grand Central Terminal (p128) This Beaux-Arts stunner, with vaulted ceilings and a stunning concourse, will transport you, even if you're not getting on a train.
- New Museum of Contemporary Art (p99) The fresh new addition from Sejima and Neshizawa/SANAA is an all-white collection of stacked aluminum cubes, towering over the Bowery.
- Perry Street Towers (Map p110; Charles & Perry Sts at West Side Hwy) Richard Meier's celeb-filled, minimalist, transparent Perry Street Towers sit perched at the edge of the West Village.
- IAC Building (Map p116; Eleventh Ave at 18th St) The milky, opaque waves of glass of this beauty, designed by Frank Gehry, wake up an unremarkable stretch of the West Side Hwy.
- Hearst Tower (Map pp134–5; 300 W 57th St at Eighth Ave) Norman Foster's soaring stack of glass triangles is a gorgeous LEED-certified ('green') tower in the heart of Midtown.
- New York Times Tower (Map pp134–5; 620 Eighth Ave at 40th St) A sleek addition to the skyline by Renzo Piano Building Workshop, the ceramic tube–draped glass changes colors depending on the shifting light throughout the day.
- 40 Bond (Map pp88–9; 40 Bond St btwn Lafayette St & the Bowery) Ian Schrager's collection of luxury townhouses, designed by Swiss architects Jacques Herzog and Pierre de Meuron, is a thoroughly unique green-glass grid.

This period ushered in the city's love affair with reaching skyward. But before steel-frame skyscrapers there were cast-iron buildings, which pioneered advances in building technology, but with facades chosen from stock books. At first, cast-iron fronts were attached to conventional brick load-bearing outer walls. Later, buildings evolved as primitive cages with interior iron framing and columns. The Venetian-style, cast-iron Haughwout Building (see the walking tour, p90), 1856, holds the first passenger elevator installed in the US. SoHo, once a manufacturing area but now home to million-dollar loft apartments and must-have shopping, flaunts the largest concentration of cast-iron buildings in the world.

After Elisha Otis perfected the elevator in 1853 and William Le Baron Jenney invented steel-frame construction in Chicago in 1885, skyscrapers really shot up. The problem for architects was how to cover those steel skeletons; the answer was to suit them up in historic clothing. The 21-story Flatiron Building (p119), 1902, by Daniel Burnham, owes its distinctive shape to the triangular site. A wavy midsection is clad in white terracotta, decorated with Renaissance ornament. Cass Gilbert, architect of the Woolworth Building (Map pp72–3; 233 Broadway), 1913, modeled his designs on the 1830s Houses of Parliament in London and emphasized the upward thrust of his office tower with continuous vertical rows of windows.

Beloved art deco took hold in the 1930s, as architects turned away from history, creating unique buildings, configured with setbacks, required by new zoning laws, and decorated with original ornament. The Chanin Building (Map p126; 122 E 42nd St), 1929, by Sloan and Robertson, took the lead with its wedding-cake silhouette, exterior decoration of exotic plant forms and sea life, and singular lobby. The Chrysler Building (p124), 1930, by William Van Alen, a corporate headquarters for an automaker, rises with setbacks to a tower with a radiant stainless steel crown of sunbursts. Silver radiator hood caps jut out like gargoyles and cars race in the brickwork. The lobby glows with colorful marble and inlaid wood and its ceiling is covered with a mural celebrating technological progress. The Empire State Building (p128), 1931, by Shreve, Lamb and Harmon, was conceived as the world's tallest and planned for the maximum amount of rental space. The clean lines of the building need little ornament. Soaring from a series of setbacks, the tower pierces the sky with a silver mast.

NEW INFLUENCES

Architects Ludwig Mies van der Rohe, Walter Gropius and Marcel Breuer, who left Europe in the early 1930s, brought the vision and know-how of the avant-garde German Bauhaus to America. Architecture that rejected the past, it imagined future cities of functional glass towers. The United Nations building (p125), 1947–52, was the combined effort of many architects: Swiss-born Le Corbusier, Brazil's Oscar Niemeyer, Sweden's Sven Markelius and representatives from 10 other countries, coordinated by America's Wallace K Harrison. The angular slab of the Secretariat, New York's first building with all glass walls, looms over the ski-slope curve of the General Assembly. The Seagram Building (Map p126; 375 Park Ave), 1958, designed by Mies van der Rohe, a stunning amber glass and bronze slab, is set on an open plaza. Van der Rohe, given an unlimited budget, produced a masterpiece of the International Style. Cheaper glass towers that followed didn't measure up.

Rebelling against glass boxes, architects in the 1980s had a brief fling with vintage styles. Philip Johnson, who designed the pink granite AT&T Building (Map p126; 560 Madison Ave at 56th St), 1984, now headquarters for Sony, borrowed from three eras, producing a giant Romanesque revival base and Chicago skyscraper–style midsection, crowned by a neo-Georgian pediment. Most people shrugged off this phase and architecture continued to move forward with hardly a backward glance.

A wonderful guide published by the AIA Center for Architecture (Map p110; ☎ 212-683-0023; 536 LaGuardia Pl btwn Bleecker & W 3rd Sts) provides details on what seems like all the city's architecture, block by block. Architecture buffs should not be on the streets without one.

ENVIRONMENT & PLANNING
THE LAND

New York City is made up of a series of islands and this fact does not escape anyone who drives, as mapping an escape plan for a weekend getaway can get tricky once you factor in the traffic that tends to clog the various bridges and tunnels that connect you with the rest of the world. It's also why the city, especially Manhattan, which is just 13 miles long and 2.3 miles wide, can feel so damn crowded, as there is limited space to work within. That inability to spread outward is what gave rise to the building of skyscrapers. Extra-tall residential ones are gaining new popularity with developers who have no other choice (to the chagrin of many) when it comes to packing in new homebuyers.

But the area's major asset for growth and development were the waterways that inspired the city's founding. New York Harbor has 65 sq miles of inland waterways and 772 miles of direct shoreline. The rich marine life provided food to Native Americans and early colonists, and the strategic importance of the New York harbor did not go unnoticed by the British. Through the years, its waters have become ferry routes and host to some of the busiest ports in the world, and the shores, which were finally noticed as park-space assets, have become integral parts of New Yorkers' lives. Early on in the history of waterway use, the waters inevitably became polluted, with most traces of marine life disappearing (luckily, the city's drinking water, more than 1.5 billion gallons daily, comes from upstate reservoirs). Efforts to control the dumping of raw sewage in the 1970s and '80s helped a bit, as did more recent plans that also targeted the city's air quality.

The air quality in Lower Manhattan became a topic of much heated debate in the first years after September 11, with the Environmental Protection Agency (EPA), City Hall, business interests and community groups all conducting independent tests in an effort to evaluate exactly what's been floating around in the air down there. Scores of rescue workers got sick from it, cover-ups of just how unsafe the air was have been exposed and now, as part of the Lower Manhattan Development Corporation's plan to rebuild, air quality will be constantly monitored as part of the long rebuilding process.

GREEN NYC

The last couple of years have seen an incredible shift towards environmentalism in this city, with much of the credit due to Mayor Bloomberg's wide-sweeping plans and goals, which he calls Green Apple Initiatives. Unveiled to the public on Earth Day in 2007, Bloomberg's plans aim to reduce the strain on the city's water, air and land and move toward becoming more energy efficient. This is to be done through rebuilding water mains, supporting mass transit, creating more LEED-certified (green) buildings, and assisting low-income residents in public housing projects to replace lightbulbs with compact fluorescent ones. Also on the cards is to offer electricity-reduction plans to citywide customers, spruce up public playgrounds with more plants and flowers and continue to monitor the city's recycling program, the largest mandatory curbside recycling program in the United States. And, as of 2007, the green buildings law mandates green-building standards in the renovation or construction of any city-owned or city-funded buildings.

But much of the mayor's focus has been on the topic of transportation. He wants to create more support for city bicyclists by improving

top picks

GREEN SPACES BEYOND CENTRAL PARK

For a comprehensive list of city parks, both grand and obscure, visit the site of the NYC Department of Parks (www.nycgovparks.org).

- Brooklyn Botanical Garden (p184) Here is where you can relax among the miles of gardens and grassy areas, especially in spring, when the Cherry Blossom Festival (p21) brings a riot of color.
- General Theological Seminary (p114) Chelsea's secret place for peace is in an unlikely neighborhood.
- Wave Hill (p211) High up on a hill overlooking the Hudson River in the Bronx, this is the place for a picnic with a view.
- Riverside Park (p154) The Upper West Side's crowning glory is this narrow stretch of green, with gardens, statues, bike paths and many beautiful trees.
- Prospect Park (p181) Brooklyn's answer to Central Park is a massive urban oasis.
- Jamaica Bay Wildlife Refuge (p206) Bird watching is prime in the marshes of this Queens refuge.
- Inwood Hill Park (p164) The miles of trails are a joy to hike around at Manhattan's northern tip.
- New York Chinese Scholar's Garden (see p213) Here is the place for meditating, a unique garden within the Staten Island Botanical Garden.
- New York Botanical Garden (p211) Any season is right for strolling the 40 pristine acres of hemlock, oak and hickory trees, right in the Bronx.
- City Island (p211) The shoreline in the Bronx's City Island is ripe for wandering.

bike lanes (which have traditionally been too few and too unprotected), is on top of replacing or converting public buses to hybrids or those that use compressed natural gas (CNG) and strives to make sure that all taxis are hybrid vehicles by 2012. (Ironically, though, the City Council made a very anti-environmental ruling when it voted to impose strict limitations on the number of clean-air, human-powered pedicabs that operate throughout Midtown; critics blame the pro-taxi lobbyists.) The effort Bloomberg has received the most ink over, though, has been his proposed congestion-pricing plan. This would aim to reduce auto traffic in Manhattan by charging drivers $8 to go below 60th Street between 6am and 6pm, and then use that revenue (an estimated $491 million annually) to improve mass transit. While it's faced a tough road due to criticism from the large pro-commuter lobby, the proposal crossed a major hurdle in early 2008 and may be put into motion yet.

The city has also been getting behind its need for green space more than ever before. Rather than developing every last crumb of fallow land (though halting over development is clearly an uphill battle), some of it is in the process of being converted to public open space, with some of the most exciting projects including the High Line (p115), to be created from an abandoned elevated railway; Brooklyn Bridge Park (p175), to encompass 85 acres of green space; and Governor's Island (p75), in New York Harbor, which will undergo a complete restoration including bike paths and grassy knolls. Parts of Hudson River Park (p76), which stretches up the length of Manhattan's west side from Battery Park to 59th Street, are still under construction, with plans for still more lawns and activity courts in the works. The city's Million Trees initiative strives to plant and care for one million new trees across the city's five boroughs – in streets, parks and on private land – by 2017.

New York is also home to an increasing number of 'green' apartment buildings, a trend that began with the Solaire, the nation's first 'environmentally responsible' high-rise building, located in Battery Park City. The Solaire consumes 35% less energy and conserves 50% more water than traditional apartment buildings. Others that have sprouted up recently include Helena, in Hell's Kitchen, Tribeca Green (in Tribeca) and, on Roosevelt Island (p146), the Octagon. Green living at these oft-luxury places isn't for everyone, though, as rents tend to start at around $3500 a month and rise swiftly from there.

One group that has a hand in practically all green issues in the city is the Council on the Environment of New York City (www.cenyc.org), a privately funded citizens' organization in the Office of the Mayor. Its programs include Open Space Greening (community gardens), Greenmarket & New Farmer Development Project (supporting nearly 50 Greenmarket sites citywide), Environmental Education (for outreach) and Waste Prevention & Recycling, which encourages sustainable practices in schools and other institutions.

URBAN PLANNING & DEVELOPMENT

Neighborhood by neighborhood, block by block, New York City is being transformed. It's happening through a number of rezoning, redevelopment and green-initiative projects, many of which are entangled with each other, as the city tries to constantly shape and reshape itself to reflect the 21st century. The list of regions and neighborhoods slated for rezoning is quite long, including Harlem's 125th Street corridor, Brooklyn's Coney Island, Hunts Point in the Bronx and sections of the Lower East Side, but what they have in common is a desire to improve the landscape, streetscape and retail and residential offerings of a particular area. The project proposals are often contentious, opposed by folks who feel the neighborhood's character will be bulldozed. That's why a major plan to overhaul the area of Brooklyn known as Atlantic Yards, which would build a new district around a sports stadium and bring 17 skyscrapers to the heart of low-rise Brooklyn in the next ten years, has been tied up in court for years now in lawsuits.

While news coverage of rezoning proposals tends to flare up for a while and get surrounding neighborhoods into all manner of tizzies, the actual length of time it takes for any movement to occur can seem endless. Of course the best example of that would be the rebuilding of Lower Manhattan and Ground Zero, which has been mired in controversy and indecision for years now (see the boxed text, p56). The construction of private new luxury buildings, meanwhile, is happening as fast as lightning, quickly changing the urban landscape and troubling long-time, hard-working New Yorkers who see the creation of endless units of new housing; none of which, with condo prices averaging $1 million a unit, is for them.

WORLD TRADE CENTER SITE

While the physical dust of September 11 may have cleared, the dust of controversy and infighting over what to do with Ground Zero's rebuilding efforts has yet to settle. The years of discussion over what kind of redevelopment is appropriately soulful, strong, beautiful and useful has been fraught with drama and politicking, often pitting grieving and angry survivors against the artists and architects who were trying to bring some global meaning to the tragedy.

First, a little recap. Immediately following September 11, the area around Ground Zero was a war zone – covered in thick ash and the smell of death, bustling with only rescue workers, police officers and media folks, and residents trying to grab what was left of their belongings. Ad-hoc September 11 memorials sprang up everywhere – both official, such as the Ground Zero viewing platform that eventually morphed into a Viewing Wall, with display panels showing the history of the buildings' beginning and demise, and unofficial, like the mass of out-of-nowhere vendors who hawked mawkish mementos from framed photos to T-shirts. The true neighborhood spirit was gone for at least a year, until the tax-free Liberty Bond program, created by Congress, started wooing residents and business-owners back here in droves, bringing a feeling of boom to the region, which is still hot. But always looming was the site of the former towers itself; what to do with it?

At first, all seemed on track. The Lower Manhattan Development Corporation was put in place to oversee plans, and an esteemed architect, Daniel Libeskind, was chosen as the perfect man for the job after winning a design competition that many say was never clear about what was wanted in the first place. Libeskind became the 'master planner,' and drew up plans that were met with approval and included the 1776ft skyscraper that then Governor George Pataki promptly dubbed the 'Freedom Tower.' But soon after, developer Larry Silverstein realized that, whatever sort of building went up, it would need to house businesses that would turn a profit; meanwhile, the NYC Police Department demanded that a major design be changed to better defend against terrorist attacks. Then several other architects were brought on board and coerced into what many have dubbed a 'forced marriage' with Libeskind, whose original design has changed significantly and frequently.

And then there was what many New Yorkers saw as the most offensive part of the entire plan: the controversy over art and culture, and how much and what type was appropriate for the memorial. It all came to a head in September 2005, when Pataki scrapped plans for the International Freedom Center, meant to be an extensive art and cultural center that would look at human rights from a global perspective. Relatives of September 11 victims were angry that the culture wouldn't revolve solely around the World Trade Center tragedy, and Pataki, afraid that anything else would be viewed as unpatriotic, evicted the entire museum idea from the plans. Similar arguments ended plans for the relocation of the Drawing Center (see p90), and discussions over the possibility of an on-location performing arts center came to a halt.

Fast forward to August 2007, when the entire construction zone was dealt a tragic setback: the Deutsche Bank Building, a structure that sat vacant and damaged since September 11 and was in the process of being dismantled, broke out into a deadly blaze, killing two firefighters. The thick plumes of chemical-laced smoke reminded New Yorkers of the day the Twin Towers fell, and the finger pointing began over whom was to blame for the construction debacle in the first place.

Since then, construction is pretty much back on track. At the time of research, the concrete foundation had been poured for both the Freedom Tower and what officials agreed would be a National September 11th Memorial and Museum, and the WTC Transportation Hub, which would be a grand entrance to both the subway and New Jersey PATH train systems, seemed like it could be open by 2009. Fingers were crossed that no more bad luck would cause any more delays. For updates on construction, visit www.wtc.com. And to pay your respects to those who lost their lives and revisit the tragedy, head down to the WTC Tribute Visitors Center (p77), operated by the nonprofit September 11th Families Association.

Projects that generally don't see much fighting are those planning to bring more open space to people. Chief among the favorites right now is the High Line (p115). More than just an elevated park, the project will bring to further additions, including hotels, museums, condos and shops, to its connected neighborhoods of Chelsea and Hell's Kitchen.

GOVERNMENT & POLITICS

New York City's political history has been spirited, strange and oft contentious, highlighted by such characters as William 'Boss' Tweed, Fiorello LaGuardia, Nelson Rockefeller, Edward Koch and Rudy Giuliani. New Yorkers have had a long record of voting for the Democratic Party, though there are conservative pockets in the blue-collar sections of Queens and Brooklyn, and the suburban borough of Staten Island is exclusively Republican. But despite the Democratic tradition, socially liberal Republican reformers can be elected mayor, as proven by two-term leader Rudy Giuliani (considered a hero by many for his post–September 11 performance) and the city's current leader, billionaire Mayor Michael Bloomberg, who only switched his party affiliation from Democrat to Republican in order to run against a Democrat mayoral challenger. First elected in 2001 in an atmosphere of turmoil and grief, Bloomberg came under early fire for his severe fiscal policies and draconian moves as head of the beleaguered public school system; later he was criticized for pushing for the 2012 Olympic bid through a controversial West Side development plan. Still, 'Bloomie,' as he's been dubbed in the tabloids, won his re-election to a second term and, though he's still criticized for being pro-development, he's been well regarded in many areas: for being a big supporter of the arts and a proponent of environmentalism, and for taking on the challenge of reducing poverty through initiatives including one to dole out cash rewards to parents who keep their kids healthy and in school. His plan from the beginning has been to run the city like a business, which is something that, as head of Bloomberg News Services, he knows how to do well – and some

top picks

BOOKS ABOUT NYC POLITICS

- *New York City Politics: Governing Gotham* (Bruce F Berg, 2007) The author looks at economic development, relationships with state and federal government and racial factors in this first comprehensive NYC-government study to be written in decades.
- *The Full Rudy: The Man, The Myth, The Mania* (Jack Newfield, 2003) Veteran tabloid journalist Newfield looks deeper into Giuliani mania, painting him as a political opportunist with racist and homophobic tendencies.
- *The Power Broker: Robert Moses and the Fall of New York* (Robert Caro, 1975) A massive tale about planner Robert Moses written by the Pulitzer Prize winner who looks at how Moses' policies and political dealings physically shaped the New York of today.
- *The Napoleon of New York: Mayor Fiorello LaGuardia* (H Paul Jeffers, 2002) The complete biography provides much insight into a historically important leadership period in the city.
- *Boss Tweed's New York* (Seymour Mandelbaum, 1990) The corrupt leader of Tammany Hall provides a lens through which to look at the politics of America.

contend that this straightforward approach has been a success. His commercial enterprises, however, have drawn some unwanted attention for him. When he was elected, NYC's Conflict of Interest Board ruled that the mayor had to recuse himself from any daily decision-making in his company, which reports political and financial news. However, the mayor and his lawyers created much of the language in that ruling. A *New York Times* investigation found that Bloomberg speaks daily with his company's head honchos and the situation remains under scrupulous watch.

At the time of writing, the 2009 mayoral election promised to be an exciting affair, as it was widely believed that the contender with the best shot would be City Council Speaker Christine Quinn, who has become quite chummy with Bloomberg over the years. Elected in 2006 by her peers, the body of 50 other city council members who preside over the city along with the mayor, five borough presidents, city comptroller and public advocate, Quinn made history when she became the first woman and first out lesbian to serve as Speaker. It made her the second most powerful person in NYC government, and she wasted no time being outspoken (something that comes naturally to the Long Island–bred redhead) on topics as far reaching as city pedicabs (against), gay marriage (for), election term limits (for) and city hunger and homelessness (against).

In addition to being divided into council districts, each city borough is made up of community boards – 59 in total, led by unsalaried members appointed by the borough president, and meant to play an advisory role in zoning and land-use issues, community planning, municipal services and the city's budget process. Attending a local community board meeting is a good (and often wacky, gadfly-filled) way to truly get the sense of a specific community. To find information about upcoming meetings, including schedule and locations, visit the website of the Mayor's Community Affairs Unit (www.nyc.gov/html/cau/).

MEDIA

With all of its magazines, broadcast stations and publishing companies, NYC can easily stake a claim as the media capital of the world. And the history of this rise is particularly long and strong.

It was here, in fact, that the notion of 'freedom of the press' was first truly challenged and upheld. Though the first newspaper here was William Bradford's *New York Gazette*, it was the city's second paper, John Peter Zenger's *New York Weekly Journal*, founded in 1733, that had a profound effect on the future of journalism. Zenger reported some controversial truths about the colony's governor – a bold move during a time when the country's newspapers had been mostly seen as puppets of the government. The governor had Zenger arrested and jailed for seditious libel (his wife continued publishing the paper in his absence), but the journalist's lawyer, one Alexander Hamilton, passionately defended the idea of liberty through the writing of the truth. The jury found Zenger innocent, and it was a major step toward defending freedom of the press everywhere.

While journalistic standards – both of quality and integrity – have fluctuated markedly since then, the city has only risen in importance as the home of numerous and influential publications. Today's newspaper offerings are not quite as multitudinous as they were in, say, the late 1800s, when there were no less than 20 dailies published in New York – or even in 1940, when there were eight – but there's certainly no newspaper shortage. The mainstream dailies are the *Daily News* and *New York Post* tabloids, known for screaming headlines and sensationalist takes on grisly crimes or tragic downfalls; the *New York Sun*, a general-interest broadsheet with a conservative slant launched in 2002; and the definitive *New York Times*, a hefty, many-sectioned paper that's cited daily by all sorts of professionals and intellectuals. Though the *Times* has long been known by its nickname of 'the gray lady' because of its straightforward, oft-boring approach to news, it's received a major facelift in recent years, as publishers and editors have sought to keep hold of readers who may be more drawn to getting their news in quick, snappy doses delivered either on TV or via the internet. It remains the most widely read news source in the city. Many still say it's the best, although its closest rival is the more financially geared *Wall Street Journal*, which may soon look a lot different following its purchase by billionaire media mogul Rupert Murdoch, whose News Corporation already

top picks

NYC MEDIA MUSTS

Here's some direction through the city's vast media jungle; see also Getting Started (p26) for more suggestions.

- **East Village Radio** (www.eastvillageradio.com) Operated out of a tiny storefront on First Ave, the free, community-themed internet radio station presents a wide range of programming, including music from international pop to the Grateful Dead and talk shows hosted by folks like Daniel Nardicio, a favorite promoter among partying gay men.

- **NY1** (Time Warner Cable, channel 1; www.ny1 .com) It's the place for round-the-clock local headlines, political talk, arts, sports and weather.

- **New York Magazine** (www.nymag.com) The weekly glossy has the whole city covered for gossip, feature stories, fashion, social pages and all manner of listings, from theater to art exhibition openings. Its excellent website has a searchable database for restaurants and clubs.

- **Time Out New York** (www.timeoutny.com) *New York* magazine's chief rival, this weekly has exhaustive event listings in every category and plenty of service-oriented articles.

- **Gothamist** (www.gothamist.com) The edgy NYC culture website covers everything from food to sports.

- **WBAI** (99.5-FM; www.wbai.org) An excellent radio station dealing with political and social issues through shows like Amy Goodman's Democracy Now! and the weekly Out-FM gay-and-lesbian discussion program.

- **WNYC** (820-AM & 93.9-FM radio; www.wnyc.org) A local WNYC affiliate station that features great local talk shows such as the *Brian Lehrer Show*.

- **The New York Post** (www.nypost.com) Sure, everyone knows you should read the *New York Times* everyday, but this splashy tabloid, with make-no-apologies headlines and nasty judgments, also should be daily fodder.

- **WFUV** (90.7; www.wfuv.org) This gem of a radio station, part of Fordham University in the Bronx, plays a non-commercial mix of indie music, from old-school folk to undiscovered local rockers.

- **NYC-TV** (channel 25) Run by the city government, this is a surprisingly hip round-the-clock channel, with programming that looks at everything from New York restaurants and nightclubs to entire neighborhoods and their cultural offerings.

owns Fox News, the *New York Post*, Dow Jones, *TV Guide* and 27 other newspapers around the world, not to mention Random House Publishing and the National Geographic channel.

Luckily, in response to that domination of corporate media, the alternative and ethnic presses are jumping, broadening opportunities for other voices to be heard. They bring the latest count of local newspapers to about 280 and leave little room to complain that there are not enough perspectives outside the mainstream. The *New York Press* and the *Village Voice*, both weeklies, battle it out for liberal, anti-establishment people (though the *Voice* is now part of a national chain of 'alternatives') who like colorful, investigative journalism doled out of newspaper street boxes for free. The salmon-colored weekly *New York Observer* specializes on the political and social escapades of the upper class. And a slew of ethnic papers – the *Haitian Times, Polish Times, Jewish Forward, Korea Times, Pakistan Post, Irish Echo, El Diario* and the *Amsterdam News* among them – offer more comprehensive news reports from a variety of angles. Two free weeklies *Metro* and *AM New York* are thrust in front of zombie-like commuters who are heading onto the subway every morning and these papers now compete for the 'I've-got-no-time-for-news' crowd, offering easy-to-swallow tidbits daily.

In addition to all the publishing houses for trade paperback and hardcover books, New York is home to many magazine publishers. Condé Nast, one of the largest, publishes titles including *Gourmet, Vogue, Vanity Fair* and the *New Yorker* out of its Times Square headquarters. Other empires include Hearst *(Cosmopolitan, Marie Claire, Esquire, O)*, which also owns a dozen national newspapers and is housed in a gorgeous new 'green' Midtown building, and Hachette Filipacchi *(Premiere, Elle, Woman's Day)*. Then there are the self-titled empires, such as Martha Stewart Living Omnimedia. Major regional magazines focusing on entertainment and dining include *New York Magazine, Paper* and *Time Out New York* (for details on more newspapers and magazines, see p402).

Though many of these heavy hitters may not want to admit it, the blogs are really where much of it's at now. Blogs about every aspect of city life – real estate, politics, entertainment, nightlife, straight-up gossip and media itself – are thriving, widely read by both journalists and regular folks alike. Favorites include the gossip and celebrity driven Gawker.com and the real estate obsessed Curbed.com (for more, see p26).

FASHION

Contrary to the love-affair-with-fashion image stoked by New York–based films, TV shows and style magazines, it is possible to live an entire life in Manhattan without ever owning a pair of Jimmy Choos. While an improbably high number of women and men in the city do own $500 shoes, there is truth – and comfort – to be found in the fact that most paparazzi shots of local celebs show them wearing simple jeans and boots (albeit pricey ones). Considering that the US taught the rest of the world about blue jeans and that the most famous American designers – Calvin Klein, Ralph Lauren, Michael Kors and Donna Karan – have built their empires on their sportswear, it's not surprising that in NYC, chic equals sleekly casual. The worst fashion sin to commit, in fact, is to overdress or try too hard.

But the truth is also that almost everyone in New York is interested in looking stylish (see the NYC Style chapter for mastering that look, p274). This includes twenty-somethings being barely able to make rent who are willing to blow $250 on the 'right' pair of jeans. The definition of stylish is different, however, depending on the scene you hang with. What works in the uber-chic offices of Condé Nast just won't fly in the hipster dive bars of Williamsburg, and vice versa, just as the classic and conservative Upper East Side look doesn't gel with Tribeca's nuanced industrial chic.

This cult of casual wear might seem strange to someone accustomed to London, where residents are far more experimental and susceptible to fads, or Paris, where haute couture is a more serious affair. But one of the draws of this city life is anonymity, which is why New Yorkers prefer to mix their designer items with their regular clothes so that what they're wearing doesn't scream Prada or resemble a glorified ad.

While in much of NYC denim and sneakers rule the day, choice accessories are de rigueur, including proper devices such as iPhones and Sidekicks.

What New Yorkers aren't nonchalant about is their grooming. A real metrosexual expresses himself not by the foppishness of his ties but a slavish devotion to scrubs, cuticles, and perfectly coiffed just-rolled-out-of-bed hair. It takes hard work to achieve that impression of effortlessness. On the other hand, the city will always have plenty of high-maintenance types who have their roots touched up every two weeks or apply leg makeup so they can remain bare-kneed in the dead of winter.

You'll find both types – along with various pin-thin starlets and magazine editors – in the front rows of the shows during Fashion Week (p20) held every February and September in tents erected with much grandeur in Bryant Park. With almost all of America's major designers and magazines based in New York, it's no surprise the city is the nexus of the latest inspirations and trends. In recent years, Fashion Week shows have become more and more like Academy Award–type events, with folks clamoring to be a part of the celeb-studded crowd. It's strictly an industry affair, though, ensuring that most New Yorkers will never attend a runway show there.

Average Janes can get their hands on designer goods when need be. There are many opportunities to get them at deep discounts, thanks to ever-popular sample sales (see the boxed text, p217), which hawk one-of-a-kind designer samples sold directly from the showroom, though most 'sample sales' these days are just sales of overstock that never made it to the stores. They're still worthy events, held usually in the Garment District (p132) or SoHo showrooms, and are a great way to acquire famous labels for 30% to 90% off. Find out where they're happening at www.nysale.com or www.dailycandy.com. Other delicious bargains are waiting at Century 21 (p217), a designer discount department store which can be crowded with aggressive retail addicts but is worth a visit.

LANGUAGE

To get a sense of the many languages spoken in New York, check out these census figures: of the city's population aged five and over, a whopping 46% speak a language other than English at home – up 5% from 1990. The foreign-born population here reached a new all-time high as it hit 2.9 million in 2000, and a full 1.7 million residents are not proficient in English. Of those, 52% speak Spanish, 28% speak a different European language (French, German, Swedish etc) and 17% converse in an Asian or Pacific language (mainly Chinese and Korean). Another hint at the range of tongues lies in the city's newsstands: there are hundreds of foreign-language papers published in New York, for those speaking everything from Hebrew, Arabic and German to Russian, Croatian, Italian, Polish, Greek and Hungarian. Or step up to an ATM or Metrocard machine; the first question you'll be asked is what language you'd like to continue in and, depending on the neighborhood, you could find not only Spanish, but Korean, Russian and French among your options.

LOCAL PASSWORDS

Knowing the following New York lingo can help you make yourself clear – or at least understand what others are talking about:

Bridge-and-Tunnel A disdainful term for folks who come to party in NYC from New Jersey, Long Island or other suburbs that are found across the city's bridges and tunnels, as in 'Yuck, that club is so bridge-and-tunnel now!'

Hack Old-time nickname for a cabbie, or taxi-cab driver.

Hizzoner A slang term for the mayor ('his honor'), most often used by the New York Post.

New York's Finest The New York Police Department (NYPD).

Regular An old-school way to order coffee, meaning with one sugar and one splash of milk, as in 'Small coffee, regular.'

Schmear A small amount of cream cheese, used when ordering at a bagel counter, as in 'I'll have a sesame bagel with a schmear.'

Slice A serving of pizza, as in 'Let's get a slice for lunch.'

Straphangers Subway riders.

The train The subway.

Going about your day is an adventure in dialects. Listen on the street or the subway, and you're bound to overhear five different languages in an hour. You'll hear a blend of English with foreign languages: Jamaican patois peppered with NYC turns of phrase, a fast-moving concoction of Spanish and New Yorkese known locally as 'Spanglish,' young hip adults of Indian ancestry bringing Hindi words into their 'Desi' American English and, because the weak economy has been attracting so many European shoppers, plenty of French and Italian in the mix. Hail a cab and chat to the driver, hearing inflections of Pakistani, Sri Lankan, Russian, Arabic. Take that cab to one of the many ethnic 'hoods around the five boroughs and you'll find closed communities where no English is spoken: Dominican neighborhoods in the South Bronx, Korean pockets of Flushing, Queens, Chinese neighborhoods in Sunnyside, Brooklyn, and the Bukharian (Jews of Central Asian descent) areas of Rego Park, Queens.

Many American English words have been adapted by the successive waves of immigrants who arrived in New York. From the Germans came words including 'hoodlums,' from Yiddish-speaking Jews terms like 'schmuck' (fool), and from Irish words like 'galore.' And then there are all the long-time locals, speaking with that old-school Noo Yawk dialect that many natives – though they love it – still struggle to understand.

NEIGHBORHOODS

top picks

What's your recommendation? www.lonelyplanet.com/new-york-city

NEIGHBORHOODS

Manhattan might not exactly equal New York City – there are four other boroughs, after all – but truthfully, this is where visitors spend most, if not all, of their time. Manhattan is the heart and soul and pulse of the city, and the New York of people's dreams, home to everything from the bright lights of Times

'Manhattan has enough little worlds to make your head spin.'

Square and the green expanse of Central Park to the hustle-bustle of Harlem and the West Village's charms.

Manhattan is a long, skinny island surrounded by rivers – nuzzled close to the state of New Jersey on its west side, and within swimming distance of three of the city's other boroughs (Brooklyn, Queens and the Bronx) to its east and north. And tucked within its scant 23 sq miles are enough little worlds to make your head spin. Its neighborhoods are truly a collection of eclectic, homey and lively little towns, where you'll find regulars hunkered down at favorite diner tables or nodding hello to neighbors as they take their dogs for early-morning walks.

There's Midtown, where glimmering skyscrapers and mobs of worker bees give way to iconic landmarks such as the Empire State Building, Rockefeller Center, the Chrysler Building and the theaters of Broadway. There's the Lower East Side, where a clutch of old-timers blends in with hipsters who shop, dine and party with little knowledge of the area's deep Jewish roots; Chelsea, beloved by buff gay men and overflowing with low-lit lounges and top-notch art galleries; the Upper West Side, where nannies push strollers and musicians lug cellos home on the subway after orchestra gigs at nearby Lincoln Center; Harlem, home to the historic Apollo Theater and small jazz clubs and undergoing a fast-and-furious tide of gentrification; and Lower Manhattan, where Wall Street and its suited employees set the pace among the tightly woven streets, and where the frightful memory of September 11 still lingers after nearly a decade.

Cross a bridge or tunnel on any side of Manhattan, and you'll find that the city's borders stretch wider than most visitors realize. The outer boroughs (see the boxed text, p167) are heavily residential, housing folks who are either priced out of super-expensive Manhattan real estate or simply prefer the lower-key vibes and multi-ethnic makeups over 'the city's' frenetic, increasingly homogeneous feel. Each borough is unique and worth a visit – and has been, from time to time, thought of as being even cooler than Manhattan itself, thanks to the lower rents that consistently pull city hipsters into their farthest reaches. Get ready to join them in being seduced.

DIY NYC

We at Lonely Planet are dedicated to providing comprehensive and in-depth coverage of every country and city we write about. But more than that, we are dedicated to creating a sustainable global traveler culture, which is why we say that the greatest adventure is to fly by the seat of your pants. And so, as antithetical as it may seem, we want you to put the guidebook down for a day – even several – and try exploring this big, bad city on your own, in ways that you just won't find in the pages of this guide.

We'll happily jumpstart your exploration with some ideas: stroll Central Park or Prospect Park without any agenda. Jump onto a passing bus and ride it until you feel like getting off, then explore the neighborhood you've landed in. Get lost among the illogical, diagonal streets of the far West Village. Read the bulletin board at a local café and find an announcement for a performance going on that night – and then go to it. Hail a cab and ask the driver to take you to his favorite lunch spot, where you'll no doubt delight in an obscure and affordable ethnic feast. Afterward, if you've had a great, offbeat travel experience, let us know about it! Tell us your stories at www.lonelyplanet.com/feedback.

0 5 km
0 3.0 miles

With so many neighborhoods, each one chock full of attractions, planning a logical daily schedule is key if you want to try to see it all – but it can also get downright tedious! Relax for a day or two and let us take care of it. Just follow the chart below to get started.

ACTIVITIES

NEIGHBORHOODS ITINERARY BUILDER

AREA	Uptown	Midtown	Downtown
Sights	Whitney Museum of American Art (p143) Neue Galerie (p145) Solomon R Guggenheim Museum (p144)	New York Public Library (p129) Top of the Rock (p133) Museum of Arts & Design (p138)	Staten Island Ferry (p75) Museum of Jewish Heritage (p76) Trinity Church (p80)
Shops	Malcolm Shabazz Harlem Market (p241) Zabar's (p240) Penny Whistle Toys (p241)	Bergdorf Goodman (p235) Takashimaya (p236) Barneys (p235)	Century 21 (p217) Strand Book Store (p231) Other Music (p221)
Restaurants	Hacienda de Argentina (p263) Pio Pio (p264) Candle Café (p264)	Brasserie (p261) Bouchon Bakery (p263) Soba Nippon (p261)	Les Halles (p250) Thalassa (p250) Financier Patisserie (p251)
Bars & Clubs	Metropolitan Museum of Art Roof Garden Café (p295) Smoke (p306) Lenox Lounge (p305)	Campbell Apartment (p293) Jimmy's Corner (p294) 230 Fifth (p294)	Little Branch (p291) Banjo Jim's (p306) Ear Inn (p288)
Arts & Entertainment	Lincoln Center (p311) Symphony Space (p316) The Frick Collection's concert series (p315)	Wicked (p312) City Center (p316) Carnegie Hall (p315)	Trinity Church/St Paul's Chapel (p316) Film Forum (p319) Performance Space 122 (p314)
Sports & Activities	Asphalt Green (p336) West Side YMCA (p336) Columbia Lions (p327)	Chelsea Piers (p337) Rockefeller Center Ice Rink (p333) New York Knicks (p326)	Bowlmor Lanes (p331) Downtown Boathouse (p330) New York Trapeze School (p334)
Offbeat	Metropolitan Museum of Art's baseball card collection (p141) New York Academy of Medicine (p146) Yorkville (p146)	Big Button sculpture (p132) Diamond District (p132) Hell's Kitchen (p132)	Lips (p341) Dixon Place (p313) NY Tour Goddess New York Tour/Wall Street (p404)

HOW TO USE THIS TABLE

The table below allows you to plan a day's worth of activities in any area of the city. Simply select which area you wish to explore, and then mix and match from the corresponding listings to build your day. The first item in each cell represents a well-known highlight of the area, while the other items are more off-the-beaten-track gems.

Central Park	Brooklyn	Other Boroughs
Strawberry Fields (p148) Bethesda Fountain (p150) Great Lawn (p148)	Brooklyn Heights Promenade (p169) Brooklyn Museum (p184) Prospect Park (p181)	PS1 Contemporary Art Center (p202) Panorama of New York City, Queens Museum of Art (p205) Bronx Zoo (p210)
	Powerhouse Books (p242) Jacques Torres Chocolate (p242) Beacon's Closet (p243)	Arthur Avenue Market (p244) Everything Goes Clothing (p244) India Sari Palace (p243)
Central Park Boathouse Restaurant (p265)	Lucali (p271) Franny's (p272) The Farm on Adderley (p270)	Jackson Diner (p282) Donovan's Pub (p282) Roberto Restaurant (p282)
	Gutter (p297) Barcade (p176) O'Connor's (p298)	Bohemian Hall & Beer Garden (p298) Stan's Sports Bar (p298)
Joseph Papp Public Theater/ Shakespeare in the Park (p313) New York Philharmonic (p22) SummerStage (p23)	Brooklyn Public Library (p322) Brooklyn Academy of Music (p315) Bargemusic (p315)	

Central Park Tennis Center (p334)
Loeb Boathouse (p330)
Starr Saphir Tours (p331)
	Gowanus Dredgers Canoe Club
	    (p330)
	Shore Parkway Path (p329)
	Audubon Center Boathouse (p330)
		Flushing Meadows Pitch & Putt
		    (p332)
		New York Yankees (p325)
		Jamaica Bay Wildlife Refuge (p206)

Wildman Steve Brill tour (p405) Belvedere Castle (p148) Alice in Wonderland statue (p150)	Weeksville Historic Center (p193) Coney Island USA freak show (p196) Tacos stands in Red Hook (p271)	The *Taxi Driver* mohawk wig (p203) 5 Pointz Graffiti (p199) City Island (p211)

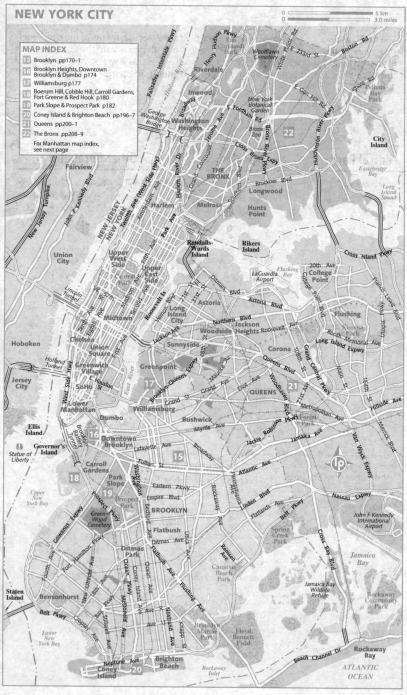

NEW YORK CITY

0 — 5 km
0 — 3.0 miles

Woodlawn Cemetery
Van Cortlandt Park
E 233rd St
Shore Rd
Boston Rd
Pelham Bay Park
White Plains Rd
Henry Hudson Pkwy
Riverdale
E Gun Hill Rd
Hutchinson River Pkwy
City Island
Inwood
New York Botanical Garden
Eastchester Bay
E Fordham Rd
Bronx River Pkwy
Long Island Sound
Bronx Zoo
22
George Washington Bridge
Washington Heights
Jerome Ave
Cross Bronx Expwy
Fairview
Amsterdam Ave
Harlem River Dr
THE BRONX
Bruckner Blvd
Longwood
Harlem
Park Ave
Melrose
Hunts Point
Cross Island Pkwy
NEW JERSEY
NEW YORK
Union City
Twelfth Ave (West Side Hwy)
Lenox Ave
Randalls-Wards Island
Rikers Island
20th Ave
College Point
Upper West Side
Central Park
Upper East Side
LaGuardia Airport
Flushing Bay
College Point Blvd
Francis Lewis Blvd
Lincoln Tunnel
W 57th
Ditmars Blvd
Astoria Blvd
Astoria
Flushing
Hoboken
Midtown
Roosevelt Is
Long Island City
Northern Blvd
Jackson Heights
Roosevelt Ave
Corona
Grand Central Pkwy
Main St
Astoria Blvd
Chelsea
Union Square
Jackson Ave
Woodside
Queens Blvd
Holland Tunnel
Greenwich Village
E Houston St
Greenpoint
Sunnyside
Maurice Ave
Eliot Ave
Woodhaven Blvd
QUEENS
21
Metropolitan Ave
Hillside Ave
Jersey City
West Side Hwy
SoHo
17
Brooklyn-Queens Expwy
Grand St
Forest Park
Van Wyck Expwy
Lower Manhattan
Dumbo
Williamsburg
Bushwick
Myrtle Ave
Jackie Robinson Pkwy
Jamaica Ave
Merrick Blvd
Ellis Island
16
Downtown Brooklyn
Lafayette Ave
Atlantic Ave
Governor's Island
Brooklyn Battery Tunnel
15
Broadway
Statue of Liberty
Fulton St
Nassau Expwy
Carroll Gardens
Park Slope
Washington Ave
Eastern Pkwy
Rockaway Ave
Linden Blvd
Belt Pkwy
John F Kennedy International Airport
18
19
Prospect Park
Bedford Ave
Empire Blvd
Flatlands Ave
Upper New York Bay
Green-Wood Cemetery
BROOKLYN
Spring Creek Park
Jamaica Bay
Flatbush
Ralph Ave
Jamaica Bay Wildlife Refuge
Rockaway Community Park
Staten Island
Ditmas Park
Flatbush Ave
Ocean Ave
Flushing Ave
Canarsie Beach Park
Bensonhurst
Fort Hamilton Pkwy
New Utrecht Ave
Ocean Pkwy
Coney Island Ave
Nostrand Ave
Knapp St
Brooklyn Marine Park
Floyd Bennett Field
Rockaway Bay
Belt Pkwy
Cropsey Ave
Stillwell Ave
McDonald Ave
Ave U
Beach Channel Dr
Lower New York Bay
Neptune Ave
Brighton Beach
Rockaway Inlet
ATLANTIC OCEAN
Coney Island
20

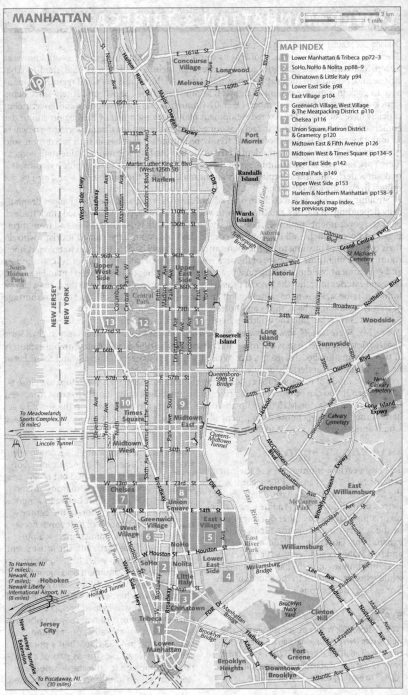

MANHATTAN

0 ____ 2 km
0 ____ 1 mile

Drinking p287; Eating p249; Shopping p217; Sleeping p349

The borough comes to a pencil point at its southern tip, forming the general swath known as Lower Manhattan. Teeming with iconic images that include Wall St, City Hall, the Brooklyn Bridge and, offshore in the near distance, the Statue of Liberty, this is a small region that manages to pack in a diverse wallop of sights. It's come back to life slowly and surely since being struck a heavy blow on September 11, 2001 (though bickering developers and government officials have seriously delayed redevelopment plans, leaving much of this region still under construction). The whole area, in fact, has gone through a recent renaissance, bringing newness in many forms – museums, hotels and trendy restaurants – that has in turn lured more and more visitors. Relatively new residents have made this the fastest growing residential 'hood in New York for several years running. Add those elements to the area's geographic narrowness – making waterfronts and sweeping views an intimate part of the fabric here – and you've got quite a lively little city corner.

Strolling the winding streets here is an adventure to be sure, and one that changes dramatically depending on the day and time of your visit. Weekdays bustle with focused stock traders, bankers, government employees, housing lawyers and politicians, who rush to and from meetings and power lunches all day long. Weekend days belong in large part to tourists, who do their own form of bustling to hit the many attractions or get back to their fab water-view hotel room. Come nighttime, the pace of the area really slows, with shops closing early, courthouses and government buildings taking on a peaceful glow and the scattered collection of late-night bars and eateries injecting the buzz of possibility into the air. An exception to these rules can be found in Tribeca, known for rambling loft apartments, an industrial-chic feel and no shortage of trendy restaurants, bars, shops and hotels.

A great way to tap into the offerings here is to check in with the Alliance for Downtown New York (Map pp72–3; ☎ 212-566-6700; www.downtownny.com; World Trade Center PATH Station, cnr Church & Vesey Sts, also at Staten Island Ferry Terminal), which hands out maps and offers neighborhood factoids to intrepid explorers at two information booths, leads a free Wall St walking tour every Thursday and Saturday at noon and runs a wonderfully detailed website.

The best mode of transport for crisscrossing the area is walking, as most stops are close by each other. Or you can opt for short cab rides or helpful buses, using the M9 to cross from west to east or vice versa, the M15 to go up and down the east side or the M20 on the west. To get here in the first place, choose from practically any subway line. Check the map (pp72–3) to see which options get you closest to your mark.

NEW YORK HARBOR

The city's earliest immigrants got their first taste of New York here at Ellis Island, with the Statue of Liberty in sharp relief nearby. Retracing their footprints is a fine idea – as is luxuriating in the many other offerings down in these parts, including the picnic-perfect expanses on Governor's Island and the fun and free Staten Island Ferry, which gives you close-up glimpses of all the harbor's highlights while whisking you off to the shores of New York's forgotten borough.

STATUE OF LIBERTY Map p68

☎ 212-363-3200; www.nps.gov/stli, www.statue cruises.com (ferry info); admission free, ferry (incl Ellis Island) adult/child/senior $12/5/10; ⏱ ferries every 15-30min 9:30am-3pm, park open till 5pm; ◉ 4, 5 to Bowling Green, 1 to South Ferry

One of the most recognizable icons in the world, the Statue of Liberty is a symbol of kinship and freedom formed out of 31 tons of copper and standing 93m from ground to torch-tip. A joint effort between America and France to commemorate the centennial of the Declaration of Independence, it was created by commissioned sculptor Frédéric-Auguste Bartholdi. The artist spent most of the next 20 years turning his dream – to create the monument and mount it in the New York Harbor – into reality. Along the way it was hindered by serious financial problems, but was helped in part by the fund-raising efforts of newspaper publisher Joseph Pulitzer, as well as poet Emma Lazarus, who in 1883 published a poem called 'The New Colossus' as part of a fund-raising campaign for the statue's pedestal. Her words have long since been associated

WATER, WATER, ALL AROUND

It can be easy for ever-distracted New Yorkers to forget that they live on an island, surrounded by water – although anyone who's ever tried to hop in a car and escape for a holiday weekend is soon reminded while trying to exit Manhattan via one of the always-clogged tunnels or bridges. Still, if you happen to remember in a good moment, it can add a wonderful dimension to your city experience. The waters – comprised of the Hudson River to the west, the East River to the east and, to the south, the New York Harbor, Upper and Lower New York Bays and the Atlantic Ocean – may not be as busy as in the days when New York was a truly bustling port, but they are still plied day in and day out by barges, freighters and tankers en route to Brooklyn's shores; water taxis going back and forth between Manhattan and New Jersey; pleasure voyages on sailboats, kayaks and the famous Circle Line; and gargantuan cruise ships (including both the QE2, which docked here many times, and its successor, the Queen Mary 2), which arrive and leave like sideways skyscrapers along the western shores of Midtown.

For more details on New York's water life of both today and the past, visit the South Street Seaport Museum (p81), which is home to a fleet of historic schooners. And then get yourself out onto the water! There are various ways for you to do it:

- For a 30-minute rush, take a ride on the Beast (☎ 212-630-8855; www.circleline42.com; $18), a tourist fave that will ferry you through the Hudson and around the Statue of Liberty at a brisk 45mph.
- Hop aboard the free and easy Staten Island Ferry (see p75), joining a crowd of commuters to enjoy great glimpses of the skyline.
- Go for a sunset sail aboard one of the South Street Seaport's historic schooners, such as the Pioneer (☎ 212-738-8786; $19).
- Take one of the various sightseeing cruises offered by New York Waterway (☎ 800-533-3779; www.nywaterway.com) or the Circle Line (see p404).
- In the summertime, hop aboard a SeaStreak (www.seastreak.com), which will ferry you 30 minutes away to the wonderful beach getaway of Sandy Hook, New Jersey (see p381).
- Sink yourself into a kayak and paddle along on a tour of the Hudson River with some equipment (and guidance) from the Manhattan Kayak Company (p330) – or do some DIY paddling from the Downtown Boathouse (p330), where use of kayaks is absolutely free!
- Experience the fabulous Floating Pool (www.brooklynbridgepark.org), a massive swimming pool atop an old barge that moves to a different docking point each summer. It's a unique way to cool off and enjoy stellar views.
- Enjoy a day at the beach at one of the many sandy spits around the city, from Rockaway Beach (p205) in Queens to Brooklyn's Coney Island (p195).

with the monument and its connection to newly arrived immigrants:

Give me your tired, your poor,
Your huddled masses yearning to breathe free,
The wretched refuse of your teeming shore.
Send these, the homeless, tempest-tost to me,
I lift my lamp beside the golden door!

Ironically, these famous words were added to the base only in 1903, over 15 years after the poet's death.

Bartholdi's work on the statue was also delayed by structural challenges – a problem resolved by the metal framework mastery of railway engineer Gustave Eiffel (of yes, the famous tower). The work of art was finally completed in France in 1884 (a

bit off schedule for that centennial). It was shipped here as 350 pieces packed in 214 crates, reassembled over a span of four months and placed on a US-made granite pedestal for a spectacular October 1886 dedication.

The statue and Liberty Island were put under the administration of the National Park Service in 1933; in 1984 a restoration began on the Lady's oxidized copper, and the UN placed it on a list of World Heritage Sites.

Unfortunately, the icon has been a bit less enjoyable in the wake of September 11, as it joined the list of many other city landmarks that became hyper-protected and off-limits to the public. The statue's interior, crown and museum were closed for three years after that fateful day, reopening with much fanfare in July 2004 following a multimillion-dollar renovation. Although you still cannot enter the statue itself – a

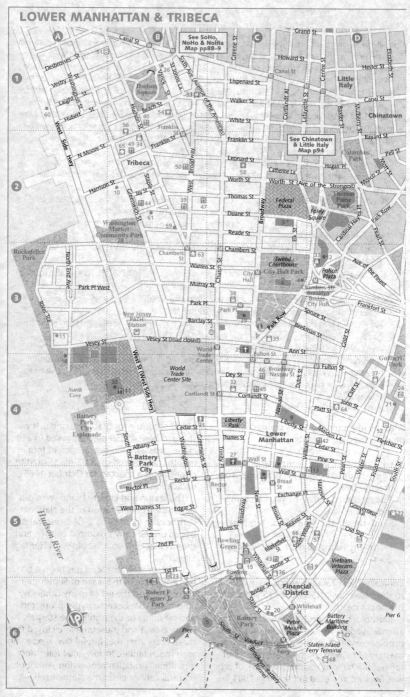

See SoHo, NoHo & Nolita Map pp88–9

See Chinatown & Little Italy Map p94

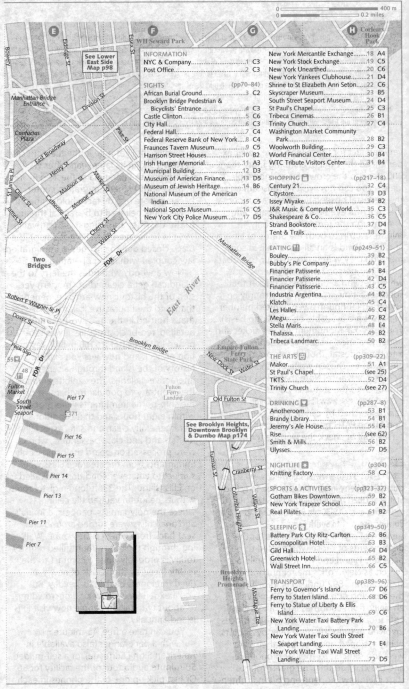

INFORMATION
NYC & Company...................................1 C3
Post Office...2 C3

SIGHTS (pp70–84)
African Burial Ground..........................3 C2
Brooklyn Bridge Pedestrian &
  Bicyclists' Entrance..........................4 C3
Castle Clinton.....................................5 C6
City Hall..6 C3
Federal Hall..7 C4
Federal Reserve Bank of New York....8 C4
Fraunces Tavern Museum....................9 C5
Harrison Street Houses.....................10 B2
Irish Hunger Memorial......................11 A3
Municipal Building.............................12 D3
Museum of American Finance...........13 D5
Museum of Jewish Heritage..............14 B6
National Museum of the American
  Indian...15 C5
National Sports Museum....................16 C5
New York City Police Museum...........17 D5

New York Mercantile Exchange........18 A4
New York Stock Exchange.................19 C5
New York Unearthed..........................20 C6
New York Yankees Clubhouse...........21 D4
Shrine to St Elizabeth Ann Seton......22 C6
Skyscraper Museum...........................23 B5
South Street Seaport Museum...........24 D4
St Paul's Chapel.................................25 C3
Tribeca Cinemas.................................26 B1
Trinity Church....................................27 C4
Washington Market Community
  Park..28 B2
Woolworth Building...........................29 C3
World Financial Center......................30 B4
WTC Tribute Visitors Center..............31 B4

SHOPPING (pp217–18)
Century 21..32 C4
Citystore...33 D3
Issey Miyake......................................34 B2
J&R Music & Computer World............35 C3
Shakespeare & Co..............................36 C5
Strand Bookstore...............................37 D4
Tent & Trails......................................38 C3

EATING (pp249–51)
Bouley..39 B2
Bubby's Pie Company.........................40 B1
Financier Patisserie............................41 B4
Financier Patisserie............................42 D4
Financier Patisserie............................43 C5
Industria Argentina...........................44 B2
Klatch...45 C4
Les Halles...46 C4
Megu..47 B2
Stella Maris..48 E4
Thalassa...49 B2
Tribeca Landmarc...............................50 B2

THE ARTS (pp309–22)
Makor...51 A1
St Paul's Chapel.........................(see 25)
TKTS...52 D4
Trinity Church ....(see 27)

DRINKING (pp287–8)
Anotheroom.......................................53 B1
Brandy Library...................................54 B1
Jeremy's Ale House............................55 E4
Rise...(see 62)
Smith & Mills......................................56 B2
Ulysses...57 D5

NIGHTLIFE (p304)
Knitting Factory.................................58 C2

SPORTS & ACTIVITIES (pp323–37)
Gotham Bikes Downtown...................59 B2
New York Trapeze School..................60 A1
Real Pilates..61 B4

SLEEPING (pp349–50)
Battery Park City Ritz-Carlton............62 B6
Cosmopolitan Hotel...........................63 B3
Gild Hall...64 D4
Greenwich Hotel................................65 B2
Wall Street Inn...................................66 C5

TRANSPORT (pp389–96)
Ferry to Governor's Island.................67 D6
Ferry to Staten Island........................68 D6
Ferry to Statue of Liberty & Ellis
  Island..69 C6
New York Water Taxi Battery Park
  Landing...70 B6
New York Water Taxi South Street
  Seaport Landing..............................71 E4
New York Water Taxi Wall Street
  Landing...72 D5

See Lower East Side Map p98

Manhattan Bridge Entrance

Confucius Plaza

Two Bridges

FDR Dr

East River

Manhattan Bridge

Robert F Wagner Sr Pl

Dover St

Peck Slip

Brooklyn Bridge

Fulton Market

South Street Seaport

Pier 17

Pier 16

Pier 15

Pier 14

Pier 13

Pier 11

Pier 7

Empire–Fulton Ferry State Park

New Dock St

Fulton Ferry Landing

Old Fulton St

See Brooklyn Heights, Downtown Brooklyn & Dumbo Map p174

Furman St

Cranberry St

Columbia Heights

Willow St

Brooklyn Heights Promenade

Montague Tce

STATUE OF LIBERTY SURVIVAL GUIDE

Deciding to spend your afternoon visiting the Statue of Liberty is kind of like heading directly into the belly of the tourism beast – not because it's not a great place to visit, but because crowds and waits can make for much anxiety. Skip all that and enjoy the icon by just following a few simple rules of thumb: first, buy your tickets online in advance and you'll get a pass with a specific entrance time, which will let you breeze onto the boat. Second, try to choose either the first or last time of the day, as these can be less mobbed than middle-of-the-day options. Finally, have an added adventure by heading out from the Jersey side instead, at Liberty State Park (☎ 201-435-9499; www.libertystatepark.org), which tends to be less crowded than the Manhattan approach. It may be a bit more complicated to get there, but you can always combine the detour with a stop in Hoboken or Jersey City, both interesting urban enclaves of New Jersey.

very sad fact for those who have never experienced the thrill of climbing more than 300 steps to the crown for an incredible view – you can now visit its museum and the pedestal observation deck, all under the watchful eye of an official park ranger.

Although the ferry ride lasts only 15 minutes, a trip to both the Statue of Liberty and Ellis Island is an all-day affair. In summer, you may wait up to an hour to embark on an 800-person ferry, and reservations, which get you a 'time pass' (a ticket that specifies a time to enter), are strongly encouraged (although a very limited number of passes are available on a walk-up basis). You'll need a 'Monument Access' ticket and undergo a special security screening to get into the pedestal, though this option is free and must be chosen while purchasing ferry tickets in advance. Note that a less crowded approach to the statue is via Liberty State Park (☎ 201-435-9499; www.libertystatepark.org), which can be reached by car, taxi or a combination of the PATH train and light rail in New Jersey; call or check the website for details.

ELLIS ISLAND Map p68

☎ 212-363-3200; www.nps.gov/elis, www.statuecruises.com (ferry info); admission free, ferry (incl Statue of Liberty) adult/child/senior $12/5/10; ferries every 15-30min 9:30am-3pm; 4, 5 to Bowling Green, 1 to South Ferry

An icon of mythical proportions for the descendents of those who passed through here, this island and its hulking building served as New York's main immigration station from 1892 until 1954, processing the amazing number of 12,000 individuals daily, from countries including Ireland, England, Germany and Austria. The process involved getting the once-over by doctors, being assigned new names if their own were too difficult to spell or pronounce, and basically getting the green light to start their new, hopeful and often frighteningly difficult lives here in the teeming city of New York. In its later years, after WWI and during the paranoia of the 'Red Scare' in this country, the immigration center became more of a de facto holding pen for newcomers believed to be radical threats to the US. After admitting its last arrival in 1954 (a Norwegian merchant seaman), the place closed due to changes in immigration law coupled with rising operating costs.

Now anybody who rides the ferry to the island can get a cleaned-up, modern version of the historic new-arrival experience, thanks to the impressive Immigration Museum that's housed in the massive, beautifully detailed, red-brick structure. It was reopened in 1990 after a $160 million restoration project, and now lets you explore the history of the island through a series of interactive galleries. The exhibits emphasize that, contrary to popular myth, most of the ship-borne immigrants were processed within eight hours and that conditions were generally clean and safe, especially for 1st- and 2nd-class passengers, who were processed on board their ships; only immigrants from the steerage class were subject to whatever conditions prevailed on Ellis Island. The 338ft-long registry room, with its beautiful vaulted tile ceiling, is where the polygamists, paupers, criminals and anarchists were turned around and sent back from whence they came. Walking through the roomy, light-filled registry today is probably quite a contrast to the reality faced by thousands of newly arrived foreigners back in its heyday. But you'll experience a new kind of crowding, as about two million people now visit Ellis Island annually.

You can take a free, 45-minute guided tour with a park ranger (also available in American Sign Language), or a self-guided, 50-minute audio tour of the facility for $6. Or just pick up one of the phones in each display area and listen to the recorded, yet affecting memories of real Ellis Island immigrants, taped in the 1980s. For even more context, you can catch daily theatrical productions based on the accounts of immigrants, as well as a free, 30-minute film about the immigrant experience called *Island of Hope, Island of Tears*.

To be sure you get onto a ferry, you should secure a 'time pass' by making advance reservations. However, if you're not one for planning in advance, you can take your chances by going for one of a limited number of time passes available to walkups on a first-come-first-served basis. Also, it should be noted that during the especially busy summer months, there is a less crowded approach to Ellis Island, via ferry from New Jersey's Liberty State Park (☎ 201-435-9499; www.libertystatepark.org).

STATEN ISLAND FERRY Map pp72–3
☎ 311; free; ☑ every 30 min; ◉ 1 to South Ferry, 4, 5 to Bowling Green

Staten Islanders know the fleet of hulking, dirty-orange ferryboats as commuter vehicles, while Manhattanites like to think of them as their secret, romantic vessels for a spring-day escape. But that secret is long out, as many a tourist has been clued into the charms of the Staten Island Ferry, which provides one of the most wonderful, free adventures in New York. In service since

1905, the city celebrated the line's centennial with great fanfare in 2005, using it as a chance to promote the idea of visiting Staten Island – a novel idea to most New Yorkers. Today, the ferry service carries more than 19 million passengers each year across the 5.2-mile stretch of the Hudson River that separates downtown Manhattan from the Staten Island neighborhood of St George. So whether you choose to simply ride it there and back in one run – enjoying grand views of the city skyline, the Verrazano-Narrows Bridge (which connects Staten Island to Brooklyn) and the Statue of Liberty – or stay and poke around the shores of the St George neighborhood before catching a later ferry, it's sure to be a memorable experience. For a great DIY adventure, take your bike aboard and head toward one of Staten Island's majestic parklands or sandy beaches (see p213).

BATTERY PARK CITY

There's a surreal sense to this corner of the city. That's because the highway-like West St cuts much of its clutch of gleaming, modern high-rises and lovely promenades and parks off from the rest of the city. Its position at sunset makes it feel like people on the street and the hovering towers are quietly aglow.

By day, you can find peace here, thanks to the 30-acre waterfront swath of parkland that stretches along the Hudson River from

GOVERNOR'S ISLAND

For decades, New Yorkers knew Governor's Island (Map p68; ☎ 212-514-8285; www.nps.gov/gois, www.govisland .com; admission free; tours twice daily Tue-Sat, summer only; ◉ 4, 5 to Bowling Green, 1 to South Ferry) only as an untouchable, mysterious patch of green out in the harbor. As of 2003, ownership of the 172-acre island was transferred from the federal government to both the National Park Service (which owns a 22-acre area) and the Governor's Island Preservation and Education Corporation, and both were charged with the job and privilege of transforming this well-trod ground into an elaborately designed public parkland.

The island's historic significance is far-reaching: besides serving as a successful military fort in the Revolutionary War, the Union Army's central recruiting station during the Civil War and the take-off point for Wilbur Wright's famous 1909 flight around the Statue of Liberty, it's where the 1988 Reagan–Gorbachev summit signaled the beginning of the end of the Cold War.

Anyone interested in relaxing on these peaceful grounds has been doing so since 2003, when the National Park Service began offering daily ferry service (a 5-minute ride from Manhattan) in summer, along with frequent walking tours. Explorers of this little gem can enjoy several highlights, including two 19th-century fortifications – Fort Jay and the three-tiered, sandstone Castle Williams – plus open lawns, massive shade trees and unsurpassed city views.

But the island's future holds many more landscaped pleasures, as the new development plan – arrived at through many public meetings and incorporating the input of various civic and community groups – adds to the 22 acres of national park land a sweeping 90 acres of recreational open space, including a botanic forest, concert amphitheater, bike trails and a waterfront promenade, all designed by some of the city's most renowned architects. (The plan was still in discussion phases at this writing.)

Chambers St to Pier 1 on the southern tip of the island, encompassing Rockefeller Park, the plaza of the World Financial Center, the tree-lined Battery Park City Esplanade, Robert F Wagner Jr Park and Battery Park. It's a great opportunity for escape, with glorious sunsets and Statue of Liberty views, outdoor concerts and films in summer, Frisbee and soccer games, and smooth paths for cycling, running, strolling or rollerblading. Kids will love romping in the playgrounds and climbing on the whimsical bronze sculptures by Tom Otterness. Plus, the Battery Park City Parks Conservancy (☎ 212-267-9700; www.bpcparks.org) offers a range of free or low-fee walking tours, group swims, children's programs and classes here. Various historic sites and small museums can bring you back to earth nicely with some culture to mix in with the escapism.

HUDSON RIVER PARK Maps pp72–3 & p69
www.hudsonriverpark.org; Manhattan's west side from Battery Park to 59th St
Encompassing way more than Battery Park – though its beginning (or end) is located here – this 5-mile, 550-acre waterfront park that runs along the lower western side of Manhattan is overseen by the Hudson River Park Trust and is still in various stages of construction. It's been a beloved addition, as for many years the west side was known more for snarling highway traffic, unseemly pastimes and smoggy New Jersey vistas. With this park NYC follows the lead of most other cities that sit on bodies of water – Paris, Chicago, Miami – and turns the shoreline into something spectacular.

Among its charms are a bike/run/skate path snaking along its entire length, community gardens, basketball courts, playgrounds, dog runs, and a collection of renovated piers jutting out into the water, serving as riverfront esplanades, miniature golf courses and alfresco movie theaters and concert venues come summer. For a detailed map of the entire park, visit the Trust's website.

MUSEUM OF JEWISH HERITAGE
Map pp72–3
☎ 646-437-4200; www.mjhnyc.org; 36 Battery Pl; adult/child/student/senior $10/free/5/7, admission free 4-8pm Wed; ☽ 10am-5:45pm Sun-Tue & Thu, 10am-8pm Wed, 10am-5pm Fri; ☻ 4, 5 to Bowling Green
This 30,000-sq-ft waterfront memorial museum, with a six-sided shape and three tiers

to symbolize the Star of David and the six million Jews who perished in the Holocaust, explores all aspects of what it means to be Jewish in modern-day New York. Displays include personal artifacts, photographs and documentary films. A centerpiece of the museum is the Garden of Stones – an outdoor memorial garden created by artist Andy Goldsworthy (and his first permanent exhibition in NYC), in which 18 boulders form a narrow pathway for contemplating the fragility of life – dedicated to those who have lost loved ones in the Holocaust. The onsite, kosher Heritage Café serves light food during museum hours, and the 375-seat Safra Hall is a great venue for films, plays, ongoing lecture series and special holiday performances. Frequent, free workshops for families with children are also on offer.

SKYSCRAPER MUSEUM Map pp72–3
☎ 212-968-1961; www.skyscraper.org; 39 Battery Pl; adult/senior & student $5/2.50; ☽ noon-6pm Wed-Sun; ☻ 4, 5 to Bowling Green
Occupying the ground-floor space of the Ritz-Carlton Hotel, this wonderful ode to skyscrapers the world over features two serene, high-gloss galleries. One focuses on rotating exhibits, environmentally sustainable skyscrapers, Hong Kong's verticality versus that of New York and the creations of Frank Lloyd Wright. The other half of the museum is dedicated to a permanent study of high-rise history, including a size chart of the world's biggest buildings (Taiwan's Taipei 101, built in 2004, is currently in the lead – it's a whopping 1670ft high!), as well as exhibits on the construction of the Empire State Building and an overview of downtown architecture. The museum is also home to the cutting-edge technology known as VIVA – the Visual Index to the Virtual Archive, a visually based interface that uses a 3-D computer model of Manhattan as a clickable map, allowing users to see the city's past and present, and to explore the museum's collections through an online database (which you can access via the museum's website).

CASTLE CLINTON Map pp72–3
☎ 212-344-7220; www.nps.gov/cacl; Battery Park; ☽ 8am-5pm; ☻ 4, 5 to Bowling Green, 1 to South Ferry
Built as a fort to defend the New York Harbor during the War of 1812, the circular wall got its current moniker in 1817 to

honor then mayor DeWitt Clinton. Later, and before Ellis Island opened to immigrants, Castle Garden (as it was then known) served as the major processing center for new arrivals, welcoming more than 8 million people between 1855 and 1890. Today it's a restored national monument – after turns as an opera house, entertainment complex and aquarium – and now serves as a visitor center, with historical displays, as well as a massive performance space, where outdoor concerts are held on the roofless stage for summer shows under the stars. Rangers also lead 20-minute historic tours of the site on warm afternoons.

IRISH HUNGER MEMORIAL Map pp72–3
290 Vesey St at North End Ave; admission free; 2, 3 to Park Place
This compact labyrinth of low limestone walls and patches of grass is the creation of artist Brian Tolle, and is meant to increase awareness of the Great Irish Famine and Migration (1845–52), which led so many immigrants to leave Ireland for the opportunity of a better life in the New World. Representing abandoned cottages, stone walls and potato fields, it was created with stones from each of Ireland's 32 counties. The winning proposal in a design competition organized by the Battery Park City Authority in 2000, Tolle's sculpture is an even more fitting metaphor than he probably meant it to be: it's turned out to be a delicate piece, and has already required extensive repairs due to harsh winters that chipped away at its structure.

WORLD FINANCIAL CENTER Map pp72–3
☎ 212-945-2600; www.worldfinancialcenter.com; 200 Liberty St; E to World Trade Center, R, W to Cortlandt St
This mall-like complex consists of four office towers surrounding the Winter Garden, a palm-and-light-filled glass atrium that hosts free concerts, dance performances and art exhibits throughout the year – a program the WFC has been putting a lot of effort into in the hopes of being thought of as an arts center as well as a retail hub. Some of the more impressive performances have included gospel choirs and ballet companies. All the offerings make this a good place to head if the weather turns nasty – you can pass an hour or so by shopping at the various chain stores (Ann Taylor, Banana

Republic, Gap) or eating at the large food-court area.

SHRINE TO ST ELIZABETH ANN SETON Map pp72–3
☎ 212-269-6865; www.setonshrine.com; Our Lady of the Rosary Church, 7 State St; admission free; 6:30am-5pm Mon-Fri, before & after 12:15pm mass Sat & 9am & noon masses Sun; N, R, W to Whitehall St
This mystical, silent escape from the city is a tiny church and shrine to Mother Seton, housed in the red-brick, Federal-style home where America's first saint actually lived in 1801. Born in NYC, Elizabeth Ann married and had five children but was eventually widowed, which inspired her to become a nun and found the Sisters of Charity. Today, her devotees can often be found praying inside this spiritual space at all hours of the day.

WALL STREET & THE FINANCIAL DISTRICT
Anchored by the mile-long and world-famous Wall St, which was named for a defensive wall the Dutch built in 1653 to mark the northern line of their colony, New Amsterdam, this history-steeped area is where the US Congress first convened, where Alexander Hamilton founded the nation's first bank and where America's first president, George Washington, was inaugurated. The concentrated feel of the area is distinguished by intimate, circuitous and sometimes confusing side streets flanked by stoic Federal homes, Greek-revival temples, Gothic churches, Renaissance palazzos and a fine collection of early-20th-century skyscrapers. Though the New York Stock Exchange has been closed to visitors indefinitely 'for security purposes' since September 11, tourists still gather on the sidewalk to gawk at harried traders who scurry in and out for cigarettes and hot dogs before getting back to their frenzied business. Nearby is the Federal Reserve Bank, where just glancing at the hushed, guarded exterior is a good reminder that you have most definitely stumbled onto the seat of capitalism.

WTC TRIBUTE VISITORS CENTER
Map pp72–3
☎ 866-737-1184; www.tributewtc.org; 120 Liberty St; admission $10; Mon, Wed-Sat 10am-6pm, Tue noon-6pm, Sun noon-5pm; E to World Trade Center, R, W to Cortlandt St

Operated by the nonprofit Families' Association, this center serves as a temporary memorial to the September 11 disaster. It features a gallery of moving images and artifacts, including battered firefighting uniforms, and the opportunity to join one-hour tours of the WTC site's perimeter. For details about the WTC redevelopment efforts and plans for a permanent memorial and museum, see the boxed text on p56.

NEW YORK STOCK EXCHANGE
Map pp72–3

☎ 212-656-5168; www.nyse.com; 11 Wall St; ⊚ 2, 3, 4, 5 to Wall St, J, M, Z to Broad St

Wall Street has become the widely recognized symbol for US capitalism as home to this, the world's best-known stock exchange (NYSE). Before it closed to the public due to stepped-up security measures, more than 700,000 visitors a year passed behind the portentous Romanesque facade to see where about a billion shares valued at around $44 billion change hands daily.

Feel free to gawk outside the building, though, where you'll see dozens of brokers dressed in color-coordinated trading jackets popping out for a quick cigarette or lunch from a vendor cart; luckily for you, the street scene outside is often more entertaining than the money-swapping within.

Frantic buying and selling by those familiar red-faced traders screaming 'Sell! Sell!' goes on at the New York Mercantile Exchange (Map pp72–3; ☎ 212-299-2499; www.nymex.com; 1 North End Ave; ⊚ 2, 3 to Park Place, E to World Trade Center), near Vesey St. This exchange deals in gold, gas and oil commodities, but no longer with tourists; like the NYSE, it's closed to visitors, but encourages you to check back periodically to see if the policy has changed.

FEDERAL HALL Map pp72–3

☎ 212-825-6888; www.nps.gov/feha; 26 Wall St; admission free; ⊙ 9am-5pm Mon-Fri; ⊚ 2, 3, 4, 5 to Wall St, J, M, Z to Broad St

Following an extensive renovation, Federal Hall, which contains a museum dedicated to postcolonial New York, features exhibits on George Washington's inauguration, Alexander Hamilton's close relationship with New York City, and a visitor information hall where you can pick up information about downtown cultural happenings.

The building itself, distinguished by a huge statue of George Washington, stands on the site of New York's original City Hall, where the first US Congress convened and Washington took the oath of office as the first US president on April 30, 1789. After that structure's demolition in the early 19th century, this Greek revival building gradually rose in its place between 1834 and 1842. Considered to be one of the country's premier examples of classical architecture, it served as the US Customs House until 1862. It's also played a significant role in establishing freedom of the press, as it's where John Peter Zenger was jailed, tried and acquitted of libel for exposing government corruption in his newspaper, a history lesson that is still poignant today.

NATIONAL MUSEUM OF THE AMERICAN INDIAN Map pp72–3

☎ 212-514-3700; www.nmai.si.edu; 1 Bowling Green; admission free; ⊙ 10am-5pm Fri-Wed, to 8pm Thu; ⊚ 4, 5 to Bowling Green

This museum, an affiliate of the Smithsonian Institution, is housed in the spectacular former US Customs House (which celebrated its centennial in 2007), near the southernmost point of Manhattan. It's an ironically grand space for the country's leading museum on Native American art, established by oil heir George Gustav Heye in 1916. The facility's information center is in the former duty collection office, with computer banks located next to old wrought-iron teller booths.

The galleries are on the 2nd floor, beyond a vast rotunda featuring statues of famous navigators and murals celebrating shipping history. This museum does little to explain the history of Native Americans but instead concentrates on Native American culture, boasting a million-item collection of crafts and everyday objects. Computer touch-screens feature insights into Native American life and beliefs, and working artists offer explanations of their techniques. The museum also hosts a range of cultural programs, including dance and music performances, readings for children, craft demonstrations, films and workshops. A shop on the 1st floor is well-stocked with Native American jewelry, books, CDs and crafts.

FRAUNCES TAVERN MUSEUM Map pp72–3

☎ 212-425-1778; www.frauncestavernmuseum .org; 54 Pearl St; adult/senior, student & child $4/3; ⊙ noon-5pm Mon-Sat; ⊚ 4, 5 to Bowling Green, R, W to Whitehall St

This unique museum/restaurant combo, a complex of four early-18th-century structures, is an homage to the nation-shaping events of 1783 – when the British left New York at the end of the Revolutionary War and General George Washington gave a farewell speech to his officers – all in the context of the Queen's Head Tavern. Owned by Samuel Fraunces, this was the most popular watering hole of its day, and the site of many historic moments.

The site was originally built as a tony residence for merchant Stephen Delancey's family; barkeeper Samuel Fraunces purchased it in 1762, turning it into a tavern in honor of the American victory in the Revolutionary War. It was in the 2nd-floor dining room on December 4, 1783, that George Washington bade farewell to the officers of the Continental Army after the British relinquished control of New York City. After the war, when New York was the nation's first capital, the space was used by the Departments of War, Treasury and Foreign Affairs. The tavern was closed and fell into disuse in the 19th century – and soon after was damaged during several massive fires that destroyed most colonial buildings and Dutch-built structures in the area. In 1904, the Sons of the Revolution, a historical society, bought the building and returned it to an approximation of its colonial-era look – an act believed to be the first major attempt at historical preservation in the USA.

Today the museum hosts historical walking tours, rotating exhibits and lunchtime and evening lectures, such as the recent 'The Women of the House: The Strong, Gutsy Women of Colonial New York,' by author Jean Zimmerman.

NATIONAL SPORTS MUSEUM Map pp72–3
☎ 212-837-7950; www.thesportsmuseum.com; 26 Broadway at Bowling Green; admission adult/child/senior $27/20/24; ⏰ Mon-Fri 9am-7pm, Sat & Sun to 9pm; ⊚ 4, 5 to Bowling Green
The newest cultural offering in these parts (opened in mid-2008) is jock heaven: a 100,000-sq-ft space comprising the first-ever all-sports museum in the US. Located in the landmark former Standard Oil Building and funded (to the tune of $60 million!) by post–September 11 Liberty Bonds and private investors, it's a multimedia experience offering more than 600 artifacts, 20 original films and a slew of interactive computer exhibits that offer virtual sports ex-

periences – from driving around a NASCAR racetrack to hearing the pressured plays of an NFL official. Gallery exhibits cover every conceivable sport, from basketball, tennis and swimming to hockey, equestrian events and speed racing. Tickets must be purchased in advance as they provide you with a specific entry date and time.

MUSEUM OF AMERICAN FINANCE
Map pp72–3
☎ 212-908-4110; www.financialhistory.org; 48 Wall St; adult/child under 6/student & senior $8/free/5; ⏰ 10am-4pm Tue-Sat; ⊚ 2, 3, 4, 5 to Wall St
One of the shining new examples of Lower Manhattan's cultural renaissance is this formerly under-the-radar tribute to finance. In a stunning new location (28 Broadway was its former home) that opened in early 2008, this museum comprises 30,000 sq ft in the old Bank of New York headquarters, with a grand space featuring 30ft ceilings, high arched windows, a majestic staircase to the mezzanine, glass chandeliers, and murals depicting historic scenes of banking and commerce. Exhibits focus on historic moments in American financial history, and permanent collections include rare, 18th-century documents, stock and bond certificates from the Gilded Age, the oldest known photograph of Wall St and a stock ticker from 1867.

BOWLING GREEN Map pp72–3
cnr Broadway & State St; ⊚ 4, 5 to Bowling Green
New York's oldest – and possibly tiniest – public park is believed to have been the spot where Dutch settler Peter Minuit paid Native Americans the equivalent of $24 to purchase Manhattan Island. The tree-filled triangle was leased by the people of New York from the English crown beginning in 1733, for the token amount of one peppercorn each. But an angry mob, inspired by George Washington's nearby reading of the Declaration of Independence, descended upon the site in 1776 and tore down a large statue of King George III; a fountain now stands in its place. The 7000lb bronze Charging Bull sculpture by Arturo Di Modica, which famously sits at the northern edge of the park, was actually placed here permanently after it mysteriously appeared in front of the New York Stock Exchange in 1989, two years after a market crash. Now it's the unwitting subject of constant

tourist photos and an unintentional Wall Street icon.

TRINITY CHURCH Map pp72–3

☎ 212-602-0800; www.trinitywallstreet.org; Broadway at Wall St; ☻ 8am-6pm Mon-Fri, to 4pm Sat, 7am-4pm Sun; ⊕ 2, 3, 4, 5 to Wall St, R, W to Rector St

This former Anglican parish church was founded by King William III in 1697 and once presided over several constituent chapels, including St Paul's Chapel (below) at the corner of Fulton St and Broadway. Its huge landholdings in Lower Manhattan made it the country's wealthiest and most influential church throughout the 18th century. The current Trinity Church is the third structure on the site. Designed by English architect Richard Upjohn, this 1846 building helped to launch the picturesque neo-Gothic movement in America. At the time of its construction, its 280ft-high bell tower made it the tallest building in New York City.

The long, dark interior of the church includes a beautiful stained-glass window over the altar, plus a small museum area that hosts rotating art exhibits. Out back, a peaceful, fenced-in cemetery is filled with ancient headstones smoothed by the centuries, and it's a fascinating, serene place to wander. Trinity, like other Anglican churches in America, became part of the Episcopal faith following American independence from Britain.

One of the best times to visit Trinity Church is during weekday lunchtime services or for its excellent Concerts at One midday music series, also held at St Paul's Chapel; admission is just a $2 suggested donation. Trinity is also known for its magnificent choir concerts, especially its annual December rendition of Handel's *Messiah*.

ST PAUL'S CHAPEL Map pp72–3

☎ 212-602-0800; www.saintpaulschapel.org; Broadway at Fulton St; ⊕ 4, 5 to Fulton St

George Washington worshipped here after his inauguration in 1789, and that was the biggest claim to fame for this colonial-era chapel (affiliated with Trinity Church, which sits further down Broadway) prior to September 11. After that fateful day, when the World Trade Center destruction occurred just a block behind this classic revival brownstone, the mighty structure became a spiritual support center for all

who needed it. Volunteers worked round the clock, serving meals, setting up beds, doling out massages and counseling rescue workers.

Today a moving interactive exhibit, 'Unwavering Spirit: Hope & Healing at Ground Zero,' sits beneath the elegant cut-glass chandeliers, bringing streams of people who are still searching for healing and understanding. The chapel, which functions more as a spiritual community center, also hosts workshops, special events and a popular classical-music series with free performances on Mondays at 1pm.

FEDERAL RESERVE BANK OF NEW YORK Map pp72–3

☎ 212-720-6130; www.ny.frb.org; 33 Liberty St at Nassau St; admission free; tours hourly 9:30am-2:30pm (except 12:30pm) Mon-Fri; ⊕ 2, 3, J, M, Z to Fulton St

Attention, money worshippers: the best reason to visit the Federal Reserve Bank is to get a chance to ogle the facility's high-security vault – more than 10,000 tons of gold reserves reside here, 80ft below ground. You'll only see a small part of that fortune, but signing on to a free tour here (the only way in) will also teach you a lot about the US Federal Reserve System. You can also browse through an exhibition of coins and counterfeit currency. Beware that reservations – which need to be made an annoying full month in advance – are required for the comprehensive tour.

SOUTH STREET SEAPORT

Long known as a mandatory stop on the tourist circuit, this is a historic corner turned commercial swath – largely a mall on the water, with some cultural distractions tossed in to keep things grounded. It's worth a visit for several reasons, though, and the main one is to get an idea of New York's long and storied seafaring past. There are plenty of reminders here of the salty old days, from the docked wooden schooners to the wonderful South Street Seaport Museum. There's also the skeleton of the iconic Fulton Fish Market, beloved for 180 years but closed since 2005, its prime space now being used to host occasional farmers markets; talks of a permanent one are among the hopes for the spot's future. While the gastronomic options have been nothing worth getting excited over for years, a recent boom in new eateries has injected the area with a renewed sense of excitement. But to get a sense of the gritty history of this waterfront area, check out the writings of the late literary journalist Joseph Mitchell, who wrote about the neighborhood's myriad characters in his now famous 1952 story 'Up in the Old Hotel,' published in a collection of his writings of the same name.

SOUTH STREET SEAPORT Map pp72–3

☎ 212-732-7678; www.southstseaport.com; ⊕ 2, 3, 4, 5, J, M, Z to Fulton St

This 11-block enclave of shops, piers and sights combines the best and worst in historic preservation. It's not on the radar for most New Yorkers, but tourists are drawn to the sea air, the nautical feel, the frequent street performers and the mobbed restaurants. Pier 17, beyond the elevated FDR Dr, is a waterfront-development project that's home to several floors of shops, restaurants and a rare public bathroom. Clustered around the piers are some genuinely significant 18th- and 19th-century buildings dating from the heyday of this old East River ferry port, which fell into disuse with the building of the Brooklyn Bridge and the establishment of deep-water jetties on the Hudson River. The pedestrian malls, historic tall ships and riverside locale make the seaport a picturesque destination or detour – and create a lovely backdrop if you happen to be standing in line for discounted Broadway tickets at the downtown TKTS booth (p313). Schermerhorn Row, a block of old warehouses bordered by Fulton, Front and South Sts, contains novelty shops, upscale boutiques and the New York Yankees Clubhouse (Map pp72–3; ☎ 212-514-7182; 8 Fulton St; ⏲ 10am-9pm Mon-Sat, 11am-8pm Sun), where you can purchase fee-free game tickets and plenty of Yankees souvenirs. In the summertime, the outdoor courtyard becomes home to an often worthy series of performances from local blues, jazz and rock bands.

SOUTH STREET SEAPORT MUSEUM
Map pp72–3

☎ 212-748-8600; www.southstreetseaport.org; 207 Front St; adult/child/senior & student $8/4/6; ⏲ 8am-6pm Tue-Sun Apr-Oct, 10am-5pm Fri-Mon Nov-Mar; ⊕ 2, 3, J, M, Z to Fulton St, A, C, 4, 5, to Broadway-Nassau St

Opened in 1967, this museum offers a glimpse of the seaport's history and a survey of the world's great ocean liners, with permanent exhibits and various other sites

dotted around the 11-block area. Included in the museum are three galleries, an antique printing shop, a children's center, a maritime crafts center and historic ships: just south of Pier 17 stands a group of tall-masted sailing ships – the *Peking, Wavertree, Pioneer, Ambrose* and *Helen McAllister,* among others – and the admission price to the museum includes access to their windswept decks and intimate interiors.

For a really special treat, join a sailing tour (☎ 212-748-8786; adult/child/senior $30/15/20) aboard the gorgeous, iron-hulled *Pioneer,* built in 1885 to carry mined sand but today just perfect for holding happy humans transfixed by the views. The two-hour journeys run from late May through mid-September from Tuesday to Friday evenings and Saturday and Sunday beginning at 1pm; passengers are encouraged to bring snacks and even a bottle of wine for this relaxing, stellar sail. Reservations are essential.

NEW YORK CITY POLICE MUSEUM
Map pp72–3

☎ 212-480-3100; www.nycpolicemuseum.org; 100 Old Slip; suggested donation adult/child/senior $5/2/3; ⏲ 10am-5pm Mon-Sat; ⊕ 1 to South Ferry, 2, 3 to Wall St

This minute museum is chock full of 'New York's Finest' facts and exhibits. It's housed in a building modeled after an Italian palace located on a landfilled inlet. Check out the cool old police vehicles (some sit right in the museum while others, like a 1939 beauty, appear only in photographs), as well as mugshots and weapons of some of New York's most notorious criminals, from Willie Sutton to Al Capone. There's also a collection of police shields and uniforms from throughout the decades, NYPD leadership histories, and a moving September 11 memorial exhibit called the Hall of Heroes.

CITY HALL & CIVIC CENTER

Here lies the center of all government business, where the frenzied buzz of change and progress (even if it might take years to see its effects) is bound to sweep you up. City Council members dash from public hearings to constituent brunches at nearby diners, reporters clamor to City Hall Park for press conferences while various civic groups gather for protests, and TV satellite vans camp out across from the majestic row of courthouses – all while resentful locals drag themselves to jury duty each afternoon. Hovering along the island's eastern edge here is the floating span of the Brooklyn Bridge (see the boxed text, opposite), which has a popular pedestrian and bicyclists' entrance just across from City Hall.

South of City Hall is Park Row, known as Newspaper Row when it was the center of New York newspaper publishing from the 1840s to the 1920s. Now it's the spot of a veritable strip mall of shops, including the excellent computer and electronics purveyor J&R Music & Computer World (p218).

CITY HALL Map pp72–3

☎ 212-788-6865; City Hall Park, Park Row; tours by appointment only; ⊙ 4, 5, 6 to Brooklyn Bridge-City Hall, J, M, Z to Chambers St

This elegant, cupola-topped marble hall, located in placid City Hall Park facing the entrance to the Brooklyn Bridge, has been home to New York City's government since 1812. In keeping with the half-baked civic planning that has often plagued large-scale New York projects, officials neglected to finish the building's northern side in marble, due to objections about cost. A compromise was made by finishing the northern facade in brownstone and reducing the size of the building overall. The domed tower was rebuilt in 1917 after being damaged by two fires, and the original marble (and brownstone) facades were replaced with limestone over a granite base in 1954–56. Its beautiful restoration prompted critic Ada Louise Huxtable to call it a 'symbol of taste, excellence and quality not always matched by the policies inside.'

After climbing the formal staircase out front – the site of constant press conferences, as well as civil demonstrations (with pre-arranged permits) – you'll soon find yourself under the soaring rotunda, which is supported by 10 Corinthian columns on the second floor. One highlight inside includes the spot where Abraham Lincoln's coffin lay in state for a brief time in 1865 (look at the top of the staircase on the 2nd floor). The Governor's Room, a reception area where the mayor entertains important guests, contains 12 portraits of the founding fathers by John Trumbull, George Washington's old writing table and other examples of Federal-style furniture, and the remnants of a flag flown at the first president's 1789 inaugural ceremony. If you take a quick peek into the City Council chambers, you might even see lawmakers of the 51-member body deliberating over issues such as urban development, the budget or civil rights.

You can also explore the grand interior of City Hall through free guided tours (☎ 311, from outside NYC 212-NEW-YORK; tours weekdays by appt only) offered by the Art Commission of the City of New York (call for reservations).

Out front is bustling City Hall Park, graced with gas lamps, fountains, lovely landscaping, chess tables and benches, making it a nice place to sit with a sandwich for some prime people-watching. Hot months brings Summerfest, a concert series of live R&B and jazz, on weekends. Adding to the excitement here is the fact that it's often edged by protestors of one issue or another, unless the groups have planned ahead and gotten a protest permit (required by Mayor Bloomberg for demonstrations within the actual park or on the steps of City Hall).

MUNICIPAL BUILDING Map pp72–3

1 Centre St at Chambers St; ⊙ 4, 5, 6 to Brooklyn Bridge-City Hall, J, M, Z to Chambers St

ASHES TO ASHES: THE AFRICAN BURIAL GROUND

Sitting among the financial movers and shakers and beautiful, old, official buildings is a quiet piece of very important history: the African Burial Ground (Map pp72–3; ☎ 212-637-2019; www.nps.gov/afbg; 290 Broadway btwn Duane & Elk Sts; ⌚ 9am-5pm; ⊙ 4, 5 to Wall St). During preliminary construction of a downtown office building in 1991, builders were shocked to find more than 400 stacked wooden caskets, discovered only 16 to 28ft below street level. When it became clear that the boxes held the remains of enslaved Africans (nearby Trinity Church graveyard had banned the burial of Africans at the time), construction was halted, an investigation was launched and all hell broke loose. As a result, the site became permanently protected as a National Historic Landmark, and today it's part of the National Parks Service. A visitor center provides historic background – and, as a federal site, requires airport-like security screenings, so leave your nail files in the hotel. The beautiful memorial honors an estimated 15,000 Africans buried here during the 17th and 18th centuries.

BROOKLYN BRIDGE

A New York icon, the Brooklyn Bridge (Map pp72–3; ◎ 4, 5, 6 to Brooklyn Bridge-City Hall) was the world's first steel suspension bridge. When it opened in 1883, the 1596ft span between its two support towers was the longest in history. Although its construction was fraught with disaster, the bridge became a magnificent example of urban design, inspiring poets, writers and painters. Today, the Brooklyn Bridge continues to dazzle – many regard it as the most beautiful bridge in the world.

The bridge, which spans the East River from Manhattan to Brooklyn, was designed by the Prussian-born engineer John Roebling, who was knocked off a pier in Fulton Landing in June 1869; he died of tetanus poisoning before construction of the bridge even began. His son, Washington Roebling, supervised construction of the bridge, which lasted 14 years and managed to survive budget overruns and the deaths of 20 workers. The younger Roebling himself suffered from the bends while helping to excavate the riverbed for the bridge's western tower and remained bedridden for much of the project; his wife Emily oversaw construction in his stead. There was one final tragedy to come in June 1883, when the bridge opened to pedestrian traffic. Someone in the crowd shouted, perhaps as a joke, that the bridge was collapsing into the river, setting off a mad rush in which 12 people were trampled to death.

The bridge entered its second century as strong and beautiful as ever following an extensive renovation in the early 1980s. The pedestrian walkway that begins just east of City Hall affords a wonderful view of lower Manhattan; observation points under the support towers offer brass 'panorama' histories of the waterfront. Just take care to stay on the side of the walkway marked for folks on foot – one half is designated for cyclists, who use it en masse for both commuting and pleasure rides, and frustrated pedalers have been known to get nasty with oblivious tourists who wander, camera pressed to an eye, into the bike lane. Barring any such run-ins, you should reach Brooklyn after about a 20-minute walk. Bear left to Empire-Fulton Ferry State Park or Cadman Plaza West, which runs alongside Middagh St in the heart of Brooklyn Heights, taking you to Brooklyn's downtown area; don't miss the ornate Brooklyn Borough Hall (see p173) and the Brooklyn Heights Promenade (see p168).

Built between 1913 and 1918, this massive, Federal-style skyscraper houses various city government agencies, from the city's Marriage Bureau and Office of the Comptroller to the local NPR affiliate public-radio station, WNYC. The U-shaped, 25-story behemoth sits over an open-sided, column-ringed plaza that's about three stories tall, and walking through here will surely have you rubbing elbows with all manner of government employees (an interesting, if motley, crew). The building is best admired from a distance, though, and walking or cabbing it across Chambers St, especially at night when it's all lit up, gives you such a sense of its grand immensity that you'll feel as if you're hurtling toward a mountain.

WOOLWORTH BUILDING Map pp72–3
233 Broadway at Park Pl; ◎ 4, 5, 6 to Brooklyn Bridge-City Hall, J, M, Z to Chambers St
Cass Gilbert's magnificent 60-story Woolworth Building was completed in 1913. At 792ft, it was the tallest building in the city – and the world – until it was surpassed by the Chrysler Building in 1930. It's designed in a neo-Gothic style meant to emphasize its height and constructed of masonry and terra-cotta over a steel frame. At its dedication, the building was described as a 'cathedral of commerce' – though meant as an insult, FW Woolworth, head of the five-and-dime chain store empire headquartered there, took the comment as a compliment and began throwing the term around himself. Today the building houses mainly offices, but as part of a unique program offered through the Lower Manhattan Cultural Council, the 33rd floor's open rooms recently housed a dozen artists who were allowed to work in the magnificent space – featuring 360-degree views of the city – thanks to a grant program.

Visitors are not allowed into the building (though you may be able to sneak a peek at the beautifully preserved lobby), but you can marvel at the facade and height from across the street in City Hall Park.

TRIBECA

Taking its moniker from real estate agents who noted the pocket of land sitting in a 'TRIangle BElow CAnal (St),' this intimate neighborhood is composed of landmark 19th-century buildings as well as massive former warehouses that have been pretty thoroughly converted into luxury condos. It's a quiet and unassuming place that hasn't seen a true media frenzy since the tragic death of John F Kennedy Jr in 1999, which still inspires visitors to leave flowers at his former residence on N Moore St. There are plenty of living, breathing stars living here, too – though none so prominent as Robert De Niro, who has put his 'hood on the map as NYC's new center of film with his wildly successful Tribeca Film Festival (p21), which has exploded into a destination fest that gets bigger each year. Still, local foodies know this as the place to celebspot while spending small fortunes on sushi or steak frites, and night owls love it for its sultry lounge bars.

First used as farmland for Dutch settlers, the years since have seen it become a center for the textile industry, dairy mercantile exchanges, cheap artists' lofts and, by the 1970s, an urban renewal plan that knocked down many of the old buildings and threw up high-rises, parks and educational facilities, including the Borough of Manhattan Community College. Though Tribeca has not been known as one of the top spots to see art since the '80s (most galleries have fled uptown to Chelsea), there's still plenty to see here. The best time to see what's cookin' is in late April, during the annual TOAST: Tribeca Open Artist Studio Tour (www.toastartwalk.com), when artists open up their local studios to anyone interested in what they're creating. It's fun, free and a great intro to the neighborhood.

Tribeca is bordered by Canal St (to the north), West St (west), Chambers St (south) and Broadway (east). A good way to get acquainted with the neighborhood is through the shopping, eating and entertainment listings of the Tribeca Organization (www.tribeca.org). For getting around once you're here, walking should suit you fine; otherwise try the M20 or M6 buses or the 1 train to Franklin St or the 1, 2, 3 to Chambers St.

HARRISON STREET HOUSES Map pp72–3

Harrison St; ⊕ 1, 2, 3 to Franklin St
Built between 1804 and 1828, the eight townhouses on the block of Harrison St immediately west of Greenwich St constitute the largest collection of Federal architecture left in the city. But they were not always neighbors – six of them once stood two blocks away, on a stretch of Washington St that no longer exists. In the early 1970s, that site was home to the Washington Market, a wholesale fruit and vegetable shopping complex. But development of the waterfront – which resulted in the construction of the Borough of Manhattan Community College and the Sovietstyle concrete apartment complex that

now looms over the town houses – meant the market had to move uptown and the historic row of houses had to be relocated. Only the buildings at 31 and 33 Harrison St remain where they were originally constructed.

TRIBECA CINEMAS Map pp72–3

☎ 212-941-2001; www.tribecacinemas.com; 54 Varick St at Laight St; ⊕ 1, A, C, E to Canal St
This is the physical home of the Tribeca Film Festival (p21), founded in 2002 by Robert De Niro and Jane Rosenthal. Throughout the year, the space hosts a range of screenings and educational panels, including festivals dedicated to Brazilian films (in August) or Bosnian-Herzegovinian works (in May), many of which are open to the public. Check the website for upcoming events and screening schedules.

WASHINGTON MARKET COMMUNITY PARK Map pp72–3

☎ 212-964-1133; www.washingtonmarketpark .org; cnr Greenwich & Chambers Sts; ⊙ 6am-dusk; ⊕ 1, 2, 3 to Chambers St
This 3-acre park – once the site of the world's largest food market back in 1858 – is now beloved by local families with kids, mainly because of its popular playground. But it's a great escape for anyone needing a little green space; there's also a gazebo and tennis and basketball courts.

LOWER MANHATTAN
Walking Tour
1 City Hall Stand in the confines of City Hall Park and take a gander at the elegant marble City Hall (p82), where the city's political battles are played out – sometimes to an audience, as its grand front steps serve as a stage for frequent press conferences and protest rallies.

2 Woolworth Building Across the street you'll see the lush facade of the Woolworth Building (p83), one of the city's most celebrated neoGothic structures. Built in 1913, it was then the tallest building in the world (for a while, anyway). Security is tight, but you usually can poke your head in to inspect the opulent lobby and blue-and-gold-tiled ceiling.

3 St Paul's Chapel Heading south on Broadway, cross Vesey St and you'll see St Paul's Chapel (p80) on your right – it's the only pre–Revolutionary War church left intact in the city. Its most recent claim to fame was serving as a refuge for September 11 recovery workers; a permanent memorial exhibit takes you back.

4 Century 21 Continue south, then take a right on Cortlandt St and you'll be able to take a dip inside Century 21 (p217). Many New Yorkers' favorite discount clothing store, it sells haute couture at bargain prices.

5 WTC Tribute Visitors Center A block south, at Liberty St, turn right and you'll soon arrive at the WTC Tribute Visitors Center (p77), a temporary memorial featuring photos, artifacts and personal stories about the September 11 disaster. The center also offers tours of Ground Zero's perimeter.

6 Trinity Church Continue south on Broadway and you'll come to Trinity Church (p80), another one of Old New York's most important houses of worship. The old graveyard out back, with its ancient tombstones, is a peaceful spot to visit.

7 New York Stock Exchange Head east onto the famed Wall St, home to the New York Stock Exchange (p78). Security concerns have closed it to visitors, but you can still take in its 1903 Beaux-Arts exterior, which looks rather like a Greek Temple (except on the days when it's draped with a company's logo).

8 Federal Hall Diagonally across from the Exchange you'll see Federal Hall (p78), where George Washington was sworn in as president after praying for guidance at St Paul's Chapel. It's also the place where John Peter Zenger was acquitted of seditious libel in 1735 – the first step, historians say, in establishing a democracy committed to a free press.

9 Bowling Green Follow Broad St south to quaint Stone St, where you can fuel up at Financier Patisserie (p251); then head back to Broadway and turn right, where you'll find yourself face to face with the *Charging Bull* sculpture at Bowling Green (p79), the first public park in the city.

10 National Museum of the American Indian Bowling Green is reportedly where Dutch leader Peter Minuit bought Manhattan for $24 from Lenape Indians, although that tale is often questioned. To find out why, head

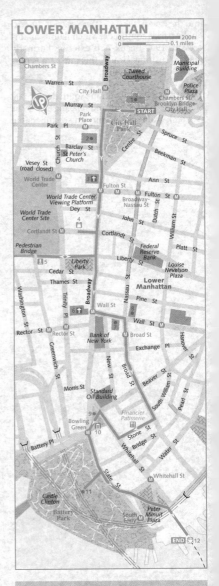

WALK FACTS

Start **Brooklyn Bridge** (④ 4, 5, 6 to Brooklyn Bridge-City Hall)

End **Staten Island Ferry Terminal** (④ 1 at South Ferry)

Distance **Two miles**

Duration **One to three hours**

Fuel stop **Financier Patisserie**

into the National Museum of the American Indian (p78) on the park's south side, which flaunts an impressive 1907 Beaux-Arts exterior. Formerly the US Customs House, this museum is now run by the Smithsonian.

11 Battery Park Continue south down State St to enter the tranquil and relaxing Battery Park (see p76), from where you can see the Statue of Liberty and get a glimpse of Ellis Island. It's the perfect place to grab a seat and reflect on the day.

12 Staten Island Ferry You can continue your adventure by simply hopping aboard the next departing Staten Island Ferry (p75), a free ride that affords stellar views of Lady Liberty and all the gems of the harbor.

SOHO, NOHO & NOLITA

Drinking p288; Eating p251; Shopping p218; Sleeping p350

This trio of cutesy acronyms, all named for geographic locales, represents three of the coolest city neighborhoods, known for their tangled thickets of hipness in the form of boutiques, bars and eateries. Real estate is through the roof in all three spots, and nights out (or days shopping) can prove to be expensive propositions. But in the end you'll be won over by the unique blend of industrial starkness and cobblestone coziness that lends these areas their character.

SoHo – the largest and most legendary of the three – stands for 'SOuth of HOuston St.' Its signature cast-iron-facade industrial buildings date from the period just after the Civil War, when this was the city's leading commercial district and filled with linen, ribbon and clothing factories. But manufacturing concerns eventually moved out of the city, and by the 1950s the huge lofts and cheap rents attracted artists, social misfits and other avant-garde types, who fought successfully to get a 26-block area declared a legally protected historic district in 1973. Unfortunately, as is always the case, the pioneers who were responsible for preserving the attractive district were pushed out by sky-high rents when SoHo became gentrified and attained hyperfashionable status as the center of New York's downtown arts scene. Though there are still some art galleries left (and a clutch of small museums), most of the top spaces have hightailed it to Chelsea, leaving mostly shoe boutiques and a growing mass of chain stores.

NoHo means 'NOrth of HOuston St,' and is a smaller blend of side streets with quirky offerings, next door to the East Village; Nolita's moniker stands for 'NOrth of Little ITAly,' and it's probably the chicest of the three, due to its preponderance of high-fashion shops. Combine both with SoHo for a great DIY experience of strolling, window-shopping and café-hopping, and you'll have quite a lovely afternoon. You can easily walk around the region (or hail a cross-town cab); to get here, take the subway on one of the following lines: 6, N, R, W or B, D, F, V.

MUSEUM OF COMIC & CARTOON ART Map pp88–9

☎ 212-254-3511; www.moccany.org; 594 Broadway btwn Houston & Prince Sts; ⏰ noon-5pm Fri-Mon, by appt Tue-Thu; adult/child $3/free; ⊕ N, R, W to Prince St

A heavenly little set of galleries for the cartoon-obsessed among us, the museum's mission is to educate the public about comic and cartoon art, and to help everyone appreciate it in all its forms – comic strips, cartoons, *anime*, animation, gag cartoons, political illustrations, caricature, graphic novels and more. Special exhibits include both well-known cartoonists and up-and-coming artists, with frequent opening parties and various festivals. Check the website for online exhibits and upcoming lecture series.

NEW YORK CITY FIRE MUSEUM
Map pp88–9

☎ 212-219-1222; www.nycfiremuseum.org; 278 Spring St btwn Varick & Hudson Sts; suggested donation adult/child under 12/senior & student $5/1/2; ⏰ 10am-5pm Tue-Sat, to 4pm Sun; ⊕ C, E to Spring St

Occupying a grand old firehouse dating from 1904, this museum houses a collection of gold, horse-drawn firefighting carriages and modern-day red firetrucks. Exhibits show the development of the NYC firefighting system (which began with the 'bucket brigades') and the museum's friendly staff (and the heavy equipment) make this a great place to bring children. The New York Fire Department (FDNY) lost half of its members in the collapse of the World Trade Center, and memorials and exhibits have become a permanent part of the collection. An excellent gift shop sells official FDNY clothing and patches and books about firefighting history.

ST PATRICK'S OLD CATHEDRAL
Map pp88–9

260-264 Prince St at Mott St; ⊕ N, R, W to Prince St

Though St Patrick's Cathedral is now famously located on Fifth Ave in Midtown, its first congregation was housed here, in the neighborhood now called Nolita, in this 1809–15 Gothic revival church designed by Joseph-François Mangin. Its soaring inner vault stands at 85ft, and the ornate interior features a marble altar and gold-leaf detailing. Back in its heyday, the church was the seat of religious life for the Archdiocese of New York, and an important community center for new immigrants, mainly from Ireland. Today it holds regular liturgies in

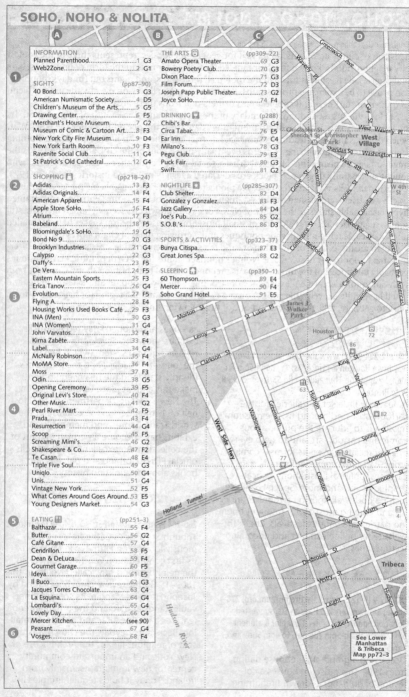

SOHO, NOHO & NOLITA

INFORMATION		
Planned Parenthood	1	G3
Web2Zone	2	G1

SIGHTS	(pp87–90)	
40 Bond	3	G3
American Numismatic Society	4	D5
Children's Museum of the Arts	5	G5
Drawing Center	6	F5
Merchant's House Museum	7	G2
Museum of Comic & Cartoon Art	8	F3
New York City Fire Museum	9	D4
New York Earth Room	10	F3
Ravenite Social Club	11	G4
St Patrick's Old Cathedral	12	G4

SHOPPING	(pp218–24)	
Adidas	13	F3
Adidas Originals	14	F4
American Apparel	15	F4
Apple Store SoHo	16	F4
Atrium	17	F3
Babeland	18	F5
Bloomingdale's SoHo	19	G4
Bond No 9	20	G3
Brooklyn Industries	21	G4
Calypso	22	G3
Daffy's	23	F5
De Vera	24	F5
Eastern Mountain Sports	25	F3
Erica Tanov	26	G4
Evolution	27	F5
Flying A	28	E4
Housing Works Used Books Café	29	F3
INA (Men)	30	G3
INA (Women)	31	G4
John Varvatos	32	F4
Kirna Zabête	33	F4
Label	34	G4
McNally Robinson	35	F4
MoMA Store	36	F4
Moss	37	F3
Odin	38	G5
Opening Ceremony	39	F5
Original Levi's Store	40	F4
Other Music	41	G2
Pearl River Mart	42	F5
Prada	43	F4
Resurrection	44	G4
Scoop	45	F5
Screaming Mimi's	46	G2
Shakespeare & Co	47	F2
Te Casan	48	E4
Triple Five Soul	49	G3
Uniqlo	50	G4
Unis	51	G4
Vintage New York	52	F5
What Comes Around Goes Around	53	E5
Young Designers Market	54	G3

EATING	(pp251–3)	
Balthazar	55	F4
Butter	56	G2
Café Gitane	57	G4
Cendrillon	58	F5
Dean & DeLuca	59	F4
Gourmet Garage	60	F5
Ideya	61	E5
Il Buco	62	G3
Jacques Torres Chocolate	63	C4
La Esquina	64	G4
Lombardi's	65	G4
Lovely Day	66	G4
Mercer Kitchen	(see 90)	
Peasant	67	G4
Vosges	68	F4

THE ARTS	(pp309–22)	
Amato Opera Theater	69	G3
Bowery Poetry Club	70	G3
Dixon Place	71	G3
Film Forum	72	D3
Joseph Papp Public Theater	73	G2
Joyce SoHo	74	F4

DRINKING	(p288)	
Chibi's Bar	75	G4
Circa Tabac	76	E5
Ear Inn	77	C4
Milano's	78	G4
Pegu Club	79	E3
Puck Fair	80	G3
Swift	81	G2

NIGHTLIFE	(pp285–307)	
Club Shelter	82	D4
Gonzalez y Gonzalez	83	F3
Jazz Gallery	84	D4
Joe's Pub	85	G2
S.O.B.'s	86	D3

SPORTS & ACTIVITIES	(pp323–37)	
Bunya Citispa	87	E3
Great Jones Spa	88	G2

SLEEPING	(pp350–1)	
60 Thompson	89	E4
Mercer	90	F4
Soho Grand Hotel	91	E5

See Lower
Manhattan
& Tribeca
Map pp72–3

See Greenwich Village, West Village & The Meatpacking District Map p110

See East Village Map p104

See Lower East Side Map p98

See Chinatown & Little Italy Map p94

89

English, Spanish and Chinese. Its ancient cemetery out back is a beautiful respite in the midst of city chaos; if it's not open when you pass by, sneak a peek through the thick, padlocked gate.

MERCHANT'S HOUSE MUSEUM
Map pp88–9

☎ 212-777-1089; www.merchantshouse.com; 29 E 4th St btwn Lafayette & Bowery; ☉ noon-5pm Thu-Mon; adult/student $8/5; ☉ B, D, F, V to Broadway-Lafayette St, 6 to Bleecker St

This elegant, red-brick row house is a family home dating from 1832 – and it's perfectly preserved both inside and out. Home to a prosperous merchant family, the Tredwells, for nearly a century, the place is in mint condition, allowing you to step back in time through the formal Greek revival parlors featuring mahogany pocket doors, bronze gasoliers and marble mantelpieces. Bedrooms reveal plenty of other luxuries, from fine antique furniture to a display of dresses, shoes and parasols.

DRAWING CENTER Map pp88–9
☎ 212-219-2166; www.drawingcenter.org; 35 Wooster St at Grand St; ☉ A, C, E, 1 to Canal St

Here since 1977, this is the only nonprofit institute in the country to focus solely on drawings, using work by masters as well as unknowns to show the juxtaposition of various styles. Historical exhibitions have included work by Michelangelo, James Ensor and Marcel Duchamp, while contemporary shows have focused on Richard Serra, Ellsworth Kelly and Richard Tuttle; exhibits can range from the whimsical to the politically controversial. Artist lectures and performance art programs are hot tickets here – as is the new Big Draw event

NEW YORK EARTH ROOM
Since 1980 the oddity of the Earth Room (Map pp88–9; www.earthroom.org; 141 Wooster St; admission free; ☉ noon-6pm Wed-Sun, closed 3-3:30pm; ☉ N, R, W to Prince St), the work of artist Walter De Maria, has been wooing the curious with something not easily found in the city: dirt (250 cu yd, or 280,000lb, of it, to be exact). Walking into the small space is a heady experience, as the scent will make you feel like you've entered a wet forest; the sight of such beautiful, pure earth in the midst of this crazy city is surprisingly moving.

(in September), which invites folks of all ages to bring a sketchpad to any of several artist-led, hands-on happenings at locations around the city.

AMERICAN NUMISMATIC SOCIETY
Map pp88–9

☎ 212-234-3130; www.numismatics.org; 1 Hudson Sq at Varick & Watts Sts; admission free; ☉ 9am-5pm Mon-Fri; ☉ 1 to Houston St

Coins can't get no respect! After bouncing around to and from various locations – beginning way uptown as part of the Audubon Terrace collection of museums in Inwood, moving to a 'permanent' Financial District location in 2004 and now to this slick new home in SoHo in 2008, this is the latest incarnation of the Society's large collection of coins, medals and paper money. Its holdings are from all over the map and throughout history, including Greek, Roman, East Asian, Medieval and Islamic items. Frequent special exhibitions and lectures focus on the history of currency.

CHILDREN'S MUSEUM OF THE ARTS
Map pp88–9

☎ 212-941-9198; www.cmany.org; 182 Lafayette St; admission $9, by donation 4-6pm Thu; ☉ noon-5pm Wed & Fri-Sun, to 6pm Thu; ☉ B, D, V, F to Broadway-Lafayette St

A place for kids to unleash their inner artist, this small but worthy stop is home to a permanent collection of paintings, drawings and photographs by local schoolkids, with exhibits getting adorable titles like 'Beyond the Refrigerator Door.' For more hands-on activities, check out the museum's vast offering of public programs for kids of all ages, including guided workshops on art forms from sculpture to collaborative mural painting, as well as movie nights and other special treats.

SOHO, NOHO & NOLITA
Walking Tour

1 Cable Building Pop out of the B, D, F, V train and get an immediate sense of old-meets-new with NoHo's Beaux-Arts Cable Building (18 W Houston St), built by famed architects McKim, Mead and White in 1894. Originally used as the power plant for the Broadway Cable Car (the nation's first), it features an oval window and caryatids on its Broadway facade. Today it houses the Angelika Film Center

(p318), a massive Crate & Barrel store and various offices.

2 St Patrick's Old Cathedral Head east across Houston St and make a right on Lafayette St. Turn left on Prince St and you'll be approaching St Patrick's Old Cathedral (p87), dating from 1809 – the original location for the famous Fifth Ave cathedral's congregation. Its ancient, peaceful cemetery is a Nolita haven that's worth a visit.

3 Elizabeth Street Gallery Continue along Prince St. If you're hungry, you can stop to fuel up at Café Gitane (p253) on Mott St. Otherwise, turn right onto Elizabeth St, where you can pause to admire the fenced-in garden of the curious Elizabeth Street Gallery (210 Elizabeth St), part of a fireplace, fountain and garden-ornament shop for the well-off homeowner. The biggest attraction in these parts, though, is the simple beauty of the small tangle of streets.

4 Singer Building Turn right on Spring St from Elizabeth St and enjoy the local neighborhood flavor until you hit Broadway; just

WALK FACTS

Start Cable Building (B, D, F, V to Broadway-Lafayette St)
End New York Earth Room (N, R, W at Prince St)
Distance 1.5 miles
Duration One to two hours
Fuel stop Café Gitane

half a block north is the Singer Building (561-563 Broadway), one of the post–Civil War cast-iron buildings that gave this area its 'Cast-Iron District' nickname. This one used to be the main warehouse for the famous sewing machine company of the same name.

5 Haughwout Building Head south down Broadway and you'll come to a garish Staples store with a fascinating history: it's located in the Haughwout Building (488 Broadway), the first structure to use the exotic steam elevator developed by Elisha Otis. Known as the 'Parthenon of Cast-Iron Architecture,' the Haughwout (pronounced *how*-out) is considered a rare structure for its two-sided design. Don't miss the iron clock that sits on the Broadway facade.

6 New York Earth Room Cross Broadway at Broome St, walking west, and continue on to Wooster St. Turn right and head up to the New York Earth Room (p90), where artist Walter De Maria's gallery filled with cool, moist soil will either thrill you or leave you scratching your head.

CHINATOWN & LITTLE ITALY

Drinking p288; Eating p254; Shopping p224

These abutting neighborhoods are feasts for the senses – though it's the sprawling and ever-expanding Chinatown, whose borders have steadily encroached upon what snippet of Little Italy remains, that is the seriously dominant force down in these parts. Strolling its streets will bring you endless exotic moments – the sight of whole roasted pigs hanging in butcher-shop windows, the whiff of fresh fish and ripe persimmons, the twangs of Cantonese and Vietnamese rising over the calls of fake-watch hawkers along Canal St. You'll have opportunities to buy not only knockoff Prada bags, but a brass gong, lacquered chopsticks, rice-paper lanterns, silk Chinese slippers and a jar of Lee Kum Kee sparerib sauce, if you wish.

More than 150,000 Chinese-speaking residents live in cramped tenements and crowded apartments in this neighborhood, the largest Chinese community outside of Asia. Many of the latest immigrants have been coming from the Fujian province, often as part of dangerous smuggling operations. In the 1990s Chinatown also attracted a growing number of Vietnamese immigrants, who set up their own shops and opened inexpensive restaurants here; depending on what street you're on, you may notice more of a Vietnamese presence than Chinese.

Call in at the official Explore Chinatown information kiosk (Map p94; ☎ 212-484-1216; www.explorechinatown.com; Baxter St btwn Canal & Walker Sts; ☾ 10am-6pm Mon-Fri & Sun, to 7pm Sat) to find helpful, multilingual folks who can guide you to specific eateries, shops, sights and festivals. But don't be afraid to explore on your own, too – this fascinating and many-layered neighborhood is ripe for DIY adventures. Duck into a random produce market and check out various oddly shaped and sometimes prickly fruits and vegetables. Buy six cakes of fresh tofu or three luscious turnip cakes for $1 from a street vendor. Try to find the biggest stock of illegal fireworks for sale, wander into one of the musty and mysterious Chinese herb shops or make a peaceful offering at one of several Buddhist temples.

In contrast to Chinatown, Little Italy's ethnic character has been largely diluted in the last 50 years. The area began as a strong Italian neighborhood (film director Martin Scorsese grew up on Elizabeth St), but in the mid-20th century it suffered a large exodus as many residents moved to more bucolic neighborhoods in Brooklyn and the city's suburbs. Still, loyal Italian Americans (mostly from the suburbs) flock here to gather around red-and-white-checked tablecloths at a handful of long-time red-sauce restaurants. That's especially true during the raucous San Gennaro Festival (p23), which honors the patron saint of Naples for 10 days starting in the second week of September.

Try to avoid taking cabs in this area – especially in Chinatown, as the traffic is almost always hellish. Let your feet do the walking instead, or head underground to the virtual alphabet of subway lines that stop at various points along Canal St: J, M, Z, N, R, W, Q or 6.

CANAL STREET Map p94

🚇 J, M, Z, N, R, W, Q, 6 to Canal St

While the hidden treasures of Chinatown are found on its tiny side streets, this wide avenue is the area's pulsing artery, and a walk along it will be an exercise not only in frustration – the crowds will leave you at constant impasses – but also in excitement. You'll pass open, stinky seafood markets hawking bloodied, slippery fish; mysterious little herb shops displaying all manner of roots and potions; storefront bakeries with steamed-up windows and the tastiest 50¢ pork buns you've ever had; restaurants with whole, roasted ducks and pigs hanging by their skinny necks in the windows; produce markets piled high with fresh lychee nuts, bok choy and Asian pears; and street vendors selling tiny, illegal turtles, as well as endless forms of knockoffs, from Gucci sunglasses and Rolex watches to faux Prada bags.

MUSEUM OF CHINESE IN AMERICA
Map p94

☎ 212-619-4785; www.moca-nyc.org; 215 Centre St; adult/senior & student $2/1; ☾ noon-6pm Tue-Sun; 🚇 J, M, Z, N, R, Q, W, 6 to Canal St

This newly relocated museum – now housed in a 12,350-sq-ft space designed by architect Maya Lin (who did the famed Vietnam Memorial in Washington DC) – will do to your mind what Canal Street can do to your senses. The exhibit galleries, book-store and visitors lounge, all serving as a national center of information, are chock

CHINATOWN & LITTLE ITALY

0 ————————— 200 m
0 ————————— 0.1 miles

INFORMATION
Chase Manhattan Bank...............................1 C4
Chinatown Tours..(see 5)
Explore Chinatown Information Kiosk
(NYC & Company)...................................2 B4

SIGHTS   (pp93–5)
Eastern States Buddhist Temple.................3 C4
Mahayana Buddhist Temple.......................4 C4
Museum of Chinese in America..................5 B3
Umberto's Clam House...............................6 B2

SHOPPING   (pp224–6)
Aji Ichiban...7 C5
Built by Wendy...8 B3
Kam Man...9 B4
Original Chinatown Ice Cream
Factory...(see 15)

EATING   (pp254–5)
Doyers Vietnamese Restaurant.................10 C5
Ferrara Bakery..11 B3
Focolare...12 B3
Great New York Noodle Town..................13 C4

New Bo Ky Restaurant.............................14 B4
Original Chinatown Ice Cream
Factory...15 C4
Vegetarian Dim Sum House......................16 C5

DRINKING   (pp288–9)
Mare Chiaro...17 B2
Winnie's...18 B4

TRANSPORT   (pp389–96)
2000 New Century Bus Stand...................19 D4
Fung Wah Bus Stand................................20 C4

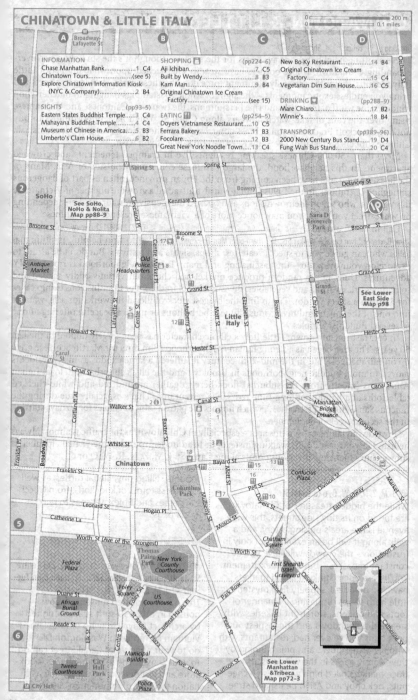

full of facts about Chinese American life. Browse through interactive multimedia exhibits, maps, timelines, photos, letters, films and artifacts, and catch rotating exhibits. Its anchor exhibit is 'The Chinese American Experience,' touching on subjects including immigration, activism and globalization.

BUDDHIST TEMPLES Map p94

Chinatown is home to Buddhist temples large and small, public and obscure. They are easily stumbled upon during a full-on stroll of the neighborhood, and at least two such temples are considered landmarks. The Eastern States Buddhist Temple (64 Mott St btwn Bayard & Canal Sts; ⓢ J, M, Z, 6 to Canal St) is filled with hundreds of Buddhas, while the Mahayana Buddhist Temple (133 Canal St at Manhattan Bridge Plaza; ⓢ B, D to Grand St) holds one golden, 16ft-high Buddha, sitting on a lotus and edged with offerings of fresh oranges, apples and flowers. Mahayana is the largest Buddhist temple in Chinatown, and its facade, right near the frenzied vehicle entrance to the Manhattan Bridge, features two giant golden lions for protection; its interior is simple, with a wooden floor, red chairs and red paper lanterns – but all these are trumped by the magnificent Buddha, thought to be the largest in the city.

MULBERRY STREET Map p94

ⓢ 6 to Spring St

Although it feels more like a theme park than an authentic Italian strip, Mulberry St is still the heart of the 'hood. It's the home of landmarks such as Umberto's Clam House (☎ 212-431-7545; 386 Broome St at Mulberry St), where mobster Joey Gallo was shot to death in the '70s, as well as the old-time bar Mare Chiaro (p288), one of the favorite haunts of the late Frank Sinatra. Just a half block off of Mulberry is the legendary Ferrara Cafe and Bakery (195 Grand St), brimming with classic Italian pastries and old-school ambience. You'll see lots of red, white and green Italian flags sold in souvenir shops, and you'll also enjoy the lovely aroma of fresh-baked pastries and pizzas wafting out of doorways. Take a gander at what was once the Ravenite Social Club (Map pp88–9; 247 Mulberry St, Nolita) to see how things have really changed around here: today the storefront is home to women's clothes boutique Amy Chan, but it was once the organized-crime hangout Ravenite (originally known as the Alto Knights Social Club), where big hitters such as Lucky Luciano and John Gotti (as well as the FBI, who kept raiding the place) logged time.

COLUMBUS PARK Map p94

Mulberry & Bayard Sts; ⓢ J, M, Z, 6 to Canal St

This is where outdoor mah-jongg and domino games take place at bridge tables while tai chi practitioners move through lyrical, slow-motion poses under shady trees. Judo-sparring folks and relaxing families are also common sights here, in this active communal space originally created in the 1890s and popular with local residents. Visitors are welcome, though (or at least ignored).

An interesting note is that the Five Points neighborhood, home to the city's first tenement slums and the inspiration for Martin Scorsese's *Gangs of New York,* was once located at the foot of where Columbus Park is now. The 'five points' were the five streets that used to converge here; now you'll find the intersection of only Mosco, Worth and Baxter Sts. (Another Columbus Park perk is its public bathroom, making it the perfect place for a pit stop.)

CHINATOWN
Walking Tour

1 Chatham Square Begin your exploration at Chatham Sq (East Broadway at Bowery), where you'll see the Kim Lau Memorial Arch, erected in 1962 as a memorial to Chinese Americans who died in WWII. There's also a statue of Lin Ze Xu, a Qing-dynasty scholar whose anti–drug trafficking stance helped lead to the First Opium War in 1839.

2 Doyers Street From the southern point of Chatham Sq head north on Bowery until you come to Doyers Street. Take a left and stroll along the short, L-shaped lane, home to many barber shops, the local post office and one of the first dim sum restaurants. Legend says the street was constructed with a 90-degree bend to hinder the movement of straight-walking ghosts.

3 Edward Mooney House At the end of Doyers take a right on Pell St, then a left on Bowery. On your left is the red-brick Edward Mooney House (18 Bowery), New York City's oldest townhouse, built in 1785 by butcher Edward

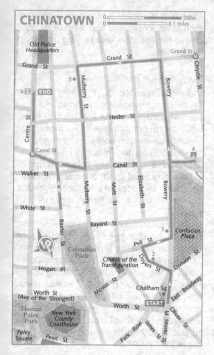

Old Police Headquarters

Grand St

Grand St

Grand St

5

Mulberry St

Bowery

6 END

Chrystie St

Centre St

Hester St

Canal St

Canal St

Walker St

Mulberry St

Mott St

Elizabeth St

Bowery

4

White St

Bayard St

Baxter St

3

Confucius Plaza

Pell St

Columbus Park

Church of the Transfiguration

Doyers St

Division St

Hogan Pl

Mosco St

Chatham Sq

Worth St (Ave of the Strongest)

Worth St

START

East Broadway

Oliver St

Thomas Paine Park

New York County Courthouse

Park Row

James St

James Pl

Foley Square

Pearl St

WALK FACTS

Start Chatham Sq (B, D to Grand St, J, M, Z, 6 to Canal St)

End Museum of Chinese in America (J, M, Z, 6 at Canal St)

Distance 1.5 miles

Duration One to two hours

Fuel stops Baxter St Vietnamese restaurants

you'll see the clogged entrance to the Manhattan Bridge and, just beyond that, the Mahayana Buddhist Temple (p95). Head on in to gaze upon the massive golden Buddha and grab a meditative moment.

5 Mulberry Street Exit the temple and head north on Bowery, turning left on Grand St. Take another left when you get to Mulberry Street (p95) and saunter along, taking in all the sights and smells to experience what remains of Little Italy.

6 Museum of Chinese in America Turn right when you hit Canal St, take your first left on Baxter St, known for its many Vietnamese restaurants. Stop for a meal, or just take a gander at the varied menus, then head back the way you came, turning left on Canal and then right on Centre St. You'll soon come to the Museum of Chinese in America (p93). Its newly constructed home – designed by artist Maya Lin – features exhibits looking at the Chinese American experience.

Mooney. The blend of Georgian–Federal architecture has housed a store, hotel, billiards parlor and Chinese social club, and today it's a bank.

4 Mahayana Buddhist Temple Continue walking north on Bowery to Canal, where

LOWER EAST SIDE

Drinking p289; Eating p255; Shopping p224; Sleeping p351

This place is just too cool for school. Wade into the grubby-turned-sleek neighborhood on any night of the week and you'll get a quick read on the place: slinky hipsters and foodies who are up on every nightlife trend there is, expensive real estate in the form of glistening new condo buildings and a veritable goldmine of chic boutiques, galleries, cafés, bars and live-music venues. But there's a silent tug-of-war going on within the high-speed swath of gentrification, and places like the Avalon Chrystie Palace – where apartments go for several million dollars and tower above land that used to house tenements and junkie flophouses – are at the center of the debate.

That's because anyone who's been here for longer than a few years tends to still be nostalgic about the history of this area. In the early 20th century, half a million Jews from Eastern Europe streamed into these parts, lending an ethnic flavor of pickles, knishes and kosher deli foods to the cramped, poverty-laden settlement. It was home to Yiddish theaters, gorgeous synagogues and yeshivas, and remained working-class for decades, also attracting Polish, Ukrainian and Puerto Rican immigrants, many in a spillover from the adjacent East Village.

More spillover came much later, in the '70s and '80s, but in the form of artists, musicians, various bohemians and, often, junkies, who found cheap rents and unguarded parks aplenty in this former ghetto. By 2000, with the blooming of trendy new eateries and bars, it became clear that cheap rents would go the way of the streetcar – and that many old-timers would be pushed out. Gentrification is a done deal here now, though the place has not stopped capturing the attention of the cool cats, mostly because high turnover and a consistent buzz keeps 'em coming. A hot new addition to the 'hood is the New Museum of Contemporary Art (p99) – a startlingly modern architectural confection that sits in stark contrast to the battered low-rises along the Bowery. The museum was formerly located on Broadway in SoHo; this new, white, seven-story structure is the first art museum to be constructed downtown in over a century.

A visit to the Lower East Side Visitors Center (Map p98; 261 Broome St btwn Allen & Orchard Sts) is a good way to orient yourself once you've arrived in the neighborhood. But don't be afraid to wander around and get lost, either. The subway's F line (Lower East Side-Second Ave or Delancey St stops) will get you there.

ELDRIDGE STREET SYNAGOGUE
Map p98

☎ 212-219-0888; www.eldridgestreet.org; 12 Eldridge St btwn Canal & Division Sts; ◉ F to East Broadway

The seemingly endless restoration of this landmark synagogue – which fell into horrifying disrepair after closing its doors in the 1950s, when many of the neighborhood's Orthodox Jews moved away – was wrapped up at the end of 2007. The makeover's great reveal has shown the city a historic temple that's been returned to its original 1887 splendor. This house of worship attracted as many as a thousand worshippers for the High Holidays at the turn of the 20th century. But membership dwindled in the 1920s following restricted immigration laws, and after its forced closure in the '50s, water damage and neglect did a number on the place. A handful of members still worship in a small basement space, but 20 years and $20 million later, the glorious sanctuary has been reopened

as a museum, its Moorish-style stained glass windows as sparkly-new as the day it opened. Same goes for the chandeliers with vintage glass, 70ft vaulted ceilings and trompe l'oeil murals that turn ordinary surfaces into marble, mahogany and stone. Stop in for a serene visit, or take advantage of one of the many cultural programs on offer, including concerts of Yiddish-film scores, cantorial music and Jewish jazz; lectures on Jewish literature and culture; and an annual Egg Rolls and Egg Cream cultural block party in the spring. Tours (adult/senior & student $10/8; ⏲ 10am-4pm Sun-Thu on the half hr, last tour 3pm) of the landmark are also available.

LOWER EAST SIDE TENEMENT MUSEUM Map p98

☎ 212-431-0233; www.tenement.org; 108 Orchard St at Delancey; adult/senior & student $17/13; ⏲ 11am-5:30pm; ◉ B, D to Grand, F to Delancey St, J, M, Z to Essex St

This museum puts the neighborhood's heartbreaking but inspiring heritage on

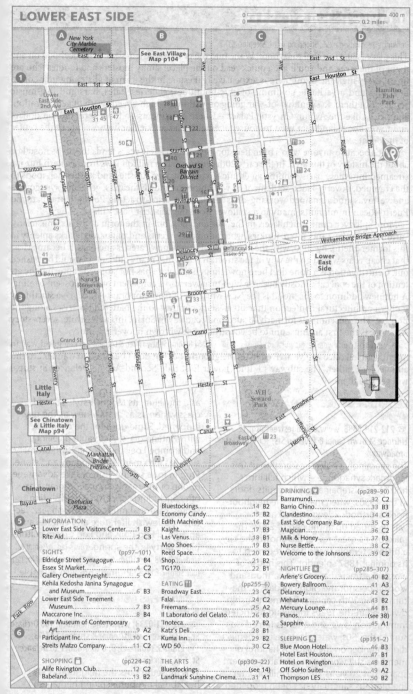

LOWER EAST SIDE

0 ———————— 400 m
0 ———————— 0.2 miles

A · New York City Marble Cemetery
East 2nd St

See East Village Map p104

East Houston St

Orchard St Bargain District

Williamsburg Bridge Approach

Lower East Side

Little Italy

See Chinatown & Little Italy Map p94

Manhattan Bridge Entrance

Chinatown

Confucius Plaza

NEW MUSEUM OF CONTEMPORARY ART

This brand-new addition to the neighborhood, the New Museum of Contemporary Art (Map p98; ☎ 212-219-1222; www.newmuseum.org; 235 Bowery btwn Stanton & Rivington Sts; adults/seniors/students/under-18s $12/8/6/free; ◉ N, R, W to Prince St, 6 to Spring St) is a sight to behold: a seven-story stack of off-kilter, white, ethereal boxes, designed by Tokyo-based architects Kazuyo Sejima and Ryue Nishizawa of SANAA and the New York-based firm Gensler. It's a long-awaited breath of fresh air along this gritty Bowery strip, and the thrills don't stop when you step inside. Its kick-off, four-part exhibit series, the group show 'Unmonumental,' was a taste of what's to come in the city's sole museum dedicated to contemporary art: edgy works in new forms, like seemingly random, discarded materials fused together and displayed in the middle of a vast room.

Founded in 1977 by Marcia Tucker and moved to five different locations over the years, the museum's mission statement is simple: 'New art, new ideas.' The institution has given gallery space to artists Keith Haring, Jeff Koons, Joan Jonas, Mary Kelly and Andres Serrano – all at the beginning of their careers – and continues to show contemporary heavy hitters. The museum also houses a small and healthy café, and has the added treat of a city viewing platform, which provides a unique perspective on the constantly changing architectural landscape.

full display in three recreations of turn-of-the-20th-century tenements, including the late-19th-century home and garment shop of the Levine family from Poland, and two immigrant dwellings from the Great Depressions of 1873 and 1929. The visitor center shows a video detailing the difficult life endured by the people who once lived in the surrounding buildings, which more often than not had no running water or electricity. Museum visits are available only as part of scheduled tours (the price of which is included in the admission), which typically operate daily. But call ahead or check the website for the schedules, which change frequently.

On weekends the museum has an interactive tour where kids can dress up in period clothes and handle items in the restored apartment of a Sephardic Jewish family from around 1916. Walking tours of the neighborhood are held from April to December, and usually include stops at the Streits Matzo Company (Map p98; 148-154 Rivington St), which opened in the 1890s, and the First Shearith Israel Graveyard (Map p98; 55-57 St James Pl btwn James & Oliver Sts, Chinatown), which was the burial ground of America's first Jewish community. Gravestones date from the late 1600s and include some who escaped the Spanish Inquisition.

ESSEX STREET MARKET Map p98

☎ 212-312-3603; www.essexstreetmarket.com; 120 Essex St btwn Delancey & Rivington Sts; ☷ 8am-7pm Mon-Sat; ◉ F to Delancey St, J, M, Z to Essex St

This 60-year-old historic shopping destination is the local place for produce, sea-food, butcher-cut meats, cheeses, Latino grocery items, and even a barber's shop and small art gallery. The stalwart stall of local and legendary Schapiro's kosher wine disappeared with the 2007 death of the company founder, and now newer spots, like Tra La La Juice Bar or Roni-Sue's Chocolates, are attracting a new-generation clientele who want to shop in an old-school environment.

LOWER EAST SIDE ART GALLERIES
Map p98

◉ F to Delancey St, J, M, Z to Essex St

Though Chelsea may be the heavy hitter when it comes to the New York art gallery scene, the LES has its very own collection of quality showplaces, thank you very much. Maccarone Inc (Map p98; ☎ 212-431-4977; www.maccarone.net; 45 Canal St btwn Ludlow & Orchard Sts) and Participant Inc (☎ 212-254-4334; www.participantinc.org; 253 E Houston St btwn Norfolk & Suffolk Sts) were both hailed as jump-starting the gallery trend here when they opened several years ago; both exhibit emerging talent, while Participant Inc has the added bonus of varied performances. Gallery Onetwentyeight (☎ 212-674-0244; www.galleryonetwentyeight.org; 128 Rivington St) is also a popular, contemporary space.

ORCHARD STREET BARGAIN DISTRICT Map p98

Orchard, Ludlow & Essex Sts btwn Houston & Delancey Sts; ☷ Sun-Fri; ◉ F to Delancey St, J, M, Z to Essex St

When the LES was still a largely Jewish neighborhood, Eastern European merchants set up pushcarts to sell their wares

top picks

IT'S FREE

- **Staten Island Ferry** (p75) Take a ride into New York Harbor and soak in the priceless views.

- **National Museum of the American Indian** (p78) The former US Customs House is gorgeous on its own, but the fascinating museum it now houses is an extra bonus.

- **Federal Hall** (p78) This historic spot was the site of George Washington's presidential inauguration, among other significant events.

- **New York Earth Room** (p90) This gallery's draw is that it's filled with moist, clean dirt – which is more moving than it sounds.

- **Brooklyn Museum** (p184) Brooklyn's stellar art museum is free on 'First Saturdays', when the whole community comes out to catch performances, dance lessons and, of course, the exhibits.

- **Japan Society** (p125) Rotating exhibits at this intimate gallery are a beautiful draw.

- **New York Public Library** (p129) Head on in to experience the stunning Reading Room, as well as diverse, museum-like exhibits.

- **Abyssinian Baptist Church** (p161) Sunday gospel services here are a raucous, soulful affair.

- **Schomburg Center for Research in Black Culture** (p161) This branch of the New York Public Library is the home of many impressive archives.

- **LGBT Community Center** (p345) A cherished resource among gay and lesbian New Yorkers, this is the place to pick up information about all the queer goings-on in town.

here. While it's no longer as quaint as that, the Lower East Side Business Improvement District (www.lowereastsideny.com) has made it a goal to bring more shoppers to this area, which sometimes gets forgotten in the trend-seeking rush. Still, bargain-hunters comb the 300-odd shops in this modern-day bazaar for sporting goods, leather belts, hats and a wide array of 'designer fashions' (which are often a bit cheesy), along with the modern-day goods of new local designers, whose boutiques tend to mix and mingle with the old-school places. Rather than searching high and low for designer label knockoffs – better found at bargain chains elsewhere, such as Century 21 (p217) or Filene's Basement (p234) – know that this is more the type of place for scoring cheap basics like bras, shoes, army-navy bags and

leather jackets. While the businesses are not exclusively owned by Orthodox Jews, they still close early on Friday afternoon and remain closed on Saturday in observance of the Sabbath.

KEHILA KEDOSHA JANINA SYNAGOGUE & MUSEUM Map p98
☎ 212-431-1619; www.kkjsm.org; 280 Broome St at Allen St; ⊙ museum 11am-4pm Sun, worship services 9am Sat; ⊙ F to Delancey St, J, M, Z to Essex St
This small synagogue is home to an obscure branch of Judaism, the Romaniotes, whose ancestors were slaves sent to Rome by ship but rerouted to Greece by a storm. This is their only synagogue in the Western Hemisphere, and includes a small museum bearing artifacts like handpainted birth certificates, an art gallery, a Holocaust memorial for Greek Jews and costumes from Janina, the Romaniote capital of Greece. An upcoming renovation has plans for a café, too.

EAST RIVER PARK Map p69
Flanked by a looming housing project and the clogged FDR Dr on one side and the less-than-pure East River on the other, you might wonder what the draw is here. But take one visit – especially if it's during spring or summer – and you'll understand. In addition to the brand-spanking-new ballparks, running and biking paths, 5000-seat amphitheater for concerts and expansive patches of green, it's got cool, natural breezes and stunning views of the Williamsburg, Manhattan and Brooklyn Bridges. A long-time renovation brought great nighttime lighting and surprisingly clean bathrooms to the mix. It's a cool spot for a picnic or a morning run.

SARA D ROOSEVELT PARK Map p98
Houston St at Chrystie St
Spiffed up just in time for the arrival of its tony new luxury-condo neighbors, this remade little park is a place that most New Yorkers will remember as more of a junkie's spot for scoring than an actual plot of green space. But it's joined the ranks of other rejuvenated 'needle parks' – such as Bryant Park and Tompkins Sq Park – and is now a three-block respite from urban chaos. Grab an ethnic picnic-to-go at any of the nearby food spots and settle into a

shady corner; if you've got kids with you, there's a nice little playground that's perfect for letting off steam.

LOWER EAST SIDE
Walking Tour
1 New Museum of Contemporary Art
Kick off your dip into the neighborhood by seeing its newest, most buzzed-about attraction: the New Museum of Contemporary Art (p99), a stunning work of architecture that towers above the gritty Bowery.

2 Freeman Alley
From the museum, walk downtown on Bowery and make a left on Rivington St, then your first left on Freeman Alley, a mysterious little crook that'll make you feel

like you've entered a spy movie. It's home to hipster hangout Freemans (p255), so if you come at night, expect a crowd.

3 Sara D Roosevelt Park
Take a left out of the alley and continue along Rivington for half a block. You're now in Sara D Roosevelt Park (p100),

WALK FACTS
Start Bowery between Rivington and Stanton Sts (Ⓢ N, R, W to Prince St)
End Oliver St at Henry St, Chinatown (Ⓢ F at East Broadway)
Distance Two miles
Duration Two to three hours
Fuel stop Essex Street Market

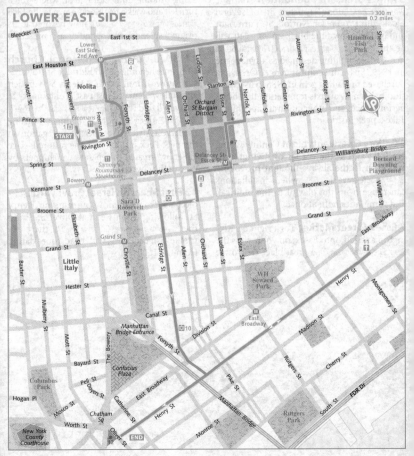

a long and skinny patch of green that looks quite spiffed up on its Houston St end. Across the street from the park's Chrystie St side, between Delancey and Rivington, is Sammy's Roumanian Steakhouse (☎ 212-673-0330; 157 Chrystie St), a famous old-world Jewish dining spot.

4 Landmark Sunshine Cinema Follow Chrystie St north to Houston St, then make a right. Just past Forsyth St, on your right, you'll see the Landmark Sunshine Cinema (p319), which was shuttered for 70 years before being reopened in its current form as an indie-movie cinema. In its heyday it was a Yiddish theater and a boxing venue, and was originally built as a Dutch church in the 1840s. The multistory lobbies have preserved some of the original interiors.

5 Angel Orensanz Foundation Continue walking east along Houston St for several blocks until you reach Norfolk St. Turn right and halfway down the block on your left will be the Angel Orensanz Foundation (172 Norfolk St), a neo-Gothic building designed as a synagogue in 1849. Spanish sculptor Angel Orensanz purchased the fading gem in 1986 to use as his studio; it's now an arts foundation that hosts performances and other cultural happenings. Take a peek inside

6 Gallery Onetwentyeight Continue along Norfolk, and at the corner of Rivington St you'll get to the always thought-provoking Gallery Onetwentyeight (p99), where installations can range from the playful to the political, and sometimes both at once.

7 Essex Street Market Turn right on Rivington and left onto Essex; on your left is the Essex Street Market (p99), a great place to browse

and indulge in gourmet treats from fresh fruit and cheese to prepared bistro fare.

8 Lower East Side Tenement Museum Continue heading down Essex, turn right onto Delancey and then left onto Orchard St. Here you'll find the visitors center for the Lower East Side Tenement Museum (p97), where a guided tour of their collection of former tenements will show you how life was for Jewish and Italian immigrants living in poverty.

9 Kehila Kedosha Janina Synagogue & Musuem From Essex St, turn right on Broome to reach the Kehila Kedosha Janina Synagogue & Museum (p100), home to the Romaniotes, an obscure branch of Greek Judaism.

10 Eldridge Street Synagogue Continue along Broome until Eldridge St, where you'll turn left and walk a few blocks down to the 1886 Eldridge Street Synagogue (p97), now restored to its original splendor and operating as a museum.

11 St Augustine's Episcopal Church Continue heading down Eldridge St (towards Chinatown), until it ends at Henry St. Turn left and follow Henry St just past Montgomery St and you'll find St Augustine's Episcopal Church (☎ 212-673-5300; 290 Henry St), an 1828 landmark housing the largest African American congregation on the LES. Peek inside to see the restored 'slave galleries,' created to separate worshippers by race in the church's early days.

12 First Shearith Israel Graveyard Double back from whence you came on Henry St, following it to its end at Oliver St. Enter the First Shearith Israel Graveyard (p99), the city's first Jewish cemetery, with headstones dating from the 1600s.

EAST VILLAGE

Drinking p290; Eating p256; Shopping p226; Sleeping p352

Welcome to the new East Village, folks. Though its image as an edgy, radical, be-yourself kind of place has been pretty unshakable for the better part of four decades, things have taken quite a turn in the past few years, putting that idea squarely in the category of nostalgic fantasy. Sure, it's still very cool – filled with endless boutiques, bars, restaurants and characters of the scruffiest, edgiest order. And it'll always have its history: this neighborhood was the inspiration for many cultural contributions, including *Rent,* the musical-turned-movie about artists trying to get by in the early days of the AIDS crisis, and Led Zeppelin's *Physical Graffiti* album cover (the building in the photograph still stands at 98 St Marks Pl). The NYC drug scene was headquartered here for much of the '70s, and the '80s ushered in a major art scene, attracting folks like photographer Nan Goldin, painter Keith Haring and poet Eileen Myles. And let's not forget the legendary CBGB, the divey little music-club gem that gave first chances to everyone from Patti Smith and Lou Reed to the Talking Heads and the Ramones.

But CBGB closed in 2006 because of skyrocketing rents – a sadly fitting time to exit, as rapidly increasing gentrification had begun to make the handful of other dives left here look like museum relics. A quick look around today proves that the moneyed residents and frantic developers are the only ones truly shaping the neighborhood now. It seems that an onslaught of luxury condo towers cannot get constructed fast enough – and that sale prices, which are now regularly topping the $10 million mark (and $8000 a month for rentals), cannot rise high enough. Also regularly seen now are new luxury restaurants and hotels – like the much-touted Bowery Hotel (p352), where rooms go for an average of $500 a night. Along with expensive residences come pricey shop rents, ushering in enough national chain stores to make a longtime local's head spin.

All that said, visitors can still have an eclectic and enjoyable day out here. Sticking to the area around Tompkins Square Park, and the lettered avenues (known as Alphabet City) to its east, is best for finding interesting little nooks in which to imbibe and ingest – as well as a collection of great little community gardens that provide leafy respites and sometimes even live performances. The streets below 14th St and east of First Ave are chock-a-block with cool little boutiques and excellent snack-food spots, offering styles and flavors from around the world. It's a mixed bag, indeed, and perhaps one of the most emblematic of today's city.

Trains don't really go far enough east to carry you to most East Village locations, but it's a quick walk (and even quicker cab or bus ride) from the 6 at Astor Pl, the F, V at Lower East Side-Second Ave or the L at First or Third Aves. The M14 bus, which goes crosstown on 14th St and then south on Aves A, B or C (depending on how the bus is marked), is particularly useful in these parts.

TOMPKINS SQUARE PARK Map p104

btwn 7th & 10th Sts & Aves A & B; ⊕ F, V to Lower East Side-2nd Ave, L to 1st Ave

This 10.5-acre park honors Daniel Tompkins, who served as governor of New York from 1807 to 1817 (and the nation's vice president after that, under James Monroe). It's like a friendly town square for locals, who gather for chess at concrete tables, picnics on the lawn on warm days and spontaneous guitar or drum jams on various grassy knolls. It's also the site of basketball courts, a fun-to-watch dog run (a fenced-in area where humans can unleash their canines), frequent summer concerts and an always-lively kids' playground.

The park wasn't always a place for such clean fun, however. In the '80s, it was a dirty, needle-strewn homeless encampment, unusable for folks wanting a place to stroll or picnic. A contentious turning point came when police razed the band shell (where the legendary and now-defunct Wigstock dragfest was founded by Lady Bunny and cohorts) and evicted more than 100 squatters living in a tent city in the park in 1988 (and again in 1991). That first eviction turned violent; the Tompkins Square Riot, as it came to be known, ushered in the first wave of yuppies in the dog run, fashionistas lolling in the grass and undercover narcotics agents trying to pass as druggie punk kids.

There's not much drama here these days, unless you count the annual Howl! Festival of East Village Arts (www.howlfestival.com), which brings Allen Ginsberg–inspired theater, music, film, dance and spoken-word events to the park and various neighborhood venues each September. The Charlie Parker Jazz Festival (www.summerstage.org) is also held here, bringing some of the biggest jazz names to the 'hood each August.

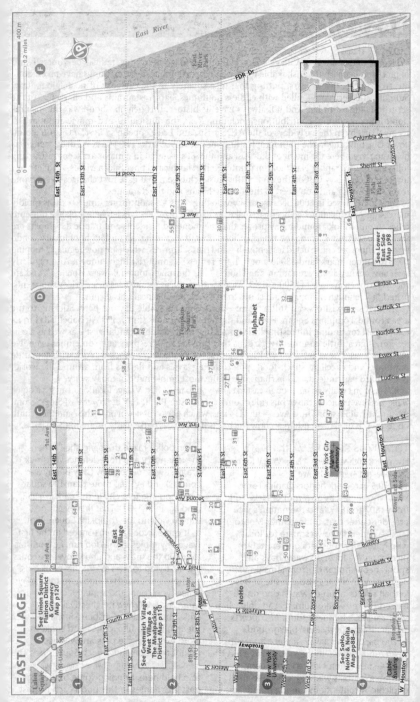

EAST VILLAGE

East River

East River Park

FDR Dr

See Union Square,
Flatiron District
& Gramercy
Map p120

See Greenwich Village,
West Village &
the Meatpacking
District Map p110

East Village

Tompkins
Square
Park

Alphabet City

NoHo

New York City
Marble Cemetery

New York
University

See SoHo,
NoHo & Nolita
Map pp88–9

Cable
Building

See Lower
East Side
Map p98

Hamilton
Fish Park

See Lower East Side
2nd Ave

EAST VILLAGE

RUSSIAN & TURKISH BATHS Map p104

☎ 212-473-8806; www.russianturkishbaths.com; 268 E 10th St btwn First Ave & Ave A; day-pass $30; ⊗ 11am-10pm Mon, Tue, Thu & Fri, 9am-10pm Wed, 7:30am-10pm Sat & Sun; ⊕ L to 1st Ave, 6 to Astor Pl

In a constantly glossed-up neighborhood, these historic Russian and Turkish steam baths remain a beloved constant. Since 1892, this has been the spa for anyone who wants to get naked (or stay in their swimsuit) and romp in steam baths, an ice-cold plunge pool, a sauna and on the sundeck. All-day access includes the use of lockers, locks, robes, towels and slippers. Extras such as Dead Sea–salt scrubs ($35) and black-mud treatments ($48) are also available. An onsite Russian café offers fresh juices, potato-olive salad, blintzes and borscht.

The baths are open to both men and women most hours (wearing shorts is required at these times), except between 9am and 2pm Wednesday (women only) and between 7:30am and 2pm Saturday (men only). These are widely considered the best times to visit, as the vibe is more open, relaxed and communal.

ST MARK'S-IN-THE-BOWERY Map p104

☎ 212-674-6377; www.stmarkschurch-in-the-bowery.com; 131 E 10th St at Second Ave; ⊗ 10am-6pm Mon-Fri; ⊕ 6 to Astor Pl, L to 3rd Ave

Though it's most popular with locals for its cultural offerings – poetry readings hosted by the Poetry Project (☎ 212-674-0910) or cutting-edge dance performances from Danspace (☎ 212-674-8194) – this is also a historic site. This Episcopal church stands on the site of the farm, or *bouwerie*, owned by Dutch Governor Peter Stuyvesant, whose crypt lies under the grounds. The 1799 church, damaged by fire in 1978, has been restored, and you can enjoy an interior view of its abstract stained-glass windows during opening hours.

UKRAINIAN MUSEUM Map p104

☎ 212-228-0110; www.ukrainianmuseum.org; 222 E 6th St btwn Second & Third Aves; adult/child under 12/senior & student $8/free/6; ⊗ 11:30am-5pm Wed-Sun; ⊕ F, V to Lower East Side-2nd Ave, L to 1st Ave

Ukrainians have a long history and still a strong presence here, hence the existence of several (though rapidly disappearing) pierogi joints – including the famous Odessa (Map p104; ☎ 212-253-1482; 119 Ave A between 7th St and St Marks Pl) and Veselka (Map p104; ☎ 212-228-9682; 144 Second Ave at 9th St) – and this interesting museum, which moved into its sleek and expansive headquarters just a few years ago. Its collection of folk art includes richly woven textiles, ceramics, metalwork and traditional Ukrainian Easter eggs, as well as the research tools needed for visitors to trace their own Ukrainian roots. Diverse courses in craftwork, from embroidery to bead stringing, are also offered, as are rotating folk-art exhibits and educational lectures.

EAST VILLAGE NOSTALGIA
Walking Tour

1 CBGB site From the Bleecker St subway, head east along leafy Bleecker St a few blocks, where you can see all that remains of CBGB (315 Bowery btwn 1st & 2nd Sts): the famous red-and-white awning and a tightly-shuttered gate (that is, if a chain store hasn't supplanted these remains already). Opened in 1973, the trashy bar launched punk rock via the Ramones, who yelled out '1-2-3-4' before launching into furious, 1950s-inspired down-strum songs that rarely broke two minutes.

2 Joey Ramone Place The corner just north of here marks the block-long Joey Ramone Place, named after the Ramones' singer, who succumbed to cancer in 2001. He was probably better off not living to see the brutal 2007 murder of Linda Stein, the Ramones' famed and original manager (who later became a real-estate agent to the stars).

3 Cooper Union Head north on the Bowery to Astor Pl. Turn right and head east through the square to come to Cooper Union (see p109), where in 1860 presidential hopeful Abraham Lincoln rocked a skeptical New York crowd with a rousing anti-slavery speech that ensured his candidacy. It's the same stage where, in 2004, AIDS activist Larry Kramer did the same for his generation with an angry speech entitled 'The Tragedy of Today's Gays.'

4 St Marks Place Continue east on St Marks Place, a block chock-full of tattoo parlors, cheap eateries and classic 'New York Fucking City' T-shirt shops that haven't changed much since the '80s. Poke your head into Trash & Vaudeville (4 St Marks Pl), a landmark goth-and-punk shop where a pre-John Yoko Ono staged happenings in the 1960s. Across the street, the modern mall-strip was once the site of the Dom (23 St Marks Pl), and later, the Electric Circus, where Andy Warhol staged his Exploding Plastic Inevitable shows in 1966, with the house band Velvet Underground providing the live soundtrack. If you're hungry, at the end of the block turn left and head north on Second Ave to the Ukrainian restaurant Veselka (144 Second Ave at 9th St), an East Village institution.

5 Love Saves the Day Continue south down Second Ave to 7th St and drop into Love Saves the Day (p228), a campy shop of Star Wars figurines and fabulous vintage clothes. It remains much like it was in 1985, when Rosanna Arquette came here for Madonna's jacket in *Desperately Seeking Susan*.

6 Fillmore East Another block south is the site of Fillmore East (105 Second Ave), a seriously big-time, 2000-seat live-music venue run by promoter Bill Graham from 1968 to 1971, where the Who premiered their rock opera *Tommy*. In the '80s the space was transformed into the Saint – the legendary, 5000-sq-ft dance club that kicked off a joyous, drug-laden, gay disco culture that continues today through a phenomenon known as circuit parties.

7 Physical Graffiti cover Cross Second Ave at 6th St and head down the block-long strip of Indian restaurants and curry shops. At First Ave, turn left, rejoin St Marks Place and turn right. The row of tenements is the site of Led Zeppelin's Physical Graffiti cover (96-98 St Marks Pl), where Mick and Keith sat in 1981 in the Stones' hilarious video for 'Waiting on a Friend.'

8 Tompkins Square Park The trees looming ahead belong to the infamous Tompkins Square Park (p103), where drag queens started the Wigstock summer festival at the bandshell where Jimi Hendrix played in the 1960s, riots broke out in 1988 when police kicked out squatters (immortalized in Lou Reed's album *New York*), and – hey – Ethan Hawke used to play pick-up basketball.

9 Charlie Parker's home Facing the park is jazz-sax great Charlie Parker's home (151 Ave B). The gifted performer died at 34 in 1955 and is remembered today through the annual Charlie Parker Jazz Festival.

10 Madonna's first New York home From the park, head south on Ave B, turning right on 4th for a worthy detour: to see Madonna's first New York home (230 E 4th St), which housed the up-and-comer in 1978.

11 Hell's Angels Motorcycle Club Continue west on 4th until Ave A, where you'll make a left. Then turn right on 3rd St and just past First Ave you'll see the mass of Harleys lined up outside the New York chapter of the Hell's Angels Motorcycle Club (77 E 3rd St). For heaven's sake, don't go inside; but know that drunken carousing still goes on here, prompting occasional busts by the police. Who says the East Village is sanitized?

12 Bowery Hotel Continue along 3rd St to the Bowery and take a left to see where rock, jazz and pop stars of today's world stay when they blow through the East Village: the upscale Bowery Hotel (p352), with $750-a-night suites and a see-and-be-seen restaurant that the gossip pages love.

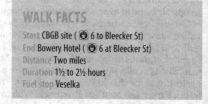

WALK FACTS

Start CBGB site (Ⓜ 6 to Bleecker St)
End Bowery Hotel (Ⓜ 6 at Bleecker St)
Distance Two miles
Duration 1½ to 2½ hours
Fuel stop Veselka

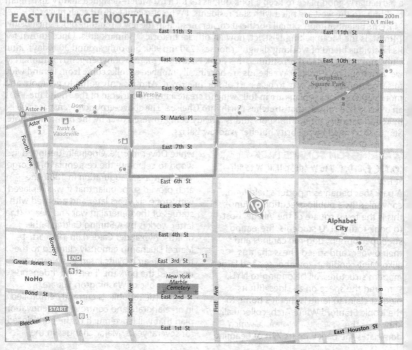

EAST VILLAGE NOSTALGIA

GREENWICH VILLAGE, WEST VILLAGE & THE MEATPACKING DISTRICT

Drinking p291; Eating p257; Shopping p228; Sleeping p352

Third Ave is the eastern boundary dividing the East Village from these three neighborhood gems, where meandering streets with low-rise buildings and a healthy sprinkling of trees eventually give way to the landscaped grounds of Hudson River Park and then the wide Hudson River itself. Once a symbol for all things artistic, outlandish and Bohemian, this storied and popular area will be forever known by visitors as 'Greenwich Village,' though locals don't use the term; they tend to refer to anything west of Sixth Ave as the West Village, and the central part between Sixth and Fourth Aves as simply 'the Village.' The neighborhood's reputation as a creative enclave can be traced back to at least the early 20th century, when artists and writers moved in; by the '40s it had become known as a gathering place for gay folk, who saw the beginning of an equal-rights movement here with the Stonewall Riots in 1969 (see p34); in the '50s, the Village's coffeehouses, bars and jazz clubs were the places to find bohemians and Beat poets such as Allen Ginsberg and Jack Kerouac.

New York University (NYU) now dominates much of the central Village, flooding the blocks around Washington Square Park with hip-looking students and gradually buying up real estate on every corner. The vibe turns mellow just west of the park, where leafy, residential blocks sport an upscale blend of townhouses, cafés and boutiques, turning carnivalesque only for the stretch of Christopher St, where you'll find a quaintly tacky collection of gay bars and tchotchke shops selling souvenirs like rainbow stickers, custom-made leather chaps and 'I'm not gay but my girlfriend is' T-shirts. The entire area is a great place for wandering, and even getting yourself happily lost, as it's just about the only place in Manhattan that's not organized in a neat grid, due to its past as a collection of navigational horse paths. There's a good chance you'll even run into a celebrity, as the chi-chi West Village is home to quite a collection of A-listers, including Sarah Jessica Parker and Matthew Broderick, Willem Dafoe, Calvin Klein and Lili Taylor. Perry St is a particularly good place to keep a look out, as its Richard Meier–designed luxury apartment buildings to the west are filled with star residents. (Who else could afford such places?)

In the neighborhood's small northern corner, nestled in the few circuitous blocks just below 14th St, is the Meatpacking District, now an official historic landmark area. Once known for its lascivious blend of working slaughterhouses (250 in 1900, but only around 30 today), kink clubs and transgendered prostitutes, this nook is now quite the picture of hyper-gentrification. (Do we see a trend here, folks?) Weekends are horrifically mobbed as folks come from far and wide to search for the latest way to be a part of the 'in' crowd. And it's only going to get more and more popular here, as plans are in full swing to create a unique park out of the High Line (p115), an old elevated railway that stretches north into Chelsea. The above-ground greenspace will be linked to various cultural hotspots and is already being towered over by the brand new hotel Standard, created by celebrity hotelier Andrew Balazs.

WASHINGTON SQUARE PARK Map p110

Ⓢ A, C, E, B, D, F, V to W 4th St, N, R, W to 8th St-NYU

A park that began as a potter's field (and, conveniently, a public-execution ground), this is the town square of the Village, host to book-toting NYU students, fire-eating street performers, dog-run canines and their owners and speed-chess champs alike. Mint-condition townhouses and large modern structures, all belonging to NYU, surround the space on all sides. But its biggest claim to fame is that it's home to the iconic Stanford White Arch, colloquially known as the Washington Square Arch, which dominates the park with its 72ft of beaming white Dover marble. Originally designed in wood to celebrate the centennial of George Washington's inauguration in 1889, the arch proved so popular that it was replaced with stone six years later and adorned with statues of the general in war and peace (the latter work is by A Stirling Calder, father of artist Alexander Calder). In 1916 artist Marcel Duchamp famously climbed to the top of the arch by its internal stairway and declared the park the 'Free and Independent Republic of Washington Square.'

This little republic is currently embroiled in an elaborate and controversial renovation plan that will leave much of the park closed for several years. Major changes in the

$16-million plan include moving the park's fountain to be in line with the arch, relocating the dog run, replacing the plaza with a lawn and, most alarmingly, the addition of a granite-and-iron fence that would be locked at night. Public-space advocates have been up in arms about the seeming privatization of the park, whose renovation has been largely privately funded, and long-time park fans are upset over the attempt to clean up the ramshackle charm of the place. Only time will tell if the new look is too sanitized to jibe with the free-spirited history here.

NEW YORK UNIVERSITY Map p110

☎ 212-998-4636; www.nyu.edu; information center 50 W 4th St

In 1831 Albert Gallatin, formerly Secretary of the Treasury under President Thomas Jefferson, founded an intimate center of higher learning open to all students, regardless of race or class background. He'd scarcely recognize the place today, as it's swelled to a student population of more than 50,000, with more than 16,000 employees and schools and colleges at six Manhattan locations. It just keeps growing, too – to the dismay of landmark activists and business owners, who have seen buildings rapidly bought out by the academic giant and replaced with ugly dormitories or administrative offices. Still, some of its crevices are charming, such as the leafy courtyard at its School of Law (Washington Sq South at MacDougal St), or impressively modern, like the Skirball Center for the Performing Arts (566 LaGuardia Pl at Washington Sq South), where top-notch dance, theater, music, spoken-word and other performers wow audiences at the 850-seat theater. NYU's academic offerings are highly regarded and wide-ranging, especially its film, theater, writing, medical and law programs. For a unique experience that'll put you on the fast track to meeting locals, sign up for a weekend or one-day class – from American history to photography – offered by the School of Professional Studies and Continuing Education (www.scps.nyu.edu), and open to all.

ASTOR PLACE Map p110

8th St btwn Third & Fourth Aves; ◉ R, W to 8th St-NYU, 6 to Astor Pl

This square and street is named after the Astor family, who built an early New York fortune on beaver pelts (check out the tiles in the wall of the Astor Pl subway platform) and lived on Colonnade Row (429-434 Lafayette St), just south of the square – four of the original nine marble-faced, Greek revival residences on Lafayette St still exist. The large, brown-stone Cooper Union, the public college founded in 1859 by glue millionaire Peter Cooper, dominates the square – now more than ever, as the school has just constructed its first new academic building in 50 years, a towering, nine-story, environmentally friendly design by architect Thom Mayne of Morphosis. It's not the first new structure to alter the character of Astor Place in recent years. That honor goes to the gleaming 'Astor Place: Sculpture for Living' steel-and-glass condo by Gwathmey Siegel architects – either an inappropriate horror or a testimony to modernity, depending on whom you ask (though most claim the former). Still, the *Alamo* cube sculpture, which sits in the middle of the square, remains a popular spot for skateboarding teens and liquored-up NYU students to hang out under. Get a group together and give it a whirl; with some powerful backs and legs you can really send it spinning.

GRACE CHURCH Map p110

802 Broadway at 10th St; ◉ N, R, W to 8th St-NYU, 6 to Astor Pl

This Gothic revival Episcopal church, designed in 1843 by James Renwick Jr, was made of marble quarried by prisoners at 'Sing Sing,' the state penitentiary in the town of Ossining, 30 miles up the Hudson River (which, legend has it, is the origin of the expression 'being sent upriver'). After years of neglect, Grace Church was spiffed up in a major way; now it's a National Landmark whose elaborate carvings, towering spire and verdant, groomed yard are sure to stop you in your tracks as you make your way down this otherwise ordinary stretch of the Village. The stained-glass windows inside are stunning, and the soaring interior makes a perfect setting for the frequent organ and choir concerts.

FORBES COLLECTION Map p110

☎ 212-206-5548; www.forbesgalleries.com; 62 Fifth Ave at 12th St; admission free; ⏲ 10am-4pm Thu-Sat; ◉ L, N, R, Q, W, 4, 5, 6 to 14th St-Union Sq

These galleries, located in the lobby of the headquarters of *Forbes* magazine, house

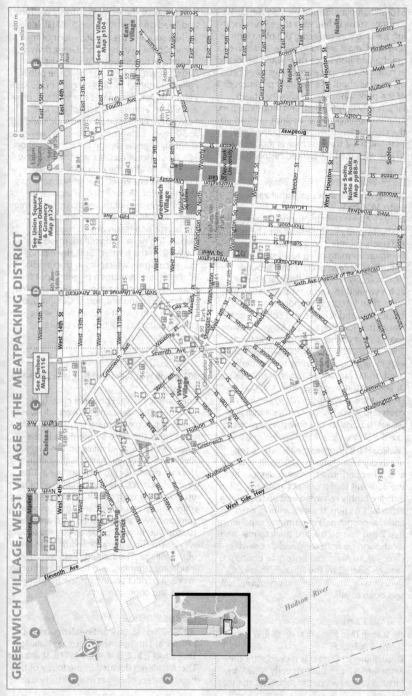

GREENWICH VILLAGE, WEST VILLAGE, CHELSEA & THE MEATPACKING DISTRICT

See East Village Map p104

See Union Square, Flatiron District & Gramercy Map p120

See Chelsea Map p116

See SoHo, NoHo & Nolita Map pp88-9

GREENWICH VILLAGE, WEST VILLAGE & THE MEATPACKING DISTRICT

rotating exhibits and curios from the personal collection of the late publishing magnate Malcolm Forbes. The eclectic mix of objects on display includes Fabergé eggs, toy boats, early versions of Monopoly and over 10,000 toy soldiers.

WEST 4TH STREET BASKETBALL COURTS Map p110

Sixth Ave btwn 3rd and 4th Sts; Ⓢ A, C, E, B, D, F, V to W 4th St

Otherwise known as 'the Cage,' the small basketball court that stands enclosed within chain-link fencing here is home to some of the best streetball in the country.

Though it's more touristy than its counterpart, Rucker Park in Harlem (see the boxed text, p325), that's also part of its charm, as the games held here in the center of the Village draw massive, excitable crowds, who often stand 10-deep to hoot and holler for the skilled, competitive guys who play here. Prime time is summer, when the W 4th St Summer Pro-Classic League, now in its 26th year, hits the scene. While the height of this court's popularity was back in 2001 – the year Nike capitalized on the raw energy of the place by shooting a commercial here – b'ball-lovin' throngs still storm the place on weekends.

ABINGDON SQUARE Map p110

Hudson St at 12th St

This historic dot on the landscape (just a quarter-acre small) is a lovely little patch of green, home to grassy knolls, beds of perennial flowers and winding bluestone paths, as well as a popular Saturday greenmarket. It's a great place to enjoy a midday picnic or rest after an afternoon of wandering the winding West Village streets. After getting horizontal, look up at the southern end of the park and you'll see the *Abingdon Doughboy*, a bronze statue dedicated to servicemen from the neighborhood who gave their lives in WWI (when soldiers were commonly known as 'doughboys').

CHRISTOPHER STREET PIER Map p110

Christopher St at Hudson River; ⓞ 1 to Christopher St-Sheridan Sq

This finger of concrete, spiffily renovated with a grass lawn, flowerbeds and tented shade shelters as part of the ongoing Hudson River Park (p76) project, is officially known as Pier 45. But with its long-time moniker it's become a magnet for downtowners of all stripes, from local families with toddlers in daylight to mobs of young gay kids who flock here at night from all over the city (and beyond) because of the pier's long-established history as a gay cruising hangout. That's been the source of ongoing conflict in the neighborhood, where moneyed West Village residents say that the clutches of youths who stream there along Christopher St are disorderly and disrespectful late into the night. The kids say they've got nowhere else to go, and deserve a claim to the pier just like anyone else. It's unclear how it'll all work out, but one thing's for sure: the spot offers sweeping views of the Hudson and cool, relieving breezes in the thick of summer.

VILLAGE RADICALS
Walking Tour

1 Oscar Wilde Bookshop To begin, disembark the subway at Christopher St and double back east about a block, where you'll find the last remaining LGBT bookstore in the city, the Oscar Wilde Bookshop (p340). A simple brick townhouse, it has bucked the mainstream by selling queer books and periodicals since 1967.

2 Christopher Park Now head back west to tiny Christopher Park, where two white, life-size

statues of same-sex couples (*Gay Liberation*, 1992) stand guard. On its north side is the legendary Stonewall Inn (p343), where a clutch of fed-up drag queens rioted for their civil rights in 1969, signaling the start of the gay revolution.

3 Little Red Square Head down Seventh Ave South and turn left onto Bleecker St, strolling for several more blocks until its intersection with Sixth Ave. To the south you'll see a plaque marking 'Little Red Square,' named not for communists but for the original site of the experimental Little Red Schoolhouse, founded by Elisabeth Irwin in 1921 and still thriving nearby.

4 Fat Black Pussycat Site Continue east on the crooked Minetta St, home to the unremarkable Panchito's Mexican Restaurant. But above its rear red facade is the faded sign for the former site of the Fat Black Pussycat (103 MacDougal St) – called The Commons in 1962 when a young Bob Dylan wrote and first performed 'Blowin' in the Wind' here.

5 Minetta Tavern Turn right on Minetta Lane and right on MacDougal St to find the historic Minetta Tavern (☎ 212-475-3850; 113 MacDougal St; ☺ noon–midnight), a great place for a pit stop. The bar and restaurant, its walls lined with photos of celebs who have visited, opened as a speakeasy in 1922. It was later frequented by one of the most famous local eccentrics, Joe Gould, who was immortalized through the writings of journalism great Joseph Mitchell (a friendship further depicted in the 2000 flick *Joe Gould's Secret*).

6 Folklore Center Also on this block is the former site of the Folklore Center (110 MacDougal St), where Izzy Young established a hangout for folk artists, including Bob Dylan, who found his first audience at the music venue Cafe Wha? (☎ 212-254-3706; 115 MacDougal St).

7 Café Reggio Further along MacDougal is another great place to take a load off. It's the cozy Café Reggio (☎ 212-475-9557; 119 MacDougal St), whose original 1927 owners claimed to be the first to bring cappuccino from Italy to the US.

8 Provincetown Playhouse Head further up MacDougal to the Provincetown Playhouse (☎ 212-998-5867; 133 MacDougal St). Founded on a wharf in Provincetown, Massachusetts, in 1915 as an experimental theater, it moved to this converted stable and was once managed by a young Eugene O'Neill.

9 Washington Square Park Beyond here is the southwest entrance to Washington Square Park (p108), which has a long history of being a magnet for radicals hosting demonstrations on topics from anti-war and pro-marijuana to dyke pride. Leave the park through the iconic arch and head up Fifth Ave.

10 Weatherman House Make a left on W 11th St, where you'll wrap up the tour with two notable townhouses. First is the infamous Weatherman House (18 W 11th St), used in 1970 as a hideout and bomb factory for the radical antigovernment group until an accidental explosion killed

WALK FACTS

Start Christopher St (⊕ 1 to Christopher St-Sheridan Sq)
End 11th St at Sixth Ave (⊕ F, V, L at Sixth Ave-14th St)
Distance 1.5 miles
Duration 1½ hours
Fuel stops Minetta Tavern, Café Reggio

three members and destroyed the house; it was rebuilt in its current angular form in 1978.

11 Oscar Wilde's House Just a bit further west, the tour comes full circle with a former, albeit brief, home of Oscar Wilde (48 W 11th St). The famed Irish wit lived here for a few weeks following a US lecture tour in 1882.

113

CHELSEA

Drinking p292; Eating p259; Shopping p232; Sleeping p354

Chelsea has a wonderful mix of everything – a great nightlife and restaurant scene, a mix of streets both intimate and industrial, an excellent location neither too far north or south, a slew of shopping opportunities and the most stellar collection of art galleries in the city. The area is perhaps best known as a 'gayborhood,' home to many beautiful men (as well as women and children, of course) who strut their stuff on the runway of Eighth Ave while running between the gym, work and various happy-hour gatherings.

During the city's Gilded Age in the late 19th century, Chelsea was the dry-goods and retail center of the city, drawing well-heeled shoppers to its varied emporia. Closer to the Hudson River, you can still find plenty of old warehouses, and many of the townhouses, especially those in the Chelsea Historic District (the low 20s between Eighth and Tenth Aves), are beautifully restored.

Cool cafés, shops and restaurants have exploded along Ninth and Tenth Aves over the past several years, and west of Tenth Ave lies the hub of the city's art gallery scene, which grows more expansive by the year. The area is absolutely crawling with reviewers and buyers on Thursday evenings, when big openings take place. For a unique DIY adventure, wander through the small but fascinating Flower District (around Sixth Ave btwn 26th & 29th Sts) on a weekday morning, when trucks unload massive amounts of fragrant, fresh flowers and plants, and where you can discover great decorative bargains, including cases of votive candles and bamboo reeds.

The best trains for getting to Chelsea are the 1 to 14th, 18th or 23rd Sts or the A, C, E to 14th or 23rd Sts. Traversing the entire area on foot is a breeze, though those cross-town treks can be doozies in winter, when the river whips up icy winds – then you'll want to hop on the M23 bus down 23rd St instead.

CHELSEA GALLERIES

Chelsea is home to the highest concentration of art galleries in the entire city – and the number of them just keeps increasing. Most lie in the 20s, on the blocks between Tenth and Eleventh Aves, and wine-and-cheese openings for their new shows are typically held on Thursday evenings. For a complete guide and map, pick up a copy of the monthly Gallery Guide (www.galleryguide.com), available for free at most art venues, or visit www.westchelseaarts.com. Also, see p117 of this guide for a Chelsea gallery walking tour. Among the showcases that create the most buzz in these parts are the Andrea Rosen Gallery (Map p116; www.andrearosengallery.com; 525 W 24th St), with gems by Katy Moran, Rita Ackerman and Felix Gonzalez-Torres; the Mary Boone Gallery (Map p116; www.maryboonegallery.com; 541 W 24th St), whose owner found fame in the '80s with her eye for Jean-Michel Basquiat and Julian Schnabel in SoHo; and the Matthew Marks Gallery (Map p116; www.matthewmarks.com; 522 W 22nd St), a Chelsea pioneer known for exhibiting big names from Jasper Johns to Ellsworth Kelly.

GENERAL THEOLOGICAL SEMINARY
Map p116

☎ 212-243-5150; www.gts.edu; 175 Ninth Ave btwn 20th & 21st Sts; ☻ noon-3pm Mon-Fri, 11am-3pm Sat

Founded in 1817, this is the oldest seminary of the Episcopal Church in America. The school, which sits in the midst of the beautiful Chelsea historic district, has been working hard lately to make sure it can preserve its best asset – the gardenlike campus snuggled in the middle its full block of buildings – even as Chelsea development sprouts up all around it. This peaceful haven is the perfect spot for finding respite, either before or after your neighborhood gallery crawl.

CHELSEA HOTEL Map p116

☎ 212-243-3700; 222 W 23rd St btwn Seventh & Eighth Aves; ☻ 1, C, E to 23rd St

It's probably not any great shakes as far as hotels go – and besides, it mainly houses long-term residents. But as a place of mythical proportions, the Chelsea Hotel is top of the line. The red-brick hotel, featuring ornate iron balconies and no fewer than seven plaques declaring its literary landmark status, has played some major roles in pop-culture history. It's where the likes of Mark Twain, Thomas Wolfe, Dylan Thomas and Arthur Miller hung out; Jack Kerouac allegedly crafted On the Road during one marathon session here, and it's where Arthur C Clarke wrote 2001: A Space Odyssey. Dylan Thomas died of alcohol poisoning while staying here in 1953, and Nancy Spungeon died here after being stabbed by her Sex Pistols boyfriend Sid Vicious in 1978. Among the many celebs who have logged time living at the Chelsea are Joni Mitchell, Arthur Miller, Stanley Kubrick, Dennis Hopper, Edith Piaf, Bob Dylan and Leonard Cohen, whose song 'Chelsea Hotel' recalls a romp with Janis Joplin (who spent time here, too). The art-filled lobby is worth a look-see, and its basement-level Star Lounge is a sexy, low-lit spot for a martini.

CHELSEA MARKET Map p116
www.chelseamarket.com; 75 Ninth Ave at 15th St; Ⓔ A, C, E to 14th St, L to 8th Ave
In a shining example of redevelopment and preservation, the Chelsea Market has taken a former factory of cookie giant Nabisco (creator of the Oreo) and turned it into an 800ft-long shopping concourse that caters to foodies. And that's only the lower part of a larger, million-sq-ft space that occupies a full city block, current home of television channels the Food Network, Oxygen Network and NY1, the local news channel. The prime draw for shoppers, though, are the more than two dozen food shops, including Amy's Bread, Fat Witch Brownies, The Lobster Place, Hale & Hearty Soup, Ronnybrook Farm Dairy and Frank's butcher shop. You can also sit down and indulge at lunch spots such as the Green Market organic-food café, and

buy nonfood items at Imports from Marrakesh (specializing in Moroccan art and design) and the expert-staffed Chelsea Wine Vault. Live music shows grace the main public space weekly.

CHELSEA PIERS Map p116
☎ 212-336-6000; www.chelseapiers.com; Twelfth Ave at 23rd St; Ⓔ C, E to 23rd St, 🚌 M23 westbound
This massive waterfront sports center caters to the athlete in everyone. You can set out to hit a bucket of golf balls at the four-level driving range, ice skate in the complex's indoor rink or rent in-line skates to cruise along the new Hudson River Park waterfront bike path – all the way down to Battery Park. There's a jazzy bowling alley, Hoop City for basketball, a sailing school for kids, batting cages, a huge gym facility with an indoor pool (day passes for nonmembers are $50), indoor rock-climbing walls – the works. There's even waterfront dining and drinking at the Chelsea Brewing Company, which serves great pub fare and delicious home-brews for you to carb-load on after your workout. Though the complex is somewhat cut off by the busy West Side Hwy (Twelfth Ave), the wide array of attractions here brings in the crowds; the M23 crosstown bus, which goes right to the main entrance, saves you the long, four-avenue trek from the subway. For more information on Chelsea Piers, see the boxed text on p337.

THE HIGH LINE COMETH

For years now, the big buzz in Chelsea and Hell's Kitchen has been all about the High Line – whose story, in the prodevelopment environment of today's New York City, is very much like a fairy tale. The High Line itself is a 30ft-high, abandoned stretch of elevated railroad track, which ranges from Gansevoort St in the Meatpacking District up to 34th St. Overgrown with thick weeds and not used since the 1960s, the blissfully empty space has inspired a group of activists to fight with the city for the right to turn it into a long ribbon of parkland – and, miracle of miracles, they won. The struggle for the site began in 1999, when a group of community activists, Friends of the High Line (www.thehighline.org), lobbied to save the track from being demolished to pave the way for salivating developers. Then-mayor Giuliani opposed the preservation effort, but Mayor Bloomberg supported it – and a heap of financial promises to the tune of $50 million didn't hurt matters, either. Construction began more or less on schedule in 2006, and the first portion of the public green space was set to open in 2008 (though had not yet at this writing). The park, which will create a peaceful continuum that sews together a long swath of the West Side, will be one of only two elevated parks in the world (the other, created atop an abandoned railroad viaduct, is the Promenade Plantée in Paris). And this one will have plenty of perks tied to it, including an Andre Balazs luxury hotel, the Standard (similar to his others in LA and Miami), under construction at W 13th St, as well as a downtown branch of the Whitney Museum. Neighborhoods alongside and under the High Line – many of which are still pretty undeveloped and even downright gritty – are expected to spiff up as the park progresses, bringing quick change to what historically has been a rather slowly evolving area.

CHELSEA

CHELSEA

RUBIN MUSEUM OF ART Map p116

☎ 212-620-5000; www.rmanyc.org; 150 W 17th St at Seventh Ave; adult/child under 12/senior & student $10/free/7; ⏰ 11am-5pm Mon & Thu, to 7pm Wed, to 10pm Fri, to 6pm Sat & Sun; ◉ 1 to 18th St

This is the first museum in the western world to dedicate itself to art of the Himalayas and surrounding regions. Its impressive collections include embroidered textiles from China, metal sculptures from Tibet, Pakistani stone sculptures, and intricate Bhutanese paintings, as well as ritual objects and dance masks from various Tibetan regions, spanning from the 2nd to the 19th centuries. Rotating exhibitions have included the educational 'BIG! Himalayan Art' and 'Bon: The Magic Word,' about the religion of the indigenous people of Tibet.

CHELSEA ART MUSEUM Map p116

☎ 212-255-0719; www.chelseaartmuseum.org; 556 W 22nd St at Eleventh Ave; adult $6 ($3 after 6pm Thu), student & senior $3; ⏰ noon-6pm Tue, Wed, Fri & Sat, to 8pm Thu; ◉ C, E to 23rd St

Occupying a three-story red-brick building dating from 1850, this popular museum stands on land once owned by writer Clement Clarke Moore (author of the famous poem 'A Visit from St Nicholas'). Its focus is on post-war abstract expressionism, especially by national and international artists, and its permanent collection includes works by Antonio Corpora, Laszlo Lakner, Jean Arp and Ellen Levy. The museum is also the headquarters of the Miotte Foundation, dedicated to archiving the works of Jean Miotte, a SoHo-based artist who has played a large role in creating the genre known as 'Informel' (Informal Art).

CHELSEA'S ART CRAWL
Walking Tour

1 Chelsea Art Museum Begin your trek on 22nd St at Eleventh Ave at the Chelsea Art Museum (left), a unique collection of 'informal art' near the Hudson River.

2 24th Street galleries Head north on Eleventh Ave and turn right on 24th St, where you'll find a trio of excellent showcases: Metro Pictures (☎ 212-206-7100; 519 W 24th St), best known for representing photographer Cindy Sherman, Luhring Augustine (☎ 212-206-9100; www.luhring augustine.com; 531 W 24th St), which often shows large-format photography, and the famous Mary Boone Gallery (see p114).

3 Gallery Group Head north on Tenth Ave and turn left on 27th St, where you'll find a

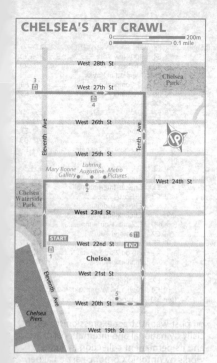

CHELSEA'S ART CRAWL

0 ————— 200m
0 ————— 0.1 mile

West 28th St

Chelsea Park

3 🏛

West 27th St

🏛 4

West 26th St

West 25th St

VP

Mary Boone Gallery · Luhring Augustine · Metro Pictures

West 24th St

2

West 23rd St

Chelsea Waterside Park

START

6 🍴

West 22nd St   END

🏛 1

Chelsea

West 21st St

Eleventh Ave

Tenth Ave

5

West 20th St

Chelsea Piers

West 19th St

WALK FACTS

Start Chelsea Art Museum (🚊 M23 westbound)
End 22nd St and Tenth Ave (🚇 C, E at 23rd St)
Distance 1.5 miles
Duration Two hours
Fuel stop Tía Pol

spots into the old loading dock bays of what used to be the Tunnel nightclub.

4 Aperture Gallery Wander back east and into the Aperture Gallery (☎ 212-505-5555; 547 W 27th St btwn Tenth & Eleventh Aves), the exhibit space of the photography-focused Aperture Foundation, which mounts shows from pros and newcomers alike.

5 529 W 20th St Now stroll south on Tenth Ave to 20th St, making a right and taking advantage of one of several multigallery spaces, which feel oddly mall-like and often exhibit newer talents. Inside the eight-floor building at 529 W 20th St you'll find ACA Galleries, Admit One Gallery, the Bill Maynes Gallery and many others.

6 Tía Pol No doubt you're famished by now, and luckily the cozy and delicious Tía Pol (p259), a scrumptious Spanish tapas bar, isn't far – you'll find it on Tenth Ave between 23rd and 22nd Sts.

buzzed-about gallery group (615 W 27th St) where, in 2006, six showcases – Derek Eller Gallery, Foxy Production, Wallspace, Oliver Kamm Gallery, Clementine Gallery and John Connelly Presents – relocated from other Chelsea

UNION SQUARE, THE FLATIRON DISTRICT & GRAMERCY

Drinking p293; Eating p259; Shopping p233; Sleeping p355

This trio of east-side neighborhoods boasts lovely architecture, diverse public spaces and a smattering of offerings that are quite hip – but in a subtle, less frenzied way than, say, the Lower East Side or the Meatpacking District. Though they each have distinct qualities, they all share that of being unpretentious – and of drawing shoppers looking for particular items or services, whether it's furniture (Flatiron District) or discount designer duds (Union Square). And all have a bounty of good restaurants and bars.

Union Square was one of New York's first business districts, providing a convenient site for many workers' rallies and political protests throughout the mid-19th century. Its name, though, has more prosaic origins, as this spot was simply the 'union' of the old Bowery and Bloomingdale (now Broadway) roads. By the 1960s, junkies and gigolos took over here, but were ushered out in the '90s during a massive revival, which was helped along by the arrival of the Greenmarket Farmers Market (p121), thriving today more than ever (despite a massive Whole Foods store that has moved in on the park's southern side). Today, shops and eateries surround Union Sq Park, whose interior hops with activity – too much, say many of the political and social activists who gather for frequent demonstrations here; they and others fear that an ever-expanding farmers market and annual holiday fair, with rows upon rows of booths, eat up too much public space with profit-making operations.

To the northwest is the Flatiron District, loaded with loft buildings and boutiques, and doing a good imitation of SoHo without the pretensions, prices or crowds. There are some fine restaurants, some performance and cocktail lounges (especially along 22nd St) and plenty of shopping opportunities. The neighborhood takes its name from the Flatiron Building (below), a thin and gorgeous work of architecture that sits just south of Madison Sq Park.

The Gramercy area, loosely comprising the 20s blocks east of Park Ave South, is named after one of New York's loveliest parks – Gramercy Park, the kind of public garden area found in London and other European cities. But while the botanical sentiment did translate across the Atlantic, the socialist sense did not: when developers transformed the surrounding marsh into a city neighborhood in 1830, admission to Gramercy Park was restricted to residents, and to this day you still need a key to get in (which, incidentally, you can procure as a guest of the Gramercy Park Hotel, p356). Other attractions in the region include stately brownstones on tranquil streets, including Irving Place, a short street named after writer Washington Irving that contains some great little cafés, eateries and the rockin' Irving Plaza (p303) live music venue. The eastern edge of the 'hood was scheduled to welcome a brand-new addition, the East River Science Park, part of Bellevue Hospital, sometime in 2009. The $400 million project will hold specialized laboratories, 500,000 sq feet of offices and a public-space component.

FLATIRON BUILDING Map p120

23rd St & Broadway; ⊙ **N, R, W, F, V, 6 to 23rd St**
Built in 1902, the 20-story Flatiron Building, designed by Daniel Burnham, has a uniquely narrow triangular footprint that resembles the prow of a massive ship, and a traditional, Beaux-Arts limestone facade, built over a steel frame, that gets more complex and beautiful the longer you stare at it. Best viewed from the traffic island north of 23rd St between Broadway and Fifth Ave, this unique structure dominated the plaza back in the skyscraper era of the early 1900s. Images of the Flatiron that were published before its official opening – many thanks to the fact that this was also

the time of the first mass-produced picture postcards – aroused a buzz of curiosity around the globe. Publisher Frank Munsey was one of the building's first tenants, and from his 18th-floor offices his firm put out *Munsey's Magazine*, which featured the writings of short-story writer O Henry ('The Gift of the Magi'). His musings, along with the paintings of John Sloan and photographs by Alfred Stieglitz, best immortalized the Flatiron back in the day – along with a famous comment by actress Katherine Hepburn, who said in a TV interview once that she'd like to be admired as much as the grand old building. Today it remains one of the most photographed architectural sites in New York.

UNION SQUARE, THE FLATIRON DISTRICT & GRAMERCY

0 — 400 m
0 — 0.2 miles

INFORMATION
Beth Israel Medical Center..........1 D5
Duggal...............................2 A3
Institute of Culinary Education......3 A3
International Center in New York....4 A3
School of Visual Arts................5 C3

SIGHTS (pp119–22)
Flatiron Building....................6 B4
Greenmarket Farmers Market........7 B5
Holocaust Memorial..................8 B3
Metropolitan Life Insurance Tower.9 B3
National Arts Club..................10 C4
New York Life Insurance Building.11 B3
Theodore Roosevelt's Birthplace...12 B4
Tibet House.........................13 A5

SHOPPING (pp233–5)
ABC Carpet & Home.................14 B4
Academy Records....................15 A4
Bed Bath & Beyond................16 A4
Books of Wonder....................17 A4

Chelsea Outdoor Market.............18 A3
Filene's Basement...................19 B5
Paragon Athletic Goods.............20 B5
Revolution Books....................21 A4
Shakespeare & Co...................22 C3
Virgin Megastore....................23 B5
Whole Foods........................(see 19)

EATING (pp259–60)
City Bakery.........................24 A4
Craft...............................25 B4
Cupcake Cafe.......................26 A4
Gramercy Tavern....................27 B4
Maoz Vegetarian....................28 B5
Max Brenner........................29 A5
Pure Food and Wine................30 C4

DRINKING (p293)
Crocodile Lounge...................31 D5
Old Town Bar & Restaurant.........32 B4
Pete's Tavern.......................33 C4

Proof...............................34 C4
Sapa...............................35 A3

NIGHTLIFE (p303)
The Fillmore at Irving Plaza........36 C5

SPORTS & ACTIVITIES (pp323–37)
Bikram Yoga NYC...................(see 6)
Jivamukti..........................37 B5
New York City Audubon Society...38 A3

GAY & LESBIAN NYC (p343)
Splash Bar.........................39 A5

SLEEPING (pp355–7)
Chelsea Inn........................40 A5
Gramercy Park Hotel...............41 C4
Hotel 17...........................42 C5
Inn at Irving Place.................43 C5
Jazz on the Town...................44 D5
W New York - Union Square........45 B4

See Midtown East & Fifth Avenue Map p126

See Chelsea Map p116

See East Village Map p104

See Greenwich Village, West Village & The Meatpacking District Map p110

UNION SQUARE Map p120

14th to 17th Sts btwn Broadway & Park Ave S; ⊕ L, N, Q, R, W, 4, 5, 6 to 14th St-Union Sq

Town square for an eclectic crowd, this park hosts loungers and local workers catching some fresh air, throngs of young skateboarders doing tricks on the southeastern stairs and frequent antiwar or general antigovernment protestors. Opened in 1831, this park soon became the central gathering place for surrounding mansions and grand concert halls and eventually an explosion of high-end shops along Broadway, which became known as the Ladies' Mile. Then, from the start of the Civil War until well into the 20th century, this became the site for protests of all kinds – for everyone from union workers to political activists. By the time of WWI, the area had become neglected and depressed, but eventually was home to all sorts of working-class headquarters, including the American Civil Liberties Union, the Communist and Socialist Parties and the Ladies' Garment Workers Union. The 1960s ushered in an era of lounging hippiedom in the park, spurred on by the fact that Andy Warhol opened his famous Factory on Union Sq West (in a building that, in a perfect sign of the times, now houses a Puma sportswear store).

Its latest transformation has been that of the yearly Christmas-holiday bazaar, with all manner of crafts hawked at festive booths, a fun shopping experience (although its annual expansion leaves less and less room for people who simply want to hang out). The weekly greenmarket (see the boxed text, below) is one of the most popular farmers markets in the city. And all can take solace in a very special bronze statue near the park's southwest edge immortalizing Mohandas K Gandhi, created by Kantilal Patel and dedicated in 1986 on the occasion of the peacemaker's 117th birthday.

MADISON SQUARE PARK Map p120
www.madisonsquarepark.org; 23rd to 26th Sts btwn Fifth & Madison Aves
This park defined the northern reaches of Manhattan until the city's population exploded just after the Civil War. It has enjoyed a rejuvenation within the past few years thanks to a renovation and re-dedication project, and now neighborhood residents head here to unleash their dogs in the popular dog-run area, as workers enjoy lunches – which can now be bought

from the hip, on-site Shake Shack (☎ 212-889-6600; 🕑 11am-11pm) – while perched on the shaded benches or sprawled on the wide lawn. These are perfect spots from which to gaze up at the landmarks that surround the park, including the Flatiron Building (p119) to the southwest, the art-deco Metropolitan Life Insurance Tower to the southeast and the New York Life Insurance Building, topped with a gilded spire, to the northeast. The space also sports 19th-century statues of folks including Senator Roscoe Conkling (who froze to death in a brutal 1888 blizzard) and Civil War admiral David Farragut. Between 1876 and 1882 the torch-bearing arm of the Statue of Liberty was on display here, and in 1879 the first Madison Square Garden arena was constructed on this spot, at Madison Ave and 26th St. In warm months, various park programs feature music performances and readings, while eclectic sculptures are shown year-round. The latest excitement, though, is over the park's new self-cleaning, coin-operated toilet, which lets you do your business for only 25¢.

TIBET HOUSE Map p120
☎ 212-807-0563; www.tibethouse.org; 22 W 15th St btwn Fifth & Sixth Aves; donations accepted; 🕑 noon-5pm Tue-Fri; ◉ F to 14th St, L to 6th Ave
With the Dalai Lama as the patron of its board, this nonprofit cultural space is dedicated to presenting Tibet's ancient traditions through art exhibits, a research library and various publications, while programs on offer include educational workshops, open meditations, retreat weekends and docent-led tours to Tibet, Nepal and Bhutan. Exhibits here tend to attract a diverse

NYC GREENMARKETS

It's not a feature most visitors expect to find in Gotham, but Greenmarket farmers markets (www.cenyc.org) are a widespread and beloved part of the culture here. There are more than 40 farmers markets scattered throughout the five boroughs, and though the cornucopia at Union Sq (held Monday, Wednesday, Friday and Saturday) remains one of the most popular destination markets, it's the smaller, more infrequent ones in tucked-away neighborhoods that may be even more appreciated by their neighbors. Regional farmers sell all manner of edibles – homemade cheeses and handmilked cream, organic fruits and vegetables, bundled herbs, maple syrup, honey and baked goods – on stretches of park and pavement including Columbus Ave at 97th St (Friday), Tompkins Square Park in the East Village (Sunday), the West Village's Abingdon Square at 12th St and Hudson (Saturday) and Grand Army Plaza in Brooklyn (Saturday). (See the website for a full list of locations.) They attract everyone from mothers wanting to feed their families the freshest veggies they can find to celebrity chefs who come to discover just-picked rarities like fiddlehead ferns, fresh curry leaves and purple broccoli. Even if you've no reason to shop, strolling through one of the greenmarkets is a great way to enjoy a true New York experience, as well as a feast for the eyes – and possibly the stomach, if you're lucky enough to happen upon some free samples of cheese or baked goods.

and passionate crowd, and have ranged from 'Sacred Earth: Places of Peace and Power,' with color photographs by Martin Gray, to 'Delicate, Dreaming Tibet: Playful Illustrations of Tibetan Children's Tales,' featuring works by Rima Fujita.

THEODORE ROOSEVELT'S BIRTHPLACE Map p120

☎ 212-260-1616; www.nps.gov/thrb; 28 E 20th St btwn Park Ave S & Broadway; adult/child $3/free; ⏱ 9am-5pm Tue-Sat; ⊕ N, R, W, 6 to 23rd St

This National Historic Site is a bit of a cheat, since the physical house where the 26th president was actually born was demolished in his lifetime. But this building is a worthy reconstruction by his relatives, who joined it with another family residence next door. If you're interested in Roosevelt's extraordinary life, which has been somewhat overshadowed by the enduring legacy of his younger cousin Franklin D, visit here, especially if you don't have the time to see his summer home in Long Island's Oyster Bay. Included in the admission price are house tours, offered on the hour from 10am to 4pm.

NATIONAL ARTS CLUB Map p120

☎ 212-475-3424; www.nationalartsclub.org; 15 Gramercy Park South; ⊕ 6 to 23rd St

This club, founded in 1898 to promote public interest in the arts, boasts a beautiful, vaulted, stained-glass ceiling above the wooden bar in its picture-lined front parlor. Calvert Vaux, who was one of the creators of Central Park, designed the building, originally the private residence of Samuel J Tilden, governor of New York and failed presidential candidate in 1876. The club holds art exhibitions, ranging from sculpture to photography, that are sometimes open to the public from 1pm to 5pm (check the website for schedules). Other events include sketch classes, jazz lunches and French lessons.

FLATIRON & UNION SQUARE
Walking Tour

1 Madison Square Park Start off in the peaceful green space of Madison Square Park (p121), dotted with historic statues, contemporary sculptures and featuring a sparkly new coin-operated toilet. Take a pee – and, if you'd like

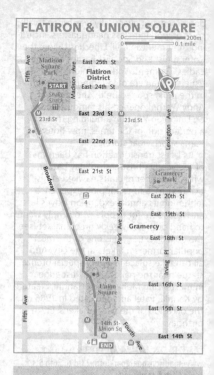

WALK FACTS

Start Madison Square Park (⊕ N, R, 6 to 23rd St)
End Filene's Basement (⊕ L, N, Q, R, W, 4, 5, 6 at 14th St-Union Sq)
Distance Two miles
Duration Two hours
Fuel stops Shake Shack, Union Square Greenmarket

to eat before the walk, hit up Shake Shack (p121) for a gourmet burger and fries.

2 Flatiron Building Before exiting the park, stand at its southwest corner and take in the lovely Flatiron Building (p119), Chicago architect Daniel Burnham's clever response to the awkward space where Fifth Ave and Broadway meet. Its Beaux-Arts style and triangular plan are mesmerizing from across the street; cross the street to stand up close to it and admire the city's oddest skyscraper from a whole new angle.

3 Gramercy Park Follow Broadway south to 21st St and take a left. Past Park Ave S you'll find yourself alongside Gramercy Park, created by Samuel Ruggles in 1831 after he drained the swamp in this area and laid out streets in an English style. You can't enter the park, as it's private, but go ahead and peer through the gate.

4 Theodore Roosevelt's Birthplace Double back west along 20th St, stopping at the reconstructed version of Theodore Roosevelt's Birthplace (opposite), which is run by the National Parks Service and offers hourly tours.

5 Union Square Head back to Broadway and continue south and you'll soon find yourself at the northwest corner of Union Square (p120). Check out the produce, cheese, baked goods and flowers of the Greenmarket farmers market (see the boxed text, p121) – or, if it happens to be a day when it's not on, amuse yourself by watching the skateboarders, visiting the Gandhi statue near the southwest corner or grabbing some food at one of the surrounding eateries for a picnic in the park.

6 Filene's Basement Standing like a beacon of retail on Union Sq South (14th St) is Filene's Basement (p234), a store offering deeply discounted designer clothing and accessories. Shop if you wish, but the real attraction is the store's massive, north-facing window, which lets you look down over the park and across to the top of the Empire State Building from a 4th-floor perch.

MIDTOWN EAST & FIFTH AVENUE

Drinking p293; Eating p260; Shopping p235; Sleeping p357

From the sophisticated shops of storied Fifth Ave to a handful of iconic sights, this quieter side of Manhattan's full belly is the slightly muted version (compared to Times Square, for example) of your New York City daydreams. It's where you'll find the Chrysler Building, the UN Building, St Patrick's Cathedral and the Beaux-Arts–style Grand Central train station – plus iconic stores like Tiffany & Co, Saks Fifth Avenue and Japanese palace of luxury goods Takashimaya, not to mention the garish Trump Tower, with an indoor waterfall and more cachet than ever thanks to the Donald upping his profile on reality TV. If you're a first- or second-time visitor, prepare to spend a bit of time in this teeming area – because even if you prefer to head off the beaten path and avoid touristy spots at all costs, you haven't gotten the full NYC experience until you've strolled through Grand Central Terminal's impressive concourse, or walked among the rush-hour crowds in the skyscraper canyons here. It can be overwhelming, and extremely crowded on weekdays, but it's also exciting, with an energy that's classic New York.

And hey, there are still off-the-beaten-track places here that are ripe for DIY adventures. Check out the ethnic enclave of Little Korea (32nd St btwn Broadway & Fifth Ave), home to karaoke bars and authentic *bulgolgi* (Korean barbecue) eateries, or the ritzy Midtown East residential corner of Sutton Place, with homes running alongside the East River in the 50s blocks. It's a bit staid over there, but the views of the Queensboro Bridge at 59th St, made famous by the poster for Woody Allen's *Manhattan*, are amazing. There's also another Little India (Lexington Ave btwn 27th & 30th Sts) in addition to the others in the East Village and Jackson Heights, Queens – a collection of wonderful Indian shops and restaurants, most featuring South Indian fare. In the east 30s is yet another small residential area called Murray Hill, home to affordable inns, more townhouses and unique little pockets such as Sniffen Court (Map p126; 150-158 E 36th St btwn Third & Lexington Aves), a preserved row of 1860 carriage houses that was used as the backdrop for the cover of the Doors' 1967 *Strange Days* LP.

There are myriad ways to get to this part of town, which is served by the 4, 5, 6 subway line running north and south, plus the 7, S, E and V lines offering some cross-town service. Buses also run cross-town, along both 34th and 42nd Sts.

MIDTOWN EAST

Slightly less buzzing than Fifth Ave or the more western reaches of Midtown is this still-worthy area, home to famous spots including Grand Central Terminal and the Chrysler Building, as well as buttoned-up hotels and cognac-and-cigar–type lounges. It can be a mellow, interesting place to stroll – except at rush hour, when the region is best avoided (unless you like getting jostled).

CHRYSLER BUILDING Map p126

Lexington Ave at 42nd St; ⊙ S, 4, 5, 6, 7 to Grand Central-42nd St

An art-deco masterpiece designed by William Van Alen in 1930, this 1048ft-high skyscraper, just across the avenue from Grand Central Terminal, has been widely named since its opening as a favorite work of architecture by laypeople and aficionados alike. The building, constructed to be the headquarters for Walter P Chrysler and his automobile empire, reigned briefly as the tallest structure in the world until superseded by the Empire State Building a few months later. Fittingly, the facade's design celebrates car culture, with gargoyles that resemble hood ornaments, radiator caps and thatched-steel designs, all best viewed with binoculars. The 200ft steel spire (known as the 'vertex'), constructed in secret, was raised through the false roof as a surprise crowning touch – which shocked and dismayed a competing architect who had hoped that his new Wall St building would turn out to be New York's tallest skyscraper at the time (now it wasn't). Nestled at the top was the famed Cloud Club, a former speakeasy. For a long time, developers have been planning to convert part of the building into a hotel, but so far that remains only a pipe dream.

The Chrysler Building has no restaurant or observation deck, but is filled with unexciting offices for lawyers and accountants. Still, it's worth wandering into the lobby to admire the elaborately veneered elevators (made from slices of Japanese ash, Oriental walnut and Cuban plum-pudding wood) and the profusion of marble, plus the ceiling mural (purportedly the world's largest at 97ft by 100ft) depicting the promise of industry. But even at a distance, there are few more poignant symbols of New York than the Chrysler Building lit up at night.

UNITED NATIONS Map p126
☎ 212-963-8687; www.un.org/tours; First Ave btwn 42nd & 48th Sts; adult/child/student/senior $13.50/6.50/7.50/9; ⏲ 9:30am-4:45pm Mon-Fri, 10am-4:30pm Sat & Sun; ⊕ S, 4, 5, 6, 7 to Grand Central-42nd St

Welcome to the headquarters of the UN, a worldwide organization that oversees international law, international security and human rights – and technically located on a patch of international territory, overlooking the East River. Take a guided tour of the facility and you'll get to see the General Assembly, where the annual convocation of member nations takes place every fall; the Security Council Chamber, where crisis management continues year-round; and the Economic & Social Council Chamber. If you're lucky you might even catch a meeting in progress. There is a serene park to the north of the complex, which is home to Henry Moore's *Reclining Figure* as well as several other sculptures with a peace theme.

English-language tours of the UN complex depart every 30 minutes; limited tours in several other languages are also available. (The visitors' entrance is at 46th St.) You may sometimes hear this area of Midtown East referred to as Turtle Bay, even though the turtles are long gone; there are also some interesting architectural examples around here, in particular among the permanent diplomatic missions, such as

those of Egypt (304 E 44th St btwn First & Second Aves) and India (245 E 43rd St btwn Second & Third Aves).

JAPAN SOCIETY Map p126
☎ 212-832-1155; www.japansociety.org; 333 E 47th St btwn First & Second Aves; admission free; ⏲ 11am-6pm Tue-Thu, to 9pm Fri, to 5pm Sat & Sun; ⊕ S, 4, 5, 6, 7 to Grand Central-42nd St

Founded in 1907 by a group of NYC businesspeople with a deep admiration for Japan, this nonprofit society has played a large role in strengthening American–Japanese relations. It expanded into a full arts and cultural center with a little help from philanthropist John D Rockefeller III, who had a strong interest in Japan. Today its main draw can be found in its galleries, which highlight Japanese art through shows like its recently hailed 'The Genius of Japanese Lacquer: Masterworks by Shibata Zeshin,' and in its theater, which hosts a range of films and dance, music and theatrical performances. Those who want to dig deeper can browse through the 14,000 volumes of the research library or attend one of its myriad lectures.

MUSEUM OF SEX Map p126
☎ 212-689-6337; www.museumofsex.org; 233 Fifth Ave at 27th St; adult/senior & student $14.50/13.50; ⏲ 11am-6:30pm Sun-Fri, to 8pm Sat; ⊕ N, R, W to 23rd St

An intriguing house of culture, this place traces the interwoven history of NYC and sex, from tittie bars and porn to street hustling and burlesque shows, and features exhibits that explore all sorts of other related subjects – from a look at people's homemade copulation machines, patent applications for various sex-related inventions, artifacts like vintage blow-up dolls and peep-show coins and lascivious documentary photography collections. Don't expect any sex parties or naked go-go dancers – though various folks do take the stage from time to time for presentations including erotica readings, one-person shows and sex-ed seminars.

PIERPONT MORGAN LIBRARY Map p126
☎ 212-685-0610; www.morganlibrary.org; 29 E 36th St at Madison Ave; adult/child & senior $12/8; ⏲ 10:30am-5pm Tue-Thu, to 9pm Fri, 10am-6pm Sat & Sun; ⊕ 6 to 33rd St

This library, recently reopened after beautiful and extensive renovations, is part of

SENSE & DIRECTION

Getting around in NYC actually can actually be a very logical affair once you know a few simple rules. First, it's important to know that Manhattan is divided into east and west sides – hence street addresses marked either 'E 27th St' or 'W 27th St.' The dividing line between east and west – above Washington Square Park in the Village, anyway – is Fifth Ave, with building numbers spreading away in either direction by 100 per block (for example, the stretch between Sixth and Seventh Aves is the 200 block, containing addresses like 227 and 280).

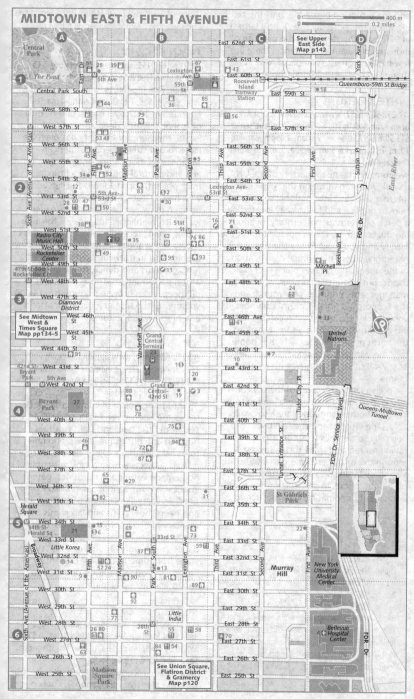

MIDTOWN EAST & FIFTH AVENUE

See Upper East Side Map p142

See Midtown West & Times Square Map pp134–5

See Union Square, Flatiron District & Gramercy Map p120

0 — 400 m
0 — 0.2 miles

Central Park

The Pond

Central Park South

West 58th St
West 57th St
West 56th St
West 55th St
West 54th St
West 53rd St
West 52nd St
West 51st St
West 50th St
West 49th St
West 48th St
West 47th St
West 46th St
West 45th St
West 44th St
West 43rd St
West 42nd St
West 40th St
West 39th St
West 38th St
West 37th St
West 36th St
West 35th St
West 34th St
West 33rd St
West 32nd St
West 31st St
West 30th St
West 29th St
West 28th St
West 27th St
West 26th St
West 25th St

5th Ave

Sixth Ave (Avenue of the Americas)
Fifth Ave
Madison Ave
Park Ave
Vanderbilt Ave

Radio City Music Hall
Rockefeller Center
47th-50th St Rockefeller Ctr
Diamond District

42nd St Bryant Park
5th Ave
Bryant Park

Herald Square
34th St Herald Sq
Little Korea
Broadway

Madison Square Park

East 62nd St
East 61st St
East 60th St
East 59th St
East 58th St
East 57th St
East 56th St
East 55th St
East 54th St
Lexington Ave-53rd St
East 52nd St
East 51st St
East 50th St
East 49th St
East 48th St
East 47th Ave
East 46th Ave
East 45th St
East 44th St
East 43rd St
East 42nd St
East 41st St
East 40th St
East 39th St
East 38th St
East 37th St
East 36th St
East 35th St
East 34th St
East 33rd St
East 32nd St
East 31st St
East 30th St
East 29th St
East 28th St
East 27th St
East 26th St
East 25th St

5th Ave-53rd St
5th Ave-53rd St

Lexington Ave
59th St

Roosevelt Island Tramway Station

Grand Central Terminal
Grand Central-42nd St

Little India

Little Square

Third Ave
Second Ave
First Ave
Sutton Pl
Beekman Pl
FDR Dr
Tudor City Pl
Tunnel Entrance St
FDR Dr Service Rd West
York Ave

East River

Queensboro-59th St Bridge

Mitchell Pl

United Nations

Queens-Midtown Tunnel

St Gabriel's Park

Murray Hill

New York University Medical Center

Bellevue Hospital Center

FDR Dr

the 45-room mansion once owned by steel magnate JP Morgan. His collection features a phenomenal array of manuscripts, tapestries and books (with no fewer than three Gutenberg Bibles), a study filled with Italian Renaissance artwork, a marble rotunda and the three-tiered East Room main library. The rotating art exhibits here – like the recent portraits of poets and writers by portrait photographer Irving Penn, or masterpieces of Renaissance drawing from the Uffizi – are really top-notch.

LITTLE KOREA Map p126
btwn 31st & 36th Sts & Broadway & Fifth Ave; ◎ B, D, F, N, Q, R, V, W to 34th St-Herald Sq
Herald Sq is a bit on the tasteless side when it comes to finding foodie treats; luckily, you can head for quality refueling at

nearby Little Korea, a small enclave of Korean-owned restaurants, shops, salons and spas that is mainly concentrated on 32nd St, with some spillover into the surrounding streets both south and north of this strip. Over the past few years this neighborhood has seen an explosion of eateries serving Korean fare, with authentic BBQ available around the clock at many of the all-night spots on 32nd St, some with the added treat of karaoke.

BRIDGEMARKET Map p126
☎ 212-980-2455; 409 E 59th St at First Ave; ◎ N, R, W, 4, 5, 6 to 59th St-Lexington Ave
After decades under restoration, Bridgemarket – a vaulted, Guastavino-tiled space under the 59th St Bridge that served as a farmers market in the early 20th century –

GRAND CENTRAL TERMINAL

Completed in 1913, Grand Central Terminal (www.grandcentralterminal.com; 42nd St at Park Ave; ⊕ S, 4, 5, 6, 7 to Grand Central-42nd St) – more commonly, if technically incorrectly, called Grand Central Station – is another of New York's stunning Beaux-Arts buildings, boasting 75ft-high, glass-encased catwalks and a vaulted ceiling bearing a mural of the constellations streaming across it – backwards (the designer must've been dyslexic). The balconies overlooking the main concourse afford an expansive view; perch yourself on one of these at around 5pm on a weekday to get a glimpse of the grace that this terminal commands under pressure. It's quite amazing how this dramatic space evokes the romance of train travel at the turn of the 20th century while also enduring the bustle of present-day New York.

There are no teary good-byes for people traveling across the country from here today, though, as Grand Central's underground electric tracks serve only commuter trains en route to northern suburbs and Connecticut. But whether you're traveling somewhere or not, the station merits a special trip for the architecture alone – not to mention the fine-dining restaurants and gourmet food court, cool bars, funky shops (including a gift shop of the Brooklyn-based Transit Museum, p173), holiday craft fairs and occasional music performances.

The Municipal Art Society (p404) leads weekly walks (⏰ 12:30pm Wed; $15) through Grand Central, during which you'll get to cross the glass catwalk high above the concourse (which is usually off-limits). Tours meet at the passenger information booth in the middle of the main concourse.

---

was brought back to life in 1999 by design guru Sir Terence Conran. Now it's a thriving retail and dining complex, anchored by the Terence Conran Shop, alive with ingenious modern design accessories, and Food Emporium, a regional, upscale supermarket chain. Guastavino's, a former restaurant (now reserved for private functions) in a magnificent space, is also worth peeking into.

FIFTH AVENUE

Whatever first pops into your head when you think of 'Fifth Avenue' – wealth, shopping, sophistication, mansions, you name it – you'll find it here. This major stretch first developed its high-class reputation in the early 20th century, when it was considered desirable for its 'country' air and open spaces. Now it's the battleground for society folks who want to retain their class status without allowing too many others in – but also a place where regular folks flock, struck starry-eyed by the offerings of shops, hotels and just general grandeur.

Most of the heirs to the millionaire mansions on Fifth Ave above 59th St sold them for demolition or converted them to the cultural institutions that now make up what's called 'Museum Mile' (p141). The Villard Houses, on Madison Ave behind St Patrick's Cathedral at 50th St, are a stunning exception. Financier Henry Villard built the six adjacent four-story town houses in 1881, and they flaunt artistic details by the likes of Louis Comfort Tiffany, John LaFarge and Augustus St-Gaudens; the mansion and neighboring townhouses were later owned by the Catholic church and then sold to a series of hotel magnates.

Today, the avenue's Midtown stretch offers the famous Trump Tower, where the Big D himself was renowned for firing folks each week on *The Apprentice*, and the endearing anchor of the Plaza Hotel, which recently underwent a $400 million renovation that converted most of its rooms to high-end condos but restored remaining guest rooms to their old splendor. While a number of the more exclusive boutiques have migrated to Madison Ave, several superstars still reign over Fifth Ave above 50th St, including Cartier, Henri Bendel (p236) and the movie-famous Tiffany & Co (p236). Sites included in this section are either on Fifth Ave or within the blocks to either side of it.

EMPIRE STATE BUILDING Map p126

☎ 212-736-3100; www.esbnyc.com; 350 Fifth Ave at 34th St; adult/child/senior & student $17/12/16; ⏰ 8:30am-2am; ⊕ B, D, F, N, Q, R, V, W to 34th St-Herald Sq

Featured prominently in almost a hundred Hollywood films over the years, the Empire State Building – actually a very glorified office building – is the most famous member of the New York skyline. It's a limestone classic built in just 410 days (using seven million hours of labor) during the Great Depression, at the astounding cost of $41 million. Located on the site of the original Waldorf-Astoria Hotel, the 102-story, 1472ft-high (to the top of the antenna) Empire State Building opened in 1931 after the laying of 10 million bricks, installation of 6400 windows and setting of 328,000 sq ft of marble. The famous antenna was originally meant to be a mooring mast for zeppelins, but the *Hindenberg* disaster slammed the brakes on that plan. Later an aircraft did (accidentally) meet up with the building: a B-25 bomber crashed into the 79th floor on a foggy day in 1945, killing 14 people.

The view of the vast city from the Empire State Building is just exquisite, but be prepared – the lines to get to the observation decks, found on the 86th and 102nd floors, are notorious. And the basement area where you must buy tickets and queue up for the elevator ride is a shabby, poorly ventilated waiting pen, especially in the summer. Getting here very early or very late will help you avoid delays – as will buying your tickets ahead of time, online (see the boxed text, below). Sunset is one of the most magical times to be up here because you can see the city don its nighttime cloak in dusk's afterglow. Once up here, you can stay as long as you like. Coin-operated telescopes offer an up-close glimpse of the city, and diagrams map out the major sights. You can even smoke up top, to the great dismay of many non-Europeans.

Since 1976, the building's top 30 floors have been floodlit in seasonal and holiday colors: green for St Patrick's Day in March, black for World AIDS Day on December 1, red and green for Christmas, lavender for Gay Pride weekend in June, etc – visit the website for each day's lighting scheme and meaning. This tradition has now been copied by many other skyscrapers, notably the Metropolitan Life Tower at Madison Sq Park and the Con Edison Tower near Union Sq, lending elegance to the night sky.

NEW YORK PUBLIC LIBRARY Map p126
☎ 212-930-0830; www.nypl.org; Fifth Ave at 42nd St; ⏱ 11am-6pm Mon, to 7:30pm Tue & Wed, 10am-6pm Thu-Sat, 1-5pm Sun; Ⓜ B, D, F, V to 42nd St-Bryant Park, 7 to Fifth Ave

This main branch of NYC's public library system is called the Humanities & Social Sciences Library, one of several specialist research libraries in the NYPL system. It's also one of the best free attractions in the city – a monument to learning, housed in a grand, Beaux-Arts building that reflects its big-money industrialist roots. When it was dedicated in 1911, New York's flagship library ranked as the largest marble structure ever built in the US, with a vast, 3rd-floor reading room designed to hold 500 patrons – not to mention the famous marble lions ('Patience' and 'Fortitude') at the entrance, profligate use of gold leaf throughout, chandeliers, carved porticoes and ceiling murals.

On a rainy day, hide away with a book in the airy Reading Room and admire the original Carre-and-Hastings lamps, or stroll through the Exhibition Hall, which contains precious manuscripts by just about every author of note in the English language, including an original copy of the Declaration of Independence and a Gutenberg Bible. Also worth getting lost in is the incredible Map Division, with a collection that holds some 431,000 maps and 16,000 atlases and books on cartography, dating from the 16th century to the present. The free guided tour (⏱ 11am & 2pm, Tue-Sat) is a bonanza of interesting tidbits; it leaves from the information desk in Astor Hall.

PALEY CENTER FOR MEDIA Map p126
☎ 212-621-6800; www.paleycenter.org; 25 W 52nd St btwn Fifth & Sixth Aves; adult/child/senior & student $10/5/8; ⏱ noon-6pm Tue, Wed & Fri-Sun, to 8pm Thu; Ⓜ E, V to Fifth Ave-53rd St

Formerly called the Museum of Television and Radio, the institution changed its name both to honor its founder, William S Paley, and to reflect both its changing mission and collection in this day of shifting media forms. But it's still a couch potato's smorgasbord, with more than 50,000 American TV and radio programs available from the museum's computer catalog with the click of a mouse. It's a great place to hang out when it's raining or when you're simply fed up with the real world. Nearly everybody checks out their favorite childhood TV programs and watches them on one of the museum's 90 consoles, but the radio-listening room is an unexpected pleasure – as are the excellent screenings, festivals and speakers presented on a regular basis.

ST PATRICK'S CATHEDRAL Map p126

☎ 212-753-2261; www.saintpatrickscathedral.org; Fifth Ave btwn 50th and 51st Sts; ☉ 6am-9pm; ⊚ B, D, F, V to 47th-50th Sts-Rockefeller Center
The largest Gothic-style Catholic cathedral in the country, this is the seat of the Archbishop of New York, Edward Cardinal Egan, and the place that's been largely recognized as the center of Catholic life in the United States – drawing a steady stream of both revelers and protesters alike. Built at a cost of nearly $2 million during the Civil War, the church did not originally include the two front spires; those were added in 1888. Although it seats a modest 2400 worshippers, most of New York's 2.2 million faithful will have been inside at one time or another. Though it may seem like each and every one is there when you show up, muddle through to see some of the exquisite details inside.

After you enter, walk by the eight small shrines along the side of the cathedral, past the shrine to Nuestra Señora de Guadalupe and the main altar, to the quiet Lady Chapel, dedicated to the Virgin Mary. From here, you can see the stunning stained-glass Rose Window above the 7000-pipe church organ. A basement crypt behind the altar contains the coffins of every New York cardinal and the remains of Pierre Touissant, a champion of the poor and the first black American up for sainthood (he emigrated from Haiti).

Know that St Patrick's is not a place for truly restful, spiritual contemplation because of the constant buzz from loud, videotaping and generally disrespectful visitors. Also, while frequent masses take place on the weekend, with New York's archbishop presiding over the Sunday service at 10:15am, casual visitors are allowed in only between services – so dress up and plan on staying for the long haul if you're interested.

MIDTOWN EAST & FIFTH AVENUE
Walking Tour

1 Empire State Building Start your tour with a little perspective from the top of the Empire State Building (p128), which provides a beautiful, bird's-eye view of the neighborhood you're about to explore – plus a few eyefuls more.

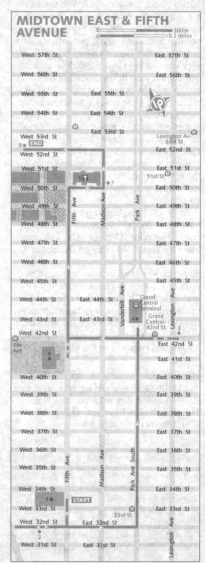

2 Little Korea Exit on Fifth Ave and head south, where you can explore the fascinating enclave of Little Korea (p127) around 32nd St. Check out the shops, try some karaoke or, if you're hungry, tuck into some Korean barbecue.

3 Chrysler Building From 32nd St, head north on Park Ave South and take a good gander as you walk, catching sight of the gorgeous Chrysler Building (p124), William Van Alen's 1930 masterpiece. Take a right at 42nd St to see it up close.

4 Grand Central Terminal At 42nd and Park is the stunning Grand Central Terminal (p128), where you'll want to check out the grand concourse and other Beaux-Arts details, as well as do some serious crowd-watching. If you're hungry, head to the impressive collection of eateries in the basement – it's not your usual food court.

5 New York Public Library Exit the terminal on 42nd St and head west, taking a left onto Fifth Ave. Here you'll find the stately New York Public Library (p129), guarded by a pair of regal lions named Patience and Fortitude.

6 St Patrick's Cathedral Eight blocks up Fifth Ave is St Patrick's Cathedral (opposite), a Gothic stunner that looks as if it's been there a million years while this modern city has popped up around it. Head in for a look at the heavenly ceilings.

7 Villard Houses Head around behind the Cathedral, onto Madison Ave, and take a gander at the lovely Villard Houses (p128), a collection of six townhouses built by financier Henry Villard in 1881.

8 Paley Center for Media Continuing north from here, turn left on 52nd St and walk until you pass Fifth Ave. You'll soon come to the Paley Center for Media (p129), where you might catch a stellar screening or choose to hunker down with some old-school TV shows.

MIDTOWN WEST & TIMES SQUARE

Drinking p294; Eating p262; Shopping p237; Sleeping p360

This is, in some ways, the heart of Manhattan – the New York most outsiders thrill over in films or daydream about before they ever set foot in the city. It's classic NYC, home to Broadway and larger-than-life billboards, seas of taxis and crushing crowds, skyscraping icons and an inimitable, frenzied energy. Midtown West is a general term that refers to any part of midtown (between 34th and 59th Sts) that's west of Fifth Ave, the east–west dividing line. Its collection of neighborhoods includes the far-west reaches of Hell's Kitchen, the office-worker crush of food carts and harried suit-wearers along Sixth Ave, the bustle of Times Square, and Columbus Circle, with its gleaming Time Warner Center, located at the southwest corner of Central Park.

Spiffed up Times Square, whose name once evoked images of drug peddlers, porn theaters and various other dregs of society, is now an utterly safe and clean tourist area, bursting at the seams with massive chain stores, famed Broadway theaters and the gaudy billboards and marquees that this area has long been synonymous with. This area sits at the intersection of Broadway and Seventh Ave, smack in the middle of Midtown. With over 60 mega-billboards and 40 miles of neon, it's startling how it always looks like daytime here. Once called Longacre Sq, Times Sq took its present name from the famous *New York Times* newspaper, whose headquarters are still located nearby, albeit now in a sparkly new tower just across Eighth Ave from the Port Authority bus terminal. Today, Times Sq draws more than 27 million annual visitors, who spend more than $12 billion in Midtown. For maps and event details, pop into the Times Square Information Center (Map pp134-5; ☎ 212-869-5667; www .timessquarenyc.org; 1560 Broadway btwn 46th & 47th Sts; ⏱ 8am-8pm; ⊕ N, Q, R, W, S, 1, 2, 3, 7 to Times Sq-42nd St), located in the beautifully restored landmark Embassy Theater.

Times Sq is also home to New York's Theater District (see p310), with dozens of Broadway and off-Broadway theaters located in an area that stretches from 41st to 54th Sts between Sixth and Ninth Aves. Unless there's a specific show you're after, the best – and most affordable – way to score tickets is at the TKTS Booth (Map pp134-5; ☎ 212-768-1818; www.tdf.org/tkts; ⏱ 3-8pm Mon-Sat, 11am-8pm Sun), where you can line up and get same-day half-price tickets for top Broadway and off-Broadway shows. It's temporarily housed at the Marriot Marquis Hotel (W 46th St btwn Broadway & Eighth Ave) until the Duffy Square location (Broadway at 47th St), under renovation until 2009, has been completed. Up to a million people gather in Times Sq every New Year's Eve to watch an illuminated Waterford Crystal ball descend from the roof of One Times Sq at midnight. While this event garners international coverage, it lasts just 90 seconds (after hours of standing in the cold) and, frankly, is something of an anticlimax.

Though at first this whole area may seem overwhelming, there are tucked-away riches within. Try wandering around Hell's Kitchen, found west of Eighth Ave between 34th and 57th Sts. For years this working-class district of tenements and food warehouses inspired films romanticizing the district's gritty, criminal character (*West Side Story* was set here); by the 1960s, though, the population of junkies and prostitutes had made it a forbidding place that few cared to enter. But the economic boom of the late '90s profoundly changed Hell's Kitchen, and developers reverted to using the cleaned-up name 'Clinton,' a moniker originating from the 1950s; locals prefer the original term. An explosion of nightspots and restaurants and an influx of cool, young (and largely gay) residents have since moved in, attracted by what were (but are no longer) cheap rents.

Or try the specialty districts that make NYC unique: the frenzied Diamond District (www.47th-street .com; 47th St btwn Fifth & Sixth Aves), packed with newly engaged couples shopping for rings and folks in the biz buying wholesale. It's home to more than 2600 independent businesses selling all manner of diamonds, gold, pearls, gemstones and watches, and offering engraving and repair services. Then there's the famed Garment District (around Seventh Ave btwn 34th St & Times Sq), sometimes called the Fashion District – an unremarkable-looking stretch of designers' offices and wholesale and retail shops both on and off the avenue, where you'll find a huge selection of fabrics, buttons, sequins, lace and more. Look at the sidewalk when you hit Seventh at 39th St and you'll see the cool Fashion Walk of Fame, honoring Betsey Johnson, Marc Jacobs, Geoffrey Beene, Bill Blass, Halston, Calvin Klein and other fashion visionaries. It's on the same corner as Claes Oldenburg's sculpture of the world's largest button, held upright by a 31ft-tall steel needle; it hovers over the Fashion Center information kiosk (Map pp134-5; www.fashioncenter.com; 249 W 39th St), which doles out maps and other details.

ROCKEFELLER CENTER Map pp134–5

☎ 212-632-3975; www.rockefellercenter.com; from Fifth to Seventh Aves & 48th to 51st Sts; ⊖ B, D, F, V to 47th-50th Sts-Rockefeller Center

Built during the height of the Great Depression in the 1930s, the 22-acre Rockefeller Center, named after developer John D Rockefeller Jr, was the first project to combine retail, entertainment and office space in what is often referred to as a 'city within a city.' Built over nine years by 70,000 workers, this complex features several outdoor plazas and 19 buildings (14 of which are the original art-deco structures), and spans from 48th to 50th Sts and Fifth to Seventh Aves. In 1987 it was declared a National Landmark, recognized for its unique combination of modernist architecture with a concentration of commercial and business enterprises. Most popular highlights include Radio City Music Hall (p138), the GE Building (30 Rockefeller Plaza at 49th St), the ice-skating plaza and the Top of the Rock (right) observation deck.

Perhaps most impressively, though, is the slew of public artwork – commissioned around the theme 'Man at the Crossroads Looks Uncertainly But Hopefully at the Future' – created by 30 great artists of the day. Mexican muralist Diego Rivera was looking skeptically at the future, though, and after he was persuaded to paint the lobby of the 70-story RCA Building (now the GE Building), became outraged, along with the rest of the art world, when the Rockefeller family rejected his painting for containing 'Communist imagery' – namely, the face of Lenin. The fresco was destroyed and replaced with a José Maria Sert work depicting the more 'acceptable' faces of Abraham Lincoln and Ralph Waldo Emerson.

Original creations still in existence, though, include Prometheus overlooking the ice-skating rink, Atlas doing his thing in front of the International Building (630 Fifth Ave), and News by Isamu Noguchi above the entrance to the Associated Press Building (50 Rockefeller Plaza). Anyone interested in artworks within the complex should pick up the Rockefeller Center Visitors Guide in the GE Building lobby, which describes many of them in detail.

Perhaps the best-known feature of Rockefeller Center, though, is its gigantic Christmas tree, which overlooks the skating rink during the holidays. It's a tradition that dates back to the 1930s, when construction workers set up a small Christmas tree on the site. Today the annual lighting of the tree, held after Thanksgiving, attracts thousands of visitors to the area to cram around the felled spruce, selected each year with fanfare from an unlucky upstate forest. The scene is too crowded to be believed, but skating at the Rink at Rockefeller Center (☎ 212-332-7654; www.therinkatrockcenter.com; off Fifth Ave btwn 49th & 50th Sts; adult/child $10/7.50 Mon-Fri, $14/8.50 Sat & Sun, skate rental $8; ☽ Oct-Apr) under the gaze of Prometheus is quite an experience (thought it's crowded, too). Opening hours change weekly, so call for the schedule.

NBC STUDIOS Map pp134–5

☎ 212-664-3700; www.nbc.com; 30 Rockefeller Plaza at 49th St; tours adult/senior & child 6-16 yrs $18.50/15.50 (under 6 not admitted); ☽ tours 8:30am-5:30pm Mon-Sat, 9:30am-4:30pm Sun (extended hrs Nov & Dec); ⊖ B, D, F, V to 47th-50th Sts-Rockefeller Center, E, V to Fifth Ave-53rd St

The NBC TV network has its headquarters in the 70-story GE Building that looms over the Rockefeller Center ice-skating rink (which is transformed into a café in the summer months). The Today show broadcasts live, 7am to 10am daily, from a glass-enclosed, street-level studio near the fountain, drawing plenty of admirers below who thrill over waving to and hamming it up for the camera. You're free to join them – or instead opt for a tour of the NBC studios, which leaves the lobby of the GE Building every half hour; the walkabout lasts for about one hour and 10 minutes, but be advised that there is a strict policy of 'no bathrooms,' so be sure to empty your bladder beforehand! Call ☎ 212-664-6298 to make a reservation.

Competition is stiff for TV show tapings (eg Saturday Night Live, Late Night with Conan O'Brien etc). For details on how to obtain tickets, see the boxed text, p319.

TOP OF THE ROCK Map pp134–5

☎ 212-698-2000; www.topoftherocknyc.com; 30 Rockefeller Plaza at 49th St; adult/child/senior $17.50/11.25/16; ☽ 8:30am-midnight; ⊖ B, D, F, V to 47th-50th Sts-Rockefeller Center, E, V to Fifth Ave-53rd St

This open-air observation deck at the top of Rockefeller Center first wowed New Yorkers back in 1933. Designed in homage to ocean liners popular in the day, it was an incredible place – 70 stories above Midtown – from which to view the city. But it became off-limits for almost two

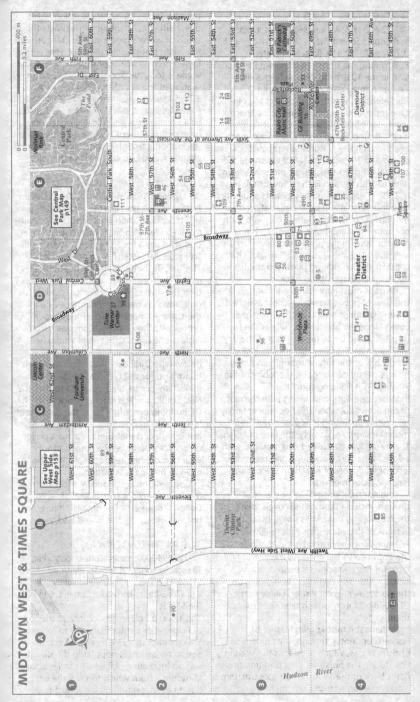

400 m
0.2 miles
0

See Upper
West Side
Map p153

See Central
Park Map p149

Lincoln
Center

Fordham
University

Time
Warner
Center

Central
Park

Wollman
Rink

The
Pond

Worldwide
Plaza

DeWitt
Clinton
Park

Theater
District

Times
Square

Diamond
District

Rockefeller
Plaza

Rockefeller
Center

Radio City
Music Hall

GE Building

St Patrick's
Cathedral

47th-50th Sts-
Rockefeller Center

Hudson River

Twelfth Ave (West Side Hwy)
Eleventh Ave
Tenth Ave
Ninth Ave
Eighth Ave
Broadway
Central Park West
Columbus Ave
Amsterdam Ave
Columbus Circle
West Dr
East Dr
Fifth Ave
5th Ave
Madison Ave
Sixth Ave (Avenue of the Americas)
Seventh Ave
57th St-7th Ave
50th St
49th St
Times Square

West 61st St
West 60th St
West 59th St
West 58th St
West 57th St
West 56th St
West 55th St
West 54th St
West 53rd St
West 52nd St
West 51st St
West 50th St
West 49th St
West 48th St
West 47th St
West 46th St
West 45th St

East 60th St
East 59th St
East 58th St
East 57th St
East 55th St
East 54th St
East 53rd St
East 52nd St
East 51st St
East 50th St
East 49th St
East 48th St
East 47th St
East 46th St
East 45th St

5th Ave-59th St
57th St
5th Ave-53rd St

134

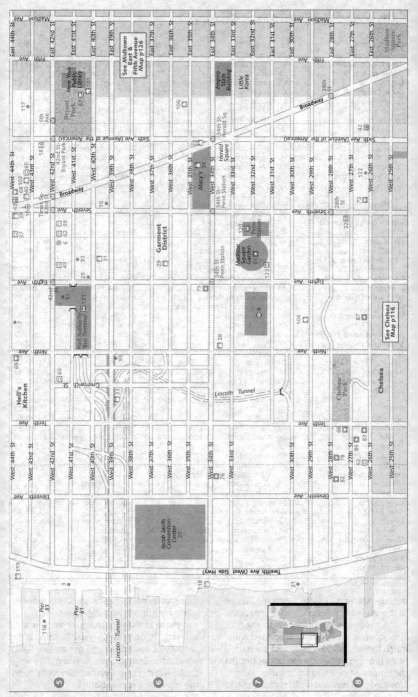

Madison Ave

East 44th St
East 42nd St
East 41st St
East 40th St
East 39th St
East 37th St
East 36th St
East 35th St
East 34th St
East 33rd St
East 32nd St
East 31st St
East 30th St
East 28th St
East 27th St
East 26th St

Madison Ave

Fifth Ave

Madison Square Park

See Midtown East & Fifth Avenue Map p126

New York Public Library
67 ⬛ 10 🏛

Bryant Park

117

5th Ave

Empire State Building
Little Korea

28th St

34th St-Herald Sq

Broadway

Sixth Ave (Avenue of the Americas)

Sixth Ave (Avenue of the Americas)

West 44th St
West 43rd St
West 42nd St
West 41st St
West 40th St
West 39th St
West 38th St
West 37th St
West 36th St
West 35th St
West 34th St
West 33rd St
West 32nd St
West 31st St
West 30th St
West 29th St
West 28th St
West 27th St
West 26th St
West 25th St

102
40 65
18

42nd St-Bryant Park

Broadway

106

Herald Square

Macy's

34th St-Penn Station

122
72

42nd St
39 57
6 62 59
49
92
25

Times Sq-42nd St

Seventh Ave

Garment District

115

31

29

Seventh Ave

28th St

22

120

Penn Station

Eighth Ave

91
121

Port Authority Bus Terminal

Madison Square Garden
91
123

34th St-Penn Station

Eighth Ave

7
69

Hell's Kitchen

60

Greenwich St

95

33

79

28

104

87

Ninth Ave

Lincoln Tunnel

Ninth Ave

Chelsea Park

Chelsea

See Chelsea Map p116

Tenth Ave

Tenth Ave

West 44th St
West 43rd St
West 42nd St
West 41st St
West 40th St
West 39th St
West 38th St
West 37th St
West 36th St
West 35th St
West 34th St
West 33rd St
West 30th St
West 29th St
West 28th St
West 27th St
West 26th St
West 25th St

Eleventh Ave

Eleventh Ave

66
52 86 83
82 78
76

Jacob Javits Convention Center
20

119

3

118

21

Twelfth Ave (West Side Hwy)

Pier 83
Pier 81
116

Lincoln Tunnel

⑤
⑥
⑦
⑧

135

decades starting in 1986, when renovation of the stunning Rainbow Room restaurant five floors below cut off access to the roof. The observation deck was reopened with much fanfare in 2005, and since then it's been proving to be an even better bet than the Empire State Building: it's much less crowded and has wider observation decks

that span several levels – some are indoors, some are outside with Plexiglass walls and those at the very top are completely alfresco. Though the Chrysler Building is partially obscured, you do get an excellent view of the Empire State Building. The very cool, multimedia-enhanced elevator ride to the top is an exciting bonus.

MUSEUM OF MODERN ART Map pp134–5

☎ 212-708-9400; www.moma.org; 11 W 53rd St btwn Fifth & Sixth Aves; adult/child/student/senior $20/free/12/16, Fri 4-8pm free; ⏱ 10:30am-5:30pm Sat-Mon, Wed & Thu, to 8pm Fri; ◉ E, V to Fifth Ave-53rd St

Founded in 1929, MoMA is one of NYC's most popular museums, home to more than 100,000 pieces of modern artwork, most by heavy hitters – Matisse, Picasso, Cezanne, Rothko, Pollock and many others. It's dedicated to showcasing artwork based on the emerging creative ideas of the late 19th century through to those that dominate today. It's easy to get lost in the vast collection for an entire day; if you want to maximize your time and create a plan of attack ahead of time, download the museum's floor plan and visitor guide (available in several languages) from the website beforehand.

Since its grand reopening in 2004 following the most extensive renovation project in its 75-year history, the Museum of Modern Art has been widely hailed for its physical design, with a central, five-story atrium housing peaceful, airy galleries with works in areas such as painting, sculpture, architecture and design, drawings, prints, illustrated books, and film and media. The reconstruction, by architect Yoshio Taniguchi, doubled the museum's capacity and restored the museum's peaceful sculpture garden to the original, larger vision of Philip Johnson's 1950s design. You can look over this area as you dine in high style at the Modern, a much-lauded foodie paradise of French-American cuisine courtesy of head chef Gabriel Kreuther (though you'll find more affordable cafés onsite, too).

The museum's cinema hosts a rich film program, with rotating screenings from its collection of more than 19,000 films, including the works of the Maysles Brothers and every Pixar animation film ever produced. Recent special exhibitions inside the high-ceilinged galleries have included 'Lucien Freud: The Painter's Etchings' and 'Take Your Time: Olafur Eliasson.'

BRYANT PARK Map pp134–5

☎ 212-768-4242; www.bryantpark.org; 42nd St btwn Fifth & Sixth Aves; ◉ B, D, F, V to 42nd St-Bryant Park, 7 to Fifth Ave

Nestled behind the grand New York Public Library building is this lovely square of green – once a patch of squalor, referred to as 'Needle Park' throughout the '80s – where local Midtown workers gather for lunchtime picnics on warm afternoons. Among its offerings are impressive skyscraper views, European-style coffee kiosks, a Brooklyn-constructed carousel offering rides for $2, and frequent special events. This is where the famed Fashion Week tent goes up every winter, and is also the site of the wonderful, outdoor Bryant Park Summer Film Festival (see the boxed text, p317), which packs the lawn with post-work crowds lugging cheese-and-wine picnics. Bryant Park Grill & Café (p295), a lovely restaurant and bar situated at the eastern end of the park, is the site of many a New York wedding come springtime. When it's not closed for a private event, the patio bar is a perfect spot for a twilight cocktail or two. And if you've got your laptop and it's a nice day, grab a seat and surf the web in the park, which is a free wi-fi hotspot.

top picks

FOR CHILDREN

- Statue of Liberty (p70) The boat ride, the big lady, the views – it's plenty of excitement for the little ones.
- Skyscraper Museum (p76) Building lovers will appreciate this small museum with displays on the world's tallest constructs.
- National Sports Museum (p79) Turn your little athlete loose in this new museum filled with interactive exhibits.
- South Street Seaport (p80) Old ships, outdoor performances and plenty of kid-friendly shops and eateries take care of many needs at once.
- New York City Fire Museum (p87) Nothing beats sliding down the pole and climbing on the trucks for kids of a certain excitable age.
- Children's Museum of the Arts (p90) This place makes your own little Picasso the star of the day.
- Lower East Side Tenement Museum (p97) Certain hands-on tours here are just for children.
- Socrates Sculpture Park (p202) This waterfront spread in Queens is filled with massive, climbable works of art.
- American Museum of Natural History (p152) It's the home of the big dinosaur skeletons, a slew of taxidermy, a cool planetarium and excellent IMAX films – among many other draws.
- Children's Museum of Manhattan (p155) Everything's pint-sized at this virtual kids' universe.

An impressive palace of design and handicrafts, from blown glass and carved wood to elaborate metal jewelry, the real buzz around the Museum of Arts & Design (Map pp134–5; ☎ 212-956-3535; www.madmuseum.org; 2 Columbus Circle btwn Eighth Ave & Broadway; adult/child under 13/senior $9/free/7; 🕙 10am-6pm Tue, Wed & Fri-Sun, to 8pm Thu; ⊕ A, C, B, D, 1 to 59th St-Columbus Circle), for now, is about its new location. Formerly housed around the corner on 53rd St, the museum moved into this Columbus Circle building after much controversy from folks who wanted the long-empty building landmarked to prevent it from being altered. It had originally opened as the Gallery of Modern Art in 1964, and had a unique, all-white design by Edward Durell Stone. But the Museum of Arts & Design won out, drastically changed the shape of the place and moved into the space in late 2008. But it still has the same displays of innovative and traditional items, and recent shows have included 'Pricked: Extreme Embroidery,' and 'Cheers! A MAD Collection of Goblets.'

INTERNATIONAL CENTER OF PHOTOGRAPHY Map pp134–5
☎ 212-857-0000; www.icp.org; 1133 Sixth Ave at 43rd St; adult/senior & student $12/8, by donation Fri 5-8pm; 🕙 10am-6pm Tue-Thu, Sat & Sun, to 8pm Fri; ⊕ B, D, F, V to 42nd St-Bryant Park
The two-level, soothing and airy ICP is the city's most important showcase for major photographers, especially photojournalists. Its past exhibitions have included work by Henri Cartier-Bresson, Man Ray, Matthew Brady, Weegee and Robert Capa, and have explored a wide range of themes through creative shows such as the recent 'Collections of Barbara Bloom,' a designer and photographer, and 'Archive Fever: Uses of the Document in Contemporary Art.' It's also a photography school, offering coursework (for credit) and a public lecture series. Its gift shop is an excellent place to stock up on quality photo books or quirky, photo-themed gifts.

AMERICAN FOLK ART MUSEUM
Map pp134–5
☎ 212-265-1040; www.folkartmuseum.org; 45 W 53rd St btwn Fifth & Sixth Aves; adult/child/senior & student $9/free/7; 🕙 10:30am-5:30pm Tue-Thu, Sat & Sun, to 7:30pm Fri; ⊕ E, V to Fifth Ave-53rd St
Housed in a beautiful, eight-story building designed by the noted Billie Tsien and Tod Williams, the focus here is on traditional arts tied to moments in history or personal milestones. The expansive collection features objects such as flags, liberty figures, textiles, weather vanes and decorative arts, and recent visiting exhibits have ranged from 'Gilded Lions and Jeweled Horses: The Synagogue to the Carousel,' which traced the journey of Jewish woodcarvers from Eastern Europe, and 'Darger-ism: Contemporary Artists and Henry Darger,' looking at the artist's

influence on others. The museum also runs several worthy programs, including lectures and Free Music Fridays, which feature up-and-coming talents covering various genres.

RADIO CITY MUSIC HALL Map pp134–5
☎ 212-247-4777; www.radiocity.com; 51st St at Sixth Ave; tours adult/child/senior $17/10/14; ⊕ B, D, F, V to 47th-50th Sts-Rockefeller Center
The interior of this 6000-seat, art-deco movie palace is a protected landmark, and one peek inside tells you why: the sea of restored velvet seats and furnishings, the lush curtains, the famous pipe organ and the decorative detailing are just as gorgeous as when the building opened in 1932. Be warned, though: the vibe of concerts here does not match the theater's splendor now that it's managed by the folks from Madison Square Garden; latecomers are allowed, which disrupts performances, and tacky glow-in-the-dark cocktails are sold in the lobby – and allowed into the theater, creating an ugly sea of purple drinks that's more akin to a stadium rock concert than a classy show in a classy joint. Still, there are often some fabulous talents on the lineup – Rufus Wainwright, Aretha Franklin, Dolly Parton – but the annual Christmas Spectacular, starring the Rockettes, is a hokey rip-off, and is best avoided (unless you believe you just haven't lived until you've seen those Rockettes kick).

For a real treat, take a guided tour of the interior. You can join one every half-hour between 11am and 3pm, Monday to Sunday.

HERALD SQUARE Map pp134–5
⊕ B, D, F, N, Q, R, V, W to 34th St-Herald Sq
This crowded convergence of Broadway, Sixth Ave and 34th St is best known as the home of Macy's (p238) department store, where you can still ride some of the remain-

ing original wooden elevators to floors ranging from women's casualwear and home furnishings to lingerie. The busy square gets its name from a long-defunct newspaper, the New York Herald, and the small, leafy park here bustles during business hours thanks to a recent and much-needed facelift. Don't bother with the two indoor malls south of Macy's on Sixth Ave, where you'll find a boring and suburban array of chain stores – the exception being Daffy's (p221), which offers great discounts on big labels.

TIME WARNER CENTER Map pp134–5

☎ 212-869-1890; www.shopsatcolumbuscircle.com; Columbus Circle at 59th St; ⏰ 9am-9pm; ⊖ A, C, B, D, 1 to 59th St-Columbus Circle

This pair of sleek towers, built for $1.8 billion on the site of the former New York Coliseum, is a highly visible retail center on the edge of Central Park. The seven-floor atrium, which affords grand views of the park from behind its glass facade and features a wonderful collection of Fernando Botero sculptures in its common spaces, is a basically a mall, albeit a rarely crowded one. That's probably because its stores – which include Williams-Sonoma, J Crew, Borders Books and Hugo Boss – can be found in so many other places, NYC and otherwise. Same goes for the basement's 59,000-sq-ft Whole Foods organic supermarket, now one of several in the city. This is also the home of luxury condos, a Mandarin Oriental Hotel (p360), Equinox Sports Club, Jazz at Lincoln Center (below) and the corporate headquarters of Time Warner, as well as CNN offices and some very pricey eateries (see p262).

INTREPID SEA, AIR & SPACE MUSEUM Map pp134–5

☎ 212-245-0072; www.intrepidmuseum.org; Pier 86, Twelfth Ave at 46th St; call for hr & admission costs; ⊖ A, C, E to 42nd St, 🚌 M42 bus westbound

This military museum is housed in a hulking aircraft carrier that survived both a WWII

bomb and kamikaze attacks. The flight deck of the USS Intrepid, which served in WWII and Vietnam, features fighter planes and military helicopters, while the pier area contains the guided-missile submarine Growler, an Apollo space capsule, Vietnam-era tanks, the 900ft destroyer Edson and a decommissioned Concorde. The Intrepid is the nexus for the Fleet Week (p21) celebrations each May, when thousands of the world's sailors descend on Manhattan for shore leave.

The museum is back after being gone from its spot for a full two years for an extensive renovation. (Because the Intrepid had not yet reopened at the time of writing, new hours and pricing information were not yet available.) The ship's removal in 2006 caused a flurry of media attention when it got stuck in the mud during the first attempted removal; the tugboats were able to move it only 15 feet before having to stop and wait till the next high tide.

JACOB JAVITS CONVENTION CENTER Map pp134–5

☎ 212-216-2000; www.javitscenter.com; Eleventh Ave btwn 34th & 38th Sts; ⊖ A, C, E to 34th St-Penn Station, 🚌 M34 bus westbound

NYC's sole convention center is a four-block construction located way on the outer reaches of Manhattan's west side. Designed by IM Pei, the behemoth of glass and steel – either loved or reviled by most New Yorkers – hosts hundreds of events each year, from auto shows and dentist conventions to travel expos and an annual Gay Life Expo (in November).

MUSEUM AT FIT Map pp134–5

☎ 212-217-5800; www.fitnyc.edu; Seventh Ave at 27th St; admission free; ⏰ noon-8pm Tue-Fri, 10am-5pm Sat; ⊖ 1 to 28th St

The Fashion Institute of Technology is a fashion, design and fine arts school located on the edge of Manhattan's Garment District

JAZZ AT LINCOLN CENTER

Back in 2004 Jazz at Lincoln Center (www.jazzatlincolncenter.com) left its old home for its grand new digs at the Frederick P Rose Hall in the Time Warner Center, a 100,000-sq-ft, $128-million facility built specifically for jazz music. The multiroom space, with a sleek and soaring glass design from Rafael Viñoly Architects, hosts opera, dance, theater and symphony shows, but its main theme is jazz, in the form of education, historical archiving and, of course, performance, with shows curated by its artistic director – none other than Wynton Marsalis. The place is perched above Columbus Circle, and a glimmering skyline and the magnificent views over Central Park serve as a backdrop for jazz shows in glass-backed spaces such as the intimate Allen Room and Dizzy's Club Coca-Cola nightclub.

(see p132). It's also the site of the popular Bravo TV series *Project Runway*. The best way for a visitor to access its unique riches is to visit its museum, which showcases rotating exhibits on fashion and style, including works by students. Its new permanent collection is the country's first gallery of fashion and textile history, which showcases rotating items from its collection of more than 50,000 garments and accessories dating from the 18th century to the present.

MIDTOWN WEST
Walking Tour

1 Bryant Park Start at the midtown oasis known as Bryant Park (p137), which you'll find sitting just west of the New York Public Library on Fifth Ave. It's a perfect place to sit and watch the swirl of people passing through – or even go for a spin on the carousel.

2 International Center of Photography
Head up and across Sixth Ave to find the International Center of Photography (p138) at 43rd St. Head in to explore the two airy levels of top-notch images.

3 Diamond District Continue north up Sixth Ave to 47th St, which features the Diamond District (see p132) between Sixth and Fifth Aves. Take a stroll up one side and back along the other and head inside some of the shops, rubbing elbows with folks seeking engagement rings and aggressive hawkers looking to make you a deal.

4 Rockefeller Center & Top of the Rock
Walk a few more blocks north on Sixth Ave and turn right on to 49th St to reach Rockefeller Center (p133), an art deco–inspired center of commerce and industry, where you can explore the plazas, outdoor sculptures, shops and interesting jumble of architecture. Also here is Top of the Rock (p133), an amazing observatory that rivals the Empire State Building with its 360-degree views, including stellar eyefuls of Central Park below.

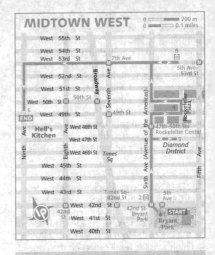

WALK FACTS
Start Bryant Park (⊕ B, D, V, F to 42nd St-Bryant Park, 7 to Fifth Ave)
End Hell's Kitchen (⊕ C, E at 50th St or A, C, E at 42nd St)
Distance **1.5 miles**
Duration **2½ hours**
Fuel stops **Hell's Kitchen**

5 Museum of Modern Art Head up Sixth Ave and turn right on 53rd St to find the Museum of Modern Art (p137), home to more than 100,000 pieces of heavy hitting modern artwork in a much-lauded, recently renovated building.

6 Hell's Kitchen Wind up your tour by continuing west to Ninth Ave and heading downtown, which will take you through Hell's Kitchen (see p132). Though there's not a specific sight to seek out, it's a great neighborhood for strolling and exploring – and noshing, as this stretch of Ninth down to about 42nd St is chock-full of eateries from all over the world. Pick the place that looks best and chow down.

Drinking p295; Eating p263; Shopping p239; Sleeping p363

The Upper East Side (often abbreviated UES) is home to New York's greatest concentration of cultural centers, including the grand dame that is the Metropolitan Museum of Art – a long section of Fifth Ave north of 79th St has even been officially designated 'Museum Mile.' But beyond museums, you'll find intellectual draws such as the 92nd Street Y (p320), as well as plenty of less high-minded attractions in the form of seriously high-end shops. The neighborhood – whose residents, by the way, are in a never-ending contest with those of the Upper West Side, just across the park (see the boxed text, p154) – also includes many of the city's most exclusive hotels and residences (not to mention many of the city's most moneyed celebrities, from Woody Allen to Shirley MacLaine). The side streets from Fifth Ave to Third Ave between 57th and 86th Sts feature some stunning townhouses and brownstones – walking through this area at night offers opportunities to see how the other half lives. (Go ahead, peer inside those grand libraries and living rooms!)

The UES runs roughly from about 59th St to 96th St, between Fifth Ave and the East River. The sole subway lines here are the 4, 5, and 6 up Lexington Ave, which explains why it's so damned crowded at rush hour – riders often wait for two packed trains to pass them by until they can squeeze into one. Crosstown buses at 67th, 72nd, 79th, 86th and 96 Sts take you to the Upper West Side.

METROPOLITAN MUSEUM OF ART
Map p142

☎ 212-535-7710; www.metmuseum.org; Fifth Ave at 82nd St; suggested donation adult/child/senior & student $20/free/15; ⏱ 9:30am-5:30pm Tue-Thu & Sun, to 9pm Fri & Sat; ⊙ 4, 5, 6 to 86th St

With more than five million visitors per year, the Met is New York's most popular single-site tourist attraction, with one of the richest coffers in the arts world. The Met is a self-contained cultural city-state, with two million individual objects in its collection and an annual budget of over $120 million. Since completing a multi-million-dollar remodeling project that brought works out of storage, renovated the halls of 19th- and early 20th-century paintings and sculptures and expanded the Ancient Hellenistic and Roman areas, the place is looking more divine than ever. Even more changes can be expected in the coming years, as 2008 saw the retirement of museum director Philippe de Montebello, who reigned over the institution for three decades.

Once inside the Great Hall, pick up a floor plan and head to the ticket booths, where you'll find a list of any exhibitions closed that day, along with a lineup of special museum talks. The Met presents more than 30 special exhibitions and installations each year and it's best to target exactly what you want to see on the floor plan and head there first, before museum fatigue sets in (usually after two hours). Then you can put the plan away and get lost trying to get back to the main entrance. It's a virtual certainty that you'll stumble across something interesting along the way.

To the right of the Great Hall, an information desk offers guidance in several languages (which change depending on the volunteers) and audio tours ($6) of the special exhibitions. The Met also offers free guided tours of museum highlights and specific galleries. (Check the calendar, given away at the information desk, for specific schedules.) Families will want to grab the children-specific brochure and events calendar (both free at the information booth).

If you can't make it to Cooperstown, New York, home of America's Baseball Hall of Fame, then exit the gallery through the door behind the Egyptian wing's Temple of Dendur to behold the Met's collection of baseball cards, which includes the rarest and most expensive card in the world – a 1909 Honus Wagner that's worth some $200,000. Continue on to the left and you'll enter the American Wing of furniture and architecture, with a quiet, enclosed garden space that's a perennial favorite as a respite from the hordes. Several stained-glass works by Louis Comfort Tiffany frame the garden, as does an entire two-story facade of the Branch Bank of the US, preserved when the downtown building was destroyed in the early 20th century.

Past the popular American Wing, you'll find the pyramid-like addition that houses

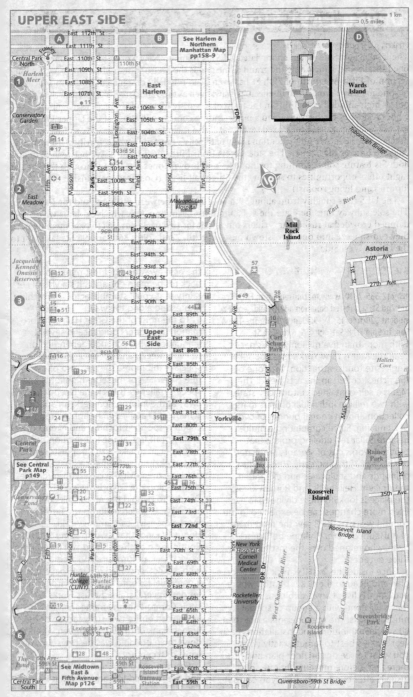

East 112th St
East 111th St
East 110th St
East 109th St
East 108th St
East 107th St
East 106th St
East 105th St
East 104th St
East 103rd St
East 102nd St
East 101st St
East 100th St
East 99th St
East 98th St
East 97th St
East 96th St
East 95th St
East 94th St
East 93rd St
East 92nd St
East 91st St
East 90th St
East 89th St
East 88th St
East 87th St
East 86th St
East 85th St
East 84th St
East 83rd St
East 82nd St
East 81st St
East 80th St
East 79th St
East 78th St
East 77th St
East 76th St
East 75th St
East 74th St
East 73rd St
East 72nd St
East 71st St
East 70th St
East 69th St
East 68th St
East 67th St
East 66th St
East 65th St
East 64th St
East 63rd St
East 62nd St
East 61st St
East 60th St
East 59th St

East Harlem

Upper East Side

Yorkville

See Harlem & Northern Manhattan Map pp158-9

Central Park North
Harlem Meer
Conservatory Garden
East Meadow
Jacqueline Kennedy Onassis Reservoir
Central Park

See Central Park Map p149

Conservatory Pond
The Pond

See Midtown East & Fifth Avenue Map p126

Central Park South

Metropolitan Hospital
Wards Island
Mill Rock Island
Astoria
Hallets Cove
Roosevelt Island
Rainey Park
Roosevelt Island Bridge
Carl Schurz Park
John Jay Park
New York Hospital Cornell Medical Center
Rockefeller University
Queensbridge Park
Queensboro-59th St Bridge
Roosevelt Island Tramway Station
Hunter College (CUNY)

East River
Triborough Bridge
FDR Dr
East End Ave
York Ave
First Ave
Second Ave
Third Ave
Lexington Ave
Park Ave
Madison Ave
Fifth Ave
East Dr

0 ___ 1 km
0 ___ 0.5 miles

UPPER EAST SIDE

the Robert Lehman Collection of impressionist and modern art, featuring several works by Renoir (including *Young Girl Bathing*), Georges Seurat and Pablo Picasso (including *Portrait of Gertrude Stein*). An unexpected bonus in this gallery is the rear terra-cotta facade of the original 1880 museum building, now completely encased by later additions and standing mutely on view as its own architectural artifact.

The Rockefeller Collection contains arts of Africa, Oceania and the Americas, then leads to the Greek and Roman art section. The museum has recently restored much of its Greek and Roman work, including the 2nd-floor Cypriot Gallery, which contains some of the finest pieces outside Cyprus.

Elsewhere on the 2nd floor, you'll see the Met's famous collection of European paintings, located in some of the museum's oldest galleries, found beyond colonnaded entryways. The exhibition features works by every artist of note, including self-portraits by Rembrandt and Van Gogh and *Portrait of Juan de Pareja* by Velázquez. An entire suite of rooms focuses on impressionist and postimpressionist art. The new collection of modern masters is housed on this level, as well as the photographs recently purchased by the Met, and the museum's exquisite

musical-instrument holdings. Also of interest up here are the treasures from Japan, China and Southeast Asia.

If you can't stand crowds, avoid a rainy Sunday afternoon in summer. But during horrible winter weather, you might try viewing the 17-acre museum, deserted, from the outside at night – a real NYC image. The roof garden (p295) is also a find, especially in the summer, when it adds a wine bar on weekend evenings.

WHITNEY MUSEUM OF AMERICAN ART Map p142

☎ 212-570-3600, 800-944-8639; www.whitney.org; 945 Madison Ave at 75th St; adult/child/senior $15/free/10; ⏰ 11am-6pm Wed, Thu, Sat & Sun, 1-9pm Fri; ⊖ 6 to 77th St

Established in the 1930s by Gertrude Vanderbilt Whitney, who began a Greenwich Village salon for prominent artists, the stellar art collection here features works by famous folk such as Edward Hopper, Jasper Johns, Georgia O'Keeffe, Jackson Pollock and Mark Rothko. Known for its blockbuster shows, recent exhibits have included 'Polaroids: Mapplethorpe,' and 'Danny Lyon: Montage, Film and Still Photography.'

The Whitney makes no secret of its mission to provoke, which starts with the most brutal of structures housing the collection. Designed by Bauhaus architect Marcel Breuer, the rock-like edifice is a fitting setting for the Whitney's style of cutting-edge American art. The collection is highlighted every two years in the much ballyhooed Whitney Biennial, an ambitious survey of contemporary art that rarely fails to generate controversy – even if it's over the mediocrity of the works. It last hit town in 2008.

FRICK COLLECTION Map p142

☎ 212-288-0700; www.frick.org; 1 E 70th St at Fifth Ave; adult/student/senior $15/5/10, children under 10 not admitted; ⏰ 10am-6pm Tue-Sat, 11am-5pm Sun; ⊕ 6 to 68th St-Hunter College
This spectacular collection sits in a mansion built by businessman Henry Clay Frick in 1914, one of the many such residences that made up 'Millionaires' Row.' Most of these mansions proved too expensive for succeeding generations and were eventually destroyed, but the wily and very wealthy Frick, a Pittsburgh steel magnate, established a trust to open his private art collection as a museum. It's a shame that the 2nd floor of the residence is not open for viewing, though the 12 rooms on the ground floor are grand enough and the garden beckons visitors on nice days.

The Frick's Oval Room is graced by Jean-Antoine Houdon's stunning figure *Diana the Huntress;* the intimate museum also displays works by Titian and Vermeer, and portraits by Gilbert Stuart, El Greco, Goya and John Constable. An audio tour (available in several languages) is included in the price of admission and helps visitors appreciate the art more fully; you can also dial up information on paintings and sculptures of your choosing on the Art-Phone. Perhaps the best asset here is that it's never crowded, providing a welcoming break from the swarms of gawkers at larger museums, especially on weekends. Also, classical music fans will no doubt be drawn here for the frequent piano and violin concerts that take place on Sundays (see p315).

COOPER-HEWITT NATIONAL DESIGN MUSEUM Map p142

☎ 212-849-8400; www.si.edu/ndm; 2 E 91st St at Fifth Ave; adult/child/senior & student $15/free/10; ⏰ 10am-5pm Mon-Thu, to 9pm Fri, to 6pm Sat, noon-6pm Sun; ⊕ 4, 5, 6 to 86th St
This museum is in the 64-room mansion built by billionaire Andrew Carnegie in 1901

in what was, in those days, *way* uptown. Within 20 years, the bucolic surroundings that Carnegie craved disappeared as other wealthy men followed his lead and built palaces nearby. Carnegie was an interesting character: an avid reader and generous philanthropist, he dedicated many libraries around the country and donated some $350 million in his lifetime. To learn more, take the 45-minute guided tour (⏰ noon & 3pm Mon-Fri, 12:30pm & 2pm Sat & Sun), included in the admission price.

Part of the Smithsonian Institution in Washington, this house of culture is a must for anyone interested in architecture, engineering, jewelry or textiles. Exhibitions have examined everything from advertising campaigns to Viennese blown glass. Even if none of this grabs you, the mansion is stunning and the museum's garden and terrace are well worth a visit.

SOLOMON R GUGGENHEIM MUSEUM Map p142

☎ 212-423-3500; www.guggenheim.org; 1071 Fifth Ave at 89th St; adult/child under 12/senior & student $18/free/15; ⏰ 10am-5:45pm Sat-Wed, to 7:45pm Fri; ⊕ 4, 5, 6 to 86th St
A sculpture in its own right, Frank Lloyd Wright's sweeping spiral building almost overshadows the collection of 20th-century art housed in this museum. Because of its unusual design, the building sparked controversy during its construction in the 1950s, but today it's a distinctive landmark that architects fiddle with at their peril. An unpopular 1992 renovation added an adjoining, 10-story tower that does indeed bear a striking resemblance to a toilet – just as the critics feared – despite being based on Wright's original drawings. Most recently, the Wright-designed exterior, whose concrete had been plagued by surface cracks practically since the day it opened, went through a lengthy restoration and repair project.

After admiring the new exterior, head inside to view some of the museum's 5000 permanent works (plus changing exhibitions) on a path that coincides with Wright's coiled design – take the elevator to the top and wind your way down. The Guggenheim's collection includes works by Picasso, Chagall, Pollock and Kandinsky. In 1976 Justin Thannhauser's major donation of impressionist and modern works added paintings by Monet, Van Gogh and Degas. In 1992, the Robert Mapplethorpe Foundation gave 200 photographs to the museum, spurring curators to devote the 4th floor to photography exhibitions. Note that you can purchase tickets online in advance via the museum's website, which lets you avoid the sometimes-brutal lines to get in.

JEWISH MUSEUM Map p142

☎ 212-423-3200; www.jewishmuseum.org; 1109 Fifth Ave at 92nd St; adult/child/student/senior $12/free/7.50/10, by donation 5-8pm Thu; ⏰ 11am-5:45pm Sat-Wed, to 8pm Thu; ⊕ 6 to 96th St

This homage to Judaism primarily features artwork examining 4000 years of Jewish ceremony and culture; it also has a wide array of children's activities (storytelling hour, arts and crafts workshops etc). The building, a gorgeous banker's mansion from 1908, houses more than 30,000 items of Judaica, as well as works of sculpture, paintings, numismatics, antiquities, prints, decorative arts and photography. Watch for occasional blockbuster exhibitions, such as the recent 'From the *New Yorker* to *Shrek*: The Art of William Steig' and 'Archaeology Zone: Discovering Treasures from Playgrounds to Palaces' shows, which drew large turnouts. The institution also offers frequent lectures and film screenings – especially in January, when it collaborates with Lincoln Center to present the annual New York Jewish Film Festival.

MUSEUM OF THE CITY OF NEW YORK Map p142

☎ 212-534-1672; www.mcny.org; 1220 Fifth Ave btwn 103rd & 104th Sts; suggested donation family/adult/senior & student $20/9/5; ⏰ 10am-5pm Tue-Sun; ⊕ 6 to 103rd St

For a look behind the intriguing facade of NYC, head here, where exhibits focus solely on the city's past, present and future. Housed in a 1932 Georgian-Colonial mansion, the Museum of the City of New York offers plenty of stimulation, both old-school and technology-based. You'll find internet-based historical resources and a decent scale model of New Amsterdam shortly after the Dutch arrival; the notable 2nd-floor gallery includes entire rooms from demolished homes of New York grandees, an exhibition dedicated to Broadway musicals and a collection of antique dollhouses, teddy bears and toys.

Rotating exhibitions cast a clever eye on the city, with past subjects ranging from 19th-century illustrations of the city to Catholics in New York.

ASIA SOCIETY & MUSEUM Map p142

☎ 212-288-6400; www.asiasociety.org; 725 Park Ave at 70th St; ⊕ 6 to 68th St-Hunter College

Founded by John D Rockefeller in 1956 – he was quite a fan of Asia; see also his Japan Society (p125) – this cultural center is meant to strengthen Western understanding of Asia and relationships between the continent and the US. Other outposts exist in cities including Los Angeles, San Francisco, Hong Kong and Shanghai, though the New York branch is the headquarters. You'll find an array of reasons to visit the place, including educational lectures and events, but the biggest draw is its museum (www.asiasocietymuseum.org), which features rare treasures from all across Asia, such as Jain sculptures from India, Buddhist paintings from Nepal and jade and lacquer items from China.

CARL SCHURZ PARK Map p142

☎ 212-459-4455; www.carlschurzparknyc.org; East End Ave btwn 84th and 89th Sts; ⊕ 4, 5, 6 to 86th St

The placid Carl Schurz Park is the oldest community-based volunteer park association in the city, and it's long been a favorite spot for a stroll along the East River, or to glimpse the blooming garden grounds of Gracie Mansion, the 1799 country residence where New York's mayors have always lived – with the exception of the extremely wealthy Mayor Bloomberg, who already had his own plush city digs when he landed the mayoral gig in 2002. To join one of the house tours (adult/student & child/senior $7/free/4), which take place on Wednesdays at 10am, 11am, 1pm and 2pm, you must first call the city's ☎ 311 line for a reservation.

NATIONAL ACADEMY OF DESIGN
Map p142

☎ 212-369-4880; www.nationalacademy.org; 1083 Fifth Ave at 89th St; adult/child under 16/senior & student $10/free/5; ⏰ noon-5pm Wed & Thu, 11am-6pm Fri-Sun; ◉ 4, 5, 6 to 86th St

Co-founded by painter/inventor Samuel Morse, the National Academy of Design art-school complex includes a permanent collection of paintings and sculptures housed in yet another stunning Beaux-Arts mansion, featuring a marble foyer and spiral staircase. This superb space was designed by Ogden Codman, who also designed the Breakers mansion in Newport, Rhode Island.

NEW YORK ACADEMY OF MEDICINE
Map p142

☎ 212-822-7200; www.nyam.org; 1216 Fifth Ave at 103rd St; admission free; ⏰ 9am-5pm Mon-Fri; ◉ 6 to 103rd St

With over 700,000 cataloged works, the New York Academy of Medicine has the second-largest health library in the world (and in its holdings is the world's largest cookbook collection). But if you want to skip all the books, you can head straight for the weirdly fascinating medical ephemera like the leper clapper (used by sufferers to warn a town of their arrival), a globule of the world's first penicillin culture, cupping glasses used in phlebotomy procedures, and George Washington's dentures.

ROOSEVELT ISLAND Map p142
◉ F to Roosevelt Island

Not exactly part of the Upper East Side but floating in the East River between Manhattan's eastern edge and Queens, New York's anomalous, planned neighborhood sits on a tiny island no wider than a football field. It was once known as Blackwell's Island after the farming family who lived here; the city bought the island in 1828 and constructed several public hospitals and a mental hospital. In the 1970s, New York State built housing for 10,000 people along

Roosevelt Island's Main St (the only street on the island). The planned area along the cobblestone roadway resembles an Olympic village or, as some observe more cynically, cookie-cutter college housing.

Zipping across the river via the four-minute aerial tram is a trip in itself and worth it for the stunning view of the East Side of Manhattan framed by the 59th St Bridge. Instead of heading straight back like most do, however, bring a picnic or a bike, as this quiet island is conducive to lounging and cycling. Trams leave from the Roosevelt Island tramway station (☎ 212-832-4543; www.rioc.com; 60th St at Second Ave) every 15 minutes on the quarter-hour from 6am to 2am Sunday to Thursday, and until 3:30am Friday and Saturday; the one-way fare is $2. Roosevelt Island also has a subway station.

TEMPLE EMANU-EL Map p142

☎ 212-744-1400; www.emanuelnyc.org; 1 E 65th St at Fifth Ave; ⏰ 10am-5pm; ◉ N, R, W to Fifth Ave-59th St

Founded in 1845 as the first Reform synagogue in New York, this temple was completed in 1929. It's now the largest Jewish house of worship in the world, and has a membership of some 3000 families. Stop by for a look at its notable Byzantine and Middle Eastern architecture: its facade features an arch with symbols representing the 12 tribes of Israel, which are also depicted on the grand set of bronze doors. Inside the majestic, buttressed interior are Guastavino tiles, marble wainscoting and brilliant stained-glass windows.

YORKVILLE Map p142
◉ 6 to 77th St

This area, east of Lexington Ave between 70th and 96th Sts, is known today as the one pocket of the Upper East Side with (relatively) affordable rental apartments. It was once the settling point for new Hungarian and German immigrants – the only trace left of that heritage today are places like Schaller & Weber, an old-world German grocery, Heidelberg, a homey restaurant serving sauerbraten and other traditional goodies (both are on Second Ave between 85th and 86th Sts) and the Yorkville Meat Emporium, on Second Ave at 81st St, stocked with fresh meats and prepared Hungarian dishes.

EXPLORING THE MUSEUM MILE

Walking Tour

1 Museum of the City of New York Start your Museum Mile journey at Fifth Ave and 103rd St, at the Museum of the City of New York (p145), where you can get your head around all sorts of Gotham angles.

2 Jewish Museum Continue south along grand Fifth Ave to the Jewish Museum (p145), at 92nd St, where exhibits include much Judaica but also cover all sorts of impressive artwork.

3 Solomon R Guggenheim Museum Further south, at 89th St, you'll see the spaceship-like, Frank Lloyd Wright–designed Solomon R Guggenheim Museum (p144), filled with modern art in a spiral setup.

4 Neue Galerie Home to German and Austrian furniture, design and artwork by masters including Gustav Klimt, the Neue Galerie (p145) is an intimate and lovely break from the block-buster showcases along this route – and its airy Café Sabarsky is the perfect place for a delicious pick-me-up.

5 Metropolitan Museum of Art After such a nice small collection of galleries, why not jump right in to the belly of the beast at the Metropolitan Museum of Art (p141), where the endless maze of intriguing exhibits will certainly call you back for a longer look on another day.

6 Whitney Museum of Art Continue south on Fifth Ave to 75th St and head east to high-class Madison Ave, home to the Whitney Museum of Art (p143), which provides a cutting-edge end to a decidedly classic afternoon. If you're still up for more, try exploring neighboring Central Park (see the walking tour, p151).

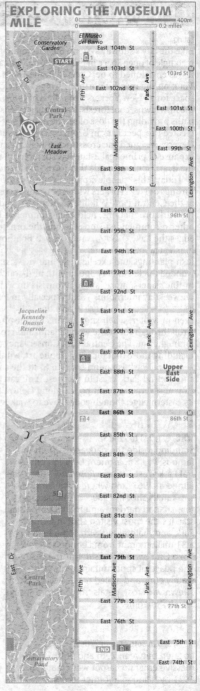

EXPLORING THE MUSEUM MILE

147

CENTRAL PARK

Eating p265

Like the city's subway system, the vast and majestic Central Park (www.centralparknyc.org), an 843-acre rectangle of open space in the middle of Manhattan, is a great class leveler – which is exactly what it was envisioned to be. Created in the 1860s and '70s by Frederick Law Olmsted and Calvert Vaux on the marshy northern fringe of the city, the immense park was designed as a leisure space for all New Yorkers, regardless of color, class or creed. And it's an oasis from the insanity: the lush lawns, cool forests, flowering gardens, glassy bodies of water and meandering, wooded paths providing the dose of serene nature that New Yorkers crave. Olmsted and Vaux (who also created Prospect Park in Brooklyn) were determined to keep foot and road traffic separate and cleverly designed the crosstown transverses under elevated roads to do so. That such a large expanse of prime real estate has survived intact for so long again proves that nothing eclipses the heart, soul and pride that forms the foundation of New York City's greatness.

Today, this 'people's park' is still one of the city's most popular attractions, beckoning throngs of New Yorkers with free outdoor concerts at the Great Lawn (below), precious animals at the Central Park Wildlife Center (p150) and top-notch drama to the annual Shakespeare in the Park productions, held each summer at the open-air Delacorte Theater (see p313). Some other recommended stops include the ornate Bethesda Fountain (Map p149; mid-park at 72nd St), which edges the Lake (Map p149) and its Loeb Boathouse (p330), where you can rent rowboats or enjoy lunch at an outdoor café (p265); the Shakespeare Garden (Map p149; west side btwn 79th & 80th Sts), which has lush plantings and excellent skyline views; and the Ramble (Map p149; mid-park from 73rd to 79th Sts), a wooded thicket that's popular with bird-watchers. While parts of the park swarm with joggers, in-line skaters, musicians and tourists on warm weekends, you'll find the whole place quieter on weekday afternoons – but especially in less well-trodden spots above 72nd St such as the Harlem Meer (Map p149; at 110th St) and the North Meadow (Map p149; north of 97th St). Folks flock to the park even in winter, when snowstorms can inspire cross-country skiing and sledding or a simple stroll through the white wonderland, and crowds turn out every New Year's Eve for a popular midnight run. The Central Park Conservancy also offers ever-changing guided tours of the park, including those that focus on public art, wildlife and places of interest to kids.

Central Park is bound by 59th St to the south, 110th St to the north, Fifth Ave to the east and Central Park West to the west. You can get to its west side via the B and C trains, which stop at several different points along Central Park West; the 6 train is as close as you'll get to its eastern edge, though you'll have to walk west a bit from Lexington Ave.

STRAWBERRY FIELDS Map p149

🚇 B, C, 1, 2, 3 to 72nd St

Standing inside the park across from the famous Dakota apartment building on Central Park West – where *Rosemary's Baby* was filmed in 1967, and where John Lennon was fatally shot in 1980 – is this poignant, tear-shaped garden, a memorial to the slain star. It's the most visited spot in Central Park, and maintained with some help from a $1 million grant from Lennon's widow Yoko Ono (who still resides at the Dakota). The peaceful spot contains a grove of stately elms and a tiled mosaic that's often strewn with rose petals from visitors. It says, simply, 'Imagine.'

GREAT LAWN Map p149

🚇 4, 5, 6 to 86th St, 6 to 77th St

Located between 79th and 86th Sts, this massive emerald carpet was created in 1931 by filling in a former reservoir. It's the

place for outdoor concerts – this is where Paul Simon played his famous comeback show, and also where you can catch the New York Philharmonic Orchestra (p22) each summer – and there are also eight softball fields, basketball courts and a canopy of London plane trees. Not far from the actual lawn are several other big sites: the Delacorte Theater (see p313), which is home to the annual Shakespeare in the Park festival, and its lush Shakespeare Garden; the panoramic Belvedere Castle; the leafy Ramble (the epicenter of both birding and gay-male cruising); and the Loeb Boathouse (p330), where you can rent rowboats for a romantic float in the middle of this urban paradise.

JACQUELINE KENNEDY ONASSIS RESERVOIR Map p149

🚇 4, 5, 6 to 86th St

Don't miss your chance to run or walk around this 1.58-mile track, which draws a

CENTRAL PARK

0 — 400 m
0 — 0.2 miles

INFORMATION		
Information	1	B3
Visitor Center	2	C6

SIGHTS	(pp148–51)	
Arsenal	3	C6
Belvedere Castle	4	C4
Bethesda Fountain	5	C5
Central Park Wildlife Center	6	C6
Loeb Boathouse	(see 17)	
Merchants' Gate	7	B6
Shakespeare Garden	8	C4
Starr Saphir Bird-Watching Tours	9	B4
Starr Saphir Bird-Watching Tours	10	B3
Strawberry Fields	11	B5
Wollman Skating Rink	12	C6

EATING 🍴	(p265)	
Central Park Boathouse Restaurant	13	C5

THE ARTS 🎭		
Central Park Summerstage	14	C5
Delacorte Theater	15	C4

SPORTS & ACTIVITIES	(pp323–37)	
Arsenal	(see 3)	
Central Park Bicycle Tours & Rentals	(see 7)	
Central Park Tennis Center	16	C2
Loeb Boathouse	17	C5
Safari Playground	18	B3
Wollman Skating Rink	(see 12)	

slew of joggers in the warmer months. The 106-acre body of water no longer distributes drinking water to residents, but serves as a gorgeous reflecting pool for the surrounding skyline and flowering trees. Take a turn around the reservoir's perimeter and you may very well spot the elderly, white-haired Albert Arroyo, the friendly and self-appointed 'Mayor of Central Park,' who used to run laps here and now makes his slow way around and around with the aid of a cane. The most beautiful time to be here is at sunset, when you can watch the sky turn from a brilliant shade of pink and orange to cobalt blue, just as the city's lights slowly flicker to life.

CENTRAL PARK WILDLIFE CENTER
Map p149

☎ 212-861-6030; www.centralparknyc.org; 64th St at Fifth Ave; ⊙ 10am-5pm; ⊚ N, R, W to 5th Ave-59th St

The penguins are the main attraction at this modern zoo, though you'll find more than two dozen other species to visit, including polar bears and the endangered tamarin monkeys and red pandas. Feeding times are especially rowdy, fun times to stroll through: watch the sea lions chow down at 11:30am, 2pm and 4pm and see the penguins gobble fish at 10:30am and 2:30pm. The attached Tisch Children's Zoo, between 65th and 66th Sts, is perfect for smaller children.

STATUARY IN THE PARK
Scattered among the many natural sculptures otherwise known as trees are a host of wonderful, freestanding, crafted works of art. If you enter the park at the Merchants' Gate (Map p149; Columbus Circle), you'll see the mighty Maine Monument, a tribute to the sailors killed in the mysterious explosion in Havana Harbor in 1898 that sparked the Spanish-American War. Further east, toward the Seventh Ave entrance, there are statues of Latin America's greatest liberators, including José Martí, 'The Apostle of Cuban Independence' (history buffs will find Martí's proximity to the Maine Monument ironic, to say the least). Further east still, at the Scholars' Gate (Map p149; Fifth Ave at 60th St), there is a small plaza dedicated to Doris Chanin Freedman, the founder of the Public Art Fund, where you can see a new sculpture every six months or so.

While almost everyone is familiar with Angel of the Waters atop Bethesda Fountain (Map p149), even those who know Central Park like the back of their hand may have overlooked the Falconer Statue, tucked away on a rise overlooking the 72nd St Transverse nearby. This 1875 bronze recreates the remarkable moment of flight, and the connection between master and charge is regal and palpable. Literary Walk (Map p149), between Bethesda Fountain and the 65th St Transverse, is lined with statues, including the requisite Christopher Columbus and literati such as Robert Burns and Shakespeare.

East and north of here is the Conservatory Water (Map p149), where model sailboats drift lazily by and kids crawl over the giant toadstools of the Alice in Wonderland statue. Replete with Alice of flowing hair and dress, a dapper Mad Hatter and mischievous Cheshire Cat, this is a Central Park treasure and a favorite of kids of all ages. Nearby is the Hans Christian Andersen statue, where Saturday story hour (⊙ 11am Jun-Sep) is an entertaining draw.

The obelisk Cleopatra's Needle, a gift from Egypt to the US in 1877 for helping to build the Suez Canal, is located on the hillock above 82nd St and East Dr, near the Metropolitan Museum of Art (p141). Drop down to East Dr and look up to see the crouching cat sculpture, poised to pounce on unsuspecting in-line skaters.

At the northeastern edge of the park is the soaring Duke Ellington statue (Map p142), depicting the man and his piano. An oft-overlooked site because of its northern location at 110th St and Fifth Ave, this stunning tribute to the jazz master, featuring a 25ft bronze tableau, was unveiled in 1997 after being conceived and funded by the late jazz-pianist Bobby Short.

WOLLMAN SKATING RINK Map p149
☎ 212-439-6900; www.wollmanskatingrink.com; btwn 62nd & 63rd Sts; ⊙ Oct-Apr; ⊚ F to 57 St, N, R, W to 5th Ave-59th St

Located in the park's southeast corner, this is a romantic and popular skating rink to strap on rented ice skates and glide around, especially at night under the stars. Just try to tune out the blaring pop music, which tends to dampen the peaceful mood. For more information see p333.

ARSENAL Map p149
off 65th St and Fifth Ave
Built between 1847 and 1851 as a munitions supply depot for the New York State

National Guard, the landmark brick building was designed to look like a medieval castle, and its construction predates the actual park. Today the building houses the NYC Department of Parks & Recreation (www.nycgovparks.org) and the Central Park Wildlife Center (opposite). The reason to visit here is not to see the building, though, but to view Olmsted's original blueprint for the park, treasured here under glass in a 3rd-floor conference room.

CENTRAL PARK
Walking Tour

1 Strawberry Fields Fittingly, Strawberry Fields (p148), the memorial garden for John Lennon, is located in the area of Central Park that's just across the street from the Dakota, the building where he lived (and died). Head in and hang for a while; you'll most likely find yourself in the company of guitar players, flower bearers and other assorted mourners and fans.

2 Delacorte Theater From here, head just a bit deeper into the park and head north; you'll soon come to the spectacular, alfresco Delacorte Theater (see p313), home to summertime Shakespeare in the Park productions, where the main scenery is the verdant park itself.

3 Belvedere Castle Just south of here is the 19th-century Belvedere Castle, which rises up out of Vista Rock and provides breezy, beautiful views of the surrounding parkland.

4 Ramble Beyond the castle to the south is the Ramble, a lush, wooded expanse that serves as a decent bird-watching pocket. Be sure to note your surroundings so you don't get hopelessly turned around in your hike.

5 Bethesda Fountain On the other side of the Lake is Bethesda Fountain, with the uplifting *Angel of the Waters* sculpture at the center. In warm weather, you'll find a vendor near here doling out warm, fresh crepes and empanadas, providing the perfect opportunity for a snack break.

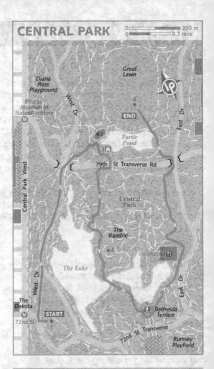

CENTRAL PARK

6 Great Lawn North of here is the grand (and appropriately named) Great Lawn (p148), where free concerts are occasionally held. Pick a corner, spread out and enjoy. If you're up for more, try the walking tours for the Upper East Side (p147) or the Upper West Side (p155).

UPPER WEST SIDE

Home to aging liberals, wealthy young families and an eclectic mix of actors and musicians, this lengthy neighborhood stretches up along the western side of Central Park and contains pockets that range from leafy parkland – Riverside Park runs along the Hudson River here – to quaint residential blocks and even bustling sections of Broadway that have been hyperdeveloped into strips of high-rise condos, drugstore chains and ugly banks. Much of the area is still an architectural wonderland, though, with everything from opulent apartment buildings – such as Dorilton (171 W 71st St at Broadway), the Dakota (see p148) at 72nd St and Central Park West and the Ansonia (2109 Broadway btwn 73rd & 74th Sts) – to functional public buildings with succulent detail, such as the former McBurney School (63rd St) and the Frederick Henry Cossitt Dormitory (64th St), both off Central Park West.

The best way to access the Upper West Side is via the 1, 2, 3 subway line along Broadway, or the B, C line up Central Park West. The M100 bus runs up and down Broadway, and the M10 runs up and down the western edge of the park.

AMERICAN MUSEUM OF NATURAL HISTORY Map p153

☎ 212-769-5100; www.amnh.org; Central Park West at 79th St; suggested donation adult/child/senior & student $15/8.50/11, last hr free; ☽ 10am-5:45pm (Rose Center to 8:45pm first Fri of the month); ❹ B, C to 81st St-Museum of Natural History, 1 to 79th St

Founded in 1869, this classic museum for kids of all ages contains halls of fascinating wonderlands holding more than 30 million artifacts; its interactive exhibits, both in the original museum and its newest section, the Rose Center for Earth & Space, are also out of this world. The most famous attractions are its three large dinosaur halls, with various skeletons for ogling, and the enormous (fake) blue whale that hangs from the ceiling of the Hall of Ocean Life. Kids of all ages will find something to be intrigued by, whether it's the stuffed Alaskan brown bear, the Star of India sapphire in the Hall of Minerals & Gems, the IMAX film on jungle life, or the skullcap of a pachycephelasaurus, a plant-eating dinosaur that roamed the earth 65 million years ago. No matter what section of the museum you're in, you'll find enthusiastic volunteer guides who are excited to answer questions.

It's the Rose Center for Earth & Space, though, that has really been the star attraction since its much-heralded opening a decade ago. Just gazing at its facade – a massive glass box that contains a silver globe, home to space-show theaters and the planetarium – is mesmerizing, especially at night when all of its otherworldly features are aglow. Step inside to trace the origins of the planets (especially Earth), and to grab a cushy seat in the high-tech planetarium, where you can watch either *The Search For Life: Are We Alone?*, narrated by Harrison Ford, or *Passport to the Universe*, with soothing voiceover by Tom Hanks. Another, smaller theater explores the Big Bang Theory with Maya Angelou's voice as your guide.

Visiting exhibitions at the museum are also popular, especially the recurring Butterfly Conservancy (☽ Nov-May), which lets you stroll through a house of glass with more than 600 butterflies from all over the world. It provides an amazing opportunity to truly hang out with – and sometimes serve as a perch for – the creatures. Other special exhibits have recently included 'Dinosaurs Alive!,' 'Cosmic Collisions' and 'Water: H2O=Life,' all of which packed the museum, more so than usual, for months. You'll also find a great, multilevel gift shop here, which is packed to the brim with unique kids' gifts, books from current exhibits and specialty items from jewelry to chocolates.

A nice evening treat for adults is the Starry Nights Live Jazz program, which takes place in the Rose Center on the first Friday of every month, with sets at 6pm and 7:30pm. Tapas, drinks and top jazz acts are all included with museum admission at these monthly gigs.

LINCOLN CENTER Map p153

☎ 212-875-5456; www.lincolncenter.org; Columbus Ave at 64th St; ❹ 1 to 66th St-Lincoln Center
The 16-acre Lincoln Center complex includes a dozen large performance spaces

UPPER WEST SIDE

See Harlem & Northern Manhattan Map pp158–9

See Central Park Map p149

See Midtown West & Times Square Map pp134–5

built in the 1960s, which controversially replaced a group of tenements called San Juan Hill, where exterior shots for the movie *West Side Story* were filmed. During the day Lincoln Center presents a demure face, but at night the interiors glow and sparkle with crystal chandeliers and well-heeled patrons of the arts.

If you have just a shred of culture vulture in you, Lincoln Center is a must-see, since it contains the Metropolitan Opera House (p321), its lobby adorned by two colorful murals (viewable from the plaza beneath) by Marc Chagall, and the New York State Theater (p321), home to both the New York City Ballet and the New York City Opera (the low-cost and more-daring alternative to the Met). The New York Philharmonic holds its season in Avery Fisher Hall (see the boxed text, p311), and you'll find constant high-quality theatrical productions at both the Mitzi E Newhouse and Vivian Beaumont Theaters.

To the right of those theaters stands the New York Public Library for the Performing Arts (☎ 212-870-1630), which houses the city's largest collection of recorded sound, video and books on film and theater. And then there's the Walter Reade Theater (p320), the city's most comfortable film-revival space and the major screening site for the New York Film Festival, held there each September. On any given night, there are at least 10 per-formances happening throughout Lincoln Center – and even more in summer, when Lincoln Center Out of Doors (a series of dance and music concerts) and Midsummer Night Swing (ballroom dancing under the stars) lure those who love parks *and* culture.

Visiting over the next few years, though, expect to see this vast entertainment center looking a bit out of sorts. It's be-cause of a massive redevelopment that began in 2007, not slated to have its first of several phases wrapped up until sometime in 2009 – just in time for Lincoln Center's

50th anniversary celebration. The end result, though – designed by New York 'starchitects' Diller Scofidio + Renfro – should prove stunning; it's set to include a Street of the Arts lined with new building facades, a public roof lawn, a large new retail shop, dramatic new entryways, a landscaped promenade and main entrance, and a complete overhaul for Alice Tully Hall, which was scheduled to be closed until at least some time in 2009. You can see excit-ing renderings of the new design on the Lincoln Center website.

Daily tours (☎ 212-875-5350; adult/child/senior & student $12.50/6/9) of the complex explore at least three of the theaters (which three you visit depends on production schedules). It's a good idea to call ahead for a space. They leave from the tour desk on the concourse level at 10:30am, 12:30pm, 2:30pm and 4:30pm.

RIVERSIDE PARK Map p153

from 72nd to 125th Sts along Hudson River; ⊕ 1, 2, 3 to 72nd St or higher
This skinny, lively greenspace is a great place to stroll, bike, run or sit back and watch all those active types pass by. It's lined with cherry trees that blossom into puffs of pink in the spring, community gardens that are lovingly tended by vol-unteers, 14 playgrounds that are popular with the local eight-and-under set, basket-ball courts and baseball fields. Its barren trees look lovely with a freshly-fallen coat of snow in winter. There are well-placed benches and a popular dog run, the seasonal Boat Basin Café at 79th St, and various works of public art, including an inspiring statue of Eleanor Roosevelt at the 72nd St entrance. It's a gem worth trekking to, especially at sunset, when the Hudson River is bathed in soft gold tones and the city seems like a peaceful place at last.

NEW-YORK HISTORICAL SOCIETY

Map p153

☎ 212-873-3400; www.nyhistory.org; 2 W 77th St at Central Park West; suggested donation adult/senior & student $10/6, Fri 6-8pm free; ☺ 10am-6pm Tue-Sat, 11am-5:45pm Sun; ◉ B, C to 81st St-Museum of Natural History, 1 to 79th St

As the antiquated hyphenated name implies, the New-York Historical Society is the city's oldest museum, founded in 1804 to preserve the city's historical and cultural artifacts. It was also New York's only public art museum until the Metropolitan Museum of Art was founded in the late 19th century. Though it's often overlooked by visitors tramping to the nearby American Museum of Natural History (p152), it shouldn't be, as its collection of more than 60,000 objects is as quirky and fascinating as NYC itself. Only here can you see 17th-century cowbells and baby rattles and the mounted wooden leg of colonial-era statesman Gouverneur Morris. The Henry Luce III Center for the Study of American Culture, which opened in 2000, is a 21,000-sq-ft showcase of more than 40,000 objects from the museum's permanent collection, and features items such as fine portraits, Tiffany lamps and model ships. The place always hosts unique special exhibits, too, with recent examples including 'Here is New York: Remembering 9/11' and 'Audubon's Aviary: Portraits of Endangered Species.'

CHILDREN'S MUSEUM OF MANHATTAN Map p153

☎ 212-721-1234; www.cmom.org; 212 W 83rd St btwn Amsterdam Ave & Broadway; adult & child over 1/senior $9/6, first Fri of the month 5-8pm free; ☺ 10am-5pm Tue-Sun; ◉ 1 to 86th St, B, C to 81st St-Museum of Natural History

Always crowded and not all that thrilling – though a perpetual rainy-day saver for neighborhood mommies – is this play center, where interactive exhibits are scaled down for little people. It features discovery centers for toddlers, a postmodern media center where technologically savvy kids can work in a TV studio, and the Inventor Center, where all the latest, cool tech stuff like digital imaging and scanners is made available. Expect the kids' stuff to be filtered through a sophisticated city lens, though, as recent exhibitions showed the art of Andy Warhol and shaped interactive art projects around the works of William Wegman, Elizabeth Murray and Fred Wilson. During summer months, kids can splash around with outdoor waterwheels and boats for lessons on buoyancy and currents. The museum also runs craft workshops on weekends and sponsors special exhibitions. (The Brooklyn Children's Museum, p193, is an affiliated children's museum.)

EXPLORING THE UPPER WEST SIDE
Walking Tour

1 Riverside Park Begin your walk in the lovely stretch of green called Riverside Park (opposite), on the western edge of the neighborhood. Be sure to visit the wonderful bronze statue of native New Yorker Eleanor Roosevelt, by sculptor Penelope Jencks, added to the park at 72nd St with some pomp and circumstance in 1996.

2 Lincoln Center Walk east on 72nd St and turn right on Broadway, heading downtown to 66th St and the grand entrance of Lincoln Center (p152), the vast campus of performance spaces. It's undergoing a major redesign, but is still worth taking a gander at – if only to catch a glimpse of the large and lovely Chagall paintings in the windows of the Metropolitan Opera House.

3 Dakota Head back up Columbus Ave to 72nd St and turn right, continuing east until you hit Central Park West. On your left you will see the grand Dakota, the exterior of which was used for the film *Rosemary's Baby*. It's also where John Lennon lived, and the site of his 1980 murder; his widow Yoko Ono still resides here. Across the street and just inside Central Park is Strawberry Fields (p148), a touching shrine to the late star.

4 New-York Historical Society Continue up along Central Park West to 77th St, where you'll come to the New-York Historical Society (left), a fascinating collection of city ephemera from both the distant and more recent pasts.

5 American Museum of Natural History One block north is the American Museum of Natural History (p152), filled with wildlife, geological and astronomical exhibits. If you don't feel like exploring it all now (it could take an entire day to see it all), at least gaze at the ethereal Rose Center for Earth & Space, on the 79th St side.

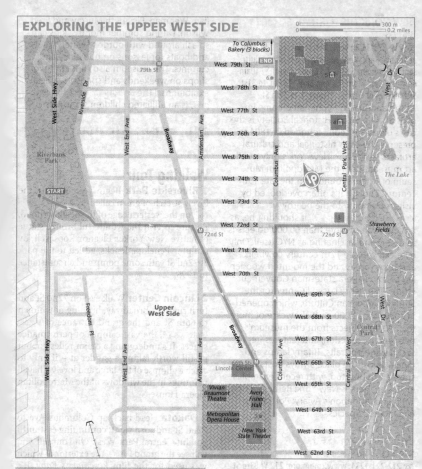

EXPLORING THE UPPER WEST SIDE

To Columbus Bakery (3 blocks)

END

West 79th St
West 78th St
West 77th St
West 76th St
West 75th St
West 74th St
West 73rd St
West 72nd St
West 71st St
West 70th St
West 69th St
West 68th St
West 67th St
West 66th St
West 65th St
West 64th St
West 63rd St
West 62nd St

Riverside Dr
West Side Hwy
West End Ave
Broadway
Amsterdam Ave
Columbus Ave
Central Park West
West Dr

Riverbank Park

START

Freedom Pl
Amsterdam Ave
West End Ave
West Side Hwy

Upper West Side

Broadway

66th St
Lincoln Center
Vivian Beaumont Theatre
Avery Fisher Hall
Metropolitan Opera House
New York State Theater

72nd St

The Lake

Strawberry Fields

Central Park

West Dr

0 ____ 300 m
0 ____ 0.2 miles

WALK FACTS

Start Riverside Park (1, 2, 3 to 72nd St)
End Columbus Ave (B, C at 81st St-Museum of Natural History, 1 at 79th St)
Distance 1.5 miles
Time One to two hours
Fuel stop Columbus Bakery

6 Columbus Avenue Head east to Columbus Avenue, where you can stroll the bustling stretch of shops and eateries and get a nice sense of the rhythm of life in this family-filled 'hood. If you're hungry, try Columbus Bakery (474 Columbus Ave at 83rd St), a casual café serving sandwiches, salads and scrumptious baked goods. If you're still up for more, try the Central Park walking tour (p151).

Drinking p296; Eating p266; Shopping p241; Sleeping p366

There's a whole other world north of the Upper West and Upper East Sides – one that's often ignored by more downtown-centric New Yorkers and visitors, but quite worthy of exploration, whether you're into parkland, historic sites, excellent music, ethnic foods or all of the above. The southernmost swatch of the island's top end is Harlem; East Harlem is filled primarily with Latino residents, while in the west you'll find Morningside Heights, home to Columbia University, p159; moving north from there will take you to sub-regions called Hamilton Heights & Sugar Hill and on to Washington Heights and Inwood. Strolling through Morningside Heights can feel like you've stumbled onto a very hip campus, as invigorated students and briefcase-toting professors alike gather in cafes and bookstores for intellectual tête-à-têtes. Washington Heights is mainly known for its large Dominican community, while Inwood comprises the northernmost tip of Manhattan. It's filled with peaceful blocks and edged by a mass of lovely waterfront parkland – and home to a lovely outpost of the Metropolitan Museum of Art, the Cloisters (p164).

Harlem eclipses its northern neighbors because of its famous history and recent 'renaissance.' From its origins as a 1920s African American enclave, the heart of black culture has always beat in this neighborhood north of Central Park; it has been the setting for extraordinary accomplishments in art, music, dance, education and letters, from the likes of Frederick Douglass, Paul Robeson, Thurgood Marshall, James Baldwin, Alvin Ailey, Billie Holiday, Jessie Jackson and many other African American luminaries. In recent years the big news here has been affordable real estate and the usual tensions of gentrification, which has been moving slowly but surely through this now-white-inclusive 'hood. It's also a great place to add to your touring agenda, for reasons cultural (museums, theaters, jazz, historic architecture and gospel churches) and gastronomical (Southern US fare at its best).

First-time visitors will probably be surprised to discover that Harlem is just one subway stop away from the 59th St-Columbus Circle station. The trip on the express A and D trains takes only five minutes, and both lines stop just one block from the Apollo Theater (p162) and two blocks from Malcolm X Blvd (Lenox Ave). Other areas of Harlem and Northern Manhattan are reached by the 1, A, B, C, D, 2, 3, 4, 5 and 6 trains.

MORNINGSIDE HEIGHTS

This area between the Upper West Side and Hamilton Heights area is generally the province of Columbia University, as is immediately evident from the scores of students and professors chilling in cafés like the Hungarian Pastry Shop (see the top picks, p265) – a classic favorite for the laptop-toting set – and darting to and from classes on the beautiful urban campus. But it's got other draws, too: namely, good bookstores, great park areas and some delicious new dining options. Morningside Heights extends north from 110th to 125th Sts, between St Nicholas Ave and the Hudson River. To get here by subway, take the 1 line to 110th or 116th Sts.

CATHEDRAL CHURCH OF ST JOHN THE DIVINE Map pp158–9

☎ 212-316-7540; www.stjohndivine.org; Amsterdam Ave at 112th St; ⏱ 7:30am-6pm; ◉ B, C, 1 to 110th St-Cathedral Pkwy

This is the largest place of worship in the US – and it's not done yet. When it's finally completed, the 601ft-long Episcopal cathedral will rank as the third-largest church in the world (after St Peter's Basilica in Rome and Our Lady of Peace at Yamoussoukro in Côte d'Ivoire). Design highlights include the Great Rose Window, the largest stained-glass window in the country, and the Great Organ, which dates from 1911 and was due to be returned and ready for playing after being silenced by smoke damage during a devastating church fire in 2001. At this writing, a five-year cleaning and restoration project was scheduled to end soon, so you can expect to see this beauty and its 8035 pipes.

To pay for its unending construction and repair projects, the cathedral has recently entered into some controversial deals with various devils – otherwise known as developers. One project involves working with Columbia University, which holds an option to lease and develop an academic building on the north site of the cathedral's 11.3-acre campus. The other partnership is with AvalonBay Communities, a condominium

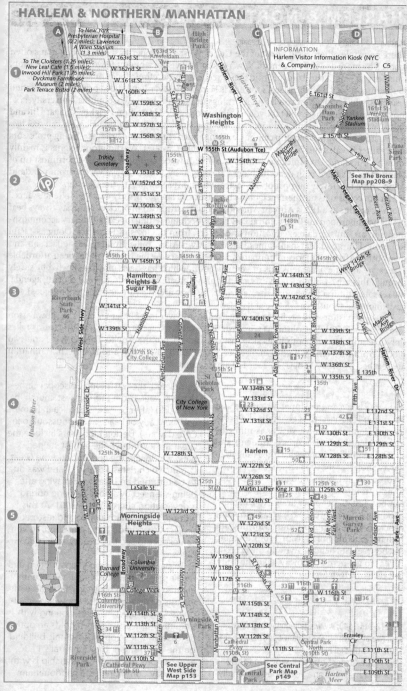

See Upper East Side Map p142

developer with ubiquitous projects in regions across the country. It recently entered into a 99-year lease with the cathedral, and plans to construct various residential buildings on the south side of the property.

Controversies aside, St John the Divine is a flourishing place of worship and community activity. Holiday concerts, lectures and memorial services for famous New Yorkers take place here. Two quirky services worth seeing are the annual Blessing of the Animals, a pilgrimage for pet owners that's held on the first Sunday of October, and the Blessing of the Bikes, on May 1, which draws helmeted folks with clunkers, sleek 10-speeds and mountain bikes. There's a Poet's Corner to the left of the front entrance but, unlike at Westminster Abbey in London, no one is actually buried here. Also see the altar designed and built by the late Keith Haring, a popular artist in the 1980s pop-art world.

Other sights are the whimsical Children's Sculpture Garden on the south side, and the Biblical Garden, containing plants that are historically correct for the era, out back. An intriguing Ecology Trail wends its way through the cathedral and its grounds, tracing the creation cycles (birth, life, death and rebirth) from a multicultural perspective. Cathedral tours (per person $5) are offered at 11am and 1pm Tuesday to Saturday and at 1pm on Sunday.

COLUMBIA UNIVERSITY Map pp158–9

☎ 212-854-1754; www.columbia.edu; Broadway at 116th St; ◉ 1 to 116th St-Columbia University
One of the top academic research universities in the world, Columbia includes three undergraduate schools, 13 graduate and professional schools and a school of continuing education. It conducts groundbreaking studies in the fields of medicine, science, the arts and humanities, and is known for having a student body that thrives on demonstrations and political involvement (as was evidenced to the world during the controversial 2008 campus visit by Iranian president Mahmoud Ahmadinejad). The university, located between 114th and 121st Sts, and the independent, but affiliated, Barnard College (located across Broadway), moved from lower Manhattan to this site in 1897, as their founders wanted a spot that was far removed from the downtown bustle. Today, the neighborhood has enveloped Columbia's gated

campus with great vigor, but the school's main courtyard, with its statue Alma Mater perched on the steps of Low Library, is still a beautifully quiet place to take some sun and read a book. Hamilton Hall, south of the main thoroughfare College Walk on the Amsterdam Ave side, was the site of the infamous student takeover in 1968, and has been the place for periodic protests and plenty of wild student parties since then. The university also offers endless opportunities for doses of culture through its itinerary of top-notch events; check the school's website or bulletin boards around campus to find out about readings, film screenings, dance and theater performances, art exhibits and sports competitions (see p327).

RIVERSIDE CHURCH Map pp158–9
☎ 212-870-6700; www.theriversidechurchny.org; 490 Riverside Dr at 120th St; ⏱ 7am-10pm; ⊕ 1 to 116th St-Columbia University
Built by the Rockefeller family in 1930, this Gothic beauty overlooks the Hudson River, and in good weather you can climb 355ft to the observation deck for expansive river views. The church rings its 74 carillon bells, the largest grouping in the world, with an extraordinary 20-ton bass bell (also the world's largest), at noon and 3pm on Sunday. Interdenominational services are held at 10:45am on Sunday, and there are frequent high-quality events such as concerts and lectures held here, many with an activist, multi-culti, queer-friendly and anti-war bent.

GENERAL ULYSSES S GRANT NATIONAL MEMORIAL Map pp158–9
☎ 212-666-1640; www.nps.gov/gegr; Riverside Dr at 122nd St; admission free; ⏱ 9am-5pm; ⊕ 1 to 125th St
Popularly known as Grant's Tomb ('Who's buried in Grant's Tomb?' 'Who?' 'Grant, stupid!' goes a classic gotcha joke), this landmark holds the remains of Civil War hero and 18th president Ulysses S Grant and his wife, Julia. Completed in 1897 – 12 years after his death – the granite structure cost $600,000 to build and is the largest mausoleum in the country. Though it plagiarizes Mausolus' tomb at Halicarnassus, this version doesn't qualify as one of the Seven Wonders of the World. The building languished as a graffiti-scarred mess for years until Grant's relatives shamed the National

Park Service into cleaning it up by threatening to move his body elsewhere.

MORNINGSIDE PARK Map pp158–9
www.morningsidepark.org; 110th to 123rd Sts btwn Manhattan Ave, Morningside Ave & Morningside Dr
The park that gives this neighborhood its name is a lovely, 13-block finger of green that has much to recommend it. In the region behind the Cathedral Church of St John the Divine you'll find a pond and waterfall, and walking north from here will lead you to several public sculpture memorials, including the Seligman (Bear and Faun) Fountain (1914) by Edgar White and the Carl Schurz Memorial (1913) by Carl Bitter and Henry Bacon. Other draws are playgrounds, shaded pathways and the lush Dr Thomas Kiel Arboretum, near 116th St. An ongoing revitalization of the park by neighborhood activists makes the once-scruffy park look better and better each year.

HARLEM

More than a decade ago, two catalysts spurred the rebirth of this neighborhood that had been all but left for dead by much of the city: the entire neighborhood was declared an Economic Redevelopment Zone in 1996, and shortly thereafter, foreign tourists began flocking here to check out the area's music and spiritual scene. Now there's another big plan afoot: the rezoning of 125th St, a sweeping proposal that seeks to transform this artery into a corridor of hotels, bookstores, nightclubs and high-rise condos. It's controversial in the neighborhood, as the plan would surely force many longtime businesses out and, many fear, turn the iconic street into the kind of cookie-cutter strip that's ubiquitous throughout today's Manhattan. Though the city promises it will not be a generic redevelopment, only time will tell.

Meanwhile, today's Harlem has a tourism business that has attracted buckets of dollars – and with it, double-decker tour buses and disrespectful crowds clamoring for pews at Sunday services. Cheap rents for amazing spaces have also given rise to a gay (and very white) ghetto, and tensions between the old and new residents are always in the air, as a balance that benefits everyone has yet to be struck.

In this 'hood – bordered roughly by 125th St to the south and 155th to the north –

you'll notice that the major avenues have been renamed in honor of prominent African Americans; however, many locals still call the streets by their original names, which makes finding your way around a little confusing. Eighth Ave (the continuation of Central Park West) is Frederick Douglass Blvd. Seventh Ave is Adam Clayton Powell Jr Blvd, named for the controversial preacher who served in Congress during the 1960s. Lenox Ave has been renamed for the Nation of Islam leader Malcolm X. The main avenue and site of many businesses, 125th St is also known as Martin Luther King Jr Blvd. Walking in Harlem can be quite tiring as the sights are pretty spread out and subway stations are few and far between; up here the crosstown buses can be handier than the train. The newly relocated Harlem Visitor Information Kiosk (Map pp158–9; ☎ 917-572-9838; 2037 Fifth Ave btwn 125th & 126th Sts; ☒ 10am-6pm) is a great source for tips, directions and history.

ABYSSINIAN BAPTIST CHURCH
Map pp158–9

☎ 212-862-7474; www.abyssinian.org; 132 Odell Clark Pl (138th St) btwn Adam Clayton Powell Jr & Malcolm X Blvds; ☒ services 9am, 11am Sun; ☻ 2, 3 to 135th St

Founded by an Ethiopian businessman, the Abyssinian Baptist Church began as a downtown institution but moved north to Harlem in 1923, mirroring the migration of the city's black population. Its charismatic pastor, Calvin O Butts III, is an important community activist whose support is sought by politicians of all parties. The church has a superb choir and the building is a beauty. If you plan on visiting with a group of 10 or more, the congregation requests that you call in advance to see if space is available.

MALCOLM SHABAZZ HARLEM MARKET Map pp158–9

☎ 212-987-8131; 52 W 116th St btwn Malcolm X Blvd & Fifth Ave; ☒ 10am-5pm; ☻ 2, 3 to 116th St

Vendors at the semi-enclosed Harlem Market, which sprawls across a large lot, do a brisk business selling tribal masks, oils, drums, traditional clothing and other assorted African bric-a-brac. You can also purchase cheap clothing, leather goods, music cassettes and bootleg videos of films that are still in first-run movie theaters. The market is operated by the nearby Malcolm

Shabazz Mosque, the former pulpit of slain Muslim orator Malcolm X.

SCHOMBURG CENTER FOR RESEARCH IN BLACK CULTURE
Map pp158–9

☎ 212-491-2200; www.nypl.org/research/sc; 515 Malcolm X Blvd at 135th St; admission free; ☒ noon-8pm Mon-Wed, to 5pm Thu-Sat; ☻ 2, 3 to 135th St

The nation's largest collection of documents, rare books, recordings and photographs relating to the African American experience resides at this center near W 135th St. Arthur Schomburg, who was born in Puerto Rico, started gathering works on black history during the early 20th century while becoming active in the movements for civil rights and Puerto Rican independence. His impressive collection was purchased by the Carnegie Foundation and eventually expanded and stored in this branch of the New York Public Library. Lectures and concerts are regularly held in the theater here. Also onsite is the recently acquired Black Gay and Lesbian Archive, a collection of books, letters, photographs and various other artifacts related to black LGBT history.

STUDIO MUSEUM IN HARLEM
Map pp158–9

☎ 212-864-4500; www.studiomuseum.org; 144 W 125th St at Adam Clayton Powell Jr Blvd; suggested donation adult/senior & student $7/3; ☒ noon-6pm Wed-Fri & Sun, 10am-6pm Sat; ☻ 2, 3 to 125th St

This showcase, a leading benefactor and promoter of African American artists for three decades, provides work and exhibition spaces for the up and coming. Its photography collection includes works by James VanDerZee, the photographer who chronicled the Harlem renaissance of the 1920s and '30s, and rotating shows feature exhibits from emerging artists in forms from painting and sculpture to video and tattoo work. Recent shows have included 'The World of Charles Ethan Porter: 19th-Century African American Artist' and 'Flow,' which focused on art by a new generation of international artists from Africa.

EAST HARLEM

Also known colloquially as Spanish Harlem or El Barrio, this is one of the biggest Latino communities in the city, and extends from

Fifth Ave to the East River above 96th St, situated to the north of the Upper East Side. Interesting stops include El Museo del Barrio (p142) and Frawley Circle (Map p142) – with a statue of jazzman Duke Ellington and his piano – at the edge of the park, where Fifth Ave and Central Park North (also known as Tito Puente Way) converge. Though La Marqueta (Map pp158–9; Park Ave btwn 112th & 115th Sts), a bustling collection of 200 vendors selling everything from tropical fruits to religious items, was the pride of the local Puerto Rican community for decades since WWII, it's recently dwindled into a calm collection of only eight vendors. All that could change in a big way, though, if a Bloomberg-proposed development project proceeds as planned. Spearheaded by the East Harlem Business Capital Corporation, the far-reaching plans call for a $20 million revival of La Marqueta, with new construction that will make way for an 85,000-sq-ft international market with pan-Latin shops, cafés and restaurants. It's years (and dollars) behind, though. So for now, stopping in and out of the many cafés and *botanicas* (religious shops carrying items such as candles and spiritual herbs) in the vicinity is a great way to find your own market adventures.

EL MUSEO DEL BARRIO Map p142
☎ 212-831-7272; www.elmuseo.org; 1230 Fifth Ave btwn 104th & 105th Sts; suggested donation adult/child/senior & student $6/free/4; 11am-5pm Wed-Sun; ⊜ 6 to 103rd St
The best starting point for exploring Spanish Harlem, this museum began in 1969 as a celebration of Puerto Rican art and culture. It has since expanded into the premiere Latino cultural institution in the city, with a dizzying collection that includes 2000 pre-Columbian ceremonial objects, 900 traditional objects from countries including Brazil and Haiti, more than 3000 Puerto Rican prints and posters, and contemporary paintings and sculptures from artists including Raul Farco, Marcos Dimas and Pepon Osorio. The film and video collection has some rare footage of life in El Barrio from the 1970s to the present, along with educational materials from Puerto Rico. Photographs document life in Puerto Rico during the Depression as well as some of the early years of Latin American migration to the US.

Temporary exhibits are a particular draw, as past showings have focused on the works of big names including Diego Rivera and Frida Kahlo, as well as themed exhibits such as 'Arte ≠ Vida: Actions by Artists of the Americas, 1960-2000' and 'The Disappeared / Los Desaparecidos,' which brought together visual responses to the tens of thousands of people who were kidnapped, killed and 'vanished' by Latin American dictatorships from the 1950s to '80s.

GRAFFITI HALL OF FAME Map p142
106th St btwn Madison & Park Aves; ⊜ 6 to 103rd St
A schoolyard that celebrates all sorts of taggers, this art gallery of the street was founded in 1980 by graffiti artist Ray Rodriguez (aka Sting Ray) and a group of community-minded supporters who saw the lasting value in an art that some politicians and business-owners tend to view as vandalism. You can visit the colorful murals at any time, though the actual Graffiti Hall of Fame event, which is when 'writers' come from all over the globe to add their art to the walls, is held in late June. For updates check the website Streets are Saying Things (www.streetsaresayingthings.com), run by a Hall of Fame organizer and a good source of graffiti-related news.

APOLLO THEATER
The Apollo Theater (Map pp158–9; ☎ 212-531-5337; www.apollotheater.com; 253 W 125th St at Frederick Douglass Blvd; admission $16 Mon-Fri, $18 Sat & Sun; tours 11am, 1pm, 3pm Mon, Tue, Thu, Fri, 11am Wed, 11am & 1pm Sat & Sun; ⊜ A, B, C, D to 125th St) has been Harlem's leading space for concerts and political rallies since 1914. Virtually every major black artist of note in the 1930s and '40s performed here, including Duke Ellington and Charlie Parker. After a desultory spell as a movie theater and several years of darkness, the Apollo was bought in 1983 and revived as a live venue. It eventually fell into disrepair again, but now, after the completion of an extensive renovation, the Apollo is more beautiful than ever, as it finally has a restored facade, marquee, glass-and-steel storefront and brand-new box office. Its famous weekly Amateur Night – 'where stars are born and legends are made' – still takes place on Wednesday, with a wild and ruthless crowd that's as fun to watch as the performers. On other nights, the Apollo hosts performances by established artists like Stevie Wonder and Joe Jackson.

HAMILTON HEIGHTS & SUGAR HILL

This area, basically an extension of Harlem that stretches from about 138th to 155th Sts west of Edgecombe Ave, is loaded with off-the-beaten path delights, including the legendary Rucker Park (Map pp158–9; W 155th St at Frederick Douglass Blvd; ◑ B, D to 155th St), home to some of the most exciting street-ball games (p325) in the city (along with the W 4th St courts in the Village). Die-hard basketball fans will want to check out the place where players as big as (pre-scandal) Kobe Bryant have even stopped in for some hoops. Sweet. And how appropriate, considering that Sugar Hill got its name by being considered the place to live the 'sweet life' during the Harlem Renaissance. (And playing hoops, to many, is high culture for sure.)

HAMILTON GRANGE Map pp158–9

☎ 212-283-5154; www.nps.gov/hagr; 141st St at St Nicholas Ave; admission free; ◷ call for more info; ◑ A, B, C, D to 145th St
(Note that this site was closed for renovations at time of writing.) Recently moved from nearby Convent Ave with a plan to reopen sometime in 2009 is what was, once upon a time, founding-father Alex-

ander Hamilton's original country retreat. Hamilton Heights was named for him, as he owned a farm and estate up here in 1802. When the Federal-style home was moved to this too-small spot from its original location, it had to be turned on its side and squeezed to fit between two buildings, so now the facade actually faces inward, making it an even more curious sight to behold. Nearby, the Hamilton Heights Historic District stretches along Convent Ave from 140th to 145th Sts: this gorgeous lineup is one of the last remaining stretches of untouched limestone and brownstone town houses in New York City. To the south, the neo-Gothic City College of New York campus (which has architectural marvels of its own) spreads down to 130th St.

STRIVERS' ROW Map pp158–9

W 138th & 139th Sts btwn Frederick Douglass & Adam Clayton Powell Jr Blvds; ◑ B, C to 135th St
Also known as the St Nicholas Historic District, Strivers' Row is so named because it was where the folks aiming to be the most successful in Harlem resided in the 1920s and '30s. Its prized row-houses and apartments, many designed by the ubiquitous McKim, Mead and White firm in the 1890s,

were distinguished additions to the neighborhood; when white residents moved out of the area, Harlem's black elite moved in. Among them, at some point or another, were architect Vertner Tandy, composer WC Handy, jazz pianist Fletcher Henderson and heavyweight contender Harry Wills. Today it's one of the most visited blocks in Harlem, so lay low, as the locals are a bit sick of gawking tourists. Plaques explain more of the area's history, while excellent alleyway signs advise visitors to 'walk your horses.'

WASHINGTON HEIGHTS & INWOOD

Located near the northern tip of Manhattan (above 155th St), Washington Heights takes its name from the first president of the US, who set up a Continental Army fort here during the Revolutionary War. An isolated rural spot until the end of the 19th century, Washington Heights has attracted lots of new blood as New Yorkers have been sniffing out its affordable rents over the past several years. Still, this neighborhood manages to retain its Latino (mainly Dominican) flavor, and now what you'll find is an interesting mix of blocks that alternate between hipster expat-downtowners and long-time residents who operate within a tight and warm community.

Inwood is at Manhattan's northern tip, from about 175th St up, and has drawn folks from downtown with its cheaper real estate, much of which offers great views of the Hudson River. Its most sparkling jewels are the Cloisters (below), an uptown, partially alfresco branch of the Met that's perched high on a hill overlooking the Hudson River, and the huge waterfront Inwood Hill Park (right), which offers a great escape between the local neighborhood and the start of the Bronx (p207).

CLOISTERS off Map pp158–9
☎ 212-923-3700; www.metmuseum.org; Fort Tryon Park; suggested donation adult/child/senior & student $20/free/10; ☒ 9:30am-4:45pm Tue-Sun Nov-Feb, to 5:15pm Mar-Oct; ◉ A to 190th St
The Met is a beautiful place to visit on any day, but if it's just too gorgeous to be indoors, you might consider heading to its outside annex instead. Set in Fort Tryon Park overlooking the Hudson River, the Cloisters museum, built in the 1930s, incorporates fragments of old French and Spanish monasteries, and houses the

Metropolitan Museum of Art's collection of medieval frescoes, tapestries and paintings. Summer is the best time to visit, when concerts take place in the grounds and more than 250 varieties of medieval flowers and herbs are on view.

Works are set in galleries – connected by grand archways and topped with Moorish terra-cotta roofs – that sit around an airy courtyard. Among the many rare treasures you'll get to gaze at are a 9th-century gold plaque of St John the Evangelist, ancient stained-glass panels depicting historic religious scenes, an English-made ivory sculpture of the Virgin and Child dating from 1290, and the stunning 12th-century Saint-Guilhem Cloister, made of French limestone and standing 30ft high.

INWOOD HILL PARK off Map pp158–9
Dyckman St at the Hudson River; ◉ A to Inwood-207th St
This gorgeous 197-acre park contains the last natural forest and salt marsh in Manhattan. It's a cool escape in summer and a great place to explore anytime, as you'll find hilly paths for hiking and mellow, grassy patches and benches for quiet contemplation. It's so peaceful and un-urban here, in fact, that the treetops serve as frequent nesting sites for bald eagles. You'll also find helpful rangers and a slew of educational programs, many geared toward children, at the Inwood Park Nature Center (☎ 212-304-2365; 218th St at Indian Rd; ☒ 11am-4pm Wed-Sun). Let your sporty side rip on basketball courts, horseback riding trails, and soccer and football fields; you can also join locals who barbecue at designated grills on summer weekends. The views of New Jersey and the Bronx from high points in the forest are wonderful.

HISPANIC SOCIETY OF AMERICA
Map pp158–9
☎ 212-926-2234; www.hispanicsociety.org; Broadway at 155th St; admission free; ☒ 10am-4:30pm Tue-Sat, 1-4pm Sun; ◉ 1 to 157th St
Housed in a two-level, ornately carved Beaux-Arts space hung with gold-and-silk tapestries, the Society lives on the serene street called Audubon Terrace (155th St), where naturalist John James Audubon once lived. Open since 1908, this is where you'll find the largest collection of Spanish art and manuscripts outside

of Spain – including a substantial collection of works by El Greco, Goya, Diego Velázquez and the formidable Joaquín Sorolla y Bastida, as well as a library with over 25,000 volumes. Head upstairs for a bird's-eye view of the lovely courtyard and its *El Cid* sculpture. All signage and brochures are in English and Spanish.

MORRIS-JUMEL MANSION Map pp158–9

☎ 212-923-8008; www.morrisjumel.org; 65 Jumel Tce at 160th St; adult/senior, student & child $4/3; ☯ 10am-4pm Wed-Sun, other times by appt; ◉ C to 163rd St-Amsterdam Ave

Built in 1765, the columned Morris-Jumel Mansion is the oldest house on the island of Manhattan. It first served as the headquarters of George Washington's Continental Army. After the war it again became a country house for Stephen Jumel and his wife Eliza, who had a somewhat sordid past – and future, as after Jumel died, she married Vice President Aaron Burr, with whom she was allegedly having an affair. Rumor has it that Eliza's ghost still flits about the place. A designated landmark, with grounds that are particularly attractive during spring, the mansion's interior contains many of the original furnishings, including a bed that reputedly belonged to Napoleon. Guided tours (per person $5) of the house are available on Saturday at noon.

You'll find other historic houses nearby on Jumel Terrace, including the fine limestone structure at No 16, which was once the home of a noted renaissance man, actor-activist-athlete-singer Paul Robeson.

DYCKMAN FARMHOUSE MUSEUM
off Map pp158–9

☎ 212-304-9422; www.dyckmanfarmhouse .org; 4881 Broadway at 204th St; admission $1; ☯ 11am-4pm Wed-Sat, noon-4pm Sun; ◉ A to Inwood-207th St

Built in 1784 on a 28-acre farm, the Dyckman House is Manhattan's lone surviving Dutch farmhouse – and is better than ever following an extensive renovation. Excavations of the property have turned up valuable clues about colonial life, and the museum includes period rooms and furniture, decorative arts, a half-acre of gardens and an exhibition on the neighborhood's history. To get to the Dyckman House, take the subway to the Inwood-207th St station (*not* Dyckman St) and walk one block south.

HARLEM & NORTHERN MANHATTAN
Walking Tour

1 Riverbank State Park From 145th St station, head west, eventually crossing a footbridge to get to Riverbank State Park (http://nysparks .state.ny.us). This 28-acre, landscaped area, perched high above the Hudson River, has ball courts, swimming pools, greenspace and an ice-skating rink in winter. You'd never even know it's built atop a sewage treatment plant.

2 Hamilton Grange Head back the way you came, and at Convent Ave you'll see the turn-of-the-last-century, Queen Anne–style townhouses that make up the Hamilton

HARLEM & NORTHERN MANHATTAN

Heights Historic District. Near the corner of 141st St, stop into the free-admission Hamilton Grange (p163) to see the home of the man on the $10 bill.

3 Strivers' Row Make a left onto 141st St and then a right onto Frederick Douglass Blvd, which will take you to Strivers' Row (p163), on the blocks of 139th and 138th Sts. Filled with 1890s townhouses, this part of Harlem got its nickname in the 1920s, when aspiring African Americans first moved here.

4 Abyssinian Baptist Church West of Adam Clayton Powell Jr Blvd on 138th St, the unsigned Abyssinian Baptist Church (p161) has its origins in 1808, when a Lower Manhattan church was formed by African Americans in response to segregated services. Its previous pastor, Adam Clayton Powell Jr, became the first African American congressional representative in 1944.

5 Mother African Methodist Episcopal Zion Church Around the corner on 137th St, you'll see the city's oldest African American church (originally in Lower Manhattan), the Mother African Methodist Episcopal Zion Church (see the boxed text, p163). The church played an important role in the Abolitionists' cause by helping to establish the Underground Railroad in the mid-1800s.

6 Harlem YMCA Walk south on Adam Clayton Powell Jr Blvd to 135th St. The Harlem YMCA (181 W 135th St), here since 1919, provided rooms for many newly arrived African Americans who were denied a room in segregated hotels elsewhere (including James Baldwin, Jackie Robinson and Malcolm X). Note the 'YMCA' in neon atop the tower. Just past the Y there are public b-ball courts with a mural that claims that 'Harlem plays the best ball in the country.'

7 Schomburg Center for Research in Black Culture Head just a block east to see

While Manhattan may be the center of the universe for most New York City visitors, for many locals, it can have a range of identities – workplace, clubland, shopping center or place of unattainable real estate, to name a few. That's because those folks make their home in one of the four outer boroughs: Brooklyn, Queens, the Bronx or Staten Island. While they all have certain aspects in common, like being calmer, more residential, more affordable and more diverse than their central counterpart, each is really quite different from the next, both in theory and reality.

Brooklyn, for example, is definitely the coolest – for some people, its hip factor has superseded that of Manhattan for years – and it's seen many of its neighborhoods rapidly gentrify, pulling in young folks with cheaper rents, sprouting pockets of destination restaurants and bars and drawing crowds of trendseekers from all over the city. Brooklyn is the home of storied nabes like Williamsburg, Park Slope and Dumbo, where art galleries, edgy theaters and amazing eclectic eats are never far away. It's also where you'll find historic Coney Island, ethnic pockets like Bay Ridge and Crown Heights, and chic blocks lined with brownstones and trees in places like Brooklyn Heights and Carroll Gardens. It's also the most populous of the five boroughs.

Queens, which also has its share of hipster enclaves – Long Island City and Astoria among them – is the largest of the boroughs, and is most known for its sheer diversity. It's got communities where you'll be challenged to hear English, as it's home to immigrants from around the world – Korea, India, South America, you name it – and thus it's your best bet for ferreting out amazing (and hard to find) ethnic eats. But Queens is also home to many wonderful museums, from the home of Corona resident Louis Armstrong to the recently renovated American Museum of the Moving Image, which is dedicated to the joy of film.

The Bronx, which sits on the mainland above the top of Manhattan like a massive wig, has an astoundingly diverse array of neighborhoods and topography – parkland, ocean beaches, hilly greenspaces, suburb-like residential enclaves, crumbling ghettos and the largest concentration of Irish immigrants in the city. Finally, there's Staten Island – the city's punching bag, a suburban city section if ever there was one. Traditionally conservative and segregated, the place seems to have more in common with its neighbor New Jersey than with the rest of NYC. Still, it's a borough for sure – and one with its own set of perks, from beautiful beaches and parklands to some seriously good cuisine. Let that be a reminder of how far the borders of this unbeatable city really stretch.

the archives and photos at the Schomburg Center for Research in Black Culture (p161).

8 Home of Langston Hughes Continue east to Fifth Ave and go south to 127th St, where turning left will get you to the last home of poet Langston Hughes (20 E 127th St), who died in 1967.

9 Marcus Garvey Park From here continue east and head south along Madison Ave to 124th St and Marcus Garvey Park, named for the Jamaica-born founder of the 'Back to Africa' movement who lived in Harlem from 1916 to 1927. There's a nice view from the fire watchtower on the central hill. From here head west on 125th St and north just slightly on Lenox Ave, where you'll find the famous Sylvia's (☎ 212-996-0660; 328 Lenox Ave; ☉ breakfast, lunch & dinner), the legendary family-owned soul

food restaurant that has grown to mythic proportions since its opening in 1962. You might be able to spot it by the tour buses parked up front.

10 Studio Museum in Harlem Back on 125th St and continuing west, stop at the Studio Museum in Harlem (p161), just across from the rather out-of-place State Office Building, built in 1973.

11 Apollo Theater Further west on 125th St is the historic Apollo Theater (p162), which hosts many performances, including Wednesday Amateurs Night. If your timing's right, head in for a historic tour of the place. Opposite the theater you'll see the sign for Blumstein's, a (now closed) store that finally began hiring African Americans following an eight-week boycott in 1934.

Drinking p296; Eating p268; Shopping p242; Sleeping p367

You have to go to Brooklyn this time. It's New York's most buzzing borough – with new buildings, parks, bars, restaurants, hotels and live venues popping up at a Manhattan-like pace. Not long ago, places like Red Hook, Fort Greene, Carroll Gardens – and even Williamsburg or Park Slope – were unknowns; now they're household names for New York's scenester crowd.

But Brooklyn's not all just 21st-century cool – you share the sidewalks with a diverse mix of locals who've loved the place for generations. As a visiting British soldier explained to the *New York Times* in 2007 about why he chose a Brooklyn dive bar during a short visit: 'You go to Manhattan to see the tourist things. But you go to Brooklyn to see the people.' Indeed, visiting Brooklyn is less about traditional 'sights' to see – outside the Brooklyn Heights Promenade (see below), Coney Island's boardwalk (p195) or perhaps the Brooklyn Museum (p184), you could argue that Queens or the Bronx has more vital 'attractions.' Brooklyn's more about diving into a residential neighborhood, exchanging a 'hello' with passersby perhaps, browsing new designers' small boutiques and having a bite to eat.

Unlike Manhattan, it's not that plausible to consider connecting many areas by foot. Like the other outer boroughs, Brooklyn's bigger, and neighboring areas are sometimes separated by un-fun avenues and industrial wastelands. It's often best to treat time in Brooklyn on a 'plus-one' method – go to the Brooklyn Heights Promenade for the views, then walk south to Boerum Hill and Cobble Hill afterwards, or perhaps visit the Brooklyn Museum and Prospect Park, then finish it off with a drink or meal on Park Slope's Fifth Ave. Take the subway to Bushwick for brunch, then walk back through what will be the next cool neighborhood to reach Williamsburg's record shops and bars. We've organized this section from the top down, starting with the northwestern entry point at Brooklyn Heights, then covering neighborhoods around it gradually, like chocolate melting over an ice-cream scoop. If you only have a day, it's not enough for much, but it's a start.

While you're exploring, listen for the lingo. Seeping into all boroughs, the glamorized working-class 'New York accent' is sometimes just called 'Brooklynese' – the popular amalgam of Italian, Yiddish, Caribbean, Spanish and even Dutch influences on English: 'da' for 'the', 'hoid' for 'heard', 'dowahg' for 'dog', 'tree' for 'three' and 'fugehdabboudit' for 'forget about it, kind sir.'

A few good Brooklyn blogs include www.freewilliamsburg.com, www.brownstoner.com and www.gowanuslounge.blogspot.com.

For more on Brooklyn, see our color feature on p186.

Orientation & Information

Located across the East River from Lower Manhattan and the Lower East Side and spreading southeast across the western end of Long Island, Brooklyn is not entirely made up of the north–south/east–west grid that makes getting around Manhattan such a breeze. This is most evident in its northern, more historic 'hoods, which are cut by diagonal roads sometimes linked to old Native American trails; one is Flatbush Ave, which connects the Manhattan Bridge with Jamaica Bay. Brooklyn's northern border with Queens begins at Newtown Creek, off the East River, then follows a jagged path east and south to Jamaica Bay, just west of JFK Airport. Brooklyn's west gets more water views, facing New York Harbor to the west and the Atlantic Ocean to the south.

In downtown Brooklyn, the Brooklyn Tourism & Visitors Center (Map p174; ☎ 718-802-3846; www.brook lyntourism.org; 209 Joralemon St; ☺ 10am-6pm Mon-Fri, plus 10am-4pm Sat in summer; ☺ 2, 3, 4, 5 to Borough Hall) has various info and sells a two-day Brooklyn Pass (www.brooklynpass.com; adult/child $25/15) that includes entry to many Brooklyn attractions.

BROOKLYN HEIGHTS

New York's oldest unchanged neighborhood, and its first designated historic district, Brooklyn Heights is, for some fogeys, what 'New York used to look like.' In the Brooklyn Heights Historic District, 19th-century brownstones of many architectural styles (Victorian Gothic, Romanesque, neo-Greco, Italianate etc) sit on quiet, tree-lined streets – some named for fruit or trees in an effort not to canonize any particular arriving migrants by name. Long gone, however, are the days when literary folks came for the cheaper housing: Thomas Wolfe wrote *Of Times and the River* in his home at 5 Montague Terrace (Map p174), while Truman Capote wrote *Breakfast at Tiffany's* at 70 Willow St (Map p174).

In the mid-19th century, Henry Ward Beecher led abolitionist sermons – and 'mock auctions' to buy a slave's freedom – at the Plymouth Church (Map p174; Orange St btwn Henry & Hicks Sts), which dates from 1849. Beecher's statue outside was created by Gutzon Borglum of Mount Rushmore fame.

All east–west lanes head to the neighborhood's number-one attraction: the Brooklyn Heights Promenade (Map p174), which hangs over the Brooklyn–Queens Expressway (BQE), offering amazing views of Lower Manhattan and New York Harbor. It will also be the place to see construction, just beneath, of the controversial waterfront Brooklyn Bridge Park (see the boxed text, p175) through 2009.

Namedropped in Bob Dylan's 'Tangled Up in Blue,' Montague Street is a rather gentrified main strip of the Heights, with a host of restaurants (Mexican, Indian, Turkish, Japanese etc). Years ago pedestrians had to watch out for streetcars rattling down the street, inspiring the borough's baseball team's name: the Brooklyn Dodgers.

top picks

OUTER BOROUGHS

- Bronx Zoo (p210) As zoos go, it's one of the best, with landmark buildings, sea-lion feeds, and the new Madagascar exhibit.
- Coney Island (p195) See the last of its still-gritty heart before Disneyfication comes.
- On the Waterfront The (changing) waterfront has the city's best harbor views, particularly around Brooklyn Heights (p172).
- Prospect Park (p181) Brooklyn's proud sequel to Central Park teems with soccer games and picnics.
- 7 Train (p202) Head off on the 'purple line' to reach Queens' diverse neighborhoods.

BROOKLYN HISTORICAL SOCIETY
Map p174

☎ 718-222-4111; www.brooklynhistory.org; 128 Pierrepont St; adult/child/student $6/free/4; ⊙ 10am-5pm Wed-Sun; Ⓜ M, R to Court St, 2, 3, 4, 5 to Borough Hall, A, C to High St
The place to go for Brooklyn's past, this 1881 Queen Anne–style landmark building (a gem in itself) houses a library and

TRANSPORTATION: BROOKLYN

Sixteen subway lines crisscross between Manhattan and Brooklyn, and the G line goes between Brooklyn and Queens. Here are a few useful stops, broken down by neighborhood:

Bay Ridge R to 77th St, 86th St or Bay Ridge-95th St

Bedford-Stuyvesant C to Kingston-Throop Aves

Bensonhurst D, M to 18th Ave

Boerum Hill F, G to Bergen St; A, C, G to Hoyt-Schermerhorn Sts

Brighton Beach B, Q to Brighton Beach

Brooklyn Heights 2, 3 to Clark St

Carroll Gardens F, G to Carroll St

Cobble Hill F, G to Bergen St

Coney Island D, F, N, Q to Coney Island-Stillwell Ave

Downtown 2, 3, 4, 5 to Borough Hall; A, C, F to Jay St-Borough Hall; M, R to Court St

Dumbo F to York St; A, C to High St

Fort Greene B, M, Q, R to DeKalb Ave; C to Lafayette Ave

Park Slope F to 7th Ave; B, Q, 2, 3, 4, 5 to Atlantic Ave; 2, 3 to Bergen St

Prospect Heights B, Q to 7th Ave; 2, 3 to Eastern Parkway-Brooklyn Museum

Prospect Park 2, 3 to Grand Army Plaza; B, Q to Prospect Park

Red Hook F to Carroll St, then bus B61

Williamsburg L to Bedford Ave

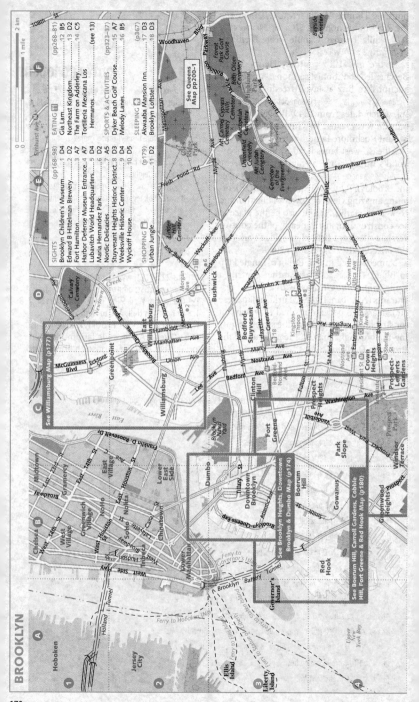

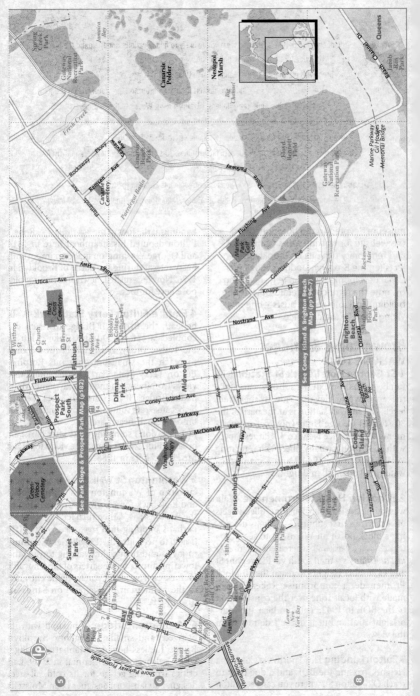

museum devoted to the borough. Check the website for walking tours (some free) and temporary exhibits on Brooklyn subjects (eg the Brooklyn Dodgers, Gowanus Canal development). If you're just walking by, note the terra-cotta details outside the building, including eight busts – one of a Viking – above the entrance.

Brownstones & Bridges
WALKING TOUR

1 St George Hotel/Clark St Station The fun begins as you exit the subway – and take the apocalyptic elevator ride to the street level. The subway station is at the base of the 30-story St George Hotel (now co-op apartments). It was once New York's largest hotel, with 2632 rooms (many filled with returning WWII vets in the 1940s) and a giant, salt-water pool open till midnight.

2 Brooklyn Heights Promenade Walk west along the leafy, brownstone-filled streets of 'America's first suburb' – perhaps detouring a block north on Willow St to see Truman Capote's home (70 Willow St), where he wrote *Breakfast at Tiffany's* – then south via Pierrepont St and Columbia Heights to reach the 10-block Promenade, a compromise Robert Moses made with locals irate over the construction of the BQE in 1942. You can hear the (out-of-sight) traffic, but it doesn't detract from the views.

3 Fulton Landing Head north via Columbia Heights, passing the BQE and a dog park to reach Old Fulton St, where you can see Fulton

Landing at the foot of the Brooklyn Bridge. Robert Fulton debuted his steamboat here in 1814 and George Washington made an important, hasty retreat during the Battle of Brooklyn in 1776. Now less-rushed, newly married couples pose here for pics.

4 Empire-Fulton Ferry State Park Walk beneath the Brooklyn Bridge to reach the cobbled streets of Dumbo. Take a left at the 19th-century, red-brick Empire Stores to reach the small-but-gorgeous Empire-Fulton Ferry State Park, with remarkable views from between the Brooklyn and Manhattan Bridges. If you sense bad vibes, it could be because rats sometimes come out at night onto the small 'beach' area of Brooklyn Bridge Park just east (don't sit on the grass after dark), or because Phil Collins filmed the video for 'Take Me Home' here in 1986.

5 Washington St Walk down the commercial strip of Washington St a couple blocks and look back for a perfectly framed shot of the Manhattan Bridge, then turn left on Front St, perhaps popping into Front Street Galleries (111 Front St) to peek into the 13 galleries. Continue to Jay St and turn right, walking toward the towering former headquarters of the Jehovah's Witnesses at Sands St; you'll see the entrance to the Manhattan Bridge, also on Sands St, to your left.

6 Manhattan Bridge Compared with its beloved (and smaller) neighbor Brooklyn Bridge, the less-heralded Manhattan Bridge, which celebrates its centennial in 2009, had critics from the get-go for its cold, all-steel design. Latvian-born designer Leon Moisseiff

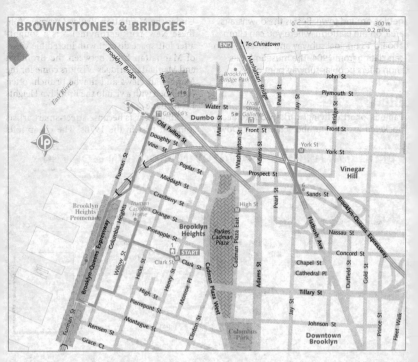

used an experimental 'deflection theory' (a flexible construction design made stronger by balancing forces of gravity with upward-pulling cables) and was able to have trains and cars (and folks) use it. As Coney Island's popularity soared, the need for such easy means to get out there did too, and it's quietly become a sturdy companion to its brother in the East River landscape. The bike/pedestrian lane finally reopened in 2001 after 60 years out of service. Once across, note the grand entrance at Canal St and Bowery.

DOWNTOWN BROOKLYN

Looming east of Cadman Plaza West and Court St from Brooklyn Heights, and continuing to Flatbush Ave, downtown Brooklyn is a functional, modern strip of busy streets where weekday workers troll sidewalks and Brooklynites come to protest towing fees in the city courts. The Brooklyn Bridge dumps traffic onto busy Adams St; east of here you'll find discount-clothing shops along the Fulton St Mall.

Housed in the Greek revival Brooklyn Borough Hall (1845) is the Brooklyn Tourism & Visitors Center (p168). Facing the old city hall is

the New York State Supreme Court, designed in 1957 by the same architects behind the Empire State Building. Across Flatbush Ave, you can walk into the gorgeous 1908 Dime Savings Bank (Map p174; 9 DeKalb Ave btwn Fulton St & Flatbush Ave) building, now a Washington Mutual bank, and get a glimpse of its Corinthian columns of red marble and bronze light fixtures.

NEW YORK TRANSIT MUSEUM Map p174

☎ 718-694-1600; www.mta.info/mta/museum; Boerum Pl at Schermerhorn St; adult/child & senior $5/3; ⏱ 10am-4pm Tue-Fri, noon-5pm Sat & Sun; 🚇 2, 3, 4, 5 to Borough Hall, M, R to Court St
Occupying an old subway station built in 1936 (and out of service since 1946), this kid-oriented museum takes on 100-plus years of

getting around town. Best is the downstairs area, on the platform, where you can climb aboard 13 original subway and elevated-train cars dating from 1904. The museum's gift shop offers popular subway-print gifts.

DUMBO

Famous for artful living/work spaces for deep-pocketed artists, Dumbo – short for Down Under the Manhattan Bridge Overpass (oh, these New York acronyms) – is a sought-after loft-space district with incredible views of Manhattan from between the Brooklyn and Manhattan Bridges. Visitors come for the Manhattan views and maybe brunch, often combined with a visit to the Brooklyn Heights Promenade (p169).

Dumbo exists because street-smart artists found it first in the 1970s. The cheap lofts

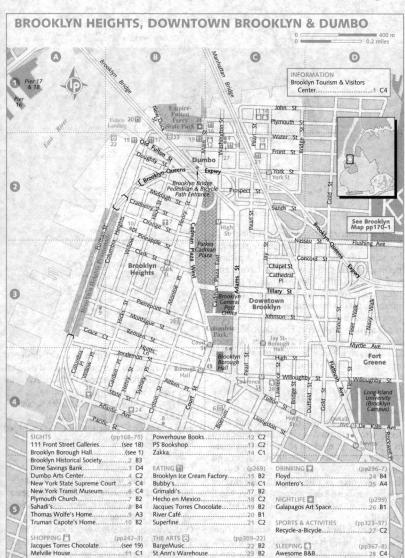

BROOKLYN HEIGHTS, DOWNTOWN BROOKLYN & DUMBO

BROOKLYN BRIDGE PARK

Mayor Michael Bloomberg famously plans to expand the city's park system so that every local would live within a '10-minute walk' of a park. The most talked-about project so far is Brooklyn's 85-acre Brooklyn Bridge Park, currently in progress, which will run alongside the river from Jay St in Dumbo to the west end of Atlantic Ave in Cobble Hill. Making public spaces out of a long-inaccessible waterfront of unused docks is certainly a popular idea, yet many are upset that the 1.3-mile-long shoreline will get divvied up for luxury condos and a hotel.

Approved in 2006, the park's first necessary demolitions – of old, unused piers and a couple of buildings – still hadn't seen a wrecking ball by early 2008. (Five piers were slated to go at research time.) But the Brooklyn Bridge Park Conservancy (www.brooklynbridgepark.org) didn't wait to get things started. In summer 2007, they hosted the first public activities here – ranging from a widely popular floating pool/beach in a barge called the *Floating Pool Lady,* plus kid-oriented puppet shows and square dancing. This was also when the first condo, One Brooklyn Bridge – converted from a 1927 warehouse formerly used by the Jehovah's Witnesses – opened to realtor walk-throughs. The 449 units, right on the water, were going for $500,000 to $7 million each. The owners of the project won no fans for flirting with the idea of a 'high-end supermarket' next door. The first real construction began in 2008, and most of Brooklyn remains watchful of how many more private projects may elbow out some of the public spaces.

The Brooklyn Paper (www.brooklynpaper.com) keeps an eye on development around the borough in its 'Not Just the Nets' section.

are long gone, but the legacy of art lives on. Look into warehouse windows as you walk the streets (particularly east of Manhattan Bridge, where graffiti-dotted buildings remain); sometimes you'll see a sculptor at work.

A good spot to pop into a gallery is 111 Front Street Galleries (Map p174; www.frontstreetgalleries .com; 111 Front St; vary by gallery; A, C to High St, F to York St), with 13 galleries keeping open hours (check the website) Wednesday through Sunday, or Dumbo Arts Center (Map p174; 718-694-0831; www.dumboartscenter.org; 30 Washington St; noon-6pm Thu-Mon; A, C to High St, F to York St). The feather in the center's cap is its Dumbo Arts Under the Bridge Festival, a three-day event in late September with sidewalk performances (art and rock music) and open doors to many galleries in the area; some 200,000 people attend.

On the water, set snugly between the bridges and backed by Civil War–era warehouses, the nine-acre Empire-Fulton Ferry State Park (Map p174; 718-858-4708; www.nysparks.state.ny.us; 26 New Dock St; 8am-dusk; A, C to High St, F to York St) has a cozy lawn on the East River. Its boardwalk has hosted a wedding or two.

Vinegar Hill, originally an Irish neighborhood (it's named for a battle in the Irish Rebellion of 1798), is just east of Dumbo, with some historic buildings along Water St between Gold St and Hudson Ave.

FORT GREENE & CLINTON HILL

Still being discovered by some, yet considered passé by some Manhattanites hoping for un-

discovered, cheap brownstone blocks, this appealing two-some neighborhood spreads east and south from the Brooklyn side of the Manhattan Bridge. It's hot to a broader mix of folk now (Erykah Badu rents a place here) than in its past, when Spike Lee grew up in the area. It's bisected by three main strips – its belly is crossed by DeKalb Avenue (between Vanderbilt and Flatbush Aves), which has a few stylish restaurants; to the south is Fulton Street, showing a bit of a renaissance with many African American businesses; while to the north, less polished Myrtle Avenue is slower to break out of its strip of discount shops and gas stations, but there are a few new bars and eateries around.

Begin a wander from the Brooklyn Academy of Music (p176) behind the art-deco clock tower of the Williamsburgh Savings Bank (1927; Map p180; cnr Flatbush Ave & Hanson Pl), Brooklyn's tallest building, which – alas – has recently been transformed into condominiums (they fixed the clock, at least). Saturday is a good day to visit, as there's a farmer's market along Washington Park on the east side of hilly Fort Greene Park, named for a Revolutionary War major-general. The centerpiece of the park is the Prison Ship Martyrs' Monument (Map p180), supposedly the world's largest Doric column (it's 149ft high); designed by Stanford White, it was built in 1905 to memorialize the 11,500 American prisoners-of-war who died in British prison ships during the Revolution.

Past the north–south Clinton Ave you'll find the area of Clinton Hill, with plenty of remarkable, century-old mansions to see along Clinton and Washington Aves. The Pratt

Institute (Map p180; ☎ 718-636-3600; www.pratt.edu; 200 Willoughby St), a noted art and design school, has some interesting courtyard sculptures created by some of its 4000-plus students.

BROOKLYN ACADEMY OF MUSIC (BAM) Map p180

☎ 718-636-4100; www.bam.org; 30 Lafayette Ave; Ⓜ 2, 3, 4, 5, B, Q to Atlantic Ave

The oldest concert center in the USA, the Brooklyn Academy of Music is known for edgier, more modern dance and music shows than its Manhattan counterparts, particularly during the autumn Next Wave festival. (Folks like Ingmar Bergman and Sufjan Stevens have staged shows here.) The complex contains a 2109-seat opera house, an 874-seat theatre and the four-screen Rose Cinemas (p319, 321), which screen indie and foreign films. At 8pm on weekend nights, the upstairs BAMCafe (☎ 718-636-4139) stages an interesting line-up of free live shows.

WILLIAMSBURG

New York's 'it' neighborhood – for rock! for drinks! for overpriced studio apartments! – of the past half-decade or more, Williamsburg has spread along the L line into Brooklyn like a cockroach problem – cockroaches, that is, with tousled hair, uncut beards, just-woke-up expressions and Deerhoof tunes on the iPod. Considering the world's 20-something 'divining rod of cool' points here, it's easy to dismiss, but impossible to skip.

Don't come expecting tree-lined brown-stones and quaint parks. 'Billyburg' is, to be frank, ugly, with its old warehouses and unas-suming build-by-numbers townhouses built to house and serve the masses with little aesthetic detail. It lights up – along with cigarettes at some rule-breaking bars – at night. The tradi-tional heart of it is Bedford Avenue, between N 10th St and Metropolitan Ave, where there are (often lame) side-by-side cafés, indie-rock stores, boutiques, cheap restaurants and bars. Things are cooler on side streets – such as 'second Bedford', N 6th St, toward the river, and parallel thoroughfares Berry and Wythe Aves – and (even cooler) in scattered eateries and bars that follow each of the next couple of L subway stops into East Williamsburg, on the other side of the Brooklyn–Queens Ex-pressway. (See right for a drunken walking tour through the area's bars.)

A priceless Williamsburg piss-take, *Hipster Olympics* (2007; www.youtube.com), was shot

at lively McCarren Park, where you'll see the neighborhood's favorite summer stage at Mc-Carren Pool (Map p177; Lorimer St btwn Driggs & Bayard Sts; tickets free–$50), a wonderful 1936 WPA project that could fit almost 7000 swimmers at once in its heyday. The water's been gone since 1984, but is now filled in August and September with indie rocksters for the super summer shows (Cat Power, Beirut, Sonic Youth).

Typical of the 'attractions' here, Brooklyn Brewery (Map p177; ☎ 718-486-7440; www.brooklyn brewery.com; 79 N 11th St; Ⓗ happy hour 6-11pm Fri, Ⓗ tours on the hr noon-4pm Sat; Ⓜ L to Bedford Ave) is where those lagers with the cute cursive logo are made. There are eight kinds of beer on tap ($4), and free, half-hour guided tours on Saturday.

South of the eponymous Williamsburg Bridge (which has an underrated pedestrian walkway to the Lower East Side), on side streets south of the intersection of Broadway and Bedford Ave, you'll find a busy Hasidic Jewish neighborhood. Follow Bedford Ave north past McCarren Park until it turns into Manhattan Ave to find Greenpoint, a tradi-tionally Polish 'hood with increasing numbers of spillover studio-apartment renters and bars. In 2007, the city opened a 'nature walk' along-side Greenpoint's Newtown Creek sewage treatment plant, a surprise hit with locals.

Free Williamsburg (www.freewilliamsburg.com) is a community-based site focusing on keeping Billyburg residents cool with a rolling list-ing of area events, bars and which albums to download.

Billyburg Booze Crawl
STUMBLING TOUR

1 Moto The Next Williamsburg is East Wil-liamsburg – a great mix of hipsters and Latin American locals and roomy bars offering free pizza and '70s arcade games: perfect for a bar-hopping night out. A good place to start is under the rattling J/M/Z subway tracks at Moto (☎ 718-599-6895; 394 Broadway at Hooper St & Division Ave; Ⓗ dinner; Ⓜ J, M, Z to Hewes St), a low-lit corner spot with creaky wood floors and live accordion music that feels like something straight out of 1920s Paris. Food's not bad – snacks and starters like panini beat the mains – but it's perfect for a glass of wine or mug of Australia's Coopers lager to kick-start the night.

2 Barcade Head up Hooper St to Grand, then left on Union for a little digestion time playing one of the two-dozen vintage arcade games

WILLIAMSBURG

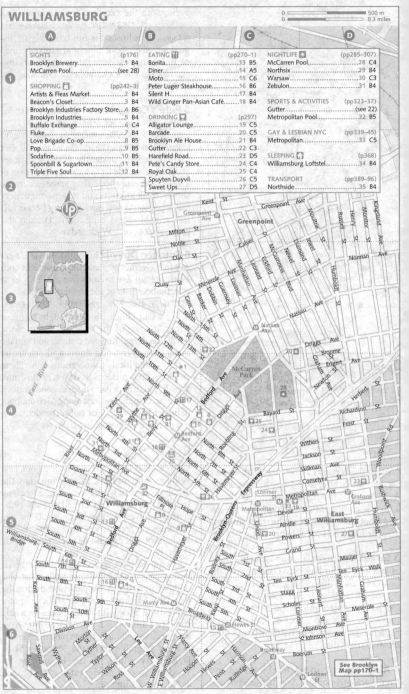

| | 0 | 500 m |
| 0 | 0.3 miles |

SIGHTS (p176)
Brooklyn Brewery...................1 B4
McCarren Pool...................(see 28)

SHOPPING (pp242–3)
Artists & Fleas Market...................2 B4
Beacon's Closet...................3 B4
Brooklyn Industries Factory Store...4 B6
Brooklyn Industries...................5 B4
Buffalo Exchange...................6 C4
Fluke...................7 B4
Love Brigade Co-op...................8 B5
Pop...................9 B5
Sodafine...................10 B5
Spoonbill & Sugartown...................11 B4
Triple Five Soul...................12 B4

EATING (pp270–1)
Bonita...................13 B5
Diner...................14 A5
Moto...................15 C6
Peter Luger Steakhouse...................16 B6
Silent H...................17 B4
Wild Ginger Pan-Asian Café...................18 B4

DRINKING (p297)
Alligator Lounge...................19 C5
Barcade...................20 C5
Brooklyn Ale House...................21 B4
Gutter...................22 C3
Harefield Road...................23 D5
Pete's Candy Store...................24 C4
Royal Oak...................25 C4
Spuyten Duyvil...................26 C5
Sweet Ups...................27 D5

NIGHTLIFE (pp285–307)
McCarren Pool...................28 C4
Northsix...................29 B4
Warsaw...................30 C3
Zebulon...................31 B4

SPORTS & ACTIVITIES (pp323–37)
Gutter...................(see 22)
Metropolitan Pool...................32 B5

GAY & LESBIAN NYC (pp339–45)
Metropolitan...................33 C5

SLEEPING (p368)
Williamsburg Loftstel...................34 B4

TRANSPORT (pp389–96)
Northside...................35 B4

See Brooklyn Map pp170–1

177

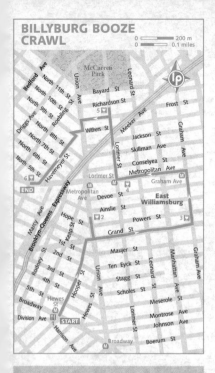

BILLYBURG BOOZE CRAWL

WALK FACTS

Start Moto (J, M to Hewes St)
End Spuyten Duyvil (L at Metropolitan Ave)
Distance 2¾ miles
Duration Four hours to ?
Fuel stop Alligator Lounge

(Asteroids, Berzerk) at Barcade (718-302-6464; 388 Union Ave; happy hour 5-8pm; L to Metropolitan Ave). It's dorky, but futile to resist. Plus there's a diverse choice of two dozen $5 microbrews and a bottle-cap mosaic in the front smoking area; drinks are $1 off at happy hour.

3 Sweet Ups Retrace your steps to Grand St and go left four blocks to Graham Ave, the heart of East Williamsburg Cool. Here, Sweet Ups (718-384-3886; 277 Graham Ave; L to Graham Ave) has no video games, no themes – just red-velvet walls and a host of Pitchfork.com readers hoisting some of Williamsburg's most creative cocktails.

4 Alligator Lounge A few blocks up and over on Metropolitan Ave, it's snack-time again, with the excellent free pizza at Alligator Lounge (718-599-4440; 600 Metropolitan Ave; L to Lorimer St), a life-is-for-fun bar with an unguarded vibe, a pool table, and a mixed crowd of Billyburg first-generation and working-class locals. There's karaoke on Thursday and live jazz on Sunday.

5 Pete's Candy Store Now that you're fed a bit (again), go see what's on at Pete's Candy Store (718-302-3770; www.petescandystore.com; 709 Lorimer St btwn N 10th & 11th Sts; L to Lorimer St). Get there by walking under the BQE via Lorimer St. The bar's made from a campy makeover of a '40s ice-cream shop. They stage free music shows (freak folksters and singer-songwritery indie-popsters) and have spelling bees on alternating Mondays, bingo every Tuesday and pub quizzes every Wednesday.

6 Spuyten Duyvil Go southwest via Union Ave to Havermeyer St and then turn right onto Metropolitan Ave to enjoy one of NYC's most eclectic beer lists at the low-key Spuyten Duyvil (718-963-4140; 359 Metropolitan Ave; L to Bedford St) – an Old Dutch phrase thought to mean either 'in spite of the devil' or 'spout of the devil'. Inside, painted-red ceilings and vintage maps look over wood floors and armchairs with chatting locals from various eras. There are cheese-and-pickle plates if you're too drunk already, plus a back patio open in good weather. From here, soldier on east along Metropolitan to busier Bedford St – or call surrender.

For more Williamsburg bars, see p297.

BUSHWICK

What's next? A couple more stops out past Williamsburg on the L from Manhattan, the grubby blocks of Bushwick – home to many Latin Americans and famed for its 19th-century brewery scene with beer vats the size of homes – is seeing increasing spillover from Williamsburg for would-be musicians seeking cheap rent.

It's fun having a walk around the industrial blocks of a changing 'hood with a bit of a dodgy rep; riots ran rampant here during the July 1977 blackout, and you still can spot a burned-out SUV with Jersey plates on a side street (we did, anyway). But crime rates have dropped considerably in the past decade.

Start a ramble from the Jefferson St or DeKalb Ave stops on the L, walking up Wyckoff Avenue; maybe catch some brunch at Northeast Kingdom (p271).

A block south down Willoughby Ave is lively Maria Hernandez Park, named for a local who struggled to rid the area of drugs (and was murdered by drug dealers in 1989). At the far end of the park is Knickerbocker Ave; follow it west several blocks (towards the visible Manhattan skyline) and cross Flushing Ave to get into East Williamsburg; at the corner of Knickerbocker Ave and Thames St are several great vintage shops, including Urban Jungle (Map pp170–1; ☎ 718-497-1331; 120 Knickerbocker Ave btwn Flushing Ave & Thames St; ☽ noon-7pm; ◎ L to Morgan Ave).

A few blocks further north into East Williamsburg, go left (west) on Meserole St, to what once was the center of Bushwick's 'Brewery's Row.' You can see the old Edward B Hittelman Brewery at the corner of Bushwick Pl. You can catch the L train back to Williamsburg two blocks southwest at Bushwick and Montrose Aves, or if you're up for a hike, follow either Bushwick Ave or (a couple blocks west) Graham Ave to the north, and then turn left (west) onto Metropolitan Ave and follow it all the way back to Williamsburg.

BOERUM HILL, COBBLE HILL & CARROLL GARDENS

Just south of Brooklyn Heights and Downtown Brooklyn, this cluster of tree-lined brownstone neighborhoods – Cobble Hill (west of Court St), Boerum Hill (east of Court St) and Carroll Gardens (south of Degraw St), sometimes called 'BoCoCa' by ambitious realtors – has become something of the 'new Park Slope.' Its locale and restaurant scene was appealing enough for the late Heath Ledger and Michelle Williams, who lived together here in Boerum Hill in 2005 and 2006.

Its two main thoroughfares – a bit more 'uptown' on Court Street, more 'downtown' on Smith Street – are short on attractions but are great strolling spots, lined with boutiques, restaurants, bars, bookshops and a cinema. Smith St's 'restaurant row' is changing with particular velocity, with increasingly higher-end restaurants (and some chains). This led Brooklyn indie-popsters Life in a Blender to lash out about the neighborhood's gentrification in their 2007 song 'What Happened to Smith?', and singer Don Ralph told *The Brooklyn Paper* that the area has been 'bitten by a poisonous snake.'

Other streets, like lovely north–south Clinton St (west of Court St) are lined with gorgeous, century-old townhouses and the quiet Cobble Hill Park (Map p180; cnr Congress & Clinton Sts). On Atlantic Ave (the area's northern border with Brooklyn Heights), west of Court St, are a handful of happening bars, as well as several Middle Eastern restaurants and the beloved delicacy shop Sahadi's (Map p174; ☎ 718-624-4550; 187 Atlantic Ave; ☽ 9am-7pm Mon-Fri, 8:30am-7pm Sat), where the olive bar boasts two-dozen options. East of Smith St (around Hoyt St), Atlantic Ave – the site of the wonderful Atlantic Antic (www.atlanticave.org) festival in September – is lined with furniture and antiques shops, plus a few boutiques.

To the south of Cobble Hill is Carroll Gardens, a long-time Italian neighborhood, which continues down to where the Brooklyn–Battery Tunnel and the Gowanus Expressway cut off the northern end of Red Hook. You'll see a few pasta shops and funeral homes about from the crustier days.

GOWANUS

Between the gentrifying, stroller-heavy neighborhoods of BoCoCa and Park Slope, you'll find some of Brooklyn's more industrial and sketchier blocks in the streets off Third Ave by Gowanus Canal (Map p180). Millionaire developers, as they do, have eyed the area in recent years, hoping to rezone it and transform warehouses into loft-like condos. Already a high-end boutique hotel, Hotel Le Bleu (p367), has opened up on nearby Fourth Ave. Meanwhile, a proud core of the 14,000 or so locals are fighting back, making Gowanus the latest battlefield in the gentrification of Brooklyn (as reported at www.gowanuslounge.com).

The best way to the canal is via Carroll St, which crosses the canal on a wood-plank, retractile bridge built in 1889. For much of the 20th century, the canal itself – a former creek named for the Gouwane Native Americans – roared with commercial life. Ships from New York Harbor came in to load and unload goods, and tens of millions of pounds of human waste were dumped in each year. But it's cleaner than it used to be, and the city signed onto a $125 million project in late 2007 to widen the canal and install pumps to allow fish to breed here. It's already been clean enough for a young whale, who briefly swam up the canal (before accidentally beaching itself and dying) in 2007. Also, the Gowanus Dredgers Canoe Club (p330), found at 2nd St, offer self-guided canoe trips of the canal.

Also in the area, Rooftop Films (www.rooftopfilms.com; ☽ Jun-Sep) stages summer film screenings

BOERUM HILL, CARROLL GARDENS, COBBLE HILL, FORT GREENE & RED HOOK

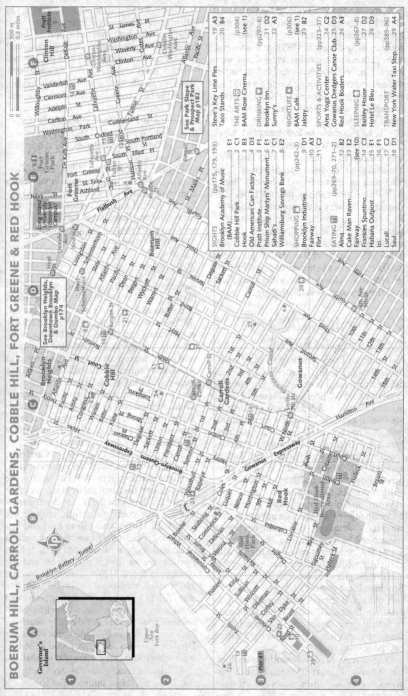

SIGHTS	(pp175, 179, 193)
Brooklyn Academy of Music	
(BAM)	1 E1
Cobble Hill Park	2 C1
Hook	3 B3
Old American Can Factory	4 D3
Pratt Institute	5 F1
Prison Ship Martyrs' Monument...6 E1	
Sahadi's	7 C1
Williamsburg Savings Bank	8 E2

SHOPPING 🛒	(pp242–3)
Brooklyn Industries	9 D1
Fairway	10 A3
Flirt	11 C2

EATING 🍴	(pp269–70, 271–2)
Alma	12 B2
Cake Man Raven	13 E2
Fairway	(see 10)
Frankies Spuntino	14 C3
Habana Outpost	15 E1
Ici	16 F1
Lucali	17 C2
Saul	18 D1

Steve's Key Lime Pies	19 A3
Taco Stands	20 B4
	(p304)
	(see 1)

THE ARTS 🎭	(pp297–8)
BAM Rose Cinema	21 D2

DRINKING 🍸	(p306)
Brooklyn Inn	22 A3
Sunny's	23 B2

NIGHTLIFE ★	(see 1)
BAM Café	(see 1)
Jalopy	24 C2

SPORTS & ACTIVITIES	(pp323–37)
Area Yoga Center	25 D3
Gowanus Dredgers Canoe Club...26 A3	
Red Hook Boaters	

SLEEPING 🛏	(pp367–8)
Baisley House	27 D2
Hotel Le Bleu	28 D3

TRANSPORT	(pp389–96)
New York Water Taxi Stop......29 A4	

See Brooklyn Heights,
Downtown Brooklyn
& Dumbo Map p174

See Park Slope
& Prospect Park
Map p182

atop the Old American Can Factory (Map p180; 232 3rd St at Third Ave).

PARK SLOPE

A bit Berkeley, a bit Upper West Side – Park Slope is the borough 'hood of choice for newbie New Yorkers or Manhattan-expat professionals seeking 19th-century brownstone homes and leafy sidewalks to push their baby strollers around on. It's gorgeous and historic, but sort of gets a 'tsk' from Brooklynites in grittier areas, even if it garnered a few street-cred points from Noah Baumbach's excellent 2005 film *The Squid & the Whale* (shot in the area). Seventh Avenue is more family-oriented, with kid-friendly pizza joints, realtors hawking million-dollar homes, and a few chainstores. Two blocks west down the gently sliding slope, Fifth Avenue is more 'downtown,' with more youthful bars and several excellent restaurants.

Once an area of farmlands known as Prospect Hill, Park Slope's upper-middle-class roots followed the construction of Prospect Park (below). Some of the finest homes here line Prospect Park West and the blocks between it and Eighth Avenue. For the best way to see both the neighborhood and the park, see right for a leisurely walking tour.

PROSPECT PARK

The creators of the 585-acre Prospect Park (Map p182; ☎ 718-965-8999; www.prospectpark.org; ◉ B, Q to Prospect Park, 2, 3 to Grand Army Plaza, F to 15th St-Prospect Park) – Frederick Law Olmsted and Calvert Vaux – considered this an improvement over their other New York project, Central Park (p148). Created in 1866, Prospect Park has many of the same activities. It's gorgeous, with a long meadow running along the western half, filled with soccer, football, cricket and baseball players (and barbecuers), and much of the rest dotted with hilly forests and a lovely boathouse on the east side; many more come to bike, skate or just lounge around. For information on activities, stop by the Audubon Center Boathouse (p330), which offers electric boat rides.

Just north of the boathouse is the Children's Corner. Here, you'll find a terrific 1912 carousel (☎ 718-282-7789; admission $1.50; ☯ noon-5pm or 6pm Thu-Sun Apr-Oct), originally from Coney Island, and a small zoo (☎ 718-399-7339; adult/child/senior $6/2/2.25; ☯ 10am-5pm Apr-Oct, to 4:30pm Nov-Mar), with sea lions, wallabies and 400 other animals. The

18th-century Lefferts Historic House (☎ 718-789-2822; www.prospectpark.org; admission free; ☯ noon-5pm Thu-Sun Apr-Nov, to 6pm Jul & Aug, noon-4pm Sat & Sun Dec-Mar) has plenty of old-fashioned toys to goof around with. South of the boathouse, on the west edge of Prospect Lake, Kate Wollman Rink (p332) has enough ice to accommodate hundreds of ice-skaters. A free weekend trolley connects points of interest around the park (including the Brooklyn Museum) from noon to 6pm.

For more on the park and its grand entry at Grand Army Plaza, see the walking tour below.

A Park & A Slope
WALKING TOUR

1 Soldiers' and Sailors' Monument Built in the 1890s, this great arch of the traffic-frenzied Grand Army Plaza solved the problem, lingering for 20 years, of what to do with the entrance to Prospect Park. Many mocked the plaza's previous tenants: a tiny Lincoln statue, followed by a gaudy Victorian fountain. But the public swooned over this memorial for the Civil War's Union soldiers. Reliefs are dedicated to the army and the navy (to the left and right as you look from the park).

2 Long Meadow After entering the 585-acre, diamond-shaped park, veer left past the gazebos and go under the Endale Arch (mistakenly changed from the original 'Enterdale') to reach the mile-long, 90-acre Long Meadow – far larger than Central Park's Great Lawn. It's a super strolling spot filled with pick-up soccer, cricket and football games, plus barbecuers and kite-fliers.

3 The Boathouse Halfway down the narrow meadow, you'll see the Picnic House to your right. Bear left on the sidewalk and follow it on a woodsy walk alongside the Lullwater creek, which leads, after 10 or 15 minutes, to this lovely white terra-cotta boathouse, built in 1904. Here you can walk across the Lullwater Bridge or hop on the *Independence,* a replica early-20th-century electric boat. There's also a small café if you want a snack.

4 Prospect Park West Follow the Lullwater path west to Terrace Bridge and continue along the road till it veers off left, but instead go to your right, continuing on the sidewalk across the park, back to Long Meadow, and north to the park exit at the Lafayette Monument on

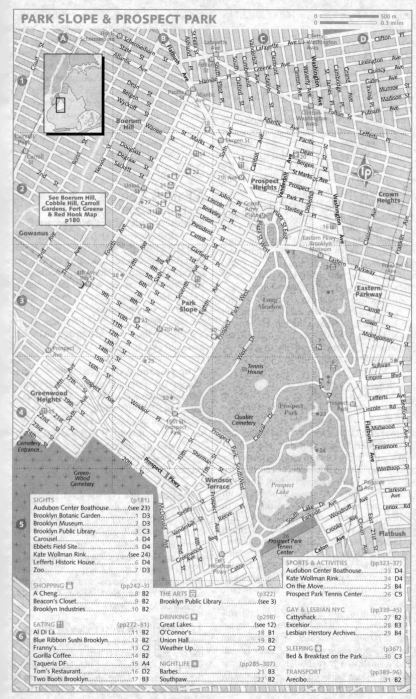

PARK SLOPE & PROSPECT PARK

0 — 500 m
0 — 0.3 miles

See Boerum Hill,
Cobble Hill, Carroll
Gardens, Fort Greene
& Red Hook Map
p180

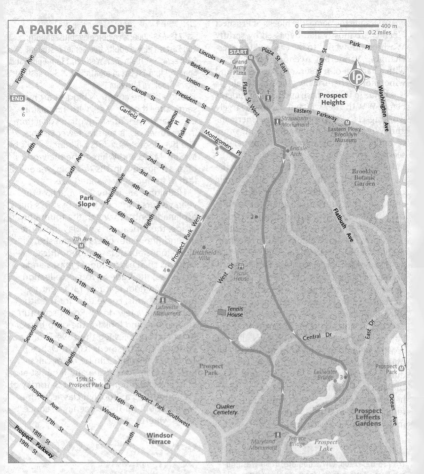

A PARK & A SLOPE

START

Grand Army Plaza

Park Pl

Lincoln Pl

Berkeley Pl

Union St

Plaza St East

Plaza St West

Prospect Heights

Underhill

Washington Ave

Carroll St

President St

Montgomery Pl

Eastern Parkway

Stranahan Monument

Eastern Pkwy-Brooklyn Museum

Garfield Pl

Prospect St

Polhemus Pl

Fiske Pl

Endale Arch

Fourth Ave

END

Fifth Ave

Sixth Ave

Seventh Ave

Eighth Ave

1st St

2nd St

3rd St

4th St

5th St

6th St

7th St

8th St

9th St

10th St

11th St

12th St

13th St

14th St

15th St

Park Slope

7th Ave

Prospect Park West

Litchfield Villa

West Dr

Picnic House

Lafayette Monument

Tennis House

Central Dr

East Dr

Brooklyn Botanic Garden

Flatbush Ave

Lullwater Bridge

Prospect Park

Prospect Lefferts Gardens

Ocean Ave

15th St-Prospect Park

Prospect Ave

16th St

17th St

18th St

19th St

Prospect Park Southwest

Windsor Pl

Tenth Ave

Eighth Ave

Seventh Ave

Windsor Terrace

Quaker Cemetery

Maryland Monument

Terrace Bridge

Prospect Lake

0 — 400 m
0 — 0.2 miles

Prospect Park West at 9th St. Turn right and walk past Romanesque revival and neo-Jacobean mansions built to impress.

5 Montgomery Place Turn left into Park Slope on shady, one-block Montgomery Place – named for a British veteran who fought in the Revolutionary War – which has one of the city's greatest displays of Beaux-Arts row-houses, most built by Paris-taught Charles Pierrepont Henry Gilbert in the 1880s. Turn left on Eighth Ave, then right on Garfield Place.

6 Old Stone House Head west, straight down the slope (pausing to count strollers along Seventh Ave), to reach Fifth Ave. To the right (north) are a handful of accessories shops and local designers' clothing boutiques. Several blocks to the left, just off the avenue, is the Old

WALK FACTS

Start Grand Army Plaza (2, 3 to Grand Army Plaza)
End Old Stone House (M, R at Union St)
Distance 3¼ miles
Duration Three to four hours
Fuel stops Boathouse Café, or Seventh or Fifth Aves

Stone House (☎ 718-768-3195; btwn 3rd & 4th Sts; admission free; 11am-4pm Sat & Sun), a restored Dutch farmhouse – a rare legacy from Brooklyn's early days as Breukelen.

PROSPECT HEIGHTS

Just across Flatbush Ave from Park Slope, Prospect Heights has always been linked more with its easterly neighbor, Crown Heights (right). Despite the name, the blocks of Prospect Heights are mostly flat, bypassed by scruffy Washington Avenue to the east and the ever-changing Vanderbilt Avenue in the center, with a handful of restaurants, bars, cafés and wine shops. Historically, Prospect Heights was home to Italian, Irish and Jewish residents before WWII, after which it became a largely working-class barrio of African Americans and West Indies immigrants – and, more recently, a growing number of cheaper-flat seekers.

Its southern boundary is marked by the start, at Grand Army Plaza, of the 2.2-mile Eastern Parkway, one of two legacies of an ambitious but unrealized plan for scenic, tree-lined roads to radiate from Prospect Park across Brooklyn and Queens (the other is Ocean Parkway). Facing Grand Army Plaza, the Brooklyn Public Library (Map p182; ☎ 718-230-2100; www.brooklynpubliclibrary.org; Grand Army Plaza) is an art-deco masterpiece from 1941 (its latest tweaks came with a basement auditorium in 2007); you can get grand plaza views from its humble third-floor café.

A new tenant on the plaza, across from the library, is architect Richard Meier's all-glass apartment building, which has attracted a new high-end crowd. The best time to come is during the raucous, all-day-and-night West Indian Day Parade (p23) on Labor Day, which has a sea of jerk-chicken stands, bright costumes, snuck-in drinks and loud drums. As many as a million participate.

BROOKLYN BOTANIC GARDEN Map p182
☎ 718-623-7200; www.bbg.org; 1000 Washington Ave; adult/child/senior & student $8/free/4, free to all Tue & 10am-noon Sat; ☽ 8am-6pm Tue-Fri, 10am-6pm Sat & Sun mid-March–Oct, 8am-4:30pm Tue-Fri, 10am-4:30pm Sat & Sun Nov–mid-March; ⊕ 2, 3 to Eastern Pkwy-Brooklyn Museum

One of Brooklyn's great attractions, this 52-acre garden – most easily accessed from the entrance next to the Brooklyn Museum – features 10,000 plants. The best area is the Japanese Hill-and-Pond garden, where you can see turtles swimming by a Shinto shrine. Other gardens are linked by trails. Try to time a visit with the beginning of May for the massive Sakuri Matsuri (Cherry Blossom Festival, p21), when trees turn pink and the festival hosts Japanese events such as *taiko* drumming and staged tales of samurai lore.

BROOKLYN MUSEUM Map p182
☎ 718-638-5000; www.brooklynmuseum.org; 200 Eastern Pkwy; adult/child/senior & student $8/free/4; ☽ 10am-5pm Wed-Fri, 11am-6pm Sat & Sun, to 11pm 1st Sat of month; ⊕ 2, 3 to Eastern Pkwy-Brooklyn Museum

Though it's the country's biggest art museum after the Met (p141), with 1.5 million pieces and the largest Egyptian collection in the Americas, it sees far fewer visitors. The five-floor Beaux-Arts building – built by McKim, Mead and White to be the world's biggest museum in 1897 – is big, yet only a fifth of its originally planned size.

Highlights are many. For much of the year, visitors linger by the museum's glass esplanade entry to watch the fountains. Inside, the African Arts display (near the ground-floor café) offers several short video loops about fascinating African customs such as traditional masks and costumes; the huge Egyptian collection on the 2nd floor features 13th-century mummy boards. Leave time for the 5th floor, where a few dozen Rodin sculptures are laid out, and look for the grab-bag of American art relics (eg the 1894 Thomas Edison film of the Sioux 'Ghost Dance'). Temporary exhibits can be hit-or-miss – lots of urban, Americana and feminist art of late. Its free night – the first Saturday of the month – is a Brooklyn classic, with a wide turnout for free screenings, concerts and a wine/beer bar.

BEDFORD-STUYVESANT & CROWN HEIGHTS

Bedford-Stuyvesant, NYC's largest African American neighborhood (where Notorious BIG grew up), gets a bad rap from its 'Bed-Stuy: Do or Die' rep. But the neighborhood – which sprawls between Flushing and Atlantic Aves beside Williamsburg and Clinton Hill – defies its infamy. Past some blocks of boarded-up townhouses and bleak housing projects are stunning historic districts. The mix 'n' match continues south of Atlantic Ave in Crown Heights, another culturally rich African American neighborhood that borders Bed-Stuy (at research time, nearly 500 buildings here were being considered for 'landmark' status). Combing the two makes for a great walk.

(Continued on page 193)

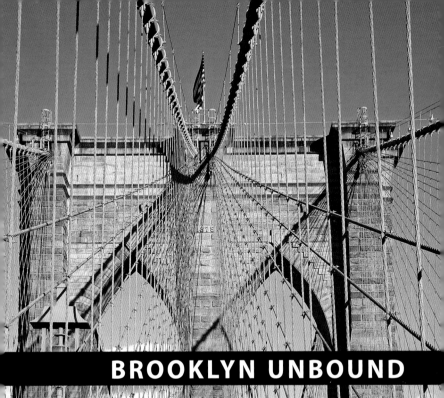

BROOKLYN UNBOUND

Strolling across the span of the Brooklyn Bridge (p83) is a summer favorite

Dramatic autumn colors in Prospect Park (p181)

When Truman Capote boasted 'I live in Brooklyn – by choice,' he was just trying to be provocative. Even just a decade ago, Brooklynites' pleas (eg 'it's *only* three stops on the A train!') could rarely entice Manhattan friends or travelers to visit. Like the other outer boroughs, Brooklyn was a clear notch or two down on the caste system of urban cool, its neighborhoods considered like ingredients of a hot dog – best left unknown. If you wanted a night out to eat good food, get drunk or see a band, you stuck with Manhattan.

Boy, has that changed in the past decade. Brooklyn's influx of Manhattan émigrés is snatching up (slightly cheaper) brownstones and rentals across Brooklyn's northern and northwestern neighborhoods. Many new arrivals bring with them the banner of indie rock. Essentially every cool New York–based band of the past several years are in Brooklyn (eg Yeah Yeah Yeahs, Beirut, Sufjan Stevens, TV on the Radio, Animal Collective, Fiery Furnaces…had enough?). Visiting cutting-edge performers eye Brooklyn too. Sonic Youth played *Daydream Nation* in full at Williamsburg's splendid McCarren Pool, Lou Reed re-created his *Berlin* at Dumbo's St Ann's Warehouse and Patrick Stewart staged a bloody *Macbeth* at Fort Greene's Brooklyn Academy of Music.

Food-wise, restaurant rows are mixing traditionally working-class roots with chi-chi eateries, like neighborhood-changers in Ditmas Park, Red Hook or strips of eateries that fill visitors' bellies along Boerum Hill's Smith St or Park Slope's Fifth Ave. Drinkers, meanwhile, have noticed that Brooklyn bars are bigger, roomier and – if you consider the trend of games (bars with bowling alleys, bocce courts, '70s arcade games) – more fun.

Good weather pulls Brooklyn outdoors – onto rooftops to see movies, onto Prospect Park's lawns (which have more lax attention to rules regarding cleats or barbecue than in Central Park), or to see raucous parades that have more elbow room than packed-tight Midtown ones.

None of this is exactly a secret anymore. Brooklyn – long famed for WWII-movie caricatures, John Travolta's disco skills and Coney Island hot dogs – is no longer just an add-on to Manhattan. Even if this place were in Ohio, people would come. By choice.

LITERARY CITY

Maybe writers need alternatives for inspiration. A sense of being outside the mainstream. Or maybe it's just the cheap rent. But for generations, Brooklyn has been something of a literary hub – where Walt Whitman, Thomas Wolfe, Norman Mailer, Truman Capote and Hubert Selby Jr wrote masterpieces. And now the new breed – born or transplanted here – write from brownstones in Park Slope or Boerum Hill (if they can afford it) or shared writers' spaces. The new list is long: Jonathan Lethem, Jonathan Safran Foer, Jennifer Egan, Paul Auster and many more. Every mid-September, some of them come out for the Brooklyn Book Festival (www.brooklynbookfestival.org) downtown. Brooklyn's now so infiltrated with folks with pad-and-pen, that one writer, Sara Gran (author of *Dope*), hilariously ranted against it in the *New York Times*: 'Brooklyn is the worst place on earth for a writer. The competition is fierce. The 'local authors' shelf... has Kathryn Harrison and Paul Auster.'

That may be so, but it's led to some good reading. Here are a few favorites:

- Jonathan Lethem's 'genre bender' *Motherless in Brooklyn* is a crime novel featuring a Brooklyn hero with Tourette's Syndrome.
- Borne from long walks and a curious eye, Francis Morrone's *An Architectural Guidebook to Brooklyn* is a detailed neighborhood-by-neighborhood listing of key buildings.
- A cult fave, Hubert Selby Jr's conversational *Last Exit to Brooklyn* (1964) explores the ugliest depths of the lower class in this six-part, anything-goes novel that was deemed 'obscene' in Britain.
- Bronx-born Chaim Potok set his classic novel *The Chosen,* about the struggle between modern and traditional Jewish families, in South Williamsburg in the 1940s.

THE PAST: BRUEKELEN TO BROOKLYN

Brooklyn's sense of independence goes way back. When the first Dutch settlers arrived with farming on their minds in the early 1600s, they mostly ignored the 2000 Lenape (or Delawarean) Indians who lived in the forests and wetlands of present-day Brooklyn. Soon, naturally, tension grew, and for protection's sake, five Dutch communities (and one British one) formed towns on existing Indian paths (including a certain route called 'Flatbush,' now Flatbush Ave). The first of the towns, Breukelen (at present-day Brooklyn Heights), was formed in 1846, a full decade before New Amsterdam was founded.

The British turned New Amsterdam into New York in 1664, but hardly any of the Dutch or British communities here cared much. Throughout the 1700s, Brooklynites quietly farmed (and

McCarren Pool in trendy Williamsburg (p176)

Classic brownstone buildings, Brooklyn Heights (p168)

A busy street scene in downtown Brooklyn (p173)

less quietly brought in slaves). When news of a Declaration of Independence crossed the East River in 1776, most shrugged their shoulders. That apathy changed when, a month later, the biggest battle of the war raged across their farms, with soldiers of both sides whoring in their taverns and killing each other around today's Prospect Park and Gowanus Canal. Led by General George Washington, the Continental Army saw 25,000 casualties, a humiliating loss.

If the 1700s were quiet in Brooklyn, the 1800s roared, as it started a more active relationship with its showy neighbor. Robert Fulton's steamboat in 1814 first turned the Brooklyn Heights area into a commuter's suburb, and Manhattan's overdeveloped waterfront sought new warehouse slots from Red Hook to Greenpoint. Gaining confidence, the 16,000 people of a wee Brooklyn proudly made themselves a city in 1834 (hilariously outraging many of New York City's 200,000 residents). But Brooklyn would soon outgrow them: by the outset of the Civil War, Brooklyn ballooned to a quarter million residents, one million by the turn of the century and – with waves of Southern blacks and European immigrants pouring in – 2.5 million by the start of the Great Depression.

Sharing secrets at the Brooklyn Museum (p184)

The period from the Civil War till the early 1900s was Brooklyn's first great boom, as its first grand institutions opened (like the Brooklyn Museum, Brooklyn Children's Museum and Brooklyn Academy of Music), and 'uptown' residential areas like Park Slope took shape. Yet the growth began tapping out the city's administration and infrastructure, and Brooklyn narrowly voted in favor of joining New York City in 1898; still remembered as a 'dark day' for the now 'demoted' borough. But its pace didn't slacken. By 1908, subway connections spurred on a mass Manhattan exit. Many Italian and Jewish people, for example, moved into new homes in deeper districts like Bay Ridge. Others came for the day, to escape the urban grind on Coney Island's rides and boardwalk, made famous nationwide by Buster Keaton films.

After WWII, Brooklyn began a long dip downward. The borough's *Daily News Eagle* stopped its presses in 1955, the hometown Dodgers packed for California in 1957, and residents with cars bolted for the suburbs of

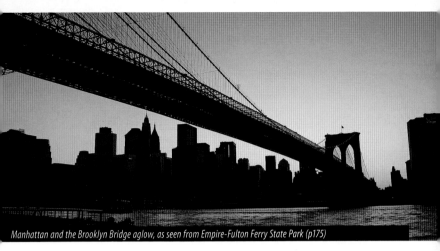
Manhattan and the Brooklyn Bridge aglow, as seen from Empire-Fulton Ferry State Park (p175)

Long Island or across the new Verrazano-Narrows Bridge (1964) to Staten Island. Increasing pockets of wasteland neighborhoods full of poverty and crime remained behind, disturbingly broadcasted nationwide in 1977 when a citywide blackout led to arson, rioting and store lootings in Bushwick.

As Manhattan bounced back in the 1990s, Brooklyn slowly followed, but it remained a step behind until the 21st century.

BROOKLYN'S BOOM!

With cheaper rents bringing Manhattan's artists and indie rockers over, Brooklyn's popularity has grown and grown. And so have the ambitions of city planners and real-estate developers. The waterfront is undergoing a (generally popular) overhaul from Dumbo to Cobble Hill (see the boxed text, p175), IKEA and cruise ships have laid stakes in once rough-and-tumble Red Hook, and debates rage over rezoning proposals to put new condos or hotels on Coney Island's long-worn amusement space (see the boxed text, p196) or along Gowanus' gritty industrial canal.

But nothing is more hotly discussed than Bruce Ratner's 22-acre 'Atlantic Yards' project, a Frank Gehry–designed complex centered at the intersection of Atlantic Ave and Flatbush Ave. Fans of the $4 billion development (approved in 2006) believe it'll bring thousands of new jobs to Brooklyn – with a new arena for the NBA Nets, plus offices and loft space for 17,000 people. Others protest that it'll worsen traffic problems (Flatbush Ave is mad as is) and that it will end up forcing many Prospect Heights and downtown locals out of their homes.

At research time, construction hadn't yet begun. A lawsuit put forth by a dozen relocated

'DEM BUMS'

It appears the NBA Nets will be Brooklyn's by 2010 and – despite the controversy of their downtown arena – they're sure to be welcomed by scores of rabid fans. It's been half a century since Brooklyn's beloved Dodgers bolted for LA – and even kids here seem to feel the scars from that dark day in 1957.

The glories of now-destroyed Ebbets Field (Map p182) – when kids put an ear to the pavement to watch from under an outfield gate for free – are told and retold to new generations, each time a little more exaggerated. Many versions, however, miss the fact that the true 'glory era' of Jackie Robinson and company was the late '40s and early '50s, when they were *losing*. Fans loved them, but called the team 'dem Bums' for their tendency to break hearts (over seven years, they lost the World Series four times, and twice they lost the pennant in a season's last inning). By the time the Dodgers finally won their first series in 1955, attendance was almost half of its '47 turnout and owner Walter O'Malley was starting to entertain can't-be-refused-offers from Los Angeles, where they ended up after the '57 season.

To read up on the legend – before a new one begins – try Roger Kahn's entertaining *The Boys of Summer*.

A greenmarket at Grand Army Plaza (p121)

property owners was appealing to the Supreme Court over the issue – but previous courts have ruled that the public benefits (transport improvements and new park space) essentially outweigh the negatives. Most believe it's a done deal, and will move ahead rapidly over the life of this book. In 2007 a local bagel shop even changed its name to 'Arena Bagels' (for the Nets' potential new home). When upset patrons stopped coming, however, the owner dropped an 'N' to become 'Area Bagels.'

BLACK BROOKLYN

Many of Brooklyn's most captivating images are linked with its rich African American history: movies like Spike Lee's *Do the Right Thing,* Chris Rock's jokes about 'Do or Die Bed-Stuy' on his TV series *Everybody Hates Chris,* or Dodgers hero Jackie Robinson stealing home plate and breaking color barriers at Ebbets Field in 1947. But the history began way before TV came to town.

After New York State emancipated slaves in 1827, the newly freed slaves – some from Brooklyn – made up nearly a third of the population here. In the tense decades leading up to the Civil War, Brooklyn Heights' Plymouth Church (p169) became something of a 'Grand Central' stop on the Underground Railroad, a network of abolitionists and sympathizers who hid runaway slaves on their journeys as they escaped from the South. Some, it's believed, settled in the long-forgotten black community of Weeksville (p193), in Bedford-Stuyvesant.

Ravishing in red: a reveler at the West Indian American Day Carnival Parade (p23)

SPECIAL EVENTS

- **Mermaid Parade** (first Saturday of summer; Coney Island) A fun, campy parade with outrageous costumes (see the boxed text, p198).
- **Nathan's Hot-Dog-Eating Contest** (Coney Island) The legendary focal point of the wild July 4 party.
- **West Indian American Day Carnival Parade** (Labor Day; Prospect Heights & Crown Heights) A summer *carnaval* on Eastern Parkway sees endless floats with drum players and dancers in bright, ruffled costumes, plus lots of good Caribbean food.
- **Atlantic Antic** (Last Sunday of September; Boerum Hill & Brooklyn Heights) Ten-block street fair with lots of greasy food, go-go and belly dancers, and overlapping rock, blues and R&B bands. Start at Atlantic Ave and walk to Brooklyn Heights.
- **Christmas Lights** (Dyker Heights) This working-class Italian neighborhood gets showy in December with power-sucking light displays that draw a quarter-million onlookers. Take the R train to 86th St and start at 1145 84th St, between 11th and 12th Aves.

Nathan's Famous Hot-Dog-Eating Contest (p22), Coney Island

Before there was a 'Brooklyn renaissance' there was a 'black renaissance' that began in Fort Greene in the early '90s, when Rosie Perez and Branford Marsalis (and later Erykah Badu) moved in. Nearby a handful of black-run businesses have helped transform the long decaying Fulton St, including Cake Man Raven (p270) with his red-velvet cupcakes. In 2008, long-time Harlem soul-food stand-out Amy Ruth's reopened the site of Gage & Tollner, a 19th-century steakhouse that ran till 2004.

Brooklyn's now home to a rising number of Caribbean immigrants (some 300,000 currently) – many of whom participate in the million-strong West Indian American Day Carnival Parade (p23) in Crown Heights on Labor Day weekend.

THE NEXT BROOKLYN?

Brooklyn used to be where downtown artists and rock bands fled for more affordable lives *and* better proximity to downtown Manhattan's nightlife; now it's providing multimillion-dollar satellite pads for the well-off – like Beyoncé, who apparently bought a penthouse in a new Richard Meier building in Prospect Heights in 2007. The dirt-cheap deals are long gone. For example, Carroll Gardens' rents went up 300% from 2005 to 2008, and a mere parking space at the controversial One Brooklyn Bridge Park condo (p175) costs about $125,000.

Where will the next 'it' neighborhood be? Pockets of Queens have a head start over the other boroughs: the Greek/Eastern European neighborhood of Astoria has a few hipsters and a popular Czech beer garden (p298), while Long Island City's Williamsburg-style industrial streets across from Midtown have long been home to an arts district (though new condo towers on the riverfront are pricing out many long-term locals these days). The great secret of Queens, particularly for family-style brick homes mixing both style and yard space, might be Sunnyside Gardens, which only became a historic district in 2007 (three-bedroom houses can be found at 30% the cost of Park Slope houses).

Yet many feel that the Bronx – with its street cred and hip-hop roots – is more 'legit' than Queens, and rezoned lofts in 'SoBro' (South Bronx, particularly along Buckner Blvd in Mott Haven) have tempted artists and space-seekers to this industrial, formerly rough-edged 'hood. Apartments go from $150,000 to $350,000 – peanuts even in Brooklyn.

Sidewalk dining on Smith St's restaurant row, Carroll Gardens (p271)

The latest intriguing buzz is Staten Island's North Shore, where an artist community has been establishing a bit of a scene near the ferry docks. Victorian homes with three bedrooms can be had for under $1000 per month – less than a junk studio in the East Village. Of course it *is* a ferry ride away. Transport's also a worry for the rise of Jersey City, with lovely historic townhouses a couple of blocks from the other side of the Hudson. Only the pokey PATH train gets you back to SoHo.

It could be that the 'next Brooklyn' is really 'Deep Brooklyn.' Some Williamsburgers have already reached the still-sketchy blocks of Bushwick, a couple of subway stops farther 'in.' Same for Ditmas Park, where there's an anarchist café and a couple of nice restaurants, on the leafy blocks of stunning-to-see *Leave It To Beaver*–style houses south of Prospect Park. What's next, East Flatbush? Either way, it's certain that New York's not over Brooklyn yet.

(Continued from page 184)

Near Bed-Stuy's southern reaches, **Stuyvesant Heights Historic District** (Map pp170–1; A, C to Utica Ave) vies with Brooklyn Heights for the best late-19th-century brownstones – something house-buyers are catching on to (prices now break $1 million). Head west from the Fulton St subway for a block and wander up Lewis Ave, then left and right on Decatur and Mc-Donough Sts; Lewis Ave has a café or two.

A block east of the Fulton St subway, Rochester Ave leads south into Crown Heights to the Weeksville Historic Center (Map pp170–1; 718-756-5250; 1698 Bergen St btwn Rochester & Buffalo Aves; adult/children $4/free; tours on the hr 1-3pm Tue-Fri, 11am-3pm Sat; A, C to Utica Ave), in a black community built (mostly) by freed slaves after New York abolished slavery in 1827. Three wooden houses (aka the Hunterfly Road Houses) can be visited.

Five blocks west on Bergen St, then south a couple on Kingston Ave, you reach the golden, L-shaped Brooklyn Children's Museum (Map pp170–1; 718-735-4400; www.brooklynkids.org; cnr Kingston & St Marks Aves; admission $5; 1-6pm Tue-Fri, 11am-6pm Sat & Sun Jul & Aug, 1-6pm Wed-Fri, 11am-6pm Sat & Sun Sep-Jun; C to Kingston-Throop Aves, 3 to Kingston Ave), a hands-on, kids' favorite. The museum – reopened in spring 2008 after a huge expansion – dates from 1899. It's known for celebrating different cultures and music and dance events on Friday nights in July and August.

Five blocks south via Kingston Ave to Eastern Parkway is the Lubavitch World Headquarters (Map pp170–1; 770 Eastern Pkwy at Kingston Ave; 3 to Kingston Ave), the center of the Chabad-Lubavitch Hasidic Jewish sect.

Follow Eastern Parkway (see p183) five blocks west to Bedford Ave, turn left and walk a few blocks to see the former site of the Brooklyn Dodgers' ballpark, Ebbets Field (Map p182; cnr Bedford Ave & Sullivan Pl; B, Q to Prospect Park, 2, 3, 4, 5 to Franklin Ave). The stadium closed in 1957 when the team moved to Los Angeles, and was replaced by the Jackie Robinson Apartments in 1960.

RED HOOK

For over a century the Statue of Liberty has fixated on this ever-gritty neighborhood of harbor warehouses and crackled brick streets. It's taken till this century for anyone else to notice. In recent years, cruise ships (including the 1132ft-long *Queen Mary 2*), Fairway supermarkets (p240) and, good golly, IKEA have set up shop in Red Hook, which remains mostly a grisly district of closed warehouses and project buildings. Many of the long-time residents remain linked with the area's gritty dock-worker rep, which inspired the film *On the Waterfront*. In recent years, an influx of Latin Americans have moved into some parts of the area, but outside of a few new-neighborhood pioneers and artists looking for studio space, Red Hook's remoteness has kept it from being transformed in a rush by new low-rent seekers.

Named by the Dutch for its shape and soil color, Red Hook has felt more like an island since the Brooklyn–Battery Tunnel and the BQE severed it from Carroll Gardens, just north. The only way here (by land, that is) is aboard the pokey B61 or B77 buses from Carroll Gardens, or an industrial-area walk from the Smith-9 Sts station on the F or G, about a mile northeast. The most fun way, however, is to take the New York Water Taxi (p391).

Red Hook

WALKING TOUR

1 Brooklyn Historic Railway Trolleys

Facing the water taxi dock, the two green trolleys (originally from Boston) that greet your Red Hook entry are legacies of the superb efforts of local history aficionado Bob Diamond in the '80s and '90s to bring back trolleys to Red Hook's streets. Initially the city backed him up, even laying tracks on Conover St (to your left), but by 2003 the Dept of Transportation withdrew support and the plan faded.

2 Post–Civil War warehouses

Facing the water are three red-brick warehouses from 1869. The one behind the trolleys once housed in-bound coffee, but is now home to Fairway supermarket (a huge success in grocery-acquisition for locals); it's a good spot to pick up a coffee or fresh bagel for a harbor-side snack. The two Beard Street Warehouses to the east are now home to the non-profit Brooklyn Waterfront Artists Coalition (www.bwac .com; 499 Van Brunt St; admission free; ☺ 1-6pm Sat & Sun), a group of private studios and galleries. Just east, notice the fire-destroyed ruins of a former sugar refinery.

3 Waterfront Museum & Showboat Barge

Head back past Fairway, along the water, then turn right on Conover St. The red barge you see to the left (marked 'Leigh 79') is the kid-oriented, floating Waterfront Museum (Map p180; ☎ 718-624-4719; www.waterfrontmuseum.org; Pier 44, 209 Conover St; admission by donation; ☺ 4-8pm Thu, 1-5pm Sat, plus special events), which stages various events (including Sunday circuses in June) aboard an old barge that a former juggler dug up from under the George Washington Bridge.

4 Coffey St Pier

Heading north on scruffy blocks near the showboat barge, turn left on Van Dyke St towards Pier 41, where you can get a chocolate-covered key lime pie at Steve's

WALK FACTS

Start Beard St Pier (via New York Water Taxi)
End Red Hook Recreational Area
Distance 2¼ miles
Duration Two to three hours
Fuel stops Fairway, Steve's Key Lime Pies, Baked café, taco stands

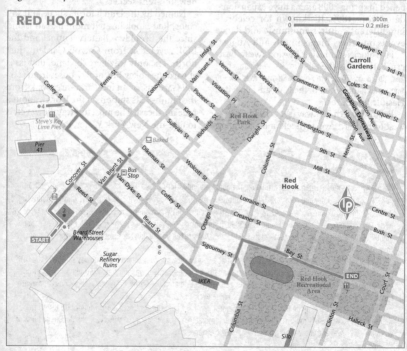

RED HOOK

Key Lime Pies (p272), then go a block north to Coffey St to reach the Coffey St Pier (Pier 39). Fishers like to come here, and there's a tiny beach that probably won't tempt you, but the pier is wonderful for its direct views towards the unsettling stare of Lady Liberty.

5 Van Brunt St Three blocks east of the pier along cobblestoned Coffey St is Van Brunt St, named for a Dutch family with roots going back to New Amsterdam. These days, it's the heart of Red Hook's bumbling renaissance – a strip of a few eateries, antique shops and a great café called Baked (☎ 718-222-0345; 359 Van Brunt St; ⏲ 7am-7pm Mon-Fri, 8am-7pm Sat & Sun).

6 Fort Defiance site Follow Van Brunt St south and turn left on Beard St. Two blocks ahead (past a school bus parking lot and towards IKEA) at the corner of Dwight St is the former site of Fort Defiance, a key part of the little-known Battle of Brooklyn during the Revolutionary War. With defeat of the young Americans certain, cannon fire from Red Hook helped General George Washington's troops retreat safely to Manhattan.

7 Soccer Field Tacos Follow the roads towards the athletic fields at the Red Hook Recreational Area. You'll see a 1922 silo ahead. Curve left then right on Bay St to reach the Central American food stalls (p271) at Clinton St. Afterwards, grab a bus to Carroll Gardens from the stop at Van Dyke St (off Van Brunt St), or walk up Columbia St.

BENSONHURST & BAY RIDGE

'Watch the hair!' At Brooklyn's southwestern tip is an almost insulated New York that garnered 15 minutes of fame when John Travolta fretted over his well-combed crown in *Saturday Night Fever* and strutted by the elevated subway tracks in Bensonhurst (Map pp170–1). That certain disco film famously starts just outside the 18th Ave subway station (take the D or M train there). There are plenty of shops and pizzerias to find along 86th St.

Known as Yellow Hook (for its clay color) until the yellow-fever epidemic of the mid-19th century, the more attractive Bay Ridge (Map pp170–1) stretches south along the water to the Verrazano-Narrows Bridge. The neighborhood is historically home to many Scandinavians and Italians, and in recent years to many Chinese. The most interesting areas are along Third Avenue from about 76th to 95th Sts (many piz-zerias and Irish pubs); take the R train to 77th, 86th or Bay Ridge-95th Sts. A few blocks west is the harbor-hugging, 2.5-mile-long Shore Parkway Promenade. Just before its south end is Verrazano-Narrows Bridge, which was built to connect Brooklyn with Staten Island in 1964.

Just below the bridge is Fort Hamilton (1826), run by future Confederate general Robert E Lee in the 1840s. The fort is still an active army base, but you can tour much of it anyway (bring a photo ID to get in). Part of the old storage area has been transformed into the Harbor Defense Museum (Map pp170–1; ☎ 718-630-4349; 101st St & Fort Hamilton Pkwy; admission free; ⏲ 10am-4pm Mon-Fri, to 2pm Sat; ⊕ R to Bay Ridge/95 St).

Most Scandinavian Americans live up in northern Bay Ridge, where you can see the Norwegian Constitution Parade at Leif Ericson Park (Fourth Ave & 66th St; ⊕ R to Bay Ridge Ave) on the first Sunday after May 17, the anniversary of Norway's first constitution. Grab some herring salad (or miniature Norwegian trolls) at Nordic Delicacies (Map pp170–1; ☎ 718-748-1874; 6909 Third Ave at Bay Ridge Ave; ⏲ 9am-6pm Mon-Fri, to 3pm Sat; ⊕ R to Bay Ridge Ave).

CONEY ISLAND & BRIGHTON BEACH

Some 50 minutes by subway from Midtown, these two beachside neighborhoods sit a mile apart on the calm Atlantic tides and are well connected by a beachside boardwalk. There the similarity ends. Coney Island is – for the time being – an anything-goes carnival district, with greasy hot dogs from Nathan's Famous (p281) and 'shoot the freak' games off the famed boardwalk; in quieter Brighton Beach, signs in Cyrillic cater to many locals born in the former Soviet Union, mostly Ukrainian Jews. It's a fun day trip to visit both (see the walking tour on p197).

The rides at Coney Island's amusement parks run on weekends only from the start of April, then daily from mid-June through Labor Day. Generally rides don't operate from September through April. All along the boardwalk, of course, is the beach. It's widely used, but still not too dirty. The water is off-limits during the low season, when lifeguards are off-duty. Plenty of shops sell water-related gear. Brighton Beach's boardwalk strip is a bit more relaxed, though it passes by a few 'banquet halls' with raucous, vodka-fueled dinner parties. A block in from the water, Brighton Beach Avenue is lined with shops

CONEY ISLAND: PAST & FUTURE

Coney Island, named by the Dutch for the wild rabbits (*konijn*) that once ran rampant here, became known as 'Sodom by the Sea' by the end of the 19th century, when it was infamous as a den for gamblers, hard drinkers, boxers, racers and other cheery sorts you'd want to introduce to Mom. In the early 1900s, the family era kicked in as amusement parks were built as diversions to the summer heat for a growing New York population. Its most famous, Luna Park, opened in 1903 – a dreamworld with live camels and elephants and 'rides to the moon' – all lit by over a million bulbs (not surprisingly, fire eventually took it down in 1946). The surviving gems from that time, the 1920 Wonder Wheel (opposite) and the 1927 Cyclone roller coaster (opposite), were then merely peripheral rides compared to the bigger players back in the park's heyday.

By the 1960s, Coney Island's pull had slipped (though long-time resident Woody Guthrie still considered nearby Mermaid Ave home) and the 'hood became a sad, crime-ridden reminder of past glories. Despite a slow, enduring comeback in the 1980s and a few promising changes in recent years – including the emergence of the wild Mermaid Parade (see the boxed text, p198), new carnival rides, a super new subway station, a minor-league baseball team (p325) and the aquarium – much of it looks like the long-abandoned site of a Siberian carnival. Derelict buildings sit in a sea of weeds behind chain-link fences, right off the boardwalk. Dennis Bourderis from Deno's Wonder Wheel told us, 'We need more rides here, more things for people to do. There've been too many empty lots for 40 years.' And David Gratt from Coney Island USA said, 'Everyone here agrees change is needed, but what kind of change?'

Earlier this decade, real-estate developer Joseph Stitt (of Thor Equities) bought up 10 acres at the heart of Coney Island for $120 million, and released a controversial $1.5 billion plan to bring a Disney-style park (plus condos and shopping centers) to the area. Most locals worried about the condos it would bring to the boardwalk area, and the city has backed up their concern. In November 2007, Mayor Michael Bloomberg offered a new plan of transforming Coney's gritty blocks into a 19-block, 47-acre project that would divide the area into separate zones, with housing allowed only north of Surf Ave. Apparently Stitt wasn't exactly giddy that his investment would be limited to rides and cinemas.

No one knows yet if and when such a plan might happen. It's likely that the clunky old Astroland and 'Shoot the Freak' paintball games could survive through the 2009 season.

---

selling imported caviar, candies and *matrushka* dolls.

CONEY ISLAND USA Map pp196–7
☎ 718-372-5159; www.coneyisland.com; 1208 Surf Ave at W 12th St; ⊕ F, D, N, Q to Coney Island-Stillwell Ave
The heart of Coney Island in many ways is this two-part, nonprofit complex. Best is

the Sideshows by the Seashore (adult/child $5/3; ⏰ 1-9pm Sat & Sun Apr-Sep, plus Wed-Fri Jul-Aug), where you can see glass-walking, a face-tattooed fire-eater, a Mormon sword-swallower and nostril nailers.

Upstairs is the small Coney Island Museum (admission $0.99; ⏰ noon-5pm Sat & Sun all year, Wed-Fri Jul-Aug), featuring local memorabilia. It also hosts a goofball Saturday night film series (ticket

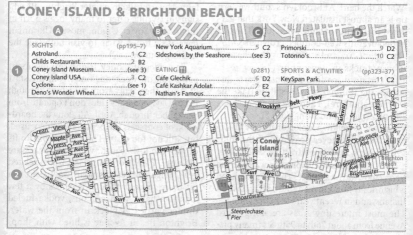

CONEY ISLAND & BRIGHTON BEACH

SIGHTS	(pp195–7)
Astroland	1 C2
Childs Restaurant	2 B2
Coney Island Museum	(see 3)
Coney Island USA	3 C2
Cyclone	(see 1)
Deno's Wonder Wheel	4 C2
New York Aquarium	5 C2
Sideshows by the Seashore	(see 3)

EATING	(p281)
Cafe Glechik	6 D2
Café Kashkar Adolat	7 E2
Nathan's Famous	8 C2

Primorski	9 D2
Totonno's	10 C2

SPORTS & ACTIVITIES	(pp323–37)
KeySpan Park	11 C2

incl free popcorn $5; ⏱ 8pm Sat May-Sep), with such campy 'classics' as cult alien romp *Forbidden Planet* and anything by John Waters.

DENO'S WONDER WHEEL Map pp196–7
☎ 718-449-8836; W 12th St near Surf Ave; ride $6, 10 kiddie rides $20; ⏱ mid-March–Oct; ◉ F, D, N, Q to Coney Island-Stillwell Ave

Safe from future development, the Wonder Wheel is a pink-and-mint-green Ferris wheel that actually predates the Cyclone by seven years (see below). There are also other kiddie rides (10-ride tickets available) and adult ones like the (surprisingly scary) Spookarama.

ASTROLAND Map pp196–7
☎ 718-265-2100; www.astroland.com; Surf Ave & W 10th St; Cyclone ride $6, Astroland per ride/10 rides $2.50/20; ⏱ Mar-Oct; ◉ F, D, N, Q to Coney Island-Stillwell Ave

The clackety, classic 1927 Cyclone roller coaster drops a dozen times and reaches the speed of 60mph on near-vertical falls. The roughly two-minute ride has been on the National Register of Historic Places since 1991 and is safe from future development. The same can't be said for its other half, a collection of kids' rides at Astroland (here since 1962), which may not survive the 2009 season.

NEW YORK AQUARIUM Map pp196–7
☎ 718-265-3474; www.nyaquarium.com; Surf Ave & W 8th St; adult/child & senior $12/8; ⏱ 10am-5pm or 6pm, see website; ◉ F to W 8th St-NY Aquarium

Right off the boardwalk, this fun, kid-friendly aquarium offers lots of opportunities to peek at creatures of the waterworld. Look for scheduled feeding times (the shark feeds are big draws) and sea lion shows (free kisses if you dare). But the biggest star these days is a baby walrus born to its 12ft-long parents in 2007. There's a virtual, 3-D 'deep sea ride' outside ($6) that kids squeal over, but it seems a bit overpriced for six minutes of bumping about.

Off the Boardwalk: Kvass & Hot Freaks
WALKING TOUR

1 Brighton Beach Avenue Just east from the subway, at the southeast corner of Coney Island Ave, the modern, 850-unit Oceana Condominium & Club opened in 2000, controversially taking up the spot of the beloved Brighton Beach Baths (opened in 1907). Double back under the tracks, browsing sidewalk stands selling fur hats and tinned caviar, or shops like M & I International (☎ 718-615-1011; 249 Brighton Beach Ave btwn Brighton 2nd & 3rd Sts; ⏱ 8am-10pm) for Czar-print chocolates, or Dom Knigi Sankt Peterburg (230 Brighton Beach Ave btwn Brighton 1st & 2nd Sts; ⏱ 10am-9pm) for ironic Soviet T-shirts and *matrushka* dolls.

2 Brighton Boardwalk Take Brighton 1st Rd to the beach boardwalk. To your left are a few beach-facing 'banquet halls' – a couple are open during the day and serve mugs of *kvass* (a barley-based drink from the heartland that takes some practice to enjoy).

3 Akituusaq the Walrus Head west on the boardwalk – the beach tends to be emptier here than at Coney – and stop at the New York Aquarium (left) to see the impossibly cute, whiskered walrus toddler 'Aki.' Born in June 2007, Akituusaq (a Siberian Yupik name), already 120 pounds at birth, is a rare walrus survivor from birth in captivity. He grows fast, but will be smaller than his 12ft-long parents for a couple of years yet.

4 Cyclone Set on the spot where the world's first roller coaster was built (in 1884), loyalists swear this 1927 coaster (left) remains the best. You must ride it. Enjoy, and prepare for a miracle: in 1948, a mute West Virginian screamed in fear the whole two minutes around the 3000ft track, suddenly finding his voice after five years of silence.

5 Surf Avenue Head along Surf Ave west. The furniture store to the right was the site of Luna Park, Coney Island's wild, Middle Eastern–styled amusement park offering 'trips to the moon.' A block west, at W 12th St, pop into Sideshows by the Seashore (p196) to see folks pound nails into their noses.

6 Steeplechase Pier Head back to the boardwalk, perhaps going for a ride on the Wonder Wheel (p197), and turn right on the boardwalk to this pier for great views of the area. To the left is KeySpan Park (opened in 2001), where Steeplechase Park – Coney Island's most-successful amusement park – flourished until the early 1960s. Woody Allen used its (now demolished) Thunderbolt rollercoaster as his childhood home in his 1977 film *Annie Hall*. Just beyond is the Parachute Jump, built for the World's Fair in Queens in 1939 and now lit up at night.

WALK FACTS

Start Brighton Beach Ave (B, Q to Brighton Beach)
End Steeplechase Pier (D, F, N, Q at Coney Island-Stillwell Ave)
Distance Two miles
Duration Two to four hours
Fuel stops Cafe Glechik (p281), Totonno's (p281)

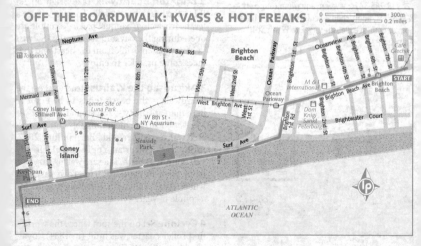

OFF THE BOARDWALK: KVASS & HOT FREAKS

Eating p281; Shopping p243

While Brooklyn barks its lore and glory to the world, Queens likes staying quiet about how great *it* is. Its popularity is growing some, though, as new condo towers shoot up in neighborhoods like Long Island City and Astoria. Typical of residents' reaction is local garage-rock band Queens Denim Rockers, whose ironic song 'Welcome to Queens' echoes their frustration with the sudden influx of new neighbors.

It's true that Queens is not always a knock-out nabe – with elevated train lines and busy streets of functional homes built to house the masses – but the borough has many pluses, thanks in no small part to its diversity. Some 46% of its 2.2 million residents were born out of the country, and some 150 nations are represented here. That makes it, with ease, the most ethnically diverse neighborhood or borough in the world. A ride on the 'International Express' (the 7 subway line, see the boxed text, p202) flies past a bewildering mix of neighborhoods – Indian, Filipino, Irish, Italian, Colombian, Korean etc – that makes for ever-rewarding and jaw-dropping strolls. Queens has also hosted the Beatles and two World Fairs, not to mention being home to two of NYC's airports and the annual US Open tennis tournament. And the other attractions, such as PS1's modern art (p202) or the Museum of the Moving Image's film props (p203), actually outnumber (and beat) Brooklyn's.

Queens was named in the 17th century for Queen Catherine of Braganza, then married to Charles II of England. (Clearly, Braganzatown didn't have the same ring to it.)

Orientation & Information

Between the Bronx and Brooklyn, Queens stretches east and south from roughly between Manhattan's 34th and 120th Sts. Queens is bounded by the East River to the north and west (where the Astoria and Long Island City neighborhoods face Manhattan), and wraps around Brooklyn to the Atlantic Ocean and Jamaica Bay (home to JFK International Airport).

Northern Blvd leads east through its northern half, passing through neighborhoods like Woodside, Jackson Heights, Corona and Flushing. Another main east–west artery is busy Roosevelt Ave, which runs under the 7 subway line from Flushing and splits into Skillman and Greenpoint Aves (which heads into Brooklyn) just east of Long Island City.

The Queens Tourism Council (☎ 718-263-0546; www .discoverqueens.info) offers information on attractions and tours, on their website or by phone. Queens Council on the Arts (☎ 718-647-3377; www.queen scouncilarts.org) promotes art in the borough, and its website has 'artMAP' and 'International Express' maps to download.

Hunter College urban-geography professor Jack Eichenbaum leads many unusual walking tours (☎ 718-961-8406; www.geognyc.com; from $13) of Queens' ethnic neighborhoods, including a full-day walk/subway ride along the 7 train.

LONG ISLAND CITY

Just over the Pulaski Bridge from Brooklyn's Greenpoint and Williamsburg and just a subway stop from Manhattan, is not surprisingly, Queens' coolest pocket these days. It's a weird mix of urban realities: elevated trains rattle by graffiti-covered warehouses while new glittering condo towers hug the waterfront by the landmark cursive 'Coca-Cola' sign that faces the UN.

Things aren't looking back. A scrubby 'hood of unused warehouses not that long ago, it's eyed by many professionals seeking the 'new Brooklyn.' The boom sprang from the unlikely 48-story Citicorp Building (1 Court Sq; ◎ 7 to 45th Rd-Court House Sq, E, V to 23rd St-Ely Ave, G to Long Island City-Court House Sq), built in 1989, and – more importantly – its growing devotion to art, particularly evidenced by the PS1 Contemporary Art Center (p202).

Across the street is Court House Square (◎ 7 to 45th Rd-Court House Sq, E, V to 23rd St-Ely Ave, G to Long Island City-Court House Sq), home to a 1904 Beaux-Arts courthouse. Nearby, standing proud and keeping it real, is 5 Pointz, one of the best collections of graffiti left anywhere in New York. Walk under the 7 subway tracks on (unsigned) Davis St, just south of Jackson Ave, to see the dazzling displays of wall-to-wall art on a cluster of industrial buildings.

A couple of arty options reachable by foot include the Sculpture Center (☎ 718-361-1750; www .sculpture-center.org; 44-19 Purves St near 43rd Ave; suggested donation $5; ◷ 11am-6pm Thu-Mon), a giant brick warehouse with rotating exhibits.

You'll find good food and café options towards the water along Vernon Boulevard between

QUEENS

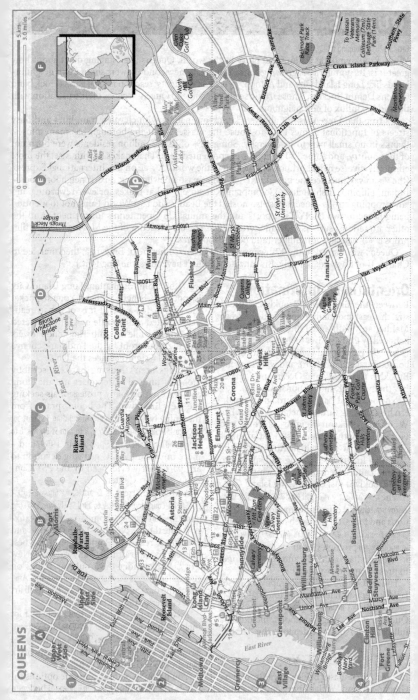

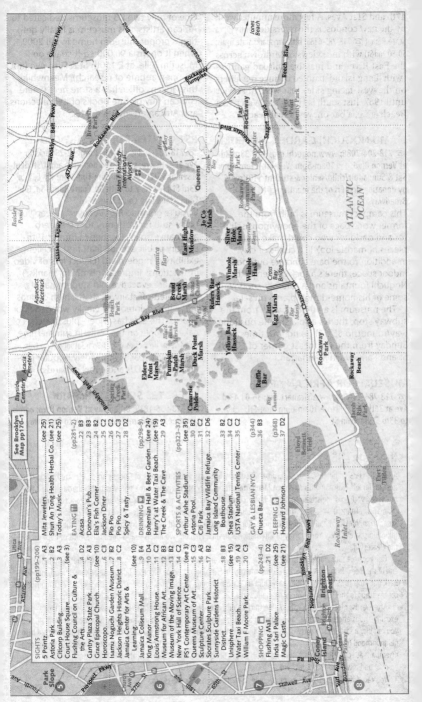

See Brooklyn Map pp170–1

47th and 51st Aves. A few more minutes west, by the new condos, is the riverside Gantry Plaza State Park (☎ 718-785-6385; http://nysparks.state.ny.us; 50-50 2nd St) with nice views of Midtown across the East River and massive railroad gantries (with 'Long Island' painted in huge red letters on the west-facing side) that were in service until 1967. Just south is Harry's at Water Taxi Beach (p298), a bar on, yes, a real beach.

ISAMU NOGUCHI GARDEN MUSEUM
☎ 718-204-7088; www.noguchi.org; 9-01 33rd Rd at Vernon Blvd; ⏰ 10am-5pm Wed-Fri, 11am-6pm Sat & Sun; adult/child/senior & student $10/free/5, by donation first Fri of the month; ◉ N, W to Broadway

This compact museum is built from the former workspace of the eponymous sculptor and designer who could make curling pieces of marble look like cubes of clay. In addition to the bare concrete outdoor/indoor space, there's a rock garden with Noguchi fountains and a café/gift shop with some of his home-design pieces on sale.

The museum is a 10-block walk from the subway stop; there's also a shuttle bus (one way/roundtrip $5/10) going four times each Sunday from the northeast corner of E 70th St and Park Ave in Manhattan.

MUSEUM FOR AFRICAN ART
☎ 718-784-7700; www.africanart.org; 36-01 43rd Ave at 36th St; ⏰ store 10am-6pm Mon-Fri; ◉ 7 to 33rd St-Rawson St

One of only two US museums dedicated to African artists, this museum is finally getting a proper museum home in fall 2009, when it opens a 90,000-sq-ft space on Museum Mile, at E 110th St & Fifth Ave (not yet open at time of research). Meanwhile, this Queens office has a store here where you can buy picture books of its collections and African art–themed gifts.

PS1 CONTEMPORARY ART CENTER
☎ 718-784-2084; www.ps1.org; 22-25 Jackson Ave at 46th Ave; suggested donation adult/student & senior $5/2; ⏰ noon-6pm Thu-Mon; ◉ E, V to 23rd St-Ely Ave, 7 to 45th Rd-Court House Sq, G to Long Island City-Court House Sq

If you're going to MoMA anyway, keep your ticket stub for free entry to this superb alternative-space location (a former 19th-century public school) featuring excellent exhibits of modern art. (Expect lots of video installations: 'Impressionism? No, thanks.') Rooms are evocative, old student haunts, with wired-off stairwell shafts, high ceilings and white-painted and creaky wooden floorboards. The café has wine – plus sketches of naked people on the walls. In summertime the 'Warm Up' Series (⏰ 3-9pm Sat Jul & Aug) fills the outside space with widely popular parties featuring DJs and a mix of bands.

SOCRATES SCULPTURE PARK
☎ 718-956-1819; Broadway at Vernon Blvd; admission free; ⏰ 10am-dusk; ◉ N, W to Broadway

RIDE ON THE INTERNATIONAL EXPRESS

A Queens classic: the elevated, ultra-urban 7 subway line cuts across the guts of Queens on an elevated track, connecting far-off Flushing with Midtown Manhattan. It not only offers views of the borough to Manhattan (and back), but takes you on a registered 'national historic trail' through the longtime immigrant neighborhoods of Sunnyside (Romanian, Turkish), Woodside (Irish), Jackson Heights (Indian, Filipino), Corona Heights (Italian, Peruvian, Colombian, Ecuadorian, Mexican) and Flushing (Chinese, Korean). A good day could be spent hopping on and off the 'purple' line, taking in some of New York's array of international flavors. Plan on two meals – and ride in the front or back car for the clearest views.

One possible tour would be to get a subway day pass and take the 7 from Times Sq or Grand Central Terminal to the end of the line (Flushing-Main St), a 35-minute trip. In Flushing, get some Chinese, Taiwanese or Korean food, and ride back one stop to Willets Point-Shea Stadium for a walk through Flushing Meadows Corona Park (p204). Then ride a couple stops to the 103 St-Corona Park station: the Louis Armstrong House (p205) is a few blocks north.

Afterwards, meander under the 7 line tracks along Roosevelt Ave for 30 blocks west (towards Manhattan) – past exciting shops and restaurants, all signed in Spanish – to 74th St, where things suddenly become quite Indian, and you can buy a sari or eat a curry (p282). Hop back on the subway to Woodside-61st St and wander through an old Irish neighborhood to the Sunnyside Gardens Historic District (opposite). Catch the train at the 46th St-Bliss St station and disembark at Long Island City's 45th Rd-Court House Sq, getting out for a look at the PS1 Contemporary Art Center (above) and a walk to the waterfront.

You can download a free 7 line map/guide at www.queenscouncilarts.org.

TRANSPORTATION: QUEENS

Here are a few useful subway stops, broken down by neighborhood:

Astoria   ⊙ N, W to 30th Ave, Astoria Blvd or Astoria-Ditmars Blvd

Flushing   ⊙ 7 to Flushing-Main St, ⊞ LIRR to Flushing

Jackson Heights   ⊙ 7 to 74th St-Broadway, E, F, G, R, V to Jackson Heights-Roosevelt Ave

Jamaica   ⊙ E, J, Z to Sutphin Blvd-Archer Ave, ⊞ LIRR to Jamaica

Long Island City   ⊙ 7 to 45th Rd-Court House Sq or Vernon Blvd-Jackson Ave, E, V to 23rd St-Ely Ave, G to Long Island City-Court Sq

Rockaway Beach   ⊙ A to Beach 90th St (among other stops)

Shea Stadium & Flushing Meadows Corona Park   ⊙ 7 to Willets Point-Shea Stadium, ⊞ LIRR to Shea Stadium

Transformed from an illegal dumping site in 1986, this open-air, 4.5-acre public space near the Noguchi museum displays sculptures, installations and superb light shows illuminating its waterfront location on the East River. Try to time a visit for the fun free movies on Wednesdays in July and August; screenings start around 8pm (food available).

ASTORIA

Named for millionaire fur merchant John Jacob Astor (1763–1848), this northwestern edge of Queens is home to the largest Greek community in NYC. Greek bakeries, diners and delis line many streets here, particularly along Broadway (⊙ N, W to Broadway); they're slightly more upscale on 31st St and Ditmars Blvd (⊙ N, W to Astoria-Ditmars Blvd). Before Greeks began moving here in the 1950s, it was primarily a neighborhood of factories (not to mention bridges – arched Hell's Gate and towering Triborough still dominate the views west). These days an influx of Eastern Europeans (Croatians, Romanians) and Middle Eastern folk, not to mention the hip kids, have added to the scene.

An easy walk northwest of the Astoria-Ditmars Blvd station, 15-acre Astoria Park is set admirably on the water, with paths looking south toward Manhattan's skyscrapers from underneath the Triborough Bridge. Near the park is the 1936 art-deco beaut Astoria Pool (p336) – the fountains at one end were used as torches when Olympic trials were held here in 1936 and 1964.

MUSEUM OF THE MOVING IMAGE

☎ 718-784-4520; www.movingimage.us; 35th Ave at 36th St; adult/child/senior & student $10/5/7.50, free to all 4-8pm Fri; ⌚ 11am-5pm Wed & Thu, noon-8pm Fri, 11am-6:30pm Sat & Sun; ⊙ G, R, V to Steinway St

Once the home of Paramount Pictures' east coast HQ, this super-fun, three-story museum is closed for a $65-million renovation until late 2009. An extension will include a new theater and screening room and add more gallery space to house the museum's 150,000 movie props and knickknacks, which include Robert De Niro's mohawk wig from *Taxi Driver* and Chewbacca's head (sorry, kids, he's not real). Another fun part is the sound-edit room, where you can re-dub the 'we're not in Kansas anymore' scene from *The Wizard of Oz*. There are lots of massive, early cameras, including a camera that records your goofy antics as a flip-book (which you can then purchase as a souvenir). A downstairs area has free arcade games and screens films on Friday, Saturday and Sunday.

SUNNYSIDE & WOODSIDE

Half way between Long Island City and Jackson Heights loom two less-visited, side-by-side classic Queens neighborhoods that stretch under and off the elevated tracks of the 7 line. Sunnyside (centered at the 46 St/Bliss St subway stop) is a long-ignored residential area that's getting attention for the Sunnyside Gardens Historic District (north of Skillman Ave btwn 43rd & 49th Sts), a 1920s 'garden district' with US flags hanging outside red-brick townhouses. Nearby Skillman Avenue is lined with many Romanian and Turkish restaurants these days.

Following Skillman Ave east toward Roosevelt Ave and the 7 tracks, you enter Woodside, a long-time Irish neighborhood. Stop by local classic Donovan's Pub (p282) for a brew and some juicy burgers.

JACKSON HEIGHTS

All riders on the 'International Express' (see the boxed text, opposite) ought to stop off in the international whirlwind found off the 7 train's 74 St-Broadway stop. It's famously home to many Indians – with many curry and Bollywood DVD shops to suit – but you can also find Bangladeshi, Vietnamese, Korean, Mexican, Colombian, Ecuadorian and other ethnic groups.

Spread out in a 50-block area to the north of the subway is one of the nicest NYC neighborhoods that next to no New Yorkers know about. Following the 1909 opening of the 59th St-Queensboro Bridge, the Jackson Heights Historic District (btwn Roosevelt & 34th Aves, from 70th to 90th Sts) was set up in 1917 as a 'garden city' (popular in England at the time), with six-story, chateau-style brick apartment buildings sharing long, well-landscaped, (still) private gardens. There are a few good vantage points – try 80th or 81st Sts from 37th to 34th Aves.

Just east of 87th St, and right out of the Amazon, Horoscopo (☎ 718-779-9391; 86-26 Roosevelt Ave; ⊖ 7 to 90th St-Elmhurst Ave) is the lively base of the 'Amazon Indian' who tells fortunes amid colored tonics, tarot cards and hanging chicken feet.

FLUSHING & CORONA

Aside from coming out to see the Mets at their new stadium (as of 2009; see the boxed text, p211) or the US Open tennis matches (p328), these two otherwise little-known neighborhoods have active streets of locals' shops signed in Chinese, Korean, Spanish and Italian. In between the two areas is the bizarre but interesting Flushing Meadows Corona Park, dotted with buildings and monuments originally built to make statements for the 1939 and 1964 World's Fairs. They still do.

In the 17th century, Quakers met in Flushing to figure out how to avoid religious persecution from Dutch governor Peter Stuyvesant (which they did through tenacity, letters and finally appealing to the Dutch West India Company in Amsterdam in 1663). Two hundred years later, many escaped slaves found freedom here via the 'Underground Railroad'. By the 20th century, Flushing (in particular) had let itself go. When F Scott Fitzgerald dissed the area as an ash heap in The Great Gatsby (1925), he was being kind. The World's Fairs helped turn things around, making the swampy area more attractive for the many jazz greats who would later live here.

Flushing – at the end of the 7 subway line – has a flourishing Chinatown that's bigger than Manhattan's. Clusters of shops and eateries center on Roosevelt Ave and Main St. A couple of subway stops west, Corona's southern reach is a quaint Italian neighborhood that looks like a town square from another era. At William F Moore Park (aka Spaghetti Park, 108th St & Corona Ave), the clink-clank of bocce balls sounds in summer while passersby eat lemon ices.

FLUSHING COUNCIL ON CULTURE & THE ARTS
☎ 718-463-7700; www.flushingtownhall.org; 137-135 Northern Blvd; ⊗ 9am-5pm Mon-Fri, gallery noon-5pm; ⊖ 7 to Flushing-Main St
Built in 1862, this Romanesque revival building hosts year-round art shows and jazz concerts, as well as leading fun, three-hour 'Queens Jazz Trail' trolley tours ($35), held on the first Saturday of the month. The tour goes by old clubs and the homes of a staggering number of greats who lived in the area: Louis Armstrong, Lena Horne, Ella Fitzgerald, John Coltrane, Billie Holiday, Count Basie, Charles Mingus and others.

FLUSHING MEADOWS CORONA PARK
☎ 718-760-6565; www.nycgovparks.org; ⊖ 7 to Willets Point-Shea Stadium
The area's biggest attraction is this 1225-acre park, built for the 1939 World's Fair and dominated by monuments such as Queens' most famous landmark, the stainless steel Unisphere (the world's biggest globe, 120ft high and weighing 380 tons). Facing it is the former New York City Building, now home to the Queens Museum of Art (see opposite page). Just south are three weather-worn, Cold War–era New York State Pavilion Towers, which were part of the New York State Pavilion for the 1964 World's Fair.

If entering the park from the subway walkway, look for the 1964 World Fair mosaics by Salvador Dali and Andy Warhol (just down from the ped bridge from the subway). Also nearby is the tall Arthur Ashe Stadium, and the rest of the USTA National Tennis Center (p328). Head west on the pedestrian bridge over the Grand Central Pkwy to find a few more attractions, including the New York Hall of Science (☎ 718-699-0055; www.nyhallsci .org; 47-01 111th St; adult/student & child $11/8, free 2-5pm Fri; ⊗ daily Apr-Aug, closed Mon Sep-Mar, call or see website for hrs).

The park actually has grounds too, on its eastern and southern edges. The top-notch AstroTurf soccer fields are popular for organized and pick-up soccer, and there's a pitch-and-putt golf course that's lit up for drunken golfers at night (p332).

QUEENS MUSEUM OF ART

☎ 718-592-9700; www.queensmuseum.org; Flushing Meadows Corona Park; adult/child/senior & student $5/free/2.50; ☯ 10am-5pm Wed-Fri, noon-5pm Sat & Sun Sep-Jun, noon-6pm Wed, Thu, Sat & Sun, to 8pm Fri Jul-Aug; ◉ 7 to 111th St

Housed in the historic building made for the '39 World's Fair (and once home to the UN), this great museum's most famous piece is the Panorama of New York City, a 9335-sq-ft miniature New York City, with all buildings accounted for in a sweeping room the size of three tennis courts. Walking around the 895,000-structure piece – and its 15-minute dusk-to-dawn light simulation of a New York day – feels like descending in a plane over New York (without the tiny bag of mixed nuts or the ear pops). It was last updated after the events of September 11. The rest of the museum isn't to be missed either – a fetching collection of modern art and an excellent World's Fair exhibit to recount the days, in '39 and '64, when the rest of the globe looked at Queens. The museum will keep open hours through an ongoing expansion, to be finished in 2010.

LOUIS ARMSTRONG HOUSE

☎ 718-478-8274; www.louisarmstronghouse.org; 34-56 107th St; adult/senior & student $8/6; ☯ 10am-5pm Tue-Fri, noon-5pm Sat & Sun; ◉ 7 to 103rd St-Corona Plaza

At the peak of his career and with worldwide fame at hand, Satchmo chose Queens. Armstrong spent his last 28 years in this quiet Corona Heights home, now a museum and regarded as a national treasure; he died in 1971. Guides offer free 40-minute tours, leaving on the hour (the last starts at 4pm), through the home and past his many gold records on the wall.

JAMAICA

Where 50 Cent and LL Cool J first penned their rhymes, Jamaica gets missed by most Manhattan residents, but it's getting attention from travelers from afar, specifically those interested in superb 'hip-hop' shopping. Home to many West Indian immigrants, Jamaica's name is only coincidentally a nod to many of the new residents' birthplaces – centuries ago the Algonquin natives named the area *jameco* (or beaver), a name altered by the first English settlers in the mid-17th century. After railways linked Jamaica with the city, the population grew. The area is also now home to many Latin Americans.

The Jamaica Center-Parsons Archer subway stop (the last along the E, J and Z lines) is a short block south of the main strip, Jamaica Ave. Near the station, amid the 11-acre King Park, is the redone, Greco-Roman–style King Manor (☎ 718-206-0545; www.kingmanor.org; Jamaica Ave at 150th St; adult/student $5/3; ☯ noon-2pm Thu & Fri, 1-5pm Sat & Sun), home to US Constitution signatory Rufus King in the early 1800s. King, an early abolitionist, made a failed run for president in 1817 (the last Federalist to run). King is buried a block east in the cemetery outside Grace Episcopal Church (155-03 Jamaica Ave).

A couple of blocks east, outside the Jamaica Center for Arts & Learning (JCAL; ☎ 718-658-7400; www.jcal.org; 161-04 Jamaica Ave; admission free; ☯ 8:30am-6pm Mon-Sat) is one of only two remaining cast-iron sidewalk clocks in NYC (this one dates from 1900). Inside is a small art gallery featuring local works. Jamaica's main draw, however, is hip-hop shopping along the 165th St pedestrian mall, just north of Jamaica Ave, where side-by-side shops hawk Phat Farm, airbrushed sweatshirts of Tupac, Bailey straw hats, pastel neo-jazz suits and African dresses. A good catch-all is Jamaica Coliseum Mall (☎ 718-657-4400; 165th St at 85th Ave; ☯ 11am-7pm Mon-Fri, 10am-7pm Sat & Sun).

ROCKAWAY BEACH

The country's largest urban beach – and New York's best – is just a $2 trip on subway line A. Immortalized by the Ramones' 1977 song 'Rockaway Beach,' this terrific four-mile beach is less crowded than Coney Island and – despite being under the jet path to nearby JFK Airport – is home to some surprisingly natural scenery and surf spots (see p334).

Much of the area is part of the 26,000-acre Gateway National Recreation Area (www.nps.gov/gate), which encompasses several parks. One, toward the southern tip of the Rockaways, is Jacob Riis Park (☎ 718-318-4300; ◉ A, S to Rockaway Park Beach-116th St), named for an advocate and photographer of immigrants in the late 19th century; it's also home to Fort Tilden, a decommissioned coastal artillery installation from WWI. The boardwalk, beach and picnic areas are popular in summer.

Extending from near JFK, at the start of the Cross Bay Veterans Memorial Bridge, the 9155-acre Jamaica Bay Wildlife Refuge (Map pp200–1; ☎ 718-318-4340; www.nps.gov/gate; Cross Bay Blvd; admission free; ☯ 8:30am-5pm; ☉ A to Broad Channel) is home to a few hundred bird species. Drop by the visitors center for trail maps (or see the website) for the two trails; the west trail loops 1¼ miles around the West Pond amid marshes, just off the bay (plenty of waterfowl to spot). See p331 for information on bird-watching tours.

THE BRONX

Eating p282; Shopping p243

North of Manhattan, the Bronx is 'X-treme' New York. Here, the horn-honking is a little louder, the graffiti a little more daring, the swagger a little sharper. (Tellingly, a sign at a recent Yankees playoff game read: 'Welcome to Da Bronx. Get ready to die!') Maybe it's that definite article preceding its name that helps make the Bronx more than just your ordinary living place. And it is. It's the place that's given us three of New York's great achievements: the men in pinstripes (the Yankees), hip-hop, and the three-pack of cool – J-Lo, C-Po and B-Jo (Jennifer Lopez, Colin Powell and, uh, Billy Joel).

More of New York is talking about the Bronx these days, and pondering a move to enormous loft spaces at (relatively) cheap rents. In 'SoBro' (or South Bronx), Mott Haven (around 138th St & Bruckner Blvd; ⊙ 6 to 3rd Ave-138th St) is starting to attract its share of artists and folks looking for more elbow room. Bruckner Blvd is lined with industrial shops, red-brick loft spaces and nearly a dozen antique shops between the Third Ave and Willis Ave Bridges. It's possible to take kayak tours of the Bronx River here, too (p330). There's also a pedestrian walkway across the Third Ave Bridge into Harlem (p157).

Rough-at-the-edges Hunts Point, in southeastern Bronx, is starting to eke out some life. Here, the stunning Bronx Academy of Arts & Dance (BAAD!; ☎ 718-842-5223; www.bronxacademyofartsanddance.org; 841 Barretto St at Garrison Ave; ⊙ 6 to Hunts Point Ave) hosts some interesting festivals – 'BAAD! Ass Women Festival' in March and 'Out Like That!' in June, with gay, lesbian and transgender artworks and plays.

Like Queens, the Bronx is home to an ethnically diverse population. Nearly a quarter of the population is Puerto Rican and another quarter is black, while there are growing numbers of Jamaicans, Indians, Vietnamese, Cambodians and Eastern Europeans.

Orientation & Information

The only borough on the US mainland, the 42-sq-mile Bronx lies just north of Manhattan and wedged between the Hudson, Harlem and East Rivers and Long Island Sound.

The Bronx Tourism Council (www.ilovethebronx.com) regularly updates its website with area events. The Bronx County Historical Society (Map pp208-9; ☎ 718-881-8900; www.bronxhistoricalsociety.org; 3309 Bainbridge Ave at 208th St; ⊙ 4 to Mosholu Pkwy), set in a 1758 farmhouse, has a book shop and small museum and schedules occasional walking tours.

If you can stomach the cost, MCs like Kurtis Blow and Grandmaster Caz (from Cold Crush Brothers) lead weekly guided 'Birthplace of Hip-Hop' tours for Hush Tours (☎ 212-209-3370; www.hushtours.com; $55).

ARTHUR AVENUE/BELMONT Map pp208–9
⊙ B, D to Fordham Rd

Called New York's 'real Little Italy,' the Belmont area – on the blocks south of Fordham University between Bronx Park (to the east) and Third Ave (to the west) – is clearly marked with 'Little Italy in the Bronx' banners. Here you'll find pizzerias, trattorias, bakeries, fishmongers, and butchers with bunnies in the window – many working without breaking into English. Many New Yorkers claim that Roberto Restaurant (p282) offers the finest Italian eating in the city.

The famous scene in *The Godfather* – where Al Pacino gets the gun from behind 'the toilet with the chain thing' and blasts

TRANSPORTATION: THE BRONX

Subway The B, D, 1, 2, 4, 5 and 6 lines connect Manhattan with the Bronx, with useful stops at Yankee Stadium (B, D, 4 to 161st St-Yankee Stadium), near the Bronx Zoo (2, 5 to E Tremont Ave) and at the corner of Grand Concourse and Fordham Rd (B, D to Fordham Rd).

Train From Grand Central, Metro-North commuter trains provide better access to some parts of the Bronx, including the New York Botanical Garden and Wave Hill.

Trolley The Bronx Tourism Council runs a useful, free 'Bronx Tour Trolley,' which leaves from the NYC Visitors Information Center (53rd St at Seventh Ave, Manhattan) at 9:30am on weekends from April through October, and offers hop-on/off stops at the Bronx Zoo, Belmont and the Botanical Garden.

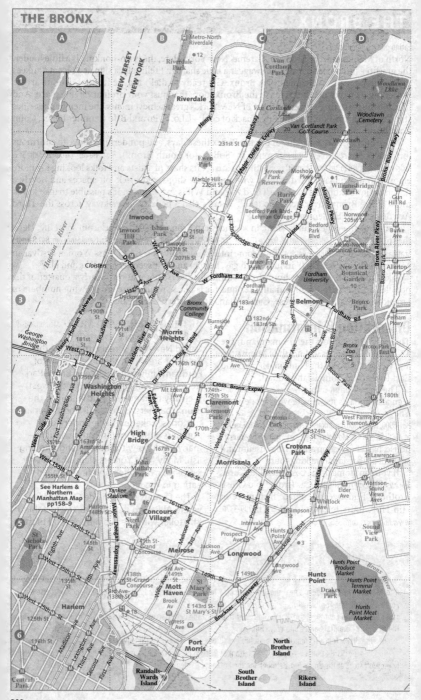

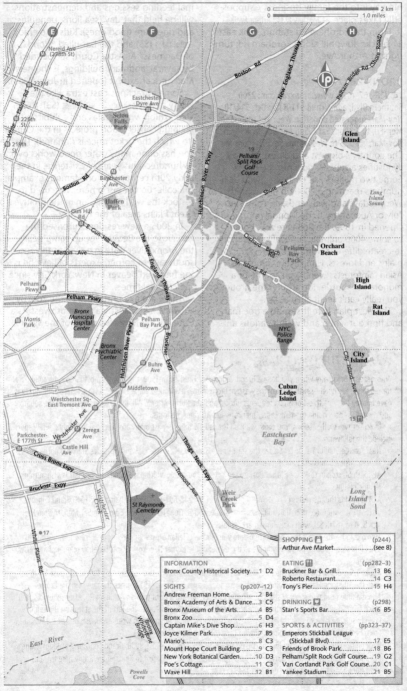

his way into the family business – supposedly takes place at Mario's (2342 Arthur Ave).

From the Fordham Rd station, walk east 11 blocks downhill along Fordham Rd; turn right at Arthur Ave.

BRONX ZOO Map pp208–9

☎ 718-367-1010; www.bronxzoo.com; 2300 Southern Blvd; adult/child $11/8 Apr-Oct, $14/10 Nov-Mar, suggested donation Wed; 10am-5pm Mon-Fri, to 5:30pm Sat & Sun Apr-Oct, to 4:30pm Nov-Mar; 2, 5 to West Farms Sq-E Tremont Ave

The country's biggest and oldest zoo easily justifies a subway ride into the Bronx. Some two million visit each year, with daily numbers reaching 35,000 on discounted Wednesdays and weekends, and any day in July or August (try to go Monday morning). Opened in 1899, the 265-acre zoo, home to some 4000 animals, has leafy areas that re-create different world habitats – African plains and forests, Himalayan mountains, Asian rainforests. Even if you spring for a monorail or shuttle ride around the grounds, you really can't see it all in a day.

The best plan is to first grab a free map and find out when and where various animal feeding sessions and demonstrations will be held that day (sea lions, penguins and tigers are good ones). Kids also enjoy camel rides ($5) and the bat-filled 'World of Darkness.' At Astor Court, surrounded by several landmark buildings, is the new Madagascar exhibit (opened in June 2008).

Some attractions cost extra, like the wildly popular Congo Gorilla Forest ($3), a 6.5-acre exhibit with gorillas and exhibits explaining conservation projects in the Congo (to which the ticket price is donated). The zoo has done many other good works over its hundred-plus years of existence. In the early 20th century, for one famous example, the collection of bison here were used to restock the wild population in their native Great Plains area of the country.

In 2005 a new resident surprised the zoo. 'Jose the Beaver' set up camp near the Bronx River Gate in a river at the zoo's southeastern corner; experts believe he is the first wild beaver in New York City since the colonial times.

There are five entrances to the zoo. By subway, it's easiest via the southwest Asia Gate (a couple blocks north of the West

WALKING THE CONCOURSE

Who needs a Broadway when you have a Grand Concourse? Finished in 1909, the Bronx's most famous thoroughfare turned this broad north–south stripe of the western Bronx into a New York Champs-Élysées, with art-deco buildings that have housed the wealthiest of Bronx residents (including Babe Ruth). After WWII, many locals rushed for the suburbs, and the area is now home to many Latin Americans and African Americans.

In one or two walk sessions, you could walk up the full 4½ miles – past many architectural highlights. A few spots include the following:

- Near Yankee Stadium at 161st St, see the start of the Bronx Walk of Fame, which includes Stanley Kubrick, Regis Philbin, Afrika Bambaataa and Rita Moreno.
- At 164th St, stop in to Joyce Kilmer Park to see Lorelei Fountain, which pays tribute to German Jewish author Heinrich Heine.
- At 165th St is the interesting Bronx Museum of Arts (☎ 718-681-6000; www.bxma.org; 1040 Grand Concourse. at 165th St; suggested donation adult/senior & student $5/3, free Fri; noon-6pm Thu, Sat-Mon, to 8pm Fri; B, D to 167th St), with many urban-art exhibits.
- Two blocks north, across the Concourse before you reach McClellan St, stands the Andrew Freedman Home, a 1924 limestone palace, previously home to the owner of the former New York Giants baseball team and a czarist general.
- About 1.5 miles north (along the tree-lined road, over the Cross Bronx Expressway, and two blocks past 176th St), note the 10-story, Flatiron Building–like Mount Hope Court Building (1914), once the tallest in the Bronx.
- About a mile (and two subway stops) north you can detour with a right turn on Fordham Rd. After six blocks, you reach Fordham University (north of Fordham Ave at Webster Ave); head to the left of the statue on the campus. lawn to see the bells of University Church, which inspired Edgar Allen Poe to write – can you guess? – *The Bells*. From here you can go on to explore Belmont (p207) or the Bronx Zoo (above).
- Back on the Concourse, and a block north, is Poe's Cottage (☎ 718-881-8900; Grand Concourse at Kingsbridge Rd; adults/students & seniors $3/2; 10am-4pm Sat, 1-5pm Sun; 4 to Kingsbridge Rd), where the author lived from 1846 till his drunken death in 1849.

Farms Sq-E Tremont Ave stop, up Boston Rd). Another option is aboard the BxM11 express bus ($5), which comes from Manhattan via Madison Ave, stopping along Madison at 26th, 47th, 54th, 84th and 99th Sts every 20 minutes or so. For transport by car, there's a parking lot ($10) near the Southern Blvd Gate on the zoo's north side.

CITY ISLAND Map pp208–9

🚇 6 to Pelham Bay Park, then 🚌 Bx29
About 15 miles and a world away from midtown Manhattan, City Island is one of New York's most surprising neighborhoods. Founded by the English in 1685, the 1.5-mile-long fishing community juts into the Long Island Sound and Eastchester Bay, connected to the mainland by a causeway. The Victorian clapboard houses here definitely look more New England than the Bronx, and the island is filled with boat slips, half a dozen yacht clubs and some rowdy seafood restaurants – notably Tony's Pier (☎ 718-885-1424; 1 City Island Ave), which fries everything but the cocktails.

If you're serious about diving, sailing or fishing, head to City Island. Island Current (☎ 917-417-7557; www.islandcurrent.com) leads fishing tours all year (from $50) and sunset tours. Captain Mike's Dive Shop (☎ 718-885-1588; www.captainmikesdiving.com; 530 City Island Ave) offers two-tank dive trips in the Long Island Sound or the ocean from May through November (from $75). Regular dives are scheduled weekends and some weeknights.

The City Island Chamber of Commerce (☎ 718-885-9100; www.cityislandchamber.org) has information on area services.

NEW YORK BOTANICAL GARDEN
Map pp208–9

☎ 718-817-8700; www.nybg.org; Bronx River Pkwy & Fordham Rd; adult/child/senior & student $6/1/3, free Wed & 10am-noon Sat; 🕙 10am-6pm Tue-Sun; 🚊 Metro-North to Botanical Garden
Spread across 50 acres of virgin forest (just north of the Bronx Zoo), the New York Botanical Garden (opened in 1891) is home to several beautiful gardens and the restored Enid A Haupt Conservatory, a grand, Victorian iron-and-glass edifice that is a New York landmark. You can also stroll through an outdoor rose garden just next to the conservatory, and a rock garden with a multi-tiered waterfall.

It's possible to take the subway via the B or D line to Bedford Park Blvd, then take bus Bx26 east, but it's easier to take the Metro-North's Harlem Line from Grand Central Terminal to the Botanical Garden stop (one way off-peak/peak $4.75/6.25).

WAVE HILL Map pp208–9

☎ 718-549-3200; www.wavehill.org; W 249th St at Independence Ave, Riverdale; adult/senior & student $6/3, free Tue & 9am-noon Sat; 🕙 9am-5:30pm Tue-Sun mid-Apr–mid-Oct, to 4:30pm mid-Oct–mid-Apr; 🚊 Metro-North to Riverdale
Built by a lawyer in 1843 as a country estate, the 28-acre, riverside Wave Hill served the needs of the wealthy and connected

until it became a city park in 1960. Other guests have included Theodore Roosevelt and Mark Twain. There are soaring views of the Hudson and a café in the stone mansion that serves as the park's centerpiece. From the Riverdale Metro-North station, it's a 15-minute walk uphill.

WOODLAWN CEMETERY Map pp208–9

☎ 718-920-0500; www.thewoodlawncemetery .org; Webster Ave at E 233rd St; ◷ 8:30am-5pm; ◉ 4 to Woodlawn

As elegant as Brooklyn's Green-Wood is this 400-acre cemetery, the top resting place in the Bronx. It dates from the Civil War and actually has more big names than Green-Wood – and it is a contest – among its 300,000 headstones, including Herman Melville and jazz greats like Miles Davis and Duke Ellington. Ask at the front for a photo pass if you want to snap pictures.

YANKEE STADIUM Map pp208–9

☎ 718-293-6000, tour info 718-579-4531; www .yankees.com; E 161st St at River Ave; tours $14-25; ◷ call for hrs; ◉ B, D, 4 to 161st St-Yankee Stadium

The Boston Red Sox like to talk about their record of two World Series championships in the last 80 years, but the Yankees have won a mere 26 in that period at this legendary ballpark. The team's banking that the magic will move with them across 161st St to the new Yankee Stadium, which will be ready by 2009 or 2010 (see boxed text, p211). The Yankees play from April to October (see p325 about tickets).

The old stadium offers hour-long guided tours of the dugout, press box, clubhouse, field and Monument Park (with plaques commemorating greats like Babe Ruth and Joe DiMaggio). Check with the new stadium after 2009 about similar tours.

STATEN ISLAND

If not for its namesake ferry – or Robert Redford and Jane Fonda's wild night out with Armenians in *Barefoot in the Park* – New York's 'forgotten borough' might be a complete unknown. Looking at a map, it's practically New Jersey; indeed, its first road connection with New York City came only with the construction of the Verrazano-Narrows Bridge in 1964, and on occasion the island's half-million residents – many of whom are middle-class Republicans (unique in a city known for its liberal politics) – have pondered secession from the city (a vote in favor in 1993 was turned down by New York State).

Of all things, an increasing number of New Yorkers are saying 'yes' to SI (no pun intended), as a steady trickle of high-rent dodgers are moving into Victorian homes in the working-class 'hoods of the North Shore, around the Staten Island pier. A two-bedroom house here goes for under a grand in monthly rent – a mansion compared to the options in Williamsburg or the East Village, which cost considerably more.

Most visitors here exit the ferry – which docks in downtown St George, on the northern tip of the 58-sq-mile island – then re-board right away. Much of the island isn't very convenient to reach (other than buses that pass less frequently than in Manhattan), but there are a few interesting things to see within walking distance of the pier.

The Staten Island Chamber of Commerce (☎ 718-727-1900; www.sichamber.com; 130 Bay St; ☼ 9am-5pm Mon-Fri), three blocks east (left, if the water's at your back) of the terminal, has a single brochure on the island's attractions. Behind the nearby police station (west of the terminal), the Staten Island Museum (☎ 718-727-1135; www.statenislandmuseum.org; 75 Stuyvesant Pl at Wall St; adult/senior & child $2/1; ☼ noon-5pm Mon-Fri, 10am-5pm Sat, noon-5pm Sun) has a permanent display about the boat you just rode in on.

For coffee, books or political talks – or later on, live music – the lively Everything Goes Book Café & Neighborhood Stage (☎ 718-447-8256; 208 Bay St; ☼ 10am-10pm Tue-Sat, noon-10pm Sun), near the chamber of commerce, has become something of the center of a growing, Berkeley-style arts community. Sports fans will want to grab a seat at a Staten Island Yankees (p326) game, which gets harbor views.

ALICE AUSTEN HOUSE

☎ 718-816-4506; www.aliceausten.org; 2 Hylan Blvd; admission $2; ☼ noon-5pm Thu-Sun; 🚌 S51 to Hylan Blvd

The harbor-side home of this early-20th-century photographer shows a bit about her life on Staten Island and many of her works. It's located just north of the Verrazano-Narrows Bridge, about a 15-minute bus ride from the ferry pier.

GREENBELT

☎ 718-667-2165; www.sigreenbelt.org; 200 Nevada Ave; 🚌 S62 & S54

In the heart of Staten Island, the 2800-acre Greenbelt – and its 32 miles of trails for hiking – crosses five ecosystems, including swamps and freshwater wetlands. One hike reaches the Atlantic seaboard's highest points south of Maine (take that, Jersey!). Check the website for the many access points. One good place is at High Rock Park, a hardwood forest spot-cut by six trails. Take bus S62 from the ferry terminal to Victory Blvd and Manner Rd (about 15 or 20 minutes), and then transfer to the S54.

HISTORIC RICHMOND TOWN

☎ 718-351-1611; www.historicrichmondtown .org; 441 Clarke Ave; adult/child $5/3.50; ☼ 1-5pm Wed-Sun Sep-Jun, 10am-5pm Wed-Sat, 1-5pm Sun Jul-Aug; 🚌 S74 to Richmond Rd & St Patrick's Pl

In the center of Staten Island, this 'town' of 27 buildings (some dating back to a 1690s Dutch community) stands in a 100-acre preservation project maintained by the Staten Island Historical Society. The town includes the former county seat of the island; its most famous building, the two-story, 300-year-old, redwood Voorlezer's House, is the USA's oldest schoolhouse. Guides lead tours (included with admission) at 2:30pm on weekdays and 2pm and 3:30pm on weekends; in July and August folks in period garb roam the grounds. It's about 40 minutes from the ferry by bus.

SNUG HARBOR CULTURAL CENTER

☎ 718-448-2500; www.snug-harbor.org; 1000 Richmond Tce; 🚌 S40 to Snug Harbor

This stunning waterfront complex of 28 buildings, a few gardens and several museums is easily the island's top attraction. Made from a lovely, 19th-century Greek

Twenty-three bus routes converge on four ramps at the St George ferry terminal. The buses, which all accept the MTA MetroCard, are timed to coincide with boat arrivals and tend to run every 20 minutes during the day. Routes loosely cover the island, though some destinations require added walks to get there. Staten Island's train service, which departs from the ferry terminal, has less useful routes for attractions.

revival old sailors' home, it almost saw the wrecking ball until Jackie Onassis and her big sunglasses intervened in 1976.

Confusingly, its separate attractions are not connected – the main 'Snug Harbor' site (now affiliated with the Smithsonian) fills the Main Hall, the central building as you enter from the road. Here you can see temporary exhibits and the excellent New-house Center for Contemporary Art (☎ 718-425-3560; www.newhousecenter.org; admission $6; ☺ 10am-5pm Tue-Sun), home to changing exhibitions of modern art.

To the left (from the entrance) is the in-dependent Noble Maritime Collection (☎ 718-447-6490; www.noblemaritime.org; adults/seniors & students $5/3; ☺ 1-5pm Thu-Sun), with period-piece reconstructions of sailors' dorms and other nautical tidbits.

Behind the front five buildings, you'll find the glasshouse of the Staten Island Botanical Garden (☎ 718-273-8200; www.sibg.org; admission free; ☺ dawn-dusk), and a maze behind it. Just west, the super-soothing New York Chinese Scholar's Garden (adult/child $5/4; ☺ 10am-5pm Tue-Sun Apr-Oct, noon-4pm Nov-Mar), built in 1999, offers a walk through ancient-style pavilions and teahouses with waterfalls running through. It gets busiest in April and May when many of the plants bloom.

You can bus it here or take a (rather grim) two-mile walk along Richmond Terrace west from the ferry terminal pier.

top picks

- **ABC Carpet & Home** (p234) This six-story emporium is a temple to home design.
- **Other Music** p221) Indie rockers, DJs and world-music heads love this cool CD and vinyl store.
- **Bergdorf Goodman** (p235) An enchanted wonderland for fashion-loving folk.
- **Reed Space** (p225) Check out this buzzy little shop for a slice of urban culture.
- **Marc Jacobs** (p229) Don't miss the West Village boutique of one of NYC's favorite designers.
- **Tokio 7** (p227) This standout vintage store has an excellent selection of top-name fashions.
- **De Vera** (p219) More museum than store, with artfully wrought jewelry, antique carvings and *objets d'art*.
- **Tiffany & Co** (p236) Audrey Hepburn's famed breakfast site is still a glittering destination for high-end jewelry.
- **Antiques Garage Flea Market** (p232) This weekend goldmine is a treasure trove of relics from the days of yore.

What's your recommendation? www.lonelyplanet.com/new-york-city

SHOPPING

New Yorkers live in a city of temptation. Candy-colored fashion boutiques, cutting-edge music shops, atmospheric antique stores, tea parlors – no matter what your weakness, you'll come face to face with all the objects your heart desires and plenty of curiosities you never knew existed. If self-control is lacking, stick to Central Park, one of the few places where you can safely battle the spending demons (although carriage rides, balloon animals and ice cream may entice). Otherwise, delve into the city. Its wide avenues and tree-lined side streets hide many surprises for the intrepid, card-wielding explorer.

Shopping here isn't just about collecting pretty, fanciful things. It's also about experiencing the city in all its variety and connecting to New York's many subcultures. Where else aside from Forbidden Planet can *manga*-lovers and Trekkies find each other so easily on a rainy afternoon? Vinyl lovers bond over the seemingly endless bins of jazz and soul albums at Academy Records, one of many LP shops in the East Village. Old-school hip-hop fans flock to well-hidden stores in the Lower East Side, while fashion insiders elbow joust over rare denim at lesser-known SoHo boutiques. There are shops for lovers of chess (with pick-up games for browsers), street art (the tagger might be working the cash register), cuddly robots, artist monographs, Danish things, handmade jewelry, Ukrainian handicrafts, old-fashioned toys, vintage boots, New York State wine (it's good!) and mosaics made by you. This is just the beginning, and there really is no end.

Shopping can also give you a taste of local history, whether you're stopping by the mom-and-pop shops still left in the Lower East Side, exploring the storefronts in Harlem or browsing the rare titles of a longtime antiquarian bookseller like Argosy. There are also the many antique sellers and several excellent flea markets where you can put your hands on those little fragments from New York's past.

While New York can seem like pure quicklime to the budget, insiders know where to find the deals. In addition to great thrift shops like Housing Works (p233), there are many discount stores (see the Top Picks, p220) that sell top fashion labels at excellent prices – though you'll have to dig. There are also superb sample sales (see the boxed text, opposite), where you can walk away looking like a million bucks without having to spend it.

SHOPPING AREAS

To the question 'Where do I shop?', NY answers 'How much you got?' Well-funded shoppers head to Midtown's Fifth Ave and the Upper East Side's Madison Ave, where high-end fashion is served in glittering Bergdorf-style department stores and famous shops like Cartier. Downtown neighborhoods are the stomping grounds of fashion-forward folk. SoHo has high-end boutiques stocking the wares of international and famous local designers, while Nolita has smaller boutiques of expensive, up-and-coming stylists. The Lower East Side and the East Village are traditional enclaves of vintage and indie fashion, with a mix of both pricey and budget-friendly shops. The West Village has tiny, well-known boutiques, while the Meatpacking District is home to designer havens like Jeffrey and Stella McCartney. Midtown is the place for big-box retailers like Macy's, multistoried H&M and other chain stores along with overflowing tourist shops selling tacky but essential souvenirs like Big Apple snow globes.

For more tips on where to shop, see the Top Picks, p230.

OPENING HOURS

With the exception of Lower Manhattan and shops run by Orthodox Jews (who close their doors on Saturdays), nearly all stores, boutiques and megastores are open daily. Few stores open before 10am, though many stay open until 7pm or 8pm. Things open a little later (at 11am or noon) in more residential pockets (such as the East Village, Lower East Side and Brooklyn). Many stores, particularly on Madison Ave, stay open later on Thursdays.

CONSUMER TAXES

Since the mayor's repeal of various consumer taxes between 2005 and 2007, there is currently no city sales tax on the purchase of clothing or footwear, regardless of price: what's on the tag is what you'll pay. For clothing or footwear items over $110, however, you'll still have to pay state sales tax of 4.375%.

LOWER MANHATTAN & TRIBECA

Manhattan's financial area doesn't have much shopping, though there is one notable clothing shop and an electronics store worth visiting. Other options include the big, chain-filled South Street Seaport (p80) and the humdrum indoor mall of the World Financial Center (p77). We mention them not for the shops (you've been to a Sunglass Hut, no?), but for the location. South Street Seaport is on the breezy East River, while the Financial Center offers bird's-eye views of the former World Trade Center site.

Tribeca offers a few more options (though no bargains), at the handful of stylish boutiques and furniture stores targeting the well-heeled residents. Try strolling the lower reaches of Hudson St and its surrounding lanes for quirky home furnishings, antiques and children's designer clothing shops.

SHAKESPEARE & CO Map pp72–3   Books
☎ 212-742-7025; 1 Whitehall St; ⏰ 8am-7pm Mon-Fri; ◉ R, W to Whitehall St, 4, 5 to Bowling Green
This popular New York bookstore chain – with other store locations in NoHo (p219), Gramercy (Map p120; ☎ 212-505-2021; 137 E 23rd St at Lexington Ave; ⏰ 10am-8pm Mon-Sun; ◉ 6 to 23rd St) and the Upper East Side (Map p142; ☎ 212-570-

0201; 939 Lexington Ave at 69th St; ⏰ 9am-8pm Mon-Fri, 10am-6pm Sat, noon-6pm Sun; ◉ 6 to 68th St) – is a great indie option, featuring a wide array of contemporary fiction and nonfiction, art books and tomes about NYC. A small but unique collection of periodicals is another great feature.

ISSEY MIYAKE Map pp72–3   Designer Clothing
☎ 212-226-0100; 119 Hudson St at N Moore St; ⏰ 10am-6pm Mon-Fri, 11am-6pm Sat, noon-5pm Sun; ◉ 1 to Franklin St
Find the designer's runway designs, by Naoki Takizawa, and several of the other collections – Pleats Please, APOC, Me and more – at this downtown showcase for the high-end silky, modern, sugary confections for both men and women.

CENTURY 21
Map pp72–3   Discount Department Store
☎ 212-227-9092; 22 Cortland St at Church St; ⏰ 7:45am-8pm Mon-Wed & Fri, 7:45am-8:30pm Thu, 10am-8pm Sat, 11am-7pm Sun; ◉ A, C, J, M, Z, 2, 3, 4, 5 to Fulton St-Broadway-Nassau St
This four-level, marble-floor department store is a favorite New Yorker 'secret.' Problem is, everyone and his mother knows about it. To beat the almost constant mobs, come early in the morning (it opens before most stores on weekdays) and then go out to breakfast. Its popularity is due to its deep discounts on men's and women's designer clothes, accessories, shoes, perfumes and linens (sometimes at less than half the original price). Big names – Donna Karen,

SAMPLE SALE SURVIVAL GUIDE

While clothing sales happen year-round, usually when the seasons change and the old stock must be moved out, sample sales are held frequently, mostly in the huge warehouses in the Fashion District of Midtown or in SoHo. While the original sample sale was a way for designers to get rid of one-of-a-kind prototypes that weren't quite up to snuff, most sample sales these days are for high-end labels to get rid of overstock at wonderfully deep discounts. The semi-annual Barneys warehouse sale, held at the Chelsea Barneys Co-op (p233), is one such frenzied event, bringing pushy crowds that resemble bread lines in their zeal for finding half-price Christian Louboutins or Diane Von Furstenburg dresses.

To truly do well at such an event, there are two golden rules: first, wear uncomplicated clothing with nice undergarments to the sale. That's because sample sales, set up in temporary, slapdash ways, have no dressing rooms, so you'll have to drop trousers and model your possible spoils in front of shared (and often way too small) mirrors placed in the middle of the room. Second, remember to hold fast to your own fashion reality. That's because, when you find yourself suddenly able to afford an item with an honest-to-goodness 'Louis Vuitton' or 'Marc Jacobs' tag in the collar, you may wind up throwing your taste out the window and purchasing something so ugly that it'll never make it out of your closet once you get it home.

To find sales that are happening when you're in town, check NY Sale (www.nysale.com), the Sample Sale Seconds page of Daily Candy (www.dailycandy.com), Lazar Shopping (www.lazarshopping.com) or the Check Out section of Time Out New York magazine.

CLOTHING SIZES

Women's clothing

Aus/UK	8	10	12	14	16	18
Europe	36	38	40	42	44	46
Japan	5	7	9	11	13	15
USA	6	8	10	12	14	16

Women's shoes

Aus/USA	5	6	7	8	9	10
Europe	35	36	37	38	39	40
France only	35	36	38	39	40	42
Japan	22	23	24	25	26	27
UK	3½	4½	5½	6½	7½	8½

Men's clothing

Aus	92	96	100	104	108	112
Europe	46	48	50	52	54	56
Japan	S		M	M		L
UK/USA	35	36	37	38	39	40

Men's shirts (collar sizes)

Aus/Japan	38	39	40	41	42	43
Europe	38	39	40	41	42	43
UK/USA	15	15½	16	16½	17	17½

Men's shoes

Aus/UK	7	8	9	10	11	12
Europe	41	42	43	44½	46	47
Japan	26	27	27½	28	29	30
USA	7½	8½	9½	10½	11½	12½

Measurements approximate only – try before you buy.

Marc Jacobs, Armani, you name it – can be found here. Be prepared for long queues for dressing rooms – and for the impulse to purchase just about everything you see.

J&R MUSIC & COMPUTER WORLD

Map pp72–3   Music & Electronics

☎ 212-238-9000; 15-23 Park Row; 🕙 9am-7:30pm Mon-Sat, 10:30am-6:30pm Sun; Ⓔ A, C, J, M, Z, 2, 3, 4, 5 to Fulton St-Broadway-Nassau St
Located on what used to be known as Newspaper Row – the center of New York's newspaper publishing biz from the 1840s to the 1920s – this is now a communications hub of a more modern sort. Occupying a full block with J&R shops and their separate entrances, this is considered by many to be the best place in the city to buy a computer of any sort. You can buy any other electronics item here, including cameras, recorders and stereos, as well as DVDs and CDs of every kind. You'll find good deals and knowledgeable staff.

CITYSTORE

Map pp72–3   NYC Gifts & Books

☎ 212-669-7452; North Plaza, Municipal Bldg, 1 Centre St; 🕙 9am-4:30pm Mon-Fri; Ⓔ 4, 5, 6 to Brooklyn Bridge-City Hall, J, M, Z to Chambers St
This small, little-known city-run shop is the perfect place to score all manner of New York memorabilia, including authentic taxi medallions, manhole coasters, silk ties and newborn baby items bearing the official 'City of New York' seal, Brooklyn Bridge posters, NYPD baseball caps, actual streets signs ('No Parking,' 'Don't Feed the Pigeons') and baseballs signed by famous Mets and Yanks. There's also a great collection of city-themed books – including the famous *Green Book*, an official directory to city agencies, published annually and not available anywhere else.

TENT & TRAILS

Map pp72–3   Outdoor Sporting Goods

☎ 212-227-1760; 21 Park Pl; 🕙 9:30am-6pm Mon-Wed & Sat, 9:30am-7pm Thu & Fri, noon-6pm Sun; Ⓔ 2, 3 to Park Pl
This fantastic outdoor outfitter – an NYC rarity – sells top-of-the-line gear like tents, backpacks and footwear, from favorite brands including North Face, Kelty and Eureka, with a small selection available to rent. Staff are knowledgeable, too.

SOHO, NOHO & NOLITA

Credit-card companies generally do quite well after you visit SoHo. There are many ways to rack up debt at this major shopping destination, with hundreds of stores, big and small, scattered along its streets. Broadway is one of the main corridors, and is lined with less expensive chain stores. Hidden west along the tree-lined streets are pricier boutiques selling clothing, shoes, accessories and housewares. During the warmer months, you'll also find street vendors hawking jewelry, art, T-shirts, hats and other crafts. Over on Lafayette, shops cater to the DJ and skate crowd with indie labels and vintage shops thrown in the mix.

If indie is your thing, continue east to Nolita, home of tiny jewel-box boutiques selling unique apparel, footwear, accessories and kitschy stuff at marginally lower prices than SoHo stores. Mott St is best for browsing, followed by Mulberry and Elizabeth.

NoHo is just a tiny little 'hood, with a few quaint little shops along Bond St.

DE VERA Map pp88–9 Antiques & Art Objects

☎ 212-625-0838; 1 Crosby St; ⏰ 11am-7pm Tue-Sat; ⊖ N, R, Q, W, 6 to Canal St

Federico de Vera travels the globe in search of rare and exquisite jewelry, carvings, lacquerware and other *objets d'art* for this jewel-box of a store. Illuminated glass cases display works like 200-year-old Buddhas, Venetian glassware and gilded inlaid boxes from the Meiji period, while tapestries and carvings along the walls complete the museum-like experience.

MCNALLY ROBINSON Map pp88–9 Books

☎ 212-274-1160; 52 Prince St at Crosby St; ⏰ 10am-10pm Mon-Sat, 10am-8pm Sun; ⊖ R, W to Prince St

A new indie bookstore – what a promising sign! Right in the heart of SoHo, this cozy spot is a gem. Find a great selection of magazines, plus sections devoted to subjects that include food writing, architecture and design, teen novels and LGBT (lesbian-gay-bi-transgender) literature. There's a great café, too, the perfect place to settle in with some reading material or just watch the shoppers of Prince St go by.

SHAKESPEARE & CO Map pp88–9 Books

☎ 212-529-1330; 716 Broadway; ⏰ 10am-11pm Sun-Thu, 10am-11:30pm Fri & Sat; ⊖ N, R, W to 8th St, 6 to Astor Pl

See p217 for the main branch in Lower Manhattan. This NoHo branch, near NYU's Tisch film school, stocks many theater and film books and scripts.

PEARL RIVER MART

Map pp88–9 Chinese Department Store

☎ 212-431-4770; 477 Broadway; ⏰ 10am-7pm; ⊖ J, M, Z, N, Q, R, W, 6 to Canal St

This one-stop Canal St classic, now in its fancier Broadway location, is still Chinatown's best shop. Find everything Asian here – cheap Chinese and Japanese teapots, dragon-print dresses, paper lanterns, Chinese slippers in all colors, jars of Chinese spices and sauces, imported teas, pecking chicken wind-up clocks that look like throwbacks to the Mao era, and various (loud) Asian instruments. Eastward ho!

AMERICAN APPAREL Map pp88–9 Clothing

☎ 212-226-4880; 121 Spring St btwn Broadway & Mercer St; ⊖ R, W to Prince St

It's all blissfully simple inside these shops (visit www.americanapparel.net for more

city locations) from a Los Angeles-based company that eschews sweatshops for its conscientious in-house production. The racks are filled with the kind of basic T-shirts and sweatshirts you might buy with slogans or band photos printed across the chests, but here they're all free of graphics. You'll also find tanks, hoodies, underwear, bras, socks and scarves, with styles geared toward men, women, children, babies – even dogs – in a huge range of colors from the primaries to pink and olive green.

FLYING A Map pp88–9 Clothing

☎ 212-965-9090; 169 Spring St; ⏰ 11am-7pm Mon-Thu, 11am-8pm Fri & Sat, noon-7pm Sun; ⊖ N, R, W to Prince St

Sporting a logo that bears a passing resemblance to those flying wings of Aerosmith, this Danish-owned store offers a little something for both rock-and-rollers and SoHo fashion mavens. You'll find vintage pieces (weathered cowboy boots, candy-colored '70s dresses, whisper-thin button-downs) as well as new apparel – jeans, graphic T-shirts and slim-fitting dresses. Books, watches, stylish air-tote bags, sunglasses and other accessories provide for more fun browsing.

UNIQLO Map pp88–9 Clothing

☎ 917-237-8811; 546 Broadway; ⏰ 10am-9pm Mon-Sat, 11am-8pm Sun; ⊖ N, R, W to Prince St

Japan's version of H&M opened its US flagship store in SoHo to much fanfare back in 2006. The enormous three-story emporium owes its success to its attractive apparel at discount prices. You'll find Japanese denim, Mongolian cashmere, graphic T-shirts, smart-looking skirts and endless racks of colorful ready-to-wear – all at the sub-$100 mark.

UNIS Map pp88–9 Clothing

☎ 212-431-5533; 226 Elizabeth St; ⏰ noon-7pm; ⊖ N, R, W to Prince St

Unis remains a Nolita favorite for its fashionable but functional basics. You'll find slim nicely cut jeans, soft button-downs and well-made jackets for the men, with feminine dresses and slender tops for the ladies.

YOUNG DESIGNERS MARKET

Map pp88–9 Clothing & Accessories

☎ 212-580-8995; 268 Mulberry St; ⏰ 11am-7pm Sat & Sun; ⊖ B, D, F, V to Broadway-Lafayette St

This large colorful market takes over the gym of Old St Patrick's on weekends. As per the name, young and indie designers rule the roost, selling handmade jewelry, unique witty T-shirts and one-of-a-kind stationery, plus dresses, hoodies and lots of other affordable items you won't find elsewhere.

ATRIUM Map pp88–9 · Clothing & Denim
☎ 212-473-9200; cnr 644 Broadway & Bleecker St; ✆ 10am-8pm; ⊕ B, D, F, V to Broadway-Lafayette St

A real standout along a particularly ho-hum stretch of retailers, Atrium has an excellent selection of funky designerwear, including shoes and accessories, for both men and women from Diesel, G-Star, Miss Sixty and other popular labels. Best, though, is the grand range of high-end denim, from folks including Joe's, Seven, Blue Cult and True Religion.

APPLE STORE SOHO
Map pp88–9 · Computers & Electronics
☎ 212-226-3126; 103 Prince St; ✆ 10am-8pm Mon-Sat, 11am-7pm Sun; ⊕ N, R, W to Prince St

Apple's uplifting, airy flagship location – with translucent stairway and upstairs walkway and fully fledged theater, used for how-to presentations – bustles with SoHo shoppers picking up iPods, iBooks and other items from the iUniverse.

BLOOMINGDALE'S SOHO
Map pp88–9 · Department Store
☎ 212-729-5900; 504 Broadway; ✆ 10am-9pm Mon-Fri, 10am-8pm Sat, 11am-7pm Sun; ⊕ R, W to Prince St

The smaller, younger outpost of the Upper East Side (p236) legend, this Bloomies sheds housewares and other department-store items for a clear focus on fashion. Find clothing, shoes and outerwear for both men and women, plus a substantial collection of cosmetics and perfume at street level. Labels run the gamut from Marc Jacobs to the totally hip clubwear of Heatherette.

LABEL Map pp88–9 · Designer Clothing
☎ 212-966-7736; 265 Lafayette St; ⊕ R, W to Prince St

This easy-to-miss boutique has a small selection of nicely cut men's and women's fashions that tend toward a vaguely futuristic look. You can find some very flattering dresses, sports coats and shoes here. As a bonus, most of the clothes are manufactured in California, so your money won't be supporting sweatshop labor overseas.

OPENING CEREMONY
Map pp88–9 · Designer Clothing
☎ 212-219-2688; 35 Howard St; ✆ 11am-8pm Mon-Sat, noon-7pm Sun; ⊕ N, R, Q, W, 6 to Canal St

Just off the beaten SoHo path, Opening Ceremony is a favorite among fashion insiders for its unique collection of indie labels. Owners Carol Lim and Humberto Leon showcase a changing roster of labels from across the globe – though the look is always avant-garde, even if the prices are decidedly uptown.

PRADA Map pp88–9 · Designer Clothing
☎ 212-334-8888; 575 Broadway; ✆ 11am-7pm Mon-Sat, noon-6pm Sun; ⊕ N, R, W to Prince St

The Italian designer's ever-chic outfits and shoes are one thing, but the space! Transformed from the old Guggenheim SoHo location by Dutch architect Rem Koolhaas, and recently restored following extensive damage from an early 2006 fire, this shop, with sweeping wooden floors and tucked-away downstairs rooms, is a marvel to see. For a thrill, try something on, as the clear glass walls of the fitting rooms fog when the door closes.

MOMA STORE Map pp88–9 · Designer Gadgets
☎ 646-613-1367; 81 Spring St; ✆ 11am-8pm Mon-Sat, 11am-7pm Sun; ⊕ N, R, Q, W to Prince St

This sleek and stylish space carries a huge collection of handsomely designed objects for the home, office and wardrobe. You'll find modernist alarm clocks, wildly shaped vases, designer kitchenware and surreal

top picks

DISCOUNT DESIGNER CLOTHES

- Century 21 (p217) Fashion insiders frequently raid this enormous vault of super-priced top labels.
- Young Designers Market (p219) Up-and-coming designers sell their wares at this weekend Nolita market.
- Loehmann's (p233) An icon on Seventh Ave, with many floors of marked-down designer gear.
- Daffy's (opposite) You can find unbelievable deals at any Daffy's store, though you'll have to dig.
- Filene's Basement (p234) Endless racks of both famous and unknown designers offer fabled rewards for label hunters.

lamps, plus brainy games, hand puppets, fanciful scarves, coffee-table books and lots of other great gift ideas.

MOSS Map pp88–9 Designer Housewares

☎ 212-204-7100; 146 Greene St; ☼ 11am-7pm Mon-Sat, noon-6pm Sun; ☺ N, R, W to Prince St
Converted from a gallery space, Moss' two showrooms prop slick, modern and fun industrial designs behind glass, but they're definitely for sale. It's easy to find something – a Yoshitomo Nara flip clock with 84 original drawings, say, or a sleek black La Cupola espresso maker – that you'll just have to own, and that you probably won't find many other places.

DAFFY'S

Map pp88–9 Discount Designer Clothing & Accessories

☎ 212-334-7444; www.daffys.com; 462 Broadway at Grand St; ☼ 10am-8pm Mon-Sat, noon-7pm Sun; ☺ A, C, E to Canal St
Although its one of many locations around the city (see the website for details), this has one of the best selections, probably due to its cool downtown location. It's got two floors of designer duds and accessories (and a random handful of housewares) for men, women and children, with prices that can be shockingly low. And the tags – like those at most discount shops – show you the item's suggested retail price on top of Daffy's price, which, at an average of 50 percent off, just gives you more incentive to buy.

OTHER MUSIC Map pp88–9 Indie Music

☎ 212-477-8150; 15 E 4th St; ☼ noon-9pm Mon-Fri, noon-8pm Sat, noon-7pm Sun; ☺ 6 to Bleecker St
This indie-run CD store has won over a loyal fan base with its informed selection of, well, other types of music: offbeat lounge, psychedelic, electronica, indie rock etc, available new and used. Friendly staffers like what they do, and may be able to help translate your inner musical whims and dreams to actual CD reality.

ORIGINAL LEVI'S STORE

Map pp88–9 Jeans & Clothing

☎ 646-613-1847; 536 Broadway at Spring St; ☼ 10am-8pm Mon-Sat, 11am-7pm Sun; ☺ R, W to Prince St
Stock up on all your favorite Levi's jeans here – 501 button-fly, super-low boot-cut,

zip-fly straight-leg cords – plus check out the great selection of Western shirts, tees, sweaters, jackets and always-evolving new styles for both men and women.

JOHN VARVATOS

Map pp88–9 Men's Clothing & Shoes

☎ 212-965-0700; 122 Spring St; ☺ R, W to Prince St
One of the city's most coveted menswear designers, John Varvatos creates a classic, timeless look – with a rock-and-roll soul – in his stylish and handsome-fitting sports coats, jeans, footwear and accessories. Head downstairs for JV's younger, edgier persona.

ODIN Map pp88–9 Men's Clothing & Accessories

☎ 212-966-0026; 199 Lafayette St; ☼ 11am-8pm Mon-Sat, noon-7pm Sun; ☺ 6 to Spring St
Named after the mighty Norse god, Odin offers a bit of magic for men seeking a new look. The large boutique carries stylish downtown labels like Trovata, Superfine and Rag & Bone, and is a great place to browse for up-and-coming designers. Other eye candy at the minimalist store includes Comme de Garçons wallets, sleek sunglasses, Sharps grooming products, Taschen coffee-table books and Common Project's dapper sneakers. There's a branch in the East Village (Map p104; ☎ 212-475-0666; 328 E 11th St; ☼ noon-9pm Mon-Sat, noon-8pm Sun; ☺ 6 to 14th St).

VINTAGE NEW YORK

Map pp88–9 New York Winery Shop

☎ 212-226-9463; 482 Broome St at Wooster St; ☼ 10am-9pm; ☺ A C, E to Canal St
This excellent wine shop and wine bar features vintages from boutique wineries all over New York State, including Long Island, the Hudson Valley and the Finger Lakes region. Popular local varieties include sparklers, chardonnay, riesling, pinot noir, merlot and cabernet sauvignon, and all are available for tasting. The best part about the place, though, is that, because it's technically a winery, it's allowed to stay open on Sunday – something no other wine shop in the city can claim. That is, of course, except for its Uptown branch (Map p153; ☎ 212-721-9999; 2492 Broadway at 93rd St; ☼ 10am-10pm).

EASTERN MOUNTAIN SPORTS

Map pp88–9   Outdoor Gear & Clothing

☎ 212-966-8730; 591 Broadway btwn Houston & Prince Sts; ⏱ 9am-9pm Mon-Sat, 11am-8pm Sun; ⊖ N, R, W to Prince St

This rugged outfitter has everything you need to tackle the great outdoors including hiking shoes, jackets, sleeping bags, camping gear, backpacks and trekking guides. You'll also find good customer service, fewer crowds than Paragon Athletic Goods (p235), and EMS' great return policy – they give full refunds (or exchanges) on anything in the store as long as you have the receipt.

BOND NO 9 Map pp88–9   Perfume

☎ 212-228-1940; 9 Bond St; ⏱ 11am-7pm Mon-Sat, noon-6pm Sun; ⊖ R, W to Prince St

'Making scents of New York' is this thoroughly unique perfume boutique, where the gimmick is NYC. Each bottle of home-brewed potion (they begin at about $100) not only comes labeled with a trademark round label inspired by an old New York subway token, it gets filled with one of 20 fragrances that are named after and inspired by local nabes. There's Riverside Drive, Chelsea Flowers, Central Park, Eau de Noho and Chinatown, none of which smells like wet pavement, exhaust fumes *or* hot pretzels. There's also a great selection of vintage bottles with squeeze balls, which can be filled with the scent of your choice.

BABELAND Map pp88–9   Sex Toys & Books

☎ 212-966-2120; www.babeland.com; 43 Mercer St; ⏱ noon-9pm Mon-Sat, noon-7pm Sun; ⊖ A, C, E to Canal St

The women-owned sex shop formerly known as Toys in Babeland has shortened its name. It's still the queen bee of sex toys, aflutter with open and supportive staffers who will gladly talk you through the chore of picking out the very best silicone dildo or butt plug, matching it with an appropriate leather harness and inspiring you to toss in a quality vibrator (such as the ever-popular High Joy Bunny) while you're at it. But it's also much more: purveyor of sex-related books, magazines, adult DVDs, flavored lube and Babeland tees, and educator, with a constant roster of how-to lectures, for all genders, from the knowledgeable staff. The original, but smaller, shop is on the Lower East Side (Map p98; ☎ 212-375-1701; 94 Rivington St; ⏱ noon-10pm Mon-Sat, noon-7pm Sun; ⊖ F, J, M, Z to Delancey St-Essex St).

ADIDAS ORIGINALS

Map pp88–9   Sports Footwear & Active Wear

☎ 212-777-2001; 136 Wooster St; ⏱ 11am-7pm Mon-Sat, noon-6pm Sun; ⊖ B, D, F, V to Broadway-Lafayette St

This ultra-hip Adidas shop stocks lots of eye-catching sneakers, sporty jackets and other retro-looking gear. It's a tech- and music-savvy place to stop by, with DJs sometimes working the decks, and lawn chairs out front on hot summer days. For the big-box retail experience, head to the 29,5000-sq-ft Adidas (Map pp88–9; ☎ 212-529-0081; 610 Broadway at Houston St; ⏱ 10am-8pm Mon-Sat, 11am-7pm Sun) sneaker emporium a few blocks away.

BROOKLYN INDUSTRIES

Map pp88–9   Streetwear

☎ 212-219-0862; www.brooklynindustries.com; 286 Lafayette St; ⏱ 11am-8pm Mon-Sat, noon-7:30pm Sun; ⊖ B, D, F, V to Broadway-Lafayette St

The Manhattan outpost of a growing Williamsburg-based den of urban wear is one of the most light and airy. Behind the massive glass storefront are smart, basic and affordable styles, including 'Made in Brooklyn' tees and sweatshirts, plus plenty of sweaters, hoodies, jackets, denim, coats, hats, bags and even laptop sleeves in earthy colors. All boast the catchy Brooklyn Industries label – an industrial skyline that prominently features a water tower. See p242 for Brooklyn-area branches and see the website for more locations.

TRIPLE FIVE SOUL Map pp88–9   Streetwear

☎ 212-431-2404; www.triple5soul.net; 290 Lafayette St; ⏱ 11am-7pm; ⊖ B, D, F, V to Broadway-Lafayette St

Born in the Lower East Side in the late 1980s, Triple Five Soul personifies urban chic. Jeans, hoodies, jackets and T-shirts were once inextricably linked to the hip-hop scene, though today their offerings have grown more eclectic (and some would say rather mainstream). It's still a fun place to browse, however, with party music playing overhead (you can buy original mixes) and a good variety of gear. You can also visit the Williamsburg store (Map p177; ☎ 718-599-5971; 145 Bedford Ave).

HOUSING WORKS USED BOOK CAFÉ

Map pp88–9   Used Books

☎ 212-334-3324; 126 Crosby St; ⏱ 10am-9pm Mon-Fri, noon-9pm Sat, noon-7pm Sun; ⊖ B, D, F, V to Broadway-Lafayette St

With the look of a real library, complete with mezzanine, this café positively crawls with locals on weekends. Browse through over 45,000 used books and CDs. Prices are good, and all proceeds benefit Housing Works, a charity serving New York City's HIV-positive and AIDS homeless communities. See also Housing Works Thrift Shop (p233).

SCREAMING MIMI'S

Map pp88–9   Vintage Clothing
☎ 212-677-6464; 382 Lafayette St; ⏰ noon-8pm Mon-Sat, 1-7pm Sun; ⓔ 6 to Bleecker St
A warm and colorful storefront that just begs to be entered; you'll find accessories and jewelry up front, and an excellent selection of clothing – organized, ingeniously, by decade, from the '40s to the '70s – in the back. It's all in great condition, from the prim, beaded wool cardigans to the suede mini-dresses and white leather go-go boots.

WHAT COMES AROUND GOES AROUND
Map pp88–9   Vintage Designer Clothing
☎ 212-343-9303; 351 West Broadway; ⏰ 11am-8pm Mon-Sat, noon-7pm Sun; ⓔ C, E to Spring St
New York feels like cowboy country – at least inside this classic SoHo vintage store. You'll find a wide selection of Levi's, cowboy boots, concert T-shirts, leather belts, wide-brimmed hats and even those snakeskin pumps you've been hunting.

INA Map pp88–9   Vintage Designer Clothing
☎ 212-334-9048; 21 Prince St; ⏰ noon-7pm Sun-Thu, noon-8pm Fri & Sat; ⓔ N, R, W to Prince St, B, D, F, V to Broadway-Lafayette St
Locals love this super consignment shop that stocks choice designer clothes for women (the men's shop is around the corner at 262 Mott St). Label hunters will find a goldmine of top labels, including Marc Jacobs, Louis Vuitton, Seven jeans, Chanel and footwear by Christian Louboutin and Manolo Blahnik. Prices are about half retail price, but still steep.

RESURRECTION

Map pp88–9   Vintage Designer Clothing
☎ 212-625-1374; www.resurrectionvintage.com; 217 Mott St; ⏰ 11am-7pm Mon-Sat, noon-7pm Sun; ⓔ 6 to Spring St
Boudoir to the eye, Resurrection is a sleek and pricey red-walled boutique that gives new life to cutting-edge designs from past decades. Striking, mint-condition pieces

cover days of mod, glam-rock and new wave design, and well-known designers like Marc Jacobs have visited the shop for inspiration. Top picks include Gucci handbags, Halston dresses and Courrèges jackets.

EVOLUTION Map pp88–9   Weird Science
☎ 212-343-1114; 120 Spring St btwn Broadway & Mercer St; ⏰ 11am-7pm; ⓔ R, W to Prince St
Partial to insects, skulls, teeth and other usual gross-outs? Then you'll be in heaven here, home to all of that and more. Filled with natural-history collectibles of the sort usually seen in museums, this is the place to buy – or just gawk at – framed beetles and butterflies, bugs frozen in amber-resin cubes, anatomical models (ear, larynx and hand skeleton, to name a few), shark teeth and animals' penis bones.

CALYPSO Map pp88–9   Women's Clothing
☎ 212-965-0990; www.calypso-celle.com; 280 Mott St; ⏰ 11:30am-7:30pm Mon-Sat, noon-6:30pm Sun; ⓔ B, D, F, V to Broadway-Lafayette St
It's summer forever at this St Bart's–born shop, which stocks tropical clothing, such as light dresses, Dr Boudoir swimwear, flip-flops and slinky blouses, year-round. Calypso has several boutiques (the jewelry shop is a few doors down on Mott St), including one on the Upper East Side (Map p142; cnr 74th St & Madison Ave).

KIRNA ZABÊTE Map pp88–9   Women's Clothing
☎ 212-941-9656; 96 Greene St; ⏰ 11am-7pm Mon-Sat, noon-6pm Sun; ⓔ C, E to Spring St
This trim, modern boutique has a small but well-curated selection of clothing, shoes, jewelry and accessories with striking pieces by Balenciaga, Stella McCartney and Requiem among other designers. Downstairs, the eye candy continues with children's fashion, doggie wear and even gumballs, games and other curiosities.

ERICA TANOV

Map pp88–9   Women's Clothing & Shoes
☎ 212-334-8020; 204 Elizabeth St btwn Prince & Spring Sts; ⏰ 11am-7pm Mon-Sat, noon-6pm Sun; ⓔ 6 to Spring St
This handsome, high-ceilinged boutique features Tanov's delicate feminine designs like hand-printed cotton tops, handsomely cut dresses and flattering lingerie. In addition to Tanov's clothing designs, you'll also find artfully crafted jewelry by other

designers, handbags, kids' wear and those comfy rubber boots by Aigle.

TE CASAN Map pp88–9   Women's Shoes

☎ 212-584-800; 382 West Broadway; ⏰ 11am-8pm Mon-Sat, noon-7pm Sun; ⊕ C, E to Spring St

Presenting certain danger to New York's many shoe fetishists, Te Casan is a lovely three-story boutique with a shimmering spiral staircase and artfully displayed footwear. Stylish heels, flats and boots are the product of seven emerging designers who aren't afraid of innovation. Niki Robinson, for instance, uses vegetable dyes and Zulu beadwork (crafted by Zulu women) in some of her designs.

CHINATOWN & LITTLE ITALY

Chinatown is a great place for wandering, particularly if you're in the market for some aromatic herbs, exotic Eastern fruits (like litchi and durian in season), fresh noodles or delicious bakery goodies. Canal St is the major thoroughfare, with lots of touristy merchandise and knock-off designer gear spilling onto the sidewalks. The backstreets are the real joy, however, with bubble-tea cafés, perfumeries, video arcades, plant shops and fishmongers all hawking their wares. Mott St has the biggest density of shops, though don't neglect tiny Pell, with its bevy of able-bodied barbers.

As far as Little Italy shopping goes, this is mostly tourist fare of the postcard and toy taxicab variety. There are, however, a few well-photographed Italian delis, stocking prosciutto, extra-virgin olive oil and other old-world treats. You'll find it all along Mulberry St and nearby blocks, just above Canal St.

AJI ICHIBAN Map p94   Candy

☎ 212-233-7650; 37 Mott St; ⏰ 10am-8:30pm; ⊕ J, M, Z, N, Q, R, W, 6 to Canal St

This Hong Kong–based chain, the name of which means 'awesome' in Japanese, is a ubiquitous sight in Chinatown, as this is just one of five locations here. And though it is a candy shop, get ready for something a bit more exciting than malted balls and peppermint sticks. Here's where you'll find sesame-flavored marshmallows, Thai durian milk candy, preserved plums, mandarin peel, blackcurrant gummies and dried guava, as well as savory snacks like crispy

spicy cod fish, crab chips, wasabi peas and dried anchovies with peanuts.

BUILT BY WENDY Map p94   Clothing

☎ 212-925-6538; 7 Centre Market Pl; ⏰ noon-7pm Mon-Sat, 1-6pm Sun; ⊕ R, W to Prince St

Hidden out of reach from the SoHo masses, Built by Wendy is a cozy boutique where sweaters, dresses and men's and women's denim sport a classic, flattering cut with interesting details. Cute, foxy and adorable are all adjectives that fit the aesthetic. You can also pick up owner-designer Wendy Mullin's clever sewing book called *Sew U* or one of her ultra-suede guitar straps.

ORIGINAL CHINATOWN ICE CREAM FACTORY Map p94   Ice Cream & T-shirts

☎ 212-608-4170; 65 Bayard St; ⏰ 11am-10pm; ⊕ J, M, Z, N, Q, R, W, 6 to Canal St

Totally overshadowing the nearby Häagen-Dazs is this busy ice-cream shop, where you can savor scoops of green tea, ginger, red bean and black sesame. The Factory also sells ridiculously cute, trademark yellow T-shirts ($15) with an ice cream-slurping happy dragon on them.

KAM MAN Map p94   Kitchenware

☎ 212-571-0330; 200 Canal St; ⏰ 9am-9pm; ⊕ J, M, Z, N, Q, R, W, 6 to Canal St

Head past hanging ducks to the basement of the classic Canal St food store for cheap Chinese and Japanese tea sets, plus kitchen products like chopsticks, stir-frying utensils and rice cookers.

LOWER EAST SIDE

The downtown fashion crowd looking for that edgy, experimental, or 'old-school hip-hop' look head to the shops in the Lower East Side. Sprinkled among the area's many bars and restaurants are dozens of stores selling vintage apparel, vegan shoes, one-of-a-kind sneakers, old-fashioned candy, sex toys, left-wing books and more. You'll find the most shops on Orchard and Ludlow Sts, between Houston and Delancey Sts, but it's worth wandering to other strips, too.

Before the neighborhood's recent hipster makeover, shopping here was generally limited to Orchard St's leather jackets and old-school lingerie and Judaica shops on Essex St, between Grand and Canal Sts. They're still there today, and can be fun to browse in, as can the few lingering pickle and bagel shops and Jewish delis sprinkled around the area.

ECONOMY CANDY Map p98 Candy

☎ 212-254-1531; 108 Rivington St at Essex St; ⏰ 9am-6pm Mon-Fri, 10am-5pm Sat; ⊖ F, J, M, Z to Delancey St-Essex St

Bringing sweetness to the 'hood since 1937, this candy shop is stocked with floor-to-ceiling goods in package and bulk, and is home to some beautiful antique gum machines. You'll find everything from the kid-worthy jellybeans, lollipops, gumballs, Cadbury imports, gummy worms and rock candy to more adult delicacies like halvah, green tea bonbons, hand-dipped chocolates, dried ginger and papaya, Brazil nuts and pistachios, and sesame-honey bars.

REED SPACE

Map p98 Clothing & Sneakers, Magazines

☎ 212-253-0588; www.thereedspace.com; 151 Orchard St; ⏰ 1-7pm Mon-Fri, noon-7pm Sat & Sun; ⊖ F, J, M, Z to Delancey St-Essex St

A laid-back space for lovers of old-school urban culture, Reed Space has a good selection of DJ-worthy jackets, T-shirts and sneakers. You'll also find eye-catching magazines covering music, art and design as it's done in the city, ie New York City. Good music plays overhead (hip-hop, dance hall), and you can pick up good mixes, shoulder bags, ugly toys and other fun gear.

top picks

EAT DRINK MAN WOMAN

- Zabar's (p240) The famed gourmet grocery has an endless variety of temptations.
- Murray's Cheese (p231) Wondrous cheese from all parts of the globe at this near-century-old *fromagerie.*
- Vintage New York (p221) A wine shop stocking surprisingly drinkable vintages from New York State, plus a bar in back to sample the goods.
- Economy Candy (above) Willy Wonka would weep: glittering jars of gummy bears, licorice and malt balls, piles of chocolate bars, Turkish delight and delicately prepared old-fashioned confections.
- Jacques Torres (p242) Forget Godiva. Jacques Torres creates NY's most beautiful chocolates, as well as otherworldly hot chocolate (available in the café).

ESSEX ST MARKET Map p98 Food Market

☎ 212-312-3603; 120 Essex St btwn Delancey & Rivington Sts; ⏰ 8am-6pm Mon-Sat; ⊖ F, V to Delancey St, J, M, Z to Delancey St-Essex St

This 60-year-old historic shopping destination is the local place for produce, seafood, butcher-cut meats, cheeses, Latino grocery items, even a barber. It's a fun place to explore, with snack stands and an attached restaurant when you really want to get down to business.

BLUESTOCKINGS

Map p98 Radical Bookstore & Café

☎ 212-777-6028; 172 Allen St; www.blue stockings.com; ⏰ 1-10pm; ⊖ F, V to Lower East Side-2nd Ave

This independent bookstore, first opened with a lesbian bent, has now expanded its turf to radicalism of all kinds. It's still women-owned, though, and its shelves have a strong selection of dyke and feminist lit and crit – along with tomes on gender studies, global capitalism, democracy studies, black liberation and police and prison systems. It's also the site of a vegan, organic, fair-trade café, as well as myriad readings and speaking events, including women's poetry readings, workshops on radical protests and even a monthly Dyke Knitting Circle (see p321 for more details on events here).

ALIFE RIVINGTON CLUB Map p98 Sneakers

☎ 212-375-8128; 158 Rivington St; ⏰ 11am-7pm Mon-Thu, 11am-8pm Fri & Sat, noon-7pm Sun; ⊖ F, J, M, Z to Delancey St-Essex St

Concealed behind an unmarked entrance (ring the buzzer), ARC feels more like the VIP lounge of a nightclub than a shoe store. You'll find royal-hued carpeting, a long leather couch and a handsome display case of rare, limited-edition sneakers. Stocks of those coveted Nikes and Adidas change often and sell out fast, so don't dawdle if you see something you like.

MOO SHOES Map p98 Vegan Shoes

☎ 212-254-6512; www.mooshoes.com; 78 Orchard St; ⏰ 11:30am-7:30pm Mon-Sat, noon-6pm Sun; ⊖ F, J, M, Z to Delancey St-Essex St

Socially and environmentally responsible fashion usually tends to entail certain sacrifices in the good-looks department. Bucking the trend is Moo Shoes, a vegan boutique where style is no small consideration in the design of inexpensive microfiber (faux leather) shoes, bags and motorcycle jackets. Look for smart-looking Novacas, Crystalyn Kae purses, Queenbee Creations messenger bags and sleek Matt & Nat wallets. For more eco-friendly designs, head across the street to the cute boutique Kaight (Map p98; ☎ 212-680-5630; www.kaightnyc.com; 83 Orchard St; ⏰ 11am-8pm Mon-Sat, noon-6pm Sun).

EDITH MACHINIST Map p98 Vintage Clothing
☎ 212-979-9992; 104 Rivington St at Essex St; ⏰ 1-8pm; ◉ F, J, M, Z to Delancey St-Essex St
To properly strut about the Lower East Side, you've got to dress the part. Edith Machinist can help you get that rumpled, classic look in a hurry – a bit of vintage glam via knee-high soft suede boots, 1930s silk dresses and ballet-style flats, with military jackets and weather-beaten leather satchels for the gents.

LAS VENUS Map p98 Vintage Furniture
☎ 212-982-0608; 163 Ludlow St; ⏰ noon-9pm Mon-Thu, noon-midnight Fri & Sat, noon-8pm Sun; ◉ F, J, M, Z to Delancey St-Essex St
Down a couple of steps from the street, this colorful shop packs in cool Danish-modern furniture (from the 1950s, '60s and '70s) and other vintage furnishings. Much of it edges toward the pricey, but some deals await the prodder (as well as old *Playboys*, if that's your thing). Las Venus also stocks chrome furnishings on the 2nd floor of ABC Carpet & Home (p234).

SHOP Map p98 Women's Clothing
☎ 212-375-0304; 105 Stanton St; ⏰ noon-7pm; ◉ F, J, M, Z to Delancey St-Essex St
Shop is a cozy boutique selling a pretty assortment of dresses, shoes, lingerie and handbags to a crowd hungry for its decidedly cute selections. The uptown prices, single dressing room and sometimes lackluster service are drawbacks.

TG170 Map p98 Women's Clothing
☎ 212-995-8660; 170 Ludlow St; ⏰ noon-8pm; ◉ F, J, M, Z to Delancey St-Essex St
One of the first boutiques to blaze the trail into the Lower East Side way back in 1992, TG170 is still a major destination for downtown style seekers. Inside the graffiti-covered storefront, you'll find both young and established designers pushing a fashion-forward look. Lauren Moffatt chiffon dresses, Cheap Monday jeans and vinyl Freitag bags look all the better beneath the wild ice planet–style chandeliers.

EAST VILLAGE
Once the archetype of underground, downtown style, the East Village is doing some soul searching (some might say 'selling') these days. You'll still find urban and outsider fashion, but new local designers, sleeker shops and even chain stores have moved into the area, blunting the neighborhood's former edginess. Still, there's more than a whiff of those rockin' '80s days at punk-rock T-shirt shops, tattoo parlors and dusty stores selling furniture and vintage clothing, and the record stores are the real deal, with New York's best selection of vinyl. You'll have to pound the pavement to see it all; the old-school stuff is on St Marks Pl between Third and First Aves, and much of the new stuff along its parallel strips, from 13th St to Houston St, and as far east as Ave C. On weekends, vendors line St Marks Pl and Ave A, and a greenmarket hits Tompkins Sq Park. The blocks of E 2nd through E 7th Sts, between Second Ave and Ave B especially, are good for finding vintage wear, curiosity shops and record stores.

KIEHL'S Map p104 Beauty Products
☎ 212-677-3171, 800-543-4571; 109 Third Ave; ⏰ 10am-7pm Mon-Sat, noon-6pm Sun; ◉ L to 3rd Ave
Making and selling skincare products since it opened in NYC as an apothecary in 1851, this Kiehl's flagship store has doubled its shop size and expanded into an international chain, but its personal touch remains – as do the coveted, generous sample sizes. Pick up some of the legendary moisturizers, masks and emollients, including Creme with Silk Groom for the hair, Creme de Corps for the body or Abyssine Serum for the face.

ST MARK'S BOOKSHOP Map p104 Books
☎ 212-260-7853; 31 Third Ave; ⏰ 10am-midnight Mon-Sat, 11am-midnight Sun; ◉ 6 to Astor Pl
Actually located around the corner from St Marks (it moved long ago), this indie bookshop specializes in political literature, poetry, new nonfiction and novels and academic journals. There's also a superior collection of cookbooks, travel guides and magazines, both glossy and otherwise. Staffers are a bit on the unsociable side, but hey, they're bookish and they really know their stuff.

TOKIO 7 Map p104   Consignment Store
☎ 212-353-8443; 64 E 7th St; ⏰ noon-8:30pm Mon-Sat, noon-8pm Sun; Ⓜ 6 to Astor Pl
This revered and hip consignment shop, down a few steps on a shady stretch of E 7th St, has good-condition designer labels for men and women at some 'come again?' prices. Best is the selection of men's suits – there's nearly always something worth trying on in the $100 to $150 range. You could try to sell off your own labels that you might be tired of, but be prepared to have them sniffed at and promptly rejected.

PATRICIA FIELD Map p104   Designer Clothing
☎ 212-966-4066; 302 Bowery at 1st St; Ⓜ F, V to Lower East Side-2nd Ave
The move from her SoHo digs to the new Bowery location brings much-needed space (4000 sq ft to be exact) to the fun, whimsical design shop. The fashion-forward stylist for *Sex and the City*, Patricia Field isn't afraid of flash, with feather boas, pink jackets, disco dresses, graphic and color-block T-shirts and leopard-print heels, plus colored frizzy wigs, silver spandex and some wacky gift ideas for good measure.

JOHN DERIAN Map p104   Home Decor & Curios
☎ 212-677-3917; 6 E 2nd St; ⏰ noon-7pm Tue-Sun; Ⓜ F, V to Lower East Side-2nd Ave
John Derian is famed for its decoupage – collages of botanical and animal prints pieced together and stamped under glass. The result is a beautiful collection of one-of-a-kind plates, paperweights, coasters, lamps, bowls and vases. The atmospheric store hides many other curiosities – T-shirts with roguish 19th-century graphics, handmade terracotta pottery, linoleum cut prints and papier-mâché figurines. For eclectic bed linens and such visit the nearby John Derian's Dry Goods (Map p104; ☎ 212-677-8408; 10 E 2nd St; ⏰ noon-7pm Tue-Sun).

GIANT ROBOT
Map p104   Illustrated Books & T-shirts, Toys
☎ 212-674-4769; www.grny.net; 437 E 9th St; ⏰ 1-8:30pm Mon-Thu, noon-9pm Fri & Sat, noon-7pm Sun; Ⓜ 6 to Astor Pl
The walls of this small shop are lined with robots and one-eyed creatures of all sizes and cuteness levels. You'll also find one-of-a-kind graphic novels, fun T-shirts for gizmo lovers, wallets, mechanized toys and molded things, plus changing art exhibitions in the adjoining gallery.

SUNRISE MART Map p104   Japanese Groceries
☎ 212-598-3040; 29 Third Ave at Stuyvesant St; ⏰ 10am-11pm Sun-Thu, 10am-midnight Fri & Sat; Ⓜ 6 to Astor Pl
A bright, 2nd-floor supermarket dedicated to all foods Japanese, this is where you'll find clutches of homesick, well-dressed NYU kids stocking up on wasabi, plus plenty of locals who have discovered a new craving for Poki sweets. Paw through aisles of pre-sliced fish, rice noodles, ponzu sauces, sushi rice, white soy sauce, fresh yuzu, miso, tofu and endless amounts of colorful candies.

ACADEMY RECORDS Map p104   Records
☎ 212-780-9166; 415 E 12th St at First Ave; Ⓜ L to 1st Ave
The East Village outpost of this excellent music store is a vinyl-lovers Valhalla with a brilliant assortment of new and used LPs. For CDs, visit the Flatiron District store (p234). The jazz and world-music collection is particularly strong, with decks to listen to used albums before buying.

DE LA VEGA Map p104   Street Art
☎ 212-876-8649; 102 St Marks Pl; ⏰ 1-8pm Mon, Tue & Thu-Sat, 1-6pm Sun; Ⓜ 6 to Astor Pl
The thirty-something artist De La Vega is sometimes described as a blend of Keith Haring and Francisco de Goya. If you don't have time to hunt for his street murals in Spanish Harlem, head to his small gallery space in the East Village. Small canvases,

EAST VILLAGE VINYL
- A-1 Records (Map p104; ☎ 212-473-2870; 439 E 6th St btwn First Ave & Ave A) A huge selection.
- Turntable Lab (Map p104; ☎ 212-677-0675; 120 E 7th St btwn First Ave & Ave A) Electronic music and DJ mixes.
- Etherea (Map p104; ☎ 212-358-1126; 66 Ave A btwn 4th & 5th Sts) A broad, well-curated range.
- Tropicalia in Furs (Map p104; ☎ 212-982-3251; 304 E 5th St btwn Second & First Aves) Specializing in '60s-era Brazilian tropicalia, with offerings of rock, soul and blues.
- Jammyland (Map p104; ☎ 212-614-0185; 60 East 3rd St btwn Second & First Aves) The tiny but wondrous reggae emporium.

T-shirts and other curios feature De La
Vega's iconic motifs like two fish gazing
at one another from opposite fish bowls
and adages like 'Sometimes, the king is a
woman' and 'Become your dream.'

DINOSAUR HILL Map p104   Toys & Baby Clothes
☎ 212-473-5850; 306 E 9th St; ⏲ 11am-7pm;
◎ 6 to Astor Pl
A small, old-fashioned toy store that's
inspired more by imagination than Disney
movies, this shop sports an amazing puppet
selection including Czech marionettes and
international finger puppets, along with
unique jack-in-the-boxes, art and science
kits, quality wooden blocks and glass mar-
bles, plus natural-fiber clothing for infants.

LOVE SAVES THE DAY
Map p104   Vintage Clothes & Kitsch
☎ 212-228-3802; 119 Second Ave; ⏲ noon-8pm
Mon-Fri, noon-9pm Sat & Sun; ◎ 6 to Astor Pl
As the waves of change engulf the East
Village, Loves Saves the Day stays true
to its original form. Its campy collection
of old polyester clothes, fake-fur coats,
glam-rock spiked boots, GI Joes, *Star Wars*
'77 figurines and other dolls and vintage
toys is not much changed since the days
when Rosanna Arquette bought Madonna's
pyramid jacket here in the viva-los-'80s film
Desperately Seeking Susan.

GREENWICH VILLAGE, WEST VILLAGE & THE MEATPACKING DISTRICT

The picturesque, tranquil streets of the West
Village are home to some lovely boutiques,
with a few antique dealers, bookstores, record
stores, and quirky gift and curio shops adding
a bit of eclecticism to an otherwise fashion-
focused 'hood. High-end shoppers stick to
top-label stores along Bleecker St between
Bank and West 10th. There's much more color
along Christopher St, with its stores selling
leather play gear and rainbow-colored T-shirts.
Tourist hordes, meanwhile, come to the more
central poster and T-shirt shops along Bleecker
between Seventh Ave and La Guardia Pl.

The Meatpacking District is all about that
new, sleek, high-ceilinged industrial-chic

vibe, with ultramodern designers reigning
at expansive boutiques that are among the
most fashionable haunts in town (some stores
indeed look like sets for futuristic and beautifully stylized Kubrick films).

AEDES DE VENUSTAS
Map p110   Bath & Beauty
☎ 212-206-8674; 9 Christopher St; ⏲ noon-8pm
Mon-Sat, 1-7pm Sun; ◎ A, C, E, B, D, F, V to W 4th
St-Washington Sq, 1 to Christopher St-Sheridan Sq
Plush and inviting, Aedes de Venustas
('Temple of Beauty' in Latin) provides more
than 30 brands of luxury European perfumes, including Chergui, Mark Birley for
Men, Costes, Nirmala and Shalini. They have
also got skincare products created by folks
such as Patyka and Jurlique, and everyone's
favorite scented candles from Diptyque.

YOYAMART Map p110   Children's Toys & Clothing
☎ 212-242-5511; www.yoyashop.com; 15 Gansevoort St; ⏲ 11am-7pm Mon-Sat, noon-6pm Sun;
◎ A, C, E to 14th St, L to 8th Ave
Ostensibly geared toward the younger
set, Yoyamart is a fun place to browse for
adults – even if you're not packing a child.
Sure, there's adorable apparel for babies
and toddlers, but there's also cuddly robots, Gloomy Bear gloves, plush ninjas,
build-your-own-ukulele kits, CD mixes
(three-year-olds apparently love Daft Punk),
and various anime-style amusement.

DESTINATION Map p110   Clothing & Accessories
☎ 212-727-2031; www.destinationny.net; 32-36
Little W 12th St at Washington St; ◎ A, C, E to
14th St, L to 8th Ave
The eclectic merchandise provides the
spots of color in this vast, all-white space.
You'll find hard-to-get jewelry from European designers including Les Bijoux de
Sophie, Serge Thoraval and Corpus Christie.
Then there are the military-chic fashion
pieces – funky leather boots with buckle
by Gianni Barbato, sailor-inspired pants by
John Rocha, cargo bags by Orca – all mixed
in with whimsical vests and jackets, bags
from Mik and Comptoirs de Trikitrixia shoes
(with scented soles, no less!).

HUS Map p110   Clothing & Accessories
☎ 212-620-5430; 11 Christopher St; ⏲ 11am-8pm
Mon-Fri, noon-7pm Sat & Sun; ◎ 1 to Christopher St
For a taste of Scandinavia that ranges
far beyond Ikea, head to Hus, home to a

colorful collection of Swedish, Finnish and Danish design. Popular selections include WeSC streetwear, printed Marimekko bags, rainbow-colored Tretorn rainboots, quirky MoLo kids' wear and sculpted jewelry by Efva Attling. You'll also find housewares, electronic gadgets and even food. The space sometimes doubles as an art gallery after hours.

MCNULTY'S TEA & COFFEE CO, INC

Map p110   Coffee & Tea

☎ 212-242-5351; 109 Christopher St; ☽ 10am-9pm Mon-Sat, 1-7pm Sun; ◉ 1 to Christopher St-Sheridan Sq

Just down from a few sex shops, sweet Mc-Nulty's, with worn wooden floorboards and fragrant sacks of coffee beans and large glass jars of tea, flaunts a different era of Greenwich Village. It's been selling gourmet teas and coffees here since 1895.

FORBIDDEN PLANET

Map p110   Comics, Books & Games

☎ 212-473-1576; 840 Broadway; ☽ 10am-10pm Mon-Sat, 11am-8pm Sun; ◉ L, N, Q, R, W, 4, 5, 6 to 14th St-Union Sq

Indulge your inner sci-fi nerd. Find heaps of comics, books, video games and figurines (ranging from *Star Trek* to Shaq). Fellow Magic and Yu-Gi-Oh! card-game lovers play upstairs in the public sitting area.

top picks

NYC INTRIGUE

- De La Vega (p227) Collectible mini-canvases and wearable art brought to you by Spanish Harlem graffiti artist De La Vega.
- Evolution (p223) Framed insects, fossils, skulls of tiny rodents, anatomical charts and other natural-history curiosities to complete your collection/frighten your neighbors.
- Bond No 9 (p222) Maker of fine fragrances, Bond No 9 offers fine scents named (but not modeled) after Manhattan 'hoods. Try the Nuits de Noho.
- John Derian (p227) An old-fashioned store with Derian's decoupage glassware, antiquated collages, woodblock prints and other handmade artifacts.
- Printed Matter (p232) A strange and wondrous collection of glossy art books, artist monographs and quirky titles found nowhere else.

APPLE STORE

Map p110   Computers & Electronics

☎ 212-444-3400; 401 W 14th St at Ninth Ave; ☽ 11am-8pm Mon-Fri, noon-7pm Sat & Sun; ◉ A, C, E to 14th St, L to 8th Ave

Apple's newest store is its biggest yet, with a gleaming glass-and-chrome presence in a rather stylish 'hood. You can play games or check your email on the MacBooks on the 1st floor, or sweep up the curving staircase to the iPods and 'genius bar' on floors two and three. Like the Apple Store SoHo (p220), it has young, attractive and totally geeky staff. They'll either answer all your questions or leave you alone to sample all those shiny new gadgets.

DERNIER CRI

Map p110   Designer Clothing

☎ 212-242-6061; 869 Washington St; ◉ A, C, E to 14th St, L to 8th Ave

An important destination when hitting the shops in the neighborhood, Dernier Cri is a hip little store with dark wood floors, cow-hide rugs and original artwork on the walls. Great finds here include well-edited selections by Sonia Rykiel, Rag & Bone, Trosman and Isabel Marant, plus jewelry by Mawi and rock photography books (owner Stacia Valle used to have deep connections to the pop-music scene). The lack of attitude among sales staff is a nice bonus.

JEFFREY NEW YORK

Map p110   Designer Clothing

☎ 212-206-1272; 449 W 14th St; ☽ 10am-8pm; ◉ A, C, E to 14th St, L to 8th Ave

One of the pioneers in the Meatpacking makeover, Jeffrey sells several high-end designer clothing lines – Versace, Pucci, Prada, Michael Kors and company – as well as accessories, shoes and a small selection of cosmetics. DJs spinning pop and indie add to the very hip vibe.

MARC JACOBS

Map p110   Designer Clothing

☎ 212-924-0026; www.marcjacobs.com; ☽ noon-8pm Mon-Sat, noon-7pm Sun; ◉ A, C, E to 14th St, L to 8th Ave

With five small shops sprinkled around the West Village, Marc Jacobs has established a real presence in this well-heeled neighborhood. Large front windows allow easy peeking – assuming there's not a sale, during which you'll only see hordes of fawning shoppers. Here's the layout: on Bleecker St, you'll find his famous leather bags and other accessories at No 385, Marc by Marc

Jacobs men's clothing is at No 382, and the women's line is at No 403-405. One block over, you have shoes, plus women's and men's accessories at 301 W 4th St, with his children's line (Little Marc) across the street at 298 W 4th.

SCOOP Map p110   Designer Clothing

☎ 212-929-1244; 430 W 14th St; ☺ 11am-8pm Mon-Fri, 11am-7pm Sat, noon-6pm Sun; ⊕ A, C, E to 14th St, L to 8th Ave

Scoop is a great one-stop destination for unearthing top contemporary fashions by Theory, Stella McCartney, Marc Jacobs, James Perse and many others. While there's nothing particularly edgy about the selections, there's a lot on offer (over 100 designers covering men's, women's and children's), and you can often score deals at season-end sales. Scoop has several branches in the city, including smaller branches in SoHo (Map pp88–9; ☎ 212-925-3539; 473 Broadway btwn Broome & Grand) and the Upper East Side (Map p142; ☎ 212-535-5577; 1273 Third Ave btwn 73rd & 74th).

VILLAGE CHESS SHOP LTD
Map p110   Games

☎ 212-475-9580; 230 Thompson St; ☺ 11am-midnight; ⊕ A, C, E, B, D, F, V to W 4th St-Washington Sq

A crusty crew of chess-o-philes frequents this hole-in-the-wall chess shop for $1 games in a no-frills sitting area. Come to play, buy a book to study up, or buy one of the chess sets (the best ones are thematic: Aztec, Crusades, Vegas etc). There's coffee on, too.

OSCAR WILDE BOOKSHOP
Map p110   Gay & Lesbian Books

☎ 212-255-8097; 15 Christopher St; ☺ 11am-7pm; ⊕ 1 to Christopher St-Sheridan Sq

The world's oldest bookshop geared to gay and lesbian literature (open since 1967) lives in a lovely redbrick town house and stocks both new and used books, a fine range of magazines, rainbow flags, bumper stickers and other gifts. It nearly closed in 2003, but was rescued from the brink of collapse by a Washington DC–based LGBT bookstore.

MXYPLYZYK Map p110   Gifts & Housewares

☎ 800-243-9810; www.mxyplyzyk.com; 125 Greenwich Ave at W 13th St; ☺ 11am-7pm Mon-Sat, noon-5pm Sun; ⊕ A, C, E to 14th St, L to 8th Ave

top picks

SHOPPING STRIPS

- **West Broadway** (Map pp88–9) These days, SoHo is one big shopping mall, with high-end fashion well represented along West Broadway between Houston and Grand Sts.
- **Mott St** (Map pp88–9) Less touristy (and somewhat cheaper) than SoHo, Nolita (Mott St between Houston and Broome Sts) has lovely little clothing, shoe and accessory shops carrying up-and-coming designers.
- **East 9th St** (Map p104) More pleasant than chaotic St Marks Pl one block south, East 9th between Second Ave and Ave A is a good intro to the vintage stores and curio shops of the East Village.
- **Ludlow St** (Map p98) For edgier fashions and urban style, begin your Lower East Side explorations on Ludlow between Houston and Delancey Sts.
- **Christopher St** (Map p110) Proudly flying the rainbow colors, Christopher St between Greenwich and W 4th Sts has its fair share of leather and sex shops, with some friendly bars and cafés along the way.
- **Bleecker St** (Map p110) Running south from Abingdon Sq, tree-lined Bleecker (between Bank and W 10th Sts) is sprinkled with eye-catching storefronts and boutiques selling very trendy apparel.
- **Fifth Ave** (Map p126) Between Central Park and Rockefeller Center, this commercial strip is the El Dorado of shopping. Stepping into Tiffany's, Bergdorf's and Takashimaya is just the beginning…
- **Madison Ave** (Map p142) To get 'the treatment' (which can be good or bad depending on the size of your expense account), head to Madison and 72nd, gateway to the bejeweled storefronts of the Upper East Side.
- **Bedford Ave** (Map p177) On another galaxy is Bedford Ave (between N 4th and N 10th Sts) – and N 6th St for that matter – with alternative fashions, record stores and lots of flashy-trashy stuff. For more Brooklyn fun, also cruise the shops of Boerum Hill's Smith St (Map p180) and Park Slope's Fifth Ave (Map p182) from St Marks Pl to 5th St.

There's nothing usual about this totally fun home shop – including its odd name. Even the cloth napkins, in vibrant, psychedelic patterns, are worth getting excited about – as are the calculators (huge, flat and in neon colors), games (like Doggie Dominoes), bath mats (topped with photos of real grass), and outdoor grill knives (with lights at the tip, for checking whether the meat is cooked to perfection at night-time).

MURRAY'S CHEESE Map p110 Gourmet Cheese

☎ 212-243-3289; www.murrayscheese.com; 254 Bleecker St btwn Sixth & Seventh Aves; ⊙ 8am-8pm Mon-Sat, 10am-7pm Sun; ⊕ 1 to Christopher St-Sheridan Sq

Founded in 1914, this is hailed repeatedly as the best cheese shop in the city. Owner Rob Kaufelt is known for his talent of sniffing out devastatingly delicious varieties from around the world. You'll find (and be able to taste) all manner of *fromage*, be it stinky, sweet or nutty, from European nations and from small farms in Vermont and upstate New York. You'll find other delectable *fromage* at the restaurant/cheese counter of Artisanal (Map p126; ☎ 212-725-8585; 2 Park Ave S at 32nd St, enter on 32nd St; ⊙ noon-11pm Mon-Thu, to midnight Fri & Sat, to 10pm Sun; ⊕ 6 to 34th St).

CO BIGELOW CHEMISTS
Map p110 Health & Beauty

☎ 212-473-7324; 414 Sixth Ave btwn 8th & 9th Sts; ⊕ A, C, E, B, D, F, V to W 4th St-Washington Sq

The 'oldest apothecary in America' is now a slightly upscale fantasyland for the beauty-product obsessed (though there's still an actual pharmacy and drugstore items on the premises, too). In addition to its own CO Bigelow label products, including lip balms, hand and foot salves, shaving creams and rosewater, you can browse through lotions, shampoos, cosmetics and fragrances from makers including Acqua di Parma, Dr Hauschka, Weleda, Frédéric Fekkai, Propoline and many more.

RICKY'S Map p110 Health & Beauty, Kitsch

☎ 212-924-3401; www.rickys-nyc.com; 466 Sixth Ave at 11th St; ⊙ 9am-11pm Mon-Sat, 9am-10pm Sun; ⊕ A, C, E to 14th St, L to 8th Ave

Ricky's may technically be a drug store, but it's not like one you've ever seen before. Here, behind the glittery hot-pink toothpaste tube that serves as the Ricky's symbol, you'll find a bright space with blaring club music. There are endless shelves of goodies, including bright wigs, a wall of hair brushes, cosmetics, imported candies and gums, aisles of both foreign and 'only in salons' hair-care products, hosiery, kitschy tees and toys and, in the back, a selection of sex props. Just browsing is pure fun – and, luckily, there are 15 other locations throughout the city (see the website for details).

EARNEST SEWN Map p110 Jeans & Clothing

☎ 212-242-3414; 821 Washington St; ⊙ 11am-7pm Sun-Fri, 11am-8pm Sat; ⊕ A, C, E to 14th St, L to 8th Ave

Wood plank floors and a shiny open-top jeep set the scene for the high-quality apparel on display. Earnest Sewn denim has become famous for its craftsmanship, and customers sign on to long waiting lists to order customized and tailored jeans. The atmospheric store is a fun place to browse, and you'll find an odd mix of delicate jewelry, outerwear and pocketknives among the antique (still working) machinery.

REBEL REBEL Map p110 Music

☎ 212-989-0770; 319 Bleecker St; ⊙ noon-8pm Sun-Wed, noon-9pm Thu-Sat; ⊕ 1 to Christopher St-Sheridan Sq

This is a tight-fit, tiny music store with CDs and rare vinyl defying the limits of space. Ask for what you don't see, as there are loads more in the back, out of view.

MATT UMANOV GUITARS
Map p110 Musical Instruments

☎ 212-675-2157; 273 Bleecker St; ⊙ 11am-7pm Mon-Sat, noon-6pm Sun; ⊕ A, C, E, B, D, F, V to W 4th St-Washington Sq, 1 to Christopher St-Sheridan Sq

A friendly guitar house that goes easy on the blaring distortion (though they do sell the pedals), this shop stocks and services an excellent collection of our fretted friends (including some mouthwatering Gibson, Fender and Gretsch guitars, plus steel guitars and banjos).

FLIGHT 001 Map p110 Travel Gear

☎ 212-691-1001; www.flight001.com; 96 Greenwich Ave; ⊙ 11am-8:30pm Mon-Fri, 11am-8pm Sat, noon-6pm Sun; ⊕ A, C, E to 14th St, L to 8th Ave

Travel's fun, sure – but getting travel gear is even more fun. Check out Flight 001's range of luggage and smaller bags by brands from Samsonite to Orla Kiely, brightly colored passport holders and leather luggage tags, wallets sized to hold international bills, travel guidebooks (Lonely Planet included, of course), toiletry cases and a range of mini toothpastes, eye masks, jetlag pills and the like.

STRAND BOOK STORE Map p110 Used Books

☎ 212-473-1452; 828 Broadway at 12th St; ⊙ 9:30am-10:30pm Mon-Sat, 11am-10:30pm Sun; ⊕ L, N, Q, R, W, 4, 5, 6 to 14th St-Union Sq

Book fiends (or even those who have casually skimmed one or two) shouldn't miss New York's most loved used bookstore. Operating since 1927, the Strand is New York's most famous bookstore, with an incredible 18 miles of books (over 2.5 million of them). Check out the staggering number of reviewers' copies in the basement, or sell off your own tomes before you get back on the plane, as the Strand buys or trades books at a side counter on weekdays. There's also a branch in Lower Manhattan (Map pp72–3; ☎ 212-732-6070; 95 Fulton St; ⏰ 9:30am-9pm Mon-Fri, 11am-8pm Sat & Sun; ⊕ A, C, 4, 5 to Broadway-Nassau St, J, M, Z, 2, 3 to Fulton St) and a kiosk on the southeastern edge of Central Park (Map p126; 60th St & Fifth Ave; ⏰ 10am-dusk Apr-Dec, weather permitting).

INTERMIX Map p110 Women's Clothing & Handbags
☎ 212-929-7180; 365 Bleecker St at Charles St; ⏰ 11:30am-8:30pm Mon-Fri, to 7:30pm Sat, to 6pm Sun; ⊕ 1 to Christopher St-Sheridan Sq
This pleasant little pop-pink storefront is packed with stylish tops, frocks and jeans from favorite designers like Chloe, Givenchy, True Religion, Stella and Splendid. It's cool, cute and sexy all at once.

CHELSEA

Better known for its dining and nightlife scenes, Chelsea has a decent selection of antiques, discount fashion, chain stores and kitsch, along with a hidden bookstore and well-edited thrift shop among the mix. The neighborhood standout is the beloved Chelsea Market (p115), a huge concourse packed with minimarkets selling fresh baked goods, wines, veggies, imported cheeses and other temptations. Eighth Ave has the densest (but not the best) selections, with chain stores like Gap and Banana Republic among the smaller stores.

ANTIQUES GARAGE FLEA MARKET
Map p116 Antiques
112 W 25th St at Sixth Ave; ⏰ 7am-5pm Sat & Sun; ⊕ F, V to 23rd St
This weekend flea market is set in a two-level parking garage, with more than 100 vendors spreading their wares. Antique-lovers shouldn't miss a browse here, as you'll find clothing, shoes, records, books, globes, furniture, rugs, lamps, glassware, paintings, artwork and many other relics from the past. You can also catch a $1 shuttle from here to the affiliated Hell's Kitchen Flea Market (p237).

192 BOOKS Map p116 Books
☎ 212-255-4022; 192 Tenth Ave btwn 21st & 22nd Sts; ⏰ 11am-7pm Tue-Sat, noon-6pm Sun & Mon; ⊕ C, E to 23rd St
Located right in the gallery district is this small indie bookstore, with sections on literature, history, travel, art and criticism. A special treat is its offerings of rotating art exhibits, during which the owners organize special displays of books that relate thematically to the featured show or artist.

BARNES & NOBLE Map p116 Books & Music
☎ 212-727-1227; www.bn.com; 675 Sixth Ave at W 22nd St; ⏰ 9am-10pm Mon-Sat, 10am-10pm Sun; ⊕ 1 to 18th St
With more than 20 locations in NYC (visit the website for more), this heavy-hitter superstore is not well loved among the city's indie bookstores. But still, *somebody's* keeping them in business. Check out the massive space, with books displayed by endless topics including travel, cooking, classic literature, memoir, biography, children, art, dance, theater, health, gay and lesbian, and new fiction. One half is dedicated to CDs of all genres, and there's a Starbucks in the back. Frequent readings from new-book authors also happen onsite.

PRINTED MATTER Map p116 Books & Zines
☎ 212-925-0325; 195 Tenth Ave btwn 21st & 22nd St; ⏰ 11am-6pm Tue & Wed, 11am-7pm Thu-Sat; ⊕ C, E to 23rd St
Printed Matter is a wondrous little two-room shop dedicated to limited-edition artist monographs and strange little zines. Here you will find nothing carried by mainstream bookstores like Barnes & Noble; instead, trim little shelves hide call-to-arms manifestos, critical essays about comic books, flip books that reveal Jesus' face through barcodes and how-to guides written by prisoners.

CHELSEA'S WEEKEND FLEA MARKETS
- 17th St Market (Map p116; cnr W 17th St & Sixth Ave; ⏰ 7am-5pm Sat & Sun; ⊕ F, V to 14th St)
- Chelsea Outdoor Market (Map p120; 29 W 25th St btwn Fifth & Sixth Aves; ⏰ 7am-5pm Sat & Sun; ⊕ F, V to 23rd St)

☎ 646-638-0115; 75 Ninth Ave at 16th St;
⏰ 11:30am-10pm Mon-Fri, 10am-10pm Sat, 10am-6pm Sun; ⊕ A, C, E to 14th St, L to 8th Ave
On the edge of Chelsea Market, this spacious wood-floored boutique and restaurant sates many appetites with its elegant glasswares and housewares, beautifully designed men's and women's clothing, trim leather armchairs – and of course those delectable fluffy pancakes served at brunch. The 202 store is the brainchild of designer Nicole Farhi, who has a similar store in London's Notting Hill.

BALENCIAGA Map p116   Designer Clothing

☎ 212-206-0872; 522 W 22nd St at Eleventh Ave;
⏰ noon-7pm Mon-Sat, noon-5pm Sun; ⊕ C, E to 23rd St
Come and graze at this cool, grey, Zen-like space, the gallery-district's showcase, appropriately enough, for the artistic, post-apocalypse avant-garde styles of this French fashion house. Expect strange lines, goth patterns and pants for very skinny (and deep-pocketed) gals.

BARNEYS CO-OP Map p116   Designer Clothing

☎ 212-593-7800; 236 W 18th St; ⏰ 11am-8pm Mon-Fri, 11am-7pm Sat, noon-6pm Sun; ⊕ 1 to 18th St
The edgier, younger, more affordable version of Barneys (p235) has (relatively) affordable deals at this expansive, loft-like space, which has a spare, very selective inventory of clothing for men and women, plus shoes and cosmetics. Its biannual warehouse sale (February and August) packs the place, both with endless merchandise and mobs of customers.

LOEHMANN'S
Map p116   Discount Department Store

☎ 212-352-0856; www.loehmanns.com; 101 Seventh Ave at 16th St; ⏰ 9am-9pm Mon-Sat, 11am-7pm Sun; ⊕ 1 to 18th St
A starting point for local hipsters looking for designer labels on the cheap (though some may not admit it), Loehmann's is a five-story department store that, it is said, inspired a wee-young Calvin Klein to make clothes good. The original store of the successful chain is in the Bronx; see the website for other locations.

BALDUCCI'S Map p116   Gourmet Food

☎ 212-741-3700; 81 Eighth Ave at 14th St;
⏰ 9am-10pm; ⊕ A, C, E to 14th St, L to 8th Ave

Newly housed in a landmark, turn-of-the-century bank building, Balducci's (which had reigned for years a bit further south in the Village) has recently arrived in Chelsea, bringing with it its highest quality gourmet produce, international cheeses, olives, bakery goods, fresh roasted coffee and packaged items from around the globe. Just walking through is a treat in itself, especially under the high ceiling of this majestic location.

HOUSING WORKS THRIFT SHOP
Map p116   Thrift Store

☎ 212-366-0820; 143 W 17th St; ⏰ 10am-6pm Mon-Sat, noon-5pm Sun; ⊕ 1 to 18th St
This thrift shop, with its swank window displays, looks more boutique than thrift, and its selections of clothes, accessories, furniture and books are great value. All proceeds benefit the charity serving the city's HIV-positive and AIDS homeless communities. There are numerous other branches around town, including the Upper West Side (Map p153; ☎ 212-579-7566; 306 Columbus Ave btwn 74th & 75th St; ⏰ 11am-7pm Mon-Fri, 10am-6pm Sat, noon-5pm Sun; ⊕ 1, 2, 3, B, C to 72nd St).

AUTHENTIQUES PAST & PRESENT
Map p116   Vintage Housewares

☎ 212-675-2179; 255 W 18th St btwn Seventh & Eighth Aves; ⏰ noon-6pm Wed-Sat, 1-6pm Sun; ⊕ 1 to 18th St
Tucked on a quiet side street is this thoroughly dramatic and kitsch-filled vintage shop. Find groovy and colorful lamps from the '50s and '60s, pastel vases and cache pots, quirky barware, nostalgic cartoon figurines and glasses and flashy costume jewelry.

UNION SQUARE, THE FLATIRON DISTRICT & GRAMERCY

There's plenty of shopping to be had in this big block of neighborhoods. First and foremost is Union Sq, home to a delightful greenmarket (see the boxed text, p121), which hits the park several times a week all year round. Meanwhile huge chain stores flank the park to the north and south, offering books, discount fashion and music. Fourteenth St, more to the west than to the east, is a shopping adventure all its own, with store upon store hawking discount electronics, cheap linens and a great range of shoes and hit-or-miss clothing, from both bargain indies and chains like Urban Outfitters and Diesel. You'll find more up-market chain stores heading up Fifth Avenue, with Paul Smith, BCBG, Anthropologie, Zara and Intermix among the standouts.

BOOKS OF WONDER
Map p120   Children's Books
☎ 212-989-3270; 16 W 18th St; ⏱ 11am-7pm Mon-Sat, 11:45am-6pm Sun; ◎ F, V to 14th St
Chelsea folks love this small, indie, fun-loving bookstore devoted to children's and young-adult titles. It's a great place to take the kids on a rainy day, especially when a kids' author is giving a reading, or a story-teller is on hand.

FILENE'S BASEMENT
Map p120   Discount Department Store
☎ 212-348-0169; 4 Union Sq S; ⏱ 9am-10pm Mon-Sat, 11am-8pm Sun; ◎ L, N, Q, R, W, 4, 5, 6 to 14th St-Union Sq
This outpost of the Boston-based chain is not actually in a basement, but three flights up, with a tremendous view of Union Sq. The best stuff to see is inside, though, where you will find labels for up to 70% less than the price at regular retail outlets. Like similar discount department stores, it's got clothing, shoes, jewelry, accessories, cosmetics and some housewares (like bedding). Fashionistas willing to go on painstaking searches could unearth many treasures, including apparel from Dolce & Gabbana, Michael Kors, Versace and more.

WHOLE FOODS Map p120 Gourmet Supermarket
☎ 212-673-5388; 4 Union Sq S; ⏱ 8am-10pm; ◎ L, N, Q, R, W, 4, 5, 6 to 14th St-Union Sq
One of several locations of the healthy food chain that is sweeping the city (there's also one in the Shops at Columbus Circle, p238), this is an overwhelming spot to shop for a picnic. Find endless rows of gorgeous produce, both organic and conventional, plus a butcher, bakery, health and beauty section, and aisles packed with natural packaged goods.

ABC CARPET & HOME
Map p120   Home Furnishings
☎ 212-473-3000; 888 Broadway; ⏱ 10am-8pm Mon-Thu, 10am-6:30pm Fri & Sat, noon-6pm Sun; ◎ L, N, Q, R, W, 4, 5, 6 to 14th St-Union Sq

Home designers and decorators stroll here to brainstorm ideas. Set up like a museum on six floors, ABC is filled with all sorts of furnishings, small and large, including easy-to-pack knick-knacks, designer jewelry, global gifts and more bulky antique furnishings and carpets. Come Christmas season, the shop is a joy to behold, as the decorators here go all out with lights and other wondrous touches.

BED, BATH & BEYOND Map p120 Housewares
☎ 212-255-3550; 620 Sixth Ave at 18th St; ⏱ 8am-9pm; ◎ F, V to 14th St
Though it's part of a national chain, this massive home-product emporium must be seen to be believed (if you've never entered one before). It's got every kitchen, bath, bed, office and outdoor home product you can imagine. There are fun shower curtains, high-threadcount sheets, plush towels, and pots and pans spread before you like a consumer ocean, and rising high on floor-to-ceiling displays. Beware of the mobs on weekends.

ACADEMY RECORDS Map p120 Music
☎ 212-242-3000; 12 W 18th St; ◎ F, V to 14th St
This tiny music shop brings in the crowds for its excellent selection of new and used CDs. There's astounding classical selections on vinyl, while real vinyl-heads should visit the East Village store (p227).

VIRGIN MEGASTORE Map p120 Music & Videos
☎ 212-598-4666; 52 E 14th St; ⏱ 9am-1am Mon-Sat, 10am-midnight Sun; ◎ L, N, Q, R, W, 4, 5, 6 to 14th St-Union Sq
This always-bustling Union Sq branch of the massive music store has serious collections of CDs and DVDs. There's another Virgin at Times Sq (Map pp134–5; ☎ 212-921-1020; 1540 Broadway; ⏱ 9am-1am Sun-Thu, 9am-2am Fri & Sat; ◎ N, Q, R, S, W, 1, 2, 3, 7 to Times Sq-42nd St); it claims to be the world's largest music store, and also hosts frequent big-name signings.

REVOLUTION BOOKS
Map p120   Radical Bookstore
☎ 212-691-3345; 9 W 19th St; ⏱ 10am-7pm Mon-Sat, noon-5pm Sun; ◎ 1 to 18th St
The Rev has New York's biggest and most outstanding radical collection of books, leaflets and journals. You will find bookshelves devoted to Lenin, Mao and Marx, many books in español, as well as cute red-star earrings. The shop also hosts radical discussions.

PARAGON ATHLETIC GOODS

Map p120 — Sporting Goods

☎ 212-255-8036; 867 Broadway; ⏰ 10am-8pm Mon-Sat, 11:30am-7pm Sun; ⓜ L, N, Q, R, W, 4, 5, 6 to 14th St-Union Sq

A maze-like, windowless behemoth, Paragon offers a comprehensive collection of sports merchandise featuring basketballs, tennis rackets, hiking gear, swim goggles, ski poles, baseball bats, all sorts of sneakers and apparel, you name it. It has better prices than the chains and an excellent selection of in-line skates. Watch for end-of-season sales, which can get devastatingly mobbed.

MIDTOWN EAST & FIFTH AVENUE

A vast sea of concrete and chaos, Midtown offers shopping delights for commoner and debutante alike. Those with cash head north to movie-famed Fifth Ave and 59th St, gateway to the Garden of Eden as far as luxury goods are concerned. Here, fabled jewelers like Tiffany & Co and Cartier hold court, alongside the gilded department stores of Bergdorf Goodman and Henri Bendel. Even if you left your Amex black card at home, it's worth going to see the artfully designed window displays, which change seasonally and get more spectacular each year.

NIKETOWN NEW YORK

Map p126 — Athletic Wear

☎ 212-891-6453; 6 E 57th St at Fifth Ave; ⏰ 10am-8pm Mon-Sat, 11am-7pm Sun; ⓜ E, V to Fifth Ave-53rd St

Leave Gotham and enter Niketown, an athletic wonderland where you'll find the full line of Nike products, including sneakers, clothing and gizmos for every sport. You can even test-drive your footwear on the in-store treadmills, making shopping even more fun than it already is.

URBAN CENTER BOOKS

Map p126 — Architecture Books

☎ 212-935-3592; 457 Madison Ave; ⏰ 10am-7pm Mon-Thu, 10am-6pm Fri, 10am-5:30pm Sat; ⓜ 6 to 51st St

This impressive shop of the Municipal Art Society (p404), in the courtyard of the historic Villard Houses at Madison Ave, carries 7000 new (and some out-of-print) books on architecture, urban planning, design, landscape, history and all aspects of NYC.

DYLAN'S CANDY BAR Map p126 — Candy

☎ 646-735-0078; 1011 Third Ave at 60th St; ⏰ 10am-10pm Mon-Fri, 11am-11pm Sat, 11am-8pm Sun; ⓜ 4, 5, 6 to 59th St

A candy junkie's worst nightmare, sweetstore Dylan's has giant swirly lollipops, crunchy candy bars, glowing jars of jelly beans, brightly colored Pez dispensers, softball-sized cupcakes and a luminescent staircase embedded with scrumptious, unattainable candy. Stay away on weekends to avoid being pummeled by small, sugar-crazed kids.

BANANA REPUBLIC Map p126 — Clothing

☎ 212-974-2350; www.bananarepublic.com; 626 Fifth Ave; ⏰ 10am-8pm Mon-Sat, 11am-7pm Sun; ⓜ B, D, F, V to 47th-50th Sts-Rockefeller Center

Good ol' Banana Republic sells its slick, stylish staid wear in no less than a dozen Manhattan stores; check the website for locations. This branch, at Rockefeller Center, has one of the bigger selections.

BARNEYS Map p126 — Department Store

☎ 212-826-8900; 660 Madison Ave; ⏰ 10am-8pm Mon-Fri, 10am-7pm Sat, 11am-6pm Sun; ⓜ N, R, W to Fifth Ave-59th St

Perhaps offering Manhattan's best designer clothing selection, Barneys justifies its occasionally raised-nose staff with its spot-on collections of the '00s' best designer duds (Marc Jacobs, Prada, Helmut Lang, Paul Smith and Miu Miu shoes). For less expensive deals (geared to a younger market), check out Barneys Co-op on the 7th and 8th floors, or on the Upper West Side, in SoHo or in Chelsea (p233).

BERGDORF GOODMAN

Map p126 — Department Store

☎ 212-753-7300; 754 Fifth Ave; ⏰ 10am-7pm Mon-Wed & Fri, 10am-8pm Thu, noon-8pm Sun; ⓜ N, R, W to Fifth Ave, F to 57th St

This classy, legendary, high-end department store is all about labels and fabulousness – the serious, not pretentious kind. Women's collections include Eli Tahari, Dolce & Gabbana, Yves Saint Laurent, Emilio Pucci, Stella McCartney, Alice + Olivia and Moschino, to name just a few. And then there are the departments selling jewelry, fragrance, shoes, handbags, housewares and menswear – with apparel from Gucci, Etro and Paul Smith – and the terrific organic Susan Ciminelli Spa on the 9th floor.

BLOOMINGDALE'S Map p126 Department Store

☎ 212-705-2000; 1000 Third Ave at 59th St; ⏰ 10am-8:30pm Mon-Thu, 9am-10pm Fri & Sat, 11am-7pm Sun; ◉ 4, 5, 6 to 59th St, N, R, W to Lexington Ave-59th St

Massive 'Bloomies' is something like the Metropolitan Museum of Art to the shopping world: historic, sprawling, overwhelming and packed with bodies, but you'd be sorry to miss it. Navigate the mass (and dodge the dozens of automaton types trying to spray you with the latest scent) to browse and buy clothing and shoes from a who's who of designers, including an increasing number of 'new-blood' collections.

HENRI BENDEL Map p126 Department Store

☎ 212-247-1100; 712 Fifth Ave; ⏰ 10am-7pm Fri-Wed, 10am-8pm Thu; ◉ E, V to Fifth Ave-53rd St, N, R, W to Fifth Ave-59th St

As boutique-cozy as a big-name, high-class department store can be, Bendel's makes for an easy pop-in-and-out. Its European collections include curious, stylish clothing by established and up-and-coming designers, as well as cosmetics and accessories. Look out for the original Lalique windows.

LORD & TAYLOR Map p126 Department Store

☎ 212-391-3344; www.lordandtaylor.com; 424 Fifth Ave; ⏰ 10am-8:30pm Mon-Fri, 10am-7pm Sat, 11am-7pm Sun; ◉ 7 to Fifth Ave, S, 4, 5, 6, 7 to Grand Central-42nd St

Staying true to its traditional roots (Ralph Lauren, Donna Karen, Calvin Klein etc), this 10-floor classic tends to let shoppers browse pressure-free (even in the cosmetics department), and has a great selection of swimwear.

SAKS FIFTH AVE Map p126 Department Store

☎ 212-753-4000; 611 Fifth Ave at 50th St; ⏰ 10am-7pm Mon-Wed, Fri & Sat, 10am-8pm Thu, noon-6pm Sun; ◉ B, D, F, V to 47th-50th Sts-Rockefeller Center

Anyone heard of Saks? Here's where it started. This lovely flagship offers its updated collection of high-end women's and men's clothing, plus other lines including Gucci, Prada, Juicy Couture, Theory, Eli Tahari and Burberry. Its January sale is

legendary. (Also note the good view of Rockefeller Center from its upper floors.)

TAKASHIMAYA Map p126 Department Store

☎ 212-350-0100; 693 Fifth Ave; ⏰ 10am-7pm Mon-Sat, noon-5pm Sun; ◉ E, V to Fifth Ave-53rd St

The Japanese owners upped the ante on Fifth Ave's elegant, minimalist style with this stunning store, which sells high-end furniture, clothing and (less costly) homewares from all over the world; the top floor's beauty emporium has classy cosmetics and a serene day spa. Purchases come gorgeously packaged. Even if you're not buying, don't miss the ground-floor floral arrangements and the chance to sip some green tea at the relaxing Tea Box café in the basement.

SALVATORE FERRAGAMO

Map p126 Designer Clothing

☎ 212-759-3822; 655 Fifth Ave at 52nd St; ⏰ 10am-7pm Mon-Sat, noon-6pm Sun; ◉ E, V to Fifth Ave-53rd St

Opened in 2003, Salvatore's flagship store fills its two floors with the Italian designer's glamorous men's and women's collections, including gold-soled shoes, ostentatious women's outerwear and boho-chic men's turtlenecks.

THE CONRAN SHOP Map p126 Home Designs

☎ 212-755-9079; 407 E 59th St at First Ave; ⏰ 11am-8pm Mon-Fri, 10am-7pm Sat, noon-6pm Sun; ◉ 4, 5, 6 to 59th St

Find slick kitchenware and tableware, linens, furniture and home accessories at this sleek emporium, nestled in a marvelous space under the Queensboro Bridge, from British design king Terence Conran. Browse through streamlined sofas, Missoni china, Ducati pens, retro Jacob Jensen alarm clocks, Rob Brandt tumblers, Mandarina Duck luggage, Lucite photo frames and much more.

TIFFANY & CO Map p126 Jewelry & Home

☎ 212-755-8000; 727 Fifth Ave; ⏰ 10am-7pm Mon-Fri, 10am-6pm Sat, noon-5pm Sun; ◉ F to 57th St

This famous jeweler, with the trademark clock-hoisting Atlas over the door, has won countless hearts with its fine diamond rings, watches, silver Elsa Peretti heart necklaces, and fine crystal vases and glassware. It's the high-end bridal registry spot of choice, and the store's little blue boxes have been known to provoke squealing from any teenage girl lucky enough to get a gift from here. The classy elevators are operated by old-school humans – and whatever you do, don't harass them with tired 'Where's the breakfast?' jokes.

NBA STORE Map p126 Sporting Goods
☎ 212-644-9400; 767 Fifth Ave; ◷ 10am-7pm Mon-Sat, 11am-6pm Sun; ◉ E, V to Fifth Ave-53rd St
Amid posh department stores and designer outlets, why not hoops? Pick up team jerseys, basketballs and other (rather marked-up) memorabilia, or shoot some free baskets inside before slam-dunking your way to Takashimaya or Saks.

FAO SCHWARTZ Map p126 Toys
☎ 212-644-9400; 767 Fifth Ave; ◷ noon-7pm Mon-Wed, noon-8pm Thu-Sat, 11am-6pm Sun; ◉ 4, 5, 6 to 59th St, N, R, W to Fifth Ave-59th St
The toystore giant, where Tom Hanks played footsy piano in the movie *Big*, is number one on the NYC wish list of most visiting kids. Why not indulge them? The magical (over-the-top consumerist) wonderland, with dolls up for 'adoption,' life-size stuffed animals, gas-powered kiddie convertibles, air-hockey sets and much more, might even thrill you, too.

ARGOSY Map p126 Used & Rare Books
☎ 212-753-4455; www.argosybooks.com; 116 E 59th St; ◷ 10am-6pm Mon-Fri, 10am-5pm Sat; ◉ 4, 5, 6 to 59th St, N, R, W to Lexington Ave-59th St
Since 1925, this landmark used-book store has stocked fine antiquarian items such as leatherbound books, old maps, art monographs and other classics picked up from high-class estate sales and closed antique shops. Books range from a 1935 copy of James Joyce's *Ulysses* illustrated by Matisse and signed by the artist – yours for only $4000 – to less expensive clearance items.

COMPLETE TRAVELLER
Map p126 Used Travel Books
☎ 212-685-9007; 199 Madison Ave at E 35th St; ◷ 10am-6:30pm Mon-Fri, 10am-6pm Sat, noon-5pm Sun; ◉ 6 to 33rd St
Stocking two rooms full with travel guides and maps from the travelways of days past, the Complete Traveller arranges its stock by destination. It's the perfect browsing ground for travel bugs: old Baedeker guides, the complete WPA series of US state guides, maps and some newer titles, too.

MIDTOWN WEST & TIMES SQUARE

The porn parlors and urban grittiness of Times Sq disappeared in the late '90s, leaving in their place a saccharine Disney World of bright, flashing lights and generic restaurants and retail stores. Most New Yorkers would rather have the pimps and cracked storefronts.

Finding unique stores isn't easy, but they do exist. On 48th St, several musical-instrument shops (such as Manny's) service rock stars who come to pick up a pedal or a new ax. Way west, in Hell's Kitchen, are a handful of boutiques along with the excellent but only-on-weekends Hell's Kitchen Flea Market (Map pp134–5; ☎ 212-243-5343; 39th St btwn Ninth & Tenth Aves; ◷ 7am-4pm Sat & Sun). Formerly in Chelsea, the many stalls here hide furnishings, accessories, CDs, clothing and unidentifiable objects from past eras, courtesy of 170 wonderfully choosy vendors.

Gem hunters should not miss the wonderful Diamond District (p132), a wild and wacky only-in-NYC experience, while self-made style mavens should hit the Garment District (p132), around Seventh Ave in the 30s and home to massive, wonderfully stocked shops selling fabric, buttons, thread, zippers, sequins and such. A few blocks away is the ever-shrinking (real estate, you know) Flower District (p114). It's basically along 28th St near Sixth Ave, with a few shops along the avenue itself. The best time to visit is early in the morning, when the wholesale deliveries of exotic blooms arrive.

Other shopping icons are the enormous, well-peopled chain stores around Herald Sq. The commercial mayhem all started with Macy's way back in the Dark Ages, and the block-long goliath is still a great place for shoppers and wanderers.

RIZZOLI Map pp134–5 Books
☎ 212-759-2424; 31 W 57th St; ◷ 10am-7:30pm Mon-Fri, 10:30am-7pm Sat, 11am-7pm Sun; ◉ F to 57th St
This handsome store of the Italian bookstore/publisher sells great art, architecture and design books (as well as general-interest titles). There's also a good collection of foreign newspapers and magazines onsite.

H&M Map pp134–5 Budget Fashions
☎ 646-473-1164; www.hm.com; 1328 Broadway at 34th St; ◷ 10am-10pm Mon-Sat, 11am-8pm Sun; ◉ B, D, F, V, N, Q, R, W to 34th St-Herald Sq

The flagship H&M at Herald Sq is one of six branches (and counting) of the Swedish clothing giant (check online for other locations). Both it and the store at 51st St and Fifth Ave have large selections of discount clothes.

B&H PHOTO-VIDEO
Map pp134–5   Cameras & Electronics

☎ photo 212-502-6200, video 212-502-6300; www.bhphotovideo.com; 420 Ninth Ave; ☯ 9am-7pm Mon-Thu, 9am-1pm Fri, 10am-5pm Sun; ◉ A, C, E to 34th St-Penn Station

Visiting the city's most popular camera shop can be an experience in itself – it's massive and crowded, and bustling with black-clad (and quite knowledgeable) Hasidic Jewish salesmen bussed in from communities in distant Brooklyn neighborhoods. Select an item and it gets whisked away from you and dropped into a bucket, which then moves up and across the ceiling to the purchase area (which requires a second queue). It's all very orderly and fascinating, and the selection of cameras, film, computers and many other electronics is outstanding.

CLOTHINGLINE/SSS SAMPLE SALES
Map pp134–5   Clothing

☎ 212-947-8748; www.clothingline.com; 2nd fl, 261 W 36th St; ☯ 10am-6pm Mon & Wed, 10am-7pm Tue & Thu; ◉ 1, 2, 3 to Penn Station

Each week this Garment District space sells pieces from a different batch of designers – both small and well-known labels, with markdowns of up to 75%. The Theory sale is rated highly, with other weeks featuring Helmut Lang, Rag & Bone, Ben Sherman and others. Check the website to see what's on the block while you're in town.

MACY'S
Map pp134–5   Department Store

☎ 212-695-4400; 151 W 34th St at Broadway; ☯ 10am-8:30pm Mon-Sat, 11am-7pm Sun; ◉ B, D, F, V, N, Q, R, W to 34th St-Herald Sq

The world's largest department store has a bit of everything – clothing, furnishings, kitchenware, sheets, cafés, hair salons. It's less high-end than many Midtown department stores but it's useful if you're looking for simpler things, like a good pair of jeans or a work shirt, not necessarily an only-from-Manhattan 21st-century outfit. Plus, riding the creaky old wooden elevators on the Broadway side is a must-do NYC experience.

WEAR ME OUT
Map pp134–5   Gay Clubwear

☎ 212-333-3047; 358 W 47th St btwn Eighth & Ninth Aves; ☯ 11:30am-8pm; ◉ C, E to 50th St

A fun little boutique for 'Hellsea boys' who need the perfect outfit to wear to HK (p343) this weekend, this is a friendly place to pick up a pec-promoting tight tee, a pair of sexy Energie jeans, provocative undies and various types of jewelry. The flirtatious staff are full of encouragement, too.

SHOPS AT COLUMBUS CIRCLE
Map pp134–5   Mall

☎ 212-823-6300; 10 Columbus Circle; ◉ A, B, C, D, 1 to 59th St-Columbus Circle

If you want to a bunch of good chain stores all in one spot, head to the four retail floors of the Time Warner Center. You'll find 50 largely upscale shops (and several restaurants) including Coach, Williams-Sonoma, Hugo Boss, Thomas Pink, Sephora, J Crew, Borders Books & Music, Armani Exchange, Esprit and Benetton. If you're bent on a Central Park picnic, visit the absolutely enormous Whole Foods (☯ 8am-10pm) in the basement for ready-to-go salads and sandwiches.

MANNY'S MUSIC
Map pp134–5   Musical Instruments

☎ 212-819-0576; 156 W 48th St; ☯ 10am-7pm Mon-Sat, noon-6pm Sun; ◉ R, W to 49th St

Guitar junkies and gear-heads should pay tribute to W 48th St's most famous music shop, Manny's. It's where Jimi Hendrix bought new guitars, the Stones bought the distortion pedal they used on 'Satisfaction,' and, before all that, where jazz greats like Benny Goodman picked up a reed or two. Wall photos tell the tale, and Manny's still stocks all the goods (guitars, basses, drums, keyboards) for you to make your band. Sam Ash (Map pp134–5; ☎ 212-719-2299; 155 W 48th St; ☯ 10am-8pm Mon-Sat, noon-6pm Sun) is another top-notch music outfitter on the block.

MUD, SWEAT & TEARS
Map pp134–5   Pottery & Ceramics

☎ 212-974-9121; 654 Tenth Ave at 46th St; ◉ C, E to 50th St

Also a popular pottery school, this small storefront sells the top work of students and local pros, with a great selection of both functional and display-worthy items from both glazed red clay and fine white ceramic. It's a down-to-earth, pleasantly intimate spot to pick up a gift (just get it wrapped well for the trip).

top picks

BOOKSHOPS

- **Strand Book Store** (p231) The mother lode of NYC bookshops, stocking 18 miles of new and used titles.
- **192 Books** (p232) Run by writers, 192 Books is one of those charmingly old-fashioned independent neighborhood bookshops.
- **St Mark's Bookshop** (p226) Well-chosen selection of magazines, books, journals and other literary fare.
- **Spoonbill & Sugartown** (p242) Quirky bookseller whose motto is 'I went to Sugartown and I shook the sugar down.'
- **Housing Works Used Book Café** (p222) The city's most atmospheric store for used books.

COLONY Map pp134–5 — Sheet Music
☎ 212-265-2050; 1619 Broadway; ⏰ 9:30am-midnight Mon-Sat, 10am-midnight Sun; ⓮ R, W to 49th St

Located in the Brill Building (the onetime home of Tin Pan Alley song crafters), the historic Colony once sold sheet music to the likes of Charlie Parker and Miles Davis. Its collection remains the city's largest. Plus there's a giant collection of karaoke CDs (show tunes, mariachi, AC/DC etc) and cases of memorabilia (Beatles gear, original Broadway posters, unused Frank and Sammy tickets etc), all for sale.

DRAMA BOOKSHOP
Map pp134–5 — Theater Books
☎ 212-944-0595; www.dramabookshop.com; 250 W 40th St; ⏰ 10am-8pm Mon-Sat, noon-6pm Sun; ⓮ A, C, E to 42nd St-Port Authority

Treasures in print for drama fans are shelved at this large bookstore, which has taken its theater (plays and musicals) seriously since 1917. Staffers can recommend worthy selections. Check out the website for regular events, such as talks with playwrights.

TOYS 'R' US Map pp134–5 — Toys
☎ 800-869-7787; 1514 Broadway; ⏰ 10am-10pm Mon-Sat, 11am-8pm Sun; ⓮ S, N, R, Q, W, 1, 2, 3, 7 to 42nd St-Times Sq

Sure you have one of these at home, but this super-size Toys 'R' Us is its greatest bastion, with three thematic floors including a huge video-game area downstairs, an alley of stuffed animals and an indoor Ferris wheel. Just avoid it like the plague before Christmas, when all hell tends to break loose here.

UPPER EAST SIDE

Shopping isn't for amateurs – or the unemployed – on the Upper East Side. The fussy, well-scrubbed neighborhood is filled with residents who shop at Gucci, Prada and Cartier as regularly as most folks hit the Gap. The main shopping is on, and just off, Madison Ave, from Midtown up to about E 75th St. You'll also find attractive one-of-a-kind boutiques, mainly on Lexington and Third Aves in the 70s and 80s, as well as gourmet food shops. For unique gifts, hit the museum shops, including those at the Met (p141), the Whitney (p143), the Jewish Museum (p145) and the Neue Galerie (see the boxed text, p145).

LITTLE SHOP OF CRAFTS Map p142 — Crafts
☎ 212-717-6636; www.littleshopny.com; 431 E 73rd St; ⏰ 11:30am-6pm Mon & Tue, 11am-10pm Wed-Fri, 10am-8pm Sat, 10am-6:30pm Sun; ⓮ 6 to 96th St

Head to New York's largest craft house when you're in the mood for something crafty, and want to make it yourself. You can opt to paint ceramics (which they provide and then fire for you), create beaded jewelry, assemble a mosaic (picture frame, mirror, etc), or even build your own stuffed animal. Friendly staff members help guide the way. Go on a weeknight (when there's wine and good tunes playing) to avoid the child-parent crush on weekends.

CANTALOUP Map p142 — Designer Clothing
☎ 212-249-3566; 1036 Lexington Ave at 74th St; ⓮ 6 to 77th St

Jeans from True Religion and Paper Denim Cloth here, on the uptight Upper East Side? Sure, why not? There are plenty of hipsters here, really, and most of them find their way into this brightly colored, pop-vibe emporium at one time or another; it also stocks sexy dresses, filmy blouses and fab accessories.

RALPH LAUREN Map p142 — Designer Clothing
☎ 212-606-2100; 867 Madison Ave; ⏰ 10am-6pm Mon-Wed & Fri, 10am-7pm Thu, noon-5pm Sun; ⓮ 6 to 68th St-Hunter College

Housed in a beautiful 1890s mansion (one of Manhattan's few remaining residences of that era), Ralph's flagship store rewards the long stroll up Madison Ave, even if you've already stocked up on Polo gear elsewhere. There's a big selection here, with an emphasis on more formal wear (particularly for men).

SHERRY-LEHMAN Map p142 Wine

☎ 212-838-7500; 679 Madison Ave; 🕑 9am-7pm Mon-Sat; Ⓜ 4, 5, 6 to 59th St

Reigning on Madison Ave since 1934, this family-run spot's founder made a name for himself during the prohibition. Over the years the place has introduced such high-end spirits as Dom Perignon and Chivas Regal to the US market, and it now offers more than 7000 items from its sprawling 65,000-sq-ft space. Expect helpful and knowledgeable staffers, and more selection than you can fathom.

OLIVE & BETTE'S Map p142 Women's Clothing

☎ 212-717-9655; www.oliveandbettes.com; 1070 Madison btwn 80th & 81st St; 🕑 10am-7pm Mon-Sat, 11am-6pm Sun; Ⓜ 6 to 77th St

Boasting four locations about town, Olive & Bette's is a cheery spot with candy-striped wallpaper and a good selection of youthful designs. Favorite labels among the teen to thirty-something shoppers include James Perse, Theory, Splendid and Nanette Lepore. First-time visitors sometimes complain about the store attitude, and find the smaller West Village branch (Map p110; ☎ 212-206-0036; 384 Bleecker St) more accommodating.

UPPER WEST SIDE

Not a fabulous shopping destination, the Upper West Side, nevertheless, has dozens of shops catering to its well-to-do, dog-loving residents. The traditionally Jewish neighborhood still has places true to its roots, like fabled sturgeon king Barney Greengrass, plus delis, bagelries, gourmet shops and such. Three main avenues (Broadway, Amsterdam and Columbus) run through the neighborhood. Best for the stroll-and-shop is by far Columbus Ave, particularly between about W 66th St and W 82nd St, where you can find high-end boutiques and shops. You'll find endless chain stores including Barnes & Noble, Banana Republic and Gap on Broadway between about 80th and 90th Sts.

TOWN SHOP Map p153 Bras & Lingerie

☎ 212-724-8160; 2273 Broadway at 82nd St; Ⓜ 1 to 79th St

Your bra doesn't fit! No, really – statistics say that 80% of women are wearing an ill-fitting bra, and here at the more-than-a-century-old Town Shop, the attentive saleswomen want to help you. They'll hustle you into a private fitting room and bring you a selection of pretty, quality bras, and not let you leave until they find you one that fits properly. You'll also find great lingerie and sleepwear from Cosabella, Wolford and Hanro.

FAIRWAY Map p153 Gourmet Food

☎ 212-595-1888; 2127 Broadway at 75th St; 🕑 6am-1am; Ⓜ 1, 2, 3 to 72nd St

Like a museum of good eats, this landmark grocery spills its lovely mounds of produce into its sidewalk bins, seducing you inside to its aisles of international goodies, fine cooking oils, nuts, cheeses, prepared foods and, upstairs, an organic market and chi-chi café. You'll find other branches in Harlem (Map pp158–9; ☎ 212-234-3883; 2328 Twelfth Ave at 132nd St) and Brooklyn (Map p180; ☎ 718-694-6868; 480 Van Brunt St, Red Hook, Brooklyn)

ZABAR'S Map p153 Gourmet Food, Kitchenware

☎ 212-787-2000; 2245 Broadway; 🕑 8:30am-7:30pm Mon-Fri, 8am-8pm Sat, 9am-6pm Sun; Ⓜ 1 to 79th St

A New York classic gourmet emporium, Zabar's is famous not only for its food – especially the amazing array of cheeses, olives, jams, coffee, caviar and smoked fish – but also its large 2nd-floor kitchenware department. A $1 Zabar's mug, with its distinctive orange lettering that reflects a kind of uptown Dodge City font, is a great insider-type gift from New York.

HARRY'S SHOES Map p153 Shoes

☎ 212-874-2035; 2299 Broadway at 83rd St; 🕑 10am-6:45pm Tue, Wed, Fri & Sat, 10am-7:45pm Mon & Thu, 11am-6pm Sun; Ⓜ 1 to 86th St

Harry's is a classic, staffed by classy gentlemen who actually measure your foot in one of those old-school metal contraptions and then wait on you patiently, making sure the shoe fits properly. You'll find mostly sturdy, quality, comfort-trumps-style labels here, such as Merrel, Dansko, Birkenstock, Ecco, New Balance and Mephisto, as well as the vegan, eco-friendly Earth brand. But fashionable types will find fun stuff, too, mainly from Ugg, Taryn Rose and the like. Harry's also has a new children's store (2315 Broadway) one block north.

TANI Map p153
Shoes

☎ 212-595-1338; 131 W 72nd St; ⏱ 10am-7:30pm Mon-Sat, 11am-7pm Sun; ⊕ 1, 2, 3, B, C to 72nd St

This dapper little store is a neighborhood favorite for its wide selection of fashionable men's and women's shoes. Prices cover the spectrum (from $85 to $425), and the variety is impressive, with designs by Jeffrey Campbell, Chie Mihara, Pour la Victoire and YMC, along with many other brands you won't find in big department stores.

WEST Map p153
Shoes & T-shirts

☎ 212-787-8595; 147 W 72nd St; ⏱ 10am-7:30pm Mon-Sat, 11am-7pm Sun; ⊕ 1, 2, 3, B, C to 72nd St

A newcomer to the rather staid 72nd St scene, West stocks unusual and eye-catching designs by Nike, Puma and Adidas plus denim Timberlands and those goofy-looking but ultra-comfortable Clarks high-top casuals. Whimsical T-shirts bear skewed logos ('Ghost Face' instead of North Face and 'LA Lovers' rather than 'LA Lakers'), while the outerwear includes extremely durable pieces by Canada Goose and Arc'teryx.

PENNY WHISTLE TOYS Map p153
Toys

☎ 212-873-9090; 448 Columbus Ave btwn 81st & 82nd Sts; ⏱ 9am-6pm Mon-Fri, 10am-6pm Sat, 11am-5pm Sun; ⊕ B, C to 81st St

A small, indie, old-fashioned toy store, this bright shop is full of quality fun stuff, including display-worthy kites, Brio train sets, Czech marionettes, puzzles, costumes and collectible dolls.

MALIA MILLS Map p153
Women's Swimwear

☎ 212-874-7200; 220 Columbus Ave; ⏱ 11am-6pm Mon-Sat, noon-5pm Sun; ⊕ 1, 2, 3, B, C to 72nd St

'If the suit doesn't fit, the suit is flawed, not the body,' goes the well-spoken maxim by swimsuit-design guru Malia Mills. At this UWS boutique (one of three in the city), Mills offers her masterfully fitting one- and two-piece swimsuits, made with European fabrics and created in the US. Indeed, the suits fit well and proffer a classic look, while still being rather easy on the eyes – her

work has appeared on the cover of *Sports Illustrated*, after all.

HARLEM & NORTHERN MANHATTAN

The once-fabled residence of many great African American artists, writers and activists, Harlem is changing fast. Gentrification has pushed out many longtime shopkeepers, with emblematic storefronts going the way of the typewriter. In their place has come big-box retailers and a scattering of new-wave indie boutiques, where young owners focus on the legend of Harlem and their own talent for fashion. The main commercial thoroughfare here is 125th St, which is lined with clothing and sneaker stores, restaurants, and vendors selling incense, handicrafts, and many other wares on warm days.

MALCOLM SHABAZZ HARLEM MARKET Map pp158–9
Arts & Crafts

☎ 212-987-8131; 52 W 116th St btwn Malcolm X Blvd & Fifth Ave; ⏱ 10am-7pm; ⊕ 2, 3 to 116th St

Enjoy some al fresco shopping at this popular marketplace, where you'll find items including African crafts, essential oils, incense, traditional clothing, CDs and bootleg videos. See also p161.

JUMEL TERRACE BOOKS
Map pp158–9
Rare Books

☎ 646-472-5938; www.jumelterracebooks.com; 426 W 160th St; ⏱ 11am-6pm Fri-Sun & by appt; ⊕ C to 163rd St-Amsterdam Ave

Housed in a historic private home is this new shop specializing in tomes on Africana, Harlem history and African American literature. You've got to call to set up an appointment outside their weekend hours, but if you're fascinated by rare books, and rare opportunities to shop at a beautiful home, then it's worth it.

NICHOLAS Map pp158–9
Rasta Shop

☎ 212-289-3628; 2035 Fifth Ave btwn 125th & 126th Sts; ⏱ 9am-8pm Mon-Sat, noon-6pm Sun; ⊕ 4, 5, 6 to 125th St

Rasta lovers of the world unite at this eye-catching storefront on a quiet stretch of Fifth Avenue. Here you'll find graphic T-shirts, jackets, hats, tote bags, belt buckles, scarves and lots of other collectible fare with Bob Marley and the vivid swash of green, yellow and red ever-present. You'll also find books, posters and, lest we forget, some rather clever rolling papers.

HARLEMADE Map pp158–9 Wearable Harlem Art

☎ 212-987-2500; 174 Lenox Ave btwn 118th & 119th Sts; ⏱ 11:30am-7pm Mon-Fri, 11am-7pm Sat, noon-6pm Sun; ⊕ 2, 3 to 116th St

Decked out with beautiful vintage tables and sporting a mellow vibe, this boutique is filled with designer-made clothing and memorabilia that celebrates the 'hood. Check out the tees and tote bags silk-screened with the profile of a woman with a 'fro, plus earth-tone messenger bags, caps, mugs and aprons that say 'Harlem'.

BROOKLYN

Travelers looking for an alternative to the Manhattan shopping scene should cross the East River to Brooklyn. There are a number of key areas here, with a good mix of shops, cafés and restaurants. Williamsburg is famed (and scorned) for its hipster attire, required wearing by nearly everyone in the 'burg. Pick up the uniform at vintage shops, thrift stores and trendier boutiques on and around Bedford Ave.

In South Brooklyn, you'll find some satisfying browsing around Boerum Hill. Atlantic Ave, running east–west near Brooklyn Heights, is sprinkled with antique shops; heading south from Atlantic, both Court and especially Smith Sts are lined with local designers' boutiques. Residential Park Slope, just west of Prospect Park, has a good selection of laidback clothing shops and bookstores along Fifth Ave (Lower East Side hip) and Seventh Ave (slightly more Upper West Side).

In the area, you should be able to pick up a shopping guide to each neighborhood you visit. Check out www.brooklynnow.com.

LITERARY DUMBO

- **PS Bookshop** (Map p174; ☎ 718-222-3340; www.psbookshop.com; 145A Front St, Dumbo; ⏱ 10am-8pm) Used and rare books.
- **Melville House** (Map p174; ☎ 718-722-9204; www.mhpbooks.com; 145 Plymouth St, Dumbo) Literary fiction, nonfiction and poetry.
- **Zakka** (Map p174; ☎ 718-801-8037; www.zakkacorp.com; 155 Plymouth St, Dumbo; ⏱ noon-7pm Wed-Sun) Graphic novels, magazines, T-shirts and futuristic toys.

SPOONBILL & SUGARTOWN Map p177 Books

☎ 718-387-7322; www.spoonbillbooks.com; 218 Bedford Ave, Williamsburg; ⏱ 10am-10pm; ⊕ L to Bedford Ave

The 'burg's favorite bookshop has an intriguing selection of art and coffee-table books, cultural journals, used and rare titles and locally made works not found elsewhere. Also in residence are several plump kitties that frighten local residents (or at least their dogs).

POWERHOUSE BOOKS Map p174 Books

☎ 718-666-3049; www.powerhousebooks.com; 37 Main St, Dumbo; ⏱ 10am-7pm Mon-Fri, 11am-7pm Sat & Sun; ⊕ A, C to High St, F to York St

An important part of Dumbo's cultural scene, Powerhouse Books hosts changing art exhibitions, book-launch parties and weird and creative events in its 5000-sq-ft space. You'll also find intriguing books on urban art, photography and pop culture – all imprints of the critically acclaimed publishing house.

LOVE BRIGADE CO-OP Map p177 Clothing

☎ 718-715-0430; 230 Grand St, Williamsburg; ⊕ L to Bedford Ave

A newcomer to Grand St, Love Brigade showcases the work of independent fashion-forward designers. The collection ranges from the classic to the futuristic, sometimes delving into new territory – like the men's T-shirts with Native American designs. A small, frowning dachshund is the boutique's mascot.

JACQUES TORRES CHOCOLATE
Map p174 Gourmet Chocolate

☎ 718-875-9772; www.mrchocolate.com; 66 Water St, Dumbo; ⏱ 9am-7pm Mon-Sat; ⊕ A, C to High St, F to York St

Serious chocolatier JT runs this small, European-style store with three-table café, filled with the most velvety and innovative chocolates ever crafted. Take a few to the nearby Empire Fulton Ferry State Park for a snack and a view between the Brooklyn and Manhattan Bridges.

BROOKLYN INDUSTRIES
Map p177 Streetwear

☎ 718-486-6464; www.brooklynindustries.com; 162 Bedford Ave at N 8th St, Williamsburg; ⏱ 11am-9pm Mon-Sat, noon-8:30pm Sun; ⊕ L to Bedford Ave

See the SoHo branch (p222) for a full description of the mini-empire that keeps on growing. There's also a factory store in South Williamsburg (Map p177; ☎ 718-218-9166; 184 Broadway at Driggs Ave) and other branches in Park Slope (Map p182; ☎ 718-789-2764; 206 Fifth Ave at Union St) and Boerum Hill (Map p180; ☎ 718-596-3986; 100 Smith St at Atlantic Ave).

BEACON'S CLOSET Map p177   Vintage Clothing
☎ 718-486-0816; 88 N 11th St, Williamsburg; ☻ noon-9pm Mon-Fri, 11am-8pm Sat & Sun; ☺ L to Bedford Ave

Twenty-something groovers find this giant Williamsburg warehouse of vintage clothing part goldmine, part grit. Lots of coats, polyester tops and '70s-era tees are handily displayed by color, but the sheer mass can take time to conquer. The smaller, more manageable branch on Fifth Ave (Map p182; ☎ 718-230-1630; 220 Fifth Ave, Brooklyn) stocks the cream of the crop only.

A CHENG Map p182   Women's Clothing
☎ 718-783-2826; www.achengshop.com; 152 Fifth Ave, Park Slope; ☻ 11am-7pm Mon-Fri, 11am-6pm Sat & Sun; ☺ M, R to Union St

This longtime East Village favorite moved to bigger digs in Park Slope in 2008, and offers a bigger selection from the collection of local designer A Cheng. Her latest collection of tailored yet funky women's wear includes trim crochet cardigans, trench coats with fun piping and big buttons, skirts with whimsical prints and cheery sundresses.

FLIRT Map p180   Women's Clothing
☎ 718-858-7931; 252 Smith St, Cobble Hill; ☺ F, G to Bergen St

VINTAGE WILLIAMSBURG
- Artists & Fleas Market (Map p177; ☎ 718-541-5760; www.artistsandfleas.com; 129 N 6th St, Williamsburg; ☻ noon-8pm Sat & Sun) Vintage clothes, plus independent designers, books and records at this weekend market.
- Buffalo Exchange (Map p177; ☎ 718-384-6901; 504 Driggs Ave, Williamsburg; ☻ 11am-7pm Mon-Sat, noon-8pm Sun)
- Fluke (Map p177; ☎ 718-486-3166; 86 N 6th St, Williamsburg; ☻ noon-9pm Mon-Fri, 11am-8pm Sat & Sun) Better selections than most Williamsburg vintage stores.

GRAND DESIGNER BOUTIQUES
- Sodafine (Map p177; ☎ 718-230-3060; 119 Grand St, Williamsburg; ☻ noon-7pm Tue-Sat, 1-6pm Sun) Quirky women's collection from about 30 local designers, plus vintage.
- Pop (Map p177; ☎ 718-486-6001; 310 Grand St, Williamsburg; ☻ noon-7pm Tue-Sat, 1-6pm Sun) Fun, stylish men's and women's urban wear, with graphic T-shirts and accessories.

The name says it all at this girlishly sexy boutique, where a trio of stylish owners (two of whom are sisters) comes up with funky but feminine creations such as adjustable-snap wrap skirts, custom-made skirts (pick your cut and fabric) and tiny tops in soft knits. It has been stationed here in Cobble Hill for several years, with a newer outpost in Park Slope (Map p182; ☎ 718-783-0364; 93 Fifth Ave).

QUEENS, THE BRONX & STATEN ISLAND

Once you leave the comfort zones of Manhattan and Brooklyn, the best way to approach shopping is by area, looking at, say, a stretch of several blocks on one street as a mini bazaar, with a collection of various shops that you can wander into aimlessly, either laying down cash or simply taking in the otherworldly vibes. In Jackson Heights, Queens, the stretch of 74th St that begins at the Roosevelt Ave subway station is a good example. The Little India strip is chock full of shops selling saris, like India Sari Palace (Map pp200–1; ☎ 718-426-2700; 37-07 74th St at 37th Ave); 24-karat-gold jewelry, at spots like Mita Jewelers (Map pp200–1; ☎ 718-507-1555; 37-30 74th St at 37th Rd); Bollywood DVDs and CDs at Today's Music (Map pp200–1; ☎ 718-429-7179; 73-09 37th Rd at 73rd St); and all manner of Indian groceries, from fresh curry leaves to jars of mango pickle. Plus, the neighborhood's beauty salons will thread your eyebrows rather than wax them; hanging out in one of these spots is a great way to spend some time around the relaxed locals.

On and around Main St in Flushing, Queens (p204), you'll find a wonderfully hectic array of items both Chinese and Korean. The Flushing Mall (Map pp200–1; ☎ 718-886-5814; 133-31 39th Ave at Prince St) is an indoor collection of East Asian items, though the excellent food court is the real draw. Browse the area outside, stopping at spots like Magic Castle (Map pp200–1; 136-82 39th Ave), packed with Korean pop culture such as stickers, CDs, hair clips and jewelry, and Shun An Tong Health Herbal Co (Map pp200–1; 135-24 Roosevelt Ave, off Main St), one of the oldest Chinese herbalists in the 'hood.

Arthur Ave (p207) in the Belmont area of the Bronx is the place to stock up on Italian delicacies, many of which – from olive oils to spices – could easily be packed for the trip back home. You'll find a series of vendors right inside the Arthur Ave Market (Map pp208–9; ☎ 718-295-5033; 2344 Arthur Ave), including purveyors of fresh-roasted coffee, olives, bakery items, imported canned goods, fruit, fresh pasta and cheeses.

In Staten Island (p213), Ganas – a rare NYC commune of about 90 people – runs one of NYC's best-kept shopping secrets: a collection of four vintage shops called Everything Goes. Run as cooperatives, each location specializes in a different sort of item: there's Everything Goes Clothing (☎ 718-273-7139; 140 Bay St; ✆ 10:30am-6:30pm Tue-Sat); Everything Goes Book Café (☎ 718-447-8256; 208 Bay St; ✆ 10am-7pm Tue-Thu, 10am-10pm Fri & Sat, noon-5pm Sun); Everything Goes Furniture (☎ 718-273-0568; 17 Brook St; ✆ 10:30am-6:30pm Tue-Sat); and Everything Goes Gallery (☎ 718-273-0568; 123 Victory Blvd; ✆ 10:30am-6:30pm Tue-Sat), which features eclectic artwork, antiques and collectibles. For directions to each store, which are all within walking distance from the Staten Island Ferry terminal, visit www.well.com/user/ganas/etgstores/.

top picks

- **Megu** (p249) This stylish shrine to Japanese cuisine will wow your senses.
- **Peasant** (p251) A local favorite, serving hearty, country-style food in a homey setting.
- **WD 50** (p255) Get adventurous with creative fusions of modern American fare.
- **Blue Hill** (p257) Slow cooking and fresh foodstuffs from local farms offer a serene alternative.
- **Momofuku Noodle Bar** (p256) The fresh ramen soups draw constant queues to this tiny, popular café.
- **Gramercy Tavern** (p259) A legend of the New York foodie set, with standout seafood and a serious wine list.
- **Dawat** (p261) Masterpieces of Indian cuisine are served in a formal, subdued setting.
- **Landmarc at the Time Warner Center** (p262) Industrial-chic decor, eclectic dishes and stellar views of Central Park.

What's your recommendation? www.lonelyplanet.com/new-york-city

EATING

Chowing down in New York City is not your standard affair. That's no surprise in a far-from-typical city, but still: lining up for an hour to consume a bowl of homemade soba noodles and some honeycomb tripe? Forking over twenty bucks for a teensy plate of foie gras *brulée*? Trolling the greenmarkets on a 90-degree summer day just to find local organic gooseberries and artisanal tofu? Hell yeah! Getting exactly what you want in your belly is what the foodie scene is all about here, folks. And approaching the task with a sense of adventure is what makes it an utterly dazzling journey.

Speaking of journeys, the range of global cuisine you'll find here is staggering, able to bring you to several countries in a week – or even a day – if you so desire. So get ready to dive your chopsticks into some authentic Cantonese or Japanese, sop up Ethiopian with a spongy shred of *injera* bread, pull apart a fresh lobster with your bare hands – and chase Turkish mezes, Spanish tapas or Mexican *torta* sandwiches with glasses of raki, sherry or *mezcal*, respectively. Some places take the international trip to the max, adding belly dancing, flamenco performances, New Orleans jazz, hookah smoking and even karaoke into the mix. And while you can always find the foreign food of your choice – especially if you're willing to travel to the outer boroughs (see the boxed text, p249) – other hankerings may be more fleetingly available. Just so you're prepared, here's a rundown of the current NYC dining trends (but keep in mind that the restaurant scene and its trends are constantly shifting here): authentic BBQ, heavy on the smoked meats; Italian small plates (paired with the perfect pour of wine); Korean fried chicken, served in whimsically designed to-go boxes; and eating locally, with an emphasis on veggies and cheeses that are grown within a 50-mile radius, thus making chic diners feel very good about themselves and their reduced carbon footprint. Try it – all of it. You're bound to love it.

OPENING HOURS

Most places are open daily. Those that do have days off usually close on Monday; those that are open Monday are not usually filled with locals, who avoid eating fresh fish and sushi because there are no deliveries on Sunday! Meal times for the varied schedules of New Yorkers are quite fluid, with restaurants complying: many diner-type spots serve breakfast all day or at least start as early as 3am, to accommodate club-goers who rely on stacks of pancakes to sober up. Loosely speaking, though, you can usually find breakfasts served till noon. Lunchtime overlaps a bit, often starting at 11:30am and ending at 4pm, and dinnertime is anywhere from 5pm or 6pm until 10pm during the week and about 11pm on weekends. That said, there are scores of eateries that serve until midnight, 1am or even 2am or 3am; many stay open around the clock. Prime time for dinner is between 8pm and 9pm. Brunch, usually limited to Sunday, is generally served from 11am until 3pm or 4pm.

BOOKING TABLES

Most restaurants take reservations for lunch and/or dinner, although some do not accept them unless you have four or more in your party. For those places that refuse reservations altogether, expect rowdy waits that could last a half-hour or more. But hey, it's all part of the experience.

To avoid disappointment, always assume that a reservation is necessary – especially on weekends, when it's almost certainly going to be the case. Cheap-eats places are the exception, as people move in and out quickly (not to mention the fact that there is probably a no-reservations policy). The hottest eateries in town require reservations, and many times you'll be told that there's nothing available for weeks; if you know way ahead of time that you want to be able to experience WD 50 (p255) and La Esquina (p253) before you leave town, for

PRICE GUIDE

The following is a guide to the pricing system in this chapter. Prices are per meal per person, excluding taxes.

$	under $15
$$	$15-30
$$$	over $30

example, reserve your table before you even get to town – or at least the second you arrive. However, as much as New Yorkers like to talk about how you'll *never* get into certain places, there's almost always a way to do it. One trick is to accept a reservation at a less-than-popular dining time – before 7pm or after 10:30pm – which is almost always available. Also, many hot spots have bars, and many of these bars have food service. Sure, it's not the same as getting lavish table service, but it's considered a cool way to experience a place, and getting a seat is rarely a problem.

TIPPING

Just as in the rest of the USA, you are expected to tip your server an average of 15% of your bill before tax. In restaurants, wait staff are paid less than the minimum wage and they rely upon tips to make a living. Tip at least 15% unless the service is terrible; most New Yorkers either tip a straight 20% or just double the 8.375% sales tax. In coffee-bar, fast-food, take-out or deli-counter joints, you'll often find a tip jar on the counter; dropping in a quarter or two is polite.

CELEBRATING WITH FOOD

While most of America sees major holiday meals in a Norman Rockwell sort of way – cozy, copious and definitely eaten at home – New Yorkers can be a bit peculiar when it comes to such special meals. Because of the nature of their always-busy lives and cramped living quarters, dining out on holidays – or at least having the complete meal prepared and even delivered by more capable, professional hands – has become a more popular way to go. And restaurants in NYC have been happy to comply, many offering special menus for every conceivable (and typically celebrated-at-home) holiday from Thanksgiving and Christmas Eve to Easter and Passover; New Year's Eve and Valentine's Day are especially big eating-out nights, with most eateries offering overpriced prix fixe meals to starry-eyed lovebirds. Even on July 4, when the rest of the country is eating burgers at outdoor grill parties, most New Yorkers are restaurant-bound for their ribs and chicken – unless they have fled the city for the country, of course, or happen to live in one of the outer boroughs, where it's not unusual to fire up a BBQ right on your building's front stoop.

VEGETARIANS & VEGANS

Though the herbivore scene here has long lagged behind that of West Coast cities, and was for years mocked by serious foodies, many former naysayers are beginning to come around. That's thanks in part to the local-food movement, which has hit NYC like a ton of potatoes, as well as a slow but steady trickle of new eateries that enticed skeptics by injecting big doses of cool ambience – and top-notch wine and liquor options – into the mix. Downtown and Brooklyn are home to most veggie places, with groovy takes on earthy-crunchy including Broadway East (Map p98; ☎ 212-228-3100; 171 E Broadway at Rutgers St; ✆ lunch, dinner & weekend brunch; ◎ F to East Broadway), Counter (Map p104; ☎ 212-982-5870; 105 First Ave btwn 6th & 7th Sts; ✆ dinner; ◎ F, V to Lower East Side-2nd Ave), Pure Food and Wine (p260), Soy Luck Club (p258) and the Wild Ginger Pan-Asian Café (Map p177; ☎ 718-218-8828; 212 Bedford Ave btwn N 5th & N 6th Sts; ✆ lunch & dinner; ◎ L to Bedford Ave). But herbivore oases now dot the entire landscape – uptown standouts include Candle Café (p264) and Café Blossom (p266) – and even the most meat-heavy four-star restaurants are figuring out the lure of legume; the market-inspired *le potager* section on the menu at Café Boulud (Map p142; ☎ 212-772-2600; 20 E 76th St; ✆ lunch & dinner Tue-Sun, brunch Sun; ◎ 6 to 77th St) is one of the most highbrow and little-known veggie gems in town.

SPECIALTIES

Unlike California or the South or even the Southwest, New York is never really referred to as having one defining cuisine. Try asking for some 'New York food,' for example, and you could wind up getting anything from a hot dog to a South Indian feast or a $500 Japanese prix fixe at the Time Warner Center's Masa. Cuisine in this multicultural town is global by definition, and constantly evolving by its very nature.

That said, it's the food items with the longest histories that folks usually have in mind when they refer to New York City specialties. Those at the top of the list were introduced by Italians and East European Jews, because these groups were among the earliest wave of immigrants here: bagels (Jewish) and slices of pizza (Italian) are integral parts of the New York food scene. But egg creams, cheesecake and hot dogs, just to name a few, are also uncontested staples of New York eats.

Hot Dogs

A derivative of sausage and one of the oldest forms of processed food, the hot dog goes back thousands of years, making its way to New York via various European butchers in the 1800s. One, Charles Feltman of Germany, was apparently the first to sell them from pushcarts along the Coney Island seashore. But Nathan Handwerker, originally an employee of Feltman's, opened his own shop across the street, offering hot dogs at half the price of those at Feltman's and putting his former employer out of business. Today the original and legendary Nathan's (p281) still stands in Coney Island, while its empire has expanded on a national scale. And there is barely a New York neighborhood that does not have at least a few hot-dog vendors on its street corners, although some locals would never touch one of those 'dirty-water dogs,' preferring the new wave of chi-chi hot-dog shops that can be found all over town. Enjoy yours, wherever it's from, with 'the works': plenty of spicy brown mustard, relish, sauerkraut and onions.

Bagels

Bagels may have been invented in Europe, but they were perfected around the turn of the 19th century in New York City – and once you've had one here, you'll have a hard time enjoying one anywhere else. Basically, it's a ring of plain-yeast dough that's first boiled and then baked, either left plain or topped with various finishing touches, from sesame seeds to chocolate chips. 'Bagels' made in other parts of the country are often just baked and not boiled, which makes them nothing more than a roll with a hole. And even if they do get boiled elsewhere, bagel-makers here claim that it's the New York water that adds an elusive sweetness never to be found anywhere else. Which baker creates the 'best' bagel in New York is a matter of (hotly contested) opinion, but most agree that H&H Bagels (www.handhbagel.com), with locations on the Upper West Side (Map p153; ☎ 212-595-8000; 2239 Broadway at 80th St; ◉ 1 to 79th St) and Upper East Side (Map p142; ☎ 212-734-7441; 1551 Second Ave at 81st St; ◉ 6 to 77th St), ranks pretty high. The most traditionally New York way to order one is by asking for a 'bagel and a schmear,' which will yield you said bagel with a small but thick swipe of cream cheese. Or splurge and add some lox – thinly sliced smoked salmon – as was originally sold from pushcarts on the Lower East Side by Jewish immigrants back in the early 1900s.

Pizza

Pizza's certainly not indigenous to Gotham. But New York–style pizza is a very particular item, and the first pizzeria in America was Lombardi's (Map pp88–9; ☎ 212-941-7994; 32 Spring St btwn Mulberry & Mott Sts; ◷ lunch & dinner; ◉ 6 to Spring St), which opened here in 1905. While Chicago-style is 'deep dish' and Californian tends to be light and doughy, New York prides itself on having pizza with thin crust and an even thinner layer of sauce – and slices that are triangular (unless they're Sicilian-style, in which case they're square). Pizza made its way over to New York in the 1900s through Italian immigrants, and its regional style soon developed, its thin crust allowing for faster cooking time in a city where everyone's always in a hurry. Today there are pizza parlors about every 10 blocks, especially in Manhattan and most of Brooklyn, where you'll find standard slices for $2. The style at each place varies slightly – some places touting cracker-thin crust, others offering slightly thicker and chewier versions, and plenty of nouveau styles throwing everything from shrimp to cherries on top.

Egg Creams

This frothy, old-fashioned beverage contains no eggs or cream – just milk, seltzer water and plenty of chocolate syrup (preferably the classic Fox's U-Bet brand, made in Brooklyn). But when Louis Auster of Brooklyn, who owned soda fountains on the Lower East Side, invented the treat back in 1890, the syrup he used was made with eggs, and he added cream to thicken the concoction. The name stuck, even though the ingredients were modified, and soon they were a staple of every soda fountain in New York. While Mr Auster sold them for 3¢ a piece, today they'll cost you anywhere from $1.50 to $3, depending on where you find one – which could be from one of the few remaining old-fashioned soda shops, such as Lexington Candy Shop (see the boxed text, p251) on the Upper East Side, or an old-school deli, like Katz's Deli (p256).

New York–Style Cheesecake

Sure, cheesecake, in one form or another, has been baked and eaten in Europe since the 1400s. But New Yorkers, as they do with many things, have appropriated its history in the form of the New York–style cheesecake. Immortalized by Lindy's restaurant in Midtown,

REAL TIME: NYC'S MOST AUTHENTIC ETHNIC FOOD

Sure, Manhattan's Little Italy and Curry Row are fine – if you like mobs of tourists desperately seeking authenticity. But you can truly find it in the outer boroughs, where the latest waves of immigrants have settled and continue to arrive. Below, a guide to going 'round the world in a few neighborhoods:

- South American *and* Indian – Jackson Heights (Map pp200–1), Queens, instead of several Manhattan 'hoods. Go on a cultural adventure filled with a tantalizing mix of Colombian *arepas*, Argentine bakeries, sari shops, *thali* plates and *dosas*, plus a true Bollywood theater. Take subway lines E, F, G, R or 7 to Roosevelt Ave.
- Mexican – Sunset Park (Map pp170–1), Brooklyn, instead of various Manhattan spots. Find honest-to-goodness *taquerías*, perfectly proportioned *tortas* and bakeries and produce shops that'll make you think you've gone south of the border. Take the N train to Eighth Ave.
- Greek – Astoria (Map pp200–1), Queens, or Bay Ridge (Map pp170–1), Brooklyn, instead of Midtown diners. While Astoria is the biggest, most well-known Greek enclave, you can also find a hefty sampling of feta-cheese shops and grilled-octopus restaurants in the formerly Italian enclave of Bay Ridge. Take the N or W train to Astoria-Ditmars Blvd for Queens, and the R to 86th St for Brooklyn.
- Irish – Woodlawn (Map pp208–9), the Bronx, instead of Manhattan's Third Ave Irish bars. Say goodbye to drunken frat boys and hello to correctly poured pints of Guinness, authentic bangers 'n' mash, just-arrived youngsters and, of course, about a dozen great pubs. Take the 4 train to Woodlawn.
- Italian – Belmont (Map pp208–9), the Bronx, instead of Little Italy. Trade in mediocre restaurants for excellent eateries, samples of fresh mozzarella in the Arthur Avenue Market (p244), to-die-for-cannoli and serious *Soprano*-character dead ringers. Sure, it's touristy, but in a much subtler way than the beaten-down patch of Manhattan. Take the B, D or 4 subway lines to Fordham Rd, then the Bx12 bus to Hoffman St.
- Jewish – Borough Park (Map p174), Brooklyn, instead of Manhattan's Lower East Side. Rather than grasping at straws with the handful of remaining bagel and appetizer shops, go for the gusto in this tight-knit, old-world Hasidic community (just be respectful, of course). Take the subway F to Ditmas Ave.
- Korean – Flushing (Map pp200–1), Queens, instead of Little Korea. Goodbye Macy's shoppers, hello kimchi buyers. Take the 7 train to Flushing-Main St.
- Russian – Brighton Beach (Map pp196–7), Brooklyn, instead of Midtown restaurants. No more vodka-tinis, please – just the rudely staffed food markets, bustling nightclubs and boardwalk that feels like Odessa on the sea. Take subway line D to Ocean Pkwy.

which was opened by Leo Lindemann in 1921, the particular type of confection served there – made of cream cheese, heavy cream, a dash of vanilla and a cookie crust – became wildly popular in the '40s. Junior's (Map pp134–5; ☎ 212-302-2000; 1515 Broadway at 44th St), which opened on Flatbush Ave in Brooklyn in 1929 and in Midtown just a few years ago, makes its own famous version of the creamy cake with a graham-cracker crust. Today, you'll find this local favorite on plentiful dessert menus, whether you're at a Greek diner or haute-cuisine hotspot.

LOWER MANHATTAN & TRIBECA

Frenzied lunch rushes for financial types fuel two extremes in Lower Manhattan: fast-food storefronts and masculine dining rooms catering to steak-chomping bigwigs. Both genres offer plenty of satisfying experiences, and if you move just a bit north into Tribeca, you'll find that hipster-catering and more fashion-forward hotspots abound.

BOULEY Map pp72–3   Classic French $$$
☎ 212-694-2525; www.davidbouley.com; 120 W Broadway at Duane St; ☽ lunch & dinner; ◉ A, C, 1, 2, 3 to Chambers St

The home base of celebrity chef David Bouley attracts an un-flashy crowd of heavyweights who drop small fortunes on sublime, creative takes on classic fare – like seared halibut with purees of persimmon and cauliflower and a trickle of almond-milk sauce, or tea-smoked organic duckling with vanilla-glazed baby turnips. Dinner tasting menus let you sample six courses of treasures for $95, or $175 with wine pairings. The Bouley Bakery, Café & Market (130 W Broadway; ☽ bakery 7:30am-7:30pm daily, dinner Tue-Sat), right next door, lets you nibble on goodies like mango-shrimp salad, *weiner-schnitzel* or soft-shell crab sandwiches, or purchase a perfect picnic to go.

MEGU Map pp72–3   Japanese $$$
☎ 212-964-7777; 62 Thomas St btwn Church St & West Broadway; ☽ lunch & dinner; ◉ A, C, 1, 2, 3 to Chambers St

A shrine to both style and substance, this is the place to have all your senses wowed. The space itself is wondrous – various levels of high ceilings, low lighting, Japanese art installations and sleek banquettes – and the food is equally exciting. Lobster salad with *yuzu* and passionfruit sauce, elegant *edamame* soup, slippery-fresh sushi and Kobe beef (grilled, carpaccio and *tartare*) are stunners. Or go for the gusto with a drawn-out tasting menu, starting with a spoonful of raw 'egg': pineapple juice, coconut milk and a yolk-ish filling.

LES HALLES Map pp72–3   French Brasserie $$$
☎ 212-285-8585; www.leshalles.net; 15 John St btwn Broadway & Nassau St; ☽ lunch & dinner; ⊖ A, C, J, M, Z, 2, 3, 4, 5 to Fulton St-Broadway-Nassau St
Celebrity chef Anthony Bourdain still reigns at this packed and serious brasserie where vegetarians need not apply. Among the elegant light-fixture balls, dark wood paneling and stiff white tablecloths you'll find a buttoned-up, meat-lovin' crowd with deep pockets. They've come for rich and decadent favorites including *cote de boeuf, choucroute garnis* and steak au poivre, as well as more standard *moules frites,* New York strip steak, salad niçoise and grilled salmon. The lists of wine, single-malt scotches and other liquors are impressive, as are the desserts, from the crème brûlée to the *tarte tatin.*

THALASSA Map pp72–3   Greek Seafood $$$
☎ 212-941-7661; 179 Franklin St btwn Hudson & Greenwich Sts; ☽ lunch & dinner; ⊖ 1 to Franklin St
A massive, high-ceilinged and high-style hangout located in a former food warehouse; its ultra-fresh and flavorful fish dishes – langoustines baked with tomatoes and homemade fettuccine, feta-crusted halibut in saffron sauce, scallop-and-shrimp studded risotto – will thrill your taste buds. But so will other well-executed menu items, like the smoked fish or artisanal cheese plates, or traditional fava bean and Greek salads. The crowd is business-classy, with a surprisingly breezy vibe.

INDUSTRIA ARGENTINA
Map pp72–3   Argentine Steakhouse $$
☎ 212-965-8560; 329 Greenwich St btwn Duane & Jay Sts; ☽ lunch daily, dinner Mon-Sat; ⊖ 1 to Franklin St

It truly feels like a Buenos Aires hotspot in here, where sleek design and masculine details blend to create a solid, confidence-inspiring setting in which to chow down on hearty steaks with *chimicurri*, mixed grills with lamb chops and sausages and heavenly starters, including a mini-empanada *amuse bouche* and a melt-in-your-mouth *tiradito*, with layers of avocado and thin slices of tuna. A lovely bar with chunky wood stools is the perfect spot to linger over a glass of spicy Malbec while waiting to be seated for the main event.

STELLA MARIS
Map pp72–3   Organic Irish-Seafood Pub $$
☎ 212-233-2417; 213 Front St; ☽ breakfast, lunch & dinner; ⊖ A, C, J, M, Z, 2, 3, 4, 5 to Fulton St-Broadway-Nassau St
One of the exciting newcomers to the otherwise chain-saturated South St Seaport area, this cozy, Irish-owned spot brings a polished and modern vibe to a cobblestoned, old-world corner of the city. Tuck into warm asparagus salad topped with a poached egg, done-right steak frites, charcuterie plates or grilled Scottish salmon; or an array of fresh shellfish from the black-onyx raw bar. The cozy café side of the place is great for breakfasts of Irish oatmeal, pastries basked at Balthazar (p252) or thick hot chocolate courtesy of local Willy Wonka Jacques Torres (p269).

BUBBY'S PIE COMPANY
Map pp72–3   Comfort Food $$
☎ 212-219-0666; 120 Hudson St at N Moore St; ☽ breakfast, lunch & dinner daily, brunch Sun; ⊖ 1 to Franklin St
One of the most consistently popular eateries in Tribeca, this low-key standby is a great draw for families with kids, who are welcome and easily sated with a special kids' menu brimming with classics from chicken fingers to buttered spaghetti. Adult draws include the mellow, high-ceilinged ambience and excellent takes on homey basics: luscious mac-and-cheese, slow-cooked BBQ including Texas-style brisket, grits, matzo-ball soup, buttermilk fried chicken and a selection of Mexican plates – all melt-in-your-mouth good. A Dumbo, Brooklyn outpost of Bubby's (Map p174; ☎ 718-222-0666; 1 Main St) has a kids' play area, swankier dining room and sweeping views of the city.

FINANCIER PATISSERIE

Map pp72–3   French Café $

☎ 212-334-5600; 62 Stone St at Mill Lane; ⊙ 7am-8:30pm Mon-Fri, 7am-7pm Sat; ⊘ 2, 3, 4, 5 to Wall St, J, M, Z to Broad St

It's a relief to find French flavors that are both affordable and delicious down in this neck of the woods, and this spot pulls it off with panache. A graceful café on the quaint and tiny Stone St, its fresh pastries – like almond-crusted fruit tarts and the signature madeleines – are truly worth raving over, but so is the heartier fare. Choose from homemade soups such as lentil and celery root, a range of fresh salads, and sandwiches like savory chicken with goat cheese on ciabatta. Other locations in this rapidly expanding empire are found at the World Financial Center (Map pp72–3; ☎ 212-786-3220; 3-4 World Financial Center, Battery Park City) and on Cedar St (Map pp72–3; ☎ 212-952-3838; 35 Cedar St at 10 Liberty Plaza).

SOHO, NOHO & NOLITA

All three of these foodie destinations will afford you a dose of fabulousness: high ceilings, stylish crowds and excited dins rising over the lovely clatter of clinking wine glasses and forks that dive into fare from French and Italian to Vietnamese, creative American and surprisingly authentic Mexican. Dress the part (downtown-chic) and enjoy.

PEASANT

Map pp88–9   Hearty Italian $$$

☎ 212-965-9511; www.peasantnyc.com; 194 Elizabeth St btwn Spring & Prince Sts; ⊙ dinner; ⊘ 6 to Spring St

This homey house of gourmet comfort grub has a vibe of old-fashioned simplicity and quality – due to a warm dining area of bare oak tables structured around a brick hearth and open kitchen, which lovingly turns out hearty, pan-Italian, mostly meat-based fare. Peasant has made it onto various best-restaurant lists in town, and always seems to be filled with a crowd of sophisticates, who want in on solid stunners like gnocchi with wild mushrooms, grilled hen or octopus and thin-crusted pizzas – not to mention the winning bread and fresh ricotta that start off every meal.

IL BUCO

Map pp88–9   Umbrian $$$

☎ 212-533-1932; 47 Bond St btwn Bowery & Lafayette; ⊙ lunch daily, dinner Tue-Sun; ⊘ B, D, F, V to Broadway-Lafayette St, 6 to Bleecker St

top picks

KIDS

For a city meal that makes everyone happy – you, your restless munchkins and the staff and fellow patrons alike – keep your family chomping to spots that welcome children with open arms, such as these:

- EJ's Luncheonette (Map p142; 1271 Third Ave) Can be found both in the Village (Map p110; 432 Sixth Ave) and the Upper West Side (Map p153; 447 Amsterdam Ave).
- Bubby's Pie Company (opposite) In Tribeca and in Dumbo, Brooklyn.
- Peanut Butter & Co (Map p110; ☎ 212-677-3995; 240 Sullivan St) All variations on the PB&J sandwich.
- Cupcake Cafe (Map p120; ☎ 212-465-1530; 18 W 18th St) The outpost of a tasty Hell's Kitchen bakery, inside the children's Books of Wonder shop.
- Landmarc at the Time Warner Center (p262) Has a special kids' menu in a chic adult setting.
- Superfine (Map p174; ☎ 718-243-9005; 126 Front St, Dumbo) is a massive and din-filled but popular spot in Brooklyn.
- Say Cheese! (Map pp134–5; ☎ 212-265-8840; 649 Ninth Ave) Grilled-cheese sandwiches and tomato soup.
- Two Boots Brooklyn (Map p182; ☎ 718-499-3252; 514 Second St, Park Slope) Has a funky design and a kids' menu – smiley-faced-topped pizzas, chicken nuggets and noodles with butter.
- Lexington Candy Shop (Map p142; ☎ 212-288-0057; 1226 Lexington Ave at 83rd St) A retro diner, with a long counter, serving chocolate malteds, lime rickeys and great burgers.

After 15 years of success, it's still tough to score a table at this NoHo fave. That's because the magical nook has charm to spare with hanging copper pots, kerosene lamps and antique furniture, plus a stunning menu courtesy of chef Ignacio Mattos. The extensive wine list has a perfect match for everything, including seasonal and ever-changing highlights like white polenta with braised broccoli rabe and anchovies, homemade *papardelle* with a mélange of mushrooms, and a succulent Dijon-crusted lamb chop.

BUTTER

Map pp88–9   American Eclectic $$$

☎ 212-253-2828; 415 Lafayette St btwn Astor Pl & E 4th St; ⊙ dinner Mon-Sat; ⊘ 6 to Astor Pl

The soothingly backlit dining room, located on the western edge of the 'hood and just a few doors down from the Public Theater, has gotten lots of play for its A-list crowds. But even more impressive at Butter (so named for owner's collection of butter plates, which sit, filled with the good stuff, on each table) is the creative, seasonal fare, courtesy of chef Alexandra Guarnaschelli. Braised organic osso bucco and long-stem artichoke salad are among the starters; grilled halibut, house-made fettuccine with mushrooms and blackened swordfish with sunchokes shine in the simple lineup of main dishes.

MERCER KITCHEN
Map pp88–9   American Eclectic $$$

☎ 212-966-5454; 99 Prince St at Mercer St; ☼ breakfast, lunch & dinner; ⊕ R, W to Prince St
Just peering into this soothing gem of a hideaway – part of chef-god Jean-Georges Vongerichten's top-echelon empire, perched below street level in the endlessly fashionable Mercer Hotel (p350) – tells you something special is going on. Basics, like fresh figs with mozzarella and basil, black truffle and fontina-cheese pizza, roast chicken with French beans and baby carrots, and a dessert of pear crisp with sour cherries, reach higher levels thanks to the freshest, most seasonal ingredients. The same can be said for the customers, who work hard to look so divine.

BALTHAZAR   Map pp88–9   French Bistro $$$
☎ 212-965-1414; 80 Spring St btwn Broadway & Crosby St; ☼ breakfast, lunch & dinner daily, brunch Sat & Sun; ⊕ 6 to Spring St
Retaining its long-held status as a superstar among the city's glut of French bistros, this bustling (OK, *loud*) spot still pulls in the discriminating mobs. That's thanks to three winning details: the location, which makes it a convenient shopping-spree rest area; the uplifting ambience, shaped by big, mounted mirrors, cozy high-backed booths and airy high ceilings and wide windows; and, of course, the stellar something-for-everyone menu, which features an outstanding raw bar, steak frites, salad niçoise, roasted beet salad and prawn risotto with sage and butternut squash. The kitchen stays open till 2am Thursday to Saturday, and weekend brunch here is a very crowded (and delicious) production.

NEW YORK'S TOP CHEFS

Some of the most famous chefs in the country – Tom Colicchio, David Bouley, Anthony Bourdain and Mario Batali among them – are known nationally, given celebrity status by books and movies and TV shows on the Food Network channel. But first they were stars in New York.

Tom Colicchio (www.craftrestaurant.com), best known now for his role as head judge on Bravo TV's *Top Chef* reality series, has been near and dear to New York foodies for years because of his collection of eateries: Craft (p260), Craftbar, Craftsteak and 'wichcraft. The first (and still favorite), Craft, focuses on perfectly prepared single dishes – braised monkfish, roasted quail, braised escarole, soft polenta – that can be grouped together as you wish. Colicchio, who learned to cook from his mom and the illustrated manuals of Jacques Pepin, was chosen as a best new chef by *Food + Wine* in the '90s; he started the famous Gramercy Tavern (p259) with partner Danny Meyer in 1994, won the James Beard Award for Best Chef NY in 2000, and eventually moved on to open Craft and the rest of his eateries.

After studying at the Sorbonne, Connecticut native David Bouley (www.davidbouley.com) entered the New York restaurant scene as a chef at high-end eateries including Le Cirque. In the late '80s he opened Bouley, which remains a vital part of the French dining world here, and has since opened several other hotspots, including Evolution in Miami. Find them all at his website.

Anthony Bourdain (www.anthonybourdain.net) is now a film and TV superstar thanks to his memoir, *Kitchen Confidential*, which was turned into a movie in 2005, and his current position as host of the Travel Channel's *Anthony Bourdain: No Reservations*. But he's been known by gastronomy-focused New Yorkers for years because of his two Les Halles (p250) brasseries, known for expertly done French classics like steak frites and grilled filet mignon with béarnaise sauce.

Mario Batali (www.mariobatali.com), meanwhile, is owner or part owner of nine NYC restaurants. Known for his red hair and colorful Croc shoes – and for his appearances on Food Network shows including *Iron Chef America* – he's known by folks in Gotham for livening up the restaurant scene here for years, with early stunners in his empire like Babbo, serving epic Italian creations in a Village townhouse, and Otto Enoteca Pizzeria (p258), a pizza-and-pasta favorite in the Village. Recent additions are the Bar Jamon tapas bar and Del Posto, a massive palace of gourmet indulgence, done with partners Lidia and Joe Bastianich.

CENDRILLON Map pp88–9   Filipino Fusion $$

☎ 212-343-9012; 45 Mercer St btwn Broome & Grand Sts; ⏱ lunch & dinner daily, brunch Sat & Sun; ⊕ J, M, Z, N, Q, R, W, 6 to Canal St

Already a fascinating fusion of Asian and Latin cuisines, Filipino foods get even more wonderfully twisted at this much-lauded, loft-like space that features exposed brick, wood booths and a semi-open kitchen. Its exotic and tangy concoctions encompass a range of flavors, with winners like chicken adobo braised in rice vinegar, udon and shrimp swimming in a Malaysian curry sauce, Chinese-smoked spare ribs with mashed taro root, and spicy black-rice paella bursting with morsels of seafood.

LA ESQUINA Map pp88–9   Mexican $$

☎ 646-613-1333; 106 Kenmare St; ⏱ 24hr; ⊕ 6 to Spring St

This mega-popular and quirky little spot is housed in a former greasy spoon that sits within the neat little triangle formed by Cleveland Pl and Lafayette St. It's three places really: a stand-while-you-eat taco window, a casual Mexican café and, downstairs, a cozy, overly hip cave of a dining room. You can't even go down the stairs unless you've got a reservation (a guard with a clipboard stands in the entryway), but once you're in you'll enjoy a feast of melt-in-your mouth chorizo tacos, rubbed pork tacos and mango and *jicama* salads, among other authentic and delicious options – most of them available upstairs at the anyone-welcome area, too.

IDEYA Map pp88–9   Pan-Latin Bistro $$

☎ 212-625-1441; 349 W Broadway btwn Broome & Grand Sts; ⏱ lunch & dinner Mon-Fri, brunch & dinner Sat & Sun; ⊕ A, C, E, 1 to Canal St

The cool, breezy vibe of this small SoHo gem is thanks to its white-brick walls, crisp white tablecloths and cheery murals depicting happy scenes of Latin life. And the happy feeling you'll leave with is due to the creative, delicious fare, which blends Spanish, African and Latin-Caribbean flavors to form one exciting menu. Crab empanadas and clams steamed with chorizo are among the clever starters, while mains of braised grouper with fennel, beef short ribs braised in pomegranate mole and a vegetable terrine with corn and goat-cheese salad really keep the flavor party going. Cuban *medianoche* sandwiches, seafood tacos and

top picks

NYC RESTAURANT COOKBOOKS

- Bubby's (p250) *Bubby's Homemade Pies* (Wiley) takes you through the details of cracker-crumb crust and real fruit fillings.
- Candle Café (p264) Learn the tricks of the vegan trade with *The Candle Café Cookbook* (Clarkson Potter).
- Mercer Kitchen (opposite) Jean-Georges Vongerichten shares some secrets from this and other eateries with *Jean-Georges: Cooking at Home With a Four-Star Chef* (Broadway).
- Café Boulud (p247) The *Café Boulud Cookbook* (Scribner) is a deliciously French challenge.
- Balthazar (opposite) Turn your home into a bistro with *The Balthazar Cookbook* (Clarkson Potter).

sofrito-marinated chicken are among the expertly done house specialties.

CAFÉ GITANE Map pp88–9   Moroccan Bistro $

☎ 212-334-9552; 242 Mott St; ⏱ 5:30-11:30pm; ⊕ N, R, W to Prince St

Gitane is the type of place you'd expect to see everywhere in, say, Paris or Lisbon – an ochre-lit space with deep banquettes and warm air, scented by baking bread and garlic hitting a pan. Outside, slouchy, wealthy artist types and high-end-label lovers surrounded by impressive shopping bags are smoking Gauloises, and everyone is drinking coffee. And the food at this perfect shopping-break spot is quite tasty, too. The diverse menu features yellowfin tuna ceviche, spicy meatballs in tomato turmeric sauce with a boiled egg, Greek salad on focaccia and a heart-of-palm salad, with plenty of lusty wines.

LOVELY DAY Map pp88–9   Pan-Asian $

☎ 212-925-3310; 196 Elizabeth St btwn Prince & Spring Sts; ⏱ lunch & dinner; ⊕ J, M, Z to Bowery St, 6 to Spring St

Everything is just precious inside this affordable and funky nook, from the cozy red booths and bedroom-appropriate wallpaper to the lovingly prepared portions of Thai-inflected food. Coconut-rich curries, noodle dishes, papaya salad and spicy tofu squares create a fascinating harmony with the soda shop–inspired decor.

CHINATOWN & LITTLE ITALY

In addition to being a long-time haven for authentically Chinese bargain meals – and for the mobs of visitors who seek them – Chinatown has also evolved into a spot for all sorts of pan-Asian fare that is, for the most part, incredibly cheap. (Find a true culinary adventure by leaving the guidebook in your bag and strolling the crammed and winding streets south of Canal, stopping in to eat at any place that tickles your fancy, including dessert-rich bubble-tea lounges or sweet Chinese bakeries.) The abutting Little Italy, whose borders are increasingly encroached upon by Chinatown and Nolita, has a minuscule culinary scene starring a handful of spots that attract mostly tourists – and have plenty of charm. Explore Mulberry St and its surrounding blocks to find old-world bakeries and food shops that'll create a picnic like no other.

FOCOLARE Map p94 — Italian $$$

☎ 212-993-5858; 115 Mulberry St btwn Canal & Hester Sts; ☽ lunch & dinner; ◉ J, M, Z, N, Q, R, W, 6 to Canal St

If you're bent on a Little Italy dinner experience, this friendly newcomer is a fine choice. With a cozy interior warmed by a fireplace in winter (and photos of Frank Sinatra et al all around), the kitchen turns out classics in fine style: homemade pasta, cooked al dente, is an excellent base for various red and cream-based sauces; crisp rice balls ooze with cheese; fried calamari zings with flavor.

VEGETARIAN DIM SUM HOUSE

Map p94 — Vegetarian Chinese $

☎ 212-577-7176; 24 Pell St btwn Bowery & Mott Sts; ☽ 10:30am-10:30pm; ◉ J, M, Z, N, Q, R, W, 6 to Canal St

Get mocked all day long with dead-ringer takes on classic Chinatown specialties: fake 'shrimp' dumplings, spicy 'spare ribs,' sweet-and-sour 'chicken' and Hunan 'pork' are realistically created with ingredients like soy, wheat gluten and yams. For those not looking to recreate the meat they shun, straight-up options like asparagus with bean curd and spinach dumplings abound.

GREAT NEW YORK NOODLE TOWN

Map p94 — Chinese Noodles $

☎ 212-349-0923; 28 Bowery St at Bayard St; ☽ 9am-4am; ◉ J, M, Z, N, Q, R, W, 6 to Canal St

The name of this Chinatown stalwart says it all, as the specialties here are endless incarnations of the long and slippery strands, offered up through an easy-to-decipher picture menu. Among the long list of options are noodle soup with roast pork or duck, rice congee with frog or sliced fish, beef chow fun, spicy Singapore mai fun, wide Cantonese noodles with shrimp and egg or Hong Kong–style lo main with ginger and onions. What the no-frills spot lacks in ambience it makes up for in characters – especially once 2am or 3am rolls around.

DOYERS VIETNAMESE RESTAURANT

Map p94 — Vietnamese $

☎ 212-513-1521; 11 Doyers St btwn the Bowery & Pell St; ☽ lunch & dinner; ◉ J, M, Z, N, Q, R, W, 6 to Canal St

Everything about this place is an adventure: its location, on the curvy little barber-shop-lined street of Doyers; its ambience, in a cave-like, below-street-level hideaway with old-school charm; and the lengthy menu, with curiously yummy dishes including crispy fried tilapia, shrimp-papaya salad, curried eel and a slew of vegetarian offerings, from fried rice stick with vegetables to curried watercress.

top picks

ICE CREAM

- Original Chinatown Ice Cream Factory (Map p94; ☎ 212-608-4170; 65 Bayard St) Avocado, red bean, durian and sesame are among the exotic options.
- Ronnybrook Milk Bar (Map p116; ☎ 212-741-6455; 75 Ninth Ave between 15th & 16th Sts) Basic flavors from a local dairy farm.
- Brooklyn Ice Cream Factory (Map p174; ☎ 718-246-3963; 1 Water St, Dumbo) Fresh peaches 'n' cream and vanilla bean with million-dollar Manhattan skyline views.
- Sundaes & Cones (Map p110; ☎ 212-979-9398; 95 E 10th St at Third Ave) Amazing flavors from corn and honeydew to ginger and wasabi.
- Il Laboratorio del Gelato (Map p98; ☎ 212-343-9922; 95 Orchard St btwn Broome & Delancey Sts) Lab-coat-wearing pros create serious Italian gelato, in endless flavors – milk chocolate, toasted sesame, grapefruit, vanilla saffron and on and on.

NEW BO KY RESTAURANT

Map p94   Chinese $

☎ 212-406-2292; 80 Bayard St btwn Mott & Mulberry Sts; ⊙ breakfast, lunch & dinner; ◉ J, M, Z, N, Q, R, W, 6 to Canal St

This place, lack of ambience be damned, is home to nearly three dozen types of cheap and delicious soup with exotic ingredients and usually featuring some form of noodle, pork or chicken (vegetarians should be wary); the fish-ball flat noodle, curry chicken rice noodle and 'combination soup' are particularly popular. Join the chattering locals who pack into the simple setting for homey meals served by brusque waiters.

LOWER EAST SIDE

It's impossible to keep up with the offerings in these parts, as slinky lounges with elaborate nouveau-fusion menus and instant A-list crowds seem to pop up and replace 'old' places on a weekly basis. But many do wind up sticking around, and are best explored after the buzz has died down, when crowds thin but quality is still high. Though visitors won't find many remnants of the classic, old-world-Jewish LES dining scene, there are a few stellar holdouts, among them the infamous Katz's Deli (p256). Otherwise, it's strictly modern, global, small-plate hipster fare.

WD 50 Map p98   American Creative $$$

☎ 212-477-2900; 50 Clinton St at Stanton St; ⊙ dinner Mon-Sat; ◉ F, J, M, Z to Delancey-Essex Sts

This early leader in chef Wylie Dufresne's empire, a sleek space with bamboo floors, exposed wood beams and a fireplace, has held strong with thrillseekers for more than five years. Now that the frenzy has slowed a bit, you'll have a better chance of getting in to savor the cutesy-clever-complicated fare: ocean trout, black beans and forbidden rice in root-beer-and-date sauce, or a slab of Wagyu beef served with coffee gnocchi, for example. Pack more flavors than you thought imaginable into one meal with the 12-course tasting menu ($125).

FREEMANS Map p98   1950s American $$

☎ 212-420-0012; 2 Freeman Alley off Rivington St btwn Bowery & Christie St; ⊙ lunch & dinner daily, brunch Sat & Sun; ◉ F, V to Lower East Side-2nd Ave

This retro-themed 'hideaway' – a former secret quickly blown wide open by trend-hunting food writers – is all about kitsch and nostalgia. You'll see that in the decor (mounted taxidermy and tacky oil paintings, anyone?) as well as in the menu options. Enjoy your rum-soaked ribs, wild-boar terrine and 'devils on horseback' (prunes stuffed with cheese and wrapped with bacon) with one of many cool cocktails, like the potent Rum Swizzle.

FALAI Map p98   Italian $$

☎ 212-253-1960; 68 Clinton St btwn Rivington & Stanton Sts; ⊙ dinner; ◉ F, J, M, Z to Delancey-Essex Sts

A small and narrow storefront shaped by white tile, open kitchen and clean lines; it didn't take long for this LES newcomer to attract legions of stylish fans. Iacopo Falai, a former high-end pastry chef, is behind the place, which presents swoon-inducing plates of pasta (cocoa-flavored *papardelle*, squid ink strands topped with lobster), meats (tender steak medallions, fennel-flavored pork) and seafood (codfish stew). And desserts, of course, are killer. Don't miss the passionfruit soufflé.

'INOTECA Map p98   Italian Small Plates $$

☎ 212-614-0473; 98 Rivington St at Ludlow St; ⊙ lunch & dinner daily, brunch Sat & Sub; ◉ F, V to Lower East Side-2nd Ave

Join the crowd waiting at the cramped bar (it's worth it) at this airy, dark-wood-paneled corner haven to choose from *tramezzini* (small sandwiches on white or whole-wheat bread), panini (pressed sandwiches) and bruschetta options, all delicious and moderately priced. The truffled egg toast, a square of bread hollowed out in its center and filled with egg, truffles and fontina cheese, is a signature favorite. But you can't go wrong, whether you choose the beet-orange-mint salad, vegetable lasagna built with layers of eggplant rather than pasta, or a plate of garlicky mussels. There's also a list of 200 wines, 25 of them available by the glass. The West Village post is 'Ino (Map p110; ☎ 212-989-5769; 21 Bedford St btwn Sixth Ave & Downing St).

KUMA INN Map p98   Pan-Asian Small Plates $$

☎ 212-353-8866; 113 Ludlow St btwn Delancey & Rivington; ⊙ dinner Tue-Sun; ◉ F, J, M, Z to Delancey-Essex Sts

Reservations are a must at this strikingly popular spot, in a secretive 2nd-floor location that feels like a reconfigured apartment.

Most of the ambience comes from a combination of low lighting and votive candles – and the super-cool, young crowd – but good flavors are copious. The Filipino- and Thai-inspired tapas run the gamut, from vegetarian summer rolls (with the unique addition of chayote) and *edamame* drizzled with basil-lime oil to an oyster omelet and grilled salmon with mung beans and pickled onions. Pair anything with some chilled sake or mango nectar.

KATZ'S DELI Map p98 Jewish Deli $
☎ 212-254-2246; 205 E Houston St at Ludlow St; ☒ breakfast, lunch & dinner; ◉ F, V to Lower East Side-2nd Ave
Meg Ryan faked her famous orgasm in the 1989 Hollywood flick *When Harry Met Sally* here; if you love classic deli grub, it just might have the same effect on you. The vast, worn-out room is infused with old-world nostalgia – especially the WWII-era 'Send a salami to your boy in the army' ads – as are the crusty guys behind the counter doling out crisp kosher dills, frothy egg creams and pastrami and corned beef piled high on fresh rye. It's a true New York experience – especially at 2am, when trendy clubbers pile in for sobering sandwiches.

EAST VILLAGE

Here lies the epitome of what's beautiful in New York's dining scene – mind-blowing variety, which can cover several continents as well as the whole gamut of budgets in just a single city block. The neighborhood's roots lie with Ukrainian traditions, and you can still find some low-key pierogi (dumpling) palaces hanging on. Pizza places are also ubiquitous, along with spots for sushi, vegetarian and Indian fare – especially on the carnivalesque strip of E 6th St between First and Second Aves, otherwise known as Curry Row, where cheap, decent Indian restaurants are a dime a dozen.

E.U. Map p104 Pan-European Pub Food $$$
☎ 212-254-2900; 235 E 4th St btwn Aves A & B; ☒ lunch & dinner Mon-Fri, brunch & dinner Sat & Sun; ◉ F, V to Lower East Side-2nd Ave
This new and sprawling space on a street that's filled with little nooks makes for a truly fun night out. It's a sophisticated gastro-pub that mixes down-home with upscale – like its menu, printed on butcher paper but bearing items like gnocchi with

braised capon, boar with swiss-chard fondue, and grilled octopus with braised quince. There's plenty of choice beyond the hearty mains, too – like a small tapas menu, a raw bar and a range of charcuterie plates. The vibe is a bit more uptown than Ave B, but it's the series of well-balanced dichotomies that makes the EU such a find.

MOMOFUKU NOODLE BAR
Map p104 Japanese $$
☎ 212-777-7773; 171 First Ave btwn 10th & 11th Sts; ☒ lunch & dinner; ◉ L to 1st Ave
With just 30 stools and a no-reservations policy, you will always have to wait to cram into this tiny phenomenon. Judging by the constant clutter of patient souls outside, no one seems to mind. Queue up for the namesake special: homemade ramen noodles in broth, served with poached eggs, shredded pork, braised oxtail, roasted rice cakes or some interesting combo (the only vegetarian option is a broth-free bowl with ginger and veggies). Other dishes include razor clams, braised pork belly and roasted brussels sprouts with bacon. The open kitchen creates quite a bit of smoke, but the crowd remains unfazed.

BAO 111 Map p104 Vietnamese $$
☎ 212-254-7773; 111 Ave C at 7th St; ☒ dinner-2am; ◉ M14 to Ave C
Spicing up the eastern border of the 'hood is this sleek oasis of warm design, serving upscale versions of Vietnamese classics to a hyper-hip, mussed and gorgeous crowd. Top-shelf sakes, warm sakes infused with fruits and dangerously delicious sake-tinis get you in the right frame of mind to enjoy celebratory dishes like lemongrass curry shrimp, iron-pot tofu or chicken, braised vegetable and curry tofu and grilled lemongrass lamb chops. Desserts, like the steamed black rice pudding with roasted mango and coconut sauce, are sublime.

ANGELICA KITCHEN Map p104 Vegetarian $$
☎ 212-228-2909; 300 E 12th St btwn First & Second Aves; ☒ lunch & dinner; ◉ L to 1st Ave
This enduring herbivore classic has a calming vibe – candles, tables both intimate and communal and a mellow, longtime staff – and enough creative options to make your head spin. Some dishes get too-cute names (Sacre-Couer Basmatica in Paris, Thai Mee Up) but all do wonders with tofu, seitan,

spices and soy products, and sometimes an array of raw ingredients. Standards like the Pantry Plate – which lets you choose from a list of a dozen or so veggie concoctions and special salads – or the Dragon Bowl, a Buddha's delight with seasonal greens, tubers, tofu, seaweed and brown rice piled high, will leave you feeling both virtuous and full. Creative puddings and cakes only sweeten the deal.

IL BAGATTO Map p104   Italian $$
☎ 212-228-3703; 192 E 2nd St btwn Aves A & B; ⏰ lunch & dinner Tue-Sat; ⊖ F, V to Lower East Side-2nd Ave
A bustling yet romantic little nook, this spot has thoroughly delicious Italian creations at exceptionally reasonable prices – plus an excellent wine list and a dedicated sommelier who will pour you tastes before you decide (a wonderful oddity in such an affordable and casual dining room). The frazzled yet warm and quirky owners will greet you like old friends – though be prepared to wait a while even if you've made a reservation; that's just the way it works at this laid-back neighborhood spot. Menu items tend toward the sinful side, with highlights that include cheese and spinach ravioli swimming in butter and sage sauce, homemade gnocchi in gorgonzola sauce, and paper-thin beef slices sautéed in olive oil and white wine.

BAMN! Map p104   Eclectic Automat $
☎ 212-888-400-2266; 37 St Marks Pl at Second Ave; ⏰ 11:30am-1am Sun-Thu, 11:30am-3am Fri & Sat; ⊖ 6 to Astor Pl
A kitschy, themed novelty spot that actually delivers some tasty food, too, this bright-pink eatery is an homage to the 1950s Automat (and a danger to bingers!). Plunk your coins into the wall-sized vending machine and enjoy immediate global treats: Chinese pork buns, hot dogs, vegetable samosas and waffles smeared with Nutella.

GREENWICH VILLAGE, WEST VILLAGE & THE MEATPACKING DISTRICT

While the West Village is known for classy, cozy, intimate spots that cause quiet envy among the most casual of passersby, the adjacent Meatpacking District's dining scene is a bit more… ostentatious, complete with nightclub-like queues behind velvet ropes, eye-popping decor and crowds of trend-obsessed young folks. The central Village falls somewhere in between, and includes the many student-geared budget options (falafel, pizza etc) of NYU-land. The entire swath, though, is bursting with quality and ambience, to say the least.

BLUE HILL Map p110   American $$$
☎ 212-539-1776; 75 Washington Pl btwn Sixth Ave & Washington Sq; ⏰ dinner; ⊖ A, C, E, B, D, F, V to W 4th St-Washington Sq
A place for Slow Food junkies with deep pockets, Blue Hill was an early crusader in the local-is-better movement. Gifted chef Dan Barber, who hails from a farm family in the Berkshires, Massachusetts, uses harvests from that land, as well as from farms in upstate New York, to create his widely praised fare. Expect barely seasoned, perfectly ripe vegetables, which serve to highlight centerpieces of cod in almond broth, Berkshire pork stewed with four types of beans, and grass-fed lamb with white beans and new potatoes. The space itself, slightly below street level and housed in a landmark former speakeasy on a quaint Village block, is sophisticated and serene.

5 NINTH Map p110   Eclectic $$$
☎ 212-929-9460; 5 Ninth Ave btwn Gansevoort & Little West 12th Sts; ⏰ lunch & dinner; ⊖ A, C, E to 14th St, L to 8th Ave
This gorgeous, unmarked, three-story townhouse harkens back to this neighborhood's long-ago quaintness, with plenty of exposed brick, wood beams and romantic fireplaces. But its vibe is strictly modern, with a high-gloss crowd savoring hearty, seasonal dishes like rabbit ravioli, Portuguese stew with cockles and chorizo, ginger-steamed lobster and a vegetarian artichoke stew. The top floor and, in summer, the back deck both serve as perfect cocktail-swilling havens.

EN JAPANESE BRASSERIE
Map p110   Modern Japanese $$$
☎ 212-647-9196; 5 Hudson St at Leroy St; ⏰ lunch & dinner; ⊖ 1 to Houston St
This high-ceilinged space is anchored by a wide sushi bar, and you'll know you've

entered some place special by the amazing earthy yet modern decor – not to mention the exuberant welcome call you'll get from the chefs in the open kitchen. Menu options are sublime and range from snow crab tempura with avocado to black cod in miso. Perhaps the biggest excitement, though, is the range of freshly made tofus, served in warm scoops on an hourly basis. A front bar provides a moody place to sip a cocktail while gazing out over Hudson St.

OTTO ENOTECA PIZZERIA
Map p110 — Pizza & Italian $$
☎ 212-995-9559; 1 Fifth Ave at 8th St; ☿ lunch & dinner; ⊕ A, C, E, B, D, F, V to W 4th St-Washington Sq
An intimate trattoria in the heart of the Village, this is (a refreshingly affordable) part of Mario Batali's empire, a pizza palace, where thin pies are cooked on flat iron griddles till they crackle perfectly. They come topped with items far beyond your standard pizza joint – fennel, goat cheese, egg, fresh chilies, capers, the best fresh mozzarella – and sauce that has the perfect balance of smoky and sweet. Pasta dishes (for just nine bucks!) veer toward the exotic, like penne with hazelnuts and butternut squash, spaghetti with zucchini, chilies and mint, and rigatoni with sausage and black Tuscan kale. And don't even think of leaving without trying the house-made gelato.

CAFÉ ASEAN Map p110 — Pan-Asian $$
☎ 212-633-0348; 117 W 10th St at Greenwich Ave; ☿ lunch & dinner; ⊕ A, C, E, B, D, F, V to W 4th St-Washington Sq
A tiny spot on a short stretch of street, this eclectic and homey crevice is easy to miss. But wouldn't that be a shame? It serves up refreshing takes on Malaysian, Thai and Vietnamese concoctions to a low-key, cool-cat crowd who know you don't need to plunk down wads of cash for authentic flavor. Try the spice-crusted scallops in coconut sauce, rice noodles with shrimp, grilled hangar steak with lemongrass or egg noodles and tofu in peanut sauce (among several meatless options).

SPOTTED PIG Map p110 — Pub Fare $$
☎ 212-620-0393; 314 W 11th St at Greenwich St; ☿ lunch & dinner till 2am; ⊕ A, C, E to 14th St, L to 8th Ave
This diminutive hideaway in a romantic, residential West Village pocket has been

quite celebrated, receiving the coveted Michelin star each of the three years it's been open. It packs in folks nightly with its hearty, upscale blend of Italian-English-Irish pub fare – but instead of the usual bangers and mash, you get Jerusalem artichoke salad with goat cheese and hazelnuts, fried duck-egg and bacon salad, sautéed quail and bar snacks like delicious deviled eggs or marinated olives. Pair anything with an icy stout and have yourself a time.

TAÏM Map p110 — Israeli $
☎ 212-691-1287; 222 Waverly St btwn Perry & W 11th Sts; ☿ lunch & dinner; ⊕ 1, 2, 3 to 14th St
Not all Middle Eastern fare is alike, and this tiny little falafel joint proves it with its smoothies, salads and sass – and its falafel, which ranges from the traditional type to those spiced up with roasted red pepper or hot harissa. Whichever fried balls you choose, you'll get them stuffed into pita with creamy tahini sauce and a generous dose of Israeli salad – or you can try them all in a platter that gets you three tasty dips. Refreshing salads include carrots spiced with garlic and cumin, and smoothies are blended with exotics from dates to tamarind, beloved by Israeli regulars who pop into this tiny storefront to chat in Hebrew with the friendly owners.

SOY LUCK CLUB Map p110 — Healthy Café $
☎ 212-229-9191; 115 Greenwich Ave at Jane St; ☿ 7am-10pm Mon-Fri, 9am-10pm Sat & Sun; ⊕ A, C, E to 14th St, L to 8th Ave
When it first opened, this storefront café seemed a bit too theme-oriented to last. Soy, after all, isn't the sexiest selling point. But here it stands, several years later – a cool corner filled with hip locals (who love the free wi-fi), a flood of sunlight, and a counter bursting with compelling snacks and creative beverages. While many of the menu items are indeed soy-based – the soy chicken and fontina (wheat-free) crepe, the tofu salad and avocado sandwich, and the mesclun, edamame and soy-nut salad, just for starters – there's plenty here for the soy-phobic. Panini, salads and brunch items, some even containing meat, abound. Best of all, everything is fresh and tasty, especially the signature drinks, which consist of soymilk, either steamed or iced, mixed with additions from dark chocolate to honey and ginger.

CHELSEA

This fun, diverse and trés gay nabe is brimming with dining options, but caters heavily to folks who like creative takes on American food and well-stocked cocktail bars. The array of options along Eighth Ave is ever changing, with plenty of bistros, Latino spots and Asian-fusion dining rooms to choose from, many of which open to the street completely in warmer months, providing a perfect place to perch while watching the always-intriguing human parade. Ninth Ave is where you'll find the newest crop of spots, drawing plenty of foodies from the rest of Manhattan. Wherever you wind up, it's bound to be a total scene.

KLEE BRASSERIE Map p116   Eclectic $$$
☎ 212-633-8033; 200 Ninth Ave btwn 22nd & 23rd Sts; ☽ dinner; ◉ C, E to 23rd St

A fun and thoroughly unique neighborhood option, this joyously designed space – with wood-paneled walls, low banquettes and whimsically colored tile detailing – does an impressive job of creating a cool scene without throwing too much 'tude. It also creates magic in its open kitchen with some wholesome, fresh ingredients: a starter salad matches crisp chicory and chanterelle mushrooms with a slow-poached egg, while chicken gets spiced with licorice, and risotto is studded with shrimp and lemon. The thoroughly unique herbivore option packs a wide-mouthed jelly jar with a cornucopia of seasonal veggies and a healthy heaping of quinoa.

O MAI Map p116   Vietnamese Fusion $$
☎ 212-633-0550; 158 Ninth Ave btwn W 19th & W 20th Sts; ☽ dinner; ◉ A, C, E to 14th St

A diminutive and romantic cubbyhole, this is a soothingly stylish haven hewn with exposed brick and oblong sconces. Flavors here are bright and complex, found most evidently in thickly spiced options like the crispy red snapper with chili-lime sauce, roasted duck with tamarind and spicy lemongrass tofu. Cocktails and desserts sparkle, and the crowd is sophisticated, mellow and largely local.

TÍA POL Map p116   Spanish Tapas $$
☎ 212-675-8805; 205 Tenth Ave btwn 22nd & 23rd Sts; ☽ dinner Tue-Sun; ◉ C, E to 23rd St

This closet-sized, authentic and romantic Spanish tapas bar is the real deal – and the hordes of locals who crowd into the front-bar waiting area to get one of six teeny tables filled with massive doses of deliciousness know it. Come on the early side and you may get seated in under a half-hour. The red-wine options will have your tongue doing backflips, as will the array of tapas – Spanish tortillas, lemony salad topped with tuna, lima bean–puree bruschetta and sautéed cockles with razor clams. It's the perfect post–gallery opening pitstop.

F&B Map p116   Belgian Street Food $
☎ 212-646-486-4441; 269 W 23rd St btwn Seventh & Eighths Aves; ☽ lunch & dinner; ◉ C, E to 23rd St

If you think the only New York hot dogs are those wiggly ones sold from street vendors, think again. This sliver of a fast-food joint, with seating limited to high stools and brushed-steel counters, doles out steamed dogs in options including beef, pork, chicken and soy, and toppings that range from the classic relish and sauerkraut to cheese, bacon, salsa and coleslaw. Other perky menu items include lobster rolls, Swedish meatballs and, of course, the source of the name's acronym: frites and beignets.

UNION SQUARE, THE FLATIRON DISTRICT & GRAMERCY

A veritable goldmine of eateries, this multi-named area stretches from E 14th St to about the mid-30s. One precious perk is the Union Sq Greenmarket (a sprawling sensory delight held Monday, Wednesday, Friday and Saturday), when discerning chefs both pro and amateur scour the wares of upstate farmers and get inspired for their next meals. But beyond this patch of green is a real range of offerings, both pricey destination dining events and low-key neighborhood gems. Lexington Ave in the high 20s is known as Curry Hill, thanks to its preponderance of spots serving South Indian fare. But the rest of the region covers all the global bases.

GRAMERCY TAVERN
Map p120   American Creative $$$
☎ 212-477-0777; 42 E 20th St btwn Broadway & Park Ave S; ☽ lunch & dinner; ◉ 6 to 23rd St

Though superstar chef Tom Colicchio (who

EATING CHELSEA

put this legendary spot on the foodie map) recently passed the torch, Michael Anthony was the capable guy who grabbed it. And so the country-chic restaurant, aglow with copper sconces, bright murals and dramatic floral arrangements, is still in the spotlight – perhaps more than ever. That's thanks to the lighter fish-and-vegetable menu that has replaced what was meat-heavy and hearty. Smoked lobster, Spanish mackerel, blackfish and tuna-and-beet tartare are packed with punches, as are the heavenly desserts and heavy-hitting wine options.

PURE FOOD & WINE
Map p120   Raw-Food Vegetarian $$$

☎ 212-477-1010; 54 Irving Pl btwn 17th & 18th Sts; ◷ dinner; ◉ L, N, Q, R, W, 4, 5, 6 to 14th St-Union Sq
The 'chef' (there's no oven in the kitchen) at this gem achieves the impossible, churning out not just edible but extremely delicious and artful concoctions, made completely from raw organics that are put through blenders, dehydrators and the capable hands of Pure's staff. Results are creative, fresh and alarmingly delicious, and include the wonderful tomato-zucchini lasagne (sans cheese and pasta); mushroom, avocado and ginger sushi rolls; and the white-corn tamales with raw cacao *mole* and salsa verde. The dining room is sleek and festive, but in warmer months don't miss a chance to settle into a table in the shady oasis of a backyard.

CRAFT Map p120   Creative American $$$
☎ 212-780-0880; 43 E 19th at Park Ave S; ◷ dinner; ◉ L, N, Q, R, W, 4, 5, 6 to 14th St-Union Sq
When super chef Tom Colicchio opened this fine-food palace in a sweeping architectural space several years ago, the concept was completely new: create your own meal with a la carte items, and enjoy the feeling that not a plate on your table was cookie cutter. Copycats sprang up around town, but this spot still reigns – and still feels fresh – as items change seasonally, and are always finely prepared. Items can be found under their appropriate subject headings – fish, 'farm egg,' meat, vegetables, salad – and it's up to you to make the matches (or ask for some expert direction). You might wind up with a plate of Spanish mackerel with fennel, mizuna with truffle vinaigrette and some roasted Jerusalem

artichoke. Or perhaps some roasted pheasant with prunes, braised escarole and beets and tarragon will float your boat. If you can't decide, you can always go for the tasting menu: a seven-course feast paired with wines. You can't lose either way.

MAOZ VEGETARIAN Map p120   Falafel $
☎ 212-260-1988; 38 Union Sq East btwn 16th & 17th Sts; ◷ 11am-1am Mon-Thu, 11am-3am Fri & Sat, 11am-11pm Sun; ◉ L, N, Q, R, W, 4, 5, 6 to 14th St-Union Sq
This new branch of an Amsterdam chain has folks patiently waiting on a line that extends out the door of this miniscule storefront each and every afternoon. Why all the fuss? You get a delicious falafel, in pita or bowl, and get to pile on the veggie fixins – fried broccoli, Israeli carrot salad, shredded cabbage, creamy tahini – as high as you like. Fresh-squeezed juices and a good spot on a bench in Union Sq, just across the street, make it the perfect meal.

MIDTOWN EAST & FIFTH AVENUE
While this midsection of Manhattan hustles and bustles during the day, thanks to strutting, high-end shoppers and busy-as-bees business folks, it tends to lose its luster when the sun goes down, turning sidewalks into oddly quiet runways. So it's all the more thrilling to enter one of the endless classy eateries to find a packed and buzzing scene. As a rule, you'll pay dearly around here (blame the corporate types and Rockefeller Center tourist grabbers) but you'll eat mighty well.

SPARKS Map p126   Steakhouse $$$
☎ 212-687-4855; 210 E 46th St btwn Second & Third Aves; ◷ lunch & dinner Mon-Fri, dinner Sat; ◉ S, 4, 5, 6, 7 to 42nd St-Grand Central
Get an honest-to-goodness New York steakhouse experience at this classic joint, a former mob hangout that's been around for nearly 50 years, and still packs 'em in. Rub elbows with red-meat lovers of all stripes and choose your cut: prime sirloin, filet mignon, steak *fromage* (topped with Roquefort) or medallions of beef, topped with bordelaise sauce. Thick chops of veal and lamb and various seafood options are also on tap, as are heaping portions of character thanks to the skilled career waiters.

BRASSERIE Map p126 — French $$$

☎ 212-333-1220; 100 E 53rd St at Park Ave;
☑ breakfast, lunch, dinner daily, brunch Sat & Sun;
◉ E, V to 5th Ave-53rd St

This stunningly sleek temple of classics –
including onion soup, wine-laden mussels,
duck confit and chocolate beignets –
is actually most impressive because of
its ultramodern design, courtesy of NYC
starchitects Diller + Scofidio, carved into
the ground floor of the historic Seagram
Building. To get just a taste of the high-
class action, perch thyself at the elegant
backlit bar, where you can enjoy a plate of
mini-burger or lobster-salad sliders with a
bracing cucumber gimlet.

BLUE SMOKE Map p126 — Southern BBQ $$$

☎ 212-447-7733; 116 E 27th St; ☑ lunch & dinner; ◉ 6 to 23rd St

Another contender in the city's ongoing
BBQ cook-off, this soulful spot presents a
potpourri of various Southern 'cue style: St
Louis, Texas, Kansas and Memphis ribs are
all representin', as is pulled pork, smoked
chicken, peel-and-eat shrimp and the classic 'salad' consisting of an iceberg-lettuce
wedge. Mouthwatering mini-cornbread
loaves and jalapeño-studded hush puppies
are gut-busting sides, and homemade pies
and cakes take you down for the count.
When you're done chowing, head downstairs to the Jazz Standard, where pros bust
out with blues, folk, rock and jazz.

SOBA NIPPON Map p126 — Japanese $$

☎ 212-489-2525; 19 W 52nd St btwn Fifth & Sixth
Aves; ☑ lunch & dinner; ◉ B, D, F, V to 47th-50th
Sts-Rockefeller Center

The chewy buckwheat soba noodle is the
star of the menu here, in this quiet and
intimate nook smack dab in the middle
of high-bustle Midtown. Try this melt-in-
your-mouth highlight in a chilled-salad or
soothing broth, flavored with sesame, soy
and other subtle stabs, including tofu, duck
and chicken. You'll also find solid sushi and
delicious little octopus-stuffed balls, called
takoyaki.

HANGAWI Map p126 — Vegetarian Korean $$

☎ 212-213-0077; 12 E 32nd St btwn Fifth & Madison Aves; ☑ lunch Mon-Sat, dinner daily; ◉ B, D,
F, V, N, Q, R, W to 34th St-Herald Sq

An oasis in Little Korea, this Zen-like dining
room is strictly no-meat and no-shoes (cub-

top picks

VEGGIE DELIGHTS

- **Hangawi** (left) Korean staples sans meat are
  served in a soothing Midtown dining room.
- **'Inoteca** (p255) Excellent wine paired with top-
  notch small plates, with plenty of choice for herbi-
  vores, from rich cheese plates to creative panini.
- **Dawat** (below) South Indian standards like *masala
  dosa* are subtly flavored and richly filling.
- **Angelica Kitchen** (p256) The East Village classic,
  serving creative vegan fare to a pierced and tattooed fan base, is still going strong.
- **EN Japanese Brasserie** (p257) There's plenty of
  sushi and meat to eschew, but it's worth it for the
  house special: warm and creamy homemade tofu.
- **Soy Luck Club** (p258) Soy milk and cheese replaces
  dairy in delicious shakes, sandwiches, crepes and
  salads.
- **F&B** (p259) For a quick bite, don't miss the veggie
  dogs, served with a range of different toppings.
- **Pure Food & Wine** (opposite) Raw food has never
  been so fabulous.
- **Maoz Vegetarian** (opposite) Join the crowd waiting to get its hands on falafel-stuffed pitas, which
  you can pile for miles with veggie toppings.
- **Candle Café** (p264) This Upper East Side vegan
  spot has fresh and simple dishes that'll make you
  feel good.

bies and bathroom slippers are provided).
Slip down into the cushiony, low seating
and feast on unique dishes that include
crispy mushrooms in sweet and sour sauce,
tofu stone bowl rice with sesame leaves
and organic vegetable stir-fries. Desserts
are creamy and dreamy.

DAWAT Map p126 — Indian $$

☎ 212-355-7555; 210 E 58th St btwn Second &
Third Aves; ☑ lunch Mon-Sat, dinner daily;
◉ N, R, W to Lexington Ave-59th St

Famed chef, cookbook author and actress
Madhur Jaffrey runs this outpost of nirvana,
which transforms Indian favorites, including spinach *bhajia* (fritter) and fish curries,
into exotic masterpieces served with fancy
flourishes. Sea bass and lamb chops each
get royal treatments with marinades made
of various blends of yogurt, mustard seeds,
saffron and ginger, and charming, carda-
mom-flecked desserts cool your palate. The
dining room is formal and subdued and the

crowd is a bit on the stuffy side (it comes with the territory in this part of town), but none of it'll matter after your first bite.

SECOND AVENUE DELI
Map p126   Jewish Deli $$
☎ 212-677-0606; 162 E 33rd St btwn Lexington & Third Aves; ⏰ 24hr, closed Passover, Rosh Hashanah & Yom Kippur holidays; ⊕ 6 to 33rd St
Originally opened in 1954 in the East Village; lifelong fans had conniptions when it closed in 2006 following a dispute with its landlord. But the late founder's 25-year-old nephew resurrected the icon in late 2007, reopening it in a Midtown location. He's brought with it many of the same longtime employees, its frenzied following and, most importantly, the classic Jewish foods: matzo-ball soup, kugel, and sandwiches of pastrami, lean turkey and roast beef piled high on wafer-thin rye.

CHENNAI GARDEN
Map p126   Kosher Indian $
☎ 212-689-1999; 129 E 27th St btwn Park Ave S & Lexington Ave; ⏰ lunch & dinner; ⊕ 6 to 28th St
Come to this low-key Curry Row standout for favorite Southern treats like long, paper-thin *dosas* (rice-flour pancakes) stuffed with spicy mixtures of potatoes and peas; spongy *utthappams* (thicker rice pancakes studded with vegetables and herbs); steamed *idli* cakes and *bhel poori*, both ubiquitous Indian street foods that make clever use of rice and chick peas; and a range of more expected northern favorites, including curries. The interior is bright and bustling – especially for the popular lunchtime buffet, which, for less than 10 bucks, lets you reload your plate again and again.

MIDTOWN WEST & TIMES SQUARE

Midtown West, like much of East, caters primarily to the power-lunching media types who work in publishing or TV, along with the tourists who flock here to tour TV studios, shop on Fifth Ave and take in the sights of Rockefeller Center. Times Sq and the theater district, meanwhile, strive to get Broadway showgoers in and out in a filling and timely manner. While finding a truly decent place to tuck into here used to be quite a challenge, recent years have brought more and more savvy, creative restaurateurs to fill the void. Perhaps the best crop of options, though, can be found far west in recently gentrified Hell's Kitchen,

where an ever-increasing crop of hot spots has added depth to the neighborhood's moniker. Wandering up and down Ninth Ave will yield all sorts of ethnic-food-market surprises, from Middle Eastern spices sold in bulk to Amish country cheeses proffered by the pound.

RUSSIAN TEA ROOM
Map pp134–5   Russian $$$
☎ 212-581-7100; 150 W 57th St btwn Sixth & Seventh Aves; ⏰ lunch & dinner; ⊕ F, N, Q, R, W to 57th St
Opened in 1927 by members of the Russian Imperial Ballet, the high-end blini-and-caviar salon became a favorite haunt for stars, artists and various wealthy eccentrics before closing in the mid-'90s. After a $30 million renovation, it was revived for a short stint in 2001, only to fail in a post–September 11 economy. But in 2007 the doors flew open again, and this time it looks like it might be here to stay. Bright-red banquettes, massive crystal bears, chandeliers and a colorful stained-glass ceiling make the various dining rooms here pop; borscht, lamb chops, blinis and chicken Kiev, meanwhile, sing with flavor.

LANDMARC AT THE TIME WARNER CENTER
Map pp134–5   Eclectic $$$
☎ 212-823-6123; 10 Columbus Circle; ⏰ lunch & dinner; ⊕ A, C, B, D, 1 to 59th St-Columbus Circle
The newest addition to the heavy-hitting lineup of dining options inside this high-

top picks

HOT CHOCOLATE

- **City Bakery** (Map p120; ☎ 212-366-1414; 3 W 18th St btwn Fifth & Sixth Aves) With or without a homemade marshmallow cube.
- **Jacques Torres Chocolate** (p269) Try the Wicked, with an ancho-and-chipotle bite.
- **Max Brenner** (Map p120; ☎ 212-388-0030; 841 Broadway btwn 13th & 14th Sts, & 141 Second Ave at 9th St) Choose from dark, milk, white or orange-zest infused.
- **La Maison du Chocolat** (Map p142; ☎ 212-744-7177; 1018 Madison Ave at 78th St) Stunningly thick and rich.
- **Vosges** (Map pp88–9; ☎ 212-625-2929; 132 Spring St at Greene St) Dark chocolate flavored with vanilla beans, or white with lemon and lavender.

rise mall, Landmarc gets high points for its spare and airy industrial-chic decor and cylindrical, private-feeling booths. There's a no-reservations policy, so while you may get in easier here than at the neighboring Masa (☎ 212-823-9800, ☽ dinner Mon-Sat) or Per Se (☎ 212-823-9335; ☽ dinner nightly, lunch Fri-Sun), it could take a long time. But your rewards include a stellar view of Central Park and a selection of high-gloss standards: grilled salmon in red-wine sauce, braised lamb shank with celery-root puree, vegetable risotto and daily pasta specials. There's even, surprisingly, a kids' menu, with chicken fingers, pigs-in-blankets and English-muffin pizzas. There's also a Tribeca Landmarc (Map pp72–3; ☎ 212-343-3883; 179 West Broadway btwn Leonard & Worth Sts; ⊕ 1 to Franklin St).

MARSEILLE Map pp134–5 French $$
☎ 212-333-3410; 630 Ninth Ave at 44th St; ☽ lunch & dinner; ⊕ A, C, E to 42nd St-Port Authority
The atmospheric art-deco dining room here is a lovely pre- or post-theater hangout, featuring fine bistro fare – with African and Italian influences – and a convivial feel. The range of options is quite impressive, covering everything from tuna niçoise and steak frites to rock-shrimp risotto and veal scallopini. When warm weather hits, snagging a lively sidewalk-café seat is a coup.

HILL COUNTRY Map pp134–5 Texan BBQ $$
☎ 212-255-4544; 30 W 26th btwn Broadway & Sixth Ave; ☽ lunch & dinner; ⊕ N, R, W to 28th St
City slickers are going gaga for good ol'-fashioned BBQ, and fast learning the difference between smoked meats of the Carolinas, Mississippi and various other Southern states. Here it's all about the sausage, fatty brisket, beef shoulder and pork ribs cooked in the Texas style (the Hill Country is a country area between Austin and San Antonio), plus an array of imaginative side dishes including smoky deviled eggs, baked beans braised with beer, and penne with three cheeses. You can also catch frequent live Texas music acts and Sunday football games on the big screens. A hoppin' bar stays open till 2am.

RICE 'N' BEANS Map pp134–5 Brazilian $$
☎ 212-265-4444; 744 Ninth Ave btwn 50th & 51st Sts; ☽ lunch & dinner daily, brunch Sat & Sun; ⊕ C, E, 1 to 50th St

The decor in this teensy storefront is nothing to speak of – but the high-flavor, low-priced Brazilian favorites that grace the small yellow tables certainly are. Start with a salad of hearts of palm or avocado, then get completely sated with picks like the coconut milk–rich and coriander-spiced Amazon fish stew, thick with chunks of white fish and green pepper. Chicken gets sautéed with okra, pork chops are spiced and grilled Brazilian style, and the classic *feijoada* – a scrumptious black-bean stew with pork loin, sausage and beef – gets served with collard greens, rice and *farofa* (fried yucca flour). Even vegetarians are well cared for, with sautéed veggies, rice and beans, and fried plantains.

BOUCHON BAKERY Map pp134–5 Eclectic Café $
☎ 212-823-9366; 50 Columbus Circle, Time Warner Center; ☽ lunch & dinner; ⊕ A, C, B, D to 59th St-Columbus Circle
One of seven restaurants in the Time Warner Center (the others are outlandishly high-end), this one, from Per Se owner Thomas Keller, brings new meaning to 'food court.' An open-air (well, mall-air) café, its fare is outstanding: beet and mache salad, three-bean soup, turkey, tuna and veggie sandwiches that soar to new gourmet heights. And the pastries – especially the feather-light macaroons and home-spun Oreo-like sandwich cookies – are to die for.

UPPER EAST SIDE
High-end diners should prepare for jacket-and-tie–wearing movers and shakers, where conversation is hushed and service is extremely white-tablecloth formal. But go a little lower on the foodie totem pole here and you'll be pleasantly surprised not only by the sheer number of eclectic options, but by the fun and breezy vibe in the dining rooms. Meat eaters, wine lovers and foreign-food seekers will all find a place at the table.

HACIENDA DE ARGENTINA
Map p142 Argentine $$$
☎ 212-472-5300; 339 E 75th St btwn First & Second Aves; ☽ dinner; ⊕ 6 to 77th St
The elegant space, with its heavy oak tables, exposed brickwork and regal high-backed chairs, might lull you into believing you'd stepped into a Buenos Aires eatery. But what really nails it is the food itself – beef-heavy, natch, with thick and juicy

grilled top loin, shell steak, filet mignon, skirt steak and short ribs. But the meat doesn't stop there, as you'll also find grilled chicken, sweetbreads and a long lineup of blood sausages and chorizo. Order a bottle of robust Malbec and be transported (until you get the bill).

JO JO Map p142 French $$$

☎ 212-223-5656; 160 E 64th St at Lexington Ave; ☽ lunch & dinner; ⊕ 6 to 68th St-Hunter College
Part of the ever-thriving Jean-Georges empire; you really can't go wrong here, where French standards get the Midas touch with the addition of a little something special. Foie gras is fashioned into crème brûlée, venison cubes are tossed with pomegranate seeds, roast chicken gets buried under green olives. The warm and gooey chocolate Valrhona cake is widely praised as the best in the city – if not the world. And it's all turned out into a dining room so precious and intimate, you feel as if you've been invited into someone's private townhouse.

BEYOGLU Map p142 Turkish Meze $$

☎ 212-650-0850; 1431 Lexington Ave at 81st St; ☽ lunch & dinner; ⊕ 6 to 77th St
A charismatic, loungy space that's just a short stroll away from the Met, this is where to prolong your cultural imbibing with traditional small plates, like yogurt soup, doner kebabs, eggplant puree and feta-flecked salads, even daily seafood specials, that are elegant and excellent. Don't forget to get really festive with a shot or two of the traditional, anisette-flavored raki as an after-meal spirit.

CANDLE CAFÉ Map p142 Vegetarian $$

☎ 212-472-0970; 1307 Third Ave btwn 74th & 75th Sts; ☽ lunch & dinner; ⊕ 6 to 77th St
In a 'hood where quality veggie selections are hard to come by, Candle is a light at the end of a carnivorous cave – it's sandwiched, in fact, between a popular steakhouse and a burger joint. Wealthy New Age types are the norm in this simple storefront, permeated by the constant, clean scent of wheatgrass due to the juice bar stationed up front. Offerings range from the most simple, such as 'good food plates,' a custom-made spread of greens, roots, grains and soy-based protein, to the more complex concoctions, such as the beloved 'paradise

casserole,' a feast of layered sweet potatoes, black beans and millet topped with mushroom gravy. Celiacs should ask for the special gluten-free menu. An outpost with a slightly more upscale take on the subject is Candle 79 (Map p142; ☎ 212-537-7179; 154 E 79th St at Lexington Ave).

PIO PIO Map p142 Peruvian $$

☎ 212-426-5800; 1756 First Ave btwn 90th & 91st Sts; ☽ lunch & dinner; ⊕ 4, 5, 6 to 86th St
This rotisserie-chicken mini-chain pulls in the crowds in all four of its locations. It's got a simple, but quite effective, formula: marinate birds (the name is Peruvian for the 'cheep cheep' of a chick) for twelve hours in a secret blend of beer and spices, roast them to tender perfection on a spit and serve. The cheerful dining room feels casual despite its white tablecloths – and maybe that's because diners can't help but drop their guard and lick their fingers clean! Tasty sides include fresh avocado, beans and fried plantains. And don't forget the Pisco sour. Other locations are on the Upper West Side (Map p153; ☎ 212-665-3000; 702 Amsterdam Ave btwn 94th & 95th Sts; ⊕ 1, 2, 3 to 96th St), in Jackson Heights, Queens (Map pp200–1; ☎ 718-426-1010; 84-13 Northern Blvd btwn 84th & 85th Sts; ⊕ 7 to 82nd St-Jackson Heights) and in Rego Park, Queens (Map pp200–1; ☎ 718-458-0606; 62-30 Woodhaven Blvd btwn Dry Harbor & 62nd Rds; ⊕ G, R, V to Woodhaven Blvd).

LE PAIN QUOTIDIEN Map p142 Café, Bakery $

☎ 212-717-4800; 883 Lexington Ave at 64th St; ☽ breakfast, lunch & dinner; ⊕ 6 to 68th St-Hunter College
A classy Belgian bakery chain, this spot is the perfect place to unwind with a croissant and a mug of thick and addictive hot chocolate. Or go for more substantial fare – an open-faced egg salad sandwich with salty capers, tartins of radish, ricotta and scallions or shrimp and avocado. Settle in for a while, watching the parade of locals who stop in to catch up with each other or to simply while away the hours over a New York Times. Choose your own table, or join the friendly communal one. The eatery is part of an empire, with 15 across the city (another right in the 'hood – at 1131 Madison Ave between E 84th and E 85th Sts) and several around the world.

CENTRAL PARK

The park has plenty of great food vendors – ice cream, crepes, empanadas, hot dogs, you name it – but sometimes you want a little something more, and we're not talking about a picnic. (The well-known Tavern on the Green is still going strong, by the way, though it's a bit of a tourist trap.)

CENTRAL PARK BOATHOUSE RESTAURANT Map p149 Seafood $$$

☎ 212-517-2233; Central Park Lake, enter Fifth Ave at 72nd St; lunch daily, brunch Sat & Sun year-round, dinner daily Apr-Nov; 6 to 68th St
Escape the city and enter this magical lakeside setting, just by taking a 10-minute walk off Central Park West. The historic Loeb Boathouse, perched on the shores of the park's lake, is one of the city's most incredible settings for a serene and romantic meal – and the food is top notch, too. Plates are artfully designed – witness the lunch of grilled chicken artfully arranged with mashed purple potatoes – and flavorful. Other seasonal treats include homemade gnocchi tossed with slow-roasted cauliflower, pine nuts and pesto, and a pan-roasted pork tenderloin with grilled sweet onions. Reserve early and aim for an outdoor table – or simply slip up to the bar and enjoy a lakeside cocktail.

UPPER WEST SIDE

This huge swath of neighborhood – from the classic-arts Lincoln Center 60s blocks to the well-heeled, residential 70s and 80s and the more eclectic 90s – has always had plenty of good grub to mine. But it wasn't deemed destination-worthy by foodies until just a few years ago, when a couple of celebrity chefs brought their high-end fare to the 'hood and everyone followed. Now not a month goes by without at least one celebrated opening, with flavors from all corners of the globe.

'CESCA Map p153 Italian $$$

☎ 212-787-6300; 164 W 75th St btwn Columbus & Amsterdam Aves; dinner; 1, 2, 3 to 72nd St
This handsome, comforting place (stained wood, candelabras and sumptuous leather banquettes) is the setting for mackerel, chicken ragout, wild game and ravioli classics, as well as clever antipasti options such as marinated baby artichokes with fresh ricotta and tiny veal meatballs with pastina. The impressive wine list offers mainly Italian

bottles and plenty of by-the-glass choices, which you could opt to sip at the classy up-front bar, while nibbling at more casual (and affordable) fare like a bowl of warm faro salad.

CAFÉ LUXEMBOURG
Map p153 French Brasserie $$$

☎ 212-580-8700; 200 W 70th St btwn Broadway & West End Ave; breakfast, lunch & dinner daily, brunch Sun; 1, 2, 3 to 72nd St

top picks

STARBUCKS ALTERNATIVES

Why come to dynamic NYC just to drink the same coffee you can drink at any other Starbucks anywhere else in the country? The chains have taken over city neighborhoods like creeping kudzu vines – but that doesn't mean you can't avoid them. Here are some suggestions for jammin' java spots:

- Joe the Art of Coffee (Map p110; ☎ 212-924-7400; www.joetheartofcoffee.com; 141 Waverly Pl) A Village favorite, this diminutive storefront has been heralded repeatedly for having the best cup around. It's also a fun place to linger.
- Irving Farm Coffee Company (Map p110; ☎ 212-475-5200; 56 Seventh Ave at 13th St) A tiny haven between the Village and Chelsea, this place roasts its own beans at its upstate farm, and serves tasty pastries, too.
- Gorilla Coffee (Map p182; ☎ 718-230-3244; 97 Fifth Ave, Park Slope) The coolest café in the Slope serves inhouse-roasted brews to hipsters with laptops. The smell is heaven.
- Jack's Stir Brewed Coffee (Map p110; ☎ 212-929-0821; 138 W 10th St) Find everything done right in this Village shop, where java is organic, Fair Trade, shade-grown and microroasted in Vermont.
- Ninth Street Espresso (Map p104; ☎ 212-358-9225; 700 E 9th St at Ave C) Cool tattooed baristas serve up lattes and espressos with a flourish at this East Village favorite.
- Hungarian Pastry Shop (Map pp158–9; ☎ 212-866-4230; 1030 Amsterdam Ave btwn 110th & 111th Sts) Now *this* is a place to linger. Join Columbia students and other academic types, all hunched over laptops and enjoying the delicious coffee and cakes at this classic hang.
- Klatch (Map pp72–3; ☎ 212-227-7276; 9 Maiden Lane) Head way downtown for cute atmosphere and friendly service – plus delicious joe and doughnuts.

The quintessential city eatery, this neighborhood stalwart has it all: an elegant setting, friendly staff, a crowd of locals and flattering lighting – with an outstanding menu, to boot. Its execution of standards, including salmon tartare, cassoulet and steak frites, is consistently excellent, as is its approach to a range of other options, from salads and fresh pasta dishes to fabulous and eggy brunch options. Its proximity to Lincoln Center makes it the perfect post-performance destination.

CAFÉ BLOSSOM Map p153   Vegetarian $$
☎ 212-875-2600; 466 Columbus Ave btwn 82nd & 83rd Sts; ⏲ lunch & dinner; ◉ 1 to 79th St
The new uptown outpost of a Chelsea veg oasis, this snazzy café offers imaginative tofu, seitan and vegetable creations, some raw, all kosher. The stellar Autumn Sweet Potato Rolls have raw strips of the orange root wrapped around tangy strips of coconut, carrots and peppers, and will leave your taste-buds reeling. Seitan picatta has a perfect blend of richness and light lemony zing, and sandwiches like the soy parmesan sub and faux BLT are perfect afternoon pick-me-ups in this shopping-friendly 'hood. It's also just a couple of blocks from the Museum of Natural History, and a much better lunch option than the crammed museum cafés. The original Chelsea location is Blossom (Map p116; ☎ 212-627-1144; 187 Ninth Ave btwn 21st & 22nd Sts; ◉ C, E to 23rd St).

BARNEY GREENGRASS
Map p153   Jewish Deli $$
☎ 212-724-2707; 541 Amsterdam Ave at 86th St; ⏲ breakfast & lunch; ◉ 1 to 86th St
Step back in time at this century-old 'sturgeon king' gourmet shop and eatery serving a long list of traditional Jewish delicacies, including bagels and lox, a kippered salmon and whitefish platter, pastrami on rye and sturgeon scrambled with eggs and onions. While the left half of the establishment feels like a pleasant enough diner, sitting in the right side, where tables are cluttered among the rickety shelves of products for sale, puts you in the thick of the neighborhood action and ambience.

KEFI Map p153   Greek $$
☎ 212-873-0200; 222 W 79th St btwn Broadway & Amsterdam Ave; ⏲ dinner; ◉ 1 to 79th St

When it opened in 2007, this taverna-style spot became an instant classic thanks to its elegant take on hearty, traditional Greek food and its intimate dining room decked out with billowy wall hangings. Settle into plates of moussaka, spanakopita, grilled octopus, lamb and rich, raisin-studded meatballs. And get there early, as the no-reservations policy creates a constant wait in its atmospheric (though cramped) front bar area. Service is harried, but this somehow only enhances the happy, excited vibe.

HUMMUS PLACE
Map p153   Hummus & Israeli Salads $
☎ 212-799-3335; 305 Amsterdam Ave btwn 74th & 75th Sts; ⏲ lunch & dinner; ◉ 1, 2, 3 to 72nd St
This little nook is nothing special in the way of ambience – about eight tables tucked just below street level, fronting a cramped, open kitchen – but what's special are the plates of hummus, falafel, chopped salads, stuffed grape leaves and other savory, top-notch treats. The convivial atmosphere has friendly Israeli servers doling out your meals, the best of which are the hummus platters – served hot and with various toppings, from whole chickpeas and mushrooms to fava-bean stew with chopped egg. It all comes with a delicious side of pickles, olives and a basket of pillow-soft pita bread. Other locations are in the East Village (Map p104; 109 St Marks Pl btwn First Ave & Ave A) and in Greenwich Village (Map p110; 99 MacDougal St btwn Bleecker St & Minetta Lane).

HARLEM & NORTHERN MANHATTAN
Above the Upper West and Upper East Sides of Manhattan, you'll stumble upon stretches of less touristy and widely diverse terrain, where authentic foods of Latin America, the Caribbean, the American South and eclectic American all reign. Just above the Upper West Side is Morningside Heights, long colonized by the students and professors of Columbia University and thus offering plenty of cheap and late-night diners mixed with convivial bistro-type hangs. Harlem is still justifiably famous for its traditional soul food, though it has branched out in recent years to offer a little bit of everything.

Further north you'll find Washington Heights, traditionally known for its preponderance of Dominican joints, and then the northernmost 'hood of Inwood, where pleasant cafés give the almost suburban-feeling blocks some lovely depth of character.

NEW LEAF CAFÉ
off Map pp158–9   American Creative $$$

☎ 212-568-5323; Fort Tryon Park, 1 Margaret Corbin Dr; ☽ lunch & dinner; ◉ A to 190th St

After feeding your mind with the artistic beauty of the Cloisters, take a peaceful stroll through Fort Tryon Park and feed your belly here, in this beautiful 1930s stone edifice with nature-lovers' views. The airy dining room features romantic archways, lots of dark wood, sexy night lighting from orange sconces and garden-patio seating for warm afternoons. The tasty food offers something for everyone – handmade *papardelle* with fava beans and ricotta, grilled halibut with risotto, and burgers and salad niçoise for lunch. Nighttime programs like movie screenings a[...] ances provide even mor[...] make the trek, with all pr[...] maintain the park thanks t[...] city program.

AMY RUTH'S RESTAURAN[...]
Map pp158–9   [...]ood $$

☎ 212-280-8779; 114 W 116th St btwn Malcolm X Blvd (Lenox Ave) & Adam Clayton Powell Jr Blvd (Seventh Ave); ☽ breakfast, lunch & dinner, 24hr Fri & Sat; ◉ B, C, 2, 3 to 116th St

Though you will have to battle other wide-eyed tourists for a seat at this classic joint, it's worth it to get a taste of the well-made classics – candied yams, smoked ham, corn pudding, fried okra, you name it – with a particularly hard-to-resist specialization in rich and pillowy waffles. Choose from chocolate, strawberry, blueberry, smothered in sautéed apples, or paired with fried chicken. Then burn it off – you'll really need to – with a walking tour of the surrounding neighborhood.

YOU CAN TAKE IT WITH YOU

Beyond NYC's restaurants is a cornucopia of gourmet food markets, where you can choose your own fresh produce, baked goods and prepared foods without the restaurant-price mark-ups. The most authentic spots lie in ethnic neighborhoods such as Chinatown, Brooklyn Heights' 'fertile crescent' of Middle Eastern shops, the Little India of Jackson Heights or Brighton Beach and Brooklyn's Russian enclave. The cheapest such options are the 24-hour Korean groceries that sport huge salad and hot-food bars that you'll find on every other corner citywide. But the most awe-inspiring are spread around Manhattan. Here's a sampling:

Chelsea Market (p115) Shop for wine, baked goods, cheese and other delicacies.

Dean & DeLuca (Map pp88–9; ☎ 212-226-6800; www.deananddeluca.com; 560 Broadway at Prince St; ◉ R, W to Prince St) It's got museum-quality produce, chocolates, baked goods, cheeses and prepared items, at exorbitant prices. Also in Greenwich Village (Map p110; ☎ 212-473-1908; 75 University Pl; ◉ L, N, Q, R, W, 4, 5, 6 to 14th St-Union Sq).

Fairway (p240) Besides the Upper West Side branch, there are also stores in Harlem (Map pp158–9; ☎ 212-234-3883; 2328 Twelfth Ave at 132nd St; ◉ 1 to 125th St) and Brooklyn (Map p180; ☎ 718-694-6868; 480 Van Brunt St, Red Hook, Brooklyn). All three have stunning arrays of produce and global goods, but the bigger Harlem spot boasts a 10,000-sq-ft 'cold room,' where you can wear a special jacket to pick out meats, flowers, dairy products and other chilly treats. And the newest addition, in Brooklyn, has a café with stunning Manhattan skyline views.

Gourmet Garage (Map pp88–9; ☎ 212-941-5850; www.gourmetgarage.com; 453 Broome St at Mercer St; ◉ R, W to Prince St, 6 to Spring St) There are other locations, including one on the Upper East Side (Map p142) and one on the Upper West Side (Map p153). Each spot varies in size, but the stellar offerings – especially the bulk-olive bar and prepared deli dinners – are equally stand-out.

Kalustyan's (Map p126; ☎ 212-685-3451; www.kalustyans.com; 123 Lexington Ave at 28th St; ◉ 6 to 28th St) An intimate yet extensive shop filled with Indian gourmet items, including endless spices and chutneys, rare produce (like fresh curry leaves), breads, dried beans and oils.

Zabar's (Map p153; ☎ 212-787-2000; www.zabars.com; 2245 Broadway at W 80th St; ◉ 1 to 79th St) A long-standing Upper West Side favorite. The gourmet cheeses, heavenly baked goods, whole-bean coffee and Jewish deli specials inspire pilgrimages from all over the New York area.

op picks

BRUNCH

- **Amy Ruth's Restaurant** (p267) Chicken 'n' waffles mixed with live gospel music make this a Harlem magnet.
- **Balthazar** (p252) Sour cream hazelnut waffles, smoked salmon with crème fraîche and brioche, and hangover drinks such as the potent Ramos Fizz… What's not to love?
- **Park Terrace Bistro** (right) Go to the ends of the earth (or at least Manhattan) for Moroccan surroundings and eclectic options from pulled pork to blueberry pancakes.
- **Café Luxembourg** (p265) An UWS charmer with everything from eggs to full-on bistro meals.
- **Community Food & Juice** (below) Columbia students and families mingle over healthy, hearty fare.
- **Brasserie** (p261) Wake up to some seriously high-gloss design.
- **Spotted Pig** (p258) And now for something completely different: spiced-pork hash, pumpkin pancakes and soft-boiled duck eggs.
- **Cendrillon** (p253) Filipino brunches include pork and eggs with garlic fried rice, soothing noodles and steamed sticky rice with mango.
- **Stella Maris** (p250) Steel-cut oats, fat omelets and top-notch pastries.
- **Rice 'n' Beans** (p263) Go Brazilian with a hearts-of-palm frittata, scrambled eggs with boiled yucca and some fresh guava juice.

GINGER Map pp158–9   Chinese $$
☎ 212-423-1111; 1400 Fifth Ave at 116th St; ⏰ lunch & dinner; ⓔ 2, 3, 6 to 116th St
It's not where you might expect to find outstanding Chinese fare but here it is. The bright and happy room, with red lanterns and bamboo ceiling beams, is the stage for organic, creative treats like ginger beer-braised short ribs with beans and cashews, house-special grilled Angus beef spare ribs, vegetarians' grilled tofu and pineapple-pork fried rice – which is a far cry from the version found at battered storefronts all around the 'hood.

COMMUNITY FOOD & JUICE
Map pp158–9   Organic American $$
☎ 212-665-2800; 2893 Broadway btwn 112th & 113th Sts; ⏰ breakfast, lunch & dinner, brunch Sat & Sun; ⓔ 1 to 110th St

A loud and lofty instant neighborhood hotspot since opening in late 2007, this is *the* place for brunch, with fans ranging from hungover Columbia students to frenzied families with double strollers in tow. Get there before 10:30am or be prepared to wait a long time for your light blueberry pancakes, veggie scramble and warm faro porridge. Or just skip the weekend rush and bop in for a no-nonsense, candle-lit lunch or dinner of warm lentil salad, 'bowl of beets' (with pistachio nuts, goat cheese and balsamic vinegar), country fried chicken or a grass-fed beef burger.

PARK TERRACE BISTRO
off Map pp158–9   French-Moroccan $$
☎ 212-567-2828; 4959 Broadway at 207th St; ⏰ dinner daily, lunch & brunch Sat & Sun; ⓔ A to Inwood-207th St
A Moroccan outpost on the tippy-top of Manhattan, this place has been widely praised for both its location (beautiful) and its food (luscious). You wouldn't expect such a crowd at these northern reaches, but slammin' it is, both with giddy locals who don't have many options and downtown folks looking for the next big dining adventure. They find it here, through lovely service and rockin' menu items including escargot with fennel confit in a puffed pastry, spicy fish *tagine du jour*, filet mignon in bordelaise sauce, chicken *tagine* with ginger and preserved lemon, and a fresh vegetable plate, served on request.

LA BAOBOB Map pp158–9   Senegalese $
☎ 212-864-4700; 120 W 116th St btwn Adam Clayton Powell Jr Blvd (Seventh Ave) & Malcolm X Blvd (Lenox Ave); ⏰ 1pm-3am; ⓔ 2, 3 to 116th St
The small and handsome space, with portraits of African American leaders and a relaxed yet classy air, provides afternoon and late-night savories, including a tomato-based fish stew called *thiebou diene* and *soupou kanja*, rich lamb stew studded with fish and okra.

BROOKLYN

Brooklyn's eats aren't just for newbie residents too lazy to cross the river for Manhattan meals. Restaurant rows like Park Slope's Fifth Ave and Boerum Hill's Smith St are home to 'destination' restaurants that bring out Manhattanites.

EATING BROOKLYN

BROOKLYN HEIGHTS, DOWNTOWN BROOKLYN & DUMBO

The polite, more upscale crowd will opt for Dumbo's Washington St, or (though a bit less formal) Brooklyn Heights' Montague St. In downtown Brooklyn, cheap slices of pizza can be had on Court St or at the Fulton Mall.

RIVER CAFÉ Map p174   American $$$
☎ 718-522-5200; 1 Water St; ☾ lunch & dinner Mon-Sat, lunch Sun; ◉ A, C to High St, 2, 3 to Clark St

Classy, expensive and popular mostly with non–New Yorkers, the River Café sits on the water under the Brooklyn Bridge, giving it one of the best views of any New York restaurant. Diners come mostly for the scene (with waiters in tuxes and a jackets-only rule), but the food's excellent. The kitchen has served as a training ground for rising chefs of area restaurants. Dinner is prix fixe only, with a $95 menu of fine steaks, lamb cutlets and seafood.

HECHO EN MEXICO Map p174   Mexican $$
☎ 718-855-5288; 111 Front St; ☾ dinner Mon-Sat; ◉ F to York St

Serving nouveaux Mexican – as in the nouveaux Mex found in well-to-do parts of Mexico City – Hecho is a great spot with live *folklorico* or *electronico* bands Thursday through Saturday set up in the corner, and fantastic tapas-style dishes: a plate of cactus tacos,

top picks

BROOKLYN

- Al Di Là (p272) Tuesday at 6pm means a wait at this tip-top *trattoria*.
- Cafe Glechik (p281) Dumplings and borscht with Russki accents in Brighton Beach.
- The Farm on Adderley (see the boxed text, p270) Buzzing neighborhood-changer in Ditmas Park, with super brunches.
- Lucali (p271) Carroll Gardens: home of New York's best pizza?
- Tacos at the Soccer Fields (see the boxed text, p271) Latin American stands in Red Hook serve big mean tacos and *pupusas*.

or *queso fundido* (fondue-style platters with mushrooms and Oaxaca cheese), or ground-corn pancakes topped with crabmeat. Don't skip on tequilas – like the *agave* one with tumblers of spicy tomato sauce to down it with ($10). During the day it's a café.

SUPERFINE Map p174   Brunch $
☎ 718-243-9005; 126 Front St; ☾ lunch & dinner Tue-Fri & Sun, dinner Sat; ◉ F to York St

This loungey redbrick corner spot is fantastic for its Sunday 'bluegrass brunch,' when a mixed group of Dumbo locals (ie tattooed yuppies) sip Bloody Marys at the bar or by the back seats near the stage. Windows line two sides, and the rumble of the subway on Manhattan Bridge puts a little bumpy thrill into the meal. Food covers American and Mexican stomach-fillers (steaks, breakfast burritos, *enchiladas*). If there's a line, you can play on the orange (!) pool table for free.

GRIMALDI'S Map p174   Pizza $
☎ 718-858-4300; 19 Old Fulton St; ☾ lunch & dinner; ◉ A, C to High St, 2, 3 to Clark St

Known as Patsy's in a previous life – and serving one of New York's most beloved pizzas – Grimaldi's, with its red-checkered tables, bring in a loyal following of local fire-fighters, guys in leather and a tourist or 10. Sometimes lines go out the door, but the brick oven churns out the pizzas fast. This is real-deal New York pizza: Frank (Sinatra – c'mon!) is on the walls and jukebox. Four hungry folk can eat two larges (it's thin).

JACQUES TORRES CHOCOLATE
Map p174   Chocolate $
☎ 718-875-9772; www.mrchocolate.com; 66 Water St; ☾ 9am-7pm Mon-Sat, 10am-6pm Sun; ◉ F to York St

Unlike some NYC hot dogs, it's OK to trace back where this chocolate comes from. This French chocolatier takes his cocoa seriously, and the small shop churns out remarkable chocolates, including a *thick* cup of hot chocolate for $3.25. Other branches are on the Upper West Side (Map p153; ☎ 212-414-2462; 285 Amsterdam Ave at 74th St) and in western SoHo (Map pp88–9; 350 Hudson St).

FORT GREENE

The past few years have seen a renaissance along Fort Greene's DeKalb and Fulton Aves, with new spots appearing and disappearing.

ICI Map p180 French-American $$

☎ 718-789-2778; www.icirestaurant.com; 246 DeKalb Ave at Vanderbilt St; ✆ breakfast, lunch & dinner Tue-Sun; ⊕ G to Clinton-Washington Aves

French by name (and chef), the simple white-brick, wood-floor Ici fuses different worlds on its menu and wine list. The seasonal menu draws heavily on all-natural ingredients from farmers markets and isn't afraid to pair *pico de gallo* with mackerel. The braised pork shoulder goes South with collard greens and grits. Breakfast is a bonus, with croissants made in the back. There's a back courtyard too.

HABANA OUTPOST

Map p180 Burritos $

☎ 718-858-9500; 757 Fulton St; ✆ lunch & dinner Wed-Mon, closed Jan & Feb; ⊕ B, Q, 2, 3, 4, 5 to Atlantic Ave

Young, fun and social, this open courtyard spot serves a good burrito ($8 to $10) or Cuban sandwich ($7.25) from a 'taco truck kitchen,' but coming here's all about sitting at communal picnic tables, slamming *mojitos* and watching Sunday-night films (May to October) shown on the neighbors' wall.

CAKE MAN RAVEN Map p180 Red Velvet Cake $

☎ 718-694-2253; www.cakemanraven.com; 708A Fulton St; ✆ 9am-10pm; ⊕ B, Q, 2, 3, 4, 5 to Atlantic Ave

No one knows why a little red dye makes regular ol' white cake with white frosting so much better, but it does. Harlem émigré 'Cake Man Raven' set up here in 2000 and took over the Brooklyn sweet tooth with his red-velvet slices ($5).

WILLIAMSBURG & BUSHWICK

The main crawl, Bedford Ave, has the most options, but they tend to be cheaper and less rewarding than the newbies on side streets such as N 6th St, or farther flung pockets of East Williamsburg and Bushwick. Many hipsters here complain about overly casual service by the hipster waitstaff – at least you won't be rushed.

PETER LUGER STEAKHOUSE

Map p177 Steakhouse $$$

☎ 718-387-7400; 178 Broadway; ✆ lunch & dinner; ⊕ J, M, Z to Marcy Ave

Here long before Williamsburg became Slackerville, New York's most famous steakhouse looks smack out of its 1887 birthday. The sirloin cuts ($40 for single steak, $77 for a two-person one) are juicy and live up to their legend (and don't the loveably brusque waitstaff in aprons know it), but you'll need to reserve a month ahead (!) to get a good dinner time. Cash only.

DINER Map p177 American $$

☎ 718-486-3077; 85 Broadway at Berry St; ✆ lunch & dinner; ⊕ L to Bedford Ave, J, M, Z to Marcy Ave

It's easy to roll your eyes over this hipster HQ, made from a well-preserved 1920s Kullman dining car, but why bother? Diner is surprisingly good. Menus for brunch and dinner are refreshingly brief, and added to by daily specials (such as braised duck or lamb shanks, plus at least one fish and veggie option), which staff hand-write on your paper 'table cloth.' It's likely your waiter may be worn out at weekend brunch (which is great for its specials, like rhubarb pancakes) as drinks flow nightly till 2am.

SILENT H Map p177 Vietnamese $$

☎ 718-218-7063; 79 Berry St at N 9th St; ✆ lunch & dinner Tue-Sun; ⊕ L to Bedford Ave

This long-overdue intro to Vietnamese food for Williamsburg occupies a snug, modern corner spot run by a friendly Vietnamese guy who insists on 'no *pho* – nothing you

WORTH THE TRIP: DITMAS PARK

Found a few long blocks south of Prospect Park, the long-neglected Ditmas Park – with *Leave it to Beaver*–style blocks of shady, two-story homes – has become a surprising food destination, particularly along Cortelyou Rd, where you can find great mom-and-pop tacos and anarchist coffee.

Nothing put Ditmas Park on the map like The Farm on Adderley (Map pp170–1; ☎ 718-287-3101; www.thefarmon adderley.com; 1108 Cortelyou Rd btwn Stratford & Westminster Rds; ✆ lunch & dinner Tue-Sun, dinner Mon; ⊕ B, Q to Cortelyou Rd). It's sceney in a good way, a tin-ceiling transformation of an old laundromat and a back patio. It can get a bit cramped inside, but nowhere serves better food for less: as chef Tom Kearney puts it, the goal is 'to keep prices gentle.' Dishes take some imaginative twists: lots of fish dishes, poached chicken done Amish style (both $16), and a big bowl of fries served with curry sauce ($5). Brunches are huge, with a meal of a Bloody Mary ($7). Bar stays open till 1am.

TACOS! BURRITOS! AT LAST!

The best thing to happen to New York since the subway is the ongoing emergence of real-deal Mexican food in the past decade. Here are a few Brooklyn standouts.

At Red Hook's open-air taco stands (Map p180; cnr Clinton & Bay Sts, Red Hook; ☾ lunch Sat & Sun Jun-Oct), beef and pork are grilled and stuffed into giant, cheese-filled quesadillas ($5) and huaraches (long cakes of cornmeal masa) in 13 tents alongside a pan–Latin American soccer league's games. (It's so loved that when a permit was nearly refused in 2007, bloggers and activists rallied to their defense.)

Another great spot for a good ol'-fashioned San Francisco Mission–style burrito is unassuming Taqueria DF (Map p182; ☎ 718-499-2969; 709 5th Ave at 22nd St, Greenwood Heights; ☾ lunch & dinner; ◉ M, R to 25th St), where you can grab a $7 burrito stuffed with steak, chorizo or carnitas. It's a couple of blocks north of the Green-Wood Cemetery.

The tequila-plus-setting crowd head to Alma (Map p180; ☎ 718-643-5400; 187 Columbia St at Degraw St, Carroll Gardens; ☾ dinner Mon-Fri, breakfast, lunch & dinner Sat & Sun; ◉ F, G to Carroll St), a rooftop spot with 20 tequilas, and dishes from $10. Food is standard Mex – good, not great – but the setting's super.

Folks in Bushwick swear by warehouse-style Tortilleria Mexicana Los Hermanos (Map pp170–1; ☎ 718-456-3422; 271 Starr, at Wyckoff Ave, Bushwick; ☾ 11am-9pm Mon-Sat; ◉ L to Jefferson St), a tortilla shop with authentic chicken and beef tacos for $2.

see on every Vietnamese menu.' The fish sauce is real and the knock-you-out Trung Nguyen coffee is straight from Ho Chi Minh City, though the menus could stand to be expanded a bit. The best option is sharing a few appetizers ($8 pork meat balls, $6 summer rolls) and a salad.

NORTHEAST KINGDOM
Map pp170–1   American $$

☎ 718-386-3864; 18 Wyckoff Ave; ☾ dinner Mon-Fri, lunch & dinner Sat & Sun; ◉ L to Jefferson St
Under the green deer sign, lodge-style Northeast Kingdom is the pioneer of rough-at-the-edges Bushwick, a couple of L stops east of Williamsburg. With its basement lounge staying open to 2am, it's a neighborhood changer for good eating and drinking. Brunch is super and cheap ($6 to $8); particularly good is the Vermont syrup–soaked crisp pieces of French toast. Dinners are pretty hearty, with a host of lighter sandwiches ($8 to $10) joining chicken pot pie, pork chops and char fillets. 'Yep, we got the Vermont thing going,' one waiter told us.

BONITA Map p177   Gringo-Mex $

☎ 718-384-9500; 338 Bedford Ave btwn S 2nd & S 3rd Sts; ☾ breakfast, lunch & dinner; ◉ L to Bedford Ave, J, M, Z to Marcy Ave
It's all indie-rock gringos pouring into this stylish, lively Mexican restaurant transformed from an old diner. The short menu is good, though, particularly the fish tacos ($7.50). Be warned: it has beer and wine only, so those $5 margaritas are made with wine.

BOERUM HILL, COBBLE HILL, CARROLL GARDENS & RED HOOK

Smith St, south of Atlantic Ave, is one of Brooklyn's famed hip eating strips (French, Thai, Cuban, American etc) with many good choices not listed here. A block west, Court St is another strip lined with eating options. Remote Red Hook remains in its crawling stages, with good new choices along Van Brunt St coming (and going).

FRANKIES SPUNTINO Map p180   Italian $$

☎ 718-403-0033; www.frankiesspuntino.com; 457 Court St; ☾ lunch & dinner; ◉ F, G to Carroll St
Away from Smith St's eating ghetto, Frankies is a neighborhood magnet, with local couples and families lining up for a seat in the brick-wall inside or, when weather's good, in the back garden. There are main dishes – hearty pasta dishes like the cavetelli with hot sausage ($15), or braised beef short ribs ($17) – but, as a spuntino, it's more about the snacking. Go family-style with some 'table antipasti' (sweet radishes and brussels sprouts), salads or a mix of formaggio (with goat and sheep cheeses).

LUCALI Map p180   Pizza $

☎ 718-858-4086; 575 Henry St at Carroll St; ☾ dinner Wed-Mon; ◉ F, G to Carroll St
Suddenly, New York's greatest pie may come from an unlikely Carroll Gardens back street. The man behind it – after years of

271

WORTH THE TRIP: SUNSET PARK

Sunset Park has Brooklyn's 'Chinatown' – a host of noodle shops and dim sum places running along Eighth Ave between 50th and 60th Sts, including local fave Gia Lam (Map pp170–1; ☎ 718-567-0800; 5414 Eighth Ave; ⏰ lunch & dinner; ⊕ R to 53rd St). It looks more like a well-lit tavern than a noodle shop, but it's Sunset Park's go-to for Vietnamese food like *pho bo* (beef noodle soup; $4.50), *canh chua ca* (sweet-and-sour fish soup; $7.75 to $12) or *mi xao do bien* (stir-fried noodles with seafood; $9).

brick-oven practice for fun – opened the doors of a pizza-and-calzone place (and nothing else…though you can bring your own wine or beer in). It's cooked in the open kitchen – one-size pie ($19) comes with perfected crusts, moist tomato sauce covered with a limited choice of toppings (the basil is fresh, just-plucked leaves) and a real Brooklyn accent.

SAUL Map p180 American $$
☎ 718-935-9844; www.saulrestaurant.com; 140 Smith St btwn Dean & Bergen Sts; ⏰ dinner; ⊕ F to Bergen St
The king of Smith St, Saul has brought out fine-dining fans from Manhattan for nearly a decade. Compact and simple, the menu goes with fresh ingredients for its tweaks on masterly prepared game-meats, such as prosciutto-wrapped rabbit with cumin and pickled cauliflower, or pan-roasted venison with celery puree and pear chutney. Reserve ahead or you'll be trolling Smith St for back-up.

STEVE'S KEY LIME PIES Map p180 Pies $
☎ 718-858-5333; www.stevesauthentic.com; 204 Van Dyke St, Pier 41; ⏰ usually daily till 6pm; ⊕ F, G to Carroll St
Steve's key-lime pies are a Red Hook institution, set up in the back of an old waterfront warehouse. Signs point the way from the water taxi. If the weather is hot, opt for the frozen, chocolate-dipped key-lime pie on a stick ($5); an 8in pie (made to feed four people) is $15.

PARK SLOPE & PROSPECT HEIGHTS

It's not hard finding food on Fifth or Seventh Aves in Park Slope. Most fancier options are

between the 'named' cross streets – particularly on Fifth Ave – with cheaper options in the 'numbered' cross streets to the south.

Most locals and visitors wander to Park Slope for meals, but Vanderbilt Ave in Prospect Heights is starting to fill its blocks between Eastern Parkway and Atlantic Ave with good choices too.

FRANNY'S Map p182 Pizza $$
☎ 718-230-0221; 295 Flatbush Ave; ⏰ dinner Tue-Fri, lunch & dinner Sat & Sun; ⊕ M, R to Union St
Unexpectedly but gloriously, Franny's – a busy modern spot, where table chatter swells in decibel – squeezes new juice from a dish long thought tired: pizza. Thin crusts bubble crisply in the brick oven, decorated with a couple of choice organic toppings such as the simple, but excellent, buffalo mozzarella and oregano ($16). Add on organic salads and a few choice pastas (spaghetti with lemon is inspired, $13). No one leaves unhappy, and everyone seems to come back.

AL DI LÀ Map p182 Trattoria $$
☎ 718-783-4565; 248 Fifth Ave at Carroll St; ⏰ dinner Wed-Mon; ⊕ M, R to Union St
No reservations and big buzz mean the excellent Al Di Là requires some pre-planning – or waiting in the wine-bar annex for an hour or more, even on 'off' nights. The soft-lit rustic spot keeps the focus on the top of the Italian boot. Many go for gamey northern Italian specialties, like braised rabbit in white wine, tripe with tomatoes and grilled bread, or the homemade ravioli.

BLUE RIBBON SUSHI BROOKLYN
Map p182 Sushi $$
☎ 718-840-0408; 278 Fifth Ave, btwn 1st St & Garfield Pl; ⏰ dinner; ⊕ M, R to Union St
Brooklynites don't like to admit it, but generally Manhattan dominates in the raw seafood tourney. This Manhattan chain's mini-outpost is the 718's best. A slick, SoHo-styled spot with sleek wood booths and friendly waiters deliver a long list of sashimi, sushi and maki rolls. Pick and choose or go for the sushi/sashimi combo ($32.50) instead.

(Continued on page 281)

NYC STYLE

New York City style isn't just about fashion – it's about life. Gotham is a city of constant re-invention, where tapping into the latest trends in the worlds of art, music, theater, dining and drinking entails little more than stepping outside your door. The classic, the cutting-edge and the wondrously strange are all characters on the NYC stage. To take part, all you have to do is join the fray.

Step out in style with a visit to Madison Ave's chic boutiques

1

THE NEW YORK LOOK

New York living means donning the costume that lets the neighborhood know you rock. SoHo fashionistas, East Village punk rockers, Upper East Side princesses and old-school MCs from the Bronx all strut the stage of this fashion-conscious town.

2

3

❶ Opening Ceremony

The downtown fashion scene marches to a different beat, with stores like Opening Ceremony (p220) spreading avant-garde allure in their ultra-hip boutiques. This is SoHo, stomping ground of style mavens who haunt the endless storefronts in search of one-of-a-kind finds.

❷ Marc Jacobs

The West Village is Marc Jacobs country (p229), where attractive couples (gay and straight) stroll the tree-lined streets wearing stylish haircuts and handsomely tailored gear. If you left the MJ uniform at home, stop by one of his neighborhood outposts.

❸ Alife Rivington Club

Something of a men's club for the hip-hop crowd, ARC (p225) is a dimly lit parlor with a leather couch and a wall of sexy and tempting one-of-a-kind sneakers.

❹ Love Saves the Day

The East Village is home to record shops, skinny jeans, eye-catching haircuts and quirky toy store/vintage shops like this. At Love Saves the Day (p228), glam rockers and Star Wars nerds dig for the missing, highly coveted piece to complete the collection.

❺ Barneys

For a glimpse into the well-coiffed world of Madison Ave, there's no better door to enter. The designer jeans, the suit, the cocktail dress – no matter the article, Barneys (p235) holds the city's most touted labels.

❻ Housing Works Used Book Café

Sating the needs of New York's up-and-coming literary types, Housing Works (p222) has fine books to read and/or buy, used records and a café in which to daydream. It's even set on a cinematic cobbled street.

❼ Brooklyn Industries

Although the bearded Billyburg hipster is gently mocked in some circles, there are plenty of other fashion ideas coming from NY's most populous borough. For a headstart on B's stylish-but-rugged look, visit Brooklyn Industries (p222).

EAT NEW YORK

Like its residents, New York restaurants do not lack for variety. Feasting here can mean gourmet hot dogs or tender sashimi, with stylish bistros, oyster bars, steakhouses, vegan cafés and ethnic eateries to satisfy NY's 170-odd resident nationalities.

① Russian Tea Room
Reborn like Stravinsky's cacophonous Firebird, the Russian Tea Room (p262) is back, and it's as exuberant as ever. Gilded eagles, golden samovars and red leather banquettes set the scene for decadent dining on caviar, poached lobster and other czar pleasers.

② Momofuku Noodle Bar
Sleek and stylish, this award-winning restaurant (p256) sets the gold standard among the world's noodle bars. Steaming bowls of house ramen come piled with mouthwatering slices of pork, crisp fresh snow peas, scallions and – holy of holies – golden corn.

③ La Esquina
Hidden inside a neon-lit taco stand, an unmarked door leads down to a cavelike dining room. With flickering candles and gleaming tequila bottles, La Esquina (p253) has obvious sex appeal – not only for its speakeasy-like entrance and attractive crowd but for its delicious cuisine.

④ 5 Ninth
It's tough to stand out among the glittering new restaurants in the Meatpacking District. 5 Ninth (p257), however, has won over the critics, with delectable fusion fare served in an 1840s

NIGHTLIFE

Cynics say NYC nightlife isn't what it used to be. Perhaps, but let's be honest: it sure beats the hell out of Kansas. This is a city of rock, jazz, hip-hop, burlesque, cabaret, Afro-pop, salsa, experimental orchestras and much, much more.

❶ Cielo
Boasting one of the best sound systems in town, Cielo (p300) throws great parties, particularly on early-in-the-week nights. Take in the scene from one of the comfy suede couches, then head for the sunken dance floor, where DJs spin deep soulful house.

❷ Knitting Factory
This three-floored temple to the audio gods (p304) features a lineup of explosive hip-hop, spirited folk music and punch-me-in-the-face punk rock. The Knitting Factory's wasteland location amid the tumble-weeds of Tribeca only adds to the appeal.

❸ Village Vanguard
This legendary club (p306) opened in 1935 and has been at the epicenter of the jazz universe ever since. While there's plenty of history, the downstairs space continues to be at the forefront of today's improvisatory scene.

❹ Galapagos Art Space
Reason enough to venture across the murky East River, Galapagos Art Space (p299) stages experimental bands, obscure art installations and strange theater/musical events. Our current favorite is Monday's amateur burlesque night. Try not to stumble into the reflecting pool at the entrance.

URBAN ARTS

Even without Broadway, New York would still rank among the world's great arts capitals. The variety is daunting: art openings, ballet, indie film screenings, opera, modern dance, poetry readings, experimental theater and plenty of strange and exciting fusions.

❶ Metropolitan Opera House
Home to one of the world's most venerated opera companies, the Met (p321) stages dazzling productions. The great divas and maestros have all appeared here, and the sets, costumes and musical accompaniment all add to the display.

❷ St Ann's Warehouse
The once barren warehouse district of Dumbo is currently a major player in the city's arts scene. St Ann's (p314) remains the queen of the avant-garde, with theatrical collaborations involving Lou Reed, the Coen Brothers, downtown jazz hound John Zorn and many others.

❸ IFC Center
While big-box movie theaters blanket much of America, New York still clings to its independent cinemas. The IFC Center (p319) is one of the city's newest art houses; enjoy great foreign, indie and cult films without sacrificing comfy seats and the high-def experience.

❹ Kitchen
Amid the galleries and industrial grit of West Chelsea, the Kitchen (p317) has attracted performance-art lovers since the 1970s. Conceptual dance troupes and experimental dramatists work the stage, often bringing video art and other multimedia into the performance.

❺ KGB Bar
Inspiring images of comrade Lenin and fist-pumping proletarians adorn the walls of this warmly lit East Village bar (p322). The real draw, however, is KGB's reading series, with poets, eroticists, journalists and graphic novelists competing for airtime in this Commie-loving drinking den.

❻ PS1 Contemporary Art Center
Hidden in the urban wilderness of Long Island City, this former public school is a castlelike wonderland of cutting-edge art. PS1 (p202) also throws great summer parties in the walled-in courtyard.

❼ Mary Boone Gallery
Center of New York's art world, Chelsea is home to more than 300 galleries. Mary Boone (p114) stands out among the crowded scene, with a taste for controversial works (Boone was even arrested once for a show involving live ammunition).

ONLY IN NEW YORK

Imaginations run wild at NYC's many festivals, with freak-show parades, surreal theater and hot-dog-eating contests. Sometimes the New York experience is about seeing the city from a wild new vantage point or visiting a place where few have trod.

❶ 5 Pointz Graffiti Building

Urban art reaches epic proportions at this magnificent, ever-changing installation (p199). Check it out from the elevated 7 train, then stop for a closer look – or if you're not too shabby with a spray can, get a permit to add your own tag.

❷ Free Kayak Rides

Although the Hudson isn't the world's prettiest river, it's a fantastic spot for spying the man-made peaks of Manhattan. Various boathouses (p330) around town offer free kayak rentals; experienced kayakers can even sign up for four- and five-mile journeys with paddling peers.

❸ Mermaid Parade

The endangered mermaid species is rarely spotted these days. At Coney Island's annual parade (see the boxed text, p198), however, the captivating water nymph makes her triumphant return amid lots of glittery mayhem.

❹ Outdoor film screenings

When summer arrives there are plenty of places to catch an outdoor film. Top picks include Bryant Park's Monday-night screenings (p317), while film gawkers wanting to escape the crowds head to bird's-nest heights at Brooklyn's rooftop film series (p179).

TOM'S RESTAURANT Map p182   Diner $

☎ 718-636-9738; 782 Washington Ave, at Sterling Pl; ☒ breakfast & lunch Mon-Sat; ⓔ 2, 3 to Eastern Pkwy-Brooklyn Museum

Three blocks from the Brooklyn Museum, this happy greasy spoon woos locals with all-day breakfasts and egg creams. Open since 1936, much of the decor has been picked up along the way. It's good and cheap: two eggs, toast, coffee, home fries or grits (go for grits) costs $3.50. Handmade signs along the walls advertise a dozen-plus varieties of pancake. Don't fret Saturday morning lines – staff bring by coffee, orange slices and cookies while you wait.

CONEY ISLAND & BRIGHTON BEACH

Most of the Coney Island boardwalk eateries are greasy deals catering to the state-fair feel of the neighboring 'shoot the freak' games and kid-oriented rides.

If you're in a Slavic mood, along Brighton Beach Ave from Brighton 1st St to Brighton 12th or 13th Sts, crisscrossing Coney Island Ave, you can find several small groceries or restaurants with menus in Cyrillic. Brighton Beach's famed, raucous supper clubs – with cheesy pop shows and spent bottles of vodka everywhere – are found here and along the boardwalk. Most have set menus that start at $50 per person. One long-timer is Primorski (Map pp196–7; ☎ 718-891-3111; 282 Brighton Beach Ave btwn Brighton 2nd & 3rd Sts; ☒ lunch & dinner; ⓔ B, Q to Brighton Beach), which looks like a 1983-cruise-ship formal dining room – in a good way.

TOTONNO'S Map pp196–7   Pizza $$

☎ 718-372-8606; 1524 Neptune Ave, Coney Island; ☒ noon-8pm Wed-Sun; ⓔ D, F to Coney Island-Stillwell Ave

A few grubby blocks back from the boardwalk, this little family spot has been serving remarkable pizza pie since 1924. The mozzarella is homemade, the tomatoes are imported from Italy and the pizzas are baked in a clay oven. The sauce itself is enough to justify that long subway ride.

CAFE GLECHIK Map pp196–7   Borscht $

☎ 718-616-0494; 3159 Coney Island Ave, Brighton Beach; ☒ breakfast, lunch & dinner; ⓔ B, Q to Brighton Beach

A welcoming break from the stuffy supper clubs, this chatty hole in the wall serves a mean borscht, fish filets ($14 to $20) and fruit compote drinks ($2). It's named for the clay pot the *vereniki* dumplings and other dishes come in. Staff may ask '*gotovie?*' (meaning 'ready?') when taking your order.

NATHAN'S FAMOUS Map pp196–7   Hot Dogs $

☎ 718-946-2202; 1310 Surf Ave, Coney Island; ☒ breakfast, lunch & dinner till late; ⓔ D, F to Coney Island-Stillwell Ave

If you eat 'em, this is *the* place to stomach the all-beef dog ($2.75) with sauerkraut and mustard (actually Nathan supposedly stole the recipe back in 1916 from another hot-dog place, but who's keeping track anymore?). A frightening time to visit is July 4, when Nathan's holds a hot-dog-eating contest (the record gets broken every year; in 2007 it was 66 dogs in 12 minutes).

CAFÉ KASHKAR ADOLAT
Map pp196–7   Uighur $

☎ 718-743-3832; 1141 Brighton Beach Ave btwn 14th & 15th Sts, Brighton Beach; ☒ lunch & dinner; ⓔ B, Q to Brighton Beach

This tasty food from far western China is similar to Uzbek – lots of kebabs. A favorite is *lagman* (a lamb soup served with noodles and vegetables). Staff in this simple spot are patient with initiates to the world of Uighur.

QUEENS

Considering its ethnic diversity – Queens is the most diverse 'hood in the world, after all – the thrill of food really can tempt a detour across the East River to this often-missed and underrated borough. Many successful mom 'n' pop eateries in Manhattan only set up shop after testing the waters in areas like Flushing first.

LONG ISLAND CITY & ASTORIA

Long Island City's Vernon Blvd, a couple of blocks west of PS1 (p202) is up and coming, with newish eating options (pizza, Thai, Chinese, Italian).

Astoria teems with Greek, Mexican and Eastern European options – particularly under the elevated subway line on 31st St. Further south, Broadway (between 31st and

35th Sts) is something of a 'Greek row' of diners. Most who make it to Astoria eye the Bohemian Hall & Beer Garden (p298) for fresh pints of Czech beer – it also has food.

ELIA'S FISH CORNER Map pp200–1 Seafood $$
☎ 718-932-1510; 24-02 31st St; 🕑 dinner; Ⓜ N, W to Astoria Blvd
Take note of the counter of fresh fish as you walk into this Greek fish place on the corner (right under the elevated subway line) – that's your dinner. The chefs don't get fussy on details – you pick your fish, they grill (whole) your fish, you eat your fish. A host of juicy appetizers are on hand (the grilled octopus is good, and the scallops are particularly tasty). It also has Greek beer and wine.

SUNNYSIDE & WOODSIDE
Off the 7 train on the way towards Shea Stadium (home of the New York Mets baseball team), these two neighborhoods get missed by many on the food trail across Queens – too bad. There are plenty of choices two blocks north of the subway stops, along Sunnyside's Skillman Ave.

ACASA Map pp200–1 Romanian $$
☎ 718-651-1364; 48-06 Skillman Ave, Sunnyside; Ⓜ 7 to 46th St-Bliss St
For fresh meaty meals straight from Transylvania, this family fun spot delights the local Romanian community with *ciorba de burta* (tripe soup) and some mean *mamaglia* (Romanian polenta), with lamb pastrami and topped with a fried egg and sour cream. It's two blocks north of the subway, then two east on Skillman.

DONOVAN'S PUB Map pp200–1 Burgers $
☎ 718-429-9339; 5724 Roosevelt Ave, at 58th St; 🕑 lunch & dinner; Ⓜ 7 to Woodside-61st St
At this Woodside classic, gray-haired bartenders of this tavern-style pub under the tracks will pour your Guinness up front, and grandmas bring the juicy burgers and chubby fries in the family-friendly seating area in back.

JACKSON HEIGHTS
A bit further 'in,' Jackson Heights is Queens' most tightly packed smorgasbord of eating options. Cheaper, quicker eats – from tacos to chow mein – can be easily found along

Roosevelt Ave. More comfortable sit-down places of all stripes – Japanese, Colombian – are a block north along 37th Ave.

JACKSON DINER Map pp200–1 Indian $
☎ 718-672-1232; 37-47 74th St btwn Roosevelt Ave & 37th Ave; 🕑 lunch & dinner; Ⓜ 7 to 74th St-Broadway, E, F, R, V to Jackson Hts-Roosevelt Ave
This stylish converted diner is one of New York's best all-you-can-eat buffets, with a daily rotation of curries (eg goat, chicken, lamb, veggie) laid out with fresh naan bread, rice and sweets. The buffet, which runs from 11:30am to 4pm daily ($9 weekdays, $10 weekends), is worth the extra dollar or two over other cheapie buffets in the area. The diner is half a block from the subway stop, on the right-hand side.

FLUSHING
Some call Flushing 'Chinatown without the tourists.' Much of the area's inviting Chinese, Vietnamese, Korean and Malaysian restaurants are around the intersection of Main St and Roosevelt Ave. Finding food's not a problem.

SPICY & TASTY Map pp200–1 Chinese $
☎ 718-359-1601; 39-07 Prince St at 39th Ave; 🕑 lunch & dinner; Ⓜ 7 to Flushing-Main St
A block west of the subway – and away from the busy Main St – this modern Sichuan restaurant is a guaranteed tongueburner. Pick from a dozen appetizer choices in the front glass case – eggplant, bean curd, beef tongue, pork stomach. You may need to point unless your Chinese is good. Then add on some noodles from the menu. During lunch S&T has $5 set meals.

THE BRONX
Belmont, the Little Italy of the Bronx, where the movie *A Bronx Tale* was filmed, is the borough's most famous culinary enclave, filled with tempting trattorias and pizzerias. The area is centered on Arthur Ave, just south of Fordham University.

ROBERTO RESTAURANT
Map pp208–9 Italian $$
☎ 718-733-9503; 603 Crescent Ave btwn Arthur & Hughes Aves, Belmont; 🕑 lunch Mon-Fri, dinner Mon-Sat; Ⓜ B, D to Fordham Rd
Just off Arthur Ave (the 'real' Little Italy), Roberto has a great reputation; its fans

swear, with frightening passion, that it's New York's – not just Belmont's – best Italian restaurant. There's a no-reservations policy, so as the night wears on, lines congregate by the bar – for hours. It's well worth it. Ask for the chef's choice, and Roberto – hilariously festive – comes by and lights up your table with dish after dish of Northern Italian specialties, including swordfish steaks and veal cutlets. In nice weather, sidewalk seating is the way to go.

BRUCKNER BAR & GRILL
Map pp208–9   Sandwiches & Salads $
☎ 718-665-2001; 1 Bruckner Blvd at Third Ave, South Bronx; ☽ lunch & dinner; ⊚ 6 to 3rd Ave-138th St
Looking like a 100-year-old classic, with chipped-wood floors and historic photos of the area, this place is actually a new version of an elevator factory, with beer, wine and some surprisingly good sandwiches and burgers; there's a pool-table room to the side with some live music and comedy. It's nearly under the Third Ave Bridge overpass.

DRINKING & NIGHTLIFE

top picks

- **Little Branch** (p291) Modern speakeasy, retro cocktails.
- **Ear Inn** (p288) A vintage dive bar in a historic setting.
- **Holiday Cocktail Lounge** (p290) Cheap booze and nostalgia galore.
- **Bohemian Hall & Beer Garden** (p298) Raise a glass to the Old World at this classic Czech bar.
- **Gutter** (p297) Brewskis and bowling in Midwestern style.
- **Campbell Apartment** (p293) A 1920s throwback set in a once-secret pied-a-terre.
- **Upright Citizens Brigade Theatre** (p300) Edgy improv and sketch comedy from old pros and rising stars alike.
- **Banjo Jim's** (p306) Bluegrass lives at this hillbilly bar.
- **St Nick's Pub** (p305) Fresh jazz jams nightly.
- **Smalls Jazz Club** (p306) A downtown dive with an eclectic nightly lineup.
- **Barbes** (p307) European style and international music at this Brooklyn wonder.
- **Galapagos Art Space** (p299) Modern vaudeville in a new-fangled Brooklyn cabaret space.

What's your recommendation? www.lonelyplanet.com/new-york-city

New York only gets going once the sun sets. Sure, for many folks nighttime NYC is all about highbrow cultural goings-on, but who said you can't learn from having a shot of Jack Daniels and singing George Strait tunes with a live country band in a sticky-floor dive? Or managing to squeeze past velvet ropes guarded by beefy bouncers to reach subterranean star-studded nightclubs? Or laughing at the raunchy jokes of local comics looking for slots on *Saturday Night Live*? Of course the boozy nights of New York aren't all so hedonistic. New York is, essentially, the home of jazz, and (despite some reports to the contrary) it's still alive and kicking in tiny Village bars and Harlem speakeasies. And no one doubts the art behind a well-mixed cocktail at one of the 'secret' boutique bars that post no signs for ill-informed passersby in scenester 'hoods. If only dawn could hold off a few hours longer.

This chapter covers late-night fun that usually involves intoxication – split into sections on plain-ol' bars and spots where it comes with song and dance or jokes. For information on opera, theater, Broadway musicals and dance, see p310. For gay- and lesbian-oriented activities del noche, see p342.

OPENING HOURS

Most bars stay open until the legal closing time of 4am, though a few stop at 2am; opening times vary, but some start as early as 8am! Nothing like starting a day of touring with a strong Bloody Mary, right?

HOW MUCH

A beer in a bottle starts with happy-hour bottles of Budweiser for $2. Most places will charge $5 or $6 for a draft of Brooklyn Lager or Samuel Adams – it can reach $10 or more in fancier places. Cocktails or glasses of wine start at $8, but at places that specialize in them, expect to pay $12 to $15 minimum.

TIPPING

If you grab a beer or gin-and-tonic at the bar, bartenders will expect at least a $1 tip *per drink* served. Sit-down bars with waitstaff may expect more of a standard 15% to 20% tip, as in restaurants, particularly if you snacked along with your boozing.

BARS

Finally, New York's greatest highlight: the bars. Bars of all shapes and eras, where you come as you are, or dress in Prada just to have a seat for a Manhattan in the city it's named for. Yes, come and drink! But know that when you raise a pint or glass or tumbler in New York, it's no simple escape – with every sip you become a part of one of the world's greatest histories of alcohol consumption.

Considering Manhattan's shape resembles a bottle, and that its name is thought by some to derive from the Munsee word *manahactadienk* (place for inebriation), it shouldn't be surprising that New York's long been a city known for bad behavior, drunkenness and other assorted late-night tomfoolery. In fact, some 20 years after the city was founded, Peter Stuyvesant lashed out that a quarter of New Amsterdam's buildings were taverns!

By the 1880s, with the help of newly arrived Irish and German immigrants, taverns lined streets like Ave A and the Bowery and over 100 breweries dotted Manhattan and Brooklyn. At the time, 'black-and-tan' underground bars were so dangerous only the armed dare go. Things got a bit chummier by the end of the century, as vaudeville sprung from the drunkenness at places like Tony Pastor's New 14th Street Theatre.

When the prohibition era came, speakeasies dotted around the city defied the ban. With a depleted male population after WWII, liberated women started joining the public world of tipsiness, though some bars tried resisting: McSorley's (p291) stuck 'no women' signs on its door until 1970. Singles and gay bars reflected the sexual experimentation of the '70s, until AIDS ended much of bars' 'don't ask, don't tell' dark-corner action. Smoking's now gone from bars, and new bars plod on with new cocktail twists, or (in a speakeasy throwback) without signs at all. Others happily add dorm-break joys like Skee-Ball or overtake rooftop decks for unrivaled skyline views.

This section only captures the rim of the glass. Things change fast, so keep an eye out for huddled smokers outside an unsigned doorway. You never know what's going on inside until you check it out.

LOWER MANHATTAN & TRIBECA

Tie-loosening financial types don't always bolt for the 'burbs when 5pm hits. Around the South St Seaport and Wall St there are a smattering of drinking holes to pop into if you need a midday break. Tribeca (and SoHo, its neighbor to the north) has always been a good place for see-and-be-seen lounges, old-fashioned pubs and candlelit nooks great for souped-up chats – and the drinks tend to be stirred with a bit more precision than over on the East side.

BRANDY LIBRARY Map pp72–3 Cocktail Bar
☎ 212-226-5545; www.brandylibrary.com; 25 N Moore St at Varick St; ⊕ 1 to Franklin St
When sipping means serious business, it's easy to settle into this library, with soothing reading lamps and club chairs facing backlit, floor-to-ceiling, bottle-filled shelves. Go for top-shelf cognac, malt scotch or 90-year-old brandies (prices range from $9 to $280). Call ahead about tastings and other events.

RISE Map pp72–3 Cocktail Bar
☎ 212-344-0800; Battery Park City Ritz-Carlton, 14th fl, 2 West St at Battery Pl; ⊕ N, R, W to Rector St
Even $18 martinis won't make you think twice about hanging at this view bar at the Ritz-Carlton (p349), where the sleek, high-up lounge affords spectacular vistas of sunsets over New York Harbor, plus tasty cocktails and a few snacks (five mini burgers costs $28).

SMITH & MILLS Map pp72–3 Cocktail Bar
☎ 212-219-8568; 71 N Moore St, btwn Hudson & Greenwich Sts; ⊕ 1 to Franklin St
Teensy and stylish, this bar feels like a kooky professor's lair for kicking back with fellow kooky professors over $12 cocktails. There's a trace of antiques, with plush booths on well-worn wood floors and a few good snack choices.

ULYSSES Map pp72–3 Irish Pub
☎ 212-482-0400; 95 Pearl St (or 58 Stone St); ⊕ 2, 3 to Wall St
Big with old-school financial types, Ulysses is an Irish/modern hybrid, with a long bar and a kitchen serving oysters and sandwiches; it's best when you're nursing your $6 Harp or Guinness on the wood picnic tables out on cobbled Stone St. The folks here run a shuttle every 20 minutes to their two other bars – Puck Fair (Map pp88–9; ☎ 212-431-1200; 298 Lafayette St btwn E Houston & Prince Sts) in SoHo and Swift (Map pp88–9; ☎ 212-242-9502; 34 E 4th St btwn Bowery & Lafayette St) in NoHo.

ANOTHEROOM Map pp72–3 Lounge
☎ 212-226-1418; 249 W Broadway btwn Beach & N Moore Sts; ⊕ 1 to Franklin St
This industrial-chic, cement-floor place with a sidewalk table or two is the sort of place you stop for an afternoon drink you hadn't been planning on. It's all beer and wine – no mixed drinks – with chalkboard scrawl advertising the daily catch for mostly middle-aged Tribeca-sters.

JEREMY'S ALE HOUSE Map pp72–3 Sports Bar
☎ 212-964-3537; 228 Front St at Dover St; ⊕ J, M, Z to Chambers St, 2, 3 to Fulton St, 4, 5, 6 to Brooklyn Bridge-City Hall
At this obnoxious, but fun, warehouse bar, ties and bras hang from the ceiling, and

---

NYC DRINKS

You'll want to enjoy mixed drinks in the city where the term 'cocktail' was born. The city buzzes on an ever-growing list of cocktails: martinis, cosmopolitans, appletinis, lycheetinis, saketinis, *mojitos* (rum, mint, sugar and lime), *margaritas* (Mexican tequila with lime and salt) and *cachaça* (Brazilian liquor with sugarcane).

After trailing off for much of the 20th century, New York's beer scene has rebounded, to a degree, with the Williamsburg-based Brooklyn Brewery and Sixpoint Craft Ales, which churn out lagers and pilsners found in bottles and taps around the city.

In the past three decades, New York State's wines have exploded in numbers – the upstate Finger Lakes region is home to more than 60 wineries, while Long Island's wineries (p375) are closer to the city. Some bars carry regional wines, or you can grab a bottle at Vintage New York (p221).

cheap pints come in Styrofoam. It gets going early – try 8am on weekdays – but is more popular for post-work goings-on and bar-food snacking (fried clams, onion rings).

SOHO, NOHO & NOLITA

SoHo tends to be more about designer shopping. If you don't find what you're looking for to tipsy up, head a few blocks east on Nolita's narrow streets.

CIRCA TABAC Map pp88–9   Cigar Bar
☎ 212-941-1781; 32 Watts St btwn Sixth Ave & Thompson St; ◉ A, C, E, 1 to Canal St
One of a few bars left in the city where you can still smoke (and are encouraged to do so), this stylish art-deco lounge offers more than 150 types of smokes, mainly global cigars. Its specialty drink includes a pucker-inducing Gingersnap (ginger-infused vodka, crystallized ginger and champagne).

PEGU CLUB Map pp88–9   Cocktail Bar
☎ 212-473-7348; 77 W Houston St btwn W Broadway & Wooster Sts; ◉ B, D, F, V to Broadway-Lafayette St
Loosely inspired by a British colonial bar from the Burma days, Pegu is a slick upstairs cocktail lounge with a touch of Asian wall-dressings, a slightly dressed-up crowd and candlelit booths. The rum- and gin-based cocktails are knockouts, particularly the inspired Earl Grey MarTEAni (cheesy name sure, but tea-infused gin plus lemon juice and egg white is tasty).

top picks

DIVES

Some places where it might not be best to drag mom along.
- Ear Inn (right) Good-clean spot in historic home of George Washington's aide.
- Holiday Cocktail Lounge (p290) Old Ukrainian guys, fake plants and vomiting NYU students in the East Village.
- Milano's (right) Old and young clink cans of Pabst in Nolita.
- Montero's (p296) This Brooklyn Heights nautical bar gives a boozy head start on sea legs.
- Subway Inn (p294) Marilyn Monroe came here once – cheap drinks forever! In Midtown East.

EAR INN Map pp88–9   Dive Bar
☎ 212-219-8026; 326 Spring St btwn Greenwich & Washington Sts; ◉ C, E to Spring St
A block from the Hudson River, this old dive isn't just great for downing beers, eating shepherd's pie or hearing live jazz. It's historic, babes. Gradually called the 'Ear' due to a decayed 'B' on an old 'Bar' sign, it's an 1817 house that used to belong to James Brown (a George Washington aide, not Soul Brother No 1) – it's said Brown is the black man seen in the famous *Crossing the Delaware* painting. Drinking game: ponder the legend, drink, ponder some more.

MILANO'S Map pp88–9   Dive Bar
☎ 212-226-8844; 51 E Houston St btwn Mulberry & Mott Sts; ◉ B, D, F, V to Broadway-Lafayette St
For nearly a century, hole-in-the-wall Milano's has withstood the hipster onslaught of Nolita and stayed true to its divey self (eg potato chips behind the worn, wooden bar and $3 Pabst Blue Ribbon beers). Grizzled vets and curious youngsters mix it up easily, bonding over pints and a great, old-school stacked jukebox with offerings from Tony Bennett to the Chieftains.

CHIBI'S BAR Map pp88–9   Sake Bar
☎ 212-274-0025; 238 Mott St btwn Prince & Spring Sts; ◉ 6 to Spring St
Named for the resident French bulldog, this tiny, romantic sake bar has a delicately curved wooden bar with ice-blue stools, plus a lounge area to one side. It works its magic through smooth jazz sounds (live on Sundays) and the dangerously delicious flavors of specialty sakes, saketinis and good snack options that go beyond the usual edamame.

CHINATOWN & LITTLE ITALY

The realm of tourists, overpriced Italian restaurants and underpriced noodle houses, the overlapping 'hoods of Chinatown and Little Italy have just a few standouts.

MARE CHIARO Map p94   Dive Bar
☎ 212-226-9345; 176½ Mulberry St btwn Broome & Grand Sts; ◉ B, D to Grand St
Frank Sinatra liked this 100-year-old Little Italy hang, which was also used as a backdrop for scenes in *The Godfather III* and *Donnie Brasco*. And you'll like it for hanging around, even as Little Italy slowly disap-

pears. The gruff, old-school bartenders add to the charm, as does the odd mix of wide-eyed tourists, crusty regulars and the overflow of hipsters.

WINNIE'S Map p94 Karaoke
☎ 212-732-2384; 104 Bayard St btwn Baxter & Mulberry Sts; ◉ J, M, Z, N, Q, R, W, 6 to Canal St

Performing drunken, embarrassing karaoke at this tiny Chinatown dive is a rite of passage for New Yorkers. The red booths are always packed, and the disgusting cocktails are ever potent (eg the Abortion, a mixture of Sambuca and Baileys). Sing your lungs out ($1 per song) before a weird karaoke movie screen playing '80s montages, certainly at odds with the Hall & Oates song you chose.

LOWER EAST SIDE

Outside Manhattan, Williamsburg continues its rise on the indie-rock scene, but the Lower East Side still hangs onto its status as coolest 'hood on the island. Some bars are overpopulated by LES tourists, but locals still adore newfound clubs that stage Manhattan's next indie-rock kings. You'll easily find something here, with booze and beer usually a lot cheaper than in much of Manhattan – just walk up and down the tiny blocks and peek in.

BARRIO CHINO Map p98 Cocktail Bar
☎ 212-228-6710; 253 Broome St btwn Ludlow & Orchard Sts; ◉ F, J, M, Z to Delancey-Essex Sts

An eatery that spills easily into a party scene, with an airy Havana-meets-Beijing vibe and a focus on fine sipping tequilas (the menu offers 50, some breaking $25 per shot). Or stick with fresh blood-orange or black-plum margaritas, guacamole and chicken tacos.

EAST SIDE COMPANY BAR
Map p98 Cocktail Bar
☎ 212-614-7408; 49 Essex St at Grand St; ◉ F, J, M, Z to Delancey-Essex Sts

Run by the owners of the overly precious 'guest-list only' Milk & Honey, this tiny speakeasy sort of joint pours inventive $11 cocktails (lots of rye). You don't need a reservation, just walk through the plywood doorway and step down into a low, tin-ceilinged bar that arches, as if you're walking onto a dream subway car. There are cozy booths and DJ action in back, an inviting industrial bar in front.

NURSE BETTIE Map p98 Cocktail Bar
☎ 917-434-9072; www.nursebettieles.com; 106 Norfolk St btwn Delancey & Rivington Sts; ◉ F, J, M, Z to Delancey-Essex Sts

Something a bit new is going on with this pint-sized, charmer: plenty of roaming space between slick '00s-modern lounges and '50s-style ice cream–shop stools and painted pin-ups on the brick walls. Cocktails get freaky: everything from fruity vodka and brandies to a bubble-gum martini. You can bring food in, and many won-over locals do.

WELCOME TO THE JOHNSONS
Map p98 Dive Bar
☎ 212-420-9911; 123 Rivington St btwn Essex & Norfolk Sts; ◉ F, J, M, Z to Delancey-Essex Sts

Set up like a '70s game room – a bit sleazier than the one on *That '70s Show* – the Johnsons' irony still hasn't worn off for the devoted 20-something crowd. It could have something to do with the $2 Buds till 9pm, the pool table, the blasting garage-rock jukebox or the plastic-covered sofas. Too bad it smells like Bigfoot's ass on occasion.

CLANDESTINO Map p98 DJ Dive
☎ 212-475-5505; 35 Canal St; ◉ F to East Broadway

Located on the edge of Chinatown, this unguarded 'polite dive' has no hidden purpose – just cheap pints (Six Point beer goes for $5), carefully centered candles along the bar and tables, and some good snacks for a less done-up East Side crew that usually drops by to meet people they know. In nice weather, there's a small patio.

MAGICIAN Map p98 Jukebox Flirts
☎ 212-673-7851; 118 Rivington St btwn Essex & Norfolk Sts; ◉ F, J, M, Z to Delancey-Essex Sts

An unassuming storefront with office-style blinds on the window opens to a great, non-grungy, under-appreciated neighborhood bar that's sometimes seen as a backup to Welcome to the Johnsons across the street. It holds its own though, with an eclectic jukebox (Duke Ellington to the Cure), mint-green wood chairs and cheap drinks.

BARRAMUNDI Map p98 Lounge
☎ 212-529-6900; 67 Clinton St btwn Stanton & Rivington Sts; ◉ F, J, M, Z to Delancey-Essex Sts

This Australian-owned arty place fills an old tenement building with convivial booths, reasonably priced drinks (including some Aussie imports) and some cool tree-trunk tables. Happy hour runs 6pm to 9pm.

MILK & HONEY Map p98 — Secret Bar
www.mlkhny.com; 134 Eldridge btwn Delancey & Broome Sts; ⊖ B, D to Grand St
You can't knock the '40s-era low-key ambience of the most infamous bar on the LES – the cocktails are superb, the staff are even friendly – it's just that you have to know people to get in. No number listed, no sign outside but a graffitied door. Go, if you can, but we can't knock the feeling that the exclusivity is pretty lame. (Or try the owners' open East Side Company Bar, p289, or Little Branch, opposite).

EAST VILLAGE
The further east you go – away from gentrifying, terrifying Third Ave – the looser it gets. You can't walk a block without happening on a dirty dive filled with NYU students or post-grads with lofty goals, or lounges pulling in interested outsiders wanting booze in New York punk rock's old HQ. On weekends, elbow space isn't an option.

D.B.A. Map p104 — Beer Nerds
☎ 212-475-5097; 41 First Ave btwn 2nd & 3rd Sts; ⊖ F, V to Lower East Side-2nd Ave
Ever tried to pick up Led Zeppelin IV at an indie CD store? You get the same jeers if you try for a Sam Adams at this testosterone-

top picks
FUN & GAMES
When sitting and sipping isn't enough, some bars offer karaoke mics, games and outright silliness.
- Barcade (p176) Vintage arcade games line the sprawling East Williamsburg bar.
- Crocodile Lounge (p293) Free pizza and Skee-ball brings out cheapskate East Villagers.
- Union Hall (p298) Behind the library books, sign up for the (two-hour) wait to try out the two indoor bocce courts at this Park Slope place.
- Iggy's (p295) No stage, just a pass-around karaoke mic for a night of Bud and howling at the Upper East's polite veneer.
- Winnie's (p289) Raunchy Chinatown bar with nightly karaoke backed by cheesy videos.

fueled, dark-wood bar built for beer nerds disguised as the hip. (We mean that as a compliment.) There are 125 beers here, plus 130 single-malt scotches and a few dozen tequilas. There's a tiny plastic-chair patio in back, but most action is near the taps.

HOLIDAY COCKTAIL LOUNGE Map p104 — Dive Bar
☎ 212-777-9637; 75 St Marks Pl btwn First & Second Aves; ⊖ 6 to Astor Pl
No $12 cocktails at this long-term classic bad-behavior HQ – just a mix of penny-pinching alcoholic guys, students on a budget and dive-hounds who find crotchety service, a mix of nostalgia and $3 beers the perfect night out.

NUBLU Map p104 — DJ Bar
☎ 212-979-9925; www.nublu.net; 62 Ave C; ⊖ F, V to Lower East Side-2nd Ave
Not at all grunge – and that's the point – Nublu is an unsigned loungy come-together (look for the blue light outside) that looks like a 1974 Brazilian version of a Japanese ryokan. It's best in summer, when the back patio's open, but live shows and spinning DJs – who go world at times, but not irritatingly – put the soundtrack to a surprisingly unpretentious dance/chat/hangout scene.

AMSTERDAM BILLIARDS Map p104 — Games & Suds
☎ 212-995-0333; 110 E 11th St at Fourth Ave; ⊖ L, N, Q, R, W, 4, 5, 6 to 14th St-Union Sq
The long-time Upper West Side icon of the cue ball moved its green-table HQ to the Village. It offers 26 tables, $24 private 'pool clinics,' tourneys and just plain ol' gaming with beer and cocktails – only some of the regulars are dorky NYU students.

11TH STREET BAR Map p104 — Irish Pub
☎ 212-982-3929; www.11thstbar.com; 510 E 11th St btwn Aves A & B; ⊖ F, V to Lower East Side-2nd Ave
When a Liverpool game's on, the place may go nuts, but at other, non-football times it's about the homiest watering hole in the 'hood, with soft sofas, exposed-brick walls, pressed-tin ceiling and candlelit tables. There's traditional Irish music jams on Sunday evening.

KGB BAR Map p104 — Lit Bar
☎ 212-505-3360; www.kgbbar.com; 85 E 4th St; ⊖ F, V to Lower East Side-2nd Ave, 6 to Bleecker St

The propaganda posters and deepest commie-red walls of KGB long pre-date the retro tongue-in-cheek of 'CCCP' T-shirts you see on St Marks Pl. Set up in a former 1930s HQ for the Ukrainian socialist party, it's a lit bar, with interesting readings for free – more new fiction than Marx – several nights a week.

MCSORLEY'S OLD ALE HOUSE
Map p104   Old-Time Bar

☎ 212-473-9148; 15 E 7th St btwn Second & Third Aves; ❻ 6 to Astor Pl

Around since 1854, McSorley's feels far removed from the East Village veneer of cool: you're more likely to drink with firemen, Wall St refugees and a few tourists. But (didn't you know?) that's become cool again. It's hard to beat the cobwebs and sawdust floors and flip waiters who slap down two mugs of the house's ale for every one ordered.

DECIBEL Map p104   Sake Bar

☎ 212-979-2733; 240 E 9th St btwn Second & Third Aves; ❻ 6 to Astor Pl

Barely signed, this dark basement sake bar is an East Village icon. Once you get past the line (on weekends: certain) you may wonder whether the chatty staff think they know you. Up front it feels like a 19th-century Japanese bar, with a few seats wrapped around the sake bottle–backed bar. In back, there are proper tables and more sake – the lychee martini pulls no punches (two and you're KO-ed).

PDT Map p104   Secret Bar

☎ 212-614-0386; www.pdtnyc.com; 113 St Marks Pl btwn First Ave & A Ave; ❻ L to 1st Ave

The worst-kept secret in New York: PDT (or 'Please Don't Tell') is a basement bar reached via a telephone booth – Superman would like it – inside tiny Crif Hot Dogs. It's a compact place. Call ahead for a reservation, or have a hot dog while waiting. It's no East Village dive – well-swirled cocktails go for $12.

STANDINGS BAR Map p104   Sports Bar

☎ 212-420-0671; 43 E 7th St; ❻ 6 to Astor Pl

Why is it always the little guy that makes the biggest plays? If you have to see a game, this step-in/step-out, box-like bar has a wall of TV screens, updated season standings on chalkboards, changing mi-crobrews on tap, and free stuff (pizza on Friday, bagels on Sunday).

GREENWICH VILLAGE, WEST VILLAGE & THE MEATPACKING DISTRICT

The word in the West Village is 'west' – the further towards the Hudson you go, the more likely you are to sidestep the frat-boy scenes found around the NYU campus. (There are a handful of exceptions, of course, as well as a few worthy gay bars, listed on p343). Generally, though, it's easier to find a panacea in the water holes on and off the crooked lanes west of Sixth Ave. Just to the north, the Meatpacking District is strictly contemporary in vibe, with sprawling, modern spaces boasting long cocktail lists, velvet-roped entrances and dins that'll rattle your brain. Maybe a drink will help.

VOL DE NUIT Map p110   Beer Nerds

☎ 212-982-3388; 148 W 4th St; ❻ A, C, E, B, D, F, V to W 4th St-Washington Sq

Even all the NYU students can't ruin this – a cozy Belgian beer bar, with a few dozen zonkers like Lindemans Framboise (strawberry beer!) and frites to share in the front patio seats, the lounge, the communal wood tables or under the dangling red lights at the bar.

BRASS MONKEY Map p110   Chill Bar

☎ 212-675-6686; 55 Little W 12th St at Washington St; ❻ A, C, E to 14th St, L to 8th Ave

While most Meatpacking District bars tend toward the chic, the Monkey is more for beer lovers than those worrying about what shoes to wear. At first step in, it's at-ease and down-to-earth, with squeaking wood floors and a nice long list of beers and scotch.

LITTLE BRANCH Map p110   Cocktail Bar

☎ 212-929-4360; 20 Seventh Ave S at Leroy St; ❻ 1 to Houston St

Down from Seventh in an unassuming, gray, triangular building, this alluring, stylish speakeasy keeps the lights and jazz low, so the focus in two- and four-person booths is on the gin, rum and scotch cocktails, all stirred with precision. If undecided, ask for a refreshing South Side, with gin straight-up, plus lime and mint.

APT Map p110 DJ Bar

☎ 212-414-4245; 419 W 13 St btwn Washington & Greenwich Sts; ◉ A, C, E to 14th St, L to 8th Ave

APT as in your ultra-stylish, ultra-rich friend's apartment – the door isn't marked (of course), but opens into a decadently decorated flat with rooms in gold, deep purple and black-and-white. It's a long-surviving haven for a DJ-fuelled Meatpacking crowd with three aims: looking good, dancing in the basement and getting drunk (in that order).

WHITE HORSE TAVERN

Map p110 Old-Time Bar

☎ 212-243-9260; 567 Hudson St at 11th St; ◉ 1 to Christopher St-Sheridan Sq

It's a bit on the tourist trail, but that doesn't dampen the century-old, pubby dark-wood, tin-ceiling atmosphere where Dylan Thomas had his last drink (too many beers led to his 1953 death), a tipsy Jack Kerouac got kicked out, and we had a friendly NBA debate with the 'South Park guys' one night. Sit at the long oak bar inside or on sidewalk tables.

PLUNGE Map p110 Rooftop Bar

☎ 212-206-6700; Hotel Gansevoort, 18 Ninth Ave at 13th St; ◉ A, C, E to 14th St, L to 8th Ave

Located in the 15th-floor penthouse of the hopelessly trendy Hotel Gansevoort, this Meatpacking District star affords great views of the Hudson River in a Miami Beach–type club with long lines. Try to get here early,

top picks

DRINKS WITH A VIEW

Occasionally it's good to have a little air with that vodka-and-tonic.

- 230 Fifth (p294) This ex-hotel penthouse's deck looks over Midtown sprawl.
- Harry's at Water Taxi Beach (p298) Summer 'beach' with mojitos and volleyball overlooking the UN from Queens.
- Plunge (above) Brave the trendy crush in the Meatpacking District for an eyeful of NJ.
- Rise (p287) Hudson views from a swanky perch at Manhattan's south tip.
- Top of the Tower (p294) Date turf for old-timers in Midtown Beekman Tower's art-deco rooftop bar.

and on a weeknight if possible, or else risk being packed like a well-dressed sardine with hordes of scenester-searching wannabes.

MARIE'S CRISIS Map p110 Sing-Along

☎ 212-243-9323; 59 Grove St btwn Seventh Ave S & Bleecker St; ◉ 1 to Christopher St-Sheridan Sq

Aging Broadway queens, wide-eyed out-of-town gay boys, giggly tourist girls and various other fans of musical theater assemble around the piano here and take turns belting out campy numbers, often joined by the entire crowd. It's old-school fun, no matter how jaded you were when you went in.

NEVADA SMITH'S Map p110 Sports Bar

☎ 212-982-2591; www.nevadasmiths.net; 74 Third Ave; ◉ L to 3rd Ave, N, Q, R, W, 4, 5, 6 to 14th St-Union Sq

New York's greatest soccer bar gets filled with European expats and other assorted fist-pumping adult males in sports jerseys. Some 100 matches get played a week on the wall-to-wall flat-screen TVs (just past the signed jersey of Ronaldinho). There's beer too.

CHELSEA

Thought to be mostly the domain of sleek cruising lounges for gorgeous gay men as well as massive mega-nightclubs for all, there is still some variety here, particularly around Ninth Ave, where you can find lit bars, Irish pubs, sophisticated martini-making lounges and dives going for the plain ol' pint.

HALF KING Map p116 Lit Bar

☎ 212-462-4300; 505 W 23rd St at Tenth Ave; ◉ C, E to 23rd St

A unique marriage of cozy beer pub, pasta kitchen and casual writers' lair; you'll often experience top-notch literary readings in this wood-accented, candlelit watering hole. (A Perfect Storm author Sebastian Junger is one of the owners.) It's best when weather allows sidewalk-seat and back-patio action.

PETER MCMANUS TAVERN

Map p116 Old-Time Bar

☎ 212-929-9691; 152 Seventh Ave at 19th St; ◉ A, C, E to 14th St

Pouring drafts since the 1930s, this family-run dive is something of a museum to the world of the McManuses: photos of yesteryear, an old telephone booth and Tiffany glass. There's also greasy bar food to eat at the cute green booths. Hurrah for the McManuses!

GYM Map p116 | Sports Bar
☎ 212-337-2439; 167 Eighth Ave btwn 18th & 19th Sts; ⊖ A, C, E to 14th St
Hey, a gay sports bar! The 3400-sq-ft space with a slick mahogany bar, brick walls and two patio areas goes for a bit more style than your average Bud Lite neon-sign place – but it is about the game. There are nine big-screen TVs, plus Foosball and pool tables.

UNION SQUARE, FLATIRON DISTRICT & GRAMERCY

In this mix-match of neighborhoods that fill the space as downtown turns midtown, look for stylish hotel lounges, fancy-eatery bars and a few down-and-dirty basics thrown in for good measure. If you need a regular-guy Irish pub, look on Third Ave north of 14th St.

SAPA Map p120 | Cocktail Bar
☎ 212-929-1800; 43 W 24th St btwn Fifth & Sixth Aves; ⊖ N, R, W, 6 to 23rd St
Thanks to an inspired, modern look by award-winning designers, the stylish bar at this French-Vietnamese eatery has become a Flatiron hotspot – drawing not only local professionals but the occasional celeb (some scenes from 2008's *The Accidental Husband* were filmed here). Cocktails tend toward the fresh and fab, with great deals at happy hour.

CROCODILE LOUNGE
Map p120 | Games & Booze
☎ 212-477-7747; 325 E 14th St btwn First & Second Aves; ⊖ L to 1st Ave
Williamsburg comes to Manhattan! The Brooklyn success story – 20-something hideout Alligator Lounge (p178) with free pizza – has set up a 14th St outpost hauling in plenty of East Villagers seeking free dinner and some Skee-Ball and a few unusual microbrews on tap.

OLD TOWN BAR & RESTAURANT
Map p120 | Old-Time Bar
☎ 212-529-6732; 45 E 18th St; ⊖ L, N, Q, R, W, 4, 5, 6 to 14th St-Union Sq

It still looks like 1892 in here, with the original tile floors and tin ceilings – the Old Town is an 'old world' drinking-man's classic (and woman's: Madonna lit up at the bar here, when lighting up was still legal, in her *Bad Girl* video). There's cocktails around, but most come for an afternoon beer and burger ($8.50), both very good.

PETE'S TAVERN Map p120 | Old-Time Bar
☎ 212-473-7676; 129 E 18th St at Irving Pl; ⊖ L, N, Q, R, W, 4, 5, 6 to 14th St-Union Sq
Around since 1864, this dark and atmospheric watering hole is a New York classic – all pressed tin and carved wood and an air of literary history. You can get a respectable burger here, plus choose from more than 15 draft beers. The crowd draws a mix of post-theater couples, Irish expats and no-nonsense NYU students.

PROOF Map p120 | Sports Bar
☎ 212-228-4200; 239 Third Ave; ⊖ L, N, Q, R, W, 4, 5, 6 to 14th St-Union Sq
All sports, but a little style despite the occasional beer pong game, this two-floor bar gets serious with all sports – we've seen Texas football fans jumping on the floor to annoy Oklahoma fans in the basement (OU won) – but isn't a completely a frat-boy hangout.

MIDTOWN EAST & FIFTH AVENUE

The massive belly of Manhattan covers about everyone – cheesy tourist, barely-legal suburbanite, high-class hipster, you name it. In the blocks east of Times Square, things get a bit more buttoned-up–businessfolk and *New Yorker*–subscriber than to the west. Some of these places rank among Manhattan's most atmospheric, though, such as bevvies in Bryant Park or a Florentine-inspired hideaway.

CAMPBELL APARTMENT
Map p126 | '20s Lounge
☎ 212-953-0409; 15 Vanderbilt Ave at 43rd St; ⊖ S, 4, 5, 6, 7 to 42nd St-Grand Central
Party like it's 1928! This hidden-away, sublime spot in Grand Central was once the home of a '20s railroad magnate fond of fussy European details, velvet, mahogany and Florentine-style carpets. Reach it from the lift beside the Oyster Bar or the stairs to the West Balcony.

KING COLE BAR Map p126   Cocktail Bar

☎ 212-753-4500; 2 E 55th St at Fifth Ave; ◉ E, V to 5th Ave-53rd St

Pretend life's posh at the St Regis Hotel's ultra-lux bar, named for the devilish 1906 mural behind the bar (you may have seen it in *The Devil Wears Prada*). The bar's still glowing from a $400K restoration in 2007. They'll get it paid back with high-priced drinks, like the $20 'Red Snapper' (apparently New York's first Bloody Mary). Dress up, kids.

SUBWAY INN Map p126   Dive Bar

☎ 212-223-8929; 143 E 60th St btwn Lexington & Third Aves; ◉ 4, 5, 6 to 59th St

Booze in this part of town for this cheap? Count us in. Occupying its own world across from Bloomingdale's (p236), this old-geezer watering hole is a classic cheap-booze spot that, despite the classic rock and worn red booths, harkens to long-past days when Marilyn Monroe dropped in.

230 FIFTH Map p126   Rooftop Bar

☎ 212-725-4300; 230 Fifth Ave at 27th St; ◉ N, R, W, 6 to 28th St

Filling up the penthouse and 22,000-sq-ft roof of a former hotel, the 230 has a Studio 54 throwback lounge look inside – but who stays there? Outside, plants line the patio's sprawl that looks north towards the Empire State Building. As a club it's a bit off – drinks come in plastic cups – but views are superb and they hand out robes if it's chilly out.

TOP OF THE TOWER Map p126   Rooftop Bar

☎ 212-980-4796; 3 Mitchell Pl at First Ave, Beekman Tower; ◉ 6 to 51st St

Hosting anniversary dates for half a century (and plenty of old-timers are still coming), the classy Beekman Tower's rooftop bar and restaurant puts its tables by the big windows that look over Queens' retro Pepsi-Cola sign and Midtown's twinkling soul. There are outdoor seats too, you smoking heathen.

GINGER MAN Map p126   Snack Pub

☎ 212-532-3740; www.gingerman-ny.com; 11 E 36th St btwn Fifth & Madison Aves; ◉ 6 to 33rd St

A great Murray Hill beer post, this high-ceilinged, handsome pub is all about good beer, good snacks and the suits who come to take part. There are well over 100 bottled beers, but opt for the five-dozen draft choices (particularly the rare cask ales).

top picks

SPORTS BARS

'I just want somewhere to watch the damn game!' A few goodies with more character than ESPN Zone in Times Sq.

- **Gym** (p293) Anything's possible in NYC: a gay sports bar that's *really* a sports bar (Chelsea).
- **Nevada Smith's** (p292) Soccer, er, real football, in the East Village.
- **Proof** (p293) Best bet for a bring-a-date sports bar (Gramercy).
- **Standings Bar** (p291) Sometimes the tiniest hearts beat the loudest (East Village).
- **Stan's Sports Bar** (see the boxed text, p298) Long live the Yankees (but not elbow room) in the Bronx.

MIDTOWN WEST & TIMES SQUARE

The Midtown West bar scene is made up of everything from sleazy dive bars to slick, cozy lounges. The ones that range around Seventh Avenue, Times Square and Hell's Kitchen are within easy striking distance of Broadway theaters – an ideal spot for your group's post-show commentary.

LOBBY LOUNGE Map pp134–5   Cocktail Bar

☎ 212-805-8876; www.mandarinoriental.com; 35th fl, Mandarin Oriental New York, 80 Columbus Circle at 60th St; ◉ A, B, C, D, 1 to 59th St-Columbus Circle

The Mandarin hotel is super swank, and its lobby bar does feel like you're in…well, in a hotel lobby, but the comfy lounge seats look out from the 35th floor, over the twinkling lights of buildings along the south end of Central Park – amazing. A martini goes for $19.

JIMMY'S CORNER Map pp134–5   Dive Bar

☎ 212-221-9510; 140 W 44th St; ◉ N, Q, R, W, 1, 2, 3, 7 to 42nd St-Times Sq, B, D, F, V to 42nd St-Bryant Park

This skinny, welcoming, completely unpretentious dive off Times Sq is run by an old boxing trainer, as if you wouldn't guess by all the framed photos of boxing greats (and lesser-known fighters too). The jukebox covers Stax to Miles Davis (plus Lionel Ritchie's most regretful moments), kept low enough for post-work gangs to chat away.

RUDY'S Map pp134-5 Dive Bar
☎ 212-974-9169; 627 Ninth Ave; ⊖ A, C, E to 42nd St-Port Authority
The big pantless pig in a red jacket out front marks Hell's Kitchen's best divey mingler, with $7 pitchers of Rudy's two beers, half-circle booths covered in red duct tape, and free hot dogs! A mix of folks come to flirt or watch muted Knicks games as classic rock plays.

KEMIA BAR Map pp134-5 DJ Bar
☎ 212-582-3200; www.kemiabarny.com; 630 Ninth Ave at 44th St; ⊖ A, C, E to 42nd St-Port Authority
Perfect for a pre- or post-theater cocktail, the laid-back Moroccan-themed Kemia displays plenty of drama with its rose-petal-strewn staircase whisking you down to the underground hideaway decked in ottomans and billowing tapestries. There are delicious cocktails, North African tapas and DJs a-spinning.

TILLMAN'S Map pp134-5 Jazz Lounge
☎ 212-627-8320; 165 W 26th St btwn Sixth & Seventh Aves; ⊖ F, V, 1 to 23rd St
Jazzy and cool, with cubby booths, candles and vintage sepia prints reviving the jazz heyday, Tillman's is a bit dressed up – they will take your jacket up front (and often help you put it on) – but this Harlem import has a 'mingle o'er early-evening martini' ($11) vibe that sucks you in.

BRITE BAR Map pp134-5 Lounge
☎ 212-279-9706; 297 Tenth Ave at 27th St; ⊖ 1 to 28th St
This polished bar has lots of color – orange walls, Lite-Brite sets – in a rather refined throw-back where you can water up before hitting the clubs or to talk over the 'what the…?' art exhibits at the nearby Chelsea galleries.

BRYANT PARK GRILL & CAFÉ
Map pp134-5 Outside Bar
☎ 212-840-6500; 25 W 40th St btwn Fifth & Sixth Aves; ⊖ B, D, F, V to 42nd St-Bryant Park

'Let's just find some place to sit outside and have a drink.' Sound familiar? If weather's behaving (and it's between April and November), head to Bryant Park, when the outdoor café sets out its wicker chairs overlooking the lovely patch of green.

UPPER EAST SIDE

Not exactly the most hoppin' area to party in, this neighborhood relies on its elegant hotel lounges and sprinkling of dives to lure the tippling set. There's a few trashy bars, but they're posers compared to the rest of Manhattan. For the following, be sure you're dressed the part.

LEXINGTON BAR & BOOKS
Map p142 Cigar Bar
☎ 212-717-3902; 1020 Lexington Ave at 73rd St; ⊖ 6 to 68th St-Hunter College
Ashtrays and elbows – sometimes stars' elbows – line the elegant bar top in an ultra-stylish space that allows sipping whiskies and $15 cocktails and cigar smoking. The shelves are lined with books (more for looks than reading), and jazzy lounge music eases the well-dressed night-outers into polite intoxication.

IGGY'S Map p142 Karaoke
☎ 212-327-3043; 1452 Second Ave; ⊖ 6 to 77th St
How much you love this skinny Irish-lite pub depends on how badly you need to misbehave in the Upper East Side. The karaoke mic certainly helps the raucous regulars, who bring on a bit of a frat atmosphere some nights. Buds are $2 from 8pm to 9pm.

BEMELMAN'S BAR Map p142 Lounge
☎ 212-570-7109; Carlyle, 35 E 76th St at Madison Ave; ⊖ 6 to 77th St
Waiters wear white jackets, a baby grand piano is always being played and Ludwig Bemelman's Madeline murals surround you. It's a classic spot for a serious cocktail – the kind of place that could easily turn up in a Woody Allen film.

METROPOLITAN MUSEUM OF ART ROOF GARDEN CAFE Map p142 Rooftop Bar
☎ 212-535-7710; 1000 Fifth Ave, at 82nd St; ⊙ 10am-4:30pm Sun & Tue-Thu, 10am-8:30pm Fri & Sat; ⊖ 4, 5, 6 to 86th St
It's nothing fancy, just a self-service area with sandwiches and drinks, but we

can't get enough of this setting, with the roof view jutting just above Central Park's tree canopy – and the presence of Coors Light. (On the Upper East Side? Sacre bleu!)

UPPER WEST SIDE

A neighborhood for grown-ups, many with children, is not exactly the No 1 destination for hardcore drinkers. But the Upper West has its moments, particularly as things get less posh in the northern reaches where Columbia students troll for dives. There's a couple of great jazz clubs here too: Smoke (p306) and Cleopatra's Needle (p305).

EMERALD INN Map p153   Irish Pub

☎ 212-874-8840; 205 Columbus Ave btwn 69th & 70th Sts; ◉ 1, 2, 3 to 72nd St

Old guys and post-work suits cloister in this pocket-sized, ever-inviting pub with a (real) Irish accent. There's plenty of good food (burgers and shepherd's pie, naturally). Seating's a bit cramped if you can't get the sofa by the front.

DING DONG LOUNGE Map p153   Punk Bar

☎ 212-663-2600; 929 Columbus Ave btwn W 105th & 106th Sts; ◉ B, C, 1 to 103rd St

It's hard to be too bad-ass in the Upper West, but this former crack-den turned punk bar (Black Flag flyers, patrons dropping the 'f bomb') stakes its own claim for streams of Columbia students and nearby hostel guests. It's not all punk – there's a pool table and some cuckoo clocks, and the DJ dips into kept-real R&B.

'CESCA Map p153   Wine Bar

☎ 212-787-6300; 164 W 75th St btwn Amsterdam & Columbus Aves; ◉ 1, 2, 3 to 72nd St

Though it's renowned for its upscale Italian fare, the cozy front lounge and bar area here are also worth a trek. With lots of dark wood, some romantic tables and a large free-floating bar in the center of the room, the front area of 'Cesca is handsome in a gentlemen's smoking lounge sort of way. There's an impressive list of wines by the glass, plus great bar food.

HARLEM & NORTHERN MANHATTAN

A world in itself, the swath of Manhattan above 125th St is ripe for wandering and

ducking into, especially if it's a neighborhood vibe or down-home jazz jams you're looking to catch. Most of the new renaissance is designed to resemble the old – where live music comes with your drink at places jazz masters have played, like Minton's Playhouse (p305), St Nick's Pub (p305) and Lenox Lounge (p305).

DEN Map pp158–9   Lounge

☎ 212-234-3045; www.thedenharlem.com; 2150 Fifth Ave near 132nd St; ◷ Tue-Sun; ◉ 2, 3 to 135th St

Harlem for the stars: this sexy, jazzy lounge has welcomed plenty of big names – Spike Lee, Rosario Dawson – plus comics like Tracey Morgan and a rowdy karaoke Tuesday night. It's a candlelit dressed-up spot with local art on the walls and plenty of nouveau soul on the menu (including a $21 Sunday brunch). Cocktails are half off 6pm to 8pm Tuesday to Saturday.

BROOKLYN

Brooklynites have little need to leave their borough for late-night antics as neighborhood bars have long outgrown the sticky-floor, sports-bar scene outsiders might expect. Grim-by-day Williamsburg and East Williamsburg, in particular, light up at night, giving New York's post-graduate crowd its most rewarding drinking ground, with more room and more fun themes than you get back in Manhattan. Elsewhere Park Slope's Fifth Ave has a host of youthful spots and lesbian bars, while there's always something happening on Fort Greene's Dekalb Ave, Boerum Hill's Smith St, Dumbo's Front St and Prospect Height's Vanderbilt Ave.

Brooklyn Heights

FLOYD Map p174   Games & Booze

☎ 718-858-5810; 131 Atlantic Ave; ◉ 2, 3, 4, 5 to Borough Hall

Floyd's a bit flaky, and we like it. Inside the glass-front bar from Atlantic Ave, young flirters cuddle on antique-style sofas while beer-swirlers congregate around a bocce court in the back.

MONTERO'S Map p174   Nautical Dive

☎ 718-624-9799; 73 Atlantic Ave; ◉ 2, 3, 4, 5 to Borough Hall

At the edge of Atlantic Ave in Brooklyn Heights, but with a seafaring gaze, this well-lit dive gives its hard-drinker crowd (including a stray hipster or two) a healthy dose of the nautical – seven life preservers hang over the bar, along with framed photos of boats picked up since the bar's 1947 birthday.

Williamsburg

Bars group around L subway stops going east, like stepping stones into the industrial warehouses and treeless streets. Visit the Brooklyn Brewery (p176), and see p176 for a walking tour that takes in some of East Williamsburg's more far-flung bars.

HAREFIELD ROAD Map p177   Beer Nerds
☎ 718-388-6870; 769 Metropolitan Ave, btwn Graham Ave & Humboldt St; ⊕ L to Graham Ave
Do the Amish have dungeons? This all-grown-up East Williamsburg bar has a cozy woodsy chic, with big plankboard tables and roaming room under the wood ceilings. Other than a few wines served by the glass ($6 to $7), its focus is beer, with 15 unique microbrews on tap (including upstate's tasty Ommegang Rare Vos; $5). A couple of beers are $3 from 4pm to 8pm. There's a small brick courtyard in back, and weekend brunch is served 11am to 4pm.

GUTTER Map p177   Bowling Bar
☎ 718-387-3585; 200 N 14th St, btwn Berry & Wythe Sts; ⊕ L to Bedford St
Calculated to fill that hip need to look unhip, this stunning bar fills an old warehouse and goes beyond the usual Pabst beers with a remarkable Midwest import: an eight-lane bowling alley with a real-deal, clunky 1970s scoring system saved from Ohio storage. Lines build for bowling, but the drinking area itself is fun, a folksy spot that looks like a townie bar at a state university town. Pitchers of Brooklyn's Six Point cost $21. For bowling info, see the boxed text, p331.

ROYAL OAK Map p177   DJ Bar
☎ 718-388-3884; 594 Union Ave at Richardson St; ⊕ L to Bedford St
On an out-of-the-way corner, and with no sign, the colorful Royal Oak smacks of a '30s-era speakeasy – with cranberry leather booths, wood floors and a lot of rich color on the walls – except the booze flows legally, flirting runs rampant and the beat goes techno and classic rock, with DJ-aided, impromptu dancing.

BROOKLYN ALE HOUSE Map p177   Flirt Pub
☎ 718-302-9811; 103 Berry St; ⊕ L to Bedford Ave
A poke into B-Burg's pre-boom era, the Ale House is a definite 'hood bar with a trace of the crustier vets amid a flow of 20-something newbies. Sure, the jukebox pays tribute to the appropriate gods of indie rock, and some local art on the walls can be eye-rollers. But the goal's unchanged for years now: times are jollier when everyone's drunker. Ain't that true?

Boerum Hill, Cobble Hill & Carroll Gardens

SUNNY'S Map p180   Bluegrass Dive
☎ 718-625-8211; 253 Conover St btwn Beard & Reed Sts; ⏰ 8pm-2am Wed, 8pm-4am Fri & Sat; ⊕ F, G to Carroll St, then transfer to 🚌 B61
Way out in Red Hook, this old, super-inviting longshoreman bar – the sign says 'bar' – comes right out of On the Waterfront, except that Brando didn't go for bluegrass as Sunny's does on a bring-your-own-banjo, foot-stomping jam on Saturday night. Take the B61 bus from the subway.

BROOKLYN INN Map p180   Jukebox Hero
☎ 718-625-9741; 138 Bergen St at Hoyt St; ⊕ F, G to Bergen St
Black on the outside, with dark-oak ornate walls inside, the laid-back, neighborhoody

top picks

VINTAGE NYC

It's the place, not just the liquor, that transports you to long-gone eras in some classic New York watering holes.

- Bohemian Hall & Beer Garden (p298) Mugs of Czech pilsner and Czech bands in the city's last great beer garden, in Queens.
- Campbell Apartment (p293) Railroad baron's '20s-era secret hideaway at Grand Central.
- Old Town Bar (p293) The classic, preserved decor here offers a turn-of-the-century vibe.
- King Cole Bar (p294) Ultra-lux birthplace of the Bloody Mary, in Midtown.
- McSorley's Old Ale House (p291) Slamming two-for-one mugs in a cobwebby, sawdust-floor East Village dive since 1852.

WORTH THE TRIP: THE BRONX

All-out Yankees, the Bronx classic Stan's Sports Bar (Map pp208–9; ☎ 718-993-5548; 836 River Ave at 158th St; ⊕ B, D, 4 to 161st St-Yankee Stadium) gets stuffed with fans with blue ballcaps or pin-stripe jerseys before and after the Yankees play across the street. You'll need elbows to fight for a beer refill or a hot dog. If you have cheap seats, drink up – there's no beer in the bleacher seats.

Brooklyn Inn is like an English pub without the smoke – or the English. Things get pretty tight most nights, best on week days when chatty locals in work clothes bring their dogs and suck down $5 pints of Six Point ale, sometimes forgetting to re-feed the indie-rock jukebox. The bar is featured in the movie *Smoke* (1995).

Park Slope & Prospect Heights

WEATHER UP Map p182   Cocktail Bar
**589 Vanderbilt Ave btwn Bergen & Dean Sts;
⏰ Tue-Sun; ⊕ 2, 3 to Bergen St, B, Q to 7th Ave**
Transforming Vandy Ave with its 2008 opening, this compact, speakeasy-style lounge – with glimmering white ceiling tiles, retro ska softly playing and a bronze bar reflecting in the soft light – mixes some of Brooklyn's finest cocktails (Old-Fashioned, Presbyterians, Gin Fizz), as trained by the Milk & Honey (p290) gurus on the Lower East Side.

UNION HALL Map p182   Games & Booze
☎ 718-638-4400; 702 Union St btwn Fifth & Sixth Aves; ⊕ M, R to Union St, 2, 3 to Bergen St, F to 7th Ave
Up front, leather settees and armchairs sit next to the masculine full-wall bookshelves and the fireplace makes the Hall feel like an Old World gentleman's club during gentler times. Things get busy-rowdy later on, with a clanking bocce court in back and an indie-rock stage in the basement. If you're thinking of clanking the bocce ball, prepare to wait an hour or two. Good snacks.

O'CONNOR'S Map p182   Irish Dive
☎ 718-783-9721; 39 Fifth Ave, btwn Bergen & Dean Sts; ⏰ noon-4am; ⊕ 2, 3 to Bergen St
With fluorescent lights, old wall paneling, and Yankees games flickering on the TV, O'Connor's is a dive that brings in hipster youth with *cheap* drinks (gin-and-tonics are

$2.50!) and a welcoming aura of its glorious 1931 roots.

GREAT LAKES Map p182   Jukebox Bar
☎ 718-499-3710; 284 Fifth Ave at 1st St; ⊕ M, R to Union St
Set in the heart of Fifth Ave action, this simple corner bar brings out indie-rockers for beer and a jukebox that pays tribute to the little bands that could. Glass windows make the front sitting-area good if you want to see who's going to Blue Ribbon Sushi (p272) next door.

QUEENS

Queens' mighty sprawl has pockets of nightlife action catering mostly to its diverse local base – with themes ranging from Greek and Croatian to Irish and Jamaican. River-hugging nabes Astoria and Long Island City tend to bring the most Manhattanites over for a curious night out.

HARRY'S AT WATER TAXI BEACH
Map pp200–1   Beach Bar
www.watertaxibeach.com; cnr 2nd St & Borden Ave, Long Island City; ⊕ 7 to Vernon Blvd-Jackson Ave; ⚓ New York Water taxi to Hunter's Point
It's easy to make fun of the name until you see it – a full sandy beach facing the UN (so no foul language people) with volleyball and a walk-up bar serving $5 beer and $7 sangria. There are DJ nights on Friday ($10 cover). Take Jackson Ave toward the 495 West signs, turn right on 51st Ave, then left on 2nd St.

THE CREEK & THE CAVE
Map pp200–1   Dive Bar
☎ 718-706-8783; www.thecreekandthecave.com; 10-93 Jackson Ave at 49th Ave, Long Island City; ⊕ 7 to Vernon Blvd-Jackson Ave
Good for a see-what-happens evening, this local bar has a burrito grill in the back and several open-mic nights (comedy on alternating Wednesdays, anything on Tuesday). The crowd is a lively mix of Queens-forever locals and newbie pioneers. Occasional live shows tend to favor the distortion pedal.

BOHEMIAN HALL & BEER GARDEN
Map pp200–1   Outside Bar
☎ 718-274-4925; 29-19 24th Ave btwn 29th & 31st Sts, Astoria; ⊕ N, W to Astoria Blvd
Easily one of New York's great happy-drinking grounds, this outdoor beer garden

is the last survivor of the city's 800 or so such beer playgrounds. Built in 1919, the building previously housed the Bohemian Citizen's Benevolent Society (founded for Czech immigrants in 1892). It's only worth coming to enjoy – in nice weather – its huge outdoor beer garden. The mouth-watering list of cold Czech imports on draft are served with Czech accents, as are the potato dumplings and burgers. Some warm nights, folk bands set up – occasionally there's a charge of $5 or so – and you're free to linger over a pitcher outside as long as you want (get there early on key nights to ensure a spot).

CABARET

Oh so New York, cabaret shows are kind of like mini musical-theater productions, performed in intimate environments and, if done right, no less thrilling. Going for an old-fashioned vibe, they usually consist of a pianist and a vocalist who rely on beloved standards by guys like Cole Porter and Ira Gershwin. Contemporary material will often be thrown in, too, and the distinction between performers can be made based on their style of interpretation as well as where they're onstage.

CAFÉ CARLYLE Map p142
☎ 212-744-1600; 35 E 76th St at Madison Ave, Upper East Side; ◉ 6 to 77th St
This swanky spot at the Carlyle hotel draws top-shelf talent, from Eartha Kitt to Woody Allen, who plays his clarinet here with his New Orleans jazz band on Mondays (September through May). Bring bucks: it's $100 per person minimum at a table!

DON'T TELL MAMA Map pp134–5
☎ 212-757-0788; 343 W 46th St btwn Eighth & Ninth Aves, Midtown West; ◉ A, C, E to 42nd St-Port Authority
This art-deco room, named for a song in the Kander & Ebb musical Cabaret, features some high-quality camp – that is, if Tommy Femia doing a jaw-dropping rendition of Judy Garland qualifies – as well as the serious stuff, such as green (but talented) performers from nearby music schools.

DUPLEX Map p110
☎ 212-255-5438; www.theduplex.com; 61 Christopher St at Seventh Ave S, West Village; ◉ 1 to Christopher St-Sheridan Sq

It's way gay at this tiny spot, where you'll find a near-constant roster of drag queens and piano-bar shows from a range of up-and-comers.

FEINSTEIN'S AT THE REGENCY Map p142
☎ 212-339-4095; 540 Park Ave at 61st St, Upper East Side; ◉ F to Lexington Ave-63rd St, N, R, W to Lexington Ave-59th St
You'll be puttin' on the ritz at this high-class joint from cabaret queen Michael Feinstein. You need reservations to get in to see Broadway greats on the small stage (including Betty Buckley, Jackie Mason, Donny Osmond and Tony Danza).

GALAPAGOS ART SPACE Map p174
☎ 718-384-4586; www.galapagosartspace.com; 16 Main St, Dumbo, Brooklyn; ◉ F to York St
Galapagos goes modern cabaret, and more. Freshly exported from Williamsburg, the new Dumbo space is all-green and eco-hugging, a superb place for the '20s forever' campy experimentation that's brought in ukelele bands, Monday-night burlesque, blood-curdling Vicious Vaude-ville, a Russian vampire/surf-rock band and some art.

OAK ROOM Map pp134–5
☎ 212-840-6800; Algonquin hotel, 59 W 44th St btwn Fifth & Sixth Aves, Midtown West; ◉ B, D, F, V to 42nd St-Bryant Park
Dress up, order a martini and get the Dorothy Parker vibe at this famous posh piano lounge, which is known for launching the careers of Harry Connick Jr and Diana Krall.

COMEDY

Laughter's always played a big part in dealing with New York's day-to-day bullshit, and budding comics on small stages (like the edgy Upright Citizens Brigade Theatre) are ever hoping their wit catches the eye of casting directors for late-night shows. Some of the smaller classic places, like Brooklyn's Pips (where Rodney Dangerfield and Woody Allen started; closed in 2005), are shutting doors. Other are bulking up, some say beyond intimacy. Long-standing comedy clubs, like Gotham (p300), have doubled in size, and the newer clubs on the scene often fit 300 or more bottoms.

A couple of festivals to watch out for: the New York Comedy Festival (www.nyccomedyfestival.com), held in November, and – if their F-bombs seem too tame – the New York Underground Comedy Festival (www.nycundergroundcomedy.com), held in late September/early October.

If you're looking to join in, look up entertainment listings for open-mic nights. Hey, it's New York: you might end up getting five minutes of fame on *Late Night with David Letterman*.

CAROLINE'S ON BROADWAY Map pp134–5

☎ 212-757-4100; www.carolines.com; 1626 Broadway at 50th St, Midtown West; ⊙ N, R, W to 49th St, 1 to 50th St

You may recognize this big, bright, mainstream classic from comedy specials filmed here on location. Big names (Jerry Seinfeld, Jon Stewart) come here.

COMEDY CELLAR Map p110

☎ 212-254-3480; www.comedycellar.com; 117 MacDougal St btwn 3rd & Bleecker Sts, Greenwich Village; ⊙ A, C, E, B, D, F, V to W 4th St-Washington Sq

This long-established basement club in Greenwich Village features mainstream material and a good list of regulars (eg Colin Quinn, SNL's Darrell Hammond, Wanda Sykes), plus an occasional high-profile drop-by like Dave Chappelle.

GOTHAM COMEDY CLUB Map p116

☎ 212-367-9000; 208 W 23rd St btwn Seventh & Eighth Aves, Chelsea; ⊙ F, V, R, W to 23rd St

Fancying itself as a NYC comedy hall of fame, and backing it up with regular big names and Gotham All-Stars shows, this expanded club opened in 2006, and still provides space for comedians who've cut their teeth on HBO, Letterman and Leno.

STAND-UP NY Map p153

☎ 212-595-0850; www.standupny.com; 236 W 78th St at Broadway, Upper West Side; ⊙ 1 to 79th St

Shows at this small club on the Upper West Side include specialized groups (gay, Latino comics) as well as showcases from the Montreal Comedy Festival or cast-offs from the *Last Comic Standing* TV show. It's pretty mainstream, but a bright spot in the mostly humorless (clubwise, at least) UWS.

UPRIGHT CITIZENS BRIGADE THEATRE Map pp134–5

☎ 212-366-9176; www.ucbtheatre.com; 307 W 26th St btwn Eighth & Ninth Aves, Chelsea; ⊙ C, E to 23rd St

Pros of comedy sketches and outrageous improvisations reign at this popular 74-seat venue, which gets drop-bys from casting directors. Getting in is cheap ($5 to $8), so is the beer (from $2 a can), and you may recognize pranksters on stage from shows like *Late Night with Conan O'Brien*; it's free Wednesday after 11pm when newbies take the reins. Check the website for popular classes on sketch and improv, now spilling over to an annex location on W 30th St.

CLUBBING

NYC's club scene is constantly changing: partly because New York partiers get bored easily, and partly because club promoters often find themselves in party-ending battles with both the city and their neighbors over noise, drug activity and myriad other quality-of-life issues. In an effort to avoid such drama, most major dance clubs locate themselves on the less populated outer edges of the city, closer to the West Side Hwy than to bustling residential areas.

Closed Monday nights (and occasionally Monday to Wednesday), clubs are generally large spaces that revolve around dance floors and hyped DJs. For up-to-the-minute listings, check out the Clubs section of the weekly *Time Out New York* magazine, *Paper* (www.papermag.com) and, for gay soirées, either *HX* (www.hx.com) or *Next* magazine (www.nextmagazine.net), two monthly bar rags found at most queer clubs. You should also keep an eye out for club and party flyers on walls and billboards while strolling the East Village; sometimes that's the best way to find out about clubs that don't have phones and don't advertise.

Be sure to dress the part if you want to get in. Bring enough cash – some places, like Pacha (opposite), have ATMs with extortionate $8 transaction fees! Oh, and don't even think about going to any of these places before midnight (even on a weeknight) as things don't truly pick up until 1am or later. Peruse the options, and even pay entrance fees, with Clubfone (☎ 212-777-2582; www.clubfone.com).

For clubs and bars geared toward an exclusively gay or lesbian clientele, see p342.

CIELO Map p110

☎ 212-645-5700; www.cieloclub.com; 18 Little W 12th St btwn Ninth Ave & Washington St, Meatpacking District; admission $10-20; ⊙ A, C, E to 14th St, L to 8th Ave

Known for its intimate space and free or low-cost parties, this Meatpacking District staple packs in a fashionable, multi-culti crowd nightly for its blend of tribal, Latin-spiced house and soulful grooves, especially on Monday with DJ Francois K's 'outerplanetary' sounds at Deep Space.

CLUB SHELTER Map pp88–9

☎ 646-862-6117; www.clubshelter.com; 150 Varick St at Vandam St, SoHo; admission $20; ⊕ 1 to Houston St, C, E to Spring St

Now relocated to a surprisingly bare-bone space in west SoHo, the ever-casual Shelter's Saturday night is still home to the beloved, long-running deep-house party with DJ legend Timmy Regisford and a fair share of homeboy breakin' some nights.

HIRO Map p116

☎ 212-242-4300; www.themaritimehotel.com; 371 W 16th St, Chelsea; ⊗ Thu–Sun; ⊕ A, C, E to 14th St, L to 8th Ave

In the Maritime Hotel, this chic Japanese space looks a little like the place where Uma kicked a lot of ass at the end of *Kill Bill: Vol 1*. It's Japanese chic, with bamboo wall dividers and low-slung banquettes – it's most popular on Thursday and Sunday nights when a gay crowd hits the dance floor.

LOTUS Map p110

☎ 212-243-4420; www.lotusnewyork.com; 409 W 14th St btwn Ninth & Tenth Aves, Meatpacking District; admission $10-20; ⊕ A, C, E to 14th St, L to 8th Ave

The big nights at this slick, VIP-crowd supper club sees legends like the Olsen twins but stays even-keeled enough that less legendary downtowners come for fun too. The three-floor space is best on Friday, when the mix of house, disco and garage brings in almost too many to find a slot on the dance floor. At least that means it's easier to get in.

MANSION Map pp134–5

☎ 212-629-9000; www.mansionnewyork.com; 530 W 28th St btwn Tenth & Eleventh Aves, Chelsea; admission $25; ⊕ C, E to 23rd St

Rushing into the now-closed Crobar space, Miami export Mansion ups the ante with a 20ft fireplace and stylish seats below billowing curtains and hanging lights in the 10,000-sq-ft space. It opened as this book

went to press, but likely will haul in Crobar's chief crowd of suburbanistas taking Manhattan on the weekend.

MARQUEE Map pp134–5

☎ 646-473-0202; www.marqueeny.com; 289 Tenth Ave btwn 26th & 27th Sts, Chelsea; admission $20; ⊕ C, E to 23rd St

Not long ago on Manhattan's clear A-list of velvet-rope lounges, Marquee is now a *bit* past its prime: such is life in clubland. Some luster may be lost, but not the luxury, as the 600-soul limit is quickly filled. If you make it in, head up to the glass-box mezzanine lounge to peek down over 1st-floor revelers.

PACHA Map pp134–5

☎ 212-209-7500; www.pachanyc.com; 618 W 46th St btwn Eleventh Ave & West Side Hwy, Midtown West; admission $20; ⊕ A, C, E to Port Authority-42nd St

A relative newcomer that's hyped for big-name visiting DJs, Pacha is definitely a massive and spectacular place: 30,000 sq ft and four levels of glowing, sleek spaces and cozy seating nooks that rise up to surround the main dance-floor atrium.

PINK ELEPHANT Map pp134–5

☎ 212-463-0000 ext 1844; www.pinkelephant club.com; 527 W 27th St, Chelsea; admission $20; ⊗ Thu–Sun; ⊕ 1 to 28th St

The name is coy, but the place is all class – so much so that it can be tough getting in the door. DJ-blasted deep house resonates throughout the tight, low-ceilinged dance floor, so don't expect to hear your taxi driver's chatter at 4am.

top picks

WEEKNIGHT EVENTS

- Monday 'Anti-folk' open mic at East Village's Sidewalk Café (p306).
- Tuesday Slavic Soul Party at Park Slope's Barbes (p307).
- Wednesday A full-blown hillbilly jam at East Village's Banjo Jim's (p306) or amateur night at Harlem's Apollo Theater (p162).
- Thursday It's 1984 once weekly at the East Village's uninhibited Pyramid (p302).

PYRAMID Map p104

☎ 212-228-4888; www.thepyramidclub.com; 101 Ave A btwn 6th & 7th Sts, East Village; admission $3-6; ⊕ F, V to Lower East Side-2nd Ave
Goth/camp has a home too. Fans of this divey two-floor club mix sexual orientations and adherences to either the lava lamp or distortion pedal. Thursday night's long-running '80s party, 1984, draws the biggest mobs ('hit me with some Mode, DJ!'), but you'll find live rock too (in the past, the wee stage has seen Nirvana's, and a certain LP researcher's, NYC rock debuts).

SAPPHIRE Map p98

☎ 212-777-5153; www.sapphirenyc.com; 249 Eldridge St at E Houston St, Lower East Side; admission $5; ⊕ F, V to Lower East Side-2nd Ave
Fun without attitude! This tiny, hoppin' venue has survived the crowds of the mid-'90s Ludlow St boom with its hip factor intact, and its $5 cover keeps snootiness at a minimum. The tightly packed dance floor gets lit with a mix of R&B, rap, disco and funk.

SULLIVAN ROOM Map p110

☎ 212-252-2151; 218 Sullivan St btwn Bleecker & W 3rd Sts, Greenwich Village; ⊕ A, C, E, B, D, F, V to W 4th St-Washington Sq
Near NYU, this unmarked, basement-level lounge roars to a DJ-spun electronic beat for late-late dance parties (usually a $20 cover) and stiff cocktails. 'We are young, we are alive, we are… can someone get me another drink?'

LIVE MUSIC

Aspiring starlets may head to Hollywood, but droves of musician wannabes (and never-wills) get off the bus in NYC, the country's capital of live music. Just about every musical taste can be catered for here (even country and western), and there's nearly an infinite range of performances to choose from on any given night of the week. For current listings, check local publications like the *Village Voice* (www.villagevoice.com), *New York Magazine* (www.nymag.com) or *Time Out New York* (www.timeout.com/newyork).

MAJOR VENUES

New York is a must-stop destination for all touring bands, so your chance of being able to see the biggest acts is good – but don't dawdle on getting tickets for the most popular ones, as even the larger places can sell out to crazed fans in under a day. To purchase, try the venue's box office or website, or else Ticketmaster.com.

BEACON THEATRE Map p153

☎ 212-465-6500; www.beacontheatre.com; 2124 Broadway btwn 74th & 75th Sts; ⊕ 1, 2, 3 to 72nd St
This historic, 1929 theater is a perfect in-between-size venue, with 2000 seats (not a terrible one in the house) and a constant flow of national acts, though many tend to be on the geriatric side. Recent performers have included Lyle Lovett, Steely Dan, the Steve Miller Band and Ringo Starr and his All-Starr Band.

JONES BEACH off Map pp200–1

☎ 516-221-1000; www.jonesbeach.com; Jones Beach, 1000 Ocean Pkwy, Wantagh, NY; ⊕ LIRR to Freeport
In the park developed by Robert Moses in the 1920s, the Nikon at Jones Beach Theater is an open, seaside amphitheatre that hosts many summer concerts (REM, Rush and other non-'R'-lettered bands) for fans happy to get beach time as well.

MADISON SQUARE GARDEN Map pp134–5

☎ 212-307-7171; www.thegarden.com; Seventh Ave btwn 31st & 33rd Sts; ⊕ 1, 2, 3 to 34th St-Penn Station
The city's major performance venue – part of the massive complex housing Penn Station and the smaller WaMu Theater – is where you'll find all the big-arena performers, from Kanye West and Kid Rock to Jimmy Buffett and Madonna. (The aesthetics are nil here, but it's not about design.) It's also a sports arena, and the place to

catch games of the New York Knicks (p326), New York Liberty (p326), New York Rangers (p327) and boxing matches – not to mention events from the World's Strongest Man Super Series and the annual Westminster Kennel Club dog competition.

MEADOWLANDS off Map p69

☎ 201-935-3900; www.meadowlands.com; Meadowlands Sports Complex, East Rutherford, NJ; 🚌 351 from Port Authority

Home to sporting teams the Giants, Jets and (for the time being) Nets and MetroStars, the Meadowlands complex is also one of the area's biggest concert and large-event arenas. Think Rolling Stones and the Boss at the outside Giants Stadium, Van Halen reunions or the Foo Fighters in the Izod Center. For directions on getting to the Meadowlands, see the boxed text, p326.

RADIO CITY MUSIC HALL Map pp134–5

☎ 212-247-4777; www.radiocity.com; 51st St at Sixth Ave; 🚇 B, D, F, V to 47th-50th Sts-Rockefeller Center

This glittering, art-deco masterpiece is a great place to see a show. Many throwback acts (eg Dolly Parton, Santana) take the stage, but new bands like Arcade Fire play, too.

TOWN HALL Map pp134–5

☎ 212-840-2824; www.the-townhall-nyc.org; 123 W 43rd St btwn Sixth & Seventh Aves; 🚇 B, D, F, V to 42nd St-Bryant Park

A nonprofit entertainment organization founded in 1921 and housed in an elegant National Landmark building, Town Hall's 2000-plus seats get filled with folks seeking eclectic musical performances. Artists are all over the map, with recent nights offering an Iranian vocalist, a Cole Porter tribute, Emmylou Harris, KT Tunstall and Judy Collins.

ROCK, HIP-HOP & INDIE

Bands like the Ramones, Talking Heads, Blondie and Sonic Youth got going in downtown, while the Bronx saw the first beats of hip-hop. Nowadays, there's as much, or more, indie-rock action to be found in Williamsburg, Brooklyn.

ARLENE'S GROCERY Map p98

☎ 212-995-1652; www.arlenesgrocery.net; 95 Stanton St at Orchard St, Lower East Side; 🚇 F, V to Lower East Side-2nd Ave

This convenience-store-turned-club was just pre-curve enough of the LES' 1990s explosion to entitle it to a bit of a self-righteous vibe. The one-room hothouse incubates local talent with live rock'n'roll karaoke (10pm Monday) and great free live shows every night.

BOWERY BALLROOM Map pp88–9

☎ 212-533-2111; www.boweryballroom.com; 6 Delancey St at Bowery, Nolita; 🚇 J, M, Z to Bowery

This terrific, medium-sized venue has the perfect sound and feel for more blown-up indie-rock acts (Shins, Stephen Malkmus, Patti Smith).

DELANCEY Map p98

☎ 212-254-9920; www.thedelancey.com; 168 Delancey St at Clinton St, Lower East Side; 🚇 F, J, M, Z to Delancey-Essex Sts

Surprisingly stylish for the Lower East Side, the Delancey hosts some popular indie bands like Clap Your Hands Say Yeah for doting indie-rock crowds. A good early-evening spot to drink too, particularly from the airy 2nd-floor patio deck.

THE FILLMORE AT IRVING PLAZA Map p120

☎ 212-777-1224; www.irvingplaza.com; 17 Irving Pl at 15th St, Gramercy; 🚇 L, N, Q, R, W, 4, 5, 6 to 14th St-Union Sq

A great in-between stage for quirky mainstream acts – from Cat Power to a reunited Animals – the Fillmore is nominally linked with San Francisco's famed Fill. There's a cozy floor around the stage, and good views from the mezzanine.

HAMMERSTEIN BALLROOM Map pp134–5

☎ 212-279-7740; www.mcstudios.com; Manhattan Center, 311 W 34th St btwn Eighth & Ninth Aves, Garment District; 🚇 A, C, E to 34th St-Penn Station

It's not the most fun place to see a show – mobs being herded through security checks, pricey drinks, oft-rowdy crowds – but the faded grandeur inside makes it a tempting place to see bands like the Flaming Lips or Coldplay.

JOE'S PUB Map pp88–9

☎ 212-539-8778; www.joespub.com; Public Theater, 425 Lafayette St btwn Astor Pl & 4th St, NoHo; 🚇 R, W to 8th St-NYU, 6 to Astor Pl

Part cabaret theater, part rock and new-indie venue, this intimate supper club stages the fringe mainstream (eg folks like Aimee Mann). It has a nice, long bar, seats cuddled around a corner stage and a bit of a dress-up atmosphere.

KNITTING FACTORY Map pp72–3

☎ 212-219-3132; www.knittingfactory.com; 74 Leonard St btwn Church St & Broadway, Tribeca; ◎ 1 to Franklin St

This Tribeca favorite has a long and influential history in the realm of NYC jazz, but today you're more likely to find an eclectic selection of folk, indie and experimental music, from cosmic space jazz to Tokyo shock rock, plus the occasional 'performance' by (yay!) the New York Depeche Mode Fan Club. At the time of research it was rumored to be moving to the East Village sometime in the next year, so check the website for the most recent info.

MERCURY LOUNGE Map p98

☎ 212-260-4700; www.mercuryloungenyc.com; 217 E Houston St btwn Ave A & Ludlow St; ◎ F, V to Lower East Side-2nd Ave

The Mercury dependably pulls in a cool new or cool comeback band everyone downtown wants to see – such as Dengue Fever or the Slits. The sound is good, with an intimate seating area and dance space.

NORTHSIX Map p177

☎ 718-599-5103; www.northsix.com; 66 North 6th St, Williamsburg, Brooklyn; ◎ L to Bedford Ave

Catch local up-and-comers, some live hip-hop artists and occasional name bands (Yo La Tengo, Sonic Youth, Deerhoof) at this old warehouse in Williamsburg.

PIANOS Map p98

☎ 212-505-3733; www.pianosnyc.com; 106 Norfolk St, Lower East Side; ◎ F, V to Lower East Side-2nd Ave

This is an old two-level piano shop turned hipster's musical haven serving mixed-genre bills (DJs, hip-hop, cowpunk, electronica, bad karaoke) and pouring plenty of Rheingold for a large and appreciative Lower East Side crowd.

SOUTHPAW Map p182

☎ 718-230-0236; www.spsounds.com; 125 Fifth Ave btwn Sterling & St John's Pl, Park Slope, Brooklyn; ◎ 2, 3 to Bergen St, M, R to Union St

Park Slope for rock? It's perplexed the stroller-pushing locals since opening in

---

2002, and helped Fifth Ave keep its crustier side alive – some good rock, funk and DJ acts here.

WARSAW Map p177

☎ 718-387-0505; www.warsawconcerts.com; Polish National Home, 261 Driggs Ave at Eckford St, Greenpoint; ◎ L to Bedford Ave, G to Nassau Ave

A burgeoning New York classic, this stage is in the Polish National Home, with good views in the old ballroom, for bands ranging from indie darlings (Yeah Yeah Yeahs) to legends (the Wailers, George Clinton). Plus Polish grandmas serve $5 pierogis and $4 beers under the disco balls.

JAZZ

Jazz lives in New York clubs, even if the cloud of cigarette smoke are gone. The days when 52nd St or Harlem's Cotton Club ruled the jazz world are past, but you'll find great choices for jams, big-band get-ups, jazz brunches and swank dress-up clubs in the Upper West Side, around Times Sq, and – in particular – Harlem and the West Village, which now share the role of New York's veritable jazz ghettos.

Jazz fans should consider timing a visit for the Queens Jazz Trail trolley tour in Flushing on the first Saturday of the month (see p204).

55 BAR Map p110

☎ 212-929-9883; www.55bar.com; 55 Christopher St at Seventh Ave, West Village; ◎ 1 to Christopher St-Sheridan Sq

Dating to the prohibition era, this friendly basement dive is great for low-key shows without high covers or dressing up. There are regular performances twice nightly by quality artists-in-residence, some blues bands and Miles Davis' super '80s guitarist Mike Stern.

BAM CAFÉ Map p182

☎ 718-636-4139; www.bam.org; 30 Lafayette Ave at Ashland Pl, Fort Greene, Brooklyn; ◎ D, M, N, R to Pacific St, B, Q, 2, 3, 4, 5 to Atlantic Ave

A high-ceilinged restaurant and lounge in the upstairs of the Brooklyn Academy of Music complex gives free shows on Friday and Saturday (some jazz, as well as R&B and experimental rock).

BIRDLAND Map pp134–5

☎ 212-581-3080; www.birdlandjazz.com; 315 W 44th St btwn Eighth & Ninth Aves, Theater District; Ⓢ A, C, E to 42nd St-Port Authority

Off Times Sq, it's got a slick look, not to mention the legend – its name dates from bebop legend Charlie Parker (or 'Bird'), who headlined at the previous location on 52nd St, along with Miles, Monk and just about everyone else. You can see their photos on the walls, and see many nostalgic shows like the Duke Ellington Orchestra (directed by Paul Mercer Ellington) on most Tuesdays. Covers run from $15 to $50.

BLUE NOTE Map p110

☎ 212-475-8592; www.bluenote.net; 131 W 3rd St btwn Sixth Ave & MacDougal St, Greenwich Village; Ⓢ A, C, E, B, D, F, V to W 4th St-Washington Sq

This is by far the most famous (and expensive) of the city's jazz clubs. Most shows are $20 at the bar, $35 at a table, but can rise for the biggest jazz stars, and a few outside the normal jazz act (um, Doobie Brothers' Michael McDonald anyone?). Go on an off night, and be quiet – all attention's on the stage!

CLEOPATRA'S NEEDLE Map p153

☎ 212-769-6969; www.cleopatrasneedleny.com; 2485 Broadway btwn W 92nd & 93rd Sts, Upper West Side; Ⓢ 1, 2, 3 to 96th St

Late-night and open-mic jams are a hallmark at Cleopatra's Needle, where the music goes until 4am. Some of the best band views are from the bar, where you can take a pint on tap and nosh on surprisingly good Mediterranean-influenced fare. There's never a cover, just an easily reached $10 drink/food minimum.

IRIDIUM JAZZ CLUB Map pp134–5

☎ 212-582-2121; www.iridiumjazzclub.com; 1650 Broadway at 51st St, Midtown West; Ⓢ 1 to 50th St

The tables are tight, but the sound is great, and there's no knocking Monday with the hilarious and talented Les Paul Trio or Tuesday with the Mingus Big Band. Lots of fogies come around – eg '50s-era vocalists –

and some new names too. Tickets start at $25 ($50 for Les Paul).

JAZZ AT LINCOLN CENTER Map p134–5

☎ 212-258-9595; www.jalc.org; Time Warner Center, Broadway at 60th St, Midtown West; Ⓢ A, C, B, D, 1 to 59th St-Columbus Circle

Of the three venues, which include the fancy Rose Theater and Allen Room, it's Dizzy's Club Coca-Cola that you'll most likely wind up in, as it's got nightly shows. And despite that awful name, the nightclub is flawless, with stunning views overlooking Central Park and excellent lineups of everything from bebop to Afro-Cuban and Brazilian jazz acts, hand-picked by director Wynton Marsalis.

JAZZ GALLERY Map pp88–9

☎ 212-242-1063; www.jazzgallery.org; 290 Hudson St btwn Dominick & Spring Sts, SoHo; Ⓢ C, E to Spring St

A cultural center rather than your typical jazz club – there's no bar here, folks – the Gallery is for fans who are really serious about their music. The small space with great acoustics hosts several shows per week, often with two sets per night. Tickets are $12 to $15.

LENOX LOUNGE Map pp158–9

☎ 212-427-0253; www.lenoxlounge.com; 288 Malcolm X Blvd btwn 124th & 125th Sts, Harlem; Ⓢ 2, 3 to 125th St

Around since 1939, this lounge has been a Harlem go-to since Billie Holiday and Miles Davis played, AND Malcolm X dropped by. It's old-school art deco inside, particularly the lux Zebra Room in back, and gets a fair share of big names. The cover is usually $20 plus a two-drink minimum.

MINTON'S PLAYHOUSE Map pp158–9

☎ 212-864-8346; www.uptownatmintons.com; 210 W 118th St btwn Adam Clayton Powell & St Nicholas Aves, Harlem; Ⓢ B, C to 116th St

Back after three decades, Minton's is a slicked-up version of the classic spot where the Bird joined Dizzy and Monk during the birth of bebop. There's a two-drink minimum daily, plus a $10 cover most days.

ST NICK'S PUB Map pp158–9

☎ 212-283-7132; 773 St Nicholas Ave at 149th St, Washington Heights; Ⓢ A, C, B, D to 145th St

You can literally take the A train to this amazing place to hear raw jazz created by musicians for musicians (beginning at 10pm nightly); the stage is taken by open jams on Monday and Saturday nights. Later in the evening, big-name jazz cats come from their bigger gigs around town, keeping it real and live here at the Pub.

SMALLS JAZZ CLUB Map p110

☎ 212-283-9728; www.smallsjazzclub.com; 183 W 10th St at Seventh Ave, West Village; ⊕ A, C, B, D to 145th St

A total dive, down the steps from the sidewalk, with a grab-bag collection of lounge seats and a host of jazz acts nightly taking the tiny stage in back. Cover for the night is $20 (including a free drink Sunday through Thursday) – with a come-and-go policy if you need to duck out for a slice.

SMOKE Map p153

☎ 212-864-6662; www.smokejazz.com; 2751 Broadway btwn 105th & 106th Sts, Upper West Side; ⊕ 1 to 103rd St

The 1999 incarnation of Augie's, this swank but laid-back lounge – with good stage views from plush sofas – brings out some old-timers, with many New York faves like George Coleman, Hank Jones and local Lea Delaria, who scatted here for her 2007 live album. There's an inventive jam on Monday hosted by John Farnsworth. No cover, but there's a $20 minimum most nights, $30 on weekends.

VILLAGE VANGUARD Map p110

☎ 212-255-4037; www.villagevanguard.com; 178 Seventh Ave at 11th St, West Village; ⊕ 1, 2, 3 to 14th St

More intimate and real than the bigger legends, the Vanguard's been around since 1935, still pushing a no-talking policy that keeps the focus on jazz. It's seen the best in its seven decades – Bill Evans, John Coltrane, Sonny Rollings and Wynton Marsalis have recorded live albums here. Tickets are $30 or $35, including a $10 drink minimum.

COUNTRY, FOLK & BLUES

New York is still recovering from when Mayor Rudy Giuliani billed August 7, 1997, as 'Garth Brooks Day.' Truth is that, down deep, away from all the high heels and Paul Smith suits, a bit of shit-kicking does get done in NYC. (And we're not talking about on the sidewalks or at dog walks.)

BANJO JIM'S Map p104

☎ 212-777-0869; 700 E 9th St at Ave C, East Village; ⊕ 6 to Astor Pl, L to 1st Ave

The latest of the nonrock scene on Ave C, Banjo Jim's – a tiny dive with a good jukebox and friendly atmosphere – hosts a nightly crew of banjo pickers and lap-steel players. Most nights have standard lineups of a few acts, but Wednesday night is a 'We Are the World' for hillbillies, with a big crew of musicians sharing the stage.

BB KING BLUES CLUB & GRILL

Map pp134–5

☎ 212-997-4144; www.bbkingblues.com; 237 W 42nd St btwn Seventh & Eighth Aves, Midtown West; ⊕ N, R, W, 1, 2, 3, 7 to 42nd St-Times Sq

Catch old-school blues performers – along with rock, folk and reggae acts and theme nights (eg Johnny Cash's birthday) at this two-tiered, horseshoe-shaped room in the heart of the new Times Sq.

JALOPY Map p180

☎ 718-395-3214; www.jalopy.biz; 315 Columbia St at Woodhull St, Red Hook; ⊕ F, G to Carroll St

This fringe Carroll Gardens/Red Hook banjo shop – which offers lessons – has a fun DIY space with cold beer for its bluegrass, country and ukulele shows, including a feel-good Roots 'n' Ruckus show on Wednesday nights.

PEOPLE'S VOICE CAFÉ Map p126

☎ 212-787-3903; www.peoplesvoicecafe.org; 45 E 33rd St btwn Madison & Park Aves, Midtown East; ⊕ 6 to 33rd St

Long live the Rads! Around since 1979, this old-fashioned peacemonger coffeehouse stages plenty of quirk-folk shows and a fair share of political folkies with a guitar and a message. It's good fun.

RODEO BAR & GRILL Map p126

☎ 212-683-6500; www.rodeobar.com; 375 Third Ave at 27th St, Midtown East; ⊕ 6 to 28th St

New York's best Texas-style honkytonk is in Murray Hill? Good shows of country, bluegrass and rockabilly are staged nightly for a foot-tappin' Manhattan crowd. There are creative margaritas and plenty of steaks, fajitas, burgers and veggie dishes too.

SIDEWALK CAFÉ Map p104

☎ 212-473-7373; www.antifolk.net; 94 Ave A at E 6th St, East Village; ⊕ 6 to Astor Pl, F, V to Lower East Side-2nd Ave

Anti-folk forever! Never mind the Sidewalk's burger-bar appearance outside; inside is the home of New York's 'anti-folk' scene, where the Moldy Peaches carved out their legacy before Juno got knocked up. The open-mic 'anti-hootenanny' is Monday night.

LATIN

Viva la música! As one of the US's major Latino population centers, New York offers everything from tango and salsa to Afro-Cuban and merengue. In addition to the following, the stylish and fun Hecho en Mexico (p269) has live music – mostly traditional Mexican or nouveau Mexican – on Friday and Saturday night.

COPACABANA BOAT RIDE Map p110
☎ 212-239-2672; www.copacabanany.com; Houston St & 12th Ave; entry $10; ⊙ Thu May-Sept; ⊕ 1 to Houston St
The famed Miami-meets-Manhattan Copacabana club closed (and is looking for a new location), but its boat takes off on a floating dance party in a cute steamboat-style ship on Thursday nights.

GONZALEZ Y GONZALEZ Map pp88–9
☎ 212-473-8787; 625 Broadway btwn Bleecker & Houston Sts, NoHo; ⊕ B, D, F, V to Broadway-Lafayette St, 6 to Bleecker St
It's just a mall-like Mexican restaurant Sunday through Wednesday, but it livens way up the diablo up Thursday to Saturday nights with live salsa and merengue nights and a big club area full of tequila drinkers. No excuse if you don't know: there's free salsa lessons Thursday and Saturday.

S.O.B.'S Map pp88–9
☎ 212-243-4940; www.sobs.com; 204 Varick St btwn King & Houston Sts, SoHo; ⊕ 1 to Houston St
SOB stands for Sounds of Brazil, but it isn't limited to samba: you can shake it to Afro-Cuban music, salsa, reggae and African pop, both live and on the turntable. SOB's

hosts dinner shows nightly but it doesn't really start jumping until 2am.

WORLD MUSIC

OK, we know what you're thinking. But 'world music' doesn't always mean those Andean pipe-flute musicians you see playing Simon & Garfunkel in public areas, or the music at those hacky-sack circles back in Boulder. The following make up some of New York's more exciting nights out.

BARBES Map p182
☎ 718-965-9177; www.barbes.com; 376 9th St at Sixth Ave, Park Slope; ⊕ F to 7th Ave
Shooting for Parisian style, and much more in musical scope, this backstreet Park Slope wonder stages local jazz and experimental acts including the irresistible Tuesday-night Slavic Soul Party with the raucous Balkan Brass Band ($10), and a Latin-infused Chicha Libre Monday.

MEHANATA Map p98
☎ 212-625-0981; www.mehanata.com; 113 Ludlow St, Lower East Side; ⊕ F, J, M, Z to Delancey-Essex Sts
It's lost its crusty, sweaty vibe from its original Canal St locale, but the 'Bulgarian Bar' is still gypsy heaven for East Euro–chic and indie-popsters. East Euro DJs spin some nights, and belly dancers and 'gypsy bands' take the small stage for jumping-in-place dancers. It helps to be drunk.

ZEBULON Map p177
☎ 718-218-6934; www.zebuloncafeconcert.com; 258 Wythe Ave, Williamsburg, Brooklyn; ⊕ L to Bedford Ave
Ever arty and experimental, the Zeb is an unlikely tight space for reliably engaging daily shows of voodoo funk, dub, jazz and poetry – even Super Bowl parties come with a DJ spinning things you don't recognize. It's wee for its draw (we've seen an 18-piece band spilling off the stage). But there's alcohol and snacks.

top picks

- **Lincoln Center** (boxed text, p311) Here's where to find all the classics, from ballet to opera, performed by folks who are top in their fields.
- **Shakespeare in the Park** (p313) It's worth getting up early to snag free tickets to these al fresco productions.
- **TKTS Booth** (boxed text, p313) See knock-your-socks-off Broadway musicals without breaking the bank.
- **Bargemusic** (p315) Chamber music in the most spectacular of settings.
- **Film Forum** (p319) The true film buff's movie house.
- **92nd St Y** (p320) Huge talents pass through here to share their writings, musical talents and brilliant thoughts.
- **City Center** (p316) A beautiful Midtown theater that presents wonderful programs of dance.
- **Joyce Theater** (p317) Downtown dance buffs head here.
- **Performance Space 122** (p314) It's a downtown legend, hosting theater, readings, dance and more.

What's your recommendation? www.lonelyplanet.com/new-york-city

For many folks, simply walking around New York City is drama enough. Others, though, need more concentrated doses of entertainment – and, lucky for them, they have come to the right place. You probably already know this city is host to some of the finest theater productions in the world – not to mention opera, symphonies, jazz jams, dance performances, art-house films and literary readings, right? But did you know that you could get many of those infusions of culture for cheap or even free, and in places as untraditional as churches, barges, private apartments, man-made beaches, museums, rooftops and empty swimming pools? That's not even counting the endless number of subway platforms and subway cars that get turned into stages each day by oft-talented (if down-on-their-luck) vocalists, saxophonists, guitarists and other types of musicians.

The sheer number of performance venues and companies, though, is testament to how in love with culture this city's residents and tourists can be. Because let's face it: while mayor Mike Bloomberg has been hailed for his unwavering support of the arts locally, the censorship-prone federal government has hardly been a friend to creative types, slashing funding more every year and leaving arts organizations (especially the edgiest ones) scrambling to keep themselves afloat through the generosity of private grants, patrons and audience members. And that's where you come in, of course.

But how are you supposed to decide where to begin? You could do like many New Yorkers and pick your favorite medium – classical music, jazz or ballet, for example – and find all of the options, becoming a one-note (but highly expert) fan. Or you could skim through everything – a poetry reading one night, followed by an indie-film matinee and a night at the opera, with perhaps an edgy off-off-Broadway show thrown in for good measure.

To get a handle on what's happening when, simply pick up either the daily Arts & Leisure section of *The New York Times* or one of the city's venerable weeklies, like *Time Out New York, New York, The Village Voice* or the *New Yorker,* all of which include thoroughly subjective reviews, to boot. But don't spend too much time obsessing over what's best; you'll most likely not be disappointed if you follow your interests. And besides, if a show is disastrous, it'll likely make a great story for you to share back home.

THEATER

From the legendary hit factories of Broadway to the scruffy black-box theaters that dot countless downtown blocks, dramatic productions can start to feel like a dime a dozen after a while around here. But for every show that's just so-so or even a downright flop, there are a dozen that'll knock your socks off.

The most celebrated scene is, of course, that of Broadway – nicknamed the Great White Way in 1902 for its bright billboard lights – where small, lavish theaters sit on side streets running off that avenue itself, which cross-crosses through the heart of Times Sq. The musicals and dramas here – including top draws *Wicked, A Chorus Line* and *Spring Awakening* – are the most commercially successful, attracting mobs that make walking through the area just before the 8pm show-time on any evening quite a challenge. But it's also quite a thrill – as is snagging a good seat in one of the playhouses, watching the lights dim and then seeing the curtain rise. For true theater fans, nothing compares.

More adventurous stage buffs should also look into what's happening off-Broadway, downtown and even in the outer boroughs (especially at BAM, p315), as some of the freshest, most accomplished stage work is happening far, far away from the renowned Theater District; some of it winds up moving to Broadway, and sometimes it's exciting to catch shows while they're still small, but generating big buzz. Still, local critics will often decry the lack of risk taking in today's productions, and offerings will have differing degrees of edginess, depending on who's in the audience and where they're from (Berliners, for example, may do a bit more yawning than Alabamans). The annual Fringe Fest (www.fringenyc.org), held each summer at various downtown theaters, can be a welcome source for fresh, less staid works.

Buying Tickets

To purchase tickets for shows, you can either head directly to the venue's box office, or use one of several ticket-service agencies (most of which add a surcharge) to order by phone

MULTI-TALENTED: LINCOLN CENTER

Every eminent performing-arts genre in the city has a stage at the massive complex of Lincoln Center (Map p153; ☎ 212-546-2656; www.lincolncenter.org; Lincoln Center Plaza, 64th St at Columbus Ave; ⊕ 1 to 66th St-Lincoln Center), built in the 1960s and currently undergoing a massive redesign and renovation that will move the famous fountain, add new public sculptures and landscaping and completely gut and rework at least one of the venerable buildings. Avery Fisher Hall is the showplace of the fine New York Philharmonic (www.newyorkphilharmonic.org), the country's oldest symphony orchestra. Alice Tully Hall (☎ 212-875-5050) houses the Chamber Music Society of Lincoln Center, and the New York State Theater (☎ 212-870-5570) is home to both the New York City Ballet (www.nycballet.com) and the New York City Opera (www.nycopera.com). You'll find quality films, as well as the annual New York Film Festival, at the Walter Reade Theater (☎ 212-875-5600; www.filminc.com); wonderful star-studded theater at both the Mitzi E Newhouse Theater and Vivian Beaumont Theater; and frequent concerts at Juilliard School and the Fiorello H LaGuardia High School of Music. But perhaps the biggest draw here – besides the outdoor fountain that was featured in Cher's film *Moonstruck* and in Mel Brooks' *The Producers*, and which hosts the popular summer series Lincoln Center Out of Doors Festival – is the Metropolitan Opera House (☎ 212-362-6000; www.metopera.org). Its spectacular decor includes the two famous Chagall paintings, visible from the street, and the double, winding red staircase that sweeps up from the grand lobby. The house is home to the Metropolitan Opera, which features top stars and mind-boggling costumes and sets, from September to May, and visiting operas from around the world during the rest of the year – except for spring, when the world-renowned American Ballet Theater takes over the stage. Jazz at Lincoln Center (see the boxed text, p305), by the way, has moved to the Time Warner Center.

THE ARTS THEATER

or online. Many of the websites have some added perks, from reviews to the entertainment news.

Broadway Line (☎ 888-276-2392; www.livebroadway.com) Run by the Broadway League, provides descriptions and good prices for shows on the Great White Way.

Playbill (www.playbill.com) The publisher of that happy little yellow-and-white program provided by ushers at Broadway plays also has an online version, offering theater news, listings and a ticket-purchase system.

Talkin' Broadway (www.talkingbroadway.com) A less formal site, with dishy reviews as well as a board for posting extra tickets to buy or sell.

Telecharge (☎ 212-239-6200; www.telecharge.com) Sells tickets for Broadway and off-Broadway shows.

Theatermania (☎ 212-352-3101; www.theatermania.com) For any form of theater, provides listings, reviews and ticketing.

Ticketmaster (www.ticketmaster.com) An old chestnut, Ticketmaster sells for every conceivable form of big-time entertainment: rock concerts, opera, ballet, Broadway and off-Broadway, museum shows and sporting events.

SmartTix.com (☎ 212-868-4444; www.smarttix.com) A great source for practically anything but Broadway, with info on comedy, cabaret, performance art, music, dance and downtown theater.

BROADWAY SHOWS

Though some longtime favorites have ended their successful runs – *Rent* and *The Produc-*ers, most notably – plenty of others are still going strong. Catch *Spamalot*, *The Color Purple*, *The Phantom of the Opera* and many other favorites that show no sign of stopping. Or just dive on in and try something new.

There are 38 'official' Broadway theaters – lavish, early-20th-century houses surrounding Times Sq and charging the highest prices for their shows, which can easily cost $100 a ticket. Luckily, there are ways around the pain (see the boxed text, p313). Evening performances begin at 8pm, with Wednesday and weekend matinees starting at 2pm.

The following list highlights specific long-running shows, rather than theaters, since it's the production, rather than the venue, that you'll be basing your Broadway decisions on.

25TH ANNUAL PUTNAM COUNTY SPELLING BEE

Circle in the Square Theatre, Map pp134-5; 1633 Broadway, entrance on 50th St, Midtown West; ⊕ N, R, W to 49th St, 1 to 50th St
Small-town America gets its crazy side exposed in this quirky musical that pits six geeky, eccentric teens (and their respective family baggage) against each other in a spelling bee. It was the surprise hit of 2005, not to mention that same year's Tony Award–winner for Best Book of a Musical and Best Featured Actor. It still packs a powerful punch, but it's a quieter, small-scale show that is not nearly as glitzy as the other Broadway musicals.

A CHORUS LINE

Schoenfeld Theatre, Map pp134-5; **236 W 45th St btwn Broadway & Eighth Ave, Midtown West;** N, R, Q, W, 1, 2, 3, 7 to Times Sq-42nd St

Another successful revival, this one is the 1980s hit about Broadway wannabes trying to make it through a grueling audition for a musical, sharing their personal baggage – being gay, tone deaf or too short – along the way. The show is a bit like a time capsule – albeit a thrilling one, thanks to the exciting score by Marvin Hamlisch and Edward Kleban, and well-delivered song-and-dance hits from 'What I Did For Love' to 'One.'

AVENUE Q

John Golden Theatre, Map pp134-5; **252 W 45th St btwn Broadway & Eighth Ave, Midtown West;** N, R, Q, W, 1, 2, 3, 7 to Times Sq-42nd St

Who knew that puppets could have such popular appeal? Playwright Jeff Whitty, for one, who created this story of pink- and green-faced muppetlike puppets who go about their business in a quirky, urban love story. Their puppeteers stand on the stage, working their magic, but they soon blend into the background. Songs about *schadenfreude* and scenes of sex have been making audiences blush – and giggle – since 2003.

CHICAGO

Ambassador Theater, Map pp134-5; **219 W 49th St btwn Broadway & Eighth Ave, Midtown West;** N, R, W to 49th St, 1 to 50th St

This beloved Bob Fosse/Kander & Ebb classic, a musical about showgirl Velma Kelly, wanna-be Roxie Hart, lawyer Billy Flynn and the fabulously sordid goings-on of the Chicago underworld, has made a great comeback; this version, revived by director Walter Bobbie, is seriously alive and kicking.

THE LION KING

New Amsterdam Theatre, Map pp134-5; **214 W 42nd St btwn Seventh & Eighth Aves, Midtown West;** N, R, Q, W, 1, 2, 3, 7 to Times Sq-42nd St

Known by many New Yorkers as the beast that took away Times Square's bite, this Disney musical is a widely hailed, magically colorful story of kings that kids of all ages love. The marvelous direction and design is by Julie Taymor, with an African-beat score by Tim Rice and Elton John.

MAMMA MIA!

Cadillac Winter Garden Theatre, Map pp134-5; **1634 Broadway at 50th St, Midtown West;** N, R, W to 49th St, 1 to 50th St

This musical revue of a mother/daughter/who's the father? story – based on nearly two dozen hits of the 1970s supergroup Abba (and not much else, honestly) – has been a sugar-pop runaway hit since arriving on the scene in 2001.

WICKED

Gershwin Theater, Map pp134-5; **221 W 51st St, Midtown West;** B, D, F, V to 47th-50th Sts-Rockefeller Center

A whimsical, mythological and extravagantly produced prequel to *The Wizard of Oz*, this pop-rock musical, a stage version of Gregory Maguire's 1995 novel, gives the story's witches a turn to tell the tale. Its followers are an insanely cultish crew, attending frequent performances and launching all sorts of fan clubs, fansites and obsessive blogs to keep themselves occupied.

XANADU

Helen Hayes Theatre, Map pp134-5; **240 W 44th St btwn Broadway & Eighth Ave, Midtown West;** N, R, Q, W, 1, 2, 3, 7 to Times Sq-42nd St

An unlikely hit, this stage version of the weird and wacky 1980 musical movie starring Olivia Newton-John and Gene Kelly has taken everyone by surprise. Douglas Carter Beane's adaptation is a deliciously saccharine spoof, featuring Greek muses on rollerskates, an airheaded hunk seeking artistic inspiration and endlessly campy nods to the original film.

OFF-BROADWAY & OFF-OFF-BROADWAY

Off-Broadway simply refers to theaters where tickets (and production costs) are slightly less, and where houses typically have 200 to 500 seats; you'll find many of them just around the corner from Broadway venues, as well as elsewhere in town. Long-running off-Broadway productions include the noisy, drum-on-anything *Stomp*, and the infinitely annoying and overrated *Blue Man Group*. For some really exciting culture, skip the shtick-based productions and see what's happening at one of these quality theaters instead.

HALF-PRICE BROADWAY TKTS

Having that much-desired Broadway experience can break the bank – but it doesn't have to. Thanks to the Theatre Development Fund, an arts advocacy group that sells 2.5 million theater seats annually, you can snag tickets to some of the most coveted seats at up to half-price discounts. Just head to the Times Sq TKTS booth (Map pp134–5; ☎ 212-768-1818; Broadway at W 47th St), which sells cut-rate, same-day tickets to Broadway and off-Broadway shows. For evening shows, queue up from 3pm to 8pm Monday to Saturday; for matinees, line up from 10am to 2pm Wednesday to Saturday and from 11am to 3pm Sunday. A downtown TKTS (Map pp72–3; cnr Front & John Sts; ☒ 11am-6pm, closed Sun in winter) can be found at the South Street Seaport, and is often much less crowded; here you must buy Wednesday matinee tickets on Tuesday. Check the electric marquee to see what shows are available, or visit the website (www .tdf.org/tkts) to see what has been available recently, to get an idea of what you might find. There are usually plenty of choices, but be flexible and have an open mind and you won't be disappointed.

DIXON PLACE Map pp88–9

☎ 212-219-0736; www.dixonplace.org; 258 Bowery btwn Houston & Prince Sts, Nolita; ⊜ B, D, F, V to Broadway-Lafayette St

An intimate showcase for experimental theater that began as a reading space in 1985, Dixon Place has been campaigning for years to move to a brand-new spot in the 'hood. For now, though, it's still in its cramped, apartment-like home, with mismatched audience chairs and no actual stage. Still, it doesn't deter the flow of exciting shows – brand-new dramas, comedy and readings, often with a queer bent – or its passionate fans. Its summer HOT! series is a great time to catch the newest works.

JOSEPH PAPP PUBLIC THEATER
Map pp88–9

☎ 212-260-2400; www.publictheater.org; 425 Lafayette St btwn E 4th St & Astor Pl, NoHo; ⊜ 6 to Astor Pl

One of the city's most important cultural centers, the Papp, which recently celebrated its 50th anniversary season, was founded by the late, expansive-minded Joseph Papp – who once returned a massive NEA grant rather than sign its conservative anti-obscenity amendment. The theater has had an almost constant roster of can't-miss productions over the years, and staged world premieres of *Hair, A Chorus Line, Plenty* and *Caroline, or Change*, all of which moved to Broadway. The East Village complex also offers the intimate Joe's Pub (p303) for top-notch musical and cabaret shows, and every summer it presents its famous and fabulous free productions of Shakespeare in the Park at Delacorte Theater (Map p149; enter Central Park West at 81st St), which Papp began back in 1954, before the lovely, leafy, open-air theater was even built. Thrilling

productions mounted there recently, with celebrities in leading roles, have included *Macbeth, Hamlet* and *Romeo and Juliet.*

LA MAMA ETC Map p104

☎ 212-475-7710; www.lamama.org; 74A E 4th St btwn Second & Third Aves, East Village; ⊜ F, V to Lower East Side-2nd Ave

Led by founder Ellen Stewart and begun in a small East Village basement, this home for onstage experimentation (the 'ETC' stands for 'experimental theater club') has grown into a complex of three theaters, a café, an art gallery and a separate rehearsal studio building. This is the place to find cutting-edge dramas, sketch-comedy acts and readings of all stripes.

LINCOLN CENTER THEATER Map p153

☎ 212-239-6200; www.lct.org; Lincoln Center, 150 W 65th St btwn Columbus & Amsterdam Aves, Upper West Side; ⊜ 1 to 66th St-Lincoln Center

The theater arm of the Lincoln Center complex includes this pair of intimate spaces: the Mitzi Newhouse Theater and the Vivian Beaumont Theater, both of which are home to Broadway-quality dramas that sport slightly lower ticket prices. Recent productions have included a real range of fare, from a revival of *South Pacific* to the heavy-hitting drama of Tom Stoppard's *The Coast of Utopia.*

NEW YORK THEATER WORKSHOP
Map p104

☎ 212-460-5475; www.nytw.org; 79 E 4th St btwn Second & Third Aves, East Village; ⊜ F, V to Lower East Side-2nd Ave

Recently celebrating its 25th year, this innovative production house is a treasure to those seeking cutting-edge, contemporary plays with purpose. It was the originator of two big Broadway hits, *Rent* and *Urinetown,* and offers a constant supply of high-quality drama, including recent works from Jessica Blank (*Liberty City*), Rinde Eckert (*Horizon*) and even Samuel Beckett, whose quartet of one-act plays was recently adapted by director JoAnne Akalaitis and composer Phillip Glass in *Beckett Shorts,* starring Mikhail Baryshnikov.

PERFORMANCE SPACE 122 Map p104
PS 122; ☎ 212-477-5288; www.ps122.org; 150 First Ave at E 9th St, East Village; ☻ R, W to 8th St-NYU, 6 to Astor Pl
This former schoolhouse has been committed to fostering new artists and their far-out ideas since its inception in 1979. Its two stages have hosted such now-known performers as Meredith Monk, Eric Bogosian and the late Spalding Gray, and it's also home to dance shows, film screenings and various festivals for up-and-coming talents.

PLAYWRIGHTS HORIZONS Map pp134–5
☎ 212-564-1235; www.playwrightshorizons.org; 416 W 42nd St btwn Ninth & Tenth Aves, Midtown West; ☻ A, C, E to Port Authority-42nd St
Sitting on a windswept, abandoned-feeling stretch of 42nd St is this excellent place to catch a new show that could very possibly be a rising hit. It's nearly 40 years old and known as a 'writers' theater,' and is dedicated to fostering contemporary American works. Notable past productions have included *Saved,* a musical by Michael Friedman that's based on the quirky film, as well as *I Am My Own Wife* and *Grey Gardens,* both of which moved on to Broadway.

ROUNDABOUT THEATRE COMPANY Map pp134–5
☎ 212-719-1300; www.roundabouttheatre.org; 227 W 42nd St btwn Seventh & Eighth Aves, Midtown West; ☻ N, R, Q, W, 1, 2, 3, 7 to Times Sq-42nd St

This main stage for the Roundabout, unfortunately called the American Airlines Theatre, has been going strong for more than four decades now. Its attention-grabbing and award-winning productions have included *Twelve Angry Men, The Pajama Game* and, more recently, revivals of *Sunday in the Park With George* and *Crimes of the Heart.*

ST ANN'S WAREHOUSE Map p174
☎ 718-254-8779; www.stannswarehouse.org; 38 Water St, Dumbo, Brooklyn; ☻ A, C to High St
Consistently named one of the edgiest theaters in the city, this cool favorite sits at the water's edge in Dumbo, Brooklyn, attracting avant-garde works from both NYC and around the world, and a very hip crowd to go with them. The big news in its 2008 season was that St Ann's would have to set up a second venue just to house its visiting multimedia production of *Macbeth* from Polish theater company TR Warszawa, and also that it would host the Druid Theatre Company of Galway, Ireland. It's also the site of many wonderful concerts and readings.

CLASSICAL MUSIC
In NYC, the choices for orchestras, chamber music, opera and ballet are abundant, with the more cutting-edge options often stealing center stage. For all things traditional on a grand scale, don't miss Lincoln Center (see the boxed text, p311), which has a stellar stage for the New York Philharmonic; the Brooklyn Academy of Music (BAM), which hosts the Brooklyn Philharmonic and other diverse talents out in Brooklyn; and the famously stunning Carnegie Hall. More intimate listens can be had at various churches (where amazing acoustics add a lot) and smaller recital halls. And come summer, you can catch one of a handful of free outdoor events from the New York Philharmonic at parks, including Central Park, in all five boroughs.

BARGEMUSIC Map p174

☎ 718-624-2083; www.bargemusic.org; Fulton Ferry Landing, Brooklyn Heights, Brooklyn; ⊜ A, C to High St, 2, 3 to Clark St

Chamber-music concerts on this 125-seat docked ferryboat are a unique and intimate affair. For almost 30 years it has been a beloved venue, with beautiful views of the East River and Manhattan and perform-ances of classical favorites throughout the year. A recent and typical week's lineup included a piano concert of Haydn, Schumann, Brahms and Bellman; the Men-delssohn string quartet playing Bartók and Elgar; and a night with a stellar jazz trio.

BROOKLYN ACADEMY OF MUSIC (BAM) Map p180

☎ 718-636-4139; www.bam.org; 30 Lafayette Ave at Ashland Pl, Fort Greene, Brooklyn; ⊜ D, M, N, R to Pacific St, B, Q, 2, 3, 4, 5 to Atlantic Ave

Kind of like Brooklyn's answer to Lincoln Center – in its all-inclusiveness rather than its vibe, which is much edgier – this popu-lar venue also hosts performances from a roster of genres in its various performance spaces. BAM's main claim to classical-music fame is that it's the home of the Brooklyn Philharmonic, known for its innovative lineups.

CARNEGIE HALL Map pp134–5

☎ 212-247-7800; www.carnegiehall.org; 154 W 57th St at Seventh Ave, Midtown West; ⊜ N, R, Q, W to 57th St-7th Ave

Since 1891, this mostly classical and world-music historic performance hall has hosted Tchaikovsky, Mahler and Prokofiev, among others. Today it welcomes visiting philharmonics from around the world, the New York Pops orchestra and CarnegieKids family concerts (as well as occasional folk and pop performers). It sometimes presents programs that are built around specific composers. The property is home to three separate venues: the main (and gorgeous) Isaac Stern Auditorium, and the smaller Joan and Sanford I Weill Recital Hall and Judy and Arthur Zankel Hall, where you can frequently catch chamber ensembles and solo performers.

FRICK COLLECTION Map p142

☎ 212-288-0700; www.frick.org; 1 E 70th St at Fifth Ave, Upper East Side; ⊜ 6 to 68th St-Hunter College

The artwork of 14th- to 19th-century mas-ters is not the only excellent offering at this opulent mansion-turned-museum (see p144). There's also a well-regarded concert series on Sunday and Tuesday evenings, which brings world-renowned performers – French pianist Cédric Tiberghien, Israeli violinist Vadim Guzman and the Dutch Calefax Reed Quintet, to name a few – to its intimate recital hall.

MERKIN CONCERT HALL Map p153

☎ 212-501-3330; 129 W 67th St btwn Amsterdam Ave & Broadway, Upper West Side; ⊜ 1 to 66th St-Lincoln Center

This 457-seat hall, part of the Kaufman Center that also runs a public arts school and public school for musically gifted kids, is one of the city's more intimate venues for classical music. Recently through with a light-and-airy $17 million renovation de-signed by local favorite architect Robert AM Stern, this space (more than 30 years old now) hosts a remarkable array of perform-ances that's mainly classical but has some avant-garde jazz and some world music tossed in. Notable series include Pianoply, which showcases innovative keyboard works on two grand pianos; Fast Forward, fusing contemporary sounds of up-and-comers with classics; and Tuesday mati-nees, which highlights classical solo artists.

top picks

FOR KIDS

- Symphony Space (p316) Home of the annual Children's Film Festival and live-performance Just Kidding! series.
- New York City Ballet's Nutcracker (p317) The classic ballet, a Christmastime tradition, is a favorite among the little-people set.
- Brooklyn Academy of Music (BAM) (left) It's home to the BAM Kids festival, in March, plus various year-round family programs.
- The Lion King (p312) It's the king of Broadway for children.
- AMC Loews 84th St 6 (Map p153; ☎ 212-721-6023; 2310 Broadway at 84th St) The six movie theaters here only show kids' films, so you never have to worry about your tot being the only one to act up.
- Wicked (p312) Older kids fall for this cult fave again and again.

METROPOLITAN MUSEUM OF ART
Map p142

☎ 212-535-7710; www.metmuseum.org; Fifth Ave at 82nd St, Upper East Side; ⏰ 9:30am-5:30pm Tue-Thu & Sun, 9:30am-9pm Fri & Sat; ◉ 4, 5, 6 to 86th St

In addition to being a palace of visual art, the Met hosts performances within the wonderfully acoustic confines of the museum. Some are free, and are offered in conjunction with special exhibits, and others require purchasing tickets and feature renowned pianists, vocalists and assorted ensembles.

ST BARTHOLOMEW'S CHURCH
Map p126

☎ 212-378-0248; www.stbarts.org; 109 E 50th St btwn Park & Lexington Aves, Midtown East; ◉ E, V to 5th Ave-53rd St, 6 to 51st St

Several free performance series (Artists at the Crossroads, Midtown Concerts and the Stecher and Horowitz Foundation Concerts) have found an extraordinary home at this landmark Anglican church, where the fine acoustics add a special touch to cello, piano, violin and ensemble performances.

SYMPHONY SPACE Map p153

☎ 212-864-1414; www.symphonyspace.org; 2537 Broadway at 95th St, Upper West Side; ◉ 1, 2, 3 to 96th St

A multigenre space with several facilities in one, this Upper West Side performance space turns out some impressive classical music along with theater, opera, jazz and readings. You'll find a diverse musical lineup, including string quartets, opera singers, classical guitarists and pianists, especially during the January Pianocentric series.

TRINITY CHURCH/ST PAUL'S CHAPEL
Map pp72–3

☎ 212-602-0747; www.trinitywallstreet.org; Broadway at Wall St, Lower Manhattan; ◉ 2, 3, 4, 5 to Wall St, N, R to Rector St

This former Anglican parish church offers an excellent series, Concerts at One, on Thursdays at Trinity and Mondays at St Paul's Chapel (Broadway at Fulton St) for a mere $2 suggested donation. Call the concert hotline, above, for the weekly schedule, which has presented a gamut of talents, from the Harlem Quartet and Trinity Chamber Choir to marimbist Makoto Nakura.

DANCE

Dance fans are quite spoiled for choice in this town – home to both the New York City Ballet and the American Ballet Theater (both of which perform at Lincoln Center), plus modern dance companies including those of masters Alvin Ailey, Paul Taylor, Merce Cunningham, Martha Graham, Bill T Jones and Mark Morris, just for starters. Even if you prefer companies from other parts of the world – whether it's the Ballet Argentino or Paris's Sankai Juku troupe – chances are they'll make appearances here. Note that there are two major dance seasons here, first in spring, from March to May, then in late fall, from October to December. But there's always someone putting on the moves – even in less expected forms, as with the annual Dance on Camera Festival, held each January at Lincoln Center's Walter Reade Theater.

BROOKLYN ACADEMY OF MUSIC (BAM) Map p180

☎ 718-636-4139; www.bam.org; 30 Lafayette Ave at Ashland Pl, Fort Greene, Brooklyn; ◉ D, M, N, R to Pacific St, B, Q, 2, 3, 4, 5 to Atlantic Ave

The Howard Gilman Opera House and Harvey Lichtenstein Theater at this varied arts complex host their share of ballet, modern and world dance performances, often hosting the Alvin Ailey American Dance Theater, the Bill T Jones/Arnie Zane Dance Company and the Mark Morris Dance Group, which is headquartered across the street. Visiting troupes have ranged from the Pina Bausch Dance Theater to DanceAfrica and Brazil's contemporary Benguelê and Breu.

CEDAR LAKE ENSEMBLE CENTER
Map pp134–5

☎ 212-868-4444; www.cedarlakedance.com; 547 W 26th St at Tenth Ave, Chelsea; ◉ C, E to 23rd St

This contemporary ballet company focuses on bringing attention to emerging choreographers and performs frequent new works in its own 190-seat theater in Chelsea. Its group of 16 dancers has been praised by critics for being 'versatile,' 'energetic' and for displaying 'raw athleticism.'

CITY CENTER Map pp134–5

☎ 212-581-1212; www.citycenter.org; 131 W 55th St btwn Sixth & Seventh Aves, Midtown West; ◉ N, R, Q, W to 57th St

This elegant Midtown venue hosts the Alvin Ailey American Dance Theater and the American Ballet Theater every December, as well as the Paul Taylor Dance Company in the spring. At other times, there's a steady stream of great dance moments, from the annual New York Flamenco Festival in February to various tango, tap dance and ballet soloist showcases.

DANCE THEATER WORKSHOP Map p116
☎ 212-924-0077; www.dancetheaterworkshop.org; 219 W 19th St btwn Seventh & Eighth Aves, Chelsea; ⊖ 1 to 18th St

You'll find a program of more than 110 experimental, modern works annually at this sleek Chelsea dance center, led by artistic director Carla Peterson. Residency showcases, First Light Commissions and various international productions bring fresh works to the stage, with shows that will often include pre- or post-show discussions with choreographers or dancers.

JOYCE SOHO Map pp88–9
☎ 212-242-0800; www.joyce.org; 155 Mercer St at Prince St, SoHo; ⊖ R, W to Prince St

The newest branch of the Joyce Theater (below) has dance studios and a performance space that seats just 74 audience members, occupying a former firehouse in SoHo.

JOYCE THEATER Map p116
☎ 212-242-0800; www.joyce.org; 175 Eighth Ave at 19th St, Chelsea; ⊖ A, C, E to 14th St, L to 8th Ave

A favorite among dance junkies because of its excellent sight lines and offbeat offerings, this is an intimate venue, seating 470, located in Chelsea. Its focus is on traditional modern companies such as Pilobolus and Parsons Dance, which make annual appearances at this renovated cinema.

KITCHEN Map p116
☎ 212-255-5793; 512 W 19th St btwn Tenth & Eleventh Aves, Chelsea; ⊖ A, C, E to 14th St, L to 8th Ave

A loft-like experimental space in west Chelsea that also produces edgy theater and readings, this is where you'll find new, progressive pieces and works in progress from local movers and shakers.

METROPOLITAN OPERA HOUSE Map p153
☎ 212-362-6000; Lincoln Center, 64th St at Columbus Ave, Upper West Side; ⊖ 1 to 66th St-Lincoln Center

The American Ballet Theatre (www.abt.org) presents its largely classical season of full-length ballets each spring at this grand and massive theater of Lincoln Center (p311), also the place to catch visiting ballets from around the world. Be sure to get as close as you can afford, as high-up seats remove you greatly from the pomp and circumstance onstage.

NEW YORK STATE THEATER Map p153
☎ 212-870-5570; Lincoln Center, 64th St at Columbus Ave, Upper West Side; ⊖ 1 to 66th St-Lincoln Center

Established by Lincoln Kirstein and George Balanchine in 1948, New York City Ballet (www.nycballet.com) features a varied season of premieres and revivals, including a production of George Balanchine's *The Nutcracker* during the Christmas holidays, all performed at this 2755-seat Lincoln Center theater, designed by Philip Johnson, featuring a grand terrace where you can gaze into the center courtyard during intermissions.

FILM & TV

Some folks might find it strange to visit NYC and head into a movie theater. But feasting on films here is quite a different experience from the blockbuster-at-the-multiplex scene you might be used to at home. Filmgoing is actually quite a serious venture to the many cinephiles here – as evidenced by the

---

FREE FUN: BRYANT PARK FILM SERIES

Summers in Bryant Park (Map pp134–5; www.bryantpark.org) take on a celluloid focus, with its annual outdoor Monday-night film series. Films, both modern and classic, are projected onto a massive screen that goes up every June on the west side of the tree-lined patch of green. Determined viewers show up as early as 3:30pm to get a good spot for their blanket, picnics and bottles of wine, with an anxious after-work crowd zipping in by 6pm to enjoy the remaining late-afternoon rays. Join them and prepare to relax and do some hardcore people-watching, as the movies don't start until about 9pm. Each summer's series has a different theme, though most films are classics or New York–based (or both). Recent gems have included *Annie Hall, Wait Until Dark* and *Psycho*.

preponderance of movie houses that show indie, classic, avant-garde, foreign and otherwise nonstandard fare. Frequent film festivals (see the boxed text, below) with various themes provide additional texture to the moviegoing scene.

If it's small-screen fare you prefer, you can do much better than holing yourself up in your hotel room with the remote control. Instead, pop in to one of the many TV-show tapings that take place here, from *Good Morning America* to *The David Letterman Show* (see the boxed text, opposite).

Buying Tickets

In general, movie tickets cost about $11. For new releases or otherwise hot screenings, unbearably long lines on evenings, especially weekends, are the norm. To ensure you'll get in – and not wind up watching from the dreaded front row – it's pretty much imperative that you either go by the box office or use the phone or internet to buy your tickets in advance (unless it's midweek, midday or for a film that has been out for months already). You can check local movie listings for phone numbers and websites for advance sales, but know that most are handled either through Movie Fone (☎ 212-777-3456; www.moviefone.com) or Fandango (www.fandango.com). You'll have to pay an extra $1.50 fee per ticket, but it's worth it to know you'll breeze in when you get there.

AMC EMPIRE 25 Map pp134–5
☎ 212-505-6397; 234 W 42nd St at Eighth Ave, Midtown West; ◎ N, Q, R, W, 1, 2, 3, 7 to 42nd St-Times Sq
At this massive, 17-screen theater in the heart of Times Sq, taking the multiple flights of elevators with the crowds so you can climb up to your movie can feel a little

overwhelming. But it's pretty cool to look out of the huge windows that overlook lit-up 42nd St – and even more exciting to settle into the stadium-style seating, which gives good views from just about any seat. Though this isn't the best place to catch mass-consumer Hollywood flicks, as the crowds can be massive and rowdy, it's the perfect off-the-radar spot for indies, which show here frequently to well-behaved, manageable numbers.

ANGELIKA FILM CENTER Map p110
☎ 212-995-2000; 18 W Houston St at Mercer St, Greenwich Village; ◎ B, D, F, V to Broadway-Lafayette St
An old favorite, the Angelika does a great job at specializing in foreign and independent films. It's often overcrowded – despite the fact that screens can be annoyingly small and you can hear the rumble of the subway going by in the middle of your movie. The roomy café here serves gourmet grub, but if you've still time to kill before a showing, check out the Stanford White–designed Beaux-Arts building that houses Angelika. Called the Cable Building (the miles of cable here moved the country's first and last cable cars ever installed), it features an oval window and caryatids on its Broadway facade.

ANTHOLOGY FILM ARCHIVES Map p104
☎ 212-505-5181; www.anthologyfilmarchives.org; 32 Second Ave at 2nd St, East Village; ◎ F, V to Lower East Side-2nd Ave
This East Village theater, opened in 1970 by film buff Jonas Mekas and a supportive crew, is dedicated to the idea of film as an art form. It screens indie works by new filmmakers and also revives classics and

FILM FESTIVALS

With more than 30 film festivals happening in New York each year, chances are you'll be able to hit one no matter when you visit. Many credit the highly publicized and quickly growing Tribeca Film Festival (p21) for upping the ante when it comes to quality of films and screening locations. Festival topics are about as varied as the city itself, with options ranging from Dance on Camera (January), a celebration of movies about dance, to the Jewish Film Festival (January), which explores Jewish culture and religion onscreen. The old fave New York Film Festival (January) highlights up-and-coming directors every year, and the African American Women in Film Festival (March) is a self-explanatory and finely focused showcase. The Williamsburg Film Festival (March) has brought the fun to that artsy-trendy Brooklyn neighborhood, and screens work by local filmmakers, while the NewFest (June), a highlight of Gay Pride month, presents an all-queer showcase. Meanwhile, the Human Rights Watch Film Festival (June) enlightens locals to the evils of society around the globe, while the New York Hawaiian Film Festival (May), the Asian American International Film Festival (June) and the Israeli Film Festival (June) focus on those varied cultures.

TV TAPINGS

You, too, can become part of a studio audience for one of the many TV shows taped in town. Though most are booked long in advance, you can always stand in line the day of the taping and keep your fingers crossed for standbys or cancellations.

Saturday Night Live, one of the most popular NYC-based shows, is known for being difficult to get into. That said, you can try your luck by getting your name into the mix in the fall, when seats are assigned by lottery. Simply send an email to snltickets@nbcuni.com in August, or line up by 7am the day of the show on the 49th St side of Rockefeller Plaza for standby lottery tickets (16 years and older only). Another late-night show that draws crowds is the *Late Show with David Letterman*. You can try to request tickets for a specific date through the online request form at www.cbs.com/lateshow, or submit a request in person by showing up at the theater (1697 Broadway between 53rd and 54th Sts) to speak to a representative; hours for requests are 9:30am to 12:30pm Monday to Friday and 10am to 6pm Saturday and Sunday. Or else try for a standby ticket by calling ☎ 212-247-6497 at 11am on the day of the taping you would like to attend; taping begins at 5:30pm Monday to Thursday. Get on the *Daily Show with John Stewart* on Comedy Central by reserving tickets at least three months ahead of time online at www.thedailyshow.com/tickets; if the day of taping you want is filled, try emailing requesttickets@thedailyshow.com to try your luck.

For more show ticket details, visit the websites of individual TV stations, or try www.tvtickets.com.

obscure oldies that are usually screened in programs organized around a specific theme or director, from Luis Buñuel to Ken Brown's psychedelia.

BAM ROSE CINEMA Map p180
☎ 718-623-2770; www.bam.org; 30 Lafayette Ave at Flatbush Ave, Fort Greene, Brooklyn; ◉ D, M, N, R to Pacific St, B, Q, 2, 3, 4, 5 to Atlantic Ave
The gorgeous theater at the Brooklyn Academy of Music shows independent and foreign films in spaces blessed with comfy seating, great sight lines, huge screens and a lovely, landmark design. You can also catch mini-festivals and revivals here.

CLEARVIEW'S CHELSEA Map p116
☎ 212-777-3456; 260 W 23rd St btwn Seventh & Eighth Aves, Chelsea; ◉ C, E to 23rd St
In addition to showing first-run films, this multiscreen complex hosts weekend midnight showings of the *Rocky Horror Picture Show*, as well as a great Thursday-night series, Chelsea Classics, which has local drag star Hedda Lettuce hosting old-school camp fare from Joan Crawford, Bette Davis, Barbra Streisand and the like.

CLEARVIEW'S ZIEGFELD THEATER
Map pp134–5
☎ 212-307-1862; 141 W 54th St; ◉ 1 to 50th St
The last true movie palace in New York City, this stunner, built in 1969, seats a whopping 1131 moviegoers and is often used for glitzy celeb-studded premieres because of its opulence. Inside, you'll find chandeliers, fancy bathrooms and a gigantic screen. It only screens mainstream Hollywood fare,

unfortunately, though occasional special series can bring classics into the lineup.

FILM FORUM Map pp88–9
☎ 212-727-8110; www.filmforum.org; 209 W Houston St btwn Varick St & Sixth Ave, SoHo; ◉ 1 to Houston St
This three-screen cinema in SoHo screens an astounding array of independent films, revivals and career retrospectives from greats like Sidney Lumet. Theaters are small, as are the screens, so get there early for a good viewing spot. Showings are often combined with director talks or other filmic discussions, and there's a great little café in the lobby.

IFC CENTER Map p110
☎ 212-924-7771; www.ifccenter.com; 323 Sixth Ave at 3rd St, West Village; ◉ A, C, E, B, D, F, V to W 4th St-Washington Sq
This art house, right in NYU-land, has a great café and a solidly curated lineup of new indies, cult classics and foreign films. Catch shorts, documentaries, '80s revivals, director-focused series, weekend classics and the monthly NewFest at IFC Center, bringing films from June's gay and lesbian film festival to the screen all year round.

LANDMARK SUNSHINE CINEMAS
Map p98
☎ 212-358-7709; www.landmarktheatres.com; 143 E Houston St at Forsyth St, Lower East Side; ◉ F, V to Lower East Side-2nd Ave
A renovated Yiddish theater, the wonderful Landmark shows foreign and first-run mainstream art films on massive screens. It also has much-coveted stadium-style seating, so

it doesn't matter what giant sits in front of you after the lights go out.

MUSEUM OF MODERN ART Map pp134–5

☎ 212-708-9480; 11 W 53rd St btwn Fifth & Sixth Aves, Midtown West; ⊙ B, D, F, V to 47th-50th Sts-Rockefeller Center

Not only a palace of visual art, MoMA hosts an incredibly well-rounded selection of celluloid gems both old and new. A recent schedule ran the gamut from the 1948 *Alice in Wonderland* to Wallace & Gromit shorts and a retrospective of works from Serbian director Goran Paskaljevic.

WALTER READE THEATER Map p153

☎ 212-875-5600; Lincoln Center, 165 W 65th St, Upper West Side; ⊙ 1 to 66th St-Lincoln Center

The Walter Reade boasts some wonderfully wide, screening room–style seats and hosts, every September, the New York Film Festival, featuring plenty of New York and world premieres. At other times of the year you can catch independent films, career retrospectives and themed series.

LECTURES

A bit stuffier than readings or spoken-word events but often just as entertaining, mind-expanding lectures can be found at virtually every cultural center in town, from universities to museums, which is not surprising for such an intellectual hub. The following is just a small sampling.

92ND ST Y Map p142

☎ 212-415-5500; www.92y.org; 1395 Lexington Ave at 92nd St, Upper East Side; ⊙ 6 to 96th St

In addition to its spectrum of wonderful readings, the Y hosts an excellent Lectures & Discussions series, which has recently featured thinkers from Christopher Hitchens and Dennis Kucinich to Mos Def and former NYC mayor Ed Koch. Makor (Map pp72–3; ☎ 212-601-1000; 200 Hudson St), the Y's newly-relocated downtown outpost for the 35-and-under crowd, has its very own energized lineup, on topics from real estate to dating.

ARCHITECTURAL LEAGUE OF NEW YORK Map p126

☎ 212-753-1722; www.archleague.org; Urban Center, 457 Madison Ave btwn 50th & 51st Sts, Midtown East; ⊙ B, D, F, V to 47th-50th Sts-Rockefeller Center

This unique nonprofit organization, founded in 1881 by a group of young architects who wanted their own venue for creative and artistic development, offers a constant supply of top-notch architecture-based lectures (as well as installations and forums) that focus on development, urbanism, design and planning, especially as it affects the landscape of New York City.

NEW SCHOOL UNIVERSITY Map p110

☎ 212-229-5880; www.newschool.edu; 66 Fifth Ave at 12th St, Greenwich Village; ⊙ F, V to 14th St

The forward-thinking university, comprised of the Parsons School of Design and various arts, music and urban-studies divisions, hosts a series of public discourses for anyone interested in attending; if you can't be there in person, the school's website has webcasts available for downloading. Recent discussions have revolved around strengthening the middle class, recovering from the mortgage crisis in NYC neighborhoods, how to organize protests, global warming and the history of the AIDS pandemic.

NEW YORK PUBLIC LIBRARY Map p126

☎ 212-930-0830; www.nypl.org/events; 42nd St at Fifth Ave, Midtown East; ⊙ 11am-7:30pm Tue & Wed, 10am-6pm Thu-Sat; ⊙ 4, 5, 6 to 42nd St-Grand Central, 7 to Fifth Ave

The public library operates a constant offering of lectures and public seminars at its myriad branch locations, including some of the best at the main Humanities & Social Sciences Library on 42nd St. Just a select sampling of recent evenings included biographer John Richardson in conversation with journalist Robert Hughes on documenting the life of Picasso, curator Isaac Gewirtz on his NYPL exhibit about Jack Kerouac, and author Colm Toíbín on the life and work of James Baldwin.

OPERA

Minds tend to go directly to the lavish images of Metropolitan Opera productions when thinking about this category. And, though it may be what most opera fans would like to see, too, it's not necessarily what everyone can afford. Luckily, you can see equally top-shelf, but less luxuriously staged productions by the New York City Opera (though rumors of its demise are in constant circulation) and at various budget options downtown.

AMATO OPERA THEATER Map p104

☎ 212-228-8200; www.amato.org; 319 Bowery at 2nd St, East Village; ◎ 6 to Bleecker St, B, D, F, V to Broadway-Lafayette St

To see classics without all (or any of) the glitz, head to this tiny, alternative opera house, which regularly puts on favorites such as *The Barber of Seville, Così Fan Tutte, The Marriage of Figaro* and *La Bohème*.

BAM ROSE CINEMA Map p180

☎ 718-623-2770; www.bam.org; 30 Lafayette Ave at Flatbush Ave, Fort Greene, Brooklyn; ◎ D, M, N, R, W to Pacific St, B, Q, 2, 3, 4, 5 to Atlantic Ave

In addition to its excellent film, dance, music and theater programming, BAM regularly presents a small program of operas, with music by the Brooklyn Philharmonic, as well as live simulcasts of the Metropolitan Opera.

METROPOLITAN OPERA HOUSE
Map p153

☎ 212-362-6000; www.metopera.org; Lincoln Center, 64th St at Columbus Ave, Upper West Side; ◎ 1 to 66th St-Lincoln Center

New York's premier opera company, the Metropolitan Opera offers a spectacular mixture of classics and premieres. This is the place to see favorites like *Carmen, Madam Butterfly, Macbeth* and *Otello*, as well as new works like *Hansel and Gretel*, unveiled in 2008. The season runs from September to April. Though ticket prices start at $70 and can get close to $300, the standing-room tickets for $15 to $20 are one of NYC's best bargains. They go on sale at 10am Saturday for the following week's performances. True, your feet will hurt and you won't see much, but you'll hear everything.

NEW YORK STATE THEATER Map p153

☎ 212-870-5630; www.nycopera.com; Lincoln Center, 64th St at Columbus Ave, Upper West Side; ◎ 1 to 66th St-Lincoln Center

This is the home of the New York City Opera, a more daring and lower-cost company than the Metropolitan Opera. It performs new works, neglected operas and revitalized old standards in the Philip Johnson–designed space. The split season runs for a few weeks in early fall and once again during early to late spring. At the time of research, however, word was that the opera would go on indefinite hiatus during the complete renovation of the New York State Theater.

READINGS

Even with the competition of various music shows, films and theatrical events around town, literary events are still popular draws for New Yorkers. Hallelujah! Though you'll find a constant lineup of big-name writers reading from their works at the multitudinous Barnes & Nobles around town, these can often feel more profit-driven than those held at smaller, independently owned shops or literary-minded pubs, theaters, libraries and museums.

92ND ST Y Map p142

☎ 212-415-5500; www.92y.org; 1395 Lexington Ave at 92nd St, Upper East Side; ◎ 6 to 96th St

The Y is a bastion of literary greatness (as well as a venue that caters for music and dance), with its Unterburg Poetry Center hosting frequent readings, plus a Biographers and Brunch lecture series on Sundays, which features top-shelf authors. Recent appearances have included Meg Wolitzer, Umberto Eco and Salman Rushdie. Almost all the big-name readings sell out, so if there's a particular author you're wanting to hear, be sure to reserve well in advance.

BLUESTOCKINGS Map p98

☎ 212-777-6028; www.bluestockings.com; 172 Allen St btwn Stanton & Rivington Sts, Lower East Side; ◎ F, V to Lower East Side-2nd Ave

A small and independent radical/feminist bookstore and café, Bluestockings hosts frequent and energizing readings, discussions and spoken-word performances, often with a focus on social or political change. Various readings series highlight new novelists, revolutionary storytellers and, on the last Tuesday of each month, women poets, with a poetry jam and open-mic hosted by 'the hardest-working guinea butch-dyke poet on the Lower East Side.'

BOWERY POETRY CLUB Map pp88–9

☎ 212-614-0505; www.bowerypoetry.com; 308 Bowery btwn Bleecker & Houston Sts, NoHo; ◎ 6 to Bleecker St

Just across from the old CBGB site on the East Village/NoHo border, this funky café and performance space has eccentric readings of all genres, from plays to fiction, plus frequent themed poetry slams and literary-focused parties that celebrate new books and their authors.

BROOKLYN PUBLIC LIBRARY Map p182

☎ 718-230-2100; www.brooklynpubliclibrary.org; Grand Army Plaza, Prospect Park; ⊕ 2, 3 to Grand Army Plaza

Located on the northeast edge of Brooklyn's Park Slope neighborhood, this grand library hosts a phenomenal reading series that highlights local authors; Brooklyn DA Charles Hynes, novelist Russell Banks and human rights activist Simon Deng have all graced the podium to share excerpts of their books here.

CORNELIA ST CAFÉ Map p110

☎ 212-989-9319; www.corneliastreetcafe.com; 29 Cornelia St btwn Bleecker & W 4th Sts, West Village; ⊕ A, C, E, B, D, F, V to W 4th St-Washington Sq

This intimate café is known for its various lit series, including monthly storytelling gatherings, open-mic poetry nights, and readings dedicated to Italian Americans, Greeks, Caribbean Americans, NYC-area grads, members of the Writers Room (a local writers collective), scribes of prose and emerging poets. There are also music performances and art exhibits here, plus a nice café menu.

KGB BAR Map p104

☎ 212-505-3360; www.kgbbar.com; 84 E 4th St btwn Second & Third Aves, East Village; ⊕ F, V to Lower East Side-2nd Ave

This Commie-themed bar, one flight above street level, hosts readings on most nights, with occasional appearances from local lit stars such as Rick Moody and Marissa Miley, plus popular theme nights that present lineups of journalists, Jewish novelists, poets, crime authors and fantasy writers.

top picks

- **Run** (p333), **bike** (p328), **ice-skate** (p332) **and bird-watch** (p331) You can do it all in Central Park.
- **NY Yankees** (p325) Help cheer on the Bronx Bombers (or boo if you're from Boston).
- **Street basketball** (boxed text, p325) Watch a dunk-athon at 'the Cage' or historic Rucker Park in Harlem.
- **Kayak the rivers** (p330) Public boathouses across New York have free kayaks to use.
- **Hit the waves** (p334) Surf's up! NYC's surf ban has finally been lifted.

Hailing cabs in New York City can feel like a game, and waiting on subway platforms in summer heat feels like a sauna, but there are more standard ways to move about and sweat, or to simply watch others do it better than you. Considering how limited the green spaces are in New York, it's surprising for some visitors how active locals are: everywhere you go you see locals jogging, riding bikes, playing pick-up hoops or soccer, or rooting on Little Leaguers on baseball diamonds that freckle the metropolis. If you need a workout, skip that claustrophobic, windowless fitness room with a jogging machine and a couple of weights in your hotel. Chelsea Piers, where the Titanic was supposed to dock, is now a catch-all activity zone, with hockey rinks, bowling alleys, virtual golf and a huge fitness center. Outdoors you can easily find ways to exercise your bones and sightsee a bit at the same time – go run where Jackie O did in Central Park, take a free kayak out on the Hudson or East River, or have a swing on a trapeze.

When New Yorkers don't play, they watch. All sports are represented here and seasons overlap all year, with particular attention going to the Yankees' baseball season, the Giants' football season, plus the New York City Marathon in early November. Dig deeper to uncover the sports of the streets – stickball is still played in the Bronx, and watching street ball played on the basketball courts at Rucker Park in Harlem is legendary.

SPECTATOR SPORTS

Don't pay too much attention to the uppity scoffing that local sports get from New York transplants in downtown bars, Chelsea galleries or at Lincoln Center – deep down, New York is as sports-mad as any town with pitch, field, court or alley. This was proven again with the delirium that followed the New York Football Giants' unlikely late-season rally in 2008 to bring the first championship to New York since September 11.

If you can't see a game in person (though it's worth trying to catch at least a Yankees game), try a little neighborhood bar when a Knicks, Giants or Yankees game is on – it can really light up. Be ready to high-five your neighbor when Eli Manning throws for a TD or Derek Jeter throws a ninth-inning third out. Even if you don't understand American sports, you'll likely find some more-than-willing tutors.

For game analysis, skip the overly polite *New York Times* and go with the no-punches-held-back sports pages of the *New York Daily News* or the *New York Post*.

BASEBALL

New York is one of the last remaining corners of the USA where baseball reigns supreme over football and basketball. With tickets starting at $10 it's a steal to see, and by 2009 there will be two new stadiums to visit (see the boxed text, p211). In the post-WWII years, New York had three teams, all powerhouses: the Yankees, the Giants and the Brooklyn Dodgers. Thirteen times, two of them met in the finals – the heralded 'Subway Series.' The unthinkable came in 1957 when both the Dodgers and Giants bolted for Los Angeles and San Francisco, respectively. The arrival of the Mets in Queens a few years later (strategically using a color combo of the departed teams) was welcomed, but didn't quite dull the sense of betrayal felt by many fans (including ones not yet born in 1957).

Major League

The two MLB (Major League Baseball) teams play 162 games during the regular season from April to October, when the playoffs begin.

NEW YORK METS

Shea Stadium; Map pp200-1; ☎ 718-507-8499; www .mets.com; 123-01 Roosevelt Ave, Flushing, Queens; tickets $5-82; ⊙ 7 to Willets Point-Shea Stadium
In 2009, the Mets are moving from Shea (where the Beatles played) to a new sta-

NYC STREET SPORTS

With all that concrete around, New York has embraced a number of sports and events played on the streets. If you have TV handy, check SportsNet New York (http://web.sny.tv) for its weekly half-hour show *Street Games*.

Handball

Irish immigrant Phil Casey built New York's first four-wall handball court in 1882, and following his rise in the sport (he challenged, and whipped, the Irish world champ in 1887), it quickly became big in New York. In the early 20th century, South Brooklyn started putting up one-wall handball courts around Coney Island. These days, you'll find one-wall courts in outdoor parks all over the city (there are 260 in Manhattan alone). See www.nycgovparks.org for a list.

Pick-up Basketball

People with hoop dreams, small and large, hit the city's courts throughout the year. The most famous is the West 4th St Basketball Courts (Map p110; cnr W 3rd St & Sixth Ave, Greenwich Village), more famously known as 'the Cage' – they draw summer audiences on the weekends, and games sometimes fade into elongated dunk-a-thons. Up in Harlem, Rucker Park (Map pp158–9; Frederick Douglass Blvd & 155th St) is where NBA stars like Dr J, Kareem Abdul-Jabbar, Kobe Bryant, Allen Iverson and Kevin Garnett have showed up to play; organized games start around 6pm Monday to Thursday in summer.

You can also find pick-up games at Tompkins Square Park (p103) in the East Village and at Riverside Park (p154) in the Upper West Side.

Stickball

Nothing is more street than stickball, New York's decades-old offshoot of English games like 'old cat' and 'town ball.' It's essentially a crude form of baseball – but the pitcher usually throws a pink Spalding ball off the bounce, batters hit with a broom handle, the bases are manhole covers, and parked cars and fire escapes serve as obstacles.

Stickball has stormed its way back in the past 20 years. The Bronx-based Emperors Stickball League (Map pp208–9; ☎ 201-658-1871; www.stickball.com) plays 10am to 2pm or 3pm at Stickball Blvd, between Seward and Randall Aves, on Sunday from mid-April through July; call for directions. Compared with baseball, one player said, 'It's more in your face; we taunt…but with respect.'

dium next door, Citi Park. Still New York's 'new' baseball team, the Mets joined the National League in 1962. Fans still hold onto the magic of '86, when the Mets last won the World Series in a miraculous comeback. Their blue-and-orange logo shows select buildings from New York's five boroughs. The stadium is 35 minutes by subway from Midtown.

NEW YORK YANKEES

Yankee Stadium; Map pp208-9; ☎ 718-293-6000, tickets 212-307-1212; www.yankees.com; cnr 161st St & River Ave, the Bronx; tickets $10-400; ⓔ B, D, 4 to 161st St-Yankee Stadium

The Bronx Bombers are the USA's greatest dynasty, with 26 World Series championships racked up since 1900. But without one since 2000, the Bronx is trembling. In 2007 the Yankee organization snubbed long-time manager Joe Torre with a flip salary offer, and will re-focus with Joe Girardi at the helm. The roster – led by Alex Rodriguez

and Derek Jeter – is something of a single-team all-star lineup. Games in 2008 are still held at the fabled Yankee Stadium (p212), but will move in 2009 or 2010 to a new $1.3 billion stadium nearby. Note: cheap seats in the bleachers are alcohol-free.

Minor League

New York is also home to a couple of minor league teams with atmospheric waterfront stadiums.

BROOKLYN CYCLONES

KeySpan Park; Map pp196-7; ☎ 718-449-8497; www .brooklyncyclones.com; 1904 Surf Ave at W 17th St, Coney Island, Brooklyn; tickets $6-13, $1 extra Fri-Sun; ⓔ D, F, N, Q to Coney Island-Stillwell Ave

The Mets' farm team brought baseball back to Brooklyn (finally) in 2001. The minor-league team, part of the New York/Penn League, plays at this beachside park a few steps from the Coney Island boardwalk.

STATEN ISLAND YANKEES

Richmond County Bank Ballpark; off Map p68;
☎ 718-720-9265; www.siyanks.com; 75 Richmond
Tce, Staten Island; tickets $10; ☺ ticket office
9am-5pm Mon-Fri, 10am-3pm Sat; ⊙ Staten Island
Ferry

These Yanks have been champions of the
New York/Penn title three times in the past
decade (including 2005). If you don't catch
a fly ball, you can at least catch some fab
Manhattan skyline views from this stylish
waterfront stadium.

BASKETBALL

Two NBA teams, the Knicks and the Nets, call
the New York metropolitan area home. The
season lasts from October to May or June.

NEW YORK KNICKS

Madison Square Garden; Map pp134-5; ☎ 212-465-
5867, tickets 212-307-7171; www.nyknicks.com;
btwn Seventh Ave & 33rd St, Midtown West; tickets
from $34.50; ⊙ A, C, E, 1, 2, 3 to 34th St-Penn
Station

They're bad and in trouble of late (coach
Isiah Thomas paid $11 million after a sexual
harassment case in 2007), but the blue-
and-orange are loved. The first rap song,
actually, gives it up for the beloved Knick-
erbockers (Sugar Hill Gang sings 'I have a
color TV so I can watch the Knicks play basketball'). Despite big crowds of Spike Lee
and 18,999 others at the Garden, the Knicks
haven't won a championship since 1973.

NEW YORK LIBERTY

Madison Square Garden; Map pp134-5; ☎ 212-564-
6622, tickets 212-307-7171; www.nyliberty.com;
btwn Seventh Ave & 33rd St, Midtown West; tickets
$10-55; ⊙ A, C, E, 1, 2, 3 to 34th St-Penn Station
Still searching for their first championship, the women's WNBA team plays a
34-game season from May to September
or October.

NEW JERSEY NETS

Izod Center, Meadowlands Sports Complex; off Map
p69; ☎ 201-935-8888, tickets 201-507-8900; www
.njnets.com; East Rutherford, NJ; tickets from $15;
☺ box office 11am-6pm Mon-Sat & till half-time
on game days; ☐ 351 from Port Authority
Overshadowed by but better than the
Knicks, the Nets play exciting ball, though
their closest championship call was being
runners-up in 2002 and 2003 finals. Per-

haps what the Nets have needed is a total
relocation. Real-estate mogul Bruce Ratner
bought the Nets in 2004 and plans to move
them to Brooklyn by 2009 (see p189).

For directions to the Meadowlands, see
the boxed text, above.

FOOTBALL

Football season runs from August to January
or February. Most of New York tunes into
its NFL teams – the Giants and Jets – both of
whom play at Giants Stadium in New Jersey.
The NFL season has 16 regular-season games
(held on Sunday or Monday night), then up to
three playoffs before the Super Bowl. Tickets
are always sold out, but you can find some
from $100 each from StubHub (☎ 866-788-2482;
www.stubhub.com), www.craigslist.com or www
.ticketsfornfl.com. If that's too tough or expensive, try the local college teams, who play
on Saturday in fall.

For information on getting to the games,
see the boxed text, above.

NFL

NEW YORK GIANTS

Giants Stadium, Meadowlands Sports Complex; off
Map p69; ☎ 201-935-8222; www.giants.com; East
Rutherford, NJ; ☐ 351 from Port Authority
One of the NFL's oldest teams, the Giants
(part of the NFC conference) shocked the
world (and themselves) with 2007-08 Super
Bowl championship off their stingy defense
and the sometimes maligned arm of quarterback Eli Manning. The same hardened
troops of fans who grew teary-eyed and
yelled 'WE DID IT' will surely be cussing for
more by the 2008 and 2009 seasons. Glory
fades fast.

NEW YORK JETS

Giants Stadium, Meadowlands Sports Complex; off Map p69; ☎ 516-560-8200 ext 1; www.new yorkjets.com; East Rutherford, NJ; 🚌 351 from Port Authority

The Jets, generally less popular than the Giants (after all, they play in *Giants* Stadium), have yet to return to the big time since the fabled 1969 Super Bowl when flashy quarterback Joe Namath 'guaranteed' a victory – and delivered. Games are always packed though, and new fans easily get swept away by the contagious, 'J-E-T-S!' chants. Now, if they can just get a quarterback who will produce…

College

COLUMBIA LIONS

Lawrence A Wien Stadium; off Map pp158-9; www.go columbialions.com; 218th St & Broadway, Inwood, Manhattan; 🚇 1 to 215th St

Harlem has its own cute baby-blue Ivy League team for Saturday college football action. The Lions will likely lose, but at least tickets aren't a problem.

RUTGERS SCARLET KNIGHTS

Rutgers Stadium; off Map p69; www.scarletknights .com; ☎ 866-445-4678; 1 Scarlet Knight Way, Piscataway, NJ; 🚆 NJ Transit from Penn Station to New Brunswick, NJ

With fiery coach Greg Schiano leading the Scarlet Knights from scapegoat to end-of-season bowls, Rutgers (college football's oldest team) is now actually turning the heads of New York football fans. Games are held just outside the university's New Brunswick campus, about 35 miles southwest of Manhattan.

Arena Football

NEW YORK DRAGONS

Nassau Veterans Memorial Coliseum; off Map pp200-1; ☎ 516-501-6700, tickets 631-888-9000; www .newyorkdragons.com; 1255 Hempstead Turnpike, Uniondale, Long Island; tickets $20-60; 🚆 LIRR to Hempstead station, then bus 🚌 N70, N71 or N72

New York's arena football team plays the far goofier mini version of gridiron in Long Island. The season for the 17-team Arena Football League (AFL) – team names include, um, Kats and Sabercats – runs February through July.

HOCKEY

Still struggling for significance following the PR fall-out of the 2004–05 strike, the National Hockey League (NHL) has three franchises in the greater New York area; each team plays three or four games weekly during the season from September to April.

NEW YORK RANGERS

Madison Square Garden; Map pp134-5; ☎ 212-465-6741, tickets 212-307-7171; www.nyrangers.com; btwn Seventh Ave & 33rd St, Midtown West; tickets from $40; 🚇 A, C, E, 1, 2, 3 to 34th St-Penn Station

Manhattan's favorite hockey squad ended a 54-year dry spell by hoisting the Stanley Cup in 1994, though a dip in play has plagued recent seasons. If only right-winger Jaromir Jagr would grow back his trademark hockey hair (aka 'business in front, party in back').

NEW YORK ISLANDERS

Nassau Veterans Memorial Coliseum; off Map pp200-1; ☎ 631-888-9000; www.newyorkislanders.com; 1255 Hempstead Turnpike, Uniondale, Long Island; tickets from $19; 🚆 LIRR to Hempstead station, then bus 🚌 N70, N71 or N72

New York City hasn't given much Islander love since their remarkable consecutive four-year Stanley Cup streak (1980–83). If you venture out to their Long Island home, give a high-five to Sparky the Dragon (www.sparky thedragon.com) for us.

NEW JERSEY DEVILS

Prudential Center; off Map p69; ☎ 201-935-6050, tickets ☎ 212-307-7171; www.newjerseydevils .com; 165 Mulberry St, Newark, NJ; tickets from $10; 🚇 NJ Transit or PATH train to Newark Penn Station

The Devils may not be New Yorkers, but they're bigger winners (hoisting the Stanley Cup three times in the past 15 years, most recently in 2003). And now they have a home in downtown Newark, the Prudential Center (opened in 2007), so they won't have to stage their next 'victory parade' at Giants Stadium's parking lot again.

HORSE RACING

The biggest local event is the Triple Crown's final race: the Belmont Stakes (early June), held at the Belmont Park Race Track (Map pp200-1; ☎ 516-488-6000; www.nyra.com; Elmont, Long Island;

admission $2-5; ☒ LIRR to the Belmont Race Track stop). The track is open May to mid-July, and September and October.

Also, thoroughbreds race from late October to early May at the Aqueduct Race Track (Map pp200–1; ☎ 718-641-4700; Howard Beach, Queens; admission $1-2; ◎ A to Aqueduct Racetrack).

The track at Meadowlands (off Map p69; ☎ 201-843-2446; www.meadowlandsracetrack.com; Meadowlands Sports Complex, East Rutherford, NJ; admission $1-5; ☒ 351 from Port Authority) has harness racing January to August (Wednesday to Saturday or Sunday) and thoroughbreds September to November (Tuesday or Wednesday to Saturday). See the boxed text on p326 for directions.

SOCCER

Yes, people in the US *do* play soccer.

NEW YORK RED BULLS

Giants Stadium, Meadowlands Sports Complex; off Map p69; **☎ 201-583-7000; www.redbulls.com; East Rutherford, NJ; tickets $18-85; ☒ 351 from Port Authority**
The Bulls are planning to have a purpose-built, $130-million soccer stadium constructed in nearby Harrison, New Jersey (perhaps by the 2009 season). Until then, you can catch star forward Juan Pablo Angel and the Red Bulls' 30-game season (from April through October) at Giants Stadium. For directions on getting there, see the boxed text on p326.

TENNIS

The pro tennis circuit's final Grand Slam event each year, the US Open (www.usopen.org), takes place over two weeks at the end of August at USTA National Tennis Center (Map pp200–1; ☎ 718-760-6200; www.usta.com; Flushing Meadows Corona Park, Queens; ◎ 7 to Willets Point-Shea Stadium). Tickets usually go on sale at Ticketmaster (www.ticketmaster.com) in April or May, but marquee games (held at Arthur Ashe Stadium) are hard to get. General admission to early rounds is easier; they run about $75 (top bleachers on Court 7 can take in five matches at once). Check out the USTA site in January or February for updates.

ACTIVITIES

Going out in New York doesn't always mean going to a bar or the opera. There are plenty of activities that vary by the season. Pretty much

PARK HOTLINE

Check www.nycgovparks.org or call ☎ 311 for New York parks info – you'll get details on park services including free pools and open basketball-court times.

anytime it's not snowing or raining, you'll find soccer and basketball players looking for extra players, or cyclists and joggers doing loop trails in many New York parks, while other parks offer bird-watching tours that point out an unexpectedly rich life lurking in the trees. New York's canals and rivers are unexpectedly good fun for kayaks and sailboats. Even winter gets in the action, with open-air skating rinks in the parks (and even one in Midtown).

BIKING

New York has never been the world's most bicycle-friendly city, but things have started to shift gears a bit in recent years. That said, you still may prefer designated bike areas (eg waterside trails, bike lanes in Central Park or across the Brooklyn Bridge) to taking on the streets, where there always seems to be a double-parked car or open door blocking your way. This happens too on the few designated bike lanes (eg Lafayette St, Broadway, Second Ave).

On streets, wear a helmet and signal your turns. It's possible to take a bike on the last door of subways, but avoid rush hours and stand with your bike. Bike racks are around to lock up a bike in some places; only use the strongest locks.

For detailed bike maps of Manhattan and the boroughs, check the Things to Do/Activities section of www.nycgovparks.org, or search for 'bike map' at www.nyc.gov.

Where to Ride

The work-in-progress, 32-mile Manhattan Waterfront Greenway (www.nyc.gov) circumnavigates Manhattan – a great ride, though it can only be done with a detour on a surface road or two. The 'greenway' is uninterrupted from Manhattan Bridge, around the tip of Manhattan at Battery Park and up the Hudson River to Riverside Park in the Upper West Side; but it's not that hard to do the whole thing.

Central Park (Map p149) has wide, well-paved roads that run north–south and in between, making excellent loops of 1.7, 5.2 and 6.1 miles. There are bike lanes. Cars access the roads 7am to 10am and 3pm to 7pm Monday to Friday.

Brooklyn's gorgeous Prospect Park (p181) has the 3.35-mile Park Dr to ride anytime. Note the road's southbound West Drive is open to motorists 5pm to 7pm weekdays and the northbound North Drive is open 7am to 9am and 5pm to 7pm.

Long cratered and eroded, the 1940s-era Shore Parkway Path in Brooklyn, which bends along the New York Harbor past the Verrazano-Narrows Bridge, now sports two slick, redeveloped miles from the bridge to the 69th St Pier in Bay Ridge. Eventually 14 miles will be developed.

Organizations

Some clubs sponsor various rides. The Five Borough Bicycle Club (Map p153; ☎ 212-932-2300 ext 115; www.5bbc.org; 891 Amsterdam Ave at 104th St, Upper West Side; ⊕ 1 to 103rd St) leads free trips for its members ($20 annual fee); the club office is at Hostelling International – New York (p365). Another good club is the New York Cycle Club (☎ 212-828-5711; www.nycc.org).

Fast & Fabulous (☎ 212-567-7160; www.fastnfab.org) is a membership-based bicycling club for gays and lesbians with frequent rides.

Several hundred cyclists (and in-line skaters) promote safer streets and bike lanes in Critical Mass, a traffic-halting ride leaving from the north side of Union Sq at 7pm the last Friday of the month. There's also a Brooklyn Critical Mass leaving at 7pm the second Friday of the month from Grand Army Plaza at Prospect Park. Time's Up (www.times-up.org) has more information.

May is NYC Bike Month; see Transportation Alternative (www.transalt.org) for scheduled events; it also organizes a 100-mile New York Century Ride around the boroughs in September.

Concerned Long Island Mountain Bicyclists (CLIMB; www.climbonline.org) offers rides on area mountain-bike trails.

Bike Rental

CENTRAL PARK BICYCLE TOURS & RENTALS Map pp134–5

☎ 212-541-8759; www.centralparkbiketours.com; Columbus Circle, Midtown West; bike hire per 2hr/day $25/40, tours adult/child $40/20; ⊕ A, C, B, D, 1 to 59th St-Columbus Circle

This place rents mountain bikes and leads various two-hour tours of the park, going three to five times daily – one tour takes in movie sites. Rental prices include lock and helmet. Open mid-March through October. Call for pick-up location info.

GOTHAM BIKES DOWNTOWN Map pp72–3

☎ 212-732-2453; 112 W Broadway btwn Duane & Reade Sts, Lower Manhattan; bike rental per 1/24 hr $10/30; ⊕ 10am-6:30pm Mon-Sat, 10:30am-5pm Sun; ⊕ A, C, 1, 2, 3 to Chambers St

Not far from the Hudson River – a good spot for riding – this affiliate of downtown's Toga (below) has a good selection of bikes and bike parts, and also rents bikes.

LOEB BOATHOUSE Map p149

☎ 212-517-2233; Central Park, btwn 74th & 75th Sts; bike hire per hr $9-15; ⊕ 10am-6pm; ⊕ B, C to 72nd St, 6 to 77th St

Various types of bikes are available (weather permitting), roughly April to October. You'll need an ID and credit card to rent one. Helmets provided.

ON THE MOVE Map p182

☎ 718-768-4998; 400 Seventh Ave btwn 12th & 13th Sts, Park Slope, Brooklyn; bike per hr $25-35, helmet rental $5; ⊕ 11am-7pm Mon & Fri, noon-7pm Tue-Thu, 10am-6pm Sat, 11am-5pm Sun; ⊕ F to 7th Ave

Brooklyn rents too! A couple of blocks from Prospect Park, On the Move rents all year, but cuts back hours from October through March.

RECYCLE-A-BICYCLE Map p104

☎ 212-475-1655; 75 Ave C btwn 5th & 6th Sts, East Village; ⊕ F, V to Lower East Side-2nd Ave

The Recycle folks offer several youth-related programs, sell good used bikes and rent a few single-speed cruisers too (no helmets available). They also run a smaller Brooklyn location (Map p174; ☎ 718-858-2972; 35 Pear St, Brooklyn; bike hire per 1/24 hr $8/25; ⊕ noon-7pm Mon-Sat; ⊕ F to York St) in Dumbo.

TOGA BIKE SHOP Map p153

☎ 212-799-9625; www.togabikes.com; 110 West End Ave btwn 64th & 65th Sts, Upper West Side; bike rental per 24hr $35; ⊕ 11am-7pm Mon-Fri, 10am-6pm Sat, 11am-6pm Sun; ⊕ 1 to 66th St-Lincoln Center

Conveniently located between Central Park and the Hudson River path, this friendly and long-standing bike shop rents bikes in good weather (typically April through October).

You'll need to leave a deposit on a credit card. Rental price includes a helmet.

BOATING & KAYAKING

The free Staten Island Ferry (p75) is New York's ultimate recreational boating trip – and it's free. Central Park and Brooklyn's Prospect Park have rowboats or pedal boats to rent, and City Island, a fishing community in the Bronx, has charter opportunities. Manhattan's Circle Line (p404) offers classic round-the-island boat cruises, while the newfangled yellow-and-black New York Water Taxis (see p391) provide hop-on/hop-off Manhattan and Brooklyn access

New York Water Fest (www.nywaterfest.org), a six-mile race from Pier 96, is held in mid October.

Private Boathouses

AUDUBON CENTER BOATHOUSE Map p182

☎ 718-287-3400; Prospect Park, Brooklyn; boat rides adult/children $5/3; ☼ noon-5:30pm Thu-Sun Apr-Sep, noon-4:30pm Sat & Sun Oct; ◉ B, Q to Prospect Park, 2, 3 to Grand Army Plaza

The lovely Venetian-style boathouse offers electric boat rides on the vintage-style *Independence*; paddleboats are available too.

LOEB BOATHOUSE Map p149

☎ 212-517-2233; www.thecentralparkboathouse .com; Central Park btwn 74th & 75th Sts; per hr $10; ☼ 9:30am-5:30pm Apr-Oct; ◉ B, C to 72nd St, 6 to 77th St

Central Park's boathouse rents row boats from April to October (weather permitting). There are Vienna-style gondolas in summer (per 30 minutes $30). The water here is really not as dirty as Woody Allen suggests in the boat scene in *Manhattan*.

MANHATTAN KAYAK COMPANY Map p116

☎ 212-924-1788; www.manhattankayak.com; Pier 66, 26th St & Twelfth Ave, Chelsea; ◉ C, E to 23rd St

Suitable for first-timers or experts, Manhattan Kayak Company offers a huge swathe of waterborne options from April to November. The five-hour 'sushi' trip leads to a Japanese-Jersey community for sushi lunch ($100, not including food). Other offerings include 90-minute full-moon tours at night ($60) and a tough full-day romp around Manhattan ($225). One-hour practice sessions are $25. Call for tour times.

SCHOONER ADIRONDACK Map p116

☎ 646-336-5270; www.sail-nyc.com; Chelsea Piers, Pier 59 at W 17th St, Chelsea; tours $40-50; ◉ A, C, E to 14th St

The two-masted 'Dack hits the New York Harbor with four two-hour sails daily from May to October. The 1920s-style, 80ft *Manhattan* yacht makes three-hour circumnavigation sunset tours at 6pm, night tours at 8:30pm and day tours at 1pm or 3:30pm. Call or check the website for tour times.

Public Boathouses

Nonprofit boathouses around New York City make the most of the protected coves and inlets around the city's waterfront. The following offer free kayaking or canoeing – including equipment and tips – from mid-May through October.

DOWNTOWN BOATHOUSE Map p110

☎ 646-613-0740; www.downtownboathouse.org; Pier 40, near Houston St, West Village; admission free; ☼ 9am-6pm Sat & Sun mid-May–mid-Oct, also open some weekday evenings; ◉ 1 to Houston St

New York's most active public boathouse offers free walk-up 20-minute kayaking (including equipment) in the protected embayment in the Hudson River on weekends and some weekday evenings from mid-June to mid-September. Longer rides (eg to Governor's Island) usually go from the Midtown location at Clinton Cove (Map pp134–5; Pier 96, west of 56th St, Midtown West; ☼ 9am-6pm Sat & Sun, 5-7pm mid-Jun–Aug; ◉ A, B, C, D, 1 to 59th St-Columbus Circle); there's another boathouse at Riverside Park (Map p153; W 72nd St; ☼ 10am-5pm Sat & Sun; ◉ 1, 2, 3 to 72nd St).

FRIENDS OF BROOK PARK Map pp208–9

☎ 646-206-5288; www.friendsofbrookpark.org; 111 Lincoln St, at Bruckner Blvd, the Bronx; kayak tours $50-150; ◉ 6 to 3rd Ave-138th St

This Bronx community organization works hard at developing the Harlem River waterfront and hosts various events, including the 'Five Borough Harbor Ramble' in September.

GOWANUS DREDGERS CANOE CLUB Map p180

☎ 718-243-0849; www.gowanuscanal.org; cnr 2nd St & Bond St, Gowanus Canal, Brooklyn; ◉ F, G to Carroll St

Self-guided canoe trips of the gritty Gowanus Canal are offered as well as 90-minute

TEN-PIN MANIA

Among retro-crazed New Yorkers, a night of bowling qualifies as quite a hoot. Maybe it's the shoes, or all the pitchers of beer.

300 New York at Chelsea Piers (Map p116; ☎ 212-835-2695; www.300newyork.com; Chelsea Piers, btwn Piers 59 & 60, Chelsea; individual games $8-11, shoe rental $6; ☺ 9am-11pm Mon-Thu & Sun, 9am-2am Fri & Sat; ◉ C, E to 23rd St) The 300 goes for martinis and disco nights Thursday through Sunday.

Bowlmor Lanes (Map p110; ☎ 212-255-8188; 110 University Pl, Greenwich Village; individual games before/after 5pm Mon-Thu $9/9.50, Fri & Sat $9.50/10, Sun $9.50, shoe rental $5.50; ☺ 11am-2am Mon & Thu, 11am-1am Tue & Wed, 11am-3:30am Fri & Sat, 11am-midnight Sun; ◉ L, N, Q, R, W, 4, 5, 6 to 14th St-Union Sq) Open since 1938, Bowlmor is Manhattan's go-to-lanes for stars, bar mitzvah parties and beer-slugging NYU students. After 10pm Monday, it goes DJ-blasting glow-in-the-dark, with unlimited bowling for $22 including shoe rental (age 21 and up).

Gutter (Map p177; ☎ 718-387-3585; 200 N 14th St btwn Berry & Wythe Sts, Williamsburg, Brooklyn; individual games before/after 8pm $6/7, shoe rental $4; ☺ 4pm-4am Mon-Thu, noon-4am Fri-Sun; ◉ L to Bedford Ave) It's hip, cheap and old school, with eight, quickly filled vintage lanes.

Leisure Time Bowling Center (Map pp134-5; ☎ 212-268-6909; 625 Eighth Ave, 2nd fl, Port Authority Bus Terminal, Midtown West; individual games before/after 5pm Mon-Fri $6.50/9.50, Sat & Sun $9.50, shoe rental $5; ☺ 10am-midnight Mon-Thu, 10am-1am Fri, 1pm-1am Sat, 1am-11pm Sun; ◉ A, C, E to 42nd St) Amid Port Authority's bus frenzy are 30 lanes for $50 to $75 per hour depending on the time of day.

Melody Lanes (Map pp170-1; ☎ 718-832-2695; 461 37th St, Sunset Park, Brooklyn; lane per 2hr $60; ☺ 9am-midnight Sun-Thu, 9am-3am Fri & Sat; ◉ D, M, N, R to 36th St) If a lane and a pitcher of beer's all you need, Melody is New York's best deal – about a quarter the price of any Manhattan lane.

'discovery tours' that take in some of the harbor (April through October). Schedules change depending on staff and demand. The club also offers some bike and walking tours.

HOBOKEN COVE BOATHOUSE
www.hobokencoveboathouse.org; Frank Sinatra Park, 5th St & Sinatra Dr, Hoboken, NJ; ☒ PATH Train to Hoboken
Just across the Hudson River, this non-profit boathouse offers occasional free kayaking days at the waterfront shown in Marlon Brando's turf in *On the Waterfront* from June to August.

LONG ISLAND COMMUNITY BOATHOUSE Map pp200-1
☎ 718-228-9214; www.licboathouse.org; 31st Ave, Hallets Cove, Queens; ☺ free kayaking 1-5pm Sun mid-May–mid-Oct; ◉ N, W to Broadway
This boathouse regularly offers walk-up kayaking, as well as other trips from its other boathouse at Anable Cove (44th Dr; ◉ E, V to 23rd St-Ely Av, 7 to Vernon Blvd-Jackson Ave); this location may be moving to 46th Dr.

RED HOOK BOATERS Map p180
☎ 917-676-6458; www.redhookboaters.org; Louis Valentino Jr Pier Park, Coffey St, Red Hook, Brooklyn; ◉ F, G to Smith-9th Sts, transfer to ☒ B77 or B61 to Red Hook

This boathouse in the remote, harborside neighborhood of Red Hook offers free kayaking and canoeing two or three times weekly.

BIRD-WATCHING

Some of the country's most important birding areas are in New York City (no, seriously). Even Central Park sees over 200 species. The best viewing times in the parks are during migrations (roughly April to June and September to October), when many birding tours welcome the uninitiated.

The best viewing spot is probably Queens' Jamaica Bay Wildlife Refuge (Map pp200-1; www.nps.gov/gate; ◉ A to Broad Channel), part of the Gateway National Recreation Area. About 350 species visit during the year, most in July and August.

One excellent option during migratory periods are the three-hour walking tours of Central Park led by ever-busy ornithologist Starr Saphir (☎ 212-304-3808) of Central Park (adult/student $6/3). These leave at 7:30am Monday and Wednesday or 9am Tuesday from W 81st St and Central Park West, or at 7:30am Saturday from W 103rd St and Central Park West.

Throughout the year, the New York City Audubon Society (Map p120; ☎ 212-691-7483; www.nycaudubon.org; 71 W 23rd St, Flatiron District; ◉ F, V to 23rd St) stages bird-watching field trips (from free to $55;

including heron-spotting rides in the Long Island Sound) and beginning birding classes ($85, including two field trips). The group also stages a City Birding Challenge in May.

In Brooklyn, Prospect Park's Audubon Center Boathouse (p330) is the set-off point for free year-round walks – including Early Bird Walks (8am, first Sunday of the month), Introduction to Bird Watching (noon Saturday) and a kid-friendly Discover Tour (3pm weekends). There are also bird-watching boat rides (adult/children 3-12 $10/6) at noon and 1:15pm on weekends.

The best in-depth guide to city bird life is *The New York City Audubon Society Guide to Finding Birds in the Metropolitan Area*. Many of the wing-flappers are captured in Carl Vornberger's photo essay *Birds of Central Park*.

Brooklyn Bird Club (www.brooklynbirdclub.org) posts detailed info on bird-watching spots and events in Brooklyn and Queens.

GOLF

Other than a driving range, all golf options are outside Manhattan. Courses have slightly higher fees at weekends and you'll need to reserve a tee-off time.

If you feel like belting a few balls without the walking, head to the driving range at Chelsea Piers (see the boxed text, p337).

See NYC Tee Times (www.nycteetimes.com) to make reservations at several courses online, or call American Golf (☎ 718-225-4653).

BETHPAGE STATE PARK off Map pp200–1
☎ 516-249-0701; Farmingdale, Long Island; green fees Mon-Fri $31, Sat & Sun $26, Black Course Mon-Fri $100, Sat & Sun $120, state residents Mon-Fri $50, Sat & Sun $60, club rental $30
Home to five great public courses: its toughest, the Black Course, was the first public course to host the US Open (2002; won by – who else? – Tiger Woods), and it will host it again in 2009. The Black Course is closed Monday, all others are open daily. There's a LIRR rail station at Farmingdale, where you can get a taxi. See http://nysparks.state.ny.us for directions.

DYKER BEACH GOLF COURSE
Map pp170–1
☎ 718-836-9722; cnr 86th St & Seventh Ave, Dyker Beach, Brooklyn; green fees before/after 3pm Mon-Fri $32.25/16.75, Sat & Sun $39.50/17.75, club rental $35; Ⓡ R to 86th St
This scenic public course in Brooklyn is the easiest to reach by subway. Call ahead

about rentals – they're sometimes not available. It's between Seventh and Tenth Aves, to the right, when approaching from the subway station.

FLUSHING MEADOWS PITCH & PUTT
Map pp200–1
☎ 718-271-8182; Flushing Meadows Corona Park, Queens; www.nycgovparks.org; green fees 8am-5pm Mon-Fri adult/child under 12/senior $12.50/7/9.50, 5-11pm $15/8/10.50, Sat & Sun surcharge $1, club rental $1 each; Ⓞ 7 to Willets Point-Shea Stadium
Good for beginners, this fun 18-hole pitch-and-putt has rentable clubs and lights for late-night antics.

LA TOURETTE off Map p68
☎ 718-351-1889; www.latourette.americangolf.com; 1001 Richmond Hill Rd, Staten Island; green fees Mon-Fri $32.25, Sat & Sun $39.50, club rental $25
This public course in the heart of Staten Island is a bit removed from public transit; it's best to just take a taxi from the ferry. It's $8 extra for nonresidents.

PELHAM/SPLIT ROCK GOLF COURSE
Map pp208–9
☎ 718-885-1258; 870 Shore Rd, the Bronx; green fees before/after 1pm Mon-Fri $32.35/16.65, Sat & Sun $39.50/17.75, club rental $25; Ⓞ 6 to Pelham Bay Park
Set in the Bronx, this is New York City's only 36-hole course and dates from 1901. Visitors to NYC pay an extra $8 for green fees.

VAN CORTLANDT PARK GOLF COURSE
Map pp208–9
☎ 718-543-4595; Bailey Ave, the Bronx; green fees Mon-Fri $30, Sat & Sun $40, club rental $25; Ⓞ 1 to Van Cortlandt Park-242nd St
This is the USA's oldest 18-hole public golf course.

ICE SKATING

Outdoor rinks are open during the winter months, though the rink at Chelsea Piers (see the boxed text, p337) is open all year. See also p204 for the Flushing Meadows Corona Park in Queens.

KATE WOLLMAN RINK Map p182
☎ 718-287-6431; near Ocean Ave, Prospect Park, Brooklyn; adult/senior & child $5/3, rental $5; ⓨ late Nov-early Mar; Ⓞ B, Q to Prospect Park

On Prospect Lake in the southeastern part of Brooklyn's park, this rink is cheaper and generally less crowded than Manhattan rinks. The Prospect Park Figure Skating Club (☎ 718-282-1226; www.prospectparkfigureskatingclub .org) holds 'freestyle' sessions and 90-minute lessons. Call for opening hours.

ROCKEFELLER CENTER ICE RINK
Map pp134–5

☎ 212-332-7654; Rockefeller Center, cnr 49th St & Fifth Ave, Midtown West; 90min sessions adult $13.50-17.50, child $9.50-12.50, skate rental $9; ⏱ roughly 8am-midnight; ◎ B, D, F, V to 47th-50th Sts-Rockefeller Center

New York's most famous rink, under the gaze of the gold statue of Prometheus in the art-deco plaza, is an incomparable location for a twirl on ice, but it's small and gets sardine-busy. Try to show up for the first skating period (from 8am or 8:30am); otherwise expect long waits.

WOLLMAN SKATING RINK Map p149

☎ 212-439-6900; www.wollmanrink.com; Central Park, near 59th St & Sixth Ave entrance; adult/child Mon-Fri $9.50/4.75, Sat & Sun $12/5, skate rental $5; ⏱ 10am-2:30pm Mon & Tue, to 10pm Wed & Thu, to 11pm Fri & Sat, to 9pm Sun; ◎ F to 57th St, N, R, W to 5th Ave-59th St

Larger than Rockefeller's, and allowing all-day skating (as if…), this rink is at the southern edge of Central Park, with nice views. It's open mid-October through April.

IN-LINE SKATING

For decades, freestyle skaters have flaunted their footwork in a disco skate circle in Central Park near the Naumberg Bandshell or along Center Dr (aka 'Skaters' Rd') along the east side of the Sheep Meadow. Other areas to show your inline-skating stuff include the counterclockwise 6-mile loop at Central Park (with no cars on weekends, or from 10am to 3pm, and 7pm to 7am on weekdays), Brooklyn's Prospect Park loop, or along Hudson River Park from Battery Park all the way up to Riverside Park.

Check NYCSK8 (www.nycsk8.com) for a detailed online guide to skating in the city.

Renting is far less common than it was a decade ago, but you can rent skates all year at Blades West (Map p153; ☎ 212-787-3911; 156 W 72nd St, Upper West Side; per 24hr incl pads $20; ⏱ 10am-8pm Mon-Sat, 10am-7pm Sun; ◎ 1, 2, 3 to 72nd St).

JOGGING

Central Park's loop roads are best during traffic-free hours (see left), though you'll be in the company of many cyclists and in-line skaters. The 1.6-mile path surrounding the Jacqueline Kennedy Onassis Reservoir (Map p149; where Jackie O used to run) is for runners and walkers only; access it between 86th and 96th Sts. Running along the Hudson River is a popular path, best from W 23rd St to Battery Park in Lower Manhattan. The Upper East Side has a path that runs along FDR Dr and the East River (from E 63rd St to E 115th St). Brooklyn's Prospect Park has plenty of paths.

The New York Road Runners Club (Map p142; ☎ 212-860-4455; www.nyrrc.org; 9 E 89th St, Upper East Side; ⏱ 10am-8pm Mon-Fri, 10am-5pm Sat, 10am-3pm Sun; ◎ 6 to 96th St) organizes weekend runs citywide, including the New York City Marathon.

New York City Marathon

As awe-inspiring as the runners chugging through New York's streets is how the world's most famous marathon grew from a $1000 budget race with 55 finishers in 1970 to a premier running event that spans New York's five boroughs. However, you need a little luck, not just conditioning and strength, to run the race. The final list of 37,000 runners is completed by lottery; applications are accepted until April or May of each year (see www .nycmarathon.org).

Held on the first Sunday of November, it's a wonderful event to witness; sign-hoisting friends and family and live bands line much of the route from Staten Island through Brooklyn, and a bit of Queens and the Bronx, to Central Park's end point.

ROCK CLIMBING

Central Park contains a couple of rocks that attract the attention of boulderers, including Chess Rock, just north of Wollman Rink, and the more challenging Rat Rock, north of Heckscher Playground (around 61st St). However, the best is City Boy, a 20-footer around 107th St, west of the Harlem Meer.

Serious climbers will want to go 90 minutes north to the Shawangunks (aka 'da Gunks'), for gravity-defying rock-climbing options up backward-tilted walls in the Catskills outside New Paltz, New York. Check www.gunks .com for more information and several local guide services.

CITY CLIMBERS CLUB Map pp134–5

☎ 212-974-2250; www.cityclimbersclub.com;
Parks & Recreation Center, 533 W 59th St, Midtown
West; ⏱ 4:30-9:30pm Mon-Fri, noon-5pm Sat;
◉ A, C, B, D, 1 to 59th St-Columbus Circle
New York's first climbing wall still serves as
a key HQ for climbers, with 11 belay stations
and 30 routes, plus a climbing cave. The club
offers 40-minute lessons for $30. Day passes
cost $15, a six-month membership $125.

SOCCER

Soccer leagues generally don't allow drop-in,
single-game players. You can find pick-up
soccer games in Central Park's East Meadow
around E 97th St and the North Meadow at
weekends during the season (April to October). Games at Flushing Meadows Corona
Park (p204) are legendary and are in action
whenever the weather allows (even Febru-
ary); Chelsea Piers (see the boxed text, p337) has organized games of the indoor variety. Riverside
Park (p154) in the Upper West Side has weekly
pick-up soccer times in its outdoor field.

SURFING

Finally that Beach Boys–style Ramones song
'Rockaway Beach' makes sense. Since the surfing ban was lifted in 2005, Queens' Rockaway
Beach (p205) has become New York's surf central, with growing crews of surfers hitting the
waves between 88th and 90th Sts, especially
August to October when hurricanes down
south prompt the biggest action. In 2007 a
new stretch was opened to surfing – between
67th and 69th Sts. Reach either by taking the
A train to Beach 90th St or Beach 67th St.

Check the surf cam for the Rockaways at
www.surfline.com. A couple of websites focus
on area waves: www.surfrider.org/nyc and
www.newyorksurf.com.

TENNIS

Playing on New York's nearly 100 public
tennis courts requires a permit (annual fee
adult/senior/child $100/20/10) from April to
November (photo required); it's free at other
times. You can pick up single-play tickets for
$7 at the Central Park permit center at Arsenal
(Map p149; ☎ 212-360-8133; www.nyc.gov/parks; Central
Park, enter at E 65th St & Fifth Ave; ⏱ 9am-4pm Mon-Fri
& 9am-noon Sat Apr-Jun; ◉ N, R, W to 5th Ave-59th St).
See www.nyc.gov/park (search 'tennis permit
locations') for a list of other locations. Also,
Paragon Athletic Goods (p235) sells permits.

Those with an annual permit can make
reservations at the Central Park Tennis Center
and Prospect Park Tennis Center. Otherwise,
take a single-play ticket to a public court,
where it's first come, first serve.

Riverbank State Park (p336) in Northern
Manhattan also has courts.

CENTRAL PARK TENNIS CENTER
Map p149

☎ 212-280-0205; www.centralpark.com; Central Park, enter at 96th St & Central Park West;
⏱ 6:30am-dusk Apr-Oct or Nov; ◉ B, C to 96th St
The daylight-hours-only facility has 26 clay
courts for public use (and four hard courts
for lessons). You can buy single-play tickets
($7) here. Those with permits can reserve
a court for $7. The least busy times are
roughly noon to 4pm on weekdays.

PROSPECT PARK TENNIS CENTER
Map p182

☎ 718-436-2500; www.prospectpark.org; cnr Parkside & Coney Island Aves, Prospect Park, Brooklyn;
⏱ 7am-11pm; ◉ F to Fort Hamilton Pkwy or Q to
Parkside Ave
Open all year, this 11-court facility takes
permits or sells single-use tickets on location from mid-May to mid-November.
Winter hourly rates range from $30 to $66
(seasonal passes start at $741).

USTA NATIONAL TENNIS CENTER
Map pp200–1

☎ 718-760-6200; www.usta.com; Flushing Meadows Corona Park; per hr outdoor court $16-24,
indoor court $18-56; ⏱ indoor 6am-midnight Mon-
Fri, 8am-midnight Sat, 8am-11pm Sun, outdoor
8am-midnight; ◉ 7 to Willets Point-Shea Stadium
Bring your headband out to the USTA for
tennis where the stars play at the annual
US Open. The USTA has 22 outdoor courts
and – in time for the 2008 US Open – a
fancy new Billie Jean King National Tennis
Center indoor facility with 12 courts. Reservations can be made up to two days in
advance. After-dark lights for outside courts
are $8 extra. Hourly lessons are $80 to $95.

TRAPEZE

NEW YORK TRAPEZE SCHOOL
Map pp72–3

☎ 917-797-1872; www.newyork.trapezeschool
.com; Pier 40 at West Side Hwy, Lower Manhattan;
classes $47-65; ◉ 1 to Canal St

Fulfill your circus dreams, like Carrie did on *Sex and the City,* flying trapeze to trapeze in this open-air tent by the river (it's covered and heated in winter). Call or check the website for daily class times. There's a one-time $22 registration fee.

HEALTH & FITNESS

If the city's wearing you down, you're not alone. Even hardened New Yorkers need a break from time to time. Around the city you'll find many spas and health clubs to get off those streets and subways and into a place to ease into a masseuse's hands, do a cannonball in an art-deco swimming pool or take it out on a racquetball court if that's your thing.

DAY SPAS

Make an appointment at the following places in advance.

BLISS49 Map p126

☎ 212-219-8970; www.blissworld.com; 541 Lexington Ave, Midtown East; 🕑 8am-10pm; 🚇 6 to 51st St, E, V to Lexington Ave-53rd St
At the ever-stylish W New York, Bliss49 is one of three Bliss locations in Manhattan. A 90-minute body smoother with carrot mulch and oil rubdown is $165; 75-minute body massages are $150. See the website for other locations.

BUNYA CITISPA Map pp88–9

☎ 212-388-1288; www.bunyacitispa.com; 474 W Broadway, SoHo; 🕑 10am-9pm Mon-Sat, 10am-7pm Sun; 🚇 N, R, W to Prince St, C, E to Spring St
The new, chic Asian-style spa has taken over SoHo's spa front. Ex-models and shopping-bag toters bring aches and pains for poking palms and thumbs in the popular 'oriental herbal compress' massages (60 minutes, $120).

CORNELIA DAY RESORT Map p126

☎ 212-871-3050; www.cornelia.com; 663 Fifth Ave, Midtown East; 🕑 9am-7pm; 🚇 F to 57th St, E, V, to 5th Ave-53rd St
Above Salvatore Ferragamo on Fifth Ave, Cornelia is a star-studded pampering spot that makes fashion and style mags all the time. Offerings include a spoonful of honey on arrival, plus facials, Watsu flow treatment in the heated salt-water pool ($225) and honey body polish ($160).

GREAT JONES SPA Map pp88–9

☎ 212-505-3185; www.greatjonesspa.com; 29 Great Jones St, NoHo; 🕑 4-10pm Mon, 9am-10pm Tue-Sun; 🚇 6 to Bleecker St, B, D, F, V to Broadway-Lafayette St
Don't skimp on the services at this newish downtown feng shui master; if you spend over $100 (not hard: hour-long massages start at $120, facials at $130) you get free time in the water lounge's hot pool, rock sauna and cold pool.

OKEANOS Map p126

☎ 212-223-6773; www.okeanosclubspa.com; 211 E 51st St, Midtown East; 🕑 noon-10pm Tue-Fri, 11am-8pm Sat; 🚇 6 to 51st St, E, V to Lexington Ave-53rd St
It's not your grandfather's tsar's Russian baths, but the slick, inviting Okeanos offers the classic experience – birch-slappings in the sauna ($50), sports massages fit for hockey players (and some do come for it; $210) – and even a shot of vodka to finish.

PAUL LABRECQUE EAST Map p142

☎ 212-988-7816; www.paullabrecque.com; 171 E 65th St, Upper East Side; 🕑 8am-9pm Mon-Fri, 9am-8pm Sat, 10am-8pm Sun; 🚇 6 to 68th St-Hunter College
Sit back with the stars at this swank uptown spa (with a salon and barbershop just for the guys). Apparently Sting has indulged in an hour-long 'indulgent shave' ($90); a haircut by Mr Paul is $400. It's not all for the guys, though. Paul also offers a glow tan ($140) seen on many Upper Eastsiders pretending to be back from *el Caribe.*

RUSSIAN & TURKISH BATHS Map p104

☎ 212-473-8806; 268 E 10th St, East Village; entry $30; 🕑 11am-10pm Mon, Tue, Thu & Fri, 9am-10pm Wed, 7:30am-10pm Sat & Sun; 🚇 6 to Astor Pl, L to 1st Ave
This grubby historic spa is past its wink-wink heyday as a gay-romp spot, but keeps its cult fans for cheap services (mud treatments $48) and *banya*-hot Russian sauna, cold pool and roof deck. Sunday mornings are for men only, Wednesday morning for women only. See p105 for the full description.

SPA AT MANDARIN ORIENTAL Map pp134–5

☎ 212-805-8880; www.mandarinoriental.com; 80 Columbus Circle at 60th St, Midtown West; 🕑 9am-9pm; 🚇 A, C, B, D, 1 to 59th St-Columbus Circle

You might not be able to afford the $15,000 suites, but a splurge at the split-level spa/fitness center might be worth the plastic. Rooms are ultra exotic – one has a modern 'Chinese wedding bed' with Hudson River views. Full-day 'journeys' run about $675, massages start at $215.

GYMS & SWIMMING POOLS

In addition to the following, there are 32 public parks with pools in Manhattan, plus 59 in the boroughs, free to use from late June through Labor Day. See www.nycgovparks.org for more information on other outdoor pools. Chelsea Piers (see the boxed text, opposite) has a massive, riverside sports center with pretty much every activity you can imagine.

ASPHALT GREEN Map p142

☎ 212-369-8890; www.asphaltgreen.org; 555 E 90 St, Upper East Side; gym & pool pass $25; ⏱ 5:30am-10pm Mon-Fri, 8am-8pm Sat & Sun; ⊕ 4, 5, 6 to 86th St

This super nonprofit fitness center in the Upper East Side is known for its excellent 50m Olympic-size pool (with an observation window for coaches to check technique). There's also a smaller pool for classes. Some hours are for members only. Many programs cater to kids.

ASTORIA POOL Map pp200–1

☎ 718-626-8620; Astoria Park, cnr 19th St & 23rd Dr, Astoria, Queens; ⏱ 11am-7pm Jun-Aug; ⊕ N, W to Astoria Blvd

This Works Progress Administration Olympic-size outdoor pool, built in 1936, is an art-deco wonder, with views of Manhattan and the Triborough Bridge. Crowds break 1000 on nice summer days.

METROPOLITAN POOL Map p177

☎ 718-599-5707; 261 Bedford Ave at Metropolitan Ave, Williamsburg, Brooklyn; 6-month/year membership $37.75/75; ⏱ 7am-10pm Mon-Fri, 7am-6pm Sat, 10am-6pm Sun; ⊕ L to Bedford Ave

This 1922 gem in Williamsburg, fully renovated in 1997, is one of New York's nicest public pools. There's a fitness room as well.

NEW YORK SPORTS CLUB Map pp134–5

☎ 646-366-9400; www.mysportsclubs.com; 230 W 41st St, Midtown West; day pass $25; ⏱ 6am-10pm Mon-Thu, 6am-9pm Fri & Sat, 8am-6pm Sun; ⊕ N, Q, R, W, S, 1, 2, 3, 7 to Times Sq-42nd St

A day pass to this popular fitness chain includes group classes on exercise bikes ('spinning') and entry to the fitness center. Visit the website for information on Manhattan's 40 locations (some with pools, including the one at 1601 Broadway at 49th St).

RIVERBANK STATE PARK Map pp158–9

☎ 212-694-3600; 679 Riverside Dr at 145th St, Sugar Hill, Northern Manhattan; pool adult/child $2/1, fitness room $8; ⏱ park 6am-11pm; ⊕ 1 to 145th St

This modern 28-acre, five-building facility, perched atop a waste refinery (not as crazy as it sounds), has an indoor Olympic-size pool, an outdoor lap pool, a fitness room, basketball courts, a running track around a soccer field and a kids' area.

TONY DAPOLITO RECREATION CENTER Map p110

☎ 212-242-5228; 1 Clarkson St, West Village; ⏱ 7am-9pm Mon-Fri, 7am-4:30pm Sat & Sun; ⊕ 1 to Houston St

This West Village center (formerly the Carmine) has one of the city's best public pools, but it's only available by annual membership ($75 not including the indoor pool, which is $50). It has an indoor and outdoor swimming pool (the latter was used for the pool scene in *Raging Bull*).

WEST SIDE YMCA Map p153

☎ 212-875-4100; www.ymcanyc.org; 5 W 63rd St, Upper West Side; day pass $25; ⏱ 5am-11pm Mon-Fri, 8am-8pm Sat & Sun; ⊕ A, B, C, D, 1 to 59th St-Columbus Circle

Near Central Park, the West Side Y – one of 20 YMCAs in the Big Apple – boasts two swimming pools, an indoor running track, a basketball court, five racquetball/squash courts and a big weight room. Membership is $79 monthly (with a $125 initiation fee). See the website for the other locations.

YOGA & PILATES

Options are everywhere, particularly around buzzing Union Sq, the (self-named) 'wheat-packing district,' for its dozen yoga centers, free yoga in the park and the wholesome greenmarket farmers market.

AREA YOGA CENTER Map p180

☎ 718-797-3699; www.areabrooklyn.com; 2nd fl, 320 Court St, Cobble Hill, Brooklyn; ⏱ classes 7:15am-6:45pm Mon-Fri, 8am-5:45pm Sat & Sun; ⊕ F, G to Carroll St

CHELSEA PIERS

New York's biggest sporting center is at the historic Chelsea Piers (Map p116; ☎ 212-336-6666; www.chelseapiers .com; West Side Hwy btwn 16th & 22nd Sts, Chelsea; ◉ C, E to 23rd St), a 30-acre sporting village where you can golf, work out, play soccer and basketball, get a massage, swim, box and bowl (see the boxed text, p331).

Opened in its current incarnation in 1995, the red-white-and-blue Chelsea Piers served as New York's chief port during the heyday of transatlantic ocean voyages. Constructed in 1910, Chelsea Piers was where the *Titanic* was hoping to dock in 1912 and was later the embarkation point for many Europe-bound WWII soldiers. Its pier days ended in 1967.

Following is a selection of activities available. Call to confirm open times, as they vary.

Batting Cages (☎ 212-336-6500; Field House, Pier 59; 10 pitches $2.50; ◔ 11am-10pm Mon-Fri, 9am-9pm Sat & Sun) Four modern cages offer fast, medium and slow-pitch baseball and softball.

Golf (☎ 212-336-6400; Golf Club, Pier 59; ball cards from $20, golf simulator games per hr $45; ◔ 6am-midnight Apr-Sep, 6:30am-11pm Oct-Mar) Manhattan's only driving range has four levels of weather-protected tees in nets – you can aim for New Jersey! Golf clubs are available ($4 for one, $6 for three).

Ice Skating & Hockey (☎ 212-336-6100; Sky Rink, Pier 61; adult/child general skating $11.50/9, skate rental $6.50, helmets $3.50) There are two year-round rinks. Schedules vary, generally 1:30pm to 4pm or 5pm daily. Open hockey hours are limited, usually weekday lunchtimes only ($30, goaltenders are free).

Soccer (☎ 212-336-6500; Field House, Pier 62) Mostly for indoor soccer and basketball leagues and gym classes, but slots open (particularly in summer) for 'open soccer.'

Spa (☎ 212-336-6780; Pier 60; massage $70-150, facials from $70, body scrubs $80-140; ◔ 10am-9pm Mon-Fri, 10am-7pm Sat & Sun) A 75-minute seaweed body wrap is $140. Package deals include a five-hour treatment for $369; a 90-minute sampler is $153.

Sports Center (☎ 212-336-6000; Pier 60; per day $50; ◔ 5:30am-11pm Mon-Thu, 5:30am-10pm Fri, 8am-9pm Sat & Sun) This big center has an indoor running track, swimming pool, workout equipment, basketball, boxing, kickboxing, volleyball, yoga classes, rock climbing and sundecks with good views.

With a spa, a couple of shops and this yoga studio, Area conquers Brooklyn's Cobble Hill area for all things mind-and-body. A single yoga class is $16.

BIKRAM YOGA NYC Map p120
☎ 212-206-9400; www.bikramyoganyc.com; 3rd fl, 182 Fifth Ave, Union Sq; per class $23; ◔ roughly 7am-8:15pm Mon-Fri, 10am-5pm Sat & Sun; ◉ N, R, W to 23rd St
So very Hollywood (but taking off in Manhattan), Bikram is hot stuff: striking the 26-pose *asana* in a heated room means you're going to sweat into shape. There are showers. Bikram has three other locations.

JIVAMUKTI Map p120
☎ 212-353-0214; www.jivamuktiyoga.com; 841 Broadway, Union Sq; per class $19; ◔ classes 8am-8pm Mon-Thu, 8am-6:45pm Fri, 9:15am-5pm Sat & Sun; ◉ L, N, Q, R, W, 4, 5, 6 to 14th St-Union Sq
The yoga spot in Manhattan, Jivamukti – now in a 12,000-sq-ft locale on Union Sq – is a posh place for *vinyasa* and *hatha* classes (chanting alert). You can study Sanskrit if you're ready to get serious; Uma's little bro Dechen Thurman teaches classes,

too. There's also a location on the Upper East Side (Map p142; ☎ 646-290-8106; 2nd fl, 853 Lexington Ave; ◉ F to 63rd St).

OM YOGA CENTER Map p104
☎ 212-254-9642; www.omyoga.com; 6th fl, 826 Broadway, East Village; per class $18; ◉ L, N, Q, R, W, 4, 5, 6 to 14th St-Union Sq
This inviting space – with redwood floors, high ceilings and showers – has popular *vinyasa* classes run by former dancer (and choreographer of videos such as 'Girls Just Want to Have Fun') Cyndi Lee, a practitioner of *hatha* yoga and Tibetan Buddhism. Classes run all levels; an hour-long 'yoga express' is $12.

REAL PILATES Map pp72–3
☎ 212-625-0777; www.realpilatesnyc.com; 177 Duane St, Lower Manhattan; ◔ roughly 8am-7pm Mon-Fri, 8am-5:15pm Fri, 9am-1pm Sat, 9:15am-2pm Sun; ◉ A, C, 1, 2, 3 to Chambers St
Pilates guru (and author) Alycea Ungaro's studio hosts Pilates courses of all levels, as well as intensive, six- to 12-hour weekend workshops with a few resident Pilates experts.

top picks

- **Oscar Wilde Bookshop** (p340) The first LGBT bookstore in the world.
- **Splash Bar** (p343) Top-notch DJs and hotties on the dance floor.
- **Cattyshack** (p344) Where the ladies are in Brooklyn.
- **LGBT Community Center** (p345) Ground zero for all things gay & lesbian.

This city can feel pretty utopian to queer visitors who hail from less tolerant spots in the world. Cultural events, bars, clubs, eateries and even inns that cater to LGBT folks are plentiful here – but you'll find that practically no neighborhood or establishment (at least in Manhattan) will bat an eye at the sight of same-sex customers holding hands or canoodling over a meal.

Credit for much of the welcoming vibe can be given to a fed-up group of drag queens and other men and women who, on a June night in 1969, bravely (if unwittingly) kicked off the official gay-rights movement. They did it by standing up for themselves outside of the Stonewall Inn bar in Greenwich Village when cops on a routine shakedown (of anti-gay harassment) pushed this bunch of customers just a bit too far. They fought back, touching off what has since become known as the Stonewall Riots, and showed the city, the country and the world that gay folks were people, too – and that they deserved equal rights.

It's comforting to remember this city's fierce history when you're here, but it's just as inspiring to take a look around at present-day victories – from the fact that the speaker of the New York City Council, Christine Quinn, is an out and proud lesbian to the existence of various local laws that criminalize anti-gay violence, forbid workplace discrimination of LGBT people and offer legal domestic partnerships to same-sex couples. Combine all of that with the vast array of gay entertainment options and trés-gay neighborhoods – Chelsea, Hell's Kitchen, Greenwich Village and Brooklyn's Park Slope among them – and you'll never want to leave.

The best way to get a handle on the goings-on here, especially when it comes to the ever-changing scope of nightlife options, is to pick up a copy of either the weekly *HX* (www.hx.com, for boys) or monthly *Go* (www.gomag.com, for girls), two magazines that stay on top of the bar, club and performance offerings around the city and are available at various street boxes and gay establishments. Another great place to start is the LGBT Community Center (p345), a helpful resource for finding anything queer in this city, or Heritage of Pride (p345), which organizes the city's annual Gay Pride, a full month of parties and rallies, culminating in the famously long and lavish parade down Fifth Avenue.

SHOPPING

It's certainly not necessary to limit your shopping to gay-themed outlets – especially with designer-stocked, aesthetically pleasing shops like Barney's and Bergdorf's – but sometimes it's just kind of nice. You'll find queer-centric faves at the following spots, most high-mindedly at Oscar Wilde, the city's lone gay bookshop.

OSCAR WILDE BOOKSHOP Map p110 Books
☎ 212-255-8097; www.oscarwildebooks.com; 15 Christopher St btwn Greenwich Ave & Waverly Pl, Greenwich Village; ⊕ 1 to Christopher St-Sheridan Sq

The one remaining LGBT bookstore in the city is a cozy, well-stocked shop located in a historic Greenwich Village townhouse. It's the oldest gay bookstore in the world, and has gone through several owners since its founding more than 40 years ago. Current proprietor Kim Brinster is a dedicated lit lover, and manager Cecilia Martin is an extremely well-read shopping guide. In addition to books new and old, you'll find magazines, DVDs, calendars, magnets and other gay-themed gift items.

RAINBOWS & TRIANGLES
Map p116 Cards & Gifts
☎ 212-627-2166; 192 Eighth Ave btwn 18th & 19th Sts, Chelsea; ⊕ A, C, E to 14th St, L to 8th Ave

Holding court along Chelsea's hoppin' Eighth Ave is this gay-obsessed card and gift shop. This is the place for buttons and magnets with rainbows or pink triangles, as well as quirky gag gifts, erotic greeting cards and, in the hushed back room, various porn items geared toward guys.

WEAR ME OUT Map pp134–5 Cards & Gifts
☎ 212-333-3047; 358 W 47th St at Ninth Ave, Midtown West; ⊕ C, E to 50th St

This Hell's Kitchen boutique is selling a lifestyle with its gay-themed jewelry, cards, unique gifts and queer-aesthetic clothing, from hats to underwear. There's nothing earth-shattering, but it's a cute, fun place to browse, and has a really friendly staff.

UNIVERSAL GEAR Map p116 Clothing

☎ 212-206-9119; www.universalgear.com; 140 Eighth Ave btwn 16th & 17th Sts, Chelsea; Ⓢ A, C, E to 14th St, L to 8th Ave

A more accurate name might be 'Chelsea Gear,' as the place is bursting with all that's *de rigueur* for handsome Chelsea boys and wannabes. Here's where you'll find uniform staples like G-Star and Diesel denim, pouch-heightening underwear by 2(x)ist and C-IN2, plus swimwear, jackets, shoes and accessories from Ben Sherman bags to D&G watches.

BABELAND Map pp88–9 Sex Toys

☎ 212-375-1701; www.babeland.com; 96 Rivington St, Lower East Side; Ⓢ F, V to Lower East Side-2nd Ave

This excellent, lesbian-owned and -run sex-toy store presents potentially embarrassing retail items – like rabbit-shaped vibrators, bright-purple dildos and black leather floggers – in a mellow and friendly can't-shock-us way. Also available are sex books, DVDs, games, cards and, on varying nights, how-to workshops by Babeland sexperts. There's also a SoHo branch (Map p98; ☎ 212-966-2120; 43 Mercer St; Ⓢ N, R, Q, W to Canal St).

EATING

Eating can be enjoyed nearly anywhere in this city, no matter how outwardly gay you are or want to be. But if you prefer to dine 'with family,' there are a number of good options, all of which offer clever takes on American cuisine.

DEBORAH Map p110 American Eclectic $$

☎ 212-242-2606; www.deborahlifelovefood.com; 43 Carmine St, West Village; Ⓢ 1 to Christopher St-Sheridan Sq

The talented Deborah Staton – local lesbian activist and active socializer – owns this cozy West Village spot, offering a diverse range of creative American fare from an *edamame*, artichoke and Portobello salad to beef carpaccio, fish 'n' chips and homemade macaroni and cheese. Deborah targets the lesbian scene with advertising, hence the heavily Sapphic crowd, but everyone's welcome.

LIPS Map p110 American $$

☎ 212-675-7710; www.lipsnyc.com; 2 Bank St at Seventh Ave, West Village; Ⓢ 1 to Christopher St-Sheridan Sq

It's a drag-show dining experience here – which, yes, brings in hoards of straight tourists seeking thrills for bachelorette parties – but it can be truly enjoyable for any queer with a sense of humor, too. The food's been named after local drag queens – Lady Bunny (oven-roasted chicken), Bianca Leigh (penne primavera), Kevin Aviance (spicy chicken wings) – but the best dish is the entertainment, which stars many of the characters whose names you'll find on the menu.

RUBYFRUIT BAR & GRILL
Map p110 American $$

☎ 212-929-3343; 531 Hudson St btwn Charles & 10th Sts, West Village; Ⓢ 1 to Christopher St-Sheridan Sq

Packing in the lesbians since it opened in 1994, this institution features an intimate (but sometimes rowdy) bar upstairs and a cozy restaurant below. Settle in near the fireplace and dine on American classics like grilled fish, burgers and fries and steak dinners, then head on up for a nightcap. Makes a complete night out easy.

ELMO Map p116 American Eclectic $$

☎ 212-387-8000; 185 Seventh Ave btwn 19th & 20th Sts, Chelsea; Ⓢ 1 to 23rd St

One of several Chelsea hotspots that have mastered the art of blending a nightclub

---

GAY PRIDE BEYOND MANHATTAN

Sure, the annual Gay Pride (p345) march and flood of parties in Manhattan is a wild and wonderful thing. But New York City's outer boroughs have queer folks, too – and their lives and cultures can often feel worlds away from the Manhattan scene. Going to one of these smaller, non-touristy celebrations can be a joyously unique experience. Queens Pride (www.queenspride.com), held the first Sunday in June, takes places in the multi-culti neighborhood of Jackson Heights, and has a strong pan-Latin flavor. Brooklyn Pride (www.brooklynpride.org) kicks off the second Sunday in June and features a street fair and nighttime parade in Park Slope, with parties radiating throughout the borough at nightfall. Staten Island usually has a family-themed waterfront stroll and festival, while the Bronx tends toward live concerts and rallies in a park; they are less established, though, and the best way to find out information is to check in with the LGBT Community Center (p345; www.gaycenter.org) in May or June.

atmosphere with a solidly good menu, this is a consistent favorite. The sweeping space is low-lit and sexy (the fact that it's almost always packed with beautiful men doesn't hurt), and the food covers all bases, from roasted beet salad to chicken pot pie and grilled tuna. Cocktails are potent, too.

EATERY NYC Map pp134–5 American Eclectic $$
☎ 212-974-2003; 789 Ninth Ave at 55th St, Hell's Kitchen; ⊕ C, E, 1 to 50th St
Another great mix of nightspot and dining room, this Hell's Kitchen restaurant is a fun, well-designed spot with an always-hoppin' attached bar, usually featuring a live DJ. The creative menu is quite diverse, even caring for vegetarians with an Asian tofu salad, but focusing on pastas, burgers and grilled fish and steak plates. Boys flock here.

HK Map pp134–5 American Eclectic $$
☎ 212-947-4208; 523 Ninth Ave at 39th St, Hell's Kitchen; ⊕ A, C, E to 42nd St-Port Authority
A bright spot on a pretty sketchy corner of Hell's Kitchen, this has fast become the hip gay spot to be – especially for post-work cocktails and dinner or Sunday brunch. The modern design is sleek and airy, with white accents and a space that gets flooded with sunlight during the day. The menu puts a creative spin on comfort foods, with plenty of salads and pastas in the mix, and a particularly impressive array of brunch items. Around the corner is its latest addition, the gay bar HK Lounge (opposite).

DRINKING & NIGHTLIFE

This is one category that is unapologetically separated from the straight version – probably because gay bars hold such an important place in gay history, as they used to be the only places where being out was free and easy. You'll find endless options here, and watering holes that appeal to all sorts of subcultures, from pierced and tattooed baby dykes to aging circuit boys. Note that places come and go very quickly around here – especially nightclubs, which frequently get shuttered by police only to reopen a few weeks later under a new moniker – so you may want to call before heading out. Places are numerous, and therefore organized by neighborhood; some parties listed here are only one-night affairs. See also p300 for clubs, and visit the websites of some of the community's favorite roving

weekly or monthly bashes to see what's next on the agenda: Shescape (www.shescape.com) for lesbians, is known for blowout Thanksgiving Eve and New Year's Eve events, and the Saint at Large (www.saintatlarge.com) for party boys busts out each March with its massive, kink-themed Black Party.

East Village

1984 AT PYRAMID CLUB Map p104 Club
☎ 212-420-1590; 101 Ave A at 6th St; ⊕ F, V to Lower East Side-2nd Ave
A legendary and cramped multilevel club that saw its heyday sometime in the late '80s, its Friday nights take you way back there with its endlessly popular 1984 night. The party, which draws a very gay crowd, focuses on icons of that decade – Madonna, Abba, Pet Shop Boys, you name it – and gives you an overdose of their music and videos all night long.

THE COCK Map p104 Gay Bar
☎ 212-777-6254; 29 Second Ave at 2nd St; ⊕ F, V to Lower East Side-2nd Ave
A dark, dank spot that's proud of its sleazy-chic reputation, this is the place to join lanky hipster boys and rage until they kick you out at 4am. Varying theme nights present popular parties with live performers, DJs, drag-queen hostesses, nearly naked go-go boys and porn videos on constant loops. It's wild and friendly.

EASTERNBLOC Map p104 Mixed Bar
☎ 212-420-8885; 505 E 6th St btwn Aves A & B; ⊕ F, V to Lower East Side-2nd Ave
A favorite among cute local boys and a handful of lesbians, this intimate space hosts rotating DJs, theme nights, go-go boys and adorable bartenders. It has a kitschy iron-curtain theme replete with Bettie Page videos and Communist-era posters, and a neighborhoody vibe.

STARLETTE AT ANGELS & KINGS
Map p104 Weekly Lounge Party
☎ 212-254-4090; 500 E 11th St btwn Aves A & B; ⊕ L to 1st Ave
Sunday nights at this small East Village lounge pack in the young, cute and trendified lesbians thanks to Wanda Acosta, a seasoned party promoter who's got the Midas touch when it comes to cooking up new ways for fun-lovin' dykes to play.

Greenwich Village & West Village

MONSTER Map p110 *Club, Piano Bar*
☎ 212-924-3558; 80 Grove St at Sheridan Sq; ⊕ 1 to Christopher St-Sheridan Sq

It's old-school gay man–heaven in here, home to a small dance floor as well as a piano bar and cabaret space. Spirited theme nights range from Latino parties to drag queen–hosted soirees.

HENRIETTA HUDSON Map p110 *Lesbian Bar*
☎ 212-924-3347; 438 Hudson St; ⊕ 1 to Houston St

All sorts of cute young dykes, many from neighboring New Jersey and Long Island, storm this sleek lounge, where varying theme nights bring in spirited DJs who stick to particular genres (hip-hop, house, rock). The owner, Brooklyn native Lisa Canistraci, is favorite promoter in the world of lesbian nightlife, and is often on hand to mix it up with her fans.

THE CUBBYHOLE Map p110 *Mixed Bar*
☎ 212-243-9041; 281 W 12th St; ⊕ A, C, E to 14th St, L to 8th Ave

A tiny hideaway festooned with brightly patterned bar stools and strings of colorful lights, this no-attitude neighborhood watering hole has that truly rare mix of lesbians and gay men who are out to make friends rather than hit the road with the first trick they find. It's got a great jukebox, friendly bartenders and plenty of regulars.

STONEWALL INN Map p110 *Mixed Bar*
☎ 212-463-0950; 53 Christopher St; ⊕ 1 to Christopher St-Sheridan Sq

Site of the Stonewall riots in 1969, this historic bar was losing its fan base to trendier spots when new owners came along, gave it a facelift and opened it to a new and welcoming crowd in late 2007. Now it pulls in varied crowds nightly for parties catering to everyone under the gay rainbow.

SNAPSHOT AT BAR 13
Map p110 *Weekly Dance Party*
☎ 212-979-6677; 35 E 13th St at University Pl; ⊕ F, V to 14th St, L to 6th Ave

Bar 13 is the place to be on Tuesday, as it's when the vast lounge and roof deck become host to Snapshot, a young-lesbian soiree (it's near NYU) where young Shane-from-L-Word protégées stay late to sip cocktails and shimmy to the scene's favorite DJs.

Chelsea

EAGLE Map pp134–5 *Leather Bar*
☎ 646-473-1866; www.eaglenyc.com; 554 W 28th St; ⊕ C, E to 23rd St

Leathermen, furry bears and other masculine subsets descend on the Eagle for cruisey fun and thematic nights that include live S&M action. Come summertime, its open-air roof deck is the place to be for raucous beer blasts.

BARRACUDA Map p116 *Lounge*
☎ 212-645-8613; 275 W 22nd St at Seventh Ave; ⊕ C, E to 23rd St

This longtime favorite has held its own even as newer, slicker places come and go. That's because it's got a simple, winning formula: affordable cocktails, a cozy rec-room vibe and free entertainment from some of the city's top drag queens.

GYM Map p116 *Sports Bar*
☎ 212-337-2439; 167 Eighth Ave at 18th St; ⊕ A, C, E to 14th St, L to 8th Ave

This popular sports bar for men is nothing like the rowdy straight sports bars that pepper Midtown side streets. Here the decor is classy – wide-plank wooden floors, high ceilings and a long, sleek bar – the men are polite, and ice-skating championships are just as popular as basketball playoffs.

Flatiron District

SPLASH BAR Map p120 *Club*
☎ 212-691-0073; 50 W 17th St; ⊕ L to 6th Ave, F, V to 14th St

As megaclubs come and go, this staple (found near Chelsea's eastern border with the Flatiron District) has become hotter than ever. It's a multilevel club that balances both a lounge and dance-club vibe, thanks to a mix of hang-out spaces, an unrivaled lineup of DJs, great special events and performances and some of the most smokin' bartenders around.

Midtown West

HK Map pp134–5 *Lounge*
☎ 212-947-4208; 523 Ninth Ave at 39th St; ⊕ A, C, E to 42nd St-Port Authority

Enter on the 39th Street side of this popular eatery (p342) and you'll find one of the sleekest, best-designed lounge spaces around. Handsome men gather here to hear mellow DJs and rub elbows with local glitterati, from drag queens to porn stars.

RITZ Map pp134–5 _Lounge_
☎ 212-333-2554; 369 W 46th St btwn Eighth & Ninth Aves; ◉ A, C, E to 42nd St-Port Authority
Gracing the western end of the city's Restaurant Row, in the Theater District, the Ritz is a relative newcomer to the Midtown gay scene. Its front bar is loud and abuzz, with a post-work, male crowd spilling onto the street in warm months. The upstairs space is a mellow retreat, while the downstairs back lounge, lined with banquettes, is often host to DJs or live vocal performers.

THERAPY Map pp134–5 _Lounge_
☎ 212-397-1700; 348 W 52nd St btwn Eighth & Ninth Aves; ◉ C, E, 1 to 50th St
This multileveled, airy and contemporary space was the first gay-man's hotspot to draw throngs to Hell's Kitchen. It presents nightly shows, from music to comedy, while the romantic 2nd-floor lounge has great fare (burgers, hummus, salads) served in front of a roaring fireplace. Drink monikers are wonderfully in keeping with the theme: Freudian Sip, Oral Fixation and Anorexic, to name a few.

VLADA LOUNGE Map pp134–5 _Lounge_
☎ 212-974-8030; 331 W 51st St btwn Eighth & Ninth Aves; ◉ C, E, 1 to 50th St
Another Hell's Kitchen favorite, this narrow, well-designed two-level lounge specializes in house-made infused vodkas and the potent cocktails they lace. Also come for well-loved DJs, drag queens and other entertainers nightly.

Brooklyn
CATTYSHACK Map p182 _Club_
☎ 718-230-5740; 249 Fourth Ave at President St, Park Slope; ◉ M, R, W to Union St
Since closing her beloved Meow Mix lesbian spot in the East Village years ago, Brooke Webster has been providing an even bigger, better vibe to the girls of Park Slope (and there are lots of 'em) with this cool, three-level space. Smokers love the rooftop deck, while everyone goes ga-ga for the hot

go-go dancers, great DJs and special theme nights. Boys are more than welcome, too.

EXCELSIOR Map p182 _Gay Bar_
☎ 718-832-1599; 390 Fifth Ave at 6th St, Park Slope; ◉ M, R, W to Union St
Who says Park Slope is all girls? This long-running boy favorite has a cute and friendly crowd, great jukebox and a refreshing back patio for summer months (and year-round smokers).

METROPOLITAN Map p177 _Mixed Bar_
☎ 718-599-4444; 559 Lorimer St at Metropolitan Ave, Williamsburg; ◉ G to Metropolitan Ave, L to Lorimer St
This friendly and low-key Williamsburg spot draws a good blend of arty fags and dykes with its cool staff, cheap drinks, outdoor patio and great DJs. It's neighborhoody, in a hipster way.

Queens
CHUECA BAR Map pp200–1 _Lesbian Club_
☎ 718-424-1171; 69-04 Woodside Ave, Woodside; ◉ 7 to 69th St
It's a bit of a trip from Manhattan, but beautiful Latina lesbians travel from all over the region – even as far as New Jersey and Connecticut – to hang with their salsa-dancing sisters. The place gets packed on weekends.

SLEEPING
Gay couples can expect to be treated with utmost respect no matter where they choose to bunk in New York. But staying at an LGBT establishment can give you the added perk of great resources and even instant friends – which is not a bad thing in a strange city. The gay inns have comparably low rates, too.

Bubba & Bean Lodges (p364)
Chelsea Pines Inn (p355)
Colonial House Inn (p355)
East Village B&B (p352)
Incentra Village House (p353)
Ivy Terrace (p359)

FURTHER RESOURCES
Gay organizations in this city are pretty plentiful, and cover the spectrum of support, activ-

ism, political, health-related and celebratory organizing. While you're probably not on holiday here to volunteer or attend coming-out meetings, you might actually want to plan for Pride, attend a queer AA meeting or give yourself a history lesson at an info-packed yet under-the-radar site such as the Lesbian Herstory Archives or the Black Gay and Lesbian Archive in Harlem.

LGBT COMMUNITY CENTER Map p110

☎ 212-620-7310; www.gaycenter.org; 230 E 58th St btwn Second & Third Aves, West Village; ◉ R, W to Lexington Ave-59th St, 4, 5, 6 to 59th St

For more than 25 years, this has been the nexus of LGBT culture in the Village. That's because it provides a surrogate home for queer folks who may not feel so comfortable in their actual one. It's host to endless groups who meet here – everything from Crystal Meth Anonymous to the Armenian Gay and Lesbian Association, Center Kids (for children of gay parents) and the Lambda Car Club. It also provides a ton of regional publications about gay events and nightlife, and hosts frequent special events – dance parties, art exhibits, Broadway-caliber performances, readings and political panels. Plus it's home to the National Archive for Lesbian, Gay, Bisexual & Transgender History, which can be used by researchers by appointment; the small National Museum of LGBT History, which has frequent exhibits; and a cyber center, which lets you use computers to surf the web for just $3 an hour.

HERITAGE OF PRIDE

☎ 212-807-74333; www.nycpride.org

These are the folks who make New York's Gay Pride happen every year, organizing the Pride March on the last Sunday in June, among many other related events throughout the month, to the delight of hundreds of thousands who come to the city especially for this event. For best viewing of the march (called a march, and not a parade, to remember the political roots of the Stonewall Riots, which is what this event commemorates), which kicks off at noon, get to Fifth Ave by 11am. Staking your claim above 14th Street will give you much more wiggle room than in the Village, where crowds get massive.

PRIDE IN THE CITY

www.prideinthecity.com

The first week of August brings Black Pride festivities to NYC, providing a more focused perspective than that of the mainstream Pride in June. Events, most held in Brooklyn, range from film screenings and family picnics to panels on HIV. And the final hurrah is a massive dance party in the sand at Riis Beach, in the Rockaways.

LESBIAN HERSTORY ARCHIVES

Map p182

☎ 718-768-4663; www.lesbianherstoryarchives.org; Park Slope, Brooklyn; ◉ F to 15th St-Prospect Park

This Brooklyn brownstone is filled to the brim with books, periodicals, videos, audiotapes, photographs and various ephemera that tell a long and storied lesbian tale. You can visit by appointment only, or during several annual open houses. Just check the website for events. Founded by Joan Nestle and Deborah Edel in 1974, this is the oldest lesbian archive in the world. Be prepared to get lost in its fascinating holdings for hours.

BLACK GAY & LESBIAN ARCHIVE

Map pp158–9

☎ 212-491-2226; www.nypl.org/research/sc /sc.html; Schomburg Center for Research in Black Culture, 515 Malcolm X Blvd, Harlem; ◉ 2, 3 to 135th St

Part of the Schomburg Center (p161) in Harlem, these holdings include books, photographs and other writings that reflect a black gay experience. It's the brainchild of local publisher and writer Steven G Fullwood, and its documents go back to the mid-1970s.

SLEEPING

top picks

- **6 Columbus** (p361) A retro-mod boutique hotel steps away from Central Park.
- **Gild Hall** (p349) European elegance in the heart of the Financial District.
- **Mercer** (p350) Modern touches combine with historical roots at this SoHo celebrity favorite.
- **Night** (p361) This slick, Midtown glam-goth hotel is a study in black and white.
- **Casablanca Hotel** (p362) Moroccan motifs abound at this nostalgic boutique hotel in Midtown.
- **Carlyle** (p364) A Fifth Avenue classic infused with old-fashioned opulence.
- **Battery Park City Ritz-Carlton** (p349) Head to the tip of Manhattan for harbor views and posh comfort.

SLEEPING

Forget that old cliché about New York being the city that never sleeps. This town is now built around giving visitors an enticing and exciting place to get some shuteye. With a rash of new boutique and luxury hotels opening up just about every month – especially along the Lower East Side and Lower Manhattan – travelers have lots of options and prices to play with.

For the adventurous, there are B&Bs in Brooklyn, the Upper West Side and Harlem to consider, many of them located in old-fashioned brownstones or Victorian-era walkups. For the budget conscious, there are nifty hostels in the heart of the city or, for the experimental-minded, oversized 'loftstels' (see the boxed text, p368) – big lofts turned into communal dorms – in Williamsburg and Bedford-Stuyvesant.

Theater lovers and business travelers always do well in midtown, right in the midst of the city's action. Those who love posh, unique, romantic and impossibly opulent lodgings can take their pick from the city's hundreds of boutique and high-end places, but downtown Manhattan is especially popular right now. Modeled along the lines of Robert De Niro's Greenwich Hotel (opposite), or the latest Wall St luxury, Gild Hall (opposite), boutique establishments are glam, glossy and oh-so-comfortable.

As a general rule, checkout is usually somewhere between 10am and noon, and check-in ranges from noon to 3pm. Most places are happy to hold your luggage for you if you arrive ahead of check-in or need a place to stash your bags before departing.

ACCOMMODATION STYLES

You can agonize over which neighborhood to stay in, but as far as the type of room in which you can hang your hat goes, you've essentially got five kinds to choose from:

B&Bs Or family-style guesthouses, with mix-and-match furnishings and some serious savings (if you don't mind some Victorian styles or eating brekky with strangers).

Boutique hotels Usually have tiny rooms decked out with fantastic amenities like Bulgari bath salts and Egyptian cotton linens, and at least one celebrity-filled basement bar, rooftop bar or hip, flashy eatery on site. Your room might not be spacious, but you'll feel like royalty none-theless.

'Classic' hotels Typified by floral patterned bedspreads and old-fashioned, small-scale European grandeur like you'll find at the Excelsior Hotel (p365), these usually cost the same as boutiques and aren't always any larger.

European-style 'travelers' hotels' Creaky floors and small but cheap and clean (if chintzily decorated) rooms, often with a shared bath; good choices include Hotel 17 (p356).

Hostels Functional (often lifeless and tight) dorms, but often oozing in life, with backyard gardens, kitchens and TV rooms.

ROOM RATES

The average room is $340 a night, with some seasonal fluctuations (lowest in January and

PRIVATE APARTMENTS

It *is* possible to live just like a New Yorker while you are here – all you have to do is rent an apartment from one. There are several agencies that coordinate apartment rentals. Some are in 'hosted' apartments or houses, meaning the owner is present (which will save you the 13.62% city hotel tax), while others leave you completely in charge of keys, doormen and early-morning curbside trash deposits.

Stay the Night Inn (☎ 212-722-8300; www.staythenight.com; apt per night $150) A B&B in a glorious townhouse, Stay the Night also has apartments for rent around the city at reasonable rates. Weekly rates also available.

CitySonnet (☎ 212-614-3034; www.westvillagebb.com; hosted s/d from $98/175, private apt $175-295) Rents private apartments or (hosted) guest rooms in an occupied apartment, many in the hippest downtown locations plus Williamsburg and Brooklyn.

Manhattan Lodgings (☎ 212-677-7616; www.manhattanlodgings.com; apt per night/month from $150/2250, hosted stays per night/month from $150/1550) A selection of studio, one-bedroom and two-bedroom apartments across Manhattan.

February, highest in September and October), and plenty of options both below and above (especially above) this rate. When you get your bill, the hotel will also tack on a 13.625% room tax and a $2 to $6 per night occupancy tax. All that said, it's still not so hard to find a budget room (that means less than $150 by New York standards) or even space for $50 in a youth hostel. It's not uncommon to find frequent special rates no matter what time of year it is, but especially in midwinter or midsummer, when weekend rates often get slashed.

LOWER MANHATTAN & TRIBECA

A formerly desolate neighborhood, the financial district is starting to get its mojo on, with several glossy additions to the local hotel stock and another 2000 rooms coming by 2012, according to city planners. It's still predominantly a place that fills with workers by day and quietens down a lot at night, but in the summer things are livelier, as crowds en route to the Statue of Liberty and South Street Seaport wander the crooked lanes dating from the days of New Amsterdam. Nearby Tribeca's a hot spot for high-end hotels like the Greenwich Hotel (below) and – coming soon – Smyth Tribeca, the latest boutique offering from the brains behind Gild Hall (right).

GREENWICH HOTEL
Map pp72–3   Deluxe Boutique $$$
☎ 212-941-8900; www.greenwichhotelny.com; 377 Greenwich St, btwn N Moore & Franklin Sts; d from $725; ⊕ 1 to Franklin St, A, C, E to Canal St; ✂ 🖥
As of research time, Robert De Niro's latest downtown venture was still in its 'soft' opening phase, but even with a few details still to be smoothed out, the place

was just about perfection. The elegant, light-infused vaulted lobby takes you to smallish but tasteful rooms lining a serene inner courtyard. Each room has floor-to-ceiling French doors that open right into the flower-filled garden; dark, aged wood lines the floors, and bathrooms covered in Carrara marble. Larger suites have bigger bathrooms and closets, but are otherwise similar. For the most luxurious experience, book the penthouse suite – a glass-enclosed, airy perch replete with private deck and hot tub.

BATTERY PARK CITY RITZ-CARLTON
Map pp72–3   Deluxe International $$$
☎ 212-344-0800; www.ritz-carlton.com; 2 West St at Battery Pl; d/ste from $575/$645; ⊕ 4, 5 to Bowling Green; ✂ 🖥
Lower Manhattan's nicest hotel – c'mon, it's the Ritz – overlooks the southern tip of Manhattan, and many of its 298 luxurious rooms come with telescopes carefully pointed toward Lady Liberty. The bottom 14 floors of the modern 38-floor tower are home to the hotel. All rooms come with marble baths – and unique 'bath butler' services, including one for kids with milk and cookies – and Bulgari soaps and lotions. Rooms are roomy and not too posh for comfort. The balcony bar Rise (p287) serves light meals and has stunning views of the harbor. There's also a spa and gym.

GILD HALL Map pp72–3   Boutique $$$
☎ 212-232-7700; www.wallstreetdistrict.com; 15 Gold St; d/ste from $319/$700; ⊕ 2, 3 to Wall St; ✂ 🖥

Step inside the lobby and curl up with a good book and a flute of bubbly; Gild Hall's sensuous entryway leads to a bi-level library and champagne bar. Rooms are part European elegance, part American comfort, with high, tin ceilings, glass-walled balconies, Sferra linens and Frette robes, and mini-bars stocked with Dean & Deluca treats. Hermes designed the leather headboards on the king-size beds, and they don't look at all out of place in these warm-hued, minimalist surroundings.

WALL STREET INN

Map pp72–3   Business Boutique $$

☎ 212-747-1500, 800-695-8284; www.thewall streetinn.com; 9 S William St at Broad St; d incl breakfast Mon-Thu from $259, Fri-Sun from $319; ⊕ 2, 3 to Broad St, 4, 5 to Bowling Green; ✗ ▢
Off cobbled Stone St in the shadows of old and new skyscrapers, the Wall Street's rooms are homey rather than stylish, with an aura of Colonial America. Beds are big and plush, with flowery coverings, glossy wood furnishings and long, swooshy drapes. The bathrooms are full of nice touches, like Jacuzzis in the deluxe rooms and deep marble tubs in the others. The building is a piece of history too – the 'LB' tile in the entry dates from the previous tenants, the Lehman Brother's banking company. There's a small fitness center.

COSMOPOLITAN HOTEL

Map pp72–3   Budget Hotel $$

☎ 212-566-1900, 888-895-9400; www.cosmohotel .com; 95 W Broadway at Chambers St; d from $175; ⊕ 1, 2, 3 to Chambers St; ✗
The most un-Tribeca choice, the cheap Cosmo is a hero for those wanting to save their bills for the area's chic eateries and boutiques. On a busy street corner, the 122-room hotel isn't much to brag about – clean carpeted rooms with private bathrooms, a double bed or two, and IKEA knock-off furnishings. Corner rooms – 422, 522 and 622 – are best, offering views of the far-off Empire State Building. All renovated inside, the Cosmo is proud of its age. A hotel has been operating here since 1852 – making it the city's oldest.

SOHO, NOHO & NOLITA

Downtown Manhattan's picturesque corners will cost you – but the posh surroundings are

top picks

HOT, HOT, HOT

If you enjoy a good soak now and again, consider these penthouse suites with private hot tubs.

- Bowery Hotel (p352) Check into suite 702 and party it up in the outdoor Jacuzzi.
- Hotel on Rivington (opposite) Eight people can pack into this terrace Jacuzzi, and if the view's not enough for you, you'll find a home theater and fully stocked bar.
- Shoreham (p362) Booking the top-level Atrium Suite will snag you a five-seater hot tub with 360-degree city views.
- Mandarin Oriental New York (p360) Stare into Central Park from the steamy depths of a marble hot tub, perfectly sized for two.

worth every penny. Hoteliers aren't blind to the popularity factor of these neighborhoods; at research time, developers were planning to bring a version of Los Angeles's famous Mondrian Hotel to Lafayette St. Expect to pay more than the average boutique price at these places because, let's face it, the mostly celebrity clientele can well afford it.

60 THOMPSON Map pp88–9   Boutique Hotel $$$

☎ 212-431-0400, 877-431-0400; www.60 thompson.com; 60 Thompson St btwn Broome & Spring Sts; s/d/ste from $619/699/775; ⊕ C, E to Spring St; ✗ ▢
Built from scratch in 2001, the snazzy 100-room 60 Thompson is definitely a place to be seen, and many locals can be overheard greeting the blue-clad-with-headsets staff. They come to dine in the futurist Thai restaurant Kittichai, or swirl cocktails on the rooftop Thom Bar. Rooms are small but comfy; beds have goose-down duvets and leather headboards, and you can watch DVDs on the flat-screen TVs from a wing-backed seat or creamy tweed sofa. If the price is within reach, the extra-luxurious suites provide a lot more space and comfort. Wi-fi and high-speed internet is free hotel-wide.

MERCER Map pp88–9   Boutique Hotel $$$

☎ 212-966-6060; 147 Mercer St at Prince St; d from $595, ste $1500-3100; ⊕ N, R, W to Prince St; ✗ ▢

Right in the heart of SoHo's brick lanes, the grand Mercer is where stars sleep. Up from the leisurely lobby with fat, plush sofas, and Jean-Georges Vongerichten's excellent basement restaurant, the 75 rooms offer a slice of chic loft life in a century-old warehouse. Flat-screen TVs, dark-wood floors and white-marble, mosaic-tile bathrooms (some with square tubs under a skylight) add a modern touch to rooms that sport the building's industrial roots – with giant oval windows, steel pillars and exposed-brick walls. Aside from standard rooms the Mercer also has several different types of suites; the best are the two that open onto the hotel's inner courtyard, or the penthouse suite, with its grandiose views. Downstairs has fine dining in the form of the Mercer Kitchen (p252).

SOHO GRAND HOTEL
Map pp88–9   Deluxe International $$$
☎ 212-965-3000, 800-965-3000; www.sohogrand.com; 310 West Broadway; d $300-500; Ⓔ A, C, E to Canal St; ✴ ⌨
Since it opened in 1997, the industrial-gone-chic Soho Grand has kept its slot as a high-status cool-folks HQ for downtown. A nondescript 17-story tower outside, the Grand is striking inside, where a glass and cast-iron stairway leads to a towering lobby (and swank Grand Lounge) topped with warehouse-like beams and 'chicken wire' ceiling. Light pours into the 363 rooms from over Chinatown or SoHo's rooftop water towers, through wide-open windows. Rooms are decorated in more somber tones, punctuated with studded leather headboards, freestanding wardrobes and plasma flat-screen tellies. There's a courtyard restaurant in summer, and the lobby's Grand Lounge bristles with action all year.

LOWER EAST SIDE

Hotels are springing up in the LES faster than the knishes at Yonah Schimmel's famous bakery on East Houston – a welcome change from the days when crashing at a dubious flophouse was the only option.

THOMPSON LES Map p98   Deluxe Boutique $$$
☎ 212-204-6485; http://thompsonles.com; 190 Allen St near Stanton St; r $429; Ⓔ F, V to Lower East Side-2nd Ave; ✴ ⌨
Another high-end offering from the brains trust behind boutique beauties Gild Hall

and 6 Columbus, Thompson LES has 18 floors of industrial, loft-like rooms that manage to look spacious even though most are just over 400 sq ft, and the beds have lightboxes for headboards. Views from the rooms are fantastic, but nothing beats the scenic sweep from the rooftop bar (for guests only). At research time, the hotel was in a 'soft opening' and plans for a 3rd-floor swimming pool were in the works.

BLUE MOON HOTEL Map p98   Boutique $$$
☎ 212-533-9080; www.bluemoon-nyc.com; 100 Orchard St; r $350-550, ste $600-1200; Ⓔ F, V to Lower East Side-2nd Ave; ✴ ⌨
You'd never guess this quaint, welcoming brick guesthouse – full of festive yellows, blues and greens – was once a foul tenement back in the day (the day being 1879). Except for a few ornate touches, like original wood shutters, wrought-iron bed frames and detailed molding, Blue Moon's clean, spare rooms are entirely modern and comfortable, with big beds, great views from large windows, and elegant marble baths.

HOTEL ON RIVINGTON
Map p98   Boutique Hotel $$$
☎ 212-475-2600, 800-915-1537; www.hotelonrivington.com; 107 Rivington St btwn Essex & Ludlow Sts; r/ste from $305/550; Ⓔ F, J, M, Z to Delancey-Essex Sts; ✴ ⌨
Opened in 2005, the 20-floor THOR – that's the hotel acronym, not the viking – looks like a shimmering new-Shanghai building towering over 19th-century tenements. It's all-glass rooms have enviable views over the East River and downtown's sprawl. Best of the barebone-minimal rooms are 'unique suites,' some with corner positions and hanging flat-screen TVs. Some have balconies. Bathrooms are a grab bag – some are window-side and outsiders can see in too (until the windows fog); others are all-lime tiled or with three-head showers for 'multi-tasking' cleaning. Plenty of hang-out space, like the 2nd-floor lounge and ground-floor restaurant.

HOTEL EAST HOUSTON
Map p98   Boutique Hotel $$
☎ 212-777-0012; http://hoteleasthouston.com; 151 E Houston St near Eldridge St; d $199-279; Ⓔ F, V to Lower East Side-2nd Ave; ✴ ⌨
A new addition to the LES boutique craze, East Houston has a chocolate-brown lobby

with vivid red chairs that sets a sexy tone from the get-go, and the romantic vibe only intensifies in the rooms, which are small but cozy and sensual. The deep, rich golds and creams on the walls, glass-tiled bathrooms, heavily shaded windows and glossy furnishings make you feel light years away from busy Houston St (even though some traffic noise might occasionally seep in). Free breakfast, wi-fi, Fiji water and Bulgari toiletries come with the room.

OFF-SOHO SUITES Map p98 Budget Hotel $
☎ 212-979-9815; www.offsoho.com; 11 Rivington St btwn Chrystie St & the Bowery; r/ste from $129/209; ⊕ J, M, Z to Bowery; ⊠ 🖵
There's more grit than glam in Off-Soho Suites' 40 unpretentious rooms, which sleep four and contain fully functional kitchenettes (including microwave, stove, oven and generously stocked shelves). Suites come with pullout sofas across from the satellite-access TV, and a private bedroom with closet. The carpets are a bit threadbare and the brown color scheme a touch dingy, but overall it's a clean, friendly spot. Lots of indie rockers have stayed here, as seen on framed promo pics in vinyl-floored hallways. There's wi-fi access in the lobby sitting area.

EAST VILLAGE

Never one to be left behind, the East Village has gotten on the high-end hotel trend that's taking over downtown Manhattan. At research time a massive, glass-encased highrise known as 27 Cooper Square was putting on its finishing touches. It had to undergo a minor redesign when several rent-controlled neighbors refused to give up their leases (you can look down at their roof from many of the rooms). Aside from that, it's still mostly B&Bs and guesthouses in the East Village – but probably not for long.

BOWERY HOTEL Map p104 Deluxe Boutique $$$
☎ 212-505-9100; www.theboweryhotel.com; 335 Bowery; d from $425; ⊕ B, D, F, V to Broadway-Lafayette St, 6 to Bleecker St; ⊠ 🖵
Pick up your old-fashioned gold room key with its red tassel in the dark, hushed lobby – filled with antique velvet chairs and faded Persian rugs – then follow the mosaic floors to your room. There you can dock your iPod, use the wi-fi, check out the 42-inch plasma,

watch some DVDs, or raid your bathroom goodies (courtesy of CO Bigelow, the Greenwich Village apothecary). Rooms have huge factory windows with unobstructed views, simple white spreads with red piping and elegant four-poster beds. Opened in 2007, the Bowery's zinc-topped bar, outside garden patio, and rustic Italian eatery, Gemma's, are always packed.

SECOND HOME ON SECOND AVE
Map p104 Guesthouse $$
☎ 212-677-3161; www.secondhomesecondavenue.com; 221 Second Ave, btwn 13th & 14th Sts; r $105-210; ⊕ L to 3rd Ave; ⊠
A great option for the downtown-bound on a budget, the Second Home has only seven artful rooms – each with wooden floors, TVs with cable, and worldly themes based on hand-made furnishings or random finds at New York antiques markets. The roomiest, perhaps best, is the Modern Suite ($210), which features French doors separating a sitting area and two double beds on frames put together with assorted pipes. Five rooms have a clean, shared bathroom.

EAST VILLAGE B&B Map p104 B&B $
☎ 212-260-1865; evbandb@juno.com; Apt 5-6, 244 E 7th St btwn Aves C & D; s incl breakfast $75, d incl breakfast $120-150; ⊕ F, V to Lower East Side-2nd Ave; ⊠ 🖵
This lesbian-owned find is a popular oasis for Sapphic couples who want peace and quiet in the midst of the noisy East Village scene. Recently renovated, its three rooms (one single and two double) are way stylish – bold linens, modern art, gorgeous wooden floors – and the shared living-room space is filled with light, beautiful paintings from around the globe, exposed brickwork and a big-screen TV. As it's beyond Ave A, though, it's a particularly long walk to the subway station.

GREENWICH VILLAGE, WEST VILLAGE & THE MEATPACKING DISTRICT

Old-school charm, intimate quarters, reasonable prices and lots of gay-friendliness are what you'll find here – not to mention a couple of slick, impressive newcomers. At research time, fancy hotelier Andre Balaz was rushing to finish StandardNY (www.standardhotels.com/new-york-city) in the Meatpacking District, and two other well-known developers were in the process of 'relocating' tenants of a nearby dump, Hotel Riverview, to turn it into a glossy boutique.

HOTEL GANSEVOORT
Map p110   Boutique Hotel $$$
☎ 212-206-6700, 877-426-7386; www.hotelgan sevoort.com; 18 Ninth Ave at 13th St; r/ste incl breakfast from $395/650; ⊜ A, C, E to 14th St, L to 8th Ave; ⊠ ▭ ⊠

Coated in zinc-colored panels, and booming up top where rooftop bar Plunge attracts block-long lines (and guests swim in the skinny pool overlooking the Hudson River), the 14-floor Gansevoort has been a swank swashbuckler of the Meatpacking District since it opened in 2004. Light pours in the windows of all of the 187 rooms – full-wall deals. Rooms are luscious and airy, with fudge-colored suede headboards, plasma-screen TVs and illuminated bathroom doors. Some have balconies. Breakfast is served in the lovely Ono restaurant, a hot spot for sushi and evening drinks.

SOHO HOUSE Map p110   Boutique Hotel $$$
☎ 212-627-9800; www.sohohouseny.com; 29-35 Ninth Ave at 13th St; d/ste $395/550; ⊜ A, C, E to 14th St, L to 8th Ave; ⊠ ▭ ⊠

A sibling of London's Soho House, this private social club for the high-fashion VIP crowd has 24 guest rooms for nonmembers – but don't expect to snag one easily. If you get a room, opt for the 'playroom' suites with loft-like space, showers that double as steam rooms, a drawer full of 'naughty' oils, and stand-alone Boffi baths on wood floors.

LAFAYETTE HOUSE Map p110   Boutique $$$
☎ 212-505-8100; www.lafayettenyc.com; 38 E 4th St; r $350-425; ⊜ B, D, F, V to Broadway-Lafayette St, 6 to Bleecker St; ⊠ ▭

A former townhouse that's been turned into homey, spacious suites, each with a working fireplace, Lafayette House feels very Victorian. The huge (by Manhattan standards) rooms can actually interconnect, making it a good choice for families and groups. Each place feels like an actual apartment (which most of them were

before renovation), with a big bed, a desk, thick drapes and old-fashioned armoires. Bathrooms are large, with claw-footed tubs, and some rooms have mini-kitchenettes. The only drawback might be the occasional bit of noise from next-door B Bar, although as a plus you can also order room service from its kitchen. Light sleepers should ask for rooms away from the street to avoid any problem.

WEST ELEVENTH TOWNHOUSE
Map p110   B&B $$$
☎ 212-675-7897; www.west-eleventh.com; 278 W 11th St, btwn W 4th & Bleecker Sts; d $249-385; ⊜ 1 to Christopher St, A, C, E, F, V to W 4th St-Washington Sq; ⊠ ▭

Ring bell 11 when you show up at this gracious West Village townhouse, which offers five spacious suites – more like small apartments than hotel rooms – with tiny kitchenettes, cozy living areas with artfully decorated nooks and crannies, and handsome four-poster beds. The El Greco suite, two flights up, was recently renovated, and makes the most of its 12-foot ceilings. If you crave anonymity, this isn't the place for you, but if quaint B&Bs are your thing, it's perfect.

ABINGDON GUEST HOUSE
Map p110   B&B $$
☎ 212-243-5384; www.abingdonguesthouse .com; 13 Eighth Ave, btwn 12th & Jane Sts; s/d incl breakfast from $189/305; ⊜ A, C, E to 14th St, L to 8th Ave; ⊠ ▭

Four-poster beds, elegant antique pieces and scads of exposed brick make Abingdon guests feel like they've landed in a New England country inn. Too bad there are only nine rooms! Occupying two three-floor, 1850 townhouses, rooms mix up the themes (the Ambassador goes safari, with a kitchenette; the Garden has private access to its small namesake out back). Internet access and private bathrooms are found in all rooms. The only catch is the four-night minimum stay over weekends, two-nights for weekdays.

INCENTRA VILLAGE HOUSE
Map p110   B&B $$
☎ 212-206-0007; 32 Eighth Ave, btwn 12th & Jane Sts; r $169-199; ⊜ A, C, E to 14th St, L to 8th Ave; ⊠ ▭

An easy walk to Chelsea clubs, these two redbrick, landmark townhouses were built in 1841 and later became the city's first gay inn. Today, the 12 rooms get booked way in advance by many queer travelers; call early to get in on its gorgeous Victorian parlor (featuring a baby grand piano that's often the site of a show-tune sing-along) and antique-filled, serious-Americana rooms (one is fully red-white-and-blue, with a possibly stunned George Washington watching over the brass bed). The 'Garden Suite' has access to a small garden in back and there's wi-fi access in the parlor.

LARCHMONT HOTEL Map p110 Indie Inn $
☎ 212-989-9333; www.larchmonthotel.com; 27 W 11th St btwn Fifth & Sixth Aves; s/d from $90/119; Ⓜ F, V to 14th St; ⊠ ▯

This European-style inn has 60 popular rooms on a leafy residential block, mid-distance from the West and East Villages. It's great cheap sleeping if you don't mind tip-toeing in the provided robe and slippers for a tinkle or shower down the hall. Rooms are small, but fine – with wicker furnishings, cable TV, wall air-con units and high-speed internet connections. For an extra $20, rooms come with queen-size beds come with flat-screen TVs and get some townhouse views of the street.

CHELSEA

If you love the nightlife, you'll love Chelsea, an upbeat and quirky area filled with nightclubs, galleries and Chelsea boys. It's also something of an indie-hotel ghetto – there's backpacker hostels, B&Bs and big-buck luxury standouts. It's easy walking distance from Chelsea to the Meatpacking District, the West Village and Midtown's theaters and restaurants.

MARITIME HOTEL Map p116 Boutique Hotel $$$
☎ 212-242-4300; www.themaritimehotel.com; 363 W 16th St btwn Eighth & Ninth Aves; r $294-425; Ⓜ A, C, E to 14th St, L to 8th Ave; ⊠ ▯

Originally the site of the National Maritime Union headquarters (and more recently a shelter for homeless teens), this white tower dotted with portholes has been transformed into a marine-themed luxury inn by a hip team of architects. It feels like a luxury *Love Boat* inside, as its 135 rooms, each with their own round window, are compact and teak-paneled, with gravy in the form of 20-inch flat-screen TVs and DVD players. The most expensive quarters feature outdoor showers, a private garden and sweeping Hudson views. Big names show up at La Bottega, a popular trattoria and bar with 6000 sq ft of patio space out front.

INN ON 23RD ST Map p116 B&B $$
☎ 212-463-0330; www.innon23rd.com; 131 W 23rd St btwn Sixth & Seventh Aves; r incl breakfast from $269; Ⓜ F, V, 1 to 23rd St; ⊠ ▯

Housed in a lone 19th-century, five-story townhouse on busy 23rd St, this 14-room B&B is a Chelsea gem. The hotel's kitchen shares its counters with the New School Culinary Arts program, meaning lots of free cakes and breads from promising students appear in the 2nd-floor, all-Victorian library/dining room. Rooms are big and welcoming, with fanciful fabrics on big brass or poster beds and TVs held in huge armoires. There's an honor-system bar and an ol' piano for you to play boogie-woogie on.

CHELSEA HOTEL Map p116 Indie Inn $$
☎ 212-243-3700; www.hotelchelsea.com; 222 W 23rd St, btwn Seventh & Eighth Aves; r/ste from $225/585; Ⓜ C, E, 1 to 23rd St; ⊠ ▯

Immortalized by poems, overdoses (Sid Vicious did the deed here, after allegedly killing Nancy Spungen) and Ethan Hawke's novel writing, the one-of-a-kind Chelsea is soon to undergo a massive overhaul that locals fear will strip it of all its color. For now you can still enjoy (if that's the

DESMOND TUTU CENTER

Imagine bedding down in a South African–inspired retreat with sprawling parklands dotted with renovated 19th-century gothic structures – right in the heart of Chelsea. That's the bizarre combination you'll find at the Desmond Tutu Center (Map p116; ☎ 212-929-3888; www.ahl-tutucenter.com; 180 Tenth Ave btwn 20 & 21st Sts; r from $285; Ⓜ A,C,W to 23rd St), a newfangled business center/romantic getaway that shares grounds and buildings with the General Theological Seminary. The 60 historic guest rooms are fully equipped with wi-fi, faxes, phones and flat-screen TVs, but they're equally inviting for those who want to tune out the modern world and enjoy the flickering lights, flower-filled walkways and sensuous decor. We think Nobel Peace Prize–winner and South African activist Desmond Tutu, the center's namesake, would approve.

right word) the mix-match of rooms lovingly showing off their decades – most are huge, with ruby-red carpets or drip-drop designs on rugs over wooden floors. Some have kitchenettes and separate living rooms. Staying here can feel like life in a film/photo shoot – probably because one's going on next door.

CHELSEA LODGE Map p116   B&B $$

☎ 212-243-4499; www.chelsealodge.com; 318 W 20th St btwn Eighth & Ninth Aves; r/ste from $119/229; ⊙ C, E to 23rd St; ✂

Housed in a landmark brownstone in Chelsea's lovely historic district, the European-style, 20-room Chelsea Lodge is a super deal, with homey well-kept rooms. Decor flies the Americana flag, with color prints of train scenes in rooms, Native American busts and hunting duck decoys propped up over doorways. Rooms are small – just a bed, with TVs (with cable) plopped on an old wooden cabinet. There are showers and sinks in rooms, but toilets are down the hall. Six suite rooms have private bathrooms, two come with private garden access.

CHELSEA PINES INN Map p116   B&B $

☎ 212-929-1023, 888-546-2700; www.chelsea pinesinn.com; 317 W 14th St btwn Eighth & Ninth Aves; r incl breakfast from $139; ⊙ A, C, E to 14th St, L to 8th Ave; ✂ ▭

With its five walk-up floors coded to the rainbow flag, the 26-room Chelsea Pines is serious gay-and-lesbian central, but guests of all stripes are welcome. It helps to be up on your Hitchcock beauties, as vintage movie posters not only plaster the walls but rooms are named for starlets like Kim Novak, Doris Day and Ann-Margret. There's a sink in the walk-in closet of standard rooms, with clean bathrooms down the hall. The small café downstairs has free wi-fi access, and opens to a tiny courtyard out back. Plenty of advice on cruising, partying and eating by the lively staff.

COLONIAL HOUSE INN Map p116   B&B $

☎ 212-243-9669, 800-689-3779; www.colonial houseinn.com; 318 W 22nd St btwn Eighth & Ninth Aves; r incl breakfast with shared/private bathroom from $105/135; ⊙ C, E to 23rd St; ✂

Friendly and simple, this 20-room gay inn is tidy but a bit worn and small. Most rooms

top picks

GAY STAYS

- Bubba & Bean Lodges (p364) A carefree, fun and affordable spot where everyone and anyone is welcome.
- Chelsea Pines Inn (left) The decor is vintage Hollywood. OK, so it's only got loads of framed film posters. But we'll bet any of the boys bunking here can belt out some lines from the big hits as well.
- Ivy Terrace (p359) Quaint, gay run and owned, located between two gay bars and close to shopping.
- East Village B&B (p352) A homey favorite among Sapphic couples.

have small walk-in closets (with a small TV and refrigerator) and sinks. The owner, Mel Cheren, ran the legendary hip-hop club Paradise Garage. He lives on the ground floor and lines the walls with his colorful paintings. Breakfast in the small café leads to chat sessions. When weather is chummy, the rooftop deck up top sees some nude sunbathing.

CHELSEA INTERNATIONAL HOSTEL
Map p116   Hostel $

☎ 212-647-0010; www.chelseahostel.com; 251 W 20th St btwn Seventh & Eighth Aves; dm/r $30/75; ⊙ C, E, 1 to 23rd St; ✂

A festive, international scene defines this hostel, where the back patio serves as party central (until midnight closing time) for up to 350 guests. Bunk rooms sleep four to six and amenities include communal kitchens and laundry facilities. It's kind of run like an urban camp – with some staff loving their jobs less than others. Everyone – even Americans – must show their passport to check in. There's a two-week maximum stay.

UNION SQUARE, THE FLATIRON DISTRICT & GRAMERCY

Even though Union Sq is a pretty bustling section of town, this often-overlooked region actually has an abundance of upscale, quiet and romantic hotel options. Full of inns and opulent boutique hotels, the leafy, residential

top picks

BOUTIQUE HOTELS

- **Bowery Hotel** (p352) Rock-star glamour in a rough-edged nabe.
- **Gild Hall** (p349) A sexy choice for Wall St power-brokers.
- **Hotel Gansevoort** (p353) Sceney rooftop pool and bar evokes Miami.
- **Mercer** (p350) It's so SoHo cool.
- **The Muse** (p361) Excellent service and dream-like surroundings whisk you away from noisy Times Sq.

streets, in close proximity (walking distance) to both Midtown and East Village attractions, will make you feel at home. But the area, while long on character, is short on space, so book early.

GRAMERCY PARK HOTEL
Map p120   Indie Boutique $$$

☎ 212-475-4320; www.gramercyparkhotel.com; 2 Lexington Ave at 21st St; r $450-800, ste $875-5000; ◉ 6 to 23rd St; ⊠ ▢

Newly renovated and sparkling from head to toe, this grand old dame looks like a young ingénue. It's worth staying here just for the easy entry into the impossibly hip Jade and Rose bars, not to mention the private rooftop sanctuary for guests only. Rooms overlook nearby Gramercy Park, and all have customized oak furnishings, 400-count Italian linens, and big, feather-stuffed mattresses on sprawling beds. Colors are rich and alluring, fit for a Spanish grandee.

W NEW YORK – UNION SQUARE
Map p120   Classy Chain Hotel $$$

☎ 212-253-9119, 888-625-5144; www.whotels.com; 201 Park Ave S at 17th St; r from $400; ◉ L, N, Q, R, W, 4, 5, 6 to 14th St-Union Sq; ⊠ ▢

The ultra-hip W demands a black wardrobe and credit card. Everything is top of the line. Lots of somber tones in rooms, like framed leather headboards and lavender duvets for the feather beds. There are DVD players for the TVs and high-speed internet connections. Rooms aren't big, but – set in a 1911, one-time insurance building – all rooms benefit from high ceilings. If rooms here are sold out, investigate W's other Manhattan hotels: W New York – Times Square (Map pp134–5; ☎ 212-930-7400; 1567 Broad-

way at 47th St; r $260-709), W New York – Court (Map p126; ☎ 212-685-1100; 130 E 39th St; r $285-709), W New York – Tuscany (Map p126; ☎ 212-686-1600; 120 E 39th St; r $285-709) and W New York (Map p126; ☎ 212-755-1200; 541 Lexington Ave btwn 49th and 50th Sts; r $269-709).

INN AT IRVING PLACE
Map p120   B&B $$$

☎ 212-533-4600, 800-685-1447; www.innat irving.com; 56 Irving Pl btwn 17th & 18th Sts; r incl breakfast from $325; ◉ L, N, Q, R, W, 4, 5, 6 to 14th St-Union Sq; ⊠ ▢

Richly Victorian, this intimate 11-room red-brick townhouse dates from 1834 and bursts with period pieces and rosy patterns of days past. Rooms are named for area writers and figures, such as the Edith Wharton, which has smooth dark-wood floors and a sitting area in front of the original (and now just decorative) fireplace. Breakfast is served in the atmospheric Lady Mendl parlor.

CHELSEA INN
Map p120   B&B $

☎ 212-645-8989, 800-640-6469; www.chelseainn .com; 46 W 17th St btwn Fifth & Sixth Aves; s/d/ste incl breakfast from $99/149/199; ◉ F, V, L to 6th Ave-14th St; ⊠

Made up of two adjoining 19th-century townhouses, this funky-charming hide-away (a four-story walk-up) has small but comfortable rooms that look like they were furnished entirely from flea markets or grandma's attic. It's character on a budget, just a bit east of the most desir-able part of this happening 'hood. Rates drop in winter.

HOTEL 17
Map p120   Budget Hotel $

☎ 212-475-2845; www.hotel17ny.com; 225 E 17th St btwn Second & Third Aves; d $120-150; ◉ N, Q, R, W, 4, 5, 6 to 14th St-Union Sq, L to 3rd Ave; ⊠

Right off Stuyvesant Sq on a leafy residential block, this popular eight-floor townhouse has old–New York charm with cheap prices. Plus Woody Allen shot a frightening dead-body scene here for his film *Manhattan Murder Mystery* (1993). Only four of the 120 rooms have private bathrooms (all are free of the film's dead bodies). Rooms are small, with traditional, basic furnishings (gray car-pet, striped wallpaper, chintzy bedspreads, burgundy blinds) and lack much natural light. If this place is booked, ask about its sister property, Hotel 31 (Map p126; ☎ 212-685-3060; 120 E 31st St btwn Lexington & Park Aves).

JAZZ ON THE TOWN Map p120 Hostel $

☎ 212-228-2780; www.jazzhostel.com; 307 E 14th St btwn First & Second Aves; dm $34-42; ⊖ L to 1st Ave; ❌ 🖳

Affiliated with the superior Jazz on the Park Hostel (p365), this crammed, four-floor walk-up is, despite the smiles, a by-the-numbers hostel with functional, slightly depressing dorm rooms of four or six beds (one dorm is females only). There's a rooftop deck with artificial turf and seats overlooking loud 14th St (it's OK to bring in beer, but note the 'no jumping' sign). There are a few computers to check email, a storage room and laundry facilities.

MIDTOWN EAST & FIFTH AVENUE

If you want to be in the heart of the action, consider Midtown East, which encompasses the area around Grand Central Terminal and the UN. It's not as crazy and eclectic as Midtown West, but options are endless and prices and conditions range from $75 cheapies with shared toilets down the hall to thousand-dollar suites with private terraces overlooking the city's blinking lights.

FOUR SEASONS
Map p126 International Chain Hotel $$$

☎ 212-758-5700, 800-819-5053; www.foursea sons.com/newyorkfs; 57 E 57th St btwn Madison & Park Aves; r/ste from $725/2150; ⊖ N, R, W to 5th Ave-59th St; ❌ 🖳

Rising like a pyramid up 52 floors, the Four Seasons has a massive lobby (designed by IM Pei) that hits you like a Gothic cathedral gone mod, with limestone arches leading to the glass-tile skylight – plus there's an adjoining bar and restaurant. Even the smallest of the 368 rooms are giant things, with latte-colored carpets and 10-inch plasma TVs in the full-marble bathrooms. The views over Central Park are practically unfair. There's a 24-hour fitness centre and top-hatted doormen will set you up for the free car service (limit: two-mile radius) from 8am to 11pm.

BENJAMIN Map p126 Business Hotel $$$

☎ 212-715-2500, 888-423-6526; www.theben jamin.com; 125 E 50th St at Lexington Ave; d/ste from $429/500; ⊖ 6 to 51st St; ❌ 🖳

Just east of the bulk of Midtown business, the Benjamin's 209 rooms aim to please

those wishing to settle in for a bit. Most rooms are suites, and all come with fully stocked kitchens (microwave and refrigerator – but no stove or oven) and a giant work desk that pulls out for more space. Four people will do better with a suite than paying $40 for a roll-away bed. Rooms have BOSE stereos. There's a 24-hour fitness center, too.

70 PARK Map p126 Business Boutique $$$

☎ 212-973-2400; 877-707-2753; www.70parkave .com; 70 Park Ave at 38th St; r/ste $425/800; ⊖ S, 4, 5, 6, 7 to 42nd St-Grand Central; ❌ 🖳

The earth-conscious aesthetic at 70 Park extends beyond the gorgeous limestone fireplace and long communal concierge/check-in table that greet you at the lobby; guests are asked to recycle and the hotel has water-saving programs in place. The rooms are packed with state-of-the-art technology (including great sound systems) and, while small, have comfy plush beds, cute sofas tucked into corner nooks, and soothing gold and brown palettes.

CARLTON HOTEL Map p126 Boutique Hotel $$$

☎ 212-532-4100, 800-601-8500; www.carlton hotelny.com; 88 Madison Ave btwn 28th & 29th Sts; r from $399; ⊖ N, R, W, 6 to 28th St; ❌ 🖳

Entering this jazzy luxury hotel feels like walking into a sepia-toned portrait of the art-deco age. In the lobby, big-band and jazz standards play as a wall of water falls gently over a fuzzy Madison Ave street scene. The rooms are traditional and homey, with brown floral carpets, creamy walls and drapes hanging over the bed headboards. In addition to TVs and work desks, in most rooms you'll also find iHouse alarm clocks for your iPod. It has free internet access and meeting rooms that will no doubt appeal to business travelers.

KITANO Map p126 Deluxe Indie Inn $$$

☎ 212-885-7000, 800-548-2666; www.kitano.com; 66 Park Ave at 38th St; d/ste from $350/750; ⊖ S, 4, 5, 6, 7 to Grand Central-42nd St; ❌ 🖳

The long-time hotel location of the Rockefellers' Murray Hill Hotel, the cool, Japanese-run Kitano was completely rebuilt in 1995, predominantly because the owners were so unhappy with Manhattan hotels. This sleek 18-floor business hotel indeed has a hushed Eastern vibe. Carpeted rooms

top picks

SINGLES SCENE

- **Bowery Hotel (p352)** The celebrity-friendly hotel has a trifecta of perfect pick-up places: a hip-and-hot eatery, a sexy French-influenced bar and a romantic, private garden terrace.
- **6 Columbus (p361)** When you do up a hotel in '60s decor, you gotta expect some shagging.
- **Gershwin Hotel (p360)** It's right next to the Museum of Sex. Need we say more?
- **Gramercy Park Hotel (p356)** Two fantastic bars serving a lot of sexy drinks makes for a very happening scene.
- **Jazz on the Park Hostel (p365)** A fun and youthful clientele turns the communal espresso bar into a speed-dating event.

are simple, with fluffy duvets, wi-fi access, flat-screen TVs and work desks. If you wish to have the whole deal, the *ryokan*-style Japanese suite (from $890) is decorated like a traditional Japanese inn, with tatami mats, tea areas and wood floors.

HOTEL GIRAFFE Map p126 Boutique Hotel $$$
☎ 212-685-7700, 877-296-0009; www.hotelgiraffe.com; 365 Park Ave South at 26th St; r/ste incl breakfast from $339/475; ◐ N, R, W, 6 to 23rd St; ✖ ▯
Up a notch in posh from most of the boutiques this far south, the new 12-floor Giraffe earns its stripes, or dots, with sleek, modern rooms in a stretch of art-deco office buildings and a sunny rooftop area for drinks or tapas. Most of the 72 rooms have small balconies. All come with flat-screen TVs (and DVD players), granite work desks, and automatic black-out shades to open and shut the (big) windows from your bed. Corner suites add a living room with pull-out sofa.

HOTEL 373 Map p126 Business Hotel $$$
☎ 212-213-3388, 888-382-7111; www.hotel373.com; 373 Fifth Ave at 35th St; r $309-439; ◐ N, Q, R, W, B, D, F, V to 34th St-Herald Sq; ✖ ▯
The claustrophobic among us will not appreciate Hotel 373's cunning, multi-use furnishings and teeny-tiny little rooms, but those who like a great deal will understand that affordable *and* clean, fun, fabulous hotels just steps from the Empire State Build-

ing always have a drawback somewhere. Hotel 373's rooms are a tight squeeze, but it's just a wee sliver of a building, and what it lacks in square footage it makes up for in charm. And can you beat the fact that the next-door Starbucks is practically in the lobby?

WALDORF-ASTORIA
Map p126 Legendary Chain $$$
☎ 212-355-3000, 800-925-3673; www.waldorfastoria.com; 301 Park Ave btwn 49th & 50th Sts; r/ste $349/519; ◐ 6 to 51st St, E, F to Lexington Ave-53rd St; ✖ ▯
An attraction in itself, the 416-room, 42-floor legendary hotel – now part of the Hilton chain – is an art-deco landmark. It's massive, occupying a full city block – with 13 conference rooms and shops and eateries keeping the ground floor buzzing with life. Elegant rooms conjure some old-world fussiness, with rose-petal rugs and embossed floral wallpaper. Staff tell us three-quarters of daily visitors come just to look. Plenty to gawk at: the *Wheel of Life* mosaic tile entry (at the Park Ave entrance) features nearly 150,000 tiles.

HOTEL ELYSÉE Map p126 Boutique $$$
☎ 212-753-1066, 800-535-9733; www.elyseehotel.com; 60 E 54th St btwn Park & Madison Aves; r/ste $295/500; ◐ E, V to 5th Ave-53rd St; ✖ ▯
It's been around for a long time, but Hotel Elysée is still fresh to the eye, thanks to a renovation that's left it sparkling. The wood-paneled lobby and long hallways lighted by gilded chandeliers give it a romantic glow, and the massive rooms, especially the suites, are stately but stylish, with silvery wallpaper matched with white and blue linens. It's no wonder Ava Gardner chose to conduct some of her legendary affairs here. Also on site is the infamous Monkey Bar, a great place for drinks.

LIBRARY HOTEL Map p126 Boutique Hotel $$
☎ 212-983-4500, 877-793-7323; www.libraryhotel.com; 299 Madison Ave at 41st St; d incl breakfast $300; ◐ S, 4, 5, 6, 7 to 42nd St-Grand Central; ✖ ▯
Each of the 10 floors in this cleverly themed space is dedicated to one of the 10 major categories of the Dewey Decimal System: Social Sciences, Literature, Philosophy and so on, with a total of 6000 volumes split up between quarters. The

handsome style here is bookish, too: mahogany paneling, hushed reading rooms and a gentlemen's-club atmosphere, thanks largely to its stately 1912 brick-mansion home. A bonus is the rooftop deck bar, where you can peek down 41st St to the real library.

DYLAN Map p126 · Boutique Hotel $$

☎ 212-338-0500, 866-553-9526; www.dylanhotel.com; 52 E 41st St btwn Madison & Park Aves; r/ste from $280/480; ⊕ S, 4, 5, 6, 7 to 42nd St-Grand Central; ✄ ▭

Now a house of style, this 108-room luxury boutique hotel was once home to the Chemists Club (seems that science nerds used to go for ornate Beaux-Arts, evident in the original swirling marble staircase and 1903 facade). Somber lighting in cushy rooms may be too dark for some, but it's hard to not be moved by full-marble bathrooms, cube-like armchairs and color schemes of sky blue, green and lavender. Best is the Alchemy Suite, created in the 1930s as a mock medieval lab. (Those are the nerds we love most.) The ground-floor Chemist Club is a classy clubhouse restaurant serving breakfast and a tower of oysters and other seafood.

ROYALTON Map p126 · Boutique Hotel $$

☎ 212-869-4400, 800-635-9013; www.royalton.com; 44 W 44th St btwn Fifth & Sixth Aves; d $279-575; ⊕ B, D, F, V to 42nd St; ✄ ▭

A funky mix of modern and classic (glam cruise-liner theme inside, Greek columns outside), this Ian Schrager and Philippe Starck creation is a mainstay chic choice in this primetime spot Midtown. Deep blue carpet rushes by curving hallways with 'porthole' numbers on doors. Short bed frames are topped with down duvets. The refurbished 44 Bar is a modern take on the Royalton's fabled round bar. Best of all are the 'Roman' baths in the rooms: round circular tubs encased in glass.

AVALON Map p126 · International Hotel $$

☎ 212-299-7000, 888-442-8256; www.avalonhotelnyc.com; 16 E 32nd St btwn Madison & Fifth Aves; r from $275; ⊕ N, Q, R, W, B, D, F, V to 34th St-Herald Sq, 6 to 33rd St; ✄ ▭

This Spanish-run 100-room hotel aims for the Old World, with a frenzy of pillars and marble in its lobby, and chintzy rooms adorned with English-landscape art on striped walls, green floral carpets and fussy

items like a TV-packing armoire and mini bar. Suites, for an extra $50, grant you wood-floor entries and a sofa-bed in the TV room by the window. The colors are bland and – unless you like olive green and basic brown – a little depressing. Only the Executive Suite has a little pizazz to it, courtesy of the private Jacuzzi.

ROGER WILLIAMS Map p126 · Boutique Hotel $$

☎ 212-448-7000, 888-448-7788; www.hotelrogerwilliams.com; 131 Madison Ave at 31st St; d from $250; ⊕ 6 to 33rd St; ✄ ▭

Here's a boutique not afraid of a little color. A geometric splash of orange, blue and green greets guests of this hotel named for the founder of Rhode Island (and the church next door). Rooms are small, but homey – with quilts folded at the end of comfy beds, and flat-screen TVs over small work desks. Garden Terrace rooms (from $295) have balconies. The 2nd-floor lounge has a great breakfast featuring the best of bakeries from all over New York.

BEDFORD HOTEL Map p126 · Traveler Hotel $$

☎ 212-697-4800, 800-221-6881; www.bedfordhotel.com; 118 E 40th St; r $240-385; ⊕ S, 4, 5, 6, 7 to 42nd St-Grand Central; ✄ ▭

The brick-covered, old-fashioned Bedford shows its age, but if you scratch beneath the surface of chintzy furnishings and faded wall colors, what you find are basic, spacious rooms with mini-kitchenettes in an unbeatable location (one block from Grand Central Station). There's nothing flash or high-end about Bedford Hotel, but it's solidly comfortable and the clerks have a relaxed, 'no fuss, no muss' attitude that suits independent types just right.

IVY TERRACE Map p126 · B&B $$

☎ 516-662-6862; www.ivyterrace.com; 58th St btwn Second & Third Aves; r Mon-Fri from $195, Sat & Sun from $320; ⊕ 4, 5, 6 to 59th St, N, R, W to Lexington Ave-59th St; ✄

This lesbian-owned urban B&B is popular with couples who don't want to stay in the fray of the downtown scene. But with gay bars – Townhouse and OW Bar – right on the block, there's still plenty of nearby entertainment, not to mention Bloomingdale's and the rest of the shopping district for all guests, straight or gay. The rooms have Victorian charm – lace curtains, sleigh beds, hardwood floors and kitchens with breakfast supplies – and fill up fast, so call ahead. As of research time, a sixth room was planned.

THIRTYTHIRTY Map p126   Boutique Hotel $$
☎ 212-689-1900, 800-497-6078; www.thirtythirty-nyc.com; 30 E 30th St btwn Park & Madison Aves; s/d from $169/179; ◉ 6 to 33rd St; ⊗ ▣
This 252-room hotel aims to be a boutique stay for cheap, but gets sidetracked by a few tacky touches – such as handmade ads in the elevators, or playing an '80s pop radio station (and their ads) in the lobby. Still, many visitors toting Macy's bags check into simple rooms, with fudge-colored rugs, TVs bolted to the walls, a small closet with safe, and teddy bears between pillows. Worth considering at under $200.

MURRAY HILL INN Map p126   Budget Hotel $
☎ 212-683-6900, 888-996-6376; www.murrayhillinn.com; 143 E 30th St btwn Lexington & Third Aves; d $109-149; ◉ 6 to 33rd St; ⊗ ▣
Named for its pleasant, leafy residential nook of Midtown, this friendly 47-room budget option is better than most in the price range. A recent renovation added wood floors and flat-screen TVs to the rooms, which also have small refrigerators and a small closet. All but two rooms have private bathrooms.

GERSHWIN HOTEL Map p126   Indie Inn $
☎ 212-545-8000; www.gershwinhotel.com; 7 E 27th St at Fifth Ave; dm $34, r $109-300; ◉ 6 to 28th St; ⊗ ▣
Next to the Museum of Sex, and four blocks north of the Flatiron Building, the 13-floor Gershwin is one of the Manhattan greats: a mostly hotel, part hostel for many younger folk (though not exclusively) not wanting to spend several hundred dollars a night. Its facade is lined with teardrop-shaped bulbs, and inside there's framed pop art in the lobby and rooms. Of the 159 rooms, a handful are carpeted dorms with four, six or 10 bunks (most co-ed, one is women only); all have private bathroom. Appealing private rooms have wooden floors, with yellow walls, clean bathrooms, vintage furnishings, cable TV and a dresser. The rooftop deck was (still) undergoing renovations as of research time.

MIDTOWN WEST & TIMES SQUARE

Light sleepers beware – Midtown West is a 24-hours-a-day kind of place. Better bring your eyeshades. If the idea of sleeping under the neon sun of Times Square excites rather than depresses you, Midtown West is your perfect location. It's go-go-go all day and night long, thanks to the juxtaposition of Broadway and all its fantastic theater with the heart of Manhattan's business district. To top it off, Hell's Kitchen's Ninth Ave has a huge range of restaurants with cuisines from all over the world.

RITZ-CARLTON – NEW YORK, CENTRAL PARK Map p134–5   International Chain Hotel $$$
☎ 212-308-9100, 800-241-3333; www.ritzcarlton.com; 50 Central Park S btwn Sixth & Seventh Aves; r from $995; ◉ N, R, Q, W to 57th St-7th Ave, F to 57th St; ⊗ ▣
It's about as lux as Manhattan goes: a landmark building with views of Central Park so giant you almost can't see New York. Inside the opulent lobby bar, a harp player plucks on strings while the ritzy set sip on cocktails. All 261 rooms are faintly French colonial, with tasseled armchairs, lovely inlaid-tile bathrooms and loads of space. If you're splurging, do go for a park view, where a *Birds of New York* field guide is set by a telescope. Three-course dinners at high-class Atelier run to about $85. There's also a great spa and business center.

MANDARIN ORIENTAL NEW YORK Map pp134–5   International Chain Hotel $$$
☎ 866-801-8880; www.mandarinoriental.com; 80 Columbus Circle at 60th St; r from $850; ◉ A, C, B, D, 1 to 59th St-Columbus Circle; ⊗ ▣ ⊠
Occupying the 35th to 54th floors of a modern 84-floor tower at the southwestern edge of Central Park, the Mandarin is the hotel all New York hotels look up to. With some suites breaking $15,000 a night, it's tip-top, Eastern-influence opulence, with superb views over the park and Midtown skyline. Even standard rooms get many of the higher-priced suite touches – with Japanese writing-box desks, TVs in the all-marble bathrooms and chaise lounges by the full-wall windows. Those without the bucks can splurge for a $17 martini or $38 tea service at the towering Lobby Lounge.

The hotel has a seriously pampering spa and a narrow lap pool in the split-level fitness center.

LONDON NYC
Map pp134–5   Deluxe Business Boutique $$$
☎ 212-307-5000, 866-690-2029; www.thelondon nyc.com; 151 W 54th St btwn Sixth & Seventh Aves; r $459-1200; ◉ B, D, E to 7th Ave; ☒ ▣
A favorite among the corporate jet set with unlimited expense accounts, the London NYC will blow you away with its gleaming, sleek furnishings and rooms, including the top-tier Atrium Suite that offers nearly 360-degree views of Times Sq. Every amenity one would expect – wi-fi, flat-screen TVs, iPods and so on – are in the rooms, but the real allure is in the parquet floors, 2000-thread-count linens, and massive, stylish bathrooms. If you want to eat in the hotel restaurant – helmed by its namesake, ce-lebrity chef Gordon Ramsay – better book well in advance.

CHAMBERS Map pp134–5   Boutique Hotel $$$
☎ 212-974-5656, 866-204-5656; www.chamber snyc.com; 15 W 56th St btwn Fifth & Sixth Aves; d from $475; ◉ F to 57th St, N, R, W to 5th Ave-59th St; ☒ ▣
This 77-room hotel – near Fifth Ave's ritziest department stores – aims for a bit of high-style class. The towering lobby has a great mezzanine lounge with anime-like art on walls and a mix of area-rugs, sofas and arm-chairs. Upstairs rooms give illusions of more space with a small hallway. Plush cushions are plopped on the duvets of wood-frame beds; bathrooms have concrete floors and giant showerheads in clear-glass showers. Business visitors will enjoy the tear-away tracing paper on the glass-top work desks. Room service is handled by the swank neighbor, Town restaurant.

BRYANT PARK HOTEL
Map pp134–5   Boutique Hotel $$$
☎ 212-869-0100; www.bryantparkhotel.com; 40 W 40th St btwn Fifth & Sixth Aves; d/ste from $365/465; ◉ B, D, F, V to 42nd St, 7 to 5th Ave; ☒ ▣
All eyes from nearby Bryant Park naturally fixate on this gem, a black-and-gold-brick tower looming to the south. Originally the American Standard Building (1934), this 130-room hotel is chic central, with bare-bone minimalist rooms, most with huge views. The lift up is padded in red leather;

rooms come with flat-screen TVs, cashmere robes, full-size soaking tubs and Pipino lotions. If you can, opt up for a suite that faces the park (higher-priced ones have terraces). The adjoining KOI is a classy sushi restaurant.

NIGHT Map pp134–5   Offbeat Boutique $$$
☎ 212-835-9600; www.nighthotelny.com; 132 West 45th St; r $329-800; ◉ B, D, F, V to 47th-50th Sts-Rockefeller Center; ☒ ▣
From the rocker-glam entrance, draped in crushed velvet, to the purely black-and-white rooms, sleeping at Night is like stepping right into an Anne Rice novel – you wouldn't be at all surprised if an otherworldly creature jumped out at you. Celebrated hotelier Vikram Chatwal's stark, two-toned establishment stands out all the more in the glare of Times Sq's neon. The lobby's a study in cool black and white marble, with white columns and black horsehair couches, and the rooms, while not spacious, manage to be welcoming even with the stark color choices. Having the hotel's signature gothic 'N' patterned on the floor and in some cases, on the wall-paper, adds a little touch of whimsy.

6 COLUMBUS Map pp134–5   Deluxe Boutique $$$
☎ 212-204-3000; www.sixcolumbuscircle.com; 6 Columbus Circle at 59th St; r $325-800; ◉ A, C, B, D, 1 at 59th St-Columbus Circle; ☒ ▣
Flash back to the 1960s at this ultra-mod boutique hotel, done by the owners of Gild Hall (p349) and 60 Thompson (p350). Designer Steven Sclaroff has tossed some faux-fur throw rugs on the floors, put up teak wall panelings and plunked down custom-made, glossy white plastic tables in the rooms. If it sounds a horror, it isn't, actually. The rooms are as fun and whimsical as the decade that inspired the decor, but with all the high-tech hook-ups and glamorous touches of today. The location, steps from Central Park, next to Time Warner and backed by a major subway hub, can't be beat. Rumor has it that the hotel offers deep discounts online during slow times; rooms have been snagged for as little as $150.

THE MUSE Map pp134–5   Boutique $$$
☎ 212-485-2400, 877-692-6873; www.themuse hotel.com; 130 W 46th St btwn Sixth & Seventh Aves; r $309-799, ste $2500; ◉ B, D, F, V to 42nd St; ☒ ▣

top picks

HOTEL BARS

- **Rose and Jade Bars, Gramercy Park Hotel** (p356) Either of these boho-chic watering holes is worth a visit, if only to star-gaze at the celebrities.
- **Bemelmans Bar, Carlyle** (p364) Head past the slick-black granite entry to the classy bar, or see Woody Allen play jazz at the café.
- **Sky Terrace, Hudson** (below) A green oasis that's great for sunbathing with cocktails in hand.
- **Lobby Lounge, Mandarin Oriental** (p360) Up a few dozen floors, sit with a $17 martini looking out towering windows onto Central Park.
- **Ritz-Carlton – New York, Central Park lobby bar** (p360) Tinkling classical music and white-gloved servers enhance the views.
- **Metro Bar, Hotel Metro** (opposite) It's a well-kept secret that atop this midrange hotel sits a great hangout spot, popular with after-work drinkers in Midtown.

A formerly dowdy midtown choice, the Muse has been taken over and jazzed up by Kimpton Hotels – and they've made it pet friendly, so bring Fido along for the stay. It's guaranteed your pet will love the cushion feather beds, and there's plenty of space – surprisingly – for four-legged friends in the rooms and suites. The modernish black-and-white decor is softened by creamy walls and delicate touches of inspiration (hence the name) like calla lilies next to Grecian urns.

HUDSON Map pp134–5   Boutique Hotel $$$
☎ 212-554-6000, 800-697-1791; www.hudson hotel.com; 356 W 58th St btwn Eighth & Ninth Aves; r $285-450; ⊕ A, C, B, D, 1 to 59th St-Columbus Circle; 🕸 💻

One of boutique-hotel king Ian Schrager's jewels, the all-too-hip Hudson is as much a nightclub as a hotel. Suites and rooms are meant to have a naval feel, with paneled walls (imported African wood), long white curtains, stainless-steel tables, brass riveted furniture and Philippe Starck–designed chairs. The 15th-floor Sky Terrace has drinks and views looking toward the namesake river. But there's also a richly colored library to hang out in, as well as Hudson Cafeteria, a high-end dining hall with long communal table and comfort food with a twist. At night, Hudson Bar is a classy pick-up joint.

BELVEDERE HOTEL
Map pp134–5   International Hotel $$
☎ 212-245-7000, 888-468-3558; 319 W 48th St btwn Eighth & Ninth Aves; d incl breakfast $199-629; ⊕ C, E to 50th St; 🕸 💻

Open since 1928, the 400-room Belvedere's roots (and facade) are art-deco originals, even if the makeover is a modern version of the era's glory. Rooms have the usual amenities (including internet access). It has a fitness centre, business centre and a café in the intentionally '20s-style lobby.

SHOREHAM Map pp134–5   Boutique Hotel $$
☎ 212-247-6700, 800-553-3347; www.shoreham hotel.com; 33 W 55th St btwn Fifth & Sixth Aves; d $259-399; ⊕ F to 57th St; 🕸 💻

Freshly renovated Shoreham is a rising scenester in the heart of Midtown. Its re-done rooms have marbled bathrooms with frosty glass doors, great big tubs and Aveda products The basic rooms are a bit boxish, just a bed and the bath, but the suites and double queens have a lot of room to play in. Of course, the ultimate stay is in the Atrium penthouse, which has 360-degree views of the city.

DREAM Map pp134–5   Boutique Hotel $$
☎ 212-247-2000, 866-437-3266; www.dreamny .com; 210 W 55th St btwn Broadway & Seventh Ave; d from $259; ⊕ N, R, Q, W to 57th St-7th Ave; 🕸 💻

Some might find it a nightmare, but for those who like minimal all-white rooms with blue lights shining from under beds and inside glass-top desks, Dream is really a dream. The hi-tech floating TV screens, iPod docks and wi-fi add to the futuristic feel. The bizarre lobby features a two-story aquarium filled with Caribbean fish and a giant three-figure statue culled from a Connecticut Russian restaurant. The rooftop hangout, Ava, is a hidden gem.

CASABLANCA HOTEL
Map pp134–5   Boutique Hotel $$
☎ 212-869-1212, 888-922-7225; www.casablanca hotel.com; 147 W 43rd St btwn Sixth Ave & Broadway; d incl breakfast from $249; ⊕ S, N, Q, R, W, 1, 2, 3, 7 to 42nd St-Times Sq; 🕸 💻

Low-key and tourist-oriented, the popular 48-room Casablanca flexes the North African motif throughout (eg tiger statues, Moroccan murals, framed tapestries and a 2nd-floor lounge named Rick's Cafe after the movie).

Rooms are pleasant and comfortable, with sisal-like carpets and a window-side seating area. You'll find free internet, all-day espresso, wine at 5pm and roll-away beds.

HOTEL METRO
Map pp134–5   International Hotel $$

☎ 212-947-2500; www.hotelmetronyc.com; 45 W 35th St btwn Fifth & Sixth Aves; d incl breakfast from $240; ◉ B, D, F, V, N, Q, R, W to 34th St-Herald Sq; ⊠ ▣

A slightly tacky, half-hearted take on 1930s art deco, the 179-room, 13-floor Metro has a rooftop deck with full-frontal looks at the nearby Empire State Building. Up from the black-and-gold lobby, rooms are rather plain but certainly comfortable, with caramel color schemes and more thinking space than most hotels at this price range. There's a library area with flat-screen TVs, next to where breakfast is served. In peak season, rates often start at $295 – a bit beyond its worth. What saves it from complete mediocrity is the rooftop bar with great views of the Empire State Building.

HOTEL QT
Map pp134–5   Boutique Hotel $$

☎ 212-354-2323; www.hotelqt.com; 125 W 45th St btwn Sixth & Seventh Aves; d incl breakfast from $235; ◉ S, N, Q, R, W, 1, 2, 3 to Times Sq-42 St, B, D, F, V to 47th-50th Sts-Rockefeller Center; ⊠ ▣ ▣

It seemed like a cool idea when Hotel QT opened in 2005: a bar/reception area merged with a bright-blue pool. Only one problem – nobody factored in the damp smell that has come to permeate the hotel. If chlorine doesn't bother you, Hotel QT is still a great boutique on the cheap, especially for the Times Sq locale. Tight rooms named by size-based grades (A to F) barely fit the beds on wall-to-wall padded platforms, and some tiled bathrooms lack shower doors. But it's clean and cool and right in the action.

414 HOTEL
Map pp134–5   Budget $$

☎ 212-399-0006; www.414hotel.com; 414 W 46th St btwn Ninth & Tenth Aves; r incl breakfast $159-249; ◉ B, D, F, V to 42nd St; ⊠ ▣

Set up like a guesthouse, this great budget deal offers 22 tidy rooms a couple of blocks west of Times Sq. Staff hand out maps and brim with tips. All rooms are simple deals – with desks, dressers, closets with mini safe, cable TV and sinks outside tiled bathrooms. There's a small courtyard between the townhouse's two buildings; breakfast is served up front, where there are a computer and a small kitchen to use.

WJ HOTEL
Map pp134–5   Bargain Hotel $$

☎ 212-246-7550, 888-567-7550; www.wjhotel .com; 318 W 51st St btwn Eighth & Ninth Aves; d from $155; ◉ C, E to 50th St; ⊠ ▣

Still proud of a 2003 scrub-up, the Washington Jefferson (gone hip now as 'WJ') offers modern, comfortable rooms with platform beds, white and beige goose-down comforters, big padded headboards to lean your head back on and watch cable TV, and state-of-the-art marbled bathrooms. The extra-large Junior Suites are a great bargain. The downstairs sushi restaurant Shimizu attracts Hell's Kitchen locals looking for low-priced lunch specials.

BIG APPLE HOSTEL
Map pp134–5   Hostel $

☎ 212-302-2603; 119 W 45th St btwn Sixth Ave & Broadway; dm $35-60, r $125-150; ◉ B, D, F, V to 42nd St; ⊠

Half a block from Times Sq, the character-less, no-frills Big Apple has clean and safe rooms and surprisingly friendly staff. Added treats are the courtyard and kitchen, plus laundry facilities in the basement. Private rooms are like the dorms – with access to shared bathroom – but add a cable TV and a couple of chairs.

CHELSEA CENTER HOSTEL
Map pp134–5   Hostel $

☎ 212-643-0214; www.chelseacenterhostel .com; 313 W 29th St btwn Eighth & Ninth Aves; dm incl breakfast $35; ◉ A, C, E to 34th St-Penn Station; ⊠

A little more personal than most hostels, this 18-bedder is a quiet, affordable favorite for backpackers and European budget travelers. It has a kitchen to use, a sitting area, and a small garden in back. Women-only dorms are available.

UPPER EAST SIDE

Ahhh…the Upper East Side. It's cozy, warm and welcoming – even though a night at most places will set you back at least $300. Some of New York's wealthiest zip codes are in this district, but that's the price you pay for living within walking distance of the Met, the Frick Collection and so many of the city's grandest cultural institutions.

CARLYLE Map p142 Deluxe Indie Inn $$$

☎ 212-744-1600; www.thecarlyle.com; 35 E 76th St btwn Madison & Park Aves; d/ste from $700/1050; ⊖ 6 to 77th St; ✖ 🖳

A classic since its 1930 opening, the 179-room Carlyle is where Woody Allen plays clarinet on Monday night, where JFK and Jackie O stayed, and where Louis XIV might feel at home. You're in good company – if you can afford it. Opulence is at notch 11 here. The lobby's black-marble floors look like a pool of oil, the Bemelmans Bar is a slick art-deco bar, and rooms are as big as suites elsewhere, with old-fashioned luxury (eg 430-thread-count linens, Jacuzzi bathtubs).

FRANKLIN Map p142 Boutique Hotel $$

☎ 212-369-1000, 800-607-4009; www.franklin hotel.com; 164 E 87th St btwn Lexington & Third Aves; s/d incl breakfast from $219/420; ⊖ 4, 5, 6 to 86th St; ✖ 🖳

Except for the small scale, the Franklin could pass for one of New York's grander hotels. Its gold and red facade, with uniformed doorman, is a gateway into an intimate lobby, full of fresh flowers. A recent renovation has infused the rooms with fresh glamour and appeal: crisp white linens, zebra-striped chairs, tan-and-black headboards and well-equipped marbled bathrooms.

BENTLEY Map p142 Boutique Hotel $$

☎ 212-644-6000, 888-664-6835; www.nychotels .com; 500 E 62nd St at York Ave; r/ste from $177/497; ⊖ F to Lexington Ave-63rd St; ✖ 🖳

A little enigmatic and way east – it's practically under the tram to Roosevelt Island and spitting distance from the riverside FDR expressway – this 197-room transformation of an old office building packs some boutique, modern style into tight spaces. Dark gray carpet and all-leather chaise lounges by the window add a somber effect. Suites grant two rooms, and some straddle corners, but the mini kitchenettes are dated afterthoughts. Best is the top-floor lounge, with food from 5pm; it's an excellent spot for after-dinner drinks under the gaze of city lights.

BUBBA & BEAN LODGES Map p142 B&B $

☎ 917-345-7914; www.bblodges.com; 1598 Lexington Ave btwn 101st & 102nd Sts; r/ste $120/220; ⊖ 6 to 103rd; ✖ 🖳

Charting new ground on the upper, upper east side, owners Jonathan and Clement have turned their double-wide town home into a very nifty B&B that won't empty your pockets. Their rooms are really more like suites or studios and some can hold up to six people. They come with private bathrooms and kitchens, except for the standard room, which uses a public kitchen off the foyer. Hardwood floors, crisp white walls and pretty navy bedspreads make the rooms feel spacious, modern and youthful. The neighborhood is right on the cusp of the Upper East Side and Spanish Harlem, and there are two excellent Latino restaurants near the B&B.

UPPER WEST SIDE

You'll discover a broad selection of midrange and budget hotels in this part of town, but little of the fanfare you would find in the fashionable inns to the south. It's strictly old-school New York – character, bargain and no-nonsense grandeur – and Central Park is no more than a couple of blocks' walk.

INN NEW YORK CITY Map p153 B&B $$$

☎ 212-580-1900, 800-660-7051; www.innnew yorkcity.com; 266 W 71st St at West End Ave; ste $476-675; ⊖ 1, 2, 3 to 72nd St; ✖

Four massive, quirky suites occupy a whole floor in this 1900 townhouse, which allows you to feel as if you're living in a mansion. It's far west, and close to both Riverside Park and Central Park, and its rooms feature antique chestnut furnishings, feather beds topped in down comforters, Jacuzzis and stained-glass panels – if just a bit too much flowered carpeting. The Opera Suite has a private terrace. All rooms have cable TV with DVD and VCR. It's stately, massive and heavy with history.

ON THE AVE Map p153 Boutique Hotel $$$

☎ 212-362-1100, 800-497-6028; www.ontheave .com; 2178 Broadway at W 77th St; r/ste from $359/509; ⊖ 1 to 79th St, 2, 3 to 72nd St; ✖ 🖳

An excellent uptown hotel, the stylish and cool 16-floor On the Ave boasts 266 rooms done up in warm earthy tones and brimming with extras from a recent renovation (eg fudge-colored suede headboards backing new featherbeds, flat-screen TVs and bedside CD players). Sunlight pours into the huge windows. All rooms have a data port with wi-fi access. There's a super glassed-in top-floor balcony with seats facing the north.

EXCELSIOR HOTEL Map p153   Classic Hotel $$$
☎ 212-362-9200; www.excelsiorhotelny.com; 45 W 81st St at Central Park W; r $320-799; ◉ B, C to 81st St; ✪ ▣
If the dramatic Beaux-Arts redbrick facade with white limestone corner wedges doesn't grab you, the heavily draped, over-styled, old-fashioned rooms surely will. Fans of French country furnishings and ruffled window treatments will be in heaven at the Excelsior, which – despite its otherwise modern amenities – stopped evolving somewhere around 1950. The large suites, with pretty French doors, gold-and-white wallpaper, and warm, cherry wood beds, are more attractive than the plainer, floral-covered basic rooms.

LUCERNE Map p153   Business Hotel $$
☎ 212-875-1000; www.thelucernehotel.com; 201 W 79th St; r $229-499; ◉ B, C to 81st St; ✪ ▣
Family-friendly Lucerne is right around the corner from Central Park, just a few doors from the American Museum of Natural History (p152) and not far from the Children's Museum of Manhattan (p155). It's a solid, three-star property with no surprises; the larger rooms have small kitchenettes in them, perfect for traveling with kids, and many connect to other rooms so one big suite can be created. While the decor is fairly bland – Laura Ashley lite – there's nothing objectionable in flowered bedspreads, drapes and multiple, plush pillows on the bed.

COUNTRY INN THE CITY Map p153   B&B $$
☎ 212-580-4183; www.countryinnthecity.com; 270 W 77th St btwn Broadway & West End Aves; apt $210-350; ◉ 1 to 79th St; ✪ ▣
Just like staying with your big-city friend: this 1891 limestone townhouse sits on a stellar, tree-lined street, and the four popular self-contained apartments are cool and sophisticated, with four-poster beds, glossed wooden floors, warm color schemes and lots of light. Most furnishings – sofa, lamps, rugs – have been picked up in local antique shops, adding to the 19th-century feel. There's some welcome food supplies for the kitchenettes in each room (including stove and microwave). Rooms are for two people only and have internet

access; there's a three-night minimum. No credit cards.

HOTEL NEWTON Map p153   Traveler Hotel $$
☎ 212-678-6500; www.newyorkhotel.com/newton; 2528 Broadway btwn 94th & 95th Sts; r from $160-360; ◉ 1, 2, 3 to 96th St; ✪ ▣
Fairly by the numbers, but super clean and well managed, this 109-room hotel has all-new furnishings and caters to a mix of international visitors and academic folk wanting a base for Columbia University, 20 blocks north. All rooms have refrigerators, microwaves, internet access and double-paned windows, but are nothing if not nondescript. Bathrooms are tiny but pretty, covered from floor to ceiling in tiles, and larger suites add a little corner nook with a sofa. There's only one tiny creaky elevator in the lobby.

HOSTELLING INTERNATIONAL – NEW YORK Map p153   Hostel $
☎ 212-932-2300; www.hinewyork.org; 891 Amsterdam Ave at 103rd St; dm $29-40, d $135; ◉ 1 to 103rd St; ✪ ▣
Occupying an impressive redbrick 1883 mansion that once served as HQ for the 'Relief of Respectable, Aged, Indigent Females.' These days, 624 well-scrubbed bunks welcome all. There's little of the history inside the rather clinical hallways and rooms, but there are heaps of public spaces (like a back lawn and brick courtyard, plus a giant communal kitchen) and a friendly help desk offering walking tours (a few are free). Because many groups stay (including girl scouts!), the hostel is alcohol-free. Three private rooms come with private bathroom. Dorm rooms have a lot of space, and have new carpet, plus lockers and air-con. We heard a rumor of a ghost here (away from the sleeping quarters, thankfully). You'll find wi-fi access and computers handy to check email.

JAZZ ON THE PARK HOSTEL
Map p153   Hostel $
☎ 212-932-1600; www.jazzhostels.com; 36 W 106th St btwn Central Park West & Manhattan Ave; dm incl breakfast $27-32, d incl breakfast $85; ◉ B, C to 103rd St; ✪ ▣
This former flophouse, located on a street renamed for Duke Ellington, is deservedly popular. In addition to simple but small rooms, there are lots of hang-out options:

two terrace sitting areas and a basement lounge (for jazz and comedy) under renovation at research time. Also, the common snack bar serves espresso and $3.50 lasagna. Dorms are co-ed and single-sex, ranging from four to 12 bunks per room with shared baths. There are locked luggage areas and an internet terminal on the main floor. Private rooms are little but walls and a bed; all but one are at a nearby annex (Map p153; 54 W 105th St).

JAZZ ON THE CITY Map p153 Hostel $
☎ 212-678-0323; www.jazzhostels.com; 201 W 95th St; dm $25, s & d from $150; ◉ 1, 2, 3 to 96th St; ✹ ▢
Yet another popular hostel run by the famous Jazz Hostels in New York (and Miami Beach), this walk-up location near Amsterdam Ave on the Upper West Side has bright-red walls, and clean dorm rooms with bunk beds (with red duvets) and shared bathrooms for under $50. Those who prefer privacy can pay a bit more and get their own room. Nearby is an excellent Cuban diner, a few grocery stores, and the much underrated Symphony Space (p316), which offers excellent readings, retrospective movies and live music performances.

HARLEM & NORTHERN MANHATTAN

For some Harlem is gentrifying too fast; for others, the change isn't fast enough. Big-name hotels are practically nonexistent, but lots of B&Bs here cater to the tourist class. The historic neighborhood's considerable charms are on full display – wide boulevards, beautiful houses, sweeping, ample parks and tree-lined streets – but at night some corners are gathering spots, and they can get loud. It's all part of the local color, but some visitors prefer to take cabs to get around after dark.

102 BROWNSTONE Map pp158–9 B&B $$
☎ 212-662-4223; www.102brownstone.com; 102 W 118th St; s/d $150/275; ◉ 2, 3 to 116th St
Drama and romance are in the air at 102 Brownstone, the first boutique-style B&B to open in Harlem. Set in a historic brownstone, 102's four rooms are really big suites, some with Jacuzzis, and come decked out in luscious colors like ruby red and mango yellow. Rooms come with DVDs, flat screens, and a few, like the Zen room, have private kitchens. Others have mini-fridges and microwaves.

SUGAR HILL HARLEM Map pp158–9 B&B $
☎ 212-234-5432, 917-464-3528; www.sugarhill harleminn.com; 460 W 141st St; s/d $125/175; ◉ 2, 3 to 116th St
A big old airy townhouse that's been restored to its turn-of-the-century elegance, with beautiful suites named after African American jazz greats. The suites all have atmospheric beds – some four-poster, some with drapes, others handcrafted sleigh frames – and most have massive bay windows to gaze from. The facility is no smoking but the back garden is at the disposal of guests (and Smoky the resident cat). Most of the rooms have private bathrooms, and some are on the third floor (no elevator).

HARLEM FLOPHOUSE
Map pp158–9 Guesthouse $
☎ 212-662-0678; www.harlemflophouse.com; 242 W 123rd St btwn Adam Clayton Powell & Frederick Douglass Blvds; s/d $100/125; ◉ A, C, B, D to 125th St
A superb alternative Manhattan base, this gorgeous four-room, 1890s townhouse conjures up the jazz era, with period-piece antiques, glossed-wood floors and vintage radios tuned to a local jazz station. There's shared bathrooms but no air-con or TVs. It's a kept-real trip to the past. The owner

HARLEM HOMESTAYS

Get a real feel for Harlem living by renting out Sankofa Guest Apartment (Map pp158–9; ☎ 212-678-0116; www.vrbo .com/123390; 157 West 121st St btwn Lenox Ave & 7th Ave; apt $175; ◉ 2, 3 to 116th or 125th Sts) – on the 3rd floor of a 19th-century brownstone on a shady, tree-lined block. Sisters Edith and Norma Garner have turned the upper floor of their house into an Afro-centric oasis, full of decorative statues, gorgeously colored walls and original art work they've collected over years of traveling. The apartment has a fully equipped kitchen and full bathroom, and can sleep three people easily. It's perfectly situated in Central Harlem, along major bus and subway lines. The sisters are easygoing and love to talk about Harlem past and present, but you'll get plenty of privacy as well.

can point out the real-deal gospel church services that the tour buses miss and good soul-food eateries nearby.

JAZZ ON LENOX Map pp158–9   Hostel $
☎ 212-222-5773; www.jazzhostels.com; 104 W 128th St; dm $15-28, r $65-100; ⊙ 2, 3 to 125th St

Jazz Hostels – same company as Jazz on the Park Hostel (p365) – has opened two new locations not far from each other near the busy and commercial 125th St. Both Jazz on Lenox and Jazz on the Villa (Map pp158–9; ☎ 212-722-6252; www.jazzhostels.com; 12 W 129th St at Fifth Ave; dm $13-32, r $80-135; ⊙ 2, 3 to 125th St) have dorm rooms with shared bathrooms for prices as low as $13, and private rooms for about $100 more. Both also have large backyards, great for making friends, and helpful, informed staff.

BROOKLYN

For the moment quaint B&Bs still reign in Brooklyn, but as of press time the Smith Hotel, a luxury boutique, was nearing completion in Carroll Gardens and the 200-room Starwood Aloft was being constructed in downtown Brooklyn. Beating them to the punch was Hotel Le Bleu (below), a snazzy newcomer on the western edge of Park Slope.

HOTEL LE BLEU Map p180 Business Boutique $$$
☎ 718-625-1500; www.hotellebleu.com; 370 4th Ave btwn 3rd & 5th Sts, Park Slope; d $389-$600; ⊙ F, M, R to 4th Ave-9th St; ⊗ ▣

A jazzy, sexy boutique hotel catering to the business class, Hotel le Bleu is trying hard to bring a touch of Manhattan to the big borough of Brooklyn. The hi-tech lobby, meant to give travelers a place to hook up, dock iPods or conduct meetings, is glass-filled and modern; rooms are much the same, with bright-blue spreads, huge windows and gadget-filled bathrooms. As of research time a restaurant/bar, tentatively named Vue, was moving into the 8th floor. The location isn't all that atmospheric; it's between a garage and a taxi stand on an industrial stretch of road. But more quaint streets are just a short walk away.

BAISLEY HOUSE Map p180   B&B $$
☎ 718-935-1959; 294 Hoyt St btwn Union & Sackett Sts, Boerum Hill; r incl breakfast $172-202; ⊙ F, G to Carroll St; ⊗

The childhood home of Hollywood starlet Susan Hayworth, the three-room Baisley House is a five-minute walk from the subway on a side-street of 18th-century townhouses – and a step back 150 years. It's lushly decorated with a Victoriana-rama of 17th- to 19th-century pieces (busts and clocks on mantels, wing-back chairs, period-piece landscapes). All rooms access a shared bathroom. Breakfast – a big, daily changing one – is served every day (and on nice days, it's in the back garden). The owner is an encyclopedia of local-area knowledge.

BED & BREAKFAST ON THE PARK
Map p182   B&B $$
☎ 718-499-6115; www.bbnyc.com; 113 Prospect Park W btwn 6th & 7th Sts, Park Slope; d incl breakfast from $165-325; ⊙ F to 7th Ave; ⊗

Across from Brooklyn's Prospect Park in yuppified Park Slope, this homey Victorian B&B has seven rooms splashed out in oriental rugs, potted plants, poster beds covered in pillows, gas-operated fireplaces and original wood floors and wall moldings. Family-style breakfasts of soufflés and kielbasa get chatty and can last hours. All rooms have private bathroom. The wi-fi signal reaches some rooms and the garden out back.

AKWAABA MANSION INN
Map pp170–1   B&B $$
☎ 718-455-5958, 866-466-3855; www.akwaaba .com; 347 MacDonough St btwn Lewis & Stuyvesant Aves, Bedford-Stuyvesant; r incl breakfast $160-175; ⊙ A, C to Utica Ave; ⊗

An 1860 mansion fenced off on a block of century-old townhouses, the four-room Awkwaaba's only drawback is its remote location in the misunderstood neighborhood of Bedford-Stuyvesant, which has a hard time escaping its 'do or die' reputation and gritty past. Awkaaba has original parquet floors and ceiling moldings accented with new African-themed touches (eg imported statuettes in bathroom nooks, safari wallpaper borders). Rooms are themed – the 'regal retreat' is the most traditional, with claw-foot tub in the bathroom. Giant Southern breakfasts are served family-style in the parlor.

AWESOME B&B Map p174   B&B $$
☎ 718-858-4859; 136 Lawrence St btwn Willoughby & Fulton Sts, Downtown Brooklyn; r incl breakfast from $140; ⊙ M, R to Lawrence St, 2, 3 to Hoyt St; ⊗ ▣

SLEEPING BROOKLYN

LOFTSTELS

Like people, open spaces and new experiences? Then you're a prime candidate for a Loftstel (www.loftstel.com) stay, which caters to young college students, while you're in town. There are currently two loftstels in New York: one in Williamsburg (Map p177; ☎ 718-486-6189, ask for Nolwenn; 112 N 6th St; ⊘ L to Bedford Ave) and one in Bedford-Stuyvesant (Map pp170–1; ☎ 347-787-1395, ask for Valerie; 580 Greene Ave; ⊘ G to Bedford-Nostrand Aves, A, C to Nostrand Ave), both in the borough of Brooklyn. Owned and run by Jeff Pan, both New York City loftstels are huge, prime lofts turned into one big happy share, with bunk beds, communal bathrooms and kitchens, and all the amenities of home: wi-fi, laundry, TV and backyard gardens often used for barbecues and parties. Although Loftstels cater to those staying weeks or months, they've also got cheap daily rates available, from $16 to $50. Both locations are a quick 15-minute subway ride into Manhattan; the Bedford-Stuyvesant property is in a 'transitioning' neighborhood, however, so late-night travels by subway should be undertaken with care. Loftstel also takes reservations through its page on Facebook.

In busy downtown Brooklyn, this basic B&B has six small rooms overflowing with detail (lots of small lamps, entry tables, textured hand-painted walls showing their smears) and a hostel-like vibe. It's fun too: 'Gothic Nights' gets medieval on your ass, while the 'Dragon Palace' room has a mural of an Asian-style dragon wrapping around three walls. Staff will print out maps based on your NYC traveling itineraries. There are two shared bathrooms. The downtown area isn't exactly Brooklyn's most atmospheric 'hood, but Smith St's restaurants and Brooklyn Heights' brownstones are a few blocks away on foot.

QUEENS

This sprawling borough has some unexciting hotel chains, catering mostly to visiting relatives of its many immigrant residents.

HOWARD JOHNSON

Map pp200–1   Chain Hotel $

☎ 718-461-3888; info@howardjohnsonny.com; 135-33 38th Ave, Flushing; r $160; ⊘ 7 to Flushing-Main St; ✂ ▯

This basic chain at the end of the 7 line won't surprise you inside, but the heart of Flushing is a safe, cheap back-up with great Chinese, Vietnamese and Korean restaurants.

DAY TRIPS & EXCURSIONS

DAY TRIPS & EXCURSIONS

The big city is great, but sometimes you just have to break free. Luckily Manhattan is backed by some of the most gorgeous upstate terrain imaginable in the Hudson Valley and Catskills area: deep sweeping mountain ravines and crags, swiftly moving rivers, and quaint and quixotic little villages slowly being turned into weekend arts-and-crafts retreats by wealthy 'second-homers' from Manhattan.

New York's also got stunning stretches of white sandy beaches and pristine wetland parks, absolutely buzzing with migratory bird life, to wade into – and most are just a short commute away. For exciting man-made pursuits, there's New Jersey, of course; its shore is home to Atlantic City, a casino-laden hotspot that contrasts sharply with sedate and stately Cape May. Or you can opt for the glitzier and tonier Hamptons, home to the rich and famous (and the thousands of working-class people who serve them). The Hamptons are much closer to the city physically than many Jersey sights, but considering how much time you'll sit in summer traffic, it's often a much longer trip. For those who like to combine culture and exploration there's Philadelphia, full of history and fun.

You can get to just about any excursion in this chapter via public transportation (which gives you even more options if combined with cycling), but if you want or need a car, be aware that rental rates here are high (upwards of $75 a day), and plan your escape during a weekday, when most of the city is stuck at work. Beating traffic is one of the advantages of being on vacation, after all.

BEACHES

Can you believe there's surfing in Queens? Yup, as if there's not enough to do in the city, now you can join the many who like to catch some waves off Rockaway Beach (p334). If you want some sun and surf without waves, head to local favorite Coney Island (p195) – but watch the powerful Atlantic riptides in these waters. Besides these two, there's also the Bronx's family-friendly Orchard Beach (Map pp208–9; ⊖ 6 to Pelham Bay Park then 🚍 Bx5, Bx12, Bx29), which has a long, curving stretch of sand and minimal waves. But not too far afield is Long Island, a generally more tranquil and relaxed setting.

Closest is hip Long Beach (p378), a quick train ride from Manhattan; then Jones Beach (p376), a sprawling city of sand; Fire Island (p376), a peaceful, car-free gem; and finally the Hamptons (p372), with miles of white beaches edging the area's tiny towns. In New Jersey you'll find the entire Jersey Shore, with highlights including Sandy Hook (p381) and Cape May (p384).

WINE

There's a whole lotta uncorking going on in the Hamptons (p372) these days, especially on the North Fork (p375) of Long Island. It used to be you had to head way upstate to the Finger Lakes to taste some local wines, but now you can find more than 30 vineyards on Long Island's eastern end.

ARTS & ANTIQUES

Antiquing is a weekend tradition among New Yorkers, who like to scour the odd flea markets that pop up around Fleischmanns (p378), around the Catskills (p378), and among the colorful streets of Hyde Park (p380), Tarrytown (p381) and Poughkeepsie (p380). Art lovers shouldn't miss the Dia Beacon (p380), and especially the fantastic outdoor installations of Storm King Art Center (p379).

OUTDOORS

New York is surrounded by an incredible number of eco-sanctuaries and blissful green havens free (at last!) from bleating car horns. Jamaica Bay/Gateway National Park (p374) in Queens is an easy day trip, but there's also Catskill Forest Preserve (p378) and Harriman State Park (p380) upstate, Hither Hills State Park (p373) and many others in the Hamptons, and Cape May Point State Park (p384) along the Jersey Shore.

LONG ISLAND

The largest island in the US (120 miles long), Long Island begins with the New York boroughs of Brooklyn (Kings County) and Queens (Queens County) on its western shore. New York City then gives way to the suburban housing, strip malls and working-class heroes in neighboring Nassau County. You might hear reference to the north and south shores here; the north is the ritzy part. The terrain

becomes flatter, less crowded and more exclusive in rural Suffolk County, which comprises the eastern end of the island. Suffolk County itself contains two peninsulas – commonly called the North and South Forks – divided by Great Peconic Bay. It's the South Fork that lures the most visitors: it's what is also known as the East End – or, commonly, the Hamptons.

THE HAMPTONS

You'll still catch glimpses of the fishers' lifestyle and artistic hideaways that once made the Hamptons such a tranquil delight – but for most of the summer, this little jut of land becomes a frenetic scene mobbed with jetsetters, celebrities and throngs of curious wannabes. Luckily there's still plenty of opportunity for outdoor activity, from kayaking to mountain biking – and yes, even a few untrammeled beaches. There's no shortage of boutique shops, trendy eateries and celeb-heavy clubs in summer, but absolutely everything costs a pretty penny out here, with most inns charging well over $300 a night. Summer is high season; prices do drop a wee bit and traffic jams disappear about a month after Labor Day. This lessening of crowds, combined with the balmy weather of the fall harvest season, make autumn the most beautiful time for a visit.

The Hamptons is actually a series of villages, most with 'Hampton' in the name. Those at the western end – or 'west of the canal,' as locals call the places that are on the other side of the Shinnecock Canal – include Hampton Bays, Quogue and Westhampton, and are less frenzied than those to the east, which start with the village of Southampton.

Southampton is an old-moneyed and rather conservative spot compared to some of its neighbors, home to sprawling old mansions, a main street with no 'beachwear' allowed, and some lovely beaches. Pick up maps and brochures about the town at the Southampton Chamber of Commerce office, squeezed among a group of high-priced artsy-crafty shops and decent restaurants. Within the town, just past Stonybrook College, is a small Native American reservation, home to the Shinnecocks, who run the tiny Shinnecock Museum (☎ 631-287-4923; Montauk Hwy, Southampton; adult/under 6yr $5/3; ⏰ 11am-4pm Fri-Sun), which has unpredictable hours. The Parrish Art Museum (☎ 631-283-2111; 25 Jobs Lane, Southampton; adult/senior & student $5/3; ⏰ 11am-5pm Mon-Sat & 1-5pm Sun late May–mid-Sep, closed Tue & Wed mid-Sep–late May) has quality exhibitions featuring great local artists and a cute gift shop stacked with glossy posters of famous Long Island landscapes.

Great winter deals can be had at the three Enclave Inns that are dotted around Southampton, all owned by a local businessman. At the time of research, a fourth and fifth Enclave Inn had gone up in Bridgehampton and nearby Wainscott, and another was planned next to the Pink Elephant Club in Southampton.

TRANSPORTATION: THE HAMPTONS

Distance from New York City 100 miles (East Hampton)

Direction East

Travel time 2¼ hours

Car Take the Midtown Tunnel out of Manhattan, which will take you onto I-495/Long Island Expressway. Follow this for about 1½ hours to exit 70, which will take you to Sunrise Highway East/Rte 24. Take it for about 10 miles and then merge onto Montauk Hwy/Rte 27, which will take you directly into Southampton. Continue along Rte 27 to get to all towns east of there.

Bus The Hampton Jitney (☎ 800-936-0440; www.hamptonjitney.com; 1-way $29, round-trip $51) is a luxury express bus. It departs from Manhattan's East Side – 86th St; 40th St between Lexington and Third Aves; 69th St; and 59th St at Lexington Ave – and makes stops at villages along Rte 27 in the Hamptons.

Train The Long Island Rail Road (LIRR; ☎ 718-217-5477; www.mta.nyc.ny.us/lirr; 1-way $14.50) leaves from Penn Station in Manhattan and the Flatbush Ave station in Brooklyn, making stops in West Hampton, Southampton, Bridgehampton, East Hampton and Montauk.

Ferry The South Ferry (☎ 631-749-1200; www.southferry.com; Rte 114, North Haven) runs between Sag Harbor and Shelter Island every 10 to 15 minutes daily between 5:45am and 1:45am June 1 to Labor Day, and 9am to 5pm Monday to Friday and 9am to 1pm Saturday between Labor Day and May 30).

The Pink Elephant and equally celebrity-heavy Cain are two Manhattan-based clubs that get transported to Southampton every summer, and are usually open Thursday to Sunday between late May/early June and Labor Day (first weekend of September). If clubbing is not your thing but socializing is, pull up to any of these three 'must-do' eateries to rub shoulders with the jet set and the locals: the Golden Pear for cappuccino; 75 Main for daily happy hours and a live band at night; and the Driver's Seat, known for fantastic clams and seafood (it also has vegetarian plates) and gut-busting Sunday brunches served on a shady outdoor patio.

To the east, Bridgehampton has the shortest of all the main drags, but it's packed with trendy boutiques and restaurants. New nightclubs blow in and bow out every season. Two good stalwart places to get a drink are World Pie – a great pizza joint/bar with outside seating – and Almond, a trendy boîte.

Seven miles north of Bridgehampton on Peconic Bay is the old whaling town of Sag Harbor. There are bunches of historic homes and points of interests here and you can pick up a historic walking tour map at the Windmill Information Center on Long Wharf at the end of Main St. Sag Harbor Whaling Museum (☎ 631-725-0770; www.sagharborwhalingmuseum.org; 200 Main St at Garden St, Sag Harbor; adult/senior & child/under 13yr $5/3/free; ◷ 10am-5pm Mon-Sat & 1-5pm Sun May 17-Oct 1) is fascinating, and the village's tiny Cape Cod–style streets are a joy to stroll; there are several excellent restaurants to discover. Bike Hampton (☎ 631-725-7329; 36 Main St, Sag Harbor) rents bicycles (per day $35 to $45) and sells maps of cycling trails. Get gourmet sustenance without going broke at the delicious new Fat Ralph's Deli. American Hotel, right on Main St, has eight luxurious rooms and a highly regarded restaurant catering to scotch-and-cigar types from the city. There's also the Sag Harbor Inn, prettier on the outside than the inside, which sits right on a briny dock at the end of Water St. Barcelona Inn, a B&B, and Baron's Cove Inn, a hybrid motel/inn, both close to town, are affordable and pleasant enough, but a little run down.

A quick ferry ride on the South Ferry (see opposite) from the edge of North Haven, which borders Sag Harbor, will take you to sleepy Shelter Island, nearly a third of which is dedicated to the Mashomack Nature Preserve (☎ 631-749-1001), dotted with biking and hiking trails.

Long Island's trendiest town is East Hampton, where you can catch readings and art exhibitions at Guild Hall (☎ 631-324-0806; www.guildhall.org; 158 Main St, East Hampton). Babette's is an outstanding organic and mostly vegetarian eatery. Restaurants where you'll most likely spot celebrities include Della Femina and Nick & Toni's, where the Italian-influenced meals are flawless. Jerry Della Femina, owner of his eponymous restaurant, is a bit of a local celebrity in his own right, in part because he knows everyone and everything, and also because every summer he does battle with an endangered bird that seems to love Long Island beaches: piping plovers. Jerry's annual July 4 beach party usually has to be delayed until September because the threatened plovers nest in the beach marshes right at the same time – a fact Jerry never fails to rail about in Hampton newspapers every July. To stay right in the thick of things, and maybe spot ol' Jerry around town, consider checking into the Mill House Inn.

More honky-tonk than the rest of the Hamptons, Montauk has relatively reasonable restaurants and a louder bar scene, largely because all the service personnel – mainly students and new Mexican immigrants – live here in communal housing. For a kitschy 'bargain,' try staying at the Memory Motel, a scruffy but comfortable spot where Mick Jagger often stayed in the 1970s and where he was inspired to write the Rolling Stones song of the same name. To get pampered, book a room at the beachfront, spa-equipped Gurney's Inn Resort. For some real beachy eatin', head to the Lobster Roll (look for the big blue 'Lunch' sign) for what else but a lobster roll – rich lobster-meat salad stuffed into a fresh hot-dog roll.

Covering the eastern tip of the South Fork is Montauk Point State Park (☎ 631-668-3781), with its impressive Montauk lighthouse. You can camp in the sand nearby at windswept Hither Hills State Park (☎ 631-668-2554, 800-456-2267; http://nysparks.state.ny.us; 50 S Fairview Ave), a fantastic nature spot that offers a bit of everything: year-round fishing for anglers, and special permits to fish at night, beach camping, the unique 'walking dunes' in Napeague Harbor (at the east end of the park) and lots of open woodlands to tramp though (and you can bring your dog, too). You can try pitching a tent at Cedar Point Park (☎ 631-244-7275) in the Springs section of East Hampton on the calm Northwest Harbor. Just be sure to call ahead, as sites tend to fill up fast. Montauk retains a strong fishing tradition and there are many

DETOUR: JAMAICA BAY

Salty, marshy Jamaica Bay Wildlife Refuge (Map pp200–1; ☎ 718-318-4340; www.nps.gov/gate; Cross Bay Blvd, Jamaica Bay, Queens; admission free; ☼ 8:30am-5pm except Thanksgiving, Christmas & New Year; ⊖ A to Broad Channel, Far Rockaway Line), a unit of the Gateway National Recreation Area, is one of the most important migratory bird and wetland habitats along the eastern seaboard – and it's just a short subway ride from the city, literally in the shadow of JFK airport. In spring and fall, more than 325 bird species stop in to rest and snack, snapping up all sorts of briny sea creatures like clams, turtles, shrimp and oysters. Each season brings different visitors: spring features warblers and songbirds, and American woodcocks in late March. In mid-August shorebirds start to move south, landing here from Canada, fueling up for the trip to Mexico. Fall is when migrating hawks and raptors get mobile, along with ducks, geese, monarch butterflies and thousands and thousands of dragonflies. Birders and naturalists get the most action around the east and west ponds; they're both about 1.5 miles in circumference and easily walkable, but wear mud-resistant shoes, bug repellent and sunscreen, carry some water and watch out for poison ivy.

To get to the visitors center, exit at Broad Channel station, walk along Noel Rd to Crossbay Blvd, turn right (north) and walk for about half a mile, and the center will be visible on the left side of the road.

opportunities to cast a line here. You can contract charter boats at the dock for a day of fishing or jump on one of the party cruises (about $45 to $65 per person for a half day). Captain Fred E Bird's Flying Cloud (☎ 631-668-2026; www.montaukflyingcloud.com; 67 Mulford Ave, Montauk) comes highly recommended for fluke fishing May to September and sea bass, porgies and striper fishing September to November.

Information

Southampton Chamber of Commerce (☎ 631-283-0402; 76 Main St, Southampton; ☼ 9am-5pm Mon-Fri)

Windmill Information Center (☎ 631-692-4664; Long Wharf at Main St, Sag Harbor; ☼ 9am-4pm Sat & Sun)

Eating

75 Main (☎ 631-283-7575; 75 Main St, Southampton; mains $12-30)

Almonds (☎ 631-537-8885; www.almondrestaurant.com; 1970 Montauk Hwy, Bridgehampton; mains $12-39)

Babette's (☎ 631-329-5377; www.babetteseasthampton.com; 66 Newtown Lane, East Hampton; mains $12-25, prix fixe $29; ☼ Thu-Tue)

Della Femina (☎ 631-329-6666; www.dellafemina.com; N Main St, East Hampton; mains $18-35)

Driver's Seat (☎ 631-283-6606; www.thedriversseatrestaurant.com; 62 Jobs Lane, Southampton; mains $12-30)

Fat Ralph's Deli (☎ 631-725-6688; 138 Division St, Sag Harbor; sandwiches $7-10)

Golden Pear (☎ 631-283-8900; www.goldenpear.com; 99 Main St, Southampton; snacks & meals $5-18)

Lobster Roll ('Lunch'; ☎ 631-267-3740; 1980 Montauk Hwy, Montauk; mains $12-20)

Nick & Toni's (☎ 631-324-3550; 136 N Main St, East Hampton; mains $18-30)

World Pie (☎ 631-537-7999; 2402 Montauk Hwy, Bridgehampton; mains $12-18)

Entertainment

Cain (☎ 631-283-0808; www.cainnyc.com; 1181 North Sea Rd, Southampton; ☼ 10pm-4am Sun-Thu summer)

Pink Elephant (☎ 631-287-9888; www.pinkelephantclub.com; 281 County Rd/Rte 27, near N Main St, Southampton; ☼ 10pm-4am Sun-Thu summer)

Sleeping

American Hotel (☎ 631-725-3535; www.theamericanhotel.com; Main St, Sag Harbor; r low season $200-300, high season $300-400)

Barcelona Inn (☎ 631-725-0714; www.thebarcelonainn.com; 765 Rte 114, Sag Harbor; r low season $80-130, high season $200)

Baron's Cove Inn (☎ 631-725-2100; www.baronscove.com; 31 West Water St, Sag Harbor; r low season $99, high season $199-250)

Bridgehampton Inn (☎ 631-537-3660; www.bridgehamptoninn.com; 2266 Main St; r low season $195-350, high season $340-480)

Enclave Inn (☎ 631-537-2900; www.enclaveinn.com; 450 County Rd, Southampton; r low season $80-145, high season $200-399)

Gurney's Inn Resort (☎ 631-668-2345; www.gurneys-inn.com; 290 Old Montauk Hwy, Montauk; r $190-600)

Memory Motel (☎ 631-668-2702; 692 Montauk Hwy, Montauk; r $95-120)

Mill House Inn (☎ 631-324-9766; www.millhouseinn.com; 31 N Main St, East Hampton; r low season $200-600, high season $550-1200)

Sag Harbor Inn (☎ 631-725-2949; www.sagharborinn
.com; West Water St, Sag Harbor; r low/high season
$99/459)

NORTH FORK WINERIES

Who knew that Long Island was grape country? Over the past three decades it has transformed from one lone winery to a thriving
industry that takes up more than 3000 acres
of land. Most vineyards are at the East End's
North Fork, where you can follow the green
'wine trail' signs along Rte 25 once you pass
Riverhead. South Fork has Duck Walk Vineyards and Wölffer Estate Vineyards, and you
can explore them if you choose before continuing on to the North Fork via Shelter Island
and two ferries.

Harvest time is in fall, which, combined
with foliage and pumpkin-picking opportunities, makes it an ideal time to visit North
Fork (although most places remain open year-
round). Several wineries offer full-scale tours
of their facilities. The following are just some
of the wineries that offer tastings:

Bedell Cellars (☎ 631-734-7537; Cutchogue)

Castello di Borghese/Hargrave Vineyard (☎ 631-734-
5158; Cutchogue)

Duck Walk Vineyards (☎ 631-726-7555; Southampton,
South Fork)

Lenz Winery (☎ 631-734-6010; Peconic)

Osprey's Dominion Vineyards (☎ 631-765-6188;
Peconic)

Palmer Vineyards (☎ 631-722-9463; Riverhead)

Paumanok Vineyards (☎ 631-722-8800; Aquebogue)

Peconic Bay Winery (☎ 631-734-7361; Cutchogue)

Pelligrini Vineyards (☎ 631-734-4111; Cutchogue)

Pindar Vineyards (☎ 631-734-6200; Peconic)

Pugliese Vineyards (☎ 631-734-4057; Cutchogue)

Schneider Vineyards (☎ 631-727-3334; Riverhead)

Wölffer Estate Vineyards (☎ 631-537-5106; Sagaponack,
South Fork)

For individual winery information, as well
as maps for touring the wine trail, contact the
Long Island Wine Council (☎ 631-369-5887; www.liwines
.com; 104 Edwards Ave, Calverton). Wineries are generally open from 11am to 5pm, with closing
time extended by an hour in summer. If you
want to taste the wine without the travel, head
right to the Tasting Room (☎ 631-765-6404; www
.tastingroomli.com; 2885 Peconic Lane, Peconic; bottles from
$24; ☷ 11am-6pm Fri-Sun). You can sit in the 1860
store, with its original tin ceiling, tin walls and
wood floors, and sip on the best from all the
local vineyards.

A drive along the back roads of the North
Fork affords some beautiful, unspoiled
vistas of farms and rural residential areas.
If you're too bushed to make the trip out
and back in one day (a doable, but tiring,
prospect), you'll find plenty of classic inns
where you can rest your head for the night.
Two good options are the Red Barn B&B, a
cozy, antique-filled inn in Jamesport, and the
Quintessentials B&B Spa, an 1840s Victorian
place in East Marion that's outfitted with a
full-service spa, plush quarters and peaceful, flowering grounds. If you do wind up
driving out, a stop in Riverhead is worthwhile
for its Polish Town, a tiny, insular community
of Polish immigrants with various ethnic
bakeries and restaurants such as the Polonez
Polish-Russian Restaurant.

TRANSPORTATION: NORTH FORK WINERIES

Distance from New York City 100 miles

Direction East

Travel Time 2¼ hours

Bus The Hampton Jitney (☎ 212-362-8400; www.hamptonjitney.com; 1-way $20, round-trip $37) picks up passengers at 44th St at Third Ave in Manhattan and makes stops in 10 North Fork villages.

Car Take the Midtown Tunnel out of Manhattan, which will take you onto I-495/Long Island Expressway. Take this
until it ends, at Riverhead, and follow signs onto Rte 25. Stay on Rte 25 for all points east.

Train The Long Island Rail Road (LIRR; ☎ 718-217-5477; www.mta.nyc.ny.us/lirr; round-trip $29) has a North Fork
line, usually called the Ronkonkoma Branch, with trips leaving from Penn Station and Brooklyn. Make sure the stop at
the end of your line is Greenport. Tickets can be bought at the station from agents or automatic machines.

Ferry To get from the North Fork to the South Fork (or vice versa), take the North Ferry (☎ 631-749-0139; www
.northferry.com) and South Ferry (☎ 631-749-1200; www.southferry.com) services to and from Shelter Island.

Eating

Aldo's (☎ 631-477-1699; 103-105 Front St, Greenport; mains $15-25)

Claudio's (☎ 631-477-0715; 111 Main St, Greenport; mains $18-30; ☻ mid-Apr–Jan 1)

Polonez Polish-Russian Restaurant (☎ 631-369-8878; 123 W Main St, Riverhead; mains $12-20)

Sleeping

Quintessentials B&B Spa (☎ 631-477-9400, 877-259-0939; www.quintessentialsinc.com; 8585 Main Rd, East Marion; r $175-275)

Red Barn B&B (☎ 631-722-3695; www.redbarnbandb.com; 733 Herricks Lane, Jamesport; r $195-295)

JONES BEACH

The offerings of Jones Beach State Park (☎ 516-785-1600) are simple: 6½ miles of clean sand covered with bodies. The type of character differs depending on which 'field' you choose – for example, 2 is for the surfers and 6 is for families, and there is a gay beach followed by a nude beach way east – but it's a definite scene no matter where you choose to spread your blanket. The ocean gets quite warm by midsummer, up to about 70°F, and there are plenty of lifeguards. In between sunning and riding waves, though, you might also hop into one of the two massive on-site pools for a swim, play shuffleboard or basketball on beachside courts, stroll the 2-mile boardwalk, visit the still waters of the bay beach or, at the museum Castles in the Sand (☎ 516-785-1600; admission $1; ☻ 10am-4pm Sat & Sun Memorial Day-Labor Day), learn how master builder Robert Moses transformed Long Island with the creation of Jones Beach in the 1940s.

The former Boardwalk Café that was a favorite hangout was demolished in 2004 and as of press time mega-developer Donald Trump was plotting to replace it with a $30 million, 70,000-sq-foot monstrosity to be called Trump on the Ocean. A permit problem has tied it up in court, and local opposition to the project grows daily, so the treasured public space may yet avoid this blight (let's hope).

When the sun goes down, you can grill at one of the many barbecues in the sand, grab burgers at the few local restaurants near the beach, or head to the Jones Beach Theater (☎ 516-221-1000; www.jonesbeach.com), where al fresco concerts under the stars feature famous pop stars from the '80s and '90s, as well as classics like Eric Clapton and James Taylor.

Information

Jones Beach State Park (☎ 516-785-1600; http://nysparks.state.ny.us; 1 Ocean Parkway, Wantagh) No pets allowed.

Eating

Pit Stop (☎ 516-223-7799; 1706 Sunrise Hwy, Wantagh; ☻ lunch & dinner)

Thom Thom (☎ 516-221-9022; 3340 Park Ave, Wantagh; ☻ lunch & dinner)

FIRE ISLAND

This skinny barrier island of sand runs parallel to Long Island, and contains much wonder, beauty and flaming adventure along its scant 32 miles. Federally protected as the Fire Island National Seashore (☎ 631-289-4810; www.nps.gov/fiis), the land offers sand dunes, forests, white beaches, camping, hiking trails, inns, restaurants, 15 hamlets and two villages. Its

TRANSPORTATION: FIRE ISLAND

Distance from New York City **60 miles**

Direction **East**

Travel Time **Two hours (including ferry ride)**

Car Take the Midtown Tunnel out of Manhattan onto I-495/Long Island Expressway. For Sayville ferries (to The Pines, Cherry Grove and Sunken Forest), get off at exit 57 onto the Vets Memorial Hwy. Make a right on Lakeland Ave and take it to the end, following signs for the ferry. For Davis Park Ferry from Patchogue (to Watch Hill) take the Long Island Expressway to exit 63 southbound (North Ocean Ave). For Bay Shore ferries (all other Fire Island destinations), take the Long Island Expressway to exit 30E, then get onto the Sagtikos Parkway to exit 42 south, to Fifth Ave terminal in Bay Shore. You can also take Tommy's Taxi Service (☎ 631-665-4800), with pick-up points in Manhattan, directly to the Bay Shore ferry for $145 1-way. To get to Robert Moses State Park by car, take exit 53 off the Long Island Expressway and travel south across the Moses Causeway.

Train The Long Island Rail Road (LIRR; ☎ 718-217-5477; www.mta.nyc.ny.us/lirr) makes stops in both Sayville and Bay Shore ($20 round-trip), and has a connecting summer-only shuttle service to the Fire Island Ferry Service (☎ 631-665-3600, Bay Shore), Sayville Ferry Service (☎ 631-589-0810, Sayville) and Davis Park Ferry (☎ 631-475-1665, Davis Park). Visit www.fireislandferries.com for more information. One-way tickets from Manhattan and Brooklyn are about $8; round-trip ferry tickets average $13.

scenes range from car-free residential villages of summer mansions and packed nightclubs to stretches of sand where you'll find nothing but pitched tents and deer (overpopulation is a big problem here). Robert Moses State Park (☎ 631-669-0449; www.nysparks.state.ny.us), the only part of the island that's accessible by car, lies at the westernmost end and features wide, soft-sand beaches with mellower crowds than those at Jones Beach. It's also home to the Fire Island Lighthouse (☎ 631-681-4876), which houses a history museum. Walk way east along the shore here and you'll stumble upon a lively nude beach.

The gemlike parts of Fire Island, though, are found further east, in the tranquil, car-free villages. Davis Park, Fair Harbor, Kismet, Ocean Bay Park and Ocean Beach combine small summer homes with tiny towns that have groceries, bars, nightclubs and restaurants – just keep in mind that almost everything in every town shuts down a couple of weeks after Labor Day. You can rely on the South Bay Water Taxi service to shuttle you between villages. To find out more, check out the town guide at www.fireisland.com.

Perhaps the most infamous villages are those that have evolved into gay resorts: Cherry Grove (☎ 914-844-7490; www.cherrygrove.com) and The Pines (www.thepinesfireisland.com). While day trips are easy to Fire Island, staying for a night or two on this car-free oasis, where boardwalks serve as pathways between the dunes and homes, is wonderful. Until recently accommodations meant a stay in someone's summer share-house or beachy basic rooms at the Belvedere (for men only) or Grove Hotel, all in the Grove (the Grove Hotel offers the main source of entertainment with its nightclub). Now you can add to it Fire Island's first 'boutique' hotel: the Madison Fire Island, which rivals anything Manhattan has to offer in terms of amenities, but also has killer views from a rooftop deck and a gorgeous pool (and pool boys).

If you want to skip the scene altogether and just get back to nature, enjoy a hike through the Sunken Forest (☎ 631-289-4810), a 300-year-old forest, with its own ferry stop (called Sailor's Haven). At the eastern end of the island, the 1300-acre preserve of Otis Pike Fire Island Wilderness (☎ 631-289-9336; campsite $25) includes a beach campground at Watch Hill (reservations are a must, as sites fill up a year in advance); just beware of the fierce mosquitoes.

Information

Fire Island Information (www.fireisland.com)

South Bay Water Taxi (☎ 631-665-8885; 133 Ocean Ave, Bay Shore; fares $10-20)

Eating

Michael's (☎ 631-597-6555; Cherry Grove; mains $12-20) Great gourmet pizza and Italian fare.

Rachel's (☎ 631-597-4174; Cherry Grove; mains $12-18) Everybody's morning coffee spot, but perfect for lunch and dinner too.

DETOUR: LONG BEACH

Beautiful Long Beach, 30 miles from New York City, much closer than either Jones Beach or Fire Island, is one of the best stretches of sand you can find. It's easily accessible by train, has clean beaches, a hoppin' main town strip with shops and eateries within walking distance of the ocean, a thriving surfing scene and many city hipsters. Lincoln Beach (☎ 516-431-1810), at the end of Lincoln Blvd, is the main spot for surfing; you can rent bikes at Buddy's (☎ 516-431-0804; 907 W Beech St; bike hire per 3hr $20).

There's plenty of good eats in the town around the beach. Stroll around and find whatever takes your fancy, or make a beeline for Baja California Grille, serving up tasty Mexican fare, or Kitchen Off Pine Street. For more info contact the City of Long Beach (☎ 516-431-1000; www.longbeachny.org; 1 W Chester St; ☺ 9am-4pm Mon-Fri). To get there by train use the Long Island Rail Road (LIRR; ☎ 718-217-5477; www.mta.nyc.ny.us/lirr; round-trip $14), which goes directly to Long Beach from both Penn Station and Flatbush Ave in Brooklyn.

Entertainment

Kismet Inn & Marina (☎ 631-583-5592; Oak Walk, Kismet) Nightly sunset social hour.

The Dock (☎ 631-583-5200; Bay Walk, Fair Harbor) Stop by for 'The Sixers,' a nightly gathering to watch the sunset.

Sleeping

Belvedere (☎ 631-597-6448; www.belvederefireisland .com; Cherry Grove; r from $125) Men only.

Grove Hotel (☎ 631-597-6600; www.grovehotel.com; Cherry Grove; r $75-500)

Madison Fire Island (☎ 631-597-6061; www.the madisonfi.com; The Pines; r $200-775)

Pines Bluff Overlook (☎ 631-597-3064; www.pines bluffoverlook.com; The Pines; r $250-300) Prices drop for three-night packages and weekly stays.

UPSTATE NEW YORK

Outside of an unfortunate stretch of industrial blight along the Hudson Valley's main corridor (mostly visible around the city of Newburgh), northern New York is a romantic delight. Its celebrated landscape – which gave birth to literary creatures like Rip Van Winkle and the Headless Horseman – starts with a long lush stretch of historic riverfront towns and thickly treed hills with ever-changing foliage colors that are shown to best advantage during the fall.

WOODSTOCK & SAUGERTIES

In the southern Catskills, the town of Woodstock symbolizes the tumultuous 1960s, when young people questioned authority, experimented with freedom and redefined popular culture. Today it's a combination of quaint and hip – an artists' colony full of young urbanites. The

Woodstock Guild is a good source for finding out the latest goings-on in the arts and culture scene – such as the annual Woodstock Film Festival, in October, which attracts film fans from all over. The famous 1969 Woodstock music festival actually occurred in Bethel, a town over 40 miles southeast, where a simple plaque marks the famous spot. Saugerties, just a few miles from the town of Woodstock, offers a similar downtown area, with a smaller offering of galleries, cafés and eateries. Hands down the best place to stay is the Saugerties Light House – once a working structure, now restored and gorgeous to behold across Esopus Creek (you have to be boated out). It's booked months in advance, though, so also consider The Villa at Saugerties as a back up.

South of Saugerties, Rte 28 crosses the Catskills west of Woodstock, then winds past the Ashokan Reservoir and through the 'French Catskills.' Along this way are excellent restaurants, camping, inexpensive lodging, antique shops and character galore. In Mt Tremper you'll find Kate's Lazy Meadow Motel, a hip, kitschy inn owned by Kate Pierson of the B52s. In Arkville, take a scenic ride on the historic Delaware and Ulster Rail Line. Nearby Fleischmanns is a door to a bygone era (the town is named after the yeast manufacturer who used to have a factory there): the woodsy hamlet is a favorite summer retreat for Orthodox Russian Jews, who shop for antiques alongside locals in their heavy, traditional garb even in the height of August's swelter.

Fantastic hiking can be found in the Catskill Forest Preserve, a huge swath of land that contains the vital watershed feeding New York City's ravenous thirst, and 300 miles of great hiking and camping. The NY/NJ Trail Conference (☎ 212-685-9699; www.nynjtc.org) has maps and information. For winter skiing head north along Rtes 23 and 23A to Windham Mountain (☎ 518-734-4300;

www.skiwindham.com; Windham), a family-friendly resort that embraces eco-friendly practices to the fullest extent – using energy from its snow-making machines to heat mountain lodges and condos, and buying wind offsets to reduce its carbon footprint. In summer, it runs all sorts of fun family outdoors activities (golf, spa treatments and mountain-biking anyone?). Nearby Belleayre Resort (☎ 800-942-6904, 845-254-5601; www.belleayre.com), a state-run facility with a warm community feel, is getting set for a major overhaul thanks to state funds for new hotels and possibly some casinos, along with other options designed to make it an entertainment hub.

For a lazy outdoor day, head to Phoenicia to go inner-tubing down the Esopus Creek, which flows near Rte 28. Town Tinker (☎ 845-688-5553; www.towntinker.com; Bridge St, Phoenicia; per tube $10) will provide life jackets, tubes and transport back to your car.

Information

Delaware and Ulster Rail Line (☎ 845-652-2821; www .durr.org; Hwy 28, Arkville; adult/senior/child $11/8/7; ☺ May-Aug)

Woodstock Guild (☎ 845-679-2079; www.woodstock guild.org; Woodstock; ☺ 9am-5pm Mon-Fri)

Eating

Blue Mountain Bistro (☎ 845-679-8519; Glasco Turnpike, Saugerties; mains $15-25)

Miss Lucy's Kitchen (☎ 845-246-9240; www.misslucys kitchen.com; 90 Partition St, Saugerties; mains $12-25)

New World Home Cooking Co (☎ 845-246-0900; Rte 212, Woodstock; mains $10-20)

Sweet Sue's (☎ 845-688-7852; 49 Main St, Phoenicia, off Rte 28) Near Belleayre Resort.

Sleeping

Kate's Lazy Meadow Motel (☎ 845-688-7200; www .lazymeadow.com; 5191 Rte 28, Mt Tremper; r $150-275)

Saugerties Lighthouse (☎ 847-247-0656; www .saugertieslighthouse.com; Saugerties; r $165-180) Book in advance.

Villa at Saugerties (☎ 845-246-0682; www.thevillaat saugerties.com; 159 Fawn Rd, Saugerties; r $145-235)

HUDSON VALLEY

Winding roads along the Hudson River take you by picturesque farms, Victorian cottages, apple orchards and old-money mansions built by New York's elite. Hudson Valley Tourism has regional information about sites and events. Painters of the Hudson River school romanticized these landscapes – you can see their work at art museums in the area as well as in the city. Autumn is a particularly beautiful time for a trip up this way, either by car or train (though having a car makes site-hopping much easier); cyclists also love the beauty and challenge of riding through the area.

ARTS & PARKS

The area around Beacon offers a great opportunity to combine a nature trip with an art outing; it's home to two fantastic museums and two unspoiled nature parks.

Storm King Art Center (☎ 845-534-3115; www.storm king.org; Old Pleasant Hill Rd; admission $10; ☺ Apr-Nov) in Mountainville, on the west side of the Hudson River, is a giant open-air museum on 500 acres, part sculpture garden and part sculpture landscape. The spot was founded in 1960, first as a museum for painters, but it soon began to acquire larger installations and monument works that were placed outside, in natural 'rooms' created by the land's indigenous breaks and curves. There's a small museum on site, formerly a 1935 residence designed like a Norman chateau, and plenty of picnic sites that visitors are encouraged to use (besides vending machines, there's no food sold here).

Open only in April through November, Storm King changes with the seasons. The entrance has five tall columns, surrounding the figure of a slim girl (flashing a thumbs-up sign), that lead to a sweeping trail of huge maples, guarded by three towering structures by Mark di Suvero. Across the expanse of meadow is the Storm King Wall, artist Andy Goldsworthy's famously sinuous structure that starts with rocks, crescendos up and across some hills, encompasses a tree, then dips down into a pond, slithering out the other side and eventually disappearing into the woods.

Other permanent pieces belong to Alexander Calder, Henry Moore, Richard Serra and Alice Aycock, to name a few. The nearby Storm King Lodge is a stately 1800s home with tasteful rooms featuring private bathrooms and fireplaces.

Another attraction on the east side of the Hudson River is the town of Beacon – a once scruffy waterfront village that's trying to spruce itself up with one very worthwhile stop: Dia Beacon (☎ 845-440-0100; www.diaart.org; Beacon; ◷ 11am-6pm Thu-Mon Apr 14-Oct 17, 11am-4pm Fri-Mon Oct 18-Apr 13), an outpost of NYC's Dia Center for the Arts. The Dia Beacon is in a former factory (there are plenty of abandoned ones on the outskirts of town) and is filled with huge ironwork Richard Serra pieces, and ever-changing installations on loan from the Manhattan outpost. Beacon so far has only one B&B, the Botsford Briar, but there are plenty of places to eat. Locals like Angelo's Seafood, Brother's Trattorie, and cute coffee-klatch hangouts Chthonic Clash and Cup & Saucer.

For hikers, Harriman State Park (☎ 845-786-5003), on the west side of the Hudson, spans 72 sq miles and provides swimming, hiking, camping and a visitors center. Adjacent Bear Mountain State Park (☎ 845-786-2701) offers great views from its 1305ft peak. The Manhattan skyline looms beyond the river and surrounding greenery. You can enjoy hiking in summer, wildflowers in spring, gold foliage in fall and cross-country skiing in winter.

HUDSON VALLEY ROAD TRIP

The largest town on the Hudson's east bank, Poughkeepsie (puh-*kip*-see) is famous for Vassar, a private liberal-arts college that admitted only women until 1969. Its modern Francis Lehman Loeb Art Center (☎ 845-437-5632; Poughkeepsie; admission free; ◷ 10am-5pm Tue-Sat, 1-5pm Sun) features paintings of the Hudson River school and contemporary work. The office of Dutchess County Tourism has regional information.

Cheap motel chains in Poughkeepsie are clustered along Rte 9, south of the Mid-Hudson Bridge. For a stay with some character, try the Copper Penny Inn, a tasteful B&B in a converted 1860s farmhouse.

Hyde Park has long been associated with the Roosevelts, a prominent family since the 19th century. The Franklin D Roosevelt Library & Museum (☎ 845-229-8114; www.fdrlibrary.marist.edu; 511 Albany

---

TRANSPORTATION: HUDSON VALLEY

Distance from New York City 95 miles (Hyde Park)

Direction North

Travel Time 1¾ hours

Car To leave Manhattan, take the Henry Hudson Parkway across the George Washington Bridge (I-95) to the Palisades Parkway. Follow this to the New York State Thruway to Rte 9W or Rte 9, the principal scenic river routes. Most towns can also be reached by taking the faster Taconic State Parkway, which runs north from Ossining and is considered one of the state's prettiest roads when the leaves turn in autumn.

Bus Short Line Buses (☎ 212-736-4700; www.shortlinebus.com) runs regular trips to Hyde Park (round-trip $46) and Rhinebeck ($50).

Train While Amtrak (☎ 212-582-6875, 800-872-7245; www.amtrak.com) trains run the length of the river and connect with several communities on the eastern shore, your best and cheapest bet from New York City is the commuter train line Metro-North (☎ 212-532-4900; 800-638-7646; www.mnr.org; 1-way off-peak $6-13), which departs from Grand Central Terminal (take the Hudson Line). On weekends, Metro-North runs special summer and autumn tourist packages that include train fare and transportation to and from specific sites such as Hyde Park and the Vanderbilt Mansion.

Boat One of the most relaxing and pleasant ways to take in several sites is by the NY Waterway (☎ 800-533-3779; www.nywaterway.com; tours from $40), which offers ferry trips up the Hudson River. Full-day tours on offer include many of the area's mansions and historic sites.

DETOUR: STONE BARNS FARM

Pumping out all the organic protein and produce used in Manhattan's delectable Blue Hill restaurant (p257) is Stone Barns (☎ general info 914-366-6200, dinner reservations 914-366-9600; www.stonebarnscenter.org; 630 Bedford Rd, Pocantico Hills near Tarrytown; ☺ visitors center 10am-5pm Wed-Sun, Stone Barn Restaurant 5-10pm Wed & Thu & 5-11pm Fri-Sun, Blue Hill Café 10:30am-4:30pm Wed-Sun), a working farm, kitchen, classroom and campus just 45 minutes from the city. Formerly a Rockefeller family site, its gracious flagstone buildings and slate walkways are a delight to stroll, and its two on-site restaurants (one a classy dinner site and the other a family- and hiker-friendly café) serve only the freshest seasonal foods from the backyard. We recommend coming during harvest time. Visitors are welcome to check out the farm year round; there are tours Wednesday through Sunday.

Post Rd/Rte 9, Hyde Park; admission $10; ☺ 9am-5pm) features exhibits on the man who created the New Deal and led the USA into WWII. Eleanor Roosevelt's cottage, Val-Kill (☎ 845-229-9115; www.nps.gov/elro; Albany Post Rd, Hyde Park; admission $8; ☺ 9am-5pm daily May-Oct, Thu-Mon Nov-Apr), was her retreat from Hyde Park, her mother-in-law and FDR himself. The Vanderbilt Mansion (☎ 800-967-2283; www.nps.gov/vama; Rte 9, Hyde Park; admission $8; ☺ 9am-5pm), a national historic site 2 miles north on Rte 9, is a spectacle of lavish Beaux-Arts and eclectic architecture. A combination ticket (☎ 800-967-2283; adult $18) is available for the three sites; reservations are recommended. There are plenty of other grand mansions to explore nearby, such as Kykuit (☎ 914-631-9491; Pocantico Hills, Tarrytown; adult/senior/child $22/20/18; ☺ tours 9:45am, 1:45pm & 3pm), a Rockefeller home with antique carriages and gardens in Tarrytown, along with the Gothic-Revival mansion Lyndhurst Castle (☎ 914-631-4481; www.lyndhurst.org; Rte 9, Tarrytown; castle/grounds $10/4; ☺ guided tours Tue-Sun 10:30am-4:15pm). Olana (☎ 518-828-0135; www.olana.org; Rte 9G, Hudson; adult/under 12yr $3/free; ☺ grounds 8am-sunset daily, tours 10am-5pm Tue-Sun), built with Moorish touches by Hudson River-school artist Frederic Church, is in Hudson; Springwood (☎ 800-967-2283; Albany Post Rd, Hyde Park; admission $14; ☺ 9am-5pm), in Hyde Park, was President Franklin D Roosevelt's boyhood country home.

Also in Hyde Park, the renowned Culinary Institute of America (☎ 800-285-4627; www.ciachef.edu) trains future chefs and can satisfy anyone's gastronomic cravings. St Andrew's Cafe (☎ 845-471-6608; dinner around $30) is casual, but reservations are required. A nearby inn, the Willows Bed & Breakfast (☎ 845-471-6115; www.willowsbnb.com; 53 Travis Rd; r $135-165) has quirky, contemporary rooms.

Information

Dutchess County Tourism (☎ 800-445-3131; www.dutchessny.gov; 3 Neptune Rd, Poughkepsie)

Hudson Valley Network (www.hvnet.com)

Hudson Valley Tourism (☎ 800-232-4782; www.hudsonvalley.org)

Eating

Angelo's (☎ 845-831-2292; www.eatatangelos.com; 47 E Main St, Beacon; mains $12-24)

Brother's Trattoria (☎ 845-838-3300; www.brotherstrattoria.com; 465 Main St, Beacon; mains $10-20)

Chthonic Clash (☎ 845-831-0359; www.chthonicclash.com; 453 Main St, Beacon; light meals $2-12)

Cup & Saucer Tea Room (☎ 845-831-6287; 165 Main St, Beacon; light meals $2-8)

Sleeping

Botsford Briar B&B (☎ 845-831-6099; 19 High St, Beacon; r $90-150; ☺ Apr-Oct)

Copper Penny Inn (☎ 845-452-3045; www.copperpennyinn.com; 2406 New Hackensack Rd, Poughkepsie; r $139-229)

Storm King Lodge (☎ 845-534-9421; www.stormkinglodge.com; Mountainville; r $150-190)

NEW JERSEY SHORE

As the old joke goes, mention a visit to New Jersey and the stock response you get is 'What exit?' The image of New York's neighboring state as a landlocked nightmare made up mostly of endless highway and hellish traffic jams is so pervasive that even some New Jerseyites don't know the beauty of their own long stretch of sparking Atlantic shore. There are plenty of natural delights on full view – once you're off the highway.

SANDY HOOK

Sandy Hook's 1665-acre natural wonderland comprises 7 miles of beach. Like Jones Beach on Long Island, the area blends massive ocean

TRANSPORTATION: SANDY HOOK

Distance from New York City **45 miles**

Direction **West**

Travel Time **One hour**

Car Take the Garden State Parkway to exit 117, then follow Rte 36 east to the beach.

Ferry The SeaStreak Ferry (☎ 800-262-8743, www.seastreak.com, 2 First Ave, Atlantic Highlands) leaves from Pier 11 near Wall St and also from a pier at E 35th St (1-way $24, round-trip $42, 1-way bike extra $3).

beaches with bay beaches and history. But here, in Sandy Hook Gateway National Recreation Area (☎ 732-872-5970), you'll also find the nation's oldest lighthouse, the Maritime Holly Forest with plentiful opportunities for observing birds (such as the endangered plover), outstanding views of Manhattan's skyline on clear days, a nude beach alongside a gay beach (area G), and a complex system of paved bike paths, which wend their way through the abandoned forts of historic Fort Hancock (what you'll see upon arrival) and white sand-dune peaks. Best of all, you can get here via a ferry from Lower Manhattan in a cool and salty 45 minutes. Bring your bike along for the ride, and you can pedal to various Jersey Shore areas, including the nearby towns of Atlantic Highlands and Highlands. The Atlantic Highlands Chamber of Commerce can provide you with information on several eating and sleeping options in the area.

If you get hungry on the beach, you'll find plenty of standard concession stands, with a rooftop option, Seagull's Nest, serving burgers, fried clams and ice-cold beers. For better grub, ride your bike over the bridge to the mellow, waterfront Inlet Café for seafood in the Highlands. The closest place to stay is the gay-owned Sandy Hook Cottage, done up with tasteful, beach-house decor. Also nearby is the Grand Lady By the Sea Bed and Breakfast, a historic, romantic inn that overlooks the beach.

Information

Atlantic Highlands Chamber of Commerce (☎ 732-872-8711; www.atlantichighlands.org; Atlantic Highlands Municipal Harbor; ⏰ 9am-4pm Mon-Fri)

Eating

Inlet Café (☎ 732-872-9764; 3 Cornwall St, Highlands; mains $8-20)

Seagull's Nest (☎ 732-872-0025; Sandy Hook Area D; mains $5-10)

Sleeping

Grand Lady By the Sea Bed and Breakfast (☎ 732-708-1900; www.grandladybythesea.com; 254 Rte 36, Highlands; r $159-259)

Sandy Hook Cottage (☎ 732-708-1923; www.sandyhookcottage.com; 36 Navesink Ave, Highlands; r $159-299)

ATLANTIC CITY

All aboard the hipster express – the formerly grimy city of Northeastern sin is prepping for its long overdue glamour makeover. Never quite able to compete with Las Vegas in terms of over-the-top tackiness that leaves you spent and breathless, Atlantic City's casinos have for years been content to settle for cheesiness (cloying all-you-can-eat buffets, shows that fall quite short of spectacular, and a clientele that consisted mostly of retirees, thrill-seeking kids and ex-cons who bus down for a night and then immediately leave).

All that is undergoing a total change, and as of research time, a major piece of the puzzle was preparing to fall into place: the Chelsea. This 'boutique' delight ushers in a bit of Manhattan chic to lowbrow Atlantic City, with 37 luxury rooms, rooftop pools and two restaurants by magician Stephen Starr, who previously put together some of Manhattan's ritziest eateries. Add to that a $400 million overhaul of the already glammed-up Borgata Hotel Casino & Spa, and a second Borgata property, the Water Club, home to Izakaya, a 'modern Japanese pub' run by famed chef Michael Schulson, and you can see why city planners are putting together an express train from Penn Station – complete with casino-designed club cars.

It's hard to believe Atlantic City was once a genteel seaside resort back in the 1900s, so complete is its dependence on gambling and casinos. If you're a gambler, you can't beat the selection of nearly 1000 blackjack tables and more than 30,000 slot machines in town. As in Las Vegas, the hotel-casinos have themes, from the Far East to Ancient Rome, but they're very superficially done here. Inside they're still all basically the same, with clanging slot machines, flashing lights and gluttonous all-you-can-eat food buffets. Donald Trump has a large presence in Atlantic City, of course – there's Trump's Marina Resort, with an art-deco theme; Trump Plaza Casino Hotel; and the Trump Taj Mahal, where nine two-ton limestone elephants welcome visitors, and 70 bright minarets crown the rooftops.

The Borgata has outstripped everyone else in terms of modern amenities and pampering (the on-site spa doles out treatments generously to gamblers who stick around a few nights), and Harrah's (one of the friendliest in town for newbie dice throwers) is upgrading too: a 44-story waterfront tower with a glass-domed tropical oasis was going up at research time. The southernmost casino, Atlantic City Hilton, has over 500 hotel rooms. Caesar's Atlantic City contains 1000 rooms and Atlantic City's Planet Hollywood theme restaurant, which is just off the gaming area. Tropicana Casino & Entertainment Resort is one of the biggest places in town, and has a slew of hip nightclubs inside.

Each of the casinos offers a full schedule of entertainment, but there is some life outside of the gambling dens. Built in 1870, the Boardwalk was the first in the world. Enjoy a walk or a hand-pushed rolling chair ride (adult $25) and drop in on the informative Atlantic City Historical Museum (☎ 609-347-5839; www.acmuseum.org; Garden Pier; admission free; ☼ 10am-4pm), run by a quirky old-timer. The Steel Pier amusement pier, directly in front of the Trump Taj Mahal, belongs to Donald Trump's empire. It used to be the place where the famous diving horse plunged into the Atlantic before crowds of spectators, but today it's a collection of small amusement rides, games of chance, candy stands and 'the biggest Go-Kart track in South Jersey!' The Visitor Information Center, under the giant tepee in the middle of the Atlantic City Expressway, can provide you with maps and accommodation deals, as can the various other information booths on or near the Boardwalk.

The Absecon Lighthouse (☎ 609-449-1360; www.absconlighthouse.org; cnr Rhode Island & Pacific Aves; adult/child $5/3; ☼ 10am-5pm daily Jul-Aug, 11am-4pm Thu-Mon Sep-Jun) dates from 1857 and, at 171ft high, ranks as the tallest in New Jersey and the third tallest in the country. It's been restored to its original specifications (including the Frensel lens) and you can climb the 228 steps to the top for phenomenal views.

Good food can be found away from the casinos. A few blocks inland from the Boardwalk, Mexico Lindo is a favorite among Mexican locals, while Angelo's Fairmount Tavern is a beloved family-owned Italian restaurant. The outdoor patio makes a nice spot to take in the sunset and have a pint and a burger. If you've got a car, try Hannah G's, an excellent breakfast and lunch spot in nearby Ventnor; or Maloney's, a popular seafood-and-steak place. Ventura's Greenhouse Restaurant, in next-door Margate City, is an Italian restaurant loved by locals. To go upscale, try the Knife and Fork Inn, a private gentlemen's club in 1912, now open to all.

Information

Visitor Information Center (☎ 609-449-7130; www.atlanticcitynj.com; Garden State Parkway; ☼ 9am-4pm)

Eating

Angelo's Fairmount Tavern (☎ 609-344-2439; Mississippi Ave at Fairmount Ave; mains $13-20)

TRANSPORTATION: ATLANTIC CITY

Distance from New York City **130 miles**

Direction **South**

Travel Time **2¼ hours**

Car Leave Manhattan via one of the Hudson River crossings (Holland Tunnel, Lincoln Tunnel, George Washington Bridge). Take the NJ Turnpike to the Garden State Parkway; Atlantic City is exit 38 off the parkway. The Atlantic City Expressway runs directly to Atlantic City from Philadelphia. Casino parking garages cost about $2 per day, but they waive the fee if you have a receipt showing you spent money inside.

Bus Greyhound (☎ 800-231-2222), Academy (☎ 800-442-7272) and New Jersey Transit (☎ 973-762-5100; www.njtransit.com) buses run from Port Authority; a round-trip costs around $51 to $57. Gray Line (☎ 212-397-2620) operates from 900 Eighth Ave between W 53rd and 54th Sts in Midtown. A casino will often refund the fare (in chips, coins or coupons) if you get a bus directly to its door. Fares are cheaper Monday to Thursday.

Train New Jersey Transit (☎ 973-762-5100; www.njtransit.com) doesn't offer direct service to Atlantic City, so a train trip requires two connections and is about twice the cost of a bus trip. From Penn Station, switch in Trenton to Philadelphia; from Philly, switch to the Atlantic City Line.

Hannah G's (☎ 609-823-1466; 7310 Ventnor Ave; mains $5-13)

Izakaya (☎ 800-800-8817; www.thewaterclubatborgata .com; One Renaissance Way)

Knife and Fork Inn (☎ 609-344-1133; www.knifeand forkinn.com; 29 South Albany Ave; mains $11-35)

Maloney's (☎ 609-823-7858; 23 S Washington Ave; mains $14-25)

Mexico Lindo (☎ 609-345-1880; 2435 Atlantic Ave; mains $5-11)

Ventura's Greenhouse Restaurant (☎ 609-822-0140; 106 Benson Ave, Margate City; mains $12-25)

Sleeping

Rates at all of the following places fluctuate hugely, from around $80 to $600 a night, depending on weekend events, time of year, vacancy etc.

Atlantic City Hilton (☎ 609-340-7111; Boston Ave at Boardwalk)

Borgata Hotel Casino & Spa (☎ 866-692-6742; One Borgata Way)

Caesar's Atlantic City (☎ 609-348-4411; Arkansas Ave at Boardwalk)

Harrah's Marina Hotel Casino (☎ 609-441-5000; Brigantine Blvd)

Tropicana Casino & Entertainment Resort (☎ 609-340-4000; Iowa Ave at Boardwalk)

Trump Plaza Casino Hotel (☎ 609-441-6000; Mississippi Ave at Boardwalk)

Trump Taj Mahal (☎ 609-449-1000; 1000 Boardwalk)

Trump's Marina Resort (☎ 609-441-2000; Huron Ave)

Water Club (☎ 800-800-8817; www.thewaterclub atborgata.com; One Renaissance Way)

CAPE MAY

Founded in 1620 on New Jersey's southern tip, Cape May is the country's oldest seashore resort. Its sweeping beaches get crowded in summer, but the stunning Victorian architecture is attractive year-round. The entire town was designated a National Historic Landmark in 1976. In addition to its attractive architecture, accommodations (many of them B&Bs in historic homes) and restaurants, Cape May boasts a lovely beach, a famous lighthouse, antique shops, and opportunities for whale-watching, fishing and superlative bird-watching. It's the only place in New Jersey where you can watch the sun both rise and set over the water. The quaint area attracts everyone from suburban families to a substantial gay crowd, drawn to the many gay-friendly inns.

While summer is high season, when places are hoppin' and beaches can be enjoyed at their full potential, the rest of the year is also great for settling into one of the romantic lodgings, strolling on the deserted beach and enjoying some fine dining. The Cape May Jazz Festival (☎ 609-884-7277; www.capemayjazz.com) is a biannual affair held in April and November, and the Cape May Music Festival (☎ 609-884-5404; www .capemaymac.org), from mid-May to early June, is highlighted by outdoor jazz, classical and chamber-music concerts. For comprehensive information on Cape May county attractions, stop at the Welcome Center.

The white, sandy beaches are the main attractions in summer months. The narrow Cape May Beach (☎ 609-884-9525; day/week pass $6/12) requires passes sold at the lifeguard station on the boardwalk at the end of Grant St. Cape May Point Beach (admission free) is accessible from the parking lot at Cape May Point State Park near the lighthouse. Sunset Beach (admission free) is at the end of Sunset Blvd and is the spot to watch the sunset with a 100% uninterrupted horizon line. Offshore, Cape May Whale Watcher (☎ 609-884-5445; www.capemaywhalewatcher.com; Miss Chris Marina, btwn Second Ave & Wilson Dr; adult $25-32, child $12-18) 'guarantees' sighting a marine mammal on one of its ocean tours.

The 190-acre Cape May Point State Park (☎ 609-884-2159; 707 E Lake Dr), just off Lighthouse Ave, has 2 miles of trails, plus the famous Cape May Lighthouse (☎ 609-884-2159; Lighthouse Ave; admission $6). Built in 1859, the 157ft lighthouse recently underwent a $2 million restoration, and its completely reconstructed light is visible as far as 25 miles out to sea. You can climb the 199 stairs to the top in the summer months. Hours change daily; call for details.

TRANSPORTATION: CAPE MAY

Distance from New York City 150 miles

Direction South

Travel Time 2¾ hours

Car Same as directions to Atlantic City, but continue on to the end of the Garden State Parkway.

Bus Vehicles to and from New York City are run by New Jersey Transit (☎ 973-762-5100; www .njtransit.com; round-trip $66.50).

The Cape May peninsula is a resting place for millions of migratory birds each year, and the Cape May Bird Observatory (☎ 609-898-2473, 609-861-0700; 701 East Lake Dr; ☻ 9am-4:30pm) maintains a hotline offering information on the latest sightings and is considered one of the country's 10 birding hot spots. Fall is the best time to glimpse some of the 400 species that frequent the area, including hawks, but from March through May you can see songbirds, raptors and other species. The bird observatory also offers tours of Reed's Beach, 12 miles north of Cape May on Delaware Bay, where migrating shorebirds swoop down to feed on the eggs laid by thousands of horseshoe crabs each May. You can also visit the 18-acre Nature Center of Cape May (☎ 609-898-8848; 1600 Delaware Ave; admission free; ☻ 9am-4pm summer, 10am-1pm winter, 10am-3pm fall & spring), which features open-air observation platforms with wonderful views of the expansive marshes and beaches.

In town, the Emlen Physick Estate, an 18-room mansion built in 1879, now houses the Mid-Atlantic Center for the Arts (☎ 609-884-5404, 800-275-4278; www.capemaymac.org; 1048 Washington St), which books tours for Cape May historic homes, the lighthouse or nearby historic Cold Spring Village. Hours change frequently at the center; call for details. You can also get a glimpse of *Atlantus*, which dates from WWI, when 12 experimental concrete ships were built to compensate for a shortage of steel. This surviving example, with its 5-inch concrete aggregate hull, began its seagoing life in 1918, but eight years later it broke free in a storm and ran aground on the western side of the Cape May Point coast. A small chunk of the hull still sits a few feet from shore on Sunset Beach at the end of Sunset Blvd.

Though you can certainly make a day trip here, Cape May is packed with excellent places to rest your weary head. If you come here during the off season many places will have closed their doors, but you'll have your pick of the ones remaining open and at a reasonably cheap price. In high season, many places have a two- to three-night minimum stay during summer weekends. The best budget option remains Hotel Clinton. Classy Virginia Hotel has gorgeous old-fashioned rooms with costs that vary wildly depending on the season. The sprawling, just-renovated Congress Hall, run by the same owners, has a range of quarters to suit various budgets, plus a long, oceanfront porch lined with rocking chairs.

The town is positively overflowing with small B&Bs; try the darling Gingerbread House, a six-room B&B where the rates include a Cape May Beach pass, Continental breakfast and scrumptious afternoon tea. Mainstay Inn, built in 1872 as a men's gambling club, features rooms furnished in opulent dark woods and large beds; all have private bathrooms and rates include breakfast.

Finding good food is not a problem at Cape May. For a beach snack, Akroteria is a collection of small fast-food shacks. Louisa's Café, a tiny, low-ceilinged dining room, is the town's prize eatery, serving up seasonal eclectic specialties; the casual Blue Pig Tavern at Congress Hall is comparable. Diners with more upscale tastes should reserve a table at the award-winning Ebbitt Room in the Virginia Hotel or at the Union Park Dining Room, at Hotel Macomber.

Information

Welcome Center (405 Lafayette St; ☻ 9am-4pm)

Eating

Akroteria (Beach Ave; mains $2-6)

Louisa's Café (☎ 609-884-5884; 104 Jackson St; mains $12-18)

Union Park Dining Room (☎ 609-884-8811; 727 Beach Ave; mains $18-30)

Sleeping

Congress Hall (☎ 609-884-8422; 251 Beach Ave; r $100-465)

Gingerbread House (☎ 609-884-0211; www.ginger breadinn.com; 28 Gurney St; r $110-29)

Holly House (☎ 609-884-7365; 20 Jackson St; r from $120)

Mainstay Inn (☎ 609-884-8690; 635 Columbia Ave; r $115-295)

Virginia Hotel (☎ 609-884-8690; www.virginiahotel .com; 25 Jackson St; r $100-445)

PHILADELPHIA

Just two short hours outside of NYC sits one of the most historic cities on the eastern seaboard, fairly overflowing with important sites from America's colonial days and its fight for independence. But for most people, Philly is famous for one thing and one thing only: it was the gritty city that served as a backdrop for fictional underdog boxer Rocky Balboa.

So popular are the locations used to film Sylvester Stallone's iconic Rocky films that entire tours are dedicated to them – and who can resist the temptation to shadow box at the top of the steps of the Philadelphia Museum of Art, just like Rocky did?

But for those who like their history from 1776 and not 1976, you should know that William Penn made Philadelphia his capital in 1682, basing its plan on a grid with wide streets and public squares – a layout copied by many US cities. For a time the second-largest city in the British Empire (after London), Philadelphia became a center for opposition to British colonial policy. It was the new nation's capital at the start of the American Revolution and again after the war until 1790, when Washington DC took over. By the 1800s, New York had superseded Philadelphia as the nation's cultural, commercial and industrial center, and Philly never regained its early preeminent status. But in the 1970s, the nation's bicentennial prompted an urban renewal program that continues to this day.

It's an easy city to get around. Most sights and accommodations are within walking distance of each other, or a short bus ride away. East–west streets are named; north–south streets are numbered, except for Broad and Front Sts. Historic Philadelphia includes Independence National Historic Park and Old City, which extend east to the waterfront.

There are many tours that display the city's highlights; among the most complete is the 90-minute narrated trolley trip by Philadelphia Trolley Works, during which you can hop on and off at designated stops and then reboard when you're ready. For a unique way of getting around, the 76 Carriage Company will take you around various areas in a horse-drawn carriage. Phlash visitor shuttle is

a one-hour, do-it-yourself tour that visits about 25 sites. You travel in a bright-purple van, which you can hop on and off of whenever you want; there is no tour guide, but you are equipped with a color-coded, easy-to-follow map of the journey. To do it yourself, make your first stop the Independence Visitor Center. Run by the knowledgeable folks of the National Park Service, the center distributes the useful *Philadelphia Official Visitors Guide*, maps and brochures. The nearby Philadelphia Convention & Visitors Bureau has information about businesses, tours, hotels and package deals.

The L-shaped 45-acre Independence National Historic Park (INHP; ☎ 215-597-8974; www.nps.gov/inde), undergoing a major renovation, along with the Old City area, has been dubbed 'America's most historic square mile,' and can feel like a stroll back through time. Concentrating your sightseeing around this area will make the city easier to tackle, and allow you to visit the most renowned sites. (Sites marked here with 'INHP' are part of the historic park.) Carpenters' Hall (INHP; btwn Chestnut & Walnut Sts; ☼ Tue-Sun), owned by the Carpenter Company, is the USA's oldest trade guild and the site of the First Continental Congress in 1774. Housed in the Second Bank of the US and modeled after the Parthenon, is the National Portrait Gallery (INHP; Chestnut St btwn S 4th & S 5th Sts), which includes several portraits of prominent figures by Charles Willson Peale. Library Hall (INHP; S 5th btwn Chestnut & Walnut Sts) is where you'll find a copy of the Declaration of Independence, handwritten in a letter by Thomas Jefferson, plus first editions of Darwin's *On the Origin of Species*, and the field notes of Lewis and Clark, who in 1803 left Pittsburgh to begin the first American overland expedition to the Pacific coast and back.

TRANSPORTATION: PHILADELPHIA

Distance from New York City 100 miles

Direction Southwest

Travel Time Two hours

Car Take the Lincoln Tunnel to the NJ Turnpike (I-95) to Rte 73 toward Philadelphia. Merge onto I-295 and then onto US-30, over the Ben Franklin Bridge and onto I-676, which has exits into Philly.

Bus Greyhound (☎ 800-229-9424) and Capitol Trailways (☎ 800-444-2877) both go from Port Authority Bus Terminal. The trip takes two hours; a round-trip fare costs about $46. 2000 New Century (p393) charges $20 round-trip.

Train Leaving from Penn Station, Amtrak (☎ 212-582-6875, 800-872-7245, www.amtrak.com, 1-way $43, round-trip $122) goes to Philly, but a better bargain is New Jersey Transit (☎ 973-762-5100, www.njtransit.com, round-trip $25), which runs a commuter service to Philly from Penn Station, requiring a transfer in Trenton.

Liberty Bell Center (INHP; Market St btwn 5th & 6th Sts), Philadelphia's premier tourist attraction, was recently moved to a brand-new location (just around the corner from its old pavilion, where it had sat since 1976) as part of the extensive Independence Park makeover. Constructed in London and tolled at the first public reading of the Declaration of Independence, the hefty 2080lb bell became famous when abolitionists decided to adopt it as a symbol of freedom. The bell is inscribed, 'Proclaim liberty throughout all the land, to all the inhabitants thereof (Leviticus 25:10).' Extensive cracking along the face eventually made the bell unusable way back in 1846.

The Franklin Court (INHP; Market St btwn S 3rd & S 4th Sts), a row of restored tenements, pays tribute to Benjamin Franklin with an underground museum displaying his inventions. At the B Free Franklin Post Office, which has a small US Postal Service Museum, mail receives a special handwritten Franklin postmark. (In addition to being a statesman, author and inventor, the multitalented Franklin was a postmaster.) Christ Church (☎ 215-922-1695; 2nd St btwn Market & Arch Sts), completed in 1744, is where George Washington and Franklin worshipped.

The Greek-revival Philadelphia Merchant's Exchange (cnr 3rd & Walnut Sts), a beautiful edifice designed by William Strickland, is the home of the country's first stock exchange (1834). It now houses government offices and is closed to the public, but you can linger at its facade.

Old City – along with Society Hill – comprises the area bounded by Walnut, Vine, Front and 6th Sts. This was early Philadelphia. The 1970s saw its revitalization, when many warehouses were converted into apartments, galleries and small businesses. Elfreth's Alley is believed to be the oldest continuously occupied street in the USA; on it, Mantua Maker's Museum House (☎ 215-574-0560; admission $2; ☽ 10am-4pm Sat, noon-4pm Sun) has displays of period furniture. Windsor Chair Maker's House (☎ 215-574-0560; 126 Elfreth's Alley; admission $2; ☽ 10am-4pm Sat, noon-4pm Sun) produced the chairs in Independence Hall. Fireman's Hall (☎ 215-923-1438; 147 N 2nd St) is where you'll find the nation's oldest fire engine and an exhibit on the rise of organized volunteers, which was led by Ben Franklin. Betsy Ross House (☎ 215-686-1252; 239 Arch St; admission by donation; ☽ 9am-5pm) is where Betsy Griscom Ross (1752–1836), upholsterer and seamstress, is believed to have sewn the first US flag.

The National Museum of American Jewish History (☎ 215-923-3811; www.nmajh.org; 55 N 5th St; admission free; ☽ 10am-5pm Mon-Thu, 10am-3pm Fri, noon-5pm Sun) features exhibits that examine the historical role of Jewish people in the USA. At the nearby US Mint (INHP; ☎ 215-408-0114; btwn 4th & 5th Sts; admission free), tours are open to the public. Arch Street Meeting House (320 Arch St; admission by donation; ☽ Mon-Sat) is the USA's largest Quaker meetinghouse, and the African American Museum in Philadelphia (☎ 215-574-0380; www.aampmuseum.org; 701 Arch St; admission $8; ☽ 10am-5pm Thu-Sun, 10:30am-5pm Tue, 10:30am-7pm Wed) has excellent collections on black history and culture.

Gay visitors to Philly will be pleased to know that the Philadelphia Convention and Visitors Bureau launched a major ad campaign in 2004 that was specifically aimed at LGBT travelers. 'Get your history straight and your nightlife gay,' the slogan urged. Though the offerings pale in comparison to what's in NYC, there is a pretty hopping nightlife scene for a small city; plus Millennium Coffee is a hip java hang-out, filled with cute boys, while Giovanni's Room (☎ 215-923-2960; 345 S 12th St) is a large, well-stocked gay bookstore on Antique Row, definitely worth a look.

If you decide to stay the night here, know that you'll mostly find upscale hotel chains and a sprinkling of quaint B&Bs; the city is sorely lacking in classy boutique-style hotels. Penn's View Hotel is an old-fashioned inn that overlooks the water. It offers a range of rooms featuring Chippendale-style furniture, many with exposed-brick walls and working fireplaces. A continental breakfast is included. Similarly, the Latham Hotel is a classy, European-style hotel with Victorian rooms. Shippen Way Inn is a 1750s colonial house containing nine rooms with quilted beds, plus free wine and cheese in the kitchen and a cozy B&B atmosphere. The Antique Row B&B has quirky, period-furnished rooms and good breakfasts on hoppin' Antique Row. Four Seasons Hotel Philadelphia is the most lavish place in town.

Eating options are plentiful, with some of the cheapest, most interesting edibles found in the city's compact Chinatown and South St areas. Two of Philadelphia's most popular spots for a cheese steak (and you can't leave without trying this regional specialty) are Geno's and Pat's King of Steaks. The indoor Reading Terminal Market is a wonderful indoor marketplace, offering everything from fresh Amish cheeses and Thai desserts to falafel, cheese steaks, salad bars, sushi, Peking duck and great Mexican. At the high end, an elegant favorite is Buddakan, serving Asian-fusion feasts. Locals list Ishkabibbles and Figs as two of the city's best Mediterranean options, and recommend Chloe's as a good place for American comfort food.

Late afternoon drinkers will find a friendly hang out at Cutters, a favorite after-work spot that's home to a towering display of liquor bottles. Lucy's Hat Shop is an atmospheric pub with pool tables and lots of beer on tap, and live-music aficionados will want to swing by Pontiac Grille to check out the local talent.

For a full rundown of all of Philly's offerings, pick up a copy of LP's *Philadelphia & the Pennsylvania Dutch Country*.

Information

The phone number for all Independence National Historic Park (INHP) stops is the same (☎ 215-597-8974). INHP sites are open 9am to 5pm unless otherwise noted.

76 Carriage Company & Philadelphia Trolley Works (☎ 215-923-8516; www.phillytour.com; cnr 6th & Chestnut Sts; adult $20-70, child $4-13)

B Free Franklin Post Office (☎ 215-592-1289; 316 Market St)

Independence Hall/Congress Hall (INHP; Chestnut St btwn S 5th & S 6th Sts)

Independence Visitor Center (☎ 215-965-7676; www .independencevisitorcenter.com; 6th St btwn Market & Arch Sts; ☺ 8:30am-5pm)

Old City Hall/Philosophical Hall (INHP; Chestnut St btwn S 5th & S 6th Sts)

Philadelphia Convention & Visitors Bureau (☎ 215-636-3300; www.pcvb.org) Please note that this is not a place to be visited; it's a marketing office for the city.

Phlash (☎ 215-474-5274; all-day pass $4)

Eating

Buddakan (☎ 215-574-9440; 325 Chestnut St; mains $20-28)

Chloe's (☎ 215-629-2337; 232 Arch St; mains $10-18)

Figs (☎ 215-978-8440; 2501 Meredith St; mains $10-25) Cash only.

Geno's (☎ 215-389-0659; 1219 S 9th St; mains $3-6)

Ishkabibbles (☎ 215-923-4337; 337 South St; mains $10)

Millennium Coffee (☎ 731-9798; 212 S 12th St; snacks $2-6)

Pat's King of Steaks (☎ 215-468-1546; 9th St at Wharton & Passyunk Aves; mains $3-7; ☺ 24hr)

Reading Terminal Market (☎ 215-922-2317; www .readingterminalmarket.org; 12th & Arch Sts; mains $2)

Drinking

Cutters (☎ 215-851-6262; 2005 Market St)

Lucy's Hat Shop (☎ 215-413-1433; 247 Market St)

Pontiac Grille (☎ 215-925-4053; 304 South St)

Sleeping

Antique Row B&B (☎ 215-592-7802; www.antique rowbnb.com; 341 S 12th St; r $65-110)

Four Seasons Hotel Philadelphia (☎ 215-963-1500; www.fourseasons.com/philadelphia; 1 Logan Sq; r $295-395)

Latham Hotel (☎ 215-563-7474; www.lathamhotel .com; 135 S 17th St; r $109-149)

Penn's View Hotel (☎ 215-922-7600; www.penns viewhotel.com; Front & Market Sts; r $200-250)

Shippen Way Inn (☎ 215-627-7266; www.shippenway .com; 416-418 Bainbridge St; r $105-150)

TRANSPORTATION

AIR

When booking tickets, note that high season in New York City runs from mid-June to mid-September (summer), and one week before and after Christmas. February and March, and from October to Thanksgiving (the fourth Thursday in November) serve as shoulder seasons, when prices drop slightly.

Among the best websites are the following:

Cheap Tickets (www.cheaptickets.com)

Expedia (www.expedia.com)

Priceline (www.priceline.com)

Travelocity (www.travelocity.com)

STA Travel (☎ 800-777-4040, reservations 212-865-2700; www.statravel.com) offers student fares and has three Manhattan offices. In New York, the ubiquitous Liberty Travel (☎ 888-271-1584; www.libertytravel.com) has nearly 30 locations.

Airlines

As a major international hub, New York is served by most airlines. Visiting airline offices is old-fashioned business these days (and most have closed Manhattan locations in recent years); to get toll-free numbers for airlines in the US, call ☎ 800-555-1212.

Airports

Three major airports serve New York City: John F Kennedy (JFK) and LaGuardia (LGA) in Queens, and Newark Liberty International Airport (EWR) in Newark, New Jersey. Only JFK has baggage storage (per day $4-16; ☺ 7am-11pm), in Terminals 1 and 4.

JFK INTERNATIONAL AIRPORT

This busy airport (JFK; Map pp200–1; ☎ 718-244-4444; www.panynj.gov, www.kennedyairport.com; Jamaica, Queens), 15 miles from Midtown in southeastern Queens, has eight terminals, serves 43 million passengers annually and hosts flights coming and going from all corners of the globe. Major renovations have been in progress for several years, including the AirTrain link with the

GETTING INTO TOWN

There are several ways of getting to and from New York's three main airports; the easiest is queuing up for a taxi at the official stands (avoid the independent drivers who approach new arrivals). Public transportation tends to take longer.

For a little extra ease, dozens of car services can offer drop-off or pick-up service to the airports, including Tel Aviv (☎ 212-777-7777, 800-222-9888; www.telavivlimo.com) and Prime Time (☎ 718-482-7900, 800-282-3227). Tel Aviv is about $5 cheaper. Note you pay toll fees (when applicable) and taxi or car-service drivers will expect a tip of about $5; one selfless LP researcher got a bear hug from a driver for tipping $10.

If you're going to JFK or LaGuardia, the New York Airport Service Express Bus (☎ 212-875-8200; www.nyairport service.com; every 20 or 30 minutes) has routes to and from both, stopping at the Port Authority Bus Terminal, Penn Station and just outside Grand Central Terminal – no reservations needed.

Super Shuttle (☎ 800-258-3826, 212-258-3826; www.supershuttle.com; one way to LaGuardia/JFK $16/21) is kind of like a shared-taxi ride that offers pick-up/drop-off service from your hotel in Manhattan to JFK or LaGuardia. It's not worth using if you're staying in Queens or Brooklyn.

To/from JFK

* A yellow taxi from Manhattan to the airport will use the meter; prices depend on traffic (often about $55) – it can take 45 to 60 minutes. From JFK, taxis charge a flat rate of $45 to any destination in Manhattan (not including tolls or tip); it can take 45 to 60 minutes for most destinations in Manhattan. To/from a destination in Brooklyn, the metered fare should be about $33 to $38.
* Car services (see above) have set fares from $48/53 (off hours/rush hour). Note that the Williamsburg, Manhattan, Brooklyn and Queensboro-59th St Bridges have no toll either way, while the Queens-Midtown Tunnel and the Brooklyn-Battery Tunnel cost $4.50 going into Manhattan.
* If you're driving from the airport, either go around Brooklyn's south tip via the Belt Parkway to US 278 (the Brooklyn-Queens Expressway, or BQE); or via US 678 (Van Wyck Expressway) to US 495 (Long Island Expressway, or LIE), which heads into Manhattan via the Queens-Midtown Tunnel.
* The New York Airport Service Express Bus (above) costs $15.
* By subway, take either the A line (bound for Rockaway Beach) to Howard Beach-JFK Airport station, or the E, J or Z line or the Long Island Rail Road to Sutphin Blvd-Archer Ave (Jamaica Station), where you can catch the Air Train to JFK. (The E express from Midtown has the fewest stops.) The overpriced Air Train finishes the tail end of a long trip for $5 one way; you can use a Metrocard to swipe yourself in. Expect it to take at least 90 minutes from Midtown.

To/from LaGuardia

* A taxi to/from Manhattan runs about $40 for the approximately half-hour ride.
* A car service (see above) to LaGuardia costs $33/38 (off hours/rush hour).

---

subway (and free service between terminals). If you go with Jet Blue, you fly from the gorgeous ex-TWA terminal (now Terminal 4), designed by Finn architect Eero Saarinen in 1962.

LAGUARDIA AIRPORT

Used mainly for domestic flights, LaGuardia (LGA; Map pp200–1; ☎ 718-533-3400; www.panynj.gov, www.laguardia airport.com; Flushing, Queens) is smaller than JFK but only eight miles from midtown Manhattan; it sees about 26 million passengers per year. It's been open to commercial use since 1939, making it considerably older, too. US Airways and Delta have their own terminals there.

NEWARK LIBERTY INTERNATIONAL AIRPORT

Don't write off New Jersey when looking for airfares to New York. The same distance from Midtown as JFK, Newark's airport (EWR; off Map p69; ☎ 973-961-6000; www.panynj.gov, www.newarkairport .com; Newark, NJ), 16 miles from Midtown, brings many New Yorkers out for flights (there's some 36 million passengers annually). Actually it became the metropolis' first major airport in 1928. Much of the action is domestic – particularly on Continental Airlines, which treats EWR as a hub – but not all. It added 'Liberty' to its name after September 11.

BICYCLE

It's not the most bike-friendly city, but New Yorkers are getting better at tolerating cyclists, thanks in part to improved road conditions, new bike paths and the efforts of bike clubs (see p328). In late 2007, the city transformed Ninth Ave between 16th and 23rd Sts with a Euro-

- The most common driving route from the airport is along Grand Central Expressway to the BQE (US 278), then to the Queens-Midtown Tunnel via the LIE (US 495); downtown-bound drivers can stay on the BQE and cross (free) via the Williamsburg Bridge.
- The New York Airport Express Bus (opposite) costs $12.
- It's less convenient to get to LaGuardia by public transportation than the other airports. The best subway link is the 74 St-Broadway station (7 line, or the E, F, G, R, V lines at the connecting Jackson Hts-Roosevelt Ave station) in Queens, where you can pick up the Q33, Q47 or Q48 bus to the airport (about 30 minutes by bus alone); more time consuming is the M60 bus, which runs east along Harlem's 125 Street and often takes more than an hour.

To/from Newark Liberty International Airport

- A car service (see opposite) runs about $48/53 (off hours/rush hour) for the 45-minute ride from Midtown – a taxi is roughly the same. You only have to pay the toll to go through the Lincoln Tunnel (at 42nd St) or Holland Tunnel (at Canal St) coming *into* Manhattan from Jersey ($7.50). There are a couple of cheap tolls on New Jersey highways too, unless you ask your driver to take Highway 1 or 9.
- Public transportation to Newark is convenient, but a bit of a rip-off. NJ Transit (☎ 800-772-2222; www .njtransit.com) runs an AirTrain between the Newark airport (EWR) and New York's Penn Station for a shocking $15 each way (hardly worth it if you're traveling with a couple of others). The trip uses a commuter train and takes 25 minutes and runs every 20 or 30 minutes from 4:20am to about 1:40am. Hold onto your ticket, which you must show upon exiting at the airport. A clumsier, 'stick-it-to-the-man' alternative is riding NJ Transit from New York's Penn to Newark's Penn Station ($4 one way), then catch bus No 62 (every 10 or 20 minutes) for the 20-minute ride to the airport ($1.35).
- The Newark Liberty Airport Express (☎ 877-863-9275, 908-354-3330; www.usacoach.com) has a bus service between the airport and Port Authority Bus Terminal, Bryant Park and Grand Central Terminal in Midtown ($14 one way). The 45-minute ride goes every 15 minutes from 6:45am to 11:15pm (and every half hour from 4:45am to 6:45am and 11:15pm to 1:15am).

Beating the Tunnel Tolls

- If you're flying into LaGuardia or JFK, you may be asked by your cab driver for your preferred route into the city. Going across the Queensboro-59th St, Williamsburg, Manhattan or Brooklyn Bridges is free (either direction), but you'll pay $4.50 to enter Manhattan via the Brooklyn-Battery Tunnel or the Queens-Midtown Tunnel (all tunnels are free leaving Manhattan). Often the Manhattan or Williamsburg Bridge is just as easy to use – and free.
- If you're coming via the airport in Newark, New Jersey, forget about it – you'll have to pay $6 to get into NYC through the Lincoln and Holland Tunnels and, further north, the George Washington Bridge (though there's no charge going back to NJ).

styled separate bike lane separated from traffic by parked cars – hopefully more will follow.

For maps of bike paths and a clearinghouse of tips, check the website of Transportation Alternatives (Map pp134–5; ☎ 212-629-8080; www.transalt .org; suite 1002, 127 W 26th St), which sponsors Bike Month NYC every May. Key Manhattan bike lanes are along 8th Ave, Broadway, and 20th, 21st, 9th and 10th Sts.

If you do ride around the city, always wear a helmet, choose a bike with wide tires to help you handle potholes and other bits of street debris and be alert so you don't get 'doored' by a passenger exiting a taxi. Unless your urban skills are well honed, stick to the pastoral paths in Central and Prospect Parks and along the Hudson River. And don't even think of pedaling on the sidewalks – it's illegal. If you must lock a bike up somewhere

in the city, forgo anything that's not the most top-of-the-line U-lock you can find – or, better yet, stick to the $100 coated chains that weigh a ton.

You're allowed to bring your bike onto the subway. Lettered subway lines (eg A, C, E, etc) have bigger stations and subway cars, and are thus easier to manage with a bike.

BOAT

If you're coming by yacht – and if you are, do you have an opening for a deck-swabber on your next trip to Bermuda? – there are ports at an exclusive boat slip at the World Financial Center and a long-term slip at the 79th St Boathouse on the Upper West Side.

The zippy yellow boats that make up the fleet of New York Water Taxi (☎ 212-742-1969; www

.nywatertaxi.com; commuter 1-way tickets $3.50-6, one-day pass adult/child $20/15, 2-day pass $25/15) provide an interesting alternative way of getting around (from mid-April through mid-October). Boats stop at 12 landings, starting at West 44th St on the Hudson River, with stops at Christopher St, World Financial Center, Battery Park, South Street Seaport and East 34th St in Manhattan, plus Brooklyn stops at Fulton Ferry Landing (near Dumbo), Red Hook, Schaefer Landing on Kent Ave (in Williamsburg), plus in Long Island City, and Queens at Hunter's Point (with its own 'Water Taxi Beach').

A good trip to consider is from E 34th St to Fulton Ferry Landing in Brooklyn ($4.50 one way). There are also water taxis to Mets baseball games ($20 round trip), hour-long 'Gateway to America' tours around the harbor (adult/senior/child $20/18/12), and fall foliage tours up the Hudson ($35/25/15).

Another bigger, brighter ferry (this one's orange) is the commuter-oriented Staten Island Ferry (p75), which makes constant free journeys across the New York Harbor.

For information on boat tours, see p403.

BUS

Many New York buses aren't too bad, and they've certainly improved in the past decade or so. They run 24 hours a day and the routes are easily navigable, going crosstown at all the major street byways – 14th, 23rd, 34th, 42nd and 72nd Sts, and all the others that are two-way roads – and uptown and downtown, depending on which avenue they serve. Stops, many with shelters, are every few blocks and all have maps and marked schedules, which are rough guides as to how often you can expect a bus to pass. That said, buses do get overcrowded at rush hour, and slow to a crawl in heavy traffic. So when you're in a hurry, stay underground.

The cost of a bus ride is the same as the subway, $2, though express bus routes cost $5 (running during rush hours; best for long

journeys from the boroughs). You can pay with a Metrocard (see the boxed text, below) or exact change but *not* dollar bills. Transfers from one line to another bus within two hours are free, as are transfers to or from the subway.

The Hampton Jitney (☎ 212-362-8400; www.hamptonjitney.com) runs buses for Long Island beach towns from Manhattan and Brooklyn.

For long-distance bus trips, you'll leave and depart from the world's busiest bus station, the Port Authority Bus Terminal (Map pp134–5; ☎ 212-564-8484; www.panynj.gov; 41st St at Eighth Ave). Bus companies leaving from here include the following:

Greyhound (☎ 800-231-2222; www.greyhound.com) Connects New York with major cities across the country.

New Jersey Transit (☎ 800-772-2222; www.njtransit.com) Serves Jersey; its No 319 bus goes 10 or 12 times daily to Atlantic City (one way/round trip $28.50/51).

Peter Pan Trailways (☎ 800-343-9999; www.peterpanbus.com) Daily express service to Boston (one way/round trip $30/55), Washington, DC ($37/69) and Philadelphia ($21/40);

ShortLine Bus (☎ 800-631-8405, 201-529-3666; www.shortlinebus.com) Goes to northern New Jersey and upstate New York (Rhinebeck for $25.30, Woodbury Common for $16.20).

Budget line Vamoose (Map pp134–5; ☎ 877-393-2828; www.vamoosebus.com) sends buses to Arlington, Virginia ($25), near Washington, DC. Buses leave from 255 W 31st St, outside Madison Square Garden.

Chinatown Buses

Crazy and cheap, Chinatown buses depart from pushy 'sidewalk terminals' at various points around Chinatown to Boston, Philadelphia, Washington, DC, and other areas on the East Coast. There are no seat reservations; often on weekends you may have to wait for the next bus, an hour later. Of the many choices around, Fung Wah (Map p94; ☎ 212-925-

---

METROCARDS FOR TRAVELERS

New York's classic subway tokens now belong to the ages: today all buses and subways use the yellow-and-blue Metrocard, which you can purchase or add value to at one of several easy-to-use automated machines at any station. You can use cash or an ATM or credit card. Just select 'Get new card' and follow the prompts.

There are two types of Metrocard. The 'pay-per-ride' is $2 per ride, though a $20 card gives you two free rides. The other is the excellent-value 'unlimited-ride' card (it's $7.50 for a one-day 'fun pass' or $25 for a seven-day pass). The unlimited-ride card is a real treat for travelers – particularly if you're jumping around to a few different places around the city in one day.

8889; www.fungwahbus.com; 139 Canal St at Bowery) offers hourly departures to Boston ($15) from 7am to 10pm or 11pm, and 2000 New Century (Map p94; ☎ 215-627-2666; www.2000coach.com; 88 E Broadway) goes almost half-hourly from 7am to 11pm to Philadelphia ($12) and a bit less often to DC ($20).

CAR & MOTORCYCLE

Driving is not recommended around Manhattan unless it's absolutely necessary. There are always drivers who don't want you hogging lanes, gas is pricey, car hire is expensive, the struggles for parking space can age even the eternally laid-back, and it's a way bigger hassle than it's worth, considering all the excellent mass-transit options.

Driving

If you're planning to do much driving, pick up a Hagstrom five-borough map, available from the Hagstrom Map & Travel Center (Map pp134–5; ☎ 212-398-1222; 51 W 43rd St; 🕐 8:30am-6pm Mon-Fri, 10:30am-4:30pm Sat; 🚇 B, D, F, V to 42 St-Bryant Park, 7 to 5th Ave). Get traffic reports from 1010 WINS on the radio, NY1 on the telly, or the fun streaming videos online at New York City Real Time Traffic Cameras (http://nyctmc.org).

Other than trying to park when and where you want, getting in and out of the city – and dealing with crosstown traffic – are the worst parts. Lanes are loosely adhered to – generally be more aware of what's next to you and before you than what's behind. Parallel parkers can back up traffic on some streets, so middle lanes go quicker on multi-laned avenues.

Remember tunnels *into* the city (not out) want money, but that most bridges are your for-free friends both ways (the George Washington charges if coming in from Jersey).

Note a few laws: no right turns on red lights and no talking on the cell phone while driving.

You'll quickly pick up on the fact that every other street alternates one-way direction.

Heavy gridlock in the city has ignited a big New York traffic debate of late. Mayor Michael Bloomberg has proposed a congestion tax to follow cities like London in charging cars/commercial vehicles $8/21 to enter Manhattan south of 86th St on weekday peak-hour periods. Opponents, who are many, have countered with ideas to create taxi stands and increase parking-meter prices. About 850,000 vehicles enter Manhattan daily. It's possible this situation may change during the life of this book.

Parking

Parking tickets and towing charges in New York probably equal some countries' national budgets. And much swearing, sweating and effort is expended by locals to keep a step ahead of ticketers. In other words, parking is a big headache.

Many streets have parking meters with one- or two-hour limits. Neighborhood streets have free parking spots, with 'no parking' signs indicating times cars must move for streetcleaners; veteran New Yorkers have mastered the knack of moving their cars back and forth to alternate sides of the street – sometimes double-parking with a note on their windshield for the hours in question. Sometimes it can feel hopeless – remember Diane Keaton's surprise at finding a spot in *Annie Hall* – and other times it depends on timing: Chinatown is an impossibility during the day, but can empty out after 7pm or 8pm. If you're lucky enough to find a spot, read and re-read every sign on the block.

Parking in lots and garages is usually what drivers must resort to. Prices average $25 a day but some have daily specials, which require early entrances and departures. Check the site of the New York City Department of Transportation (DOT;

DRIVING OUT OF MANHATTAN?

If you're going to Brooklyn, consider going over the Williamsburg Bridge on Delancey in the Lower East Side, or tempt fate with busy Canal St to cross the Manhattan Bridge. Most hours you can circle the southern tip of Manhattan via West Side Hwy for an easy hook-up with Brooklyn Bridge (or access from Lafayette St south of Chambers St).

The Queens-bound can either take the Queens-Midtown Tunnel (off 36th St between First and Second Aves) or the freebie Queensboro Bridge (from 60th St between First and Second Aves).

Beyond the metropolis, things are pretty easy (on paper, at least): I-95, which runs from Maine to Florida, cuts east to west through the city as the Cross Bronx Expressway (another nightmare, recognized locally as the worst roadway around). Outside New York City, I-95 continues south as the New Jersey Turnpike and north as the Connecticut Turnpike. Via I-95, Boston is 194 miles to the north, Philadelphia 104 miles to the south and Washington, DC, 235 miles south.

www.nyc.gov/html/dot/home.html) for traffic updates and alternate-side parking schedules.

Because so few city travelers will be driving, restaurant and hotel listings in this book will not list any parking icons – although many city hotels do have deals with local lots and garages, affording minor discounts.

Rental

Hiring a car in the city is mighty expensive, and though agencies advertise bargain rates for weekend or week-long rentals, these deals are almost always blacked out in New York. If you want to rent for a few days, perhaps for a road trip out of town, book through a travel agency or online before leaving home. Without a reservation, a midsize rental car will cost at least $100 per day once the extra charges – such as the 13.375% tax and various insurance costs – are factored in.

To rent a car, you need a valid driver's license and a major credit card; international visitors are advised to have an International Driving Permit (IDP), a far more credible ID for New York traffic police. The law no longer decrees that you need to be over 25 to rent, but companies are still allowed to charge younger folks a higher rate, making it prohibitively expensive for all but trust-fund kids.

Many locals rent the self-service Zipcar (☎ 212-691-2884, 866-494-7227; www.zipcar.com), an on-demand car-sharing service, with rates from $60/100 per day during weekdays/weekends (including gas, insurance and parking). It requires a $25 initiation fee. There are scores of locations around Manhattan and the other boroughs for easy pick-up.

Among the many rental agencies in the city are the following:

Avis (☎ 800-331-1212; www.avis.com)

Budget (☎ 800-527-0700; www.budget.com)

Dollar (☎ 800-800-4000; www.dollar.com)

Hertz (☎ 800-654-3131; www.hertz.com)

A friendly family-run rental place, Autoteam USA (☎ 866-438-8326, 732-727-7272; www.autoteamusa .com; South Amboy, NJ) has cars with weekly rates (including 100 free miles per day) from $26 per day. They'll pick you up from the South Amboy station on the NJ Transit line.

PEDICABS

A popular new addition to New York's crazed streets are bicycle taxis, often used for novelty rides by tourists. It's goofy, but at least it's green. Rides generally range from $15 to $30, depending on the distance and number of passengers (ask how much before getting in). For more information, contact Manhattan Rickshaw (☎ 212-604-4729; www.manhattanrickshaw.com).

SUBWAY

The New York subway's 656-mile system, run by the Metropolitan Transportation Authority (MTA), is iconic, cheap ($2 per ride), round-the-clock and easily the fastest and most reliable way to get around the city. It's also safer and (a bit) cleaner than it used to be (and now with overly cheerful automated announcements on some lines).

For subway updates and information, call ☎ 718-330-1234 or visit www.mta.info. It's a good idea to grab a free map, available from any attendant. When in doubt, ask someone who looks like they know what they're doing. They may not, but subway confusion (and consternation) is the great unifier in this diverse city. You're sure to get help.

TAXI

Hailing and riding in a cab are rites of passage in New York – especially when you get a driver who's a neurotic speed demon, which is often. Still, most taxis in NYC are clean and, compared to those in many international cities, pretty clean.

The Taxi & Limousine Commission (TLC; ☎ 311), the taxis' governing body, has set fares for rides (which can be paid with credit or debit card). It's $2.50 for the initial charge (first one-fifth of a mile), 40¢ each additional one-fifth mile as well as per 120 seconds of being stopped in traffic, $1 peak surcharge (weekdays 4pm to 8pm), and a 50¢ night surcharge (8pm to 6am). Tips are expected to be 10% to 15%, but give less if you feel in any way mistreated – and be sure to ask for a receipt and use it to note the driver's license number.

The TLC keeps a Passenger's Bill of Rights, which gives you the right to tell the driver which route you'd like to take, or ask your driver to stop smoking or turn off an annoying radio station. Also, the driver does not have the right to refuse you a ride based on where you are going.

To hail a cab, it must have a lit light on its roof. It's particularly difficult to score a taxi in the rain, at rush hour and around 4pm, when many drivers end their shifts.

SUBWAY CHEAT SHEET

A few tips for understanding the madness of the New York underground follows (see the boxed text on p392 for details on the Metrocard):

Numbers, Letters, Colors

Color-coded subway lines are named by a letter or number, and most carry a collection of two to four trains on its track. For example, the red-colored line in Manhattan is the 1, 2, 3 line; these three separate trains follow roughly the same path in Manhattan, then branch out in the Bronx and Brooklyn.

Express & Local Lines

A common mistake is accidentally boarding an 'express train' and passing by a local stop you want. Know that each color-coded line is shared by local trains and express trains (indicated by a white circle on subway maps); the latter make only select stops in Manhattan. For example, on the red line, the 2 and 3 are express, the slower 1 makes local stops. If you're covering a greater distance – say from the Upper West Side to Wall St – you're better off transferring to the express train (usually just across the platform from the local) to save time.

Getting In The Right Station

Some stations – such as SoHo's Spring St station on the 6 line – have separate entrances for downtown or uptown lines (read the sign carefully). If you swipe in the wrong one – as even crusty locals and certain LP researchers do on occasion – you'll either need to ride the subway to a station where you can transfer free, or just lose the $2 and re-enter the station (usually across the street). Also look for the green and red lamps above the stairs at each station entrance; green means that it's always open, while red means that particular entrance will be closed at certain hours, usually late at night.

Weekend Warriors

All the rules switch on weekends, when some lines combine with others, some get suspended, some stations gets passed, others get reached. Locals and tourists alike stand on platforms confused, sometimes irate. Check the www.mta.info website for weekend schedules. Sometimes posted signs aren't visible until after you reach a platform.

Privately run car services make up a common taxicab alternative in the outer boroughs. Fares differ depending on the neighborhood and length of ride, and must be determined beforehand, as they have no meters. Though these 'black cars' are quite common in Brooklyn and Queens, you should never get into one if a driver simply stops to offer you a ride – no matter what borough you're in. A couple of car services in Brooklyn include Northside (Map p177; ☎ 718-387-2222; 207 Bedford Ave) in Williamsburg, and Arecibo (Map p182; ☎ 718-783-6465; 170 Fifth Ave at Lincoln Pl) in Park Slope.

TRAIN

Penn Station (Map pp134–5; 33rd St btwn Seventh & Eighth Aves) is the departure point for all Amtrak (☎ 800-872-7245; www.amtrak.com) trains, including the *Metroliner* and *Acela Express* services to Princeton, NJ, and Washington, DC (note that both these express services will cost twice as much as a normal fare; one-way to DC starts at $69). All fares vary, based on the day of the

week and the time you want to travel. There is no baggage-storage facility at Penn Station.

Long Island Rail Road (☎ 718-217-5477; www.mta.nyc.ny.us/lirr/) serves some 280,000 commuters each day, with services from Penn Station to points in Brooklyn, Queens and to Long Island. Prices are broken down by zones. A peak-hour ride from Penn Station to Jamaica Station (en route to JFK via AirTrain) costs $6.65 if you buy it online (a whopping $12 on board!). New Jersey Transit (☎ 800-772-2222; www.njtransit.com) also operates trains from Penn Station, with services to the suburbs and the Jersey Shore.

Another option for getting into NJ's northern points such as Hoboken and Newark is the New Jersey PATH (☎ 800-234-7284; www.panynj.gov/path), which runs trains ($1.50) along the length of Sixth Ave, with stops at 33rd, 23rd, 14th, 9th and Christopher Sts, as well as at the reopened World Trade Center site.

The last line departing from Grand Central Terminal, Park Ave at 42nd St, the Metro-North Railroad (☎ 212-532-4900; www.mnr.org) serves Connecticut and the Hudson Valley.

WALKING

Screw the subway and the cabs and buses, the personal jet-pack and the hot-air balloon you packed in your bag – get on your feet and go green. New York, down deep, can't be seen until you've taken the time to hit the sidewalks: the whole thing, like Nancy Sinatra's boots, is made for pedestrian transport. Broadway runs the length of Manhattan, about 13.5 miles. Crossing the East River on the pedestrian planks of the Brooklyn Bridge is a New York classic. Central Park trails can get you to wooded pockets where you can't even see or hear the city.

For walking-tour operators, see p403. If you prefer to go it on your own, try this guidebook's walking tours, found throughout the Neighborhoods chapter (p64).

DIRECTORY

BUSINESS HOURS

Most offices are open 9am to 5pm Monday to Friday, while most shops are on a later clock, typically opening at 10am or 11am or even noon in downtown neighborhoods, and closing between 7pm and 9pm, often later on weekends. Restaurants serve breakfast from about 6am to noon, and then lunch till 3pm or 4pm, with just enough time to start serving dinner by 5pm – although prime dinner hour is more like 8pm (9pm on weekends). Most stores are open on public holidays (except Christmas Day) but banks, schools and offices are usually closed. Though most banks are open 9am to 4:30pm or 5pm Monday to Friday, a few in Chinatown have limited Saturday hours, and the Commerce Bank chain, with locations all over Manhattan, has daily hours that vary, with most open on Sundays from 11am to 4pm. Check www.commerce online.com for locations and hours.

CHILDREN

Contrary to popular belief, New York can be a child-friendly city – it just takes a bit of guidance to find all the little creature comforts that you're accustomed to having back home. When seeking accommodations, steer clear of the super-trendy boutique hotels that tend to have tiny rooms and single-person party-monster vibes (and, often, no-children policies); there are plenty of other options that welcome kids with open arms. At the Iroquois Hotel (Map pp134–5; ☎ 212-840-3080; www.iroquoisny .com; 49 W 44th St btwn Fifth & Sixth Aves; r from $350), kids are welcomed with robes and slippers and in-room Nintendo access, and parents can borrow DVDs, board games, strollers, cribs, baby bathtubs and baby-proof kits, all at no extra charge. A babysitting service is also available. The Gershwin Hotel (p360) also offers babysitting; Chambers (p361) offers kids' DVDs and stroller and car-seat rentals; and the Affinia Dumont (Map p126; ☎ 212-481-7600; www .mesuite.com; 150 E 34th St, Midtown East; r from $220) offers free cribs, high chairs and strollers. And, as a rule, the larger hotel chains – Sheraton, Hilton, Doubletree – are kid-friendly, offering babysitting services and other amenities.

For another list of more options, visit www .gocitykids.com.

Museums, especially those geared to kids, like the Children's Museum of Manhattan (p155) and the American Museum of Natural History (p152), are always great places to hit, as are children's theaters, movie theaters, book and toy stores, aquariums and kid-friendly restaurants (see the boxed text, p251). For more details, pick up Lonely Planet's *Travel with Children*. And when you get to town, get your hands on a copy of the weekly *Time Out Kids* magazine, available at newsstands.

The biggest pitfalls tend to revolve around public transportation, as a startling lack of subway-station elevators will have you lugging strollers up and down flights of stairs (though you'll avoid the turnstile by getting buzzed through an easy-access gate); you can visit www.mta.info/mta/ada to find a guide to subway stations with elevators and escalators. Strollers (unless they're folded up, sans child) are not allowed on public buses. Taxis are often the easiest option.

Visiting during warm weather tends to make things easier, as you can always resort to the many parks, playgrounds and zoos to let your kids expel some pent-up energy; the following are just a few of the great parks-with-playscapes options:

Battery Park (p75) Has a great waterfront location and various activities.

Central Park's 96th St Playground (Map p149; 96th St at Fifth Ave) Features a child-safe treehouse.

Central Park's Safari Playground (Map p149) Has a fun safari theme.

Glass Garden (Map p126; ☎ 212-263-6058; 400 E 34th St at First Ave, Midtown East; ☺ 8am-5:30pm Mon-Fri, 1-5:30pm Sat & Sun) A botanical garden, complete with koi and turtle ponds, plus the educational PlayGarden and truly fun sand pit.

Hudson River Park Playground (Map p110; Pier 51, West St btwn Horatio & Jane Sts) This riverside play area features sprinklers, a boat-theme area and a bouncy surface to play on.

Tompkins Square Park (p103) Join the hipster down-town parents and little ones who populate its three playgrounds.

Babysitting

While most major hotels (and a handful of boutique-style places) offer babysitting services, or can at least provide you with referrals, you could also turn to a local childcare organization. Baby Sitters' Guild (☎ 212-682-0227; www.babysittersguild.com), established back in 1940 specifically to serve travelers staying in hotels with children, has a stable of sitters who speak a range of 16 languages. All are carefully screened, most are CPR-certified and many have nursing backgrounds; they'll come right to your hotel room and even bring games and arts-and-crafts projects. Another good option is Pinch Sitters (☎ 212-260-6005). Both will set you back about $20 per hour.

CLIMATE

While global warming has brought recent oddities like 70°F January evenings, there is still a basic framework you can usually count on. Spring in New York is lovely – blossoming trees pop into reds and pinks, sunny days glimmer and even rainy days have a lovely, cleansing feel to them. The temperatures can still dip down to a chilly 40°F in early April evenings, but average temperatures hover at around 60°F, creating days that are perfect for strolling in the city.

Summers can be beastly, as temperatures in July and August can climb to the 100°F mark; usually it's between 70°F and 80°F, with occasional thunderstorms that light up the sky and cool everything down until the sun comes out again.

Winters, of course, are cold. It can be gray for days, with sleet and snow showers that quickly turn into a mucky brown film at your feet and temperatures that can easily dip down into the single digits come January. But a good snowstorm is a beautiful thing in these parts, and a cold night inspires cuddling, which can make for a damn romantic visit.

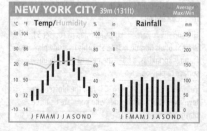

NEW YORK CITY 39m (131ft)

COURSES

New York is brimming with universities, colleges and small, focused schools where students reap the benefits of being in an artistic, culinary and cultural hotspot. Why not learn a little something while you're here? As a traveler, it's a great way to gain a different perspective on the city.

The Learning Annex (Map p126; ☎ 212-371-0280; www.learningannex.com; 16 W 53rd St btwn Fifth & Sixth Aves, Midtown East; classes $40-250), an NYC institution, is infamous for its thick catalogues, available for free in street boxes, and its wacky range of classes – feng shui, soap making, in-line skating, real estate, how to fall in love. Classes, often taught by celebs that have included Donald Trump and Suze Orman, are generally held over the course of one day or an evening.

Media Bistro (Map p126; ☎ 212-389-2000; www.media bistro.com; 475 Park Ave S btwn 31st & 32nd Sts, Midtown East; classes $65-499), a networking and educational organization for journalists and other writers, provides not only six-week courses but three-hour seminars that cover topics from Intro to Travel Writing to Pitching Your Novel and How to Write Essays about Sex. It is the perfect opportunity to rub elbows with those in the New York writers scene.

Demonstration classes at Bouley Test Kitchen (p249) enable you to learn from celeb chef David Bouley, with a single lesson ($175) that includes both food and wine tasting, plus photographs of his creations.

De Gustibus Cooking School (www.degustibusinc.com) at Macy's (p238) offers an impressive lineup of lessons at its in-store facility; subjects range from TV Inspirations (Rachael Ray and Lee Anne Wong of *Top Chef* were recent guests) and Absolutely Asian (which featured noted chef Floyd Cardoz teaching a lesson) to Knife Skills and Kosher Entertaining. Single classes average $90 per person.

You can learn to make a film in just two days at Cooper Union (Map p104; ☎ 212-353-4195; www .cooper.edu; 30 Cooper Sq btwn Fifth & Sixth Sts, East Village; $390) with Independent Filmmaking: A Crash Course, part of the Professional Development program, which takes you through writing, directing, producing and marketing.

CUSTOMS & REGULATIONS

US customs allows each person over the age of 21 to bring 1L of liquor and 200 cigarettes duty-free into the USA (smokers take note:

cigarettes cost around $8 a pack here in the big city, so take advantage of those duty-free shops). Agricultural items including meat, fruits, vegetables, plants and soil are prohibited. US citizens are allowed to import, duty-free, up to $800 worth of gifts from abroad, while non–US citizens are allowed to import $100 worth. If you're carrying more than $10,000 in US and foreign cash, traveler's checks, money orders etc, you need to declare the excess amount. There is no legal restriction on the amount that may be imported, but undeclared sums in excess of $10,000 will probably be subject to investigation. If you're bringing prescription drugs, make sure they're in clearly marked containers; and leave the illegal narcotics at home. For updates, check www.cbp.gov.

DISCOUNT CARDS

The New York City Pass (www.citypass.com), which you can purchase either online or at any major city attraction (museums, historic sites etc), buys you admission into six major attractions – the Empire State Building, the Metropolitan Museum of Art, the Museum of Modern Art, the Guggenheim Museum, the American Museum of Natural History and a Circle Line cruise, with an overall value of $131 – for just $65 ($49 for ages six to 17). New York Pass (www.newyorkpass.com), meanwhile, sells online cards for $69 ($49 for kids) and gives you daylong access to 40 top attractions (the United Nations, the Statue of Liberty, the Guggenheim etc), as well as discounts at 25 stores and restaurants. Two-, three- and seven-day passes are also available, and you can choose to collect them in NYC or have them sent to you before you leave home. The Entertainment Book (www.entertainment.com), which you can order for $20 before your arrival, is packed with passes that arm you with dining, shopping and service deals – from 20% off meals at various restaurants to free admission to the Museum of the City of New York and movie tickets for $6 (as opposed to $12).

ELECTRICITY

The US electric current is 110V to 115V, 60Hz AC. Outlets are made for flat two-prong plugs (which often have a third, rounded prong for grounding). If your appliance is made for another electrical system (eg 220V), you'll need a step-down converter, which can be bought at hardware stores and drugstores for

around $25 to $60. Most electronic devices (laptops, camera-battery chargers etc) are built for dual-voltage use, however, and will only need a plug adapter.

EMBASSIES

The presence of the UN in New York City means that nearly every country in the world maintains diplomatic offices in Manhattan. You can check the local *Yellow Pages* under 'consulates' for a complete listing. Some foreign consulates, all in Manhattan, include the following:

Australia (Map p126; ☎ 212-351-6500; www.australia nyc.org; 34th fl, 150 E 42nd St; ☙ 8:30am-5pm Mon-Fri)

Brazil (Map pp134–5; ☎ 917-777-7777; www.brazilny .org; 21st fl, 1185 Sixth Ave; ☙ 10am-noon & 2:30-4pm Mon-Fri)

Canada (Map pp134–5; ☎ 212-596-1628; www.canada -ny.org; 1251 Sixth Ave; ☙ 8:45am-5pm Mon-Fri)

France (Map p142; ☎ 212-606-3680; www.consulfrance -newyork.org; 934 Fifth Ave; ☙ 9am-1pm Mon-Fri)

Germany (Map p126; ☎ 212-610-9700; www.german .info/newyork; 871 UN Plaza; ☙ 9am-noon Mon-Fri)

India (Map p142; ☎ 212-774-0600; www.indiacny.org; 3 E 64th St; ☙ 9am-5:30pm Mon-Fri)

Japan (Map p126; ☎ 212-371-8222; www.ny.us.emb -japan.go.jp; 299 Park Ave btwn 48th & 49th Sts; ☙ 9am-5:30pm Mon-Fri)

EMERGENCIES

Poison control (☎ 800-222-1222)

Police, fire & ambulance (☎ 911)

HOLIDAYS

Following is a list of major NYC holidays and special events. These holidays may force closure of many businesses or attract crowds, making dining and accommodations reservations difficult. See p20 for a list of more specific dates.

New Year's Day January 1

Martin Luther King Day Third Monday in January

Presidents' Day Third Monday in February

Easter Mid-April

Memorial Day Late May

Gay Pride Last Sunday in June

Independence Day July 4

Labor Day Early September

Rosh Hashanah and Yom Kippur Mid-September to mid-October

Halloween October 31

Thanksgiving Fourth Thursday in November

Christmas Day December 25

New Year's Eve December 31

INTERNET ACCESS

Hotels all provide some sort of online access these days. For laptop toters, in-room services include either DSL hookups or wireless access, often for fees averaging $10 a day. Travelers without laptops can almost always find monitors available for use in a hotel's lobby or business center. Around the city, you can find service on street corners in the form of more than 100 TCC Internet Phones, found mostly in Midtown but also sprinkled throughout the East Village, SoHo, Chinatown and on the Upper East Side. They cost $1 for four minutes, though NYC information websites are free.

The mid-Manhattan branch of the New York Public Library (Map p126; ☎ 212-930-0800; 455 Fifth Ave at 40th St) offers free half-hour internet access, though there may be a wait in the afternoons; more than 80 other local branches also have free access and usually with no wait; for locations, visit www.nypl.org/branch/local. There are many wi-fi access hotspots around the city; see the boxed text, below, for a guide.

At internet cafés, you can surf the net for an hourly fee, which ranges from $1 to $12, or log onto wi-fi access, sometimes free and sometimes for a fee. Try the following places, all with their own distinct vibe:

Cyber Café (Map pp134–5; ☎ 212-333-4109; 250 W 49th St btwn Broadway & Eighth Ave, Midtown West; per 30min $6.40, minimum 30min; ☺ 8am-11pm Mon-Fri, 11am-11pm Sat & Sun) High-speed computers with color printers, scanners and web cams, plus coffee and wine bar.

Easy Internet Café (Map pp134–5; ☎ 212-398-0724; 234 W 42nd St, Midtown West; per hr $2; ☺ 24hr) This is the cheapest, and possibly the biggest, place in town.

FedEx Kinko's (www.fedexkinkos.com) Many locations of this chain of copy shops include computers with internet access. See the website for locations.

LGBT Community Center (Map p110; ☎ 212-620-7310; 208 W 13th St, West Village; suggested donation $3) The cyber-center here has 15 computers, open to all.

Web2Zone (Map pp88–9; ☎ 212-614-7300; 54 Cooper Sq btwn Astor Pl & Fourth Ave, NoHo; per hr $5; ☺ 9am-11pm Mon-Fri, 10am-11pm Sat, noon-10pm Sun) Also has extensive printing and design services, plus computer games.

LEGAL MATTERS

If you're arrested, you have the right to remain silent. There is no legal reason to speak to a police officer if you don't wish to – especially since anything you say 'can and will be used against you' – but never walk away from an officer until given permission. All persons who are arrested have the legal right to make one phone call. If you don't have a lawyer or family member to help you, call your consulate. The police will give you the number upon request.

MAPS

Lonely Planet publishes a pocket-size laminated map of New York City, available at most bookstores. You can also pick up free Manhattan maps in the lobby of any decent hotel and at tourist information booths run by NYC & Company (p408). If you want to explore the city at large, buy a five-borough street atlas, published by the Long Island City, Queens-based Hagstrom company, which also makes great maps of the individual boroughs.

Most subway stations in Manhattan have Passenger Information Centers next to the

WI-FI ACCESS

New York is not totally wired, and is frustratingly behind other cities when it comes to free access spots – especially in the area airports, with the Jet Blue terminal at JFK currently the only airport spot with free access (others charge fees) in the New York area. Once you're in the city, hotspots are not constant, but there are many. NYC Wireless (www .nycwireless.net) is a local free-wi-fi activist team and has an online map of free access points, which requires sign-in; the group has advocated for free hotspots in public parks including Bryant Park, Tompkins Square Park and Union Square Park. You'll find free hotspots on the campus of Columbia University (p159), at South Street Seaport (p80) and at businesses including Apple stores (p220 and p229), Chelsea Market (p115), Soy Luck Club (p258) and, oddly enough, the bar Fat Black Pussycat (Map p110; ☎ 212-533-4790; 130 W 3rd St), where you can surf while sipping an apple martini. Note that while all the hundreds of Starbucks in the city are wired, you'll be required to sign up for an account, which will run to about $7 an hour – not to mention that $4 latte.

token booths; they feature wonderfully large-scale, detailed maps of the surrounding neighborhood, with all points of interest clearly marked. Taking a look before heading aboveground may save you from getting lost. You can also get free subway and bus maps from the attendant inside any subway token booth.

You can buy maps at any bookstore (Barnes & Noble, p232, usually has the biggest selection); if you're on a jaunt outside of the city, gas stations sell good local road maps.

MEDICAL SERVICES

Healthcare is a major problem in this country, as there is no federal law guaranteeing medical care for all citizens, and health insurance is extremely costly. People living below the poverty line are eligible for Medicaid, which covers many costs, and seniors can apply for Medicare, which works in a similar way. But know that, as a visitor, all hospital emergency rooms are obliged to see you whether you can pay or not (you'll just be in for an insanely long and unpleasant wait, as city emergency rooms are not known for their efficiency).

Clinics

If you're sick or injured, but not in bad enough shape for an emergency room, try one of the following options:

Bolte Medical Urgent Care Center (☎ 212-588-9314; www.boltemedical.com; 141 E 55th St at Lexington Ave, Midtown East) This clinic offers same-day appointments for illness diagnosis.

Callen-Lorde Community Health Center (Map p116; ☎ 212-271-7200; www.callen-lorde.org; 356 W 18th St btwn Eighth & Ninth Aves, Chelsea) This medical center, dedicated to the LGBT community and people living with HIV/AIDS, serves people regardless of their ability to pay.

Duane Reade Walk-In Medical Care (www.drwalkin.com) A new feature of the Duane Reade drugstore chain is the walk-in clinic, where a local-hospital-affiliated doctor is available for diagnosis and treatment. Manhattan has four locations and Brooklyn has two (see the website for details); a posted care menu onsite lists all fees.

New York County Medical Society (☎ 212-684-4670; www.nycms.org) Makes doctor referrals by phone based on type of problem and language spoken.

Planned Parenthood (Map pp88–9; ☎ 212-965-7000; www.plannedparenthood.com; 26 Bleecker St, NoHo) Provides birth control, STD screenings and gynecological care.

Travel MD (☎ 212-737-1212; www.travelmd.com) A collection of physicians who specifically care for visitors

to NYC; you can call to request a house call in your hotel room, or make an appointment to visit its East Side office.

Emergency Rooms

New York City emergency rooms are like the ninth circle of hell. Avoid them at all costs. For when you really can't avoid one, consult the local phone directory for a complete listing and prepare for a miserable visit that'll average four hours (unless you're in really dire shape). Following are some major hospitals with emergency rooms that have been rated among the least horrific:

Bellevue Hospital Center (Map p126; ☎ 212-562-1000; 462 First Ave at 27th St)

Lenox Hill Hospital (Map p142; ☎ 212-434-2000; 100 E 77th St at Lexington Ave)

Mount Sinai Hospital (Map p142; ☎ 212-241-6500; 1190 Fifth Ave at 100th St)

New York-Presbyterian Hospital (Map pp158–9; ☎ 212-305-6204; 622 168th St at Ft Washington Ave)

St Vincent's Medical Center (Map p110; ☎ 212-604-7000; 153 W 11th St at Greenwich Ave)

Pharmacies

New York is practically bursting with 24-hour 'pharmacies,' which are handy all-purpose stores where you can buy over-the-counter medications anytime; the actual pharmaceutical prescription counters have more limited hours. Those with 24-hour prescription counters include a downtown Rite Aid (Map p142; ☎ 212-529-7115; 508 Grand St at Clinton St, Upper East Side) and a Midtown CVS (Map pp134–5; ☎ 212-245-0636; 400 W 58th St at Ninth Ave).

MONEY

The US dollar (familiarly called a 'buck') is divided into 100 cents (¢). Coins come in denominations of 1¢ (penny), 5¢ (nickel), 10¢ (dime), 25¢ (quarter), the practically extinct 50¢ (half-dollar), and the not-oft-seen golden dollar coin, which was introduced in early 2000, featuring a picture of Sacagawea, the Native American guide who led the explorers Lewis and Clark on their expedition through the western US. Although striking, the gold coins are prohibitively heavy and jingle conspicuously, alerting panhandlers to your well-heeled presence. These coins are often dispensed as change from ticket and stamp machines. Notes come in $1, $2 (extremely rare), $5, $10, $20, $50 and $100 denominations.

In recent years the US treasury has redesigned the $5, $10, $20, $50 and $100 bills to foil counterfeiters. Yes, they're still green, but the portraits have grown exponentially. To check the exchange rate (though it changes daily), see the Quick Reference guide inside this book's front cover.

ATMs

Automatic teller machines are on practically every corner. You can either use your card at banks – usually in a 24-hour-access lobby, filled with up to a dozen monitors at major branches – or you can opt for the lone wolves, which sit in delis, restaurants, bars and grocery stores, charging fierce service fees that go as high as $5 for foreign banks in some places. Most New York banks are linked by the New York Cash Exchange (NYCE) system, and you can use local bank cards interchangeably at ATMs – for an extra fee if you're banking outside your system. Getting money this way saves you a step – no changing money from your own currency – and is a safer way to travel, as you only take out what you need, as you go.

Changing Money

Banks and moneychangers, found all over New York City (and right in the airports where you'll land), will give you US currency based on the current exchange rate. Banks are normally open from 9am to 4:30pm or 5pm Monday to Friday. A couple of options:

American Express (Map p126; ☎ 212-421-8240, for locations 800-221-7282; 374 Park Ave at 53rd St, Midtown East; ☺ 9am-5pm Mon-Fri) American Express has plenty of branches about town.

Travelex (Map pp134–5; ☎ 212-265-6049; 1590 Broadway at 48th St, Midtown East; ☺ 9am-7pm Mon-Sat, 9am-5pm Sun) Features currency exchange at eight locations in the city, including the Times Sq office.

Credit Cards

Major credit cards are accepted at most hotels, restaurants and shops throughout New York City. In fact, you'll find it difficult to perform certain transactions, such as purchasing tickets to performances and renting a car, without one.

Stack your deck with a Visa, MasterCard or American Express, as these are the cards of choice here. Places that accept Visa and MasterCard also accept debit cards, which deduct payments directly from your check or savings account. Be sure to check with your bank to confirm that your debit card will be accepted in other states or countries – debit cards from large commercial banks can often be used worldwide.

If your cards are lost or stolen, contact the company immediately. The following are toll-free numbers for the main credit-card companies:

American Express (☎ 800-528-4800)

Diners Club (☎ 800-234-6377)

Discover (☎ 800-347-2683)

MasterCard (☎ 800-826-2181)

Visa (☎ 800-336-8472)

Traveler's Checks

This old-school option offers protection from theft or loss. Checks issued by American Express and Thomas Cook are widely accepted, and both offer efficient replacement policies. Keeping a record of the check numbers and the checks you've used is vital when it comes to replacing lost checks. Keep this record in a separate place from the checks themselves.

Bring most of the checks in large denominations. It's toward the end of a trip that you may want to change a small check to make sure you aren't left with too much local currency. Of course, traveler's checks are losing their popularity due to the explosion of ATMs and you may opt not to carry any at all.

NEWSPAPERS & MAGAZINES

There are scads of periodicals to choose from – but what else would you expect from one of the media capitals of the world? Daily newspapers include the following:

AM New York (www.amny.com) Metro's big competition, this is also a thin, weekday-only daily, geared toward subway commuters.

Metro (www.metro.us) Part of a three-city chain that includes Philadelphia and Boston, this thin, weekday-only daily, geared toward subway commuters, delivers the major news in well-written, easy-to-swallow bits.

New York Amsterdam News (www.amsterdamnews.org) This is the weekly newspaper covering African American news.

New York Daily News (www.nydailynews.com) One of two sensationalistic tabloids, this is slightly more staid in tone than the Post.

New York Observer (www.nyobserver.com) The salmon-colored broadsheet is obsessed with insidery news and gossip of the uptown sort.

New York Post (www.newyorkpost.com) The *Post* is known for screaming headlines, conservative political views and its popular Page Six gossip column.

New York Press (www.nypress.com) The alternative weekly that forced the *Voice* to go free; expect lots of first-person ramblings and a witty edge, plus lots of arts write-ups.

New York Sun (www.nysun.com) The newest broadsheet in town covers everything, with a slightly conservative slant.

New York Times (www.nytimes.com) 'The gray lady' has gotten hip in recent years, with new sections on technology, arts and dining out.

Village Voice (www.villagevoice.com) Owned by national alternative-newspaper chain New Times, the legendary *Voice* has less bite but still plenty of bark. It's home to everyone's favorite gossip columnist, Michael Musto.

The Villager (www.thevillager.com) A local neighborhood weekly, this well-reported paper is a great source of downtown news.

Wall Street Journal (www.wallstreetjournal.com) This intellectual daily has a focus on finance – though its new owner, media mogul Rupert Murdoch, plans to ratchet up the coverage to rival that of the *Times*.

Magazines that give a good sense of the local flavor include the following:

City Limits (www.citylimits.org) This monthly magazine covers planning, housing and nonprofit worlds for urban planners, organizers and anyone seriously interested in what makes this city tick.

Gotham Magazine (www.nymetro.com) This slick glossy focuses on heavy hitters and fashion and style trends.

New York Magazine (www.nymetro.com) The weekly magazine has feature stories and great listings about anything and everything in NYC, with an indispensable website.

The New Yorker (www.newyorker.com) The highbrow weekly covers politics and culture through its famously lengthy works of reportage, and also publishes fiction and poetry.

Paper (www.papermag.com) This hip monthly favors celebrities, fashion, art and film.

Time Out New York (www.timeout.com) A weekly magazine, its focus is on being complete (as you'll see from its bible-like listings on everything cultural) plus articles and interviews on arts and entertainment.

ORGANIZED TOURS

Sometimes it's nice to just follow someone blindly and learn lessons along the way.

Here are some of the city's most dynamic tour guides:

Adventure on a Shoestring (☎ 212-265-2663; $5) Shoestring founder and tour guide Howard Goldberg believes people deserve to get *more* than their money's worth, not just their money's worth. He leads neighborhood-based tours and themed walks, such as his Salute to Jacqueline Kennedy Onassis. 'We've done tours in driving rain, blackouts and subway strikes,' Goldberg says. What a perfect way to learn about NYC's fortitude.

Afoot Walking Tours (☎ 212-939-0994; www.erickwashington.com; $15) The focus here is a geographically unique one: Manhattanville, a subject that guide Eric K Washington has authored two books on. The neighborhood is an old West Harlem enclave around Broadway and 125th St; get to know it through Eric's lively walks that look at African American history. You can also choose from tours of Sugar Hill, an architecturally rich region in the northern part of Harlem, or the beautiful northern stretch of Riverside Park.

Big Apple Greeter Program (☎ 212-669-8159; www.bigapplegreeter.org; free) If you find NYC a bit overwhelming – and who wouldn't? – call to set up an intimate stroll, in the neighborhood of your choice, led by a local volunteer who just can't wait to show off his or her city to you. You'll be matched with a guide that suits your needs, whether that means speaking Spanish or American Sign Language, or knowing just where to find the best wheelchair-accessible spots in the city.

Big Onion Walking Tours (☎ 212-439-1090; www.bigonion.com; $15) 'Each tour has a very extensive script,' says Big Onion founder Seth Kamil. It's that attention to fine detail in this grand city that makes the award-winning Big Onion – whose tours 'explore the many layers of history' – stand apart, and gives it a stellar reputation. Choose from nearly 30 tours, including Brooklyn Bridge and Brooklyn Heights, the 'Official' Gangs of New York Tour, A Gay and Lesbian History Tour – Before Stonewall, and Park Slope.

Bike the Big Apple (☎ 877-865-0078; www.bikethebigapple.com; incl bike & helmet $70-80) Biking tours let you cover more ground than walking tours – and give you a healthy dose of exercise to boot. Bike the Big Apple, recommended by NYC & Company, offers five set tours. Its most popular is the six-hour Back to the Old Country – the Ethnic Apple Tour, 12 miles of riding that covers Williamsburg, Roosevelt Island and the east side of Manhattan. Other tours visit the Bronx's Little Italy, city parks, Brooklyn chocolate shops and Manhattan at night.

Chinatown Tours (Map p94; ☎ 212-619-4785; www.moca-nyc.org; Museum of Chinese in America, 215 Centre St, Chinatown; $10) To truly penetrate the layers that make up the bustling, insiders' world of Chinatown, you need a guide. And trusting one from the Chinatown-based

Museum of Chinese in America (p93) is definitely a good move. The tours, given weekly from May through December, are led by museum docents with family roots in the community, and focus on varying aspects of the 'hood that give you a sense of Chinatown's past and present.

Circle Line Boat Tours (Map pp134–5; ☎ 212-563-3200; www.circleline42.com; 42nd St at Twelfth Ave, Midtown West; $20-29.50) The classic Circle Line – whose local 1970s TV-commercial song is now the stuff of kitschy nostalgia – guides you through all the big sights from the safe distance of a boat that circumnavigates the five boroughs. It's got a bar on board and has a bit of a party reputation (especially its two-hour evening cruise); other options include a three-hour day trip and an abbreviated 75-minute journey.

Foods of New York (☎ 212-239-1124; www.foodsofny .com; $40-75) The official foodie tour of NYC & Company offers various three-hour tours that help you eat your way through gourmet shops in either Chelsea or the West Village. Prepare thyself for a moving feast of French bread, fresh Italian pasta, sushi, global cheeses, real New York pizza, local fish and fresh-baked pastries.

Gray Line (☎ 212-397-2620; www.newyorksightseeing .com; $50-75) The most ubiquitous guided tour in the city, Gray Line is responsible for bombarding New York streets with the red double-decker buses that locals love to hate. Really, though, for a comprehensive tour of the big sights, it's a great way to go. The company offers nearly 30 different options, the best being both the popular hop-on, hop-off loops of Manhattan. Tours are available in various languages, including Japanese, French, German and Italian.

Greenwich Village Literary Pub Crawl (Map p110; ☎ 212-613-5796; www.bakerloo.org/pubcrawl; White Horse Tavern, 567 Hudson Ave at 11th St, West Village; $15) Every lit-head's heard about Dylan Thomas meeting his alcoholic fate at the White Horse Tavern. But what was the real deal? Join this troupe of Bakerloo actors who take you for drinks at a lineup of neighborhood pubs; actors play the part of different writers and share stories about themselves and the surroundings from back in the day. The group meets Saturdays at 2pm at the White Horse Tavern (p292).

Hip-Hop Look at New York (Map p126; ☎ 212-714-3527; www.hushtours.com; Hush Tours, 252 Fifth Ave btwn 30th & 31st Sts, Midtown East; $15-55) Learn about the true roots of local hip-hop with a bus or walking tour led by a 'hip-hop pioneer' (Kool DJ Herc, LA Sunshine and Raheim among them) through Manhattan and the Bronx, complete with a soul-food meal, a dance performance and a freestylin' battle at the end. To really show some bling, pony up the $1500 for a private tour led by hip-hop royalty.

Kramer's Reality Tour (Map pp134–5; ☎ 212-268-5525, 800-572-6377; Producers Club Theater, 358 W 44th St,

Midtown West; $37.50) *Seinfeld* may be ancient TV history by now, but this quirky bus tour given by the real inspiration for the Kramer character is still going strong. Its focus is, of course, locales made famous by the hit series. For die-hard fans only.

Liberty Helicopter Tours (Map pp134–5; ☎ 212-967-6464; www.libertyhelicopters.com; Twelfth Ave at 30th St & East River's Pier 6; per person 2-30min $75-204, 15min Romance Over Manhattan for up to 4 people $849) Enjoy a bird's-eye view of the city in a very Donald Trump sort of way, as a helicopter whisks you high above the skyscrapers. Just get ready to shell out for the privilege.

Municipal Art Society (☎ 212-439-1049; www.mas.org; $15) With an expert focus on architecture, this nonprofit society is dedicated to championing urban design. It takes groups on walking or bus tours of structural gems, including those of Madison Ave, Bedford-Stuyvesant and Jackson Heights. Its most popular is a walk-through of the Beaux-Arts Grand Central Terminal. See the website for schedules.

New York Gallery Tours (Map p116; ☎ 212-946-1548; www.nygallerytours.com; 526 W 26th St at Tenth Ave; $20) You know you're supposed to check out the array of amazing modern-art galleries in Chelsea. But where to begin? This excellent guided tour – with additional gay and lesbian tours that focus on a 'queer aesthetic' – takes you to a slew of galleries and provides helpful commentary along the way.

NY Tour Goddess New York Tours (☎ 212-535-7798; www.nytourgoddess.com; per hr $150, negotiable with group bookings) Quirky guide Jane Marx, who's made careers of acting, writing and teaching, blends all of her talents for a huge range of tours that focus on providing intimate portraits of her city. 'I'm off the wall,' she admits. 'But I'm so knowledgeable.' Tours, which are not cheap, range from Wall St and Little Italy to Union Sq and Harlem.

On Location Tours (☎ 212-209-3370; www.screentours .com; $18-42) Face it: you want to sit on Carrie Bradshaw's apartment stoop and visit the design studio from *Will & Grace*. This company offers four tours – covering *Sex and the City, The Sopranos,* general TV and movie locations, and movie locations in Central Park – that let you live out your entertainment-obsessed fantasies. A couple of the tours are also available in German.

Phototrek Tours (☎ 212-410-2514; www.phototrek tours.com; $125-175) If the photo record of your trip is just as – if not more – important than the experience itself (you know who you are), let guide and photographer Marc Samuels (or a member of his capable staff) lead you through some of the most picturesque spots in the city, and take professional photos of you in front of each one. Choose from Central Park, Midtown and downtown; tours are for private groups or couples only.

Rock Junket New York City (☎ 212-209-3370; www .rockjunket.com; $29) Join rockin' guide Bobby Pinn each

Saturday at 11am for a two-hour tour that relives the good ol' East Village days of punk and glam rock. Learn cool tidbits about CBGB, the Ramones, the New York Dolls, the Velvet Underground, Fillmore East, Iggy Pop and others through onsite visits and in-the-know discourse. Tours sell out quickly, so buy in advance, online.

A Slice of Brooklyn Pizza Tour (☎ 212-209-3370; www .bknypizza.com; incl pizza $75) The effusive Brooklyn Borough president Marty Markowitz just loves this focused tour. And who wouldn't want to spend more than four hours downing a gut-busting range of insanely delicious slices, from the brick-oven Neapolitan style of Grimaldi's to the authentic Sicilian squares of L&B Spumoni Gardens? A guide mouths off about the neighborhoods of Bay Ridge, Red Hook, Bensonhurst and more while you're chewing.

Tours of the City with Justin Ferate (☎ 212-223-2777; www.justinsnewyork.com; free-$325) A former educator and tour director, Ferate, who also has a background in architecture, now pours all of his knowledge into his extensive tours. He offers a free trip through Grand Central Terminal and Midtown every Friday, as well as intensive walking tours that, as part of the continuing education program of the Cooper Union college, focus on a different neighborhood each week.

Watson Adventures Scavenger Hunts (☎ 212-726-1529; www.watsonadventures.com; $20-30) Go beyond walking and talking with Watson, which turns each tour into a game by making you hunt for things – be it answers to interesting questions or quirky items – as you go about your journey. Tours vary, but most are great for children, such as hunts in both the Metropolitan Museum of Art and Museum of Natural History, which have you scour the grounds for mummies, knights and bones.

Wildman Steve Brill (☎ 914-835-2153; www.wildman stevebrill.com; sliding scale $15) New York's best-known naturalist – betchya didn't know there were any! – has been leading folks on foraging expeditions through city parks for more than 20 years. He'll trek with you through Central Park, Prospect Park, Inwood Park and many more, teaching you to identify natural riches including sassafras, chickweed, ginkgo nuts, garlic and wild mushrooms along the way. It's wild.

PHOTOGRAPHY
Still lugging around that old school, film-using camera? It's okay, there are plenty of places to drop it off for developing. You can of course do the same with your digital-camera card, getting photos transferred either onto a disk or printed (or both) while you wait. Ubiquitous chains including Rite Aid, CVS and Duane Reade all have photo counters, most equipped with machines that allow you to read your digital card and edit which pho-

tos you want printed. For cameras or photo equipment, head to a photo shop such as B&H Photo-Video (p238), in Midtown, or J&R Music and Computer World (p218) in Lower Manhattan. For prints, both film and digital, you'll find several high-quality photo labs used by professionals, in the blocks of 20th to 24th Sts between Fifth and Sixth Aves; Duggal (Map p120; ☎ 212-924-8100; 29 W 23rd St btwn Fifth & Sixth Aves) is a fine example.

POST
Rates for sending mail go up every few years, and with increasing frequency it seems. With the latest increase, rates for first-class mail within the USA are 42¢ for letters up to 1oz and 27¢ for postcards. For package and international letter rates, which vary, check with the post office or with the online postal rate calculator (http://postcalc.usps.gov). For whatever postal questions you may have, call ☎ 800-275-8777 or visit the US Post Office (www.usps.com) website.

The beautiful New York General Post Office (Map pp134–5; ☎ 212-967-8585; James A Foley Bldg, 380 W 33rd St at Eighth Ave; 24hr) can help with all your postal requirements, as can the various branch offices, which are listed on the website. Alternatives to post-office mailing include various mail stores, such as the chain Mailboxes Etc (www .mbe.com), which has many options around Manhattan. The upside is there's always a much shorter wait, and there are more branches to choose from; the downside is that it's much more expensive.

RADIO
NYC has some mighty excellent radio options beyond the commercial, pop-music dreck. An excellent programming guide can be found in the *New York Times* entertainment section on Sunday. Below are some of the top station picks, all of which can be heard online:

East Village Radio (www.eastvillageradio.com) The community radio with music, talk and political chatter is available online only.

WBAI 99.5FM (www.wbai.org) Hear political talk and news with an activist bent, with highlights including shows like *Democracy Now!*, on this local Pacifica Radio affiliate.

WFUV 90.7FM (www.wfuv.org) Fordham University's radio station features excellent indie music – folk, rock and otherwise alternative-type sounds – as well as personable DJs. It has NPR news at the top of the hour.

WLIB 1190AM (www.airamericaradio.com) This Air America station, featuring 24-hour left-leaning talk, is in sharp contrast to the conservative talk shows that fill up the AM dial.

WNYC 93.9FM and 820AM (www.wnyc.org) NYC's public radio station is the local NPR affiliate, offering a blend of national and local talk and interview shows, with a switch to classical music in the day on the FM station.

WOR 710AM (www.wor710.com) A talk-show station, it features local maven Joan Hamburg, who doles out pithy advice on where to eat, shop and travel; you'll also hear the national Dr Joy Brown Show, with a call-in therapy format.

RELOCATING

Depending on where you're arriving from, moving to NYC can be a difficult experience. Sure, it's exciting to know you'll be residing in the center of the universe. But that location has a price – both financial and emotional. The financial one is not to be taken lightly because, as of this writing, the monthly rent for an average one-bedroom apartment in Manhattan was $3500. Buyers beware, too, as the median purchase price for a Manhattan one-bedroom apartment was $828,000. There are ways around this, of course, which include opting for an outer borough (though trendy parts of Brooklyn match Manhattan prices these days), finding a roommate or seeking out an illegal sublet from someone who's flown the coop but isn't quite ready to give up his or her rent-controlled pad. If you opt for an outer borough, know that, depending on where you work, you could be in for a long commute, most likely on the subway. City neighborhoods vary greatly, so getting a feel for one by hanging out in it at different times of the day is a good thing to do before plunking down any money. For overviews of what to expect, thorough neighborhood orientations and other services, speak to your real-estate broker; many have folks on staff to help out specifically with relocations. Also, the **International Center in New York** (Map p120; ☎ 212-255-9555; www.intlcenter.org; 50 W 23rd St btwn Fifth & Sixth Aves), founded in 1961 as a community resource where new immigrants, students and other newcomers can practice English and learn about American culture, can lend some helpful support.

SAFETY

Crime rates here remain at their lowest in years. There are few neighborhoods remaining where you might feel scared (and that's mainly in the outer boroughs), no matter what time of night it is. Subway stations are generally safe, too, though some in low-income neighborhoods, especially in the outer boroughs, can be dicey. There's no reason to be paranoid, but it's better to be safe than sorry, so use common sense: don't walk around alone at night in unfamiliar, sparsely populated areas, especially if you're a woman. Don't flash money around on the street, and keep your valuables somewhere safe. Unless you must accessorize with the real thing, leave the good jewelry at home. Carry your daily walking-around money somewhere inside your clothing (in a money belt, bra or sock) rather than in a handbag or an outside pocket, and be aware of pickpockets in particularly mobbed areas, like Times Sq or Penn Station at rush hour.

TAXES

Restaurants and retailers never include the sales tax – 8.375% – in their prices, so beware of ordering the $4.99 lunch special when you only have $5 to your name. Several categories of so-called 'luxury items,' including rental cars and dry-cleaning, carry an additional city surcharge of 5%, so you wind up paying an extra 13.375% in total for these services. Clothing and footwear purchases under $110 are tax-free; anything over that amount has a state sales tax of 4.375%. Hotel rooms in New York City are subject to a 13.625% tax, plus a flat $2- to $6-per-night occupancy tax. Since the US has no nationwide value-added tax (VAT), there is no opportunity for foreign visitors to make 'tax-free' purchases.

TELEPHONE

Phone numbers within the USA consist of a three-digit area code followed by a seven-digit local number. If you're calling long distance, dial ☎ 1 + the three-digit area code + the seven-digit number.

For local and national directory assistance, dial ☎ 1 + 212 + 555-1212. As part of a miraculous citywide system, you can dial ☎ 311 for any issues that are city-related – whether you have a noise complaint, have a question about parking regulations or simply want to find the nearest dog run. Operators are available 24 hours and will quickly connect you to the government office that'll best be able to serve you.

If you're calling NYC from abroad, the international country code for the USA is 1.

To dial an international number directly from NYC, dial ☎ 011, then the country code, followed by the area code and phone number. (To find country codes, check the phone book or dial ☎ 411 and ask for an international operator.) International rates vary depending on the time of day and the destination.

In New York City, Manhattan phone numbers are in the 212 or 646 area code (although cell phones and some businesses use a 917 area code) and the four outer boroughs are in the 718 or 347 zone. No matter where you're calling within New York City, even if it's just across the street in the same area code, you must *always* dial 1 + the area code first.

All toll-free numbers are prefixed with an 800, 877, 866 or 888 area code. Some toll-free numbers for local businesses or government offices only work within a limited region. But most toll-free phone numbers can be dialed from abroad – just be aware that you'll be connected at regular long-distance rates, which could become a costly option if the line you're dialing regularly parks customers on hold.

Cell Phones

Mobile phones, known in the US as 'cell phones,' have taken over the city; plans are even underway to make reception available in the subways. New Yorkers are totally in love with their phones (or, increasingly, their iPhones), which are part communication device and part status symbol here. But as a traveler, you really don't need a cell phone in the city, especially with the preponderance of pay phones. Plus, service can be less than stellar, with several silent zones around town. If you can't do without one, you'll find many tiny storefronts – most run by Verizon, T-Mobile or AT&T – where you can buy a cheap phone and load it up with prepaid minutes, thus avoiding a long-term contract.

Pay Phones

Though they seem outmoded, pay phones still exist on NYC streets and are almost always available. Just don't expect to find any phone booths like the kind that Superman changed in, unless you seek out one of the very few left in existence, such as one on the Upper West Side at West End Ave and 101st St.

To use a pay phone, you can pump in quarters, use a phone credit or debit card or make collect calls. There are thousands of pay telephones on the New York City streets,

all with a seemingly different price scheme, though most (especially the Verizon phones, which have yellow handles) are 50¢ for untimed local calls.

You can also make long-distance calls at global calling stations, which have low by-the-minute rates; you'll find them all over the city, but especially in and around Times Sq.

Phonecards

An excellent long-distance alternative is phone debit cards, which allow you to pay in advance, with access through a toll-free 800 number. In amounts of $5, $10, $20 and $50, these are available from Western Union, machines in airports and train stations, some supermarkets and nearly every corner deli. Certain cards deliver better value depending on where you're calling (eg New York Alliance is better for Brazil, while Payless is better for Ireland) and the purveyors of the cards can usually provide accurate information.

TIME

New York City is in the Eastern Standard Time (EST) zone – five hours behind Greenwich Mean Time, two hours ahead of Mountain Standard Time (including Denver, Colorado) and three hours ahead of Pacific Standard Time (San Francisco and Los Angeles, California). Almost all of the USA observes daylight-saving time: clocks go forward one hour from the second Sunday in March to the last Saturday in October, when the clocks are turned back one hour. (It's easy to remember by the phrase 'spring ahead, fall back.')

TOILETS

The most exciting toilet news to hit NYC in years has been the addition of a public pay toilet at the edge of Madison Square Park (p121). It's the first of a planned 20 for the city, and costs just a quarter to hop in and do your business. Besides this, though, New York is downright hostile to the weak of bladder or bowels. The explosion in the homeless population in the 1970s led to the closure of subway facilities, and most places turn away non-patrons from bathrooms. But there are a few public loos left, including those in Grand Central Terminal, Penn Station and Port Authority Bus Terminal, and in parks including Battery Park, Tompkins Square Park, Washington Square Park and Columbus Park in Chinatown, plus many scattered around Central Park. The best bet, though, is to pop into a Starbucks (there's one about every three blocks) and head straight to the bathroom in back.

TOURIST INFORMATION

The most reliable tourist information can be found either online or at official city kiosks and offices.

Brooklyn Tourism & Visitors Center (Map p174; ☎ 718-802-3846; Brooklyn Borough Hall, 209 Joralemon St btwn Court & Adams Sts; ⏰ 10am-6pm Mon-Fri) Get all sorts of info on the other favorite borough.

NYC & Company (Map pp134–5; ☎ 212-484-1200; www.nycvisit.com; 810 Seventh Ave btwn 52nd & 53rd Sts) The city's official tourism arm is the extremely helpful NYC & Company, which offers maps and all sorts of pamphlets at its four locations, and endless useful stuff online, from upcoming special events and various discounts to historic tidbits and security updates. Other branches include Lower Manhattan (Map pp72–3; City Hall Park at Broadway), Harlem (Map pp158–9; 163 W 125th St at Adam Clayton Powell Blvd) and Chinatown (Map p94; Canal, Walker & Baxter Sts).

Times Square Visitors Center (Map pp134–5; ☎ 212-768-1569; www.timessquarenyc.org; Seventh Ave btwn 46th & 47th Sts) This information center, run by the Times Square Business Improvement District, offers pamphlets, maps and tourism counselors who can advise you in 10 different languages.

TRAVELERS WITH DISABILITIES

Federal laws guarantee that all government offices and facilities are accessible to the disabled. For information on specific places, you can contact the mayor's Office for People with Disabilities (☎ 212-788-2830; ⏰ 9am-5pm Mon-Fri), which will send you a free copy of its *Access New York* guide if you call and request it. Another excellent resource is the Society for Accessible Travel & Hospitality (SATH; Map p126; ☎ 212-447-7284; www.sath.org; 347 Fifth Ave at 34th St; ⏰ 9am-5pm), which gives advice on how to travel with a wheelchair, kidney disease, sight impairment or deafness.

Though New York is congested and difficult to navigate, things are improving slowly but surely; buses, which all have wheelchair elevation systems and ride space, are definitely the way to go. Subways, on the other hand, are either on elevated tracks or deep below ground and there are very few elevators to access them. For detailed information

on subway and bus wheelchair accessibility, call the Accessible Line (☎ 718-596-8585) or visit www.mta.info/mta/ada for a list of subway stations with elevators or escalators. Also visit NYC & Company (www.nycvisit.com); click on 'NYC & Company' and then 'Travelers with Disabilities' for more tips.

Movie and Broadway theaters have areas reserved for wheelchairs, and sometimes the newer movie theaters even have these seats near the front, rather than stuck in the back; Broadway theaters also provide live audio description devices for blind theatergoers.

VISAS

Because of the ever-lingering fear of terrorism, foreigners needing visas to travel to the US should plan ahead. However, there is a reciprocal visa-waiver program in which citizens of certain countries may enter the USA for stays of 90 days or less with a passport but without first obtaining a US visa. There are 27 countries included in this plan, including Australia, France, Germany, Italy, Japan, the Netherlands, Switzerland and the UK (for a complete list, visit www.cbp.gov). Under this program you must have a round-trip ticket that is nonrefundable in the USA, and you will not be allowed to extend your stay beyond 90 days.

Other travelers will need to obtain a visa from a US consulate or embassy. In most countries, the process can be done by mail. Visa applicants may be required to 'demonstrate binding obligations' that will ensure their return home. Because of this requirement, those planning to travel through other countries before arriving in the USA are generally better off applying for their US visa while they are still in their home country – rather than after they're already on the road.

The Non-Immigrant Visitors Visa is the most common visa. It is available in two forms, B1 for business purposes and B2 for tourism or visiting friends and relatives. The validity period for US visitor visas depends on which country you're from. The length of time you'll be allowed to stay in the USA is ultimately determined by US immigration authorities at the port of entry. Non-US citizens with HIV should know that they can be excluded from entry to the USA.

Finally, all visa information is very likely to change, as the federal government is actively making changes all the time due to security situations. For updates on visas and other security issues, you can visit the government's visa page (www.unitedstatesvisas.gov), the US Department of State (www.travel.state.gov) and the Travel Security Administration (www.tsa.gov). Check out our website at www.lonelyplanet.com for updates as well.

WOMEN TRAVELERS

In general, New York City is a pretty safe place for women travelers, as long as common sense is used. If you are unsure which areas are considered dicey, ask at your hotel or telephone NYC & Company (☎ 212-484-1200) for advice; of course, other women are always a great source for the inside scoop. Depending on the neighborhood you're in, you are likely to encounter somewhat obnoxious behavior on the street, where men may greet you with whistles and muttered 'compliments.' Any engagement amounts to encouragement – simply walk on. Finally, if you're out late clubbing or at a venue further afield, it's a good idea to save some money for cab fare home. If you're ever assaulted, call the police (☎ 911).

WORK

To work legally in the USA you generally need both a work permit and a working visa. To apply for the correct visa at the US embassy you are generally required to obtain a work permit from the Immigration and Naturalization Service (INS) first. Your prospective employer must file a petition with the INS for permission for you to work, so you will first need to find a company that wants to hire you and is willing to file all the necessary paperwork. You can find more detailed information at the website of the US Department of State (www.travel.state.gov).

Volunteering

Though there are myriad volunteering opportunities throughout the city, most require you to first attend an orientation session – or even two or three – as well as submit to a thorough background check, which takes time. If you have the time for just one orientation while you're in town, you might want to make it with New York Cares (www.nycares.org), a nonprofit umbrella that provides information on weekly needs and volunteer events around the city; tasks can range from sprucing up a public garden to doling out meals at a soup kitchen. After being prepped, you'll be free to choose the job of your choice and then just show up.

BEHIND THE SCENES

THIS BOOK

This sixth edition of New York City was written by Ginger Adams Otis, Beth Greenfield, Robert Reid and Regis St Louis. Earlier editions were written by Conner Gorry and David Ellis. The History chapter was based on work by Kathleen Hulser, and the Architecture chapter was based on work by Joyce Mendelsohn.

This guidebook was commissioned in Lonely Planet's Oakland office, and produced by the following:

Commissioning Editors Jay Cooke, Jennye Garibaldi, Emily Wolman

Coordinating Editor Ali Lemer

Coordinating Cartographer Julie Sheridan

Coordinating Layout Designer Wibowo Rusli

Managing Editor Melanie Dankel

Managing Cartographer Alison Lyall

Managing Layout Designer Adam McCrow

Assisting Editors Melissa Faulkner, Kate James, Simon Williamson

Assisting Cartographers Ross Butler, Chandra Johan, Tadhgh Knaggs, Tom Webster

Assisting Layout Designer Aomi Hongo

Cover Designer Pepi Bluck

Project Manager Rachel Imeson

Thanks to Sasha Baskett, Jennifer Garrett, Laura Jane, Lisa Knights, Raphael Richards, Celia Wood

Cover photographs Statue of Liberty, Henryk T Kaiser/ Agefotostock (top), New York taxis in motion, pbnj productions/Brand X/Corbis (bottom)

Internal photographs p12 (#2), p13 (#2), p15 (#4, #7), p16 Ambient Images Inc/Alamy; p11 (#2) Arcaid/Alamy; p190 (top) David Grossman/Alamy; p280 (#1) dbimages/ Alamy; p275 (#6) Directphoto.org/Alamy; p7 (#4), p187 (left) Frances Roberts/Alamy; p4 (#3) Jon Hicks/Corbis; p277 (#2) Kevin Fleming/Corbis; p15 (#6), p191 Richard Levine/Alamy; p10 Ted Pink/Alamy; p14 Tracy Fahy/Alamy. All other photographs by Lonely Planet Images, and by Dan Herrick except p3, p4 (#1, #4), p5 (#2), p13 (#3), p187 (right), p188 (top), p280 (#2) Angus Osborn; p12 (#1), p186 Bill Wassman; p188 (bottom) Brent Winebrenner; p190 (bottom), p280 (#3) Corey Wise; p12 (#4) Diana Mayfield; p12 (#3) Donald C. Priscilla & Alexander Eastman; p11 (#4) Greg Gawlowski; p2 Izzet Kerribar; p8 (#1), p15 (#5), p16 (#2) Michelle Bennett; p10 (#2, #3), p11 (#3), p185, p189 Richard Cummins.

All images are copyright of the photographer unless otherwise indicated. Many of the images in this guide are available for licensing from Lonely Planet Images: www .lonelyplanetimages.com.

THANKS
GINGER ADAMS OTIS

Thanks to the unflappable Jay Cooke, the Oz editing and carto teams, all the New Yorkers who let me ask them endless questions, fellow authors Beth, Robert and Regis,

THE LONELY PLANET STORY

Fresh from an epic journey across Europe, Asia and Australia in 1972, Tony and Maureen Wheeler sat at their kitchen table stapling together notes. The first Lonely Planet guidebook, *Across Asia on the Cheap*, was born.

Travelers snapped up the guides. Inspired by their success, the Wheelers began publishing books to Southeast Asia, India and beyond. Demand was prodigious, and the Wheelers expanded the business rapidly to keep up. Over the years, Lonely Planet extended its coverage to every country and into the virtual world via lonelyplanet.com and the Thorn Tree message board.

As Lonely Planet became a globally loved brand, Tony and Maureen received several offers for the company. But it wasn't until 2007 that they found a partner whom they trusted to remain true to the company's principles of traveling widely, treading lightly and giving sustainably. In October of that year, BBC Worldwide acquired a 75% share in the company, pledging to uphold Lonely Planet's commitment to independent travel, trustworthy advice and editorial independence.

Today, Lonely Planet has offices in Melbourne, London and Oakland, with over 500 staff members and 300 authors. Tony and Maureen are still actively involved with Lonely Planet. They're traveling more often than ever, and they're devoting their spare time to charitable projects. And the company is still driven by the philosophy of *Across Asia on the Cheap*: 'All you've got to do is decide to go and the hardest part is over. So go!'

my family, my partner Michael, and a big, big thank you to Lauren Rita Carroll, whose lightning-fast hands make Derek Jeter look like a benchwarmer.

BETH GREENFIELD

Heaps of thanks to my all-around-fab commissioning editor Jay Cooke, and to my talented fellow writers Ginger Adams Otis, Robert Reid and Regis St Louis. Thank you also to my architectural genius friend Greg Wessner, to my ever-supportive parents and to my partner in love and life and travel, Kiki Herold.

ROBERT REID

Thanks to Jay Cooke of LP Oakland for his positive energy that makes the book so fun. And to Ali Lemer and the rest of the LP Melbourne production staff for deciphering my map changes and editing the text, and also to the other authors on the book – Beth, Ginger, Regis – for not yelling at my dumb questions.

REGIS ST LOUIS

Thanks to the assorted fashion designers and shopping geniuses with their tips on NY's ever-changing style scene. In particular, I'd like to thank Florence Foley, Carla Carneiro and Shannon Gooding. Thanks also to Cassandra for pounding the pavement with me on long shopping days and joining me (no arm-twisting involved) at sample sales.

OUR READERS

Many thanks to the travelers who used the last edition and wrote to us with helpful hints, useful advice and interesting anecdotes:

Allan Alfonso, Emer Allan, Stefania Antonini, Jorg Ausfelt, Lauren Barley, Jon Bates, Camilla Bhakri, Caroline Binch, Mike Brown, Hannah Carrick, Jonas Chapuis, Franzine Co, Andrew Curran, W F Doran, Kari Düwel, Deborah Ellison, Paul English, Adrian Eymann, Evelyn Faulk, Xavier Ferrer, Isabelle Garacotche, Mira Greenland, Jardena Guttmann Colm, Eric Haas, Daniel Hahn, Peter Hauser, Silvia Hensy, Stuart

SEND US YOUR FEEDBACK

We love to hear from travelers – your comments keep us on our toes and help make our books better. Our well-traveled team reads every word on what you loved or loathed about this book. Although we cannot reply individually to postal submissions, we always guarantee that your feedback goes straight to the appropriate authors, in time for the next edition. Each person who sends us information is thanked in the next edition – and the most useful submissions are rewarded with a free book.

To send us your updates – and find out about Lonely Planet events, newsletters and travel news – visit our award-winning website: www.lonelyplanet.com/contact.

Note: We may edit, reproduce and incorporate your comments in Lonely Planet products such as guidebooks, websites and digital products, so let us know if you don't want your comments reproduced or your name acknowledged. For a copy of our privacy policy visit www.lonelyplanet.com/privacy.

Hershey, Annette Holden, Katie Hotynski, Wolfgang Hürst, Brian Jenner, Joan Jennings, Kristine Kiddell-Truesdale, Julie Kirzinger, Carol Lavallee, Suzanne Lee, Albert Lemer, Rebecca Levi, Henrik Lindqvist, Kelsi Luhnow, Sarah McCormick, Idoia Mezo, Melissa Michelson, Rob Mitchell, Miles Montjuic, Marco Moretti, Gail Morse, Alex Muirhead, Wendy Mulligan, Natasha Nagina, Jane Pellowe, Mari Pääaho, Kirus Raysor, Jesse Rodriguez, Andrew Rogers, J Sabuda, Michelle Sanders, Eve Sandler, David Santer, Ulla Schwertassek, Brant Sextro, Stephen Shanasy, Arlene Shaner, Jennifer Sloan, Karen Smith, Tom Smith, Ricardo Soto, Anna De Stefano, Donna Swift, Nicoló Tamburi, Tammy Tan, Chris Tozer, Tanya Trivizas, Geoff Tyson, Peter van Marle, Richard Williamson, Chris Woods, Ursula Worms

ACKNOWLEDGMENTS

Many thanks to the Metropolitan Transportation Authority for use of their New York City and Manhattan subway and bus maps © 2008. Used with permission.

Notes

Notes

INDEX

9/11, see September 11

A

accommodations 347-68,
  see also Sleeping
  subindex
  brownstones 52, 119,
    141
  costs 348-9
  gay & lesbian 344
  online resources 349
activities 323-37, see
  also Sports & Activities
  subindex, individual
  activities
Ailey, Alvin 46
air travel
  airports 389-90
  to/from airports 390-1
ambulance 399
American Museum of
  Natural History 152
antiques 370
apartments 348, see also
  Sleeping subindex
architects
  Breuer, Marcel 144
  Burnham, Daniel 52,
    53, 119
  Foster, Norman 52
  Gehry, Frank 51
  Gropius, Walter 53
  Johnson, Philip 53, 137,
    317, 321
  Koolhaas, Rem 220
  Le Corbusier 53

Libeskind, Daniel 56
Lin, Maya 93
Lloyd Wright, Frank
  76, 144
McKim, Mead & White
  34, 36, 52, 90, 163,
  184
Meier, Richard 52, 108,
  184, 191
Mies van der Rohe,
  Ludwig 53
Saarinen, Eero 390
Stern, Robert AM 315
Taniguchi, Yoshio 137
Van Alen, William 53,
  124
White, Stanford 52, 108,
  175, 318
architecture 50-3, see also
  Sights subindex
  AIA Center for
    Architecture 53
  Beaux Arts 52
  books 53
  events 24
  Federal 51
  Georgian 51
  Greek revival 51
  Italianate 52
  skyscrapers 53
  tours 404
area codes, see inside front
  cover
art galleries, see Sights
  subindex
arts 38-50, 309-22, 370,
  see also Arts subindex,
  individual arts
arts events
  Celebrate Brooklyn 23
  Central Park
    SummerStage 23
  Dumbo Art Under the
    Bridge Festival 24
  Howl! Festival 22
  River to River Festival
    23
Astoria 203
Atlantic City 382-4
ATMs 402
Auster, Paul 48

B

B&Bs 348
babysitting 398
bagels 248
Balanchine, George 46
Baldwin, James 48
bars, see drinking
Bartholdi, Frédéric-Auguste
  70-1
Baryshnikov, Mikhail 46
baseball 324-6, see also
  Sports & Activities
  subindex
basketball 326, see also
  Sports & Activities
  subindex
Batali, Mario 252
bathrooms 407-8
Battery Park City 75-7
Bay Ridge 195
beaches 370
  Brighton Beach 195-8,
    196-7
  Cape May beaches 384
  Jones Beach 302, 376
  Long Beach 378
  Orchard Beach 370
  Rockaway Beach 205-6,
    16
  Sandy Hook beaches
    381-2
Beats, the 47-8
Bedford-Stuyvesant 184, 193
Beecher, Henry Ward 169
Bensonhurst 195
bicycling, see biking
Bike New York 21
biking 328-30, 390-1
  organizations 329
  rental 329-30
bird-watching 331-5
Blessing of the Animals 24
blogs 59
Bloomberg, Michael 37,
  38-9, 54-5, 57
boat travel 71, 391-2
boating 330-5
Boerum Hill 179, 180
  drinking 297-8
books
  architecture 53
  cookbooks 253

history 30
novels 47
politics 57
sports 189
Bouley, David 252
Bourdain, Anthony 252
bowling 331
Bridgehampton, see
  Hamptons, the
Brighton Beach 195-8,
  196-7
  food 281
  walking tour 197-8, 198
Broadway shows 311-12,
  see also Arts subindex
Bronx, the 167, 207-12,
  208-9
  food 282-3
  drinking 298
  shopping 244
  transportation 207
Bronx Zoo 210-11
Brooklyn 167, 168-98,
  170-1, 174, 177, 180,
  182, 185-192
  accommodations 367-8
  Bay Ridge 195
  Bedford-Stuyvesant
    184, 193
  Bensonhurst 195
  Boerum Hill 179, 180
  Brighton Beach 195-8,
    196-7
  Brooklyn Bridge 31, 32,
    83, 4, 185
  Brooklyn Heights 168-73,
    174, 187
  Bushwick 178-9
  Carroll Gardens 179, 180
  Clinton Hill 175-6
  Cobble Hill 179, 180
  Coney Island 195-8,
    196-7, 14
  Crown Heights 184, 193
  Ditmas Park 186, 192, 270
  Downtown Brooklyn
    173-4, 174, 188
  drinking 296-8
  Dumbo 174-5, 174
  food 268-81
  Fort Greene 175-6, 191,
    180

ARTS
BROADWAY MUSICALS

CLASSICAL MUSIC

DANCE

000 map pages
000 photographs

INDEX

INDEX

INDEX

000 map pages
000 photographs

INDEX

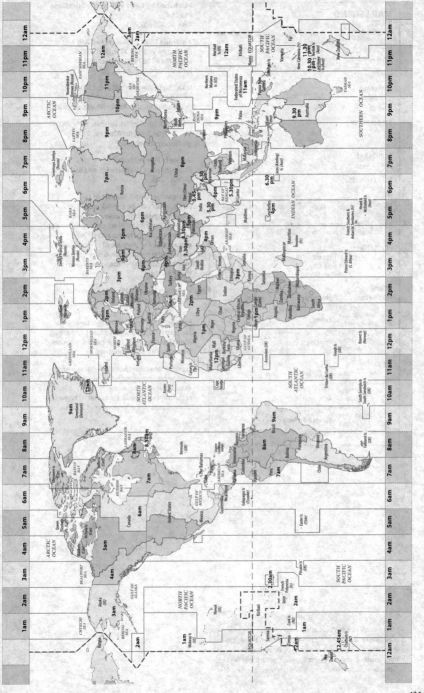

431

MAP LEGEND

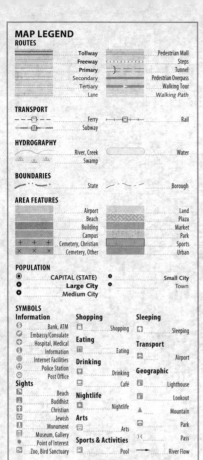

ROUTES

Tollway
Freeway
Primary
Secondary
Tertiary
Lane

Pedestrian Mall
Steps
Tunnel
Pedestrian Overpass
Walking Tour
Walking Path

TRANSPORT

Ferry
Subway
Rail

HYDROGRAPHY

River, Creek
Swamp
Water

BOUNDARIES

State
Borough

AREA FEATURES

Airport
Beach
Building
Campus
Cemetery, Christian
Cemetery, Other

Land
Plaza
Market
Park
Sports
Urban

POPULATION

CAPITAL (STATE)
Large City
Medium City

Small City
Town

SYMBOLS

Information
Bank, ATM
Embassy/Consulate
Hospital, Medical
Information
Internet Facilities
Police Station
Post Office

Sights
Beach
Buddhist
Christian
Jewish
Monument
Museum, Gallery
Point of Interest
Zoo, Bird Sanctuary

Shopping
Shopping

Eating
Eating

Drinking
Drinking
Café

Nightlife
Nightlife

Arts
Arts

Sports & Activities
Pool

Sleeping
Sleeping

Transport
Airport

Geographic
Lighthouse
Lookout
Mountain
Park
Pass
River Flow

Published by Lonely Planet Publications Pty Ltd
ABN 36 005 607 983

Australia Head Office, Locked Bag 1, Footscray, Victoria 3011, ☎03 8379 8000, fax 03 8379 8111, talk2us@lonelyplanet.com.au

USA 150 Linden St, Oakland, CA 94607, ☎510 250 6400, toll free 800 275 8555, fax 510 893 8572, info@lonelyplanet.com

UK 2nd fl, 186 City Rd, London, EC1V 2NT, ☎020 7106 2100, fax 020 7106 2101, go@lonelyplanet.co.uk

© Lonely Planet 2008
Photographs © Dan Herrick and as listed (p410) 2008

Printed by Hang Tai Printing Company. Printed in China.